FADO AND THE PLACE OF LONGING

To Maria

Fado and the Place of Longing
Loss, Memory and the City

RICHARD ELLIOTT
Newcastle University, UK

ASHGATE

Published by
Ashgate Publishing Limited
Wey Court East
Union Road
Farnham
Surrey, GU9 7PT
England

Ashgate Publishing Company
Suite 420
101 Cherry Street
Burlington
VT 05401-4405
USA

www.ashgate.com

British Library Cataloguing in Publication Data
Elliott, Richard.
Fado and the place of longing: loss, memory and the city.
– (Ashgate popular and folk music series)
1. Fados – Portugal – History and criticism.
I. Title II. Series
782.4'2162691–dc22

Library of Congress Cataloging-in-Publication Data
Elliott, Richard, 1971 June 28–
Fado and the place of longing: loss, memory and the city / Richard Elliott.
   p. cm. – (Ashgate popular and folk music series)
Includes bibliographical references and index.
ISBN 978-0-7546-6795-7 (hardcover:alk. paper)
1. Fados – Portugal – History and criticism. I. Title.
ML3718.F3E45 2009
781.62'691–dc22

                                                          2009046525

ISBN 9780754667957 (hbk)

Mixed Sources
Product group from well-managed
forests and other controlled sources
www.fsc.org Cert no. SA-COC-1565
© 1996 Forest Stewardship Council

Printed and bound in Great Britain by
MPG Books Group, UK

Contents

General Editor's Preface   *vii*

Acknowledgements and Permissions   *ix*

Introduction   1

1   Songs of Disquiet: Mythology, Ontology, Ideology, Fadology   13

2   Taking Place: The Role of the City in Fado   65

3   'Trago Fado nos Sentidos': Memory, Witnessing and
     Testimony in Fado   97

4   New Citizens of the *Fadista* World   135

5   Tudo Isto Ainda É Fado? Fado as Local and Global Practice   177

Bibliography   *217*

Discography   *229*

Videography   *235*

Index   *237*

General Editor's Preface

The upheaval that occurred in musicology during the last two decades of the twentieth century has created a new urgency for the study of popular music alongside the development of new critical and theoretical models. A relativistic outlook has replaced the universal perspective of modernism (the international ambitions of the 12-note style); the grand narrative of the evolution and dissolution of tonality has been challenged, and emphasis has shifted to cultural context, reception and subject position. Together, these have conspired to eat away at the status of canonical composers and categories of high and low in music. A need has arisen, also, to recognize and address the emergence of crossovers, mixed and new genres, to engage in debates concerning the vexed problem of what constitutes authenticity in music and to offer a critique of musical practice as the product of free, individual expression.

Popular musicology is now a vital and exciting area of scholarship, and the *Ashgate Popular and Folk Music Series* presents some of the best research in the field. Authors are concerned with locating musical practices, values and meanings in cultural context, and draw upon methodologies and theories developed in cultural studies, semiotics, poststructuralism, psychology and sociology. The series focuses on popular musics of the twentieth and twenty-first centuries. It is designed to embrace the world's popular musics from Acid Jazz to Zydeco, whether high tech or low tech, commercial or non-commercial, contemporary or traditional.

Professor Derek B. Scott
Professor of Critical Musicology
University of Leeds

Acknowledgements and Permissions

Acknowledgements

This book develops research and ideas originally explored in my doctoral thesis on loss, memory and nostalgia in popular song. That project was made possible by a scholarship from the Arts and Humanities Research Council, for which I remain deeply grateful. I would like to acknowledge once again the invaluable help, support and advice of my PhD supervisors, Richard Middleton and Ian Biddle of the International Centre for Music Studies at Newcastle University.

I have been able to present my research on fado at a number of conferences, among which I wish to note the following: 'Popular Musics of the Hispanic and Lusophone Worlds' International Conference (Newcastle, July 2006); British Forum for Ethnomusicology Annual Conference, (Newcastle, April 2007); Congreso Internacional 'Música, Ciudades, Redes' (Salamanca, March 2008); Congresso Internacional 'Fado: Percursos e Perspectivas' (Lisbon, June 2008); and the IASPM International Conference (Liverpool, July 2009). I am particularly grateful for the invitation by Salwa Castelo-Branco to speak at the Lisbon fado conference and for the opportunity to share knowledge with the participants of that event. I am also grateful for the opportunity to contribute a chapter to a forthcoming book based on the conference and edited by Salwa Castelo-Branco and Rui Vieira Nery. The chapter, entitled 'Fado's Invisible Cities', provides a condensed account of the ideas explored in Chapters 2 and 3 of the present book.

Many thanks to Heidi Bishop, Rosie Phillips and Nicole Norman at Ashgate for commissioning the book and seeing it through the editorial and production process. I am very grateful to Mary Murphy for proofreading and to Derek Scott for his kind words of encouragement on reading the manuscript.

I would like to acknowledge the advice and encouragement received from my fellow academics and friends in Newcastle, in particular Nanette de Jong, Lars Iyer, Sinéad Murphy and Paco Bethencourt. My parents Peter and Angela and my sister Liz have been a constant source of moral and intellectual support throughout and I thank them for that and much more. My partner Maria has aided me in incalculable ways. On the academic side, she helped with all the Portuguese translations, listened to or read through most sections of the book in one shape or another and advised on all kinds of matters great and small, all this while managing her own very different and busy career. In addition, she has shown endless patience when I have been lost in the place of writing and has provided the moral and practical support that allowed me to work. As with the doctoral thesis that preceded it, this book could not have been written without Maria and I dedicate it to her.

Permissions

Fados written by Amália Rodrigues

'Estranha forma de vida'
'Gostava de ser quem era'
'Lágrima'
'Trago fados nos sentidos'
'Grito'
'Ó gente da minha terra'

Translation of Fernando Pessoa's Poems by Richard Zenith

'Maritime Ode'
'Each man fulfills the destiny he must fulfill'
'Almost'
'She sings, poor reaper, perhaps'

Introduction

There is currently a significant amount of interest in fado at both national (Portuguese) and international levels. The rise in global popularity of the so-called 'new fadistas' over the last decade has led fado to a level of visibility unmatched since the heyday of the internationally-renowned performer Amália Rodrigues. Current fado performers such as Mariza have found themselves at the forefront of a star system promoted by the contemporary world music network. Fado is regularly reviewed in the Anglophone music press, with leading world music publications such as *Songlines* and *fRoots* featuring performers in prominent articles. Two films have recently been completed on the contemporary fado scene, Simon Broughton's *Mariza and the Story of Fado* (2006) and Carlos Saura's *Fados* (2007). Book-length studies of fado in English, however, have been thin on the ground. Paul Vernon's *A History of the Portuguese Fado* appeared towards the end of the 1990s, prior to the recent 'boom', and there is much to be updated in his account for those wishing to place the work of current performers such as Cristina Branco, Ana Moura and Katia Guerreiro in its proper historical context.[1] This book attempts to fill some of the gaps left in the scholarship by taking into consideration recent Portuguese work on fado and examining the continuities and discontinuities in current fado practice.

More specifically, the book presents research carried out on fado music and its role in the interlacing of mythology, history, memory and place over the second half of the twentieth century. A large proportion of the book focuses on the so-called 'new fado' which emerged in the 1990s and gained considerable popularity both domestically and internationally. My emphasis will be upon the ways in which fado acts as a cultural product for reaffirming local identity via recourse to social memory and an imagined community, while also providing a distinctive cultural export for the dissemination of a 'remembered Portugal' on the global stage. To do this will necessitate a description of fado as both local practice and 'world music' and a consideration of the role of recording technology in mediating fado's 'memory community'.

Dealing with the construction and maintenance of the local, I examine the ways in which fado songs bear witness to the city of Lisbon. Fado, often described as an 'urban folk music', emerged from the streets of Lisbon in the mid-nineteenth century and went on to become Portugal's 'national' music during the twentieth. It is known for its strong emphasis on loss, memory and nostalgia within its song texts, which often refer to absent people and places. One of the main lyrical themes of fado is the city itself, particularly those areas most associated with the

---

1   Paul Vernon, *A History of the Portuguese Fado* (Aldershot: Ashgate, 1998).

music's origins such as Mouraria, Alfama and Bairro Alto. A mythology of place is summoned up in fado song texts that attempts to trace the remembered and imagined city of the past via a poetics of haunting. At the same time certain locales of the physical city present themselves as stages in a museum of song, offering up haunted melodies of a sonic past that serve to assert the city's identity. City and song, then, bear witness to each other.

Witnessing is a productive force in that it results in the transference of a thing presented to a thing re-presented. Writing and recording are both examples of the transference from the witnessed to the re-presented: in both, something of the original event is inevitably lost in the process of 'getting it down'. Writing and recording are vital tools in allowing us the possibility to forget as much as to remember: just *what* is taken down has profound consequences for the evolution of cultural practices. Throughout this book, I suggest that it is useful to think of fado songs as performing a dynamic combination of 'fencing-off', 'framing' and 'staging' that attempts to address the processes of decadence and renewal taking place in the city. Analysis of song texts and performance strategies allied to a theory of witnessing, transcribing and testifying helps to highlight the dynamics of this process as it occurs in fado.

Another major aspect of my project is an examination of contemporary fado practice in terms of changes that take place as the genre negotiates its place in the world. This will involve dealing with the emergence of *novo fado* ('new fado') over the past two decades and an examination of what has been kept from 'traditional' fado practice and what innovations have been allowed or encouraged. While I find the '*novo fado*' tag useful for descriptive purposes, I am not sold on the claim to newness as a single event. One of the things I wish to do, then, is to suggest a spatial practice at work in such categorization whereby 'newness' is always already a part of the process of fencing-off and framing. It is important to bear in mind Portugal's place in Europe during the period covered by this account and the country's connection to a need for a distinctive cultural marker of difference from its European neighbours that would avoid the potential conflict between national and European identity. I focus on the emergence in the 1980s of what came to be known as 'world music', to which fado, as the music most associated with Portugal, was soon added, providing the genre once again with an international audience. The newly-coined 'world music' category gave a fresh image to any musics associated with it and encouraged the setting-up of a number of recording companies to release and market world music. There has been an important role played by record labels from outside of Portugal in the distribution and popularization of contemporary fado, especially in France and the Netherlands.

While a commercialized form of fado has been enjoying significant visibility in recent years, the genre has also continued as a local popular practice. Connecting to the first strand of research into the historiography of fado and cultural theoretical perspectives on memory and place, the final chapter of the book examines the relationships between fado as a local practice and a global phenomenon.

By looking at the mediation between the local and the global it will examine how myth-making and the figure of the 'star fadista' provide both the conditions of possibility for effective transmission of fado and a narrative that informs both local knowledge and media promotion of the music in equal measure. One of the more intriguing aspects of fado music is its insistence on the representation of *saudade*, a supposedly 'untranslatable' term for a yearning only Portuguese people are claimed to feel. How can fado fence off and protect *saudade* while attempting to project its musical affect to a global arena? Is the destination of *saudade* to become one of many European grammars of nostalgia, at once synonymous with and semantically distinct from each other, as suggested by Svetlana Boym?[2]

In addition to filling a gap in English language work on fado, I would hope that a project such as this has some resonance beyond its immediate subject matter by engaging with debates in the fields of memory studies, historiography and media studies. My examination of the role of the city in fado song texts bears comparison to work in other areas on what Christine Boyer has called 'the city of collective memory'.[3] By engaging with theories of witnessing, I hope to contribute to other contemporary work on the uses of memory, archival culture and the politics of reconciliation. By focusing on recent developments in fado music, I hope to extend the existing fado historiography to suggest processes of continuity and change in the mediation of highly memory-oriented cultural practices.

Chapter 1 provides an introduction to fado music via a historical overview of the genre before moving on to focus on the period 1950–2000, during which fado faced some of its greatest successes as an internationally recognized musical form as well as a number of harsh criticisms for its seeming insistence on a fatalistic lack of agency. I begin with a discussion of the central mythologies that have shaped fado's history and highlight the ways in which the music has been appropriated as an ideological tool for discussing Portugueseness. From here I move away from the specificity of fado to consider more general descriptions of loss, memory and nostalgia. The theoretical thrust of the chapter centres on fado texts as objects which fence off and privilege topics such as the city, Portugueseness, disquietude and *saudade*, the term applied to a nationally-understood yearning which fado is said to voice. The chapter also contains an overview of fado's greatest star, Amália Rodrigues, whose career spans most of the time period covered in the book and has had an enormous impact upon contemporary fado performers and fans. Amália (the use of whose surname has become redundant in most accounts of fado) will remain a constant reference point throughout the book.

Expanding on material outlined in the first chapter, Chapter 2 examines the ways that fado's witnessing 'takes place' by drawing on the work of a number of historians and theorists of memory and place. I try to show the processes by which

---

2   Svetlana Boym, *The Future of Nostalgia* (New York: Basic Books, 2001), pp. 12–13.

3   M. Christine Boyer, *The City of Collective Memory: Its Historical Legacy and Architectural Entertainments* (Cambridge, MA, and London: The MIT Press, 1996 [1994]).

fado texts provide a 'memory theatre' and to propose a description of fado which is more spatial than historical. While history plays an important part, my desire is to describe the place of fado in the contemporary musical field. I am not saying that this topic is not a historical one, for any musical genre becomes what it is (or what it seems to be) through a number of historical factors. Historical analysis is also, as Rui Vieira Nery makes clear, a vital tool in tempering the clamour of 'newness' applied to an object (or non-object) like *novo fado*.[4] However, I believe that, by focusing on place and spatial practices such as representation, categorization and framing, we can see more clearly why such claims are made. At any given moment a synchronic as well as a diachronic analysis is possible; I have tried to focus on the former while not neglecting the latter. A final note on Chapter 2: 'place' in this part of the book is very literally understood as the role of place *in* fado – the importance of toponyms in fado texts and the sense of place with which fado is infused. The broader scope of the book is to look at the place *of* fado – how fado is situated in the musical field. In my mind, these issues are interrelated and I attempt to convey this relationship at various stages.

The importance of place having been established, Chapter 3 attends to the role of transference in fado songs. Crucial to my thinking here is a theorizing of witnessing whereby the connections between the desire to remember and the imperative to testify to what one has remembered are highlighted. Witnessing is here thought of as a kind of carrying and I pursue the implications for such a carrying on the writing, memorization and voicing of song texts. The theory presented is one that has resonance beyond fado music, yet fado provides an exemplary case study given the number of song texts in the genre that focus on notions of carrying and unburdening. Bearing witness and bearing up are crucial themes in fado lyrics, while fado performance style places special emphasis on the carrying-on of tradition and the carrying-out of cathartic tasks.

Chapter 4 provides a more detailed description of the emergence of *novo fado*. It looks at a range of performers and their relationship with the wider popular music scene in Portugal. Given that relatively little information is available in English about developments in Portuguese popular music, I mention some of the main figures in its history. Such an overview, however brief, is useful for understanding how fado music has been influential upon and influenced by other national and international music genres, preparing the ground for the discussion of fado as local and global practice in Chapter 5.

The final chapter continues the discussion of *novo fado* initiated elsewhere in the book and shifts the emphasis to fado's place in the world music network. It is important to ask to what extent local and global scenes feed into each other. Is the local *casa de fado* (fado house) really as far removed from the global scene as it

---

[4]   Rui Vieira Nery, *Para uma História do Fado* (Lisbon: Corda Seca & Público, 2004). The point is made more concisely in Vieira Nery's introduction to Manuel Halpern, *O Futuro da Saudade: O Novo Fado e os Novos Fadistas* (Lisbon: Publicações Dom Quixote, 2004), pp. 11–18.

appears on first viewing? Or has the global scene created a new memory community via the ubiquity of recording and broadcast media? Contemporary local practice suggests that the archive of social memory relies as much on mass mediation as on the more localized phenomena common to earlier stages of fado history. We find in the case of mass-mediated *novo fado* a desire to stage localness and to export fado as a remembered practice and Portugal as an imagined community. At the same time, contemporary recording technology – so important to globally exported world music – paradoxically promises closeness while keeping the world at a distance. While perhaps not originally a folk music, fado, in adapting to new popular styles, leaves behind it something that seems very similar to a folk music. There is a dialectical process at work in which certain artists seek to escape one particular framework, seen as too restrictive, opening up a position from which they become subject to critique and a new hardening of the restrictions. This leads me to enquire to what extent global mediation has become 'necessary' for the memory of the local to be voiced. Globalization and detraditionalization add to the repertoire of lost objects that fado voices. In a sense, the very factors that threaten to destroy fado as a local practice are simultaneously the conditions of possibility for fado to continue.

* * *

Jorge Lima Barreto excludes fado from *Musa Lusa*, his study of modern Portuguese music, on the basis that analysis of the genre would require an ethnomusicological methodology for which he is not trained.[5] The implication here is that fado, as a locally rooted urban song form, needs to be studied 'in the flesh', to be witnessed at the point where it was created and where it still lives. Furthermore, it should be given a specialist's attention rather than a generalist's. This may be generally (but not absolutely) true for Portuguese folk music, which has a fairly scant recorded presence outside specialist circles. But fado has been a part of the recording industry in Portugal since the latter's inception and is as much a product of that industry as any of the other musics that Barreto catalogues. Indeed I would say it is more of a product of that industry than Portuguese classical musical (which gets its own chapter in *Musa Lusa*).

Discussing recordings inevitably leads to a focus on particular performers – Amália being a classic example, Mariza a more recent one – which in turn can be seen to detract from what fado really 'is' for many people, a local, living tradition that grants as much space to its amateur practitioners as it does to its stars. This is a point made by one of those very stars, Mísia: 'Fado with a capital "F" is not Amália, Mísia or Mariza; it is this river of anonymous souls who sing and play in the taverns.'[6] Should we take this as the false modesty of a successful artist

---

5   Jorge Lima Barreto, *Musa Lusa* (Lisbon: Hugin, 1997), p. 183.

6   Mísia, interview in Hervé Pons, *Os Fados de Mísia: Conversas com Hervé Pons*, tr. António Carlos Carvalho (Lisbon: Oceanos, 2007), p. 73. Unless otherwise stated, all translations from the Portuguese in this book are my own.

or as a useful reminder that the stars of the fado recording industry are a small and inevitably compromised sample of what fado 'is'? My response focuses on the nature of this 'is'. Certainly, Mísia is right to acknowledge the vitality of the community of fado performers in Portugal and in Portuguese communities outside the country. Fado emerged from the sources she mentions and has continued as a living localized practice for around two centuries. During that time it has resisted numerous attempts to co-opt it to a variety of agendas (romantic, socialist, nationalist and more). And one could argue that it could have done so without any help from star performers, who in fact may have been partly responsible for those co-optations.

But this is not all that fado 'is' and it would be unrealistic to downplay the importance of the recording industry in keeping the music at the forefront of public awareness. As with many other modern musical forms, recording is both hero and villain. It threatens loss of authenticity, takes away from the local and gives to the global, diluting and disfiguring as it does so. But it also fixes and maintains, serves as archive and reminder and sustains the music beyond its immediate point of production and reception. With this in mind, it is worth quoting another star performer, Carlos do Carmo, who maintains that 'the history of fado, deep down, is nothing more or less than the history of its interpreters'.[7] Carmo does not specify amateurs or professionals but the comment comes in a discussion of his career as a recording artist, so it seems reasonable that he is hinting at the responsibility that such artists have in producing this history.

This book is unapologetically about recorded music. This is not to belittle the magical experience of hearing the music performed live, whether in a Lisbon *tasca* (cheap eating place) or a concert hall thousands of miles from the city. Nor does it belittle the work of ethnomusicologists who have sought to represent, whether from within the culture or without, the music in its immediate time and space. It will at times critique a number of practices that have sought to fence the music off, to fix it to a particular experience that a mass mediated and globalized world denies it. But the book is not a celebration of globalization or of the processes of fusion and dispersal that many critics say have followed in globalization's wake. It is written from a belief that the processes of globalization cannot be ignored. It examines them from a dialectical approach, which means that contradictions are embraced when they arise; there is not merely a wish to replace one set of thoughts with another. At one point I will critique the practices of fencing fado off as a way of ignoring debates outside the specialized sphere of local knowledge. At other times, I will praise this very same quality as a form of refusal, aware also that I am doing my own 'fencing-off' by writing a book about fado in the first place. Fado, after all, is far from the 'biggest' music in Portugal (that title goes, as in so many places, to Anglo-American pop, rock and hip hop or to national models closely

[7] Carlos do Carmo, interview in Viriato Teles, *Carlos do Carmo: Do Fado e do Mundo* (Lisbon: Garrido Editores, 2003), p. 26.

derived from them), though it is often presented on the national and international stages as though it were.

Such contradictions are woven deep within the material of fado discourse, allowing the music to be appropriated by various political regimes and to be one minute accused of an overidentification with nostalgia (the latter assumed only in its conservative guise), the next praised for its potential to engage with the vernacular and to represent the people. The contemporary formulation of these contradictions merely reflects globalization itself, which is nothing if not contradictory. In short, I am trying to write about fado as a localized form of music which nonetheless exists in a globalized society, one in which specific musical forms are mass mediated via a world music network. My hope is that such an approach does justice both to the specifics of fado's identity as local music and its more general appeal to a wider audience who know it primarily through the mediation of the world music network.

These contradictions also extend into other areas of methodology, most notably perhaps the clash between objectivity and subjectivity. Thomas Nagel discusses the problem of trying to bring these viewpoints together: 'How, given my personal experiential perspective, can I form a conception of the world as it is independent of my perception of it? And how can I know that this conception is correct?' The problem with objective viewpoints is 'how to accommodate, in a world that simply exists and has no perspectival center, any of the following things: (a) oneself; (b) one's point of view; (c) the point of view of other selves, similar and dissimilar; and (d) the objects of various types of judgment that seem to emanate from these perspectives.'[8] Nagel argues that it is still worth staking a commitment on the pursuit of objectivity given the advances in knowledge it can bring. The problem, then, is how to deal with this 'view from nowhere'.

Views, perspectives and 'scapes' are all tropes I wish to keep in play in this book. As my use of Michel de Certeau's work in Chapter 2 suggests, it is instructive to position oneself on a continuum of perspective that allows both distant and close-up views. As someone interested in both the sonic spaces of musical texts and the contextual spaces in which music operates, I believe it is vital to maintain the possibility and the flexibility to move between these spaces. A number of thinkers have influenced me in considering how such flexibility might be possible, among them Henri Lefebvre, whose work on the 'production of space' sets out an agenda whereby dialectical thinking makes way for a 'third possibility', and Gaston Bachelard, whose 'poetics of space' indicates how it can be possible to move from intimacy of a printed text to the often unobserved intimacy of the domestic living space. Paul Carter's exploration of 'spatial history' is relevant here, too. In the following section from Carter's *The Road to Botany Bay*, he describes historical accounts of the colonizing of Australia, but his highlighting of perspective carries resonances far beyond his subject matter:

---

8   Thomas Nagel, *The View from Nowhere* (New York and Oxford: Oxford University Press, 1986), p. 27.

What we see is what the firstcomers did not see: a place, not a historical space. A place, a historical fact, detached from its travellers; static, at anchor, as if it was always there, bland, visible. Standing at this well-known point, the spatial event is replaced by a historical stage. Only the actors are absent. Even as we look towards the horizon or turn away down fixed routes, our gaze sees through the space of history, as if it was never there. In its place, nostalgia for the past, cloudy time, the repetition of facts. The fact that where we stand and how we go is history: this we do not see.[9]

Carter's point applies both to the writing of history and the perception of historical space. What Carter calls 'diorama history', an illusory history built upon the fantasy of a theatre in which history is performed for an 'all-seeing spectator', is another description of the view from nowhere.[10]

'Diorama history' is often at the centre of the kind of discourse that would allow a cultural form to be appropriated and used for nationalist ends. Fado has been appropriated towards such ends by politicians, historians, poets, fado performers and musicologists, to tell a variety of stories that have the nation and some form of nationalism as their common denominator. Sometimes they have been thoroughly convincing; on other occasions rhetoric has greatly outdistanced fact. It can be very difficult, when responding to such accounts, to be both 'scientific' and 'poetic'. One constantly runs the risk of projecting a kind of disproval via positivism, while still finding value in a rather more imaginative frame of reference. As Carter observes:

a spatial history does not go confidently forward. It does not organize its subject matter into a nationalist enterprise. It advances exploratively, even metaphorically, recognizing that the future is invented … It runs the risk of becoming as intangible as distant views. Its objects are intentions and, suggesting the plurality of historical directions, it constantly risks escaping into poetry, biography or a form of immaterialism positivists might think nihilistic. After all, what can you do with a horizon?[11]

I proceed via two approaches. One is a phenomenology of experience, presented as a description of the stages of an encounter between a listener and a genre. The other is the long-established academic exercise of what Slavoj Žižek, drawing on Hegel, calls the 'positing of presuppositions', in other words the putting in place of a narrative that retroactively accounts for, measures, defines and bounds the object

---

[9]   Paul Carter, *The Road to Botany Bay: An Exploration of Landscape and History* (New York: Alfred A. Knopf, 1988), p. xiv.

[10]   Carter, p. xv.

[11]   Carter, p. 294.

of study.[12] Such narratives, while basking in the security of the scientific gaze, are sometimes disguised formulations of the first phenomenological approach, presenting a situation as if it has always been. My hope is that these two approaches act as useful correctives to each other.

There are a number of trajectories which unfold over the course of the book. One is a gradual moving from theory to music; the proportion of theory to musical example is greater in the first three chapters than in the last two, meaning that the music gradually 'takes over', hopefully leaving the reader with a sense of how the (recorded) fado scene appeared at the time of writing. A second trajectory is from mainly literary representation to more 'sounded' representations, meaning simply that more use is made of lyrics in the first part of the book. Thirdly, we travel from the life and career of the dominant figure of twentieth-century fado, Amália Rodrigues, to a post-Amália world in which Amália is a constant posthumous presence. By focusing on Amália and not on the myriad of other performers, it could be argued that I am reinforcing the stereotypical way in which the story of fado is told, in which Amália is invariably the star. However, there is still much ground to clear in the Anglophone reception of fado and I believe those of us interested in fado as a recorded practice still need to grant Amália a prominent place in our narrative.[13] Hopefully, future work will focus on other performers such as Ercília Costa, Alfredo Marceneiro, Hermínia Silva, Maria Teresa de Noronha and many more. I have tried to ensure that some of these performers have at least a brief presence in this book. Finally, there is a sort of historical progression, though it is ultimately a history of representation. I begin with a representation from the beginning of the twentieth century and end with a number of representations from the early twenty-first.

It could be argued that the phonographic era (to use Evan Eisenberg's formulation[14]) demands its own kind of field work. Rather than seeing recordings as the enemy of local tradition, we can posit them as objects to be sought out, objects which reveal their own histories, memories and forgettings. In my case, this kind of field work has involved searching out recordings, attending concerts, and following a variety of music-related media in Portugal and abroad. In the same way that 'classic' ethnographic field work involves a greater measure of participation than that required for passing 'general' knowledge of a culture, so too does phonographic field work. Whether this is a regular acquaintanceship with record shops in Portugal, or knowing what to look for at the *feira da ladra* (the sprawling Lisbon flea market), or searching the seemingly limitless resources of the internet, the level of involvement is specialist, time-consuming and intense.

---

[12]   See Slavoj Žižek, *For They Know Not What They Do: Enjoyment as a Political Factor*, 2nd edn (London and New York: Verso, 2002), pp. 214–22.

[13]   On a more theoretical note, we could say that Amália posthumously 'posits the presuppositions' of what fado is (and is not).

[14]   Evan Eisenberg, *The Recording Angel: Music, Records and Culture from Aristotle to Zappa* (London: Picador, 1988 [1987]).

There are other issues in this book which will doubtless prove problematic for some readers. A charge may well be made that what is said for fado here could just as well be said for other musics. A related charge will state that what is done with cultural theory here could just as well be done with other (or even with no) case studies. Such claims are familiar enough, but it is questionable what they actually say. One thing they seem to say is that localizable genres can or should only be theorized according to localized theories. To claim otherwise is not to deny the importance of contextual study. Rather, it is to deny a condemnation-to-the-local that would reassert the 'universality' of certain privileged musics while refusing any such recognition to others. For my own part, I am not sure I can work otherwise: my understanding of theory is always already informed by music and vice versa. The result may be more a poetics than a theory; if so, it both accords with the sense of recognition I feel when reading Paul Carter's 'spatial history' and also seems entirely appropriate for a study of a musical genre steeped in poetry.

This brings me to the issue of words and music. I do not wish to rehearse the debates about the usefulness (or otherwise) of discussing words in songs when songs are not actually poems. There can be no absolute decree on this issue; different song forms place different levels of emphasis on words. Fado, as a rule, places a great deal of emphasis on them, whether in the traditional practice of verbal improvisation, ridicule and everyday poetics, or in the more 'erudite' practice whereby the work of noted poets is set to music by separate composers. When traditional song forms are used, it is the music that stays the same and the lyrics which are changed. Paying attention to the words takes us a long way towards interpreting the meaning of the song. This is certainly the case for those versed in Portuguese, but it seems to be challenged by one of the very qualities I am highlighting in this book, fado's ability in recent years to once again travel beyond its national borders. I have lost count of the number of English-language reviews of fado recordings and concerts which claim that the music 'transcends language barriers', that 'emotion is universal', and so on. There is truth in these claims but it is not the whole truth. Our ability to differentiate between different songs, or between 'good' and 'bad' performances of songs, suggests that we have already gone some way down the road of understanding. Different listeners will be at different stages of this journey and will have different desires as to whether to proceed further. Some will wish to fully understand the lyrics they are hearing by finding a translation or learning some words of the language; others will decide they do not wish or need to know. The importance of toponyms associated with Lisbon, such as those I discuss in Chapter 2, may be of no interest to the latter group, but they will surely be aware, if they listen to much fado, that they are hearing a music that reiterates certain sounds (words) almost obsessively. When I discuss songs about the city – or about fate or nostalgia or witnessing – by focusing on the words in the songs, the point is precisely that we hear these words endlessly repeated; they make up a large part of the sound world of fado.

This also means that when I move on to sound, I am focusing primarily on singers. In doing so I am following the popular practice of valorizing singers over musicians. I therefore risk continuing the process of obscuring the role of other musicians, particularly guitarists, in the making of fado music. As Salwa Castelo-Branco has pointed out, guitarists have been very much 'hidden musicians' in accounts of fado.[15] My omission would be notable enough if I were dealing only with amateur music-making. It is doubly notable in that I am dealing with professional recording artists who have relied on their musicians to compose the songs included on their records and in their concerts. Hopefully, other work on the cultural importance of the guitar and guitarists in the shaping of contemporary fado will be forthcoming. Meanwhile, let us at least begin our journey with a sighting of the instrument.

[15] Salwa Castelo-Branco, '"Músicos Ocultos": Percursos dos Instrumentistas do Fado', paper presented at the conference 'Fado: Percursos e Perspectivas', Lisbon, 18–21 June 2008. Castelo-Branco's title is taken from Ruth Finnegan's *The Hidden Musicians: Music-Making in an English Town* (Middletown: Wesleyan University Press, 2007).

Chapter 1
Songs of Disquiet:
Mythology, Ontology, Ideology, Fadology

Introduction: Mythology

A cheap café in the Mouraria district, at the entrance to the Rua do Capelão.
An assortment of herdsmen, cattle traders, merchants and prostitutes. Stage
left, a small staircase leading to the guest rooms, where the Count of Marialva
is lodged. A balcony stage right. At the rear a doorway with three stone steps
leading to the alley. On one of the tables lies a guitar.

– Júlio Dantas[1]

With these lines the scene is set for the first act of Júlio Dantas's 1901 play *A
Severa*, the story of the Lisbon *fadista* Maria Severa (1820–46) and her affair
with the slumming Count of Marialva.[2] The blurring of myth and history that is
illustrated in their story – framed in novels, songs, films and history books – serves
as an appropriate starting point for a study of Portuguese fado. The character of
Severa that Dantas presented – firstly as the heroine of a novel that made its
appearance just prior to its theatrical dramatization – was based on a real *fadista*
of the mid-nineteenth century, whose affair with a count (Vimiosa, not Marialva)
and whose tragic death passed into local and then national lore as the epitome
of fado and the *fadista*'s world. From this point on Severa became a recurring
figure in the cultural world of Lisbon, not least as the subject of numerous songs
(some preceding, some derived from or influenced by Dantas's play). The play
itself was performed on a number of occasions throughout the twentieth century,
with many notable actresses taking the part of Severa, including, in 1955, fado's
greatest star and one of the main subjects of this chapter, Amália Rodrigues.
A Severa was also adapted by the filmmaker Leitão de Barros in 1931 to become

---

[1] Júlio Dantas, *A Severa (Peça em Quatro Actos)*, 4th edn (Lisbon: Sociedade Editora
Portugal-Brasil, c. 1920), p. 9.

[2] The word *fadista* is used in a variety of ways in this book, as it is in fado discourse:
it is used to describe the mixture of 'roughs' (an analogy made by Pinto de Carvalho,
one of the first serious historians of fado, in 1903), criminals, prostitutes and aristocratic
libertines who made up the bohemian fado milieu of the nineteenth century; in a later set
of developments it comes to refer to performers and writers of fados, as well as to fans and
aficionados of the music. The inferred meaning will, I trust, be clear from the context.

the first Portuguese sound film.[3] The film, scored by Frederico de Freitas, produced a handful of songs which, through performances by Amália ('Rua do Capelão', 'O Timpanas', 'Novo Fado da Severa') and more recently by 'new fadistas' such as Dulce Pontes ('Novo Fado da Severa') and Lula Pena ('Rua do Capelão'), have served to keep the story of Severa alive.

The Dantas quotation above is also notable for the presence of a number of what we might call 'fado mythemes'.[4] I use this term to reflect the elements of fado stories – those expressed via acts of speech and song and via the written word (novel, play, lyric, history) – that, through constant repetition, come to represent, in however varied or mutated a fashion, a large part of the 'fado-ness' of fado (its ontology, as it were). I am not thinking here so much of the musical expression of fado, which comes from a particular set of instrumental and vocal styles; I will return to these aspects later. From the short scene-setting paragraph quoted we can already detect a number of such mythemes.

The Cheap Café

The reference to a bohemian space and its concomitant possibility of transgression is of vital importance when considering the character of Marialva and how and why he has come to be lodging here. For the other characters present, the café provides an obvious meeting place for urban and rural types to mix with each other in a relaxed environment and to come together in appreciation of various pleasures, not least fado music.

Mouraria

The Mouraria and Alfama districts of Lisbon are the clearest remnants of the Moorish occupation of the city, their maze-like alleyways and steep steps covering the hillsides below the Castelo de São Jorge. Known as the birthplace of fado, these areas have been associated with the genre ever since its emergence in the mid-nineteenth century. Rodney Gallop, writing in 1933, noted:

> [fado's] true home is Alfama and Mouraria, the poor quarters of the city, which flaunt their picturesque squalor on the slopes below St George's Castle. A walk through these steep, narrow streets on a moonlit night is likely to be rewarded

---

[3]   *Canção de Lisboa*, (dir. José Cottinelli Telmo, Portugal, 1933) was the first sound film made completely within Portugal; *A Severa* was produced partly in France. For a discussion of Telmo's film, which also featured fado prominently, see Lisa Shaw, 'A Canção de Lisboa / Song of Lisbon', in Alberto Mira (ed.), *The Cinema of Spain and Portugal* (London & New York: Wallflower Press, 2005), pp. 23–9.

[4]   I am taking the notion of the mytheme from the work of Claude Lévi-Strauss; see chapter 11 ('The Structural Study of Myth') of his *Structural Anthropology*, tr. Claire Jacobson & Brooke Grundfest Schoepf (New York: Basic Books, 1963), pp. 206–31.

with the sound of a guitar and the mournful cadences of the *triste canção do sul* [sad song of the south]. But to hold it surely in one's grasp it is best to go to one of the popular cafés such as the 'Luso' and the 'Victoria' where it is regularly performed by semi-professional *fadistas*.[5]

Gallop was writing shortly after the enforced professionalization of fado introduced by the government of António Salazar, a move that encouraged the development of venues such as *O Luso* that took fado away from its 'true home' and placed it in the more respectable bourgeois environs of the grand Avenida da Liberdade. This move was crucial in forming the split between (clandestine) amateur fado performance and its professional counterpart, with the latter becoming more or less delimited as a new song style (and therefore easier to 'hold ... surely in one's grasp'). At the same time this move away from the Mouraria area only enhanced the romantic mythology that has sprung up around the latter's 'picturesque squalor', a romanticization that would increase with the literal disappearance of much of the lower Mouraria through urban renovation projects undertaken by the Estado Novo, the name given to the 'New State' ushered in by Salazar in 1933.

The Popular Classes

This phrase is used here not to denote a distinct working class but to signal the plurality of 'low others', perhaps better understood as a lumpen proletariat, often found in romantic-mythical accounts of fado history. Fado's origins, as most writers on the subject have been keen to make clear, were very much bound up in the experiences of the popular classes centred in the city of Lisbon. Whether born into the Lisbon underclass or newly arrived from the countryside, from nearby coastal villages or from Portugal's colonial outposts, these people, living in the poor areas that had flourished in the shadow of the grandly designed post-earthquake city – the modern Lisbon conceived by the Marquês de Pombal in the eighteenth century[6] – came together to form the crucible from which fado would emerge. As a mytheme – a single feature which can signify without recourse to further reduction – one would be hard pushed to better the symbolic character of the street vendor, who features in so many descriptions of fado and Lisbon life through the nineteenth and twentieth centuries. A central mytheme – or, following Roland Barthes, 'biographeme' – of fado's greatest star, Amália Rodrigues, is

---

5   Rodney Gallop, 'The Fado: The Portuguese Song of Fate', *The Musical Quarterly*, 19/2 (1933): 199.

6   Lisbon suffered a catastrophic earthquake in 1755, which led to massive loss of life and the destruction of much of the city. Marquês de Pombal was the authoritarian chief minister tasked with rebuilding the city. He imposed on the downtown area a grid system such as that being adopted in the new cities of South America, making this a much more 'readable' part of the city than the neighbouring Mouraria and Alfama areas.

the image of her selling fruit on the streets of Lisbon in the years immediately preceding her discovery and subsequent fame.[7]

Marialvismo

This concept stems not from the fictionalized character of Dantas's work but from the eighteenth century Marquês de Marialva, author of a treatise on horsemanship. Marialva's son, a bullfighter whose death in the ring was famously avenged by the Marquês, was known, like Vimiosa, to frequent the bars and dark alleyways of the Mouraria district of Lisbon. *Marialvismo* became associated with a certain representation of masculinity that, as Miguel Vale de Almeida points out, was very much connected to processes of change within Portugal:

> Marialvismo is a cultural text that was very important in the transition from *ancien régime* to modernity in Portugal ...[It] establishes a close relationship between a vision of social hierarchy together with a vision of gender, providing a grid for understanding constructs of masculinity, emotions, social hierarchy and national identity. It is recurrently called upon in situations of crisis and change in the social organisation of those aspects. It is the only coherent text in Southern Portuguese culture tying them together, but it can also be seen as marginal, in the sense that it is put down by modern bourgeois discourses. Still, even modern bourgeois visions of nation, morals, emotions and gender, occasionally call upon Marialvismo (and the arenas where it occurs: *Fado*, Bullfighting, and the messianic discourse of *Sebastianismo*) as epytomes [*sic*] of national identity, as the link between the 'now' (a modern country in the European Union) and the 'always' ('Portugueseness').[8]

---

[7]   An obvious correlative mytheme is the figure of the prostitute, included in Dantas's opening stage directions and embodied in the figure of Maria Severa. The prostitute, while providing essential colour to the stories of fado's bohemian beginnings and its accompanying world of *fadistas*, has not survived as a significant association with fado, however. For more on the 'biographeme', see Chapter 3. The word makes its appearance in Roland Barthes, *Sade, Fourier, Loyola*, tr. Richard Miller (Baltimore: Johns Hopkins University Press, 1997 [1971]), p. 9.

[8]   Miguel Vale de Almeida, 'Marialvismo: A Portuguese Moral Discourse on Masculinity, Social Hierarchy and Nationhood in the Transition to Modernity' (1995), Série Antropologia, No. 184, Departamento de Antropologia, Universidade de Brasília, http://www.unb.br/ics/dan/Serie184empdf.pdf (2 December 2004), pp. 2–3. *Sebastianismo* refers to a belief that the slain King Sebastião, who fell at the battle of Alcácer-Quibir in 1578 and whose body was never recovered, will one day return to lead Portugal to glory. There are clear links here with the legend of King Arthur and other messiah-king discourses.

The Alleyway/Shadows

Alleyways in fado work, as in many modern narratives, as locations of urban secrecy. The roles of the dingy ill-lit bar and bustling public street become reversed at night-time – when so many of these stories take place – and the alleyway, plunged into shadows through its contrast with other sources of light, becomes a place of otherness. Also, like the 'dark end of the street' of Dan Penn and Chips Moman's classic soul song, the alleyway becomes a locus for transgression, for acting out a series of relationships not possible under the symbolic scriptural (daytime) law. Added to this are a whole set of tropes regarding light and dark, public and private, safety and danger, life and death. Shadows are regularly featured in fado discourse, as evidenced by the book *Fado: Vozes e Sombras* and the documentary *Fado: Ombre et Lumière*, as well as in fado iconography (see, for example, the cover photograph of David Cohen's book *Fado Português*).[9]

The Guitar

One of the most notable features of fado music is its use of the *guitarra portuguesa*, an aspect of the music that has tended to lead to a virtual synonymy between fado and *guitarra*. From this brief reference in Dantas's introduction we are left in little doubt that fado music has been, or is about to be, played. The imagery of the *guitarra* has proven irresistible to fadologists since the concretization of the style, and much space has been given over to the history of the instrument and its possible origins, leading to often explicitly ideological positions of ownership and appropriation. The *guitarra* is a central feature of José Malhoa's much-reproduced painting *O Fado*, which shows a man playing the instrument while a woman leans on a table gazing at him.[10] Many early paintings, prints and publicity photos featured women singers playing *guitarras*, as Severa was supposed to do, something that is not reflected in most modern fado practice, however, where women players are as unusual as female guitarists in flamenco.

---

9   Joaquim Pais de Brito (ed.), *Fado: Vozes e Sombras* (Milan/Lisbon: Electa/Museu Nacional de Etnologia, 1994), is a collection of essays accompanying an exhibition devoted to fado. *Fado: Ombre et Lumière*, dir. Yves Billon (France, 1989), is a French documentary on the Lisbon fado scene. *Fado Português: Songs from the Soul of Portugal*, by Donald Cohen (London: Wise Publications, 2003), is a collection of sheet music and lyrics to a number of well-known fados, accompanied by useful contextualizing essays.

10   Malhoa's painting was the inspiration, in its turn, for a fado recorded by Amália Rodrigues. José Galhardo's 'Fado Malhoa' describes the work as 'the most Portuguese of oil paintings' and the guitarist as 'a real local/a real Lisboan/a bohemian and a *fadista*'. In 1947, a short film was shot of Amália and the *guitarrista* Jaime Santos recreating Malhoa's scene. An extract from this 'promo video' can be seen in the documentary *The Art of Amália* (Bruno de Almeida, Portugal/USA, 2000).

Tudo Isto É Fado: Ontology

Another oft-quoted introduction to fado's ontology is a song made famous by Amália Rodrigues entitled 'Tudo Isto É Fado' [All of This Is Fado], in which the narrator initially claims not to know what fado is before going on to list a number of its features: 'defeated souls, lost nights, bizarre shadows in the Mouraria'. The list continues as it leads to the famous refrain:

Amor, ciúme	[Love, jealousy
Cinzas e lume	Ashes and fire
Dor e pecado	Sorrow and sin
Tudo isto existe	All of this exists
Tudo isto é triste	All of this is sad
Tudo isto é fado.[11]	All of this is fado.]

Sonically, the song provides as good an introduction as any to fado, opening with the distinctive tinkle of the *guitarra*, leading into the interplay between *guitarra* and *viola* (the Portuguese name for the Spanish guitar which is the other main accompanying instrument in fado) and providing an excellent example of Amália's art as, within the space of the first short verse, she displays her famous melisma ('perguntaste-me') and hovers majestically on the word 'fado'. The song, originally recorded by Rodrigues at Abbey Road in 1952, became one of those on which her reputation as the 'queen of fado' would rest.

Clearly, to elaborate on what fado 'is' will require further discussion of its musical features; I will return to these later after saying more about the interface of mythology and historiography that makes up fadology. For now, I wish to detail the account given so far by recourse to some more examples. The first comes from a book of poetry with the simple title *Fado*, produced by José Régio in 1941. Its most famous poem 'Fado Português' recounts the maritime myth of fado's origins, identifying the strong connection to the sea found in Portugal's history and the loneliness of the mariner in the midst of the watery expanse. 'Fado', we are told, 'was born ... In the breast of a sailor / Who, feeling sad, sang'.[12]

Régio's poem was, perhaps inevitably, set to music and became part of Amália's repertoire. The maritime myth is taken to arguably its greatest extreme in Maria Luísa Guerra's *Fado, Alma de um Povo* [Fado, Soul of a People], in which the music is presented as an 'existential cry' born of the loneliness of the

---

[11] 'Tudo Isto É Fado', lyric by Aníbal Nazaré, music by Fernando de Carvalho, recorded by Amália Rodrigues, *Tudo Isto É Fado: O Melhor de Amália Vol. II* (CD, EMI/ Valentim de Carvalho 724353007829, 2000).

[12] José Régio, *Fado* (Lisbon: Portugal Editora, 1969 [1941]), p. 35. A shortened and slightly reworded version of the poem was set to music by Alain Oulman and recorded by Amália Rodrigues, *Estranha Forma de Vida: O Melhor de Amália* (Valentim de Carvalho/ EMI 724383444229, 1995).

high seas.[13] One of the reasons for the popularity of the maritime origin of fado is the connection to Portugal's proud seafaring past and its significant colonial endeavours. While one searches in vain in narratives such as Guerra's for any proof that what we know now as fado really owes its existence to these sailors, the connection to the sea cannot be dismissed. Lisbon has been an important port for centuries and has been witness to the comings and goings of myriad cultures; most commentators agree that it is this mixing of cultural practices along the banks of the Tejo River that most likely gave birth to fado and that, contrary to the nationalist insistence on Portuguese purity, Brazilians and Africans most likely had some involvement in the process.

Whatever the shortcomings of descriptions which lean towards mythology, many are excellent at delineating the world of fado texts, the basis of fado poetics. One could do worse than consult the chapter titles of Mascarenhas Barreto's *Fado: Lyrical Origins and Poetic Motivation* to gain an insight into what fado is: *Saudade, Bullfighting, Places, Street Cries, Windows/Eyes/Kisses, Sailors, Jealousy, Guitarras,* and *Destiny* are among his principle topics.[14] Guerra, meanwhile, provides her own 'thematic profile' of fado: love, hate, shame, separation, hurt, sadness, despair, betrayal, destiny, disgrace, solitude, luck, travel, memory, anxiety, bitterness, fatalism, forgetting, politics, tears, hope, passion, happiness, the human condition, time, life, death, *saudade* and fado itself.[15] This seems an extensive list and one which might well be applied to other song genres. Certainly, as one works through it and through the ensuing pages that Guerra devotes to each of these themes, one wonders if there is anything that fado is not about; Guerra herself suggests that it represents a phenomenology of life.[16] Yet the list is also specific enough to give a fairly good demarcation of the world of fado songs. I would wish to add at least the following to it: an obsession with the city of Lisbon, which I will discuss further in the next chapter; a sense of witnessing, carrying and unburdening, connected to a number of the emotions listed above and explored further in Chapter 3; and the act of being a *fadista*. This latter is summed up in Artur Ribeiro's 'O Fado de Ser Fadista' [The Fado/Fate of Being a Fadista[17]],

---

13   Maria Luísa Guerra, *Fado: Alma de um Povo* (Lisbon: Imprensa Nacional-Casa da Moeda, 2003).

14   Mascarenhas Barreto, *Fado: Origens Líricas e Motivação Poética/Fado: Lyrical Origins and Poetic Motivation*, illus. José Pedro Sobreiro, parallel English text by George Dykes (Frankfurt am Main: TFM, 1994).

15   These words should be witnessed in their original language too: amor, ódio, ciúme, separação, dor, tristeza, despedida, traição, destino, desgraça, solidão, sorte, viagem, lembrança, ansiedade, amargura, fatalismo, esquecimento, política, lágrimas, esperança, paixão, felicidade, condição humana, tempo, vida, morte, saudade, fado. Guerra, *Fado*, pp. 130–31.

16   Ibid., p. 172.

17   'Fado', as well as referencing a musical genre, is also the Portuguese word for 'fate', allowing a potential double meaning in many songs that use the word.

in which fado is described as 'everything that happens / When we laugh or cry / When we recall or forget / When we hate or love'.[18] The question of whether fado was happy or sad was also addressed – poetically, if indecisively – by the great modernist poet Fernando Pessoa:

> All poetry – and song is an assisted poetry – reflects what the soul lacks. For this reason, the song of sad people is happy and the song of happy people is sad. Fado is neither happy nor sad. It is an episode of the interval … Fado is the weariness of the strong soul, the gaze of contempt that Portugal directs to the God in whom it believed and who abandoned it.[19]

The desire of the empirical historian to disentangle 'truth' from myth can be a difficult one to fulfil. In the words of Raphael Samuel, 'It is a fact familiar to all those, like field anthropologists or ethnologists, who have studied the storyteller's arts that myth and history are not mutually incompatible, but coexist as complementary and sometimes intersecting modes of representing the past.' Myths change with history, add new characters and mythemes, while 'historians, however wedded to empirical enquiry, will take on, without knowing it, the deep structures of mythic thought'. Whether tempted by 'lines of continuity', 'grand permanences of national life', or 'an unargued-for but pervasive teleology', we find ourselves falling prey to the traps laid out for us by mythology.[20] This chapter and those which follow proceed with these observations very much in mind.

While it is possible to find accounts of fado dating back to the eighteenth century, and while writers such as Guerra have been keen to highlight an archaeology of fado discourse stretching even further, the debates described here are generally sourced from a number of works that have appeared in the twentieth century.[21] In many ways, the fadology alluded to in this book can be said to have been born with the twentieth century for two important reasons. Firstly, the appearance of

---

[18] 'O Fado de Ser Fadista', lyric and music by Artur Ribeiro, recorded by Joana Amendoeira, *Joana Amendoeira* (Companhia Nacional de Música CNM103, 2003).

[19] Fernando Pessoa, *Notícias Ilustrado* (14 April 1929), cited in *Fado: Ombre et Lumière* (Billon).

[20] Raphael Samuel, *Island Stories: Unravelling Britain (Theatres of Memory, Volume II)*, ed. Alison Light, Sally Alexander & Gareth Stedman Jones (London & New York: Verso, 1998), p. 14.

[21] See José Pinto de Carvalho, *História do Fado* (Lisbon: Publicações Dom Quixote, 2003 [1903]); Alberto Pimentel, *A Triste Canção do Sul: Subsídios para a História do Fado* (Lisbon: Livraria Central de Gomes de Carvalho, n.d. [1904]); Avelino de Sousa, *O Fado e os Seus Censores* (Lisbon: self-published, 1912); Frederico de Freitas 'O Fado, Canção da Cidade de Lisboa: Suas Origens e Evolução', *Língua e Cultura*, 3/3 (1973): 325–37; António Osório, *A Mitologia Fadista* (Lisbon: Livros Horizonte, 1974); José Ramos Tinhorão, *Fado: Dança do Brasil, Cantar de Lisboa* (Lisbon: Caminho, 1994); Eduardo Sucena, *Lisboa, o Fado e os Fadistas*, 2nd edn (Lisbon: Vega, 2002); Rui Vieira Nery, *Para uma História do Fado* (Lisbon: Corda Seca & Público, 2004).

José Pinto de Carvalho's history of fado in 1903 serves as a major source for subsequent histories and thus casts a giant shadow across the historiography of the genre. Secondly, and more controversially, in considering fado as a durable musical genre from the perspective of the twenty-first century, I will be suggesting that fado, like so many musical genres we are now accustomed to, is an invention of the phonographic era. It is this era, and in particular its twentieth-century formulation, that has 'fixed' musical styles and genres like no other before it, even as it has allowed for seemingly endless new experimentation, cross-genre fusion and deconstruction.

The phonographic era has also made possible dissemination of the music to a much wider audience than ever before. While English-language descriptions of fado practice from the nineteenth century are invariably sourced from travel literature, and while twentieth-century folklorists and ethnomusicologists have continued to provide accounts from the field, it has nevertheless been possible for many to indulge in the virtual tourism of experiencing fado via its mediation in films and recordings, a point I will return to in subsequent chapters. This has created a desire for information about the music in languages other than Portuguese. A comprehensive fado history in English has yet to be completed, although Paul Vernon's *A History of the Portuguese Fado* goes part of the way towards achieving this goal. Vernon's work leans heavily on Rodney Gallop's analysis of fado from the 1930s and is somewhat lacking in translations of subsequent Portuguese scholarship. To find other work on fado in English, it has been necessary to seek out scholarly articles in music encyclopaedias and general accounts in world music guidebooks, magazines and websites, although this situation is starting to change.[22]

Establishing Portugueseness

The story of Severa and her importance in the mythology of fado has already been noted, as has the preponderance of fado mythemes. It is now worth considering the ways in which Portugueseness has been written into the history of fado. For if it is the case that the fado bibliography is one in which, as Joaquim Pais de Brito says, 'ideological discourse is the dominant key', then it is equally true that the nature of that discourse has more often than not centred itself on aspects of national identity.[23] Brito, in his introduction to the 1982 republication of Pinto de Carvalho's *História do Fado* (1903), divides the more notable studies into those which seek to draw a positive connection between fado and Portugueseness and those which attempt to distance the two. Of the former he includes Avelino de Sousa's *O Fado e os Seus Censores* (1912), an attempt to portray fado as an

---

22   Paul Vernon, *A History of the Portuguese Fado* (Aldershot: Ashgate, 1998).

23   Joaquim Pais do Brito, introduction to Pinto de Carvalho, *História do Fado* (Lisbon: Publicações Dom Quixote, 2003), p. 10.

authentically socialist music under threat from antidemocratic cultural elitists, and Álvaro Ribeiro's view of fado as 'a crystallization of the essence of the national soul', a view which is situated rather differently to de Sousa's.[24] For Ribeiro, the Herderesque notion of the musical expression of a national soul is predicated on the desire to preserve a purity in danger of being lost through foreign influence; for de Sousa, who was perhaps more familiar with the bohemian themes of fado songs, it was precisely the lack of refinement and purity in the music that made it the expression of the oppressed *par excellence*. Yet, whether the connection is made via an appeal to Romanticism or to Romantic Socialism, these writers are unequivocal in their claims for fado as a song worthy of the responsibility of representing Portugueseness.

One aspect of the focus on fado's connections to nation and nationality is the ongoing debate over the origins of the music. While many contemporary scholars such as Rui Vieira Nery seem more or less content with the conclusion reached by Rodney Gallop in 1933,[25] that fado is a reflection of the cultural interchange

Others saw fado as a negative reflection of the national character, both an unfortunate stain on the country's past and an unsuitable representation of its present. This response can be found in commentators of quite different political views. Luís Moita, broadcasting a series of lectures on national radio at the outset of the Salazar regime, spoke of fado as the 'song of the defeated' (a phrase which provided a title to the collected lectures, published in 1936 and dedicated to the fascist Mocidade Portuguesa [Portuguese Youth] movement). This concern over the suggestion of defeat reflected the attitude of the Estado Novo ideologues who were seeking at this time to arrest what was perceived as a process of decline emanating from the defeatism of *saudosismo*, the nostalgic view that Portugal's days of glory were gone, never to be recovered. From the other end of the political spectrum and nearly forty years after the publication of Moita's lectures, in the crucial revolutionary year of 1974, António Osório published *A Mitologia Fadista*, in which he lambasted fado and its followers for, once again, submitting to defeatism. For Osório, this defeatism was tied to the recent regime and was not suited to a newly democratic state where poverty should be eliminated rather than idealized and where women should be treated as equals and not as sexual objects. That fado could be seen as indicative of the previous regimes by both Moita and Osório says much about the changes imposed on the genre during the period of the Estado Novo, such as the decisions to professionalize the fado industry and monitor song content, steps which for many meant a drawing together of the ideological worlds of the Estado Novo and of fado, of which more will be said later. For now it is enough to note the distaste both Moita and Osório clearly felt for fado and their desire to downplay its importance in representing the nation as an ideal.

One aspect of the focus on fado's connections to nation and nationality is the ongoing debate over the origins of the music. While many contemporary scholars such as Rui Vieira Nery seem more or less content with the conclusion reached by Rodney Gallop in 1933,[25] that fado is a reflection of the cultural interchange

---

[24]   Brito in Carvalho, *História*, p. 11.
[25]   Gallop, 'The Fado'. This article, only very slightly revised, appeared three years later as a chapter in Gallop's *Portugal: A Book of Folk-Ways* (Cambridge University Press, 1961 [1936]).

inevitable in a port city such as Lisbon (a city, we should add, as crucial to the formation of a Black Atlantic as the Anglophone countries Paul Gilroy concentrates on in his work), there are still popular works of recent vintage that seek to essentialize certain national traces. Eduardo Sucena begins his 1992 book *Lisboa, o Fado e os Fadistas* with a summary of the most frequently suggested origins of fado. Of the suggestion made originally by Teófilo Braga (in 1885), that fado originated from Moorish influences, Sucena is dismissive, as was Gallop before him, for the reason that neither fado nor any plausible variant was to be found at an analogous time in areas subject to more prolonged Moorish occupation, such as the Algarve or Andalusia. Moving his focus to claims that fado traces its origins to Afro-Brazilian sources imported to Lisbon during the early nineteenth century – claims which are lent much credence in contemporary fadology – Sucena is equally unhappy. Yet, where his rebuttal of Arabic influence appeals to empiricism, such a process seems absent from his desire to disprove such tightly argued theses as José Ramos Tinhorão's *Fado: Dança do Brasil, Cantar de Lisboa* (1994), in which the latter author traces the initial musicological uses of the word 'fado' to Brazil. Tinhorão's work finds concurrence with Gallop's earlier conclusion and Vieira Nery's subsequent (2004) presentation of fado origins, which again points to the lack of sources using 'fado' in any other than its literal meaning ('fate') within Portugal prior to its Brazilian use. The 'Brazilian account' is that fado made its appearance in Lisbon with the return of the royal court from Brazil in 1821, following a period of exile in Rio de Janeiro dating from the Napoleonic invasion of 1807. At one point Sucena cites Frederico de Freitas's observation that, while fado may have been born in Brazil, it was 'legitimately Portuguese' by dint of having taken root in Portugal and having been accepted and assimilated into Portuguese culture. Sucena follows up with the claim that fado 'was always Portuguese, given that Brazil had not yet become independent' at the time of the court's return, a comment which seems to suggest that Portugal and Brazil were therefore culturally identical.[26]

Sucena veers even further from serious, historically-informed debate when contemplating the suggestion that African slaves might have contributed to the formation of fado, whether in Brazil or Portugal:

> However, if the relationship between fado and *cantos de São João* [popular songs performed during one of Portugal's Saints' days] fails to excite major objections, given that that relationship, in Rodney Gallop's words, was no more than a 'synthesis, shaped by centuries of slow evolution, of all the musical

---

[26] Sucena, *Lisboa*, p. 20. The de Freitas quotation that Sucena uses is: 'whether or not the fado was born in Brazil, it took root in the old country, just as the *modinha*, born in Portugal, took root in Brazil, and became by rights Brazilian. Is it not the case that what legitimizes, justifies and defines a popular creation is its adaptation to, acceptance by and identification with the character of a particular people? If so, fado is legitimately Portuguese.' Ibid., p. 19.

influences that affected the people of Lisbon', the same does not necessarily follow for the hypothesis that the 'languorous song' of the freed blacks of Alfama was the genesis of the fado. Those blacks, by the sheer fact of having been freed, ought to have been singing happy songs, and if they were singing such a 'languorous song', it must have been from a different root, for obvious culturally-defined reasons, i.e. due to their indolent nature and to the ancestral influences of their race.[27]

Quite apart from the rather confusing clash of culture and nature that we find here, what is clearly at stake in such narratives is how one wishes to imagine the nation – one's own and that of the other – and its cultural products. Mascarenhas Barreto, author of a number of fado lyrics and the voluminous *Fado: Origens Líricas e Motivação*, falls into a similar trap when he writes:

> It is not surprising that *Severa* and other gipsy singers became familiar in Portugal with the *Fado* of Moorish influence, just as they had made the acquaintance of bullfighting on foot. There is something atavistic in the blood which makes it easy for them to interpret this nostalgic song, and thieve and cheat though they may throughout those Christian lands, Iberian tolerance has allowed them to camp indefinitely ... because they dance and sing![28]

Related to the above debates is another strand that runs through the published work on fado, namely the relationship between fado and folk music. Rodney Gallop remarked on the 'resentment at the manner in which foreigners, and indeed many Portuguese, have accepted the *fado* as the only popular musical expression of the Portuguese nation', and it is no doubt from such resentment that many writers have sought to distance themselves from fado while promoting the lesser-known folk musics of the remainder of the country.[29] Notable among these was the composer and musicologist Fernando Lopes-Graça, who believed passionately in the value of Portuguese folk music and its need to be both archived as it existed and worked into the framework of a national art music. The politically committed Lopes-Graça – who had been involved with the Popular Front in France and the Republicans in Spain and was later imprisoned in Portugal by the Salazar regime – never made any secret of his distaste for fado, describing it as 'the cancer of the national culture'.[30] Another composer, Frederico de Freitas, was more tolerant of popular music, urban and rural, and composed in all genres, including scores for the films *A Severa* (1931) and *Fado, História D'uma Cantadeira* (1948), which starred Amália Rodrigues. This identification between fado and the cinema was no doubt another reason

---

[27]   Ibid., p. 16.

[28]   Barreto, *Fado*, p. 173.

[29]   Gallop, 'The Fado': 201.

[30]   Fernando Lopes-Graça, *Disto e Daquilo* (Lisbon: Cosmos, 1973), p. 150.

for the fear expressed by both Gallop and Lopes-Graça that mass culture would suffocate the more authentic culture of the rural regions. Such a view was, we should remember, being expressed elsewhere about other mass cultural forms in other cultural contexts at precisely the same time.

Fado, then, much like other popular or folk musics, has been subject to a rigorous battle of representation vis-à-vis its place as *the* national song, to the kind of debates on origins that tend to lead less careful commentators towards dangerous essentializations of nation and race, and to a familiar battle waged around the notion of authenticity under the inconstant banners of 'folk' and 'popular'. To say this is merely to situate the music within its most common set of discourses. In Chapter 2, I will return to questions of place but I will be moving away from the establishment of Portugueseness to focus on the mythology of fado as it relates to the city of Lisbon. While the fado of the university city of Coimbra has established itself as a quite distinct form and there is a strong need for further research into the role of fado in Porto (and vice versa), it is undoubtedly Lisbon fado that has proved the most dominant in terms of underscoring the debates alluded to above and in contributing to the key mythemes of fado throughout its history, from its early incarnation in the nineteenth century through its 'classic' period in the early decades of the twentieth century to its reinvention in the work of Amália Rodrigues and the more recent *fadistas* who have been influenced by that work. For now, I wish to move forward by assuming a common acceptance of fado in its contemporary incarnation as a music inextricably – though clearly not unproblematically – linked to Portugal (what Rui Vieira Nery calls 'a Portuguese way of looking at the world, at others and at ourselves'[31]).

Music

Now that I have sketched out the mythological world to which fado attaches, it will be necessary to give a brief overview of the musical style that had become established by the early part of the twentieth century, creating a 'tradition' into which the artists discussed in this book were born into. In doing so, I hope to highlight some of the changes and continuations these artists brought to their practice.

Instrumentally, as mentioned above, fado is distinguished by the *guitarra portuguesa*, a pear-shaped lute- or cittern-like instrument with twelve steel strings (tuned DDAABBEEAABB, from low to high, in the Lisbon style to which I will be mostly referring). The *guitarra* is played via a combination of strumming and plucking, using mostly the thumb and index finger, on which are worn *unhas* ('nails'). Although in the past the *guitarra* had provided only harmony, by the period covered in this book it had taken a more dominant role as provider of the

---

31 Rui Vieira Nery, liner notes to Katia Guerreiro, *Fado Maior* (Ocarina OCA 002, 2001).

melody in instrumental numbers or melodic counterpart to the voice in songs. The other constant accompaniment is provided by the *viola* (Spanish guitar), which provides harmony and rhythm predominantly but may occasionally lead. In addition, especially in contemporary practice, a *viola baixo* (acoustic bass guitar) is often added. Additional percussion is rarely used.

The fado singer, or *fadista*, tends to take the centre stage in a performance of gesture, phrasing and verbal improvisation that serves to heighten the drama of the lyric and lead the song to an appropriately momentous conclusion. Drama is often emphasized by alternating between registers and songs invariably close on a vocal climax that repeats the last part of the final verse or chorus and is punctuated by a two-chord full stop, or exclamation mark, from the guitars (generally, V–I). Lyrics are of vital importance in fado and, while some are improvised (especially in amateur settings), most are the work of fado lyricists who are not normally involved in the performing group. Adaptations of so-called 'erudite poetry' are common and mix with more down-to-earth variations of a range of lyrical themes such as those discussed above.

Stylistically, Lisbon fado can generally be divided into *fado castiço* ('authentic fado', also known as *fado fado*, *fado clássico* and *fado tradicional*) and *fado canção* ('song fado'). *Fado castiço* styles were concretized in the mid-to-late eighteenth century and include *fado corrido* ('running fado'), *fado mouraria* (named after the Lisbon district discussed earlier) and *fado menor* ('minor fado'), together with numerous variations of these three basic styles often named after particular guitarists and composers. Salwa Castelo-Branco provides a useful and concise description of the *castiço* styles:

> All three fados have fixed rhythmic and harmonic schemes (I–V) and a fixed accompaniment pattern consisting of a melodic motif that is constantly repeated, at times with slight variation. Using these patterns as a basis, the melody is either composed or improvised. Texts are usually set to one of the most common poetic structures, such as the quatrain or five-, six- and ten-verse stanzas. The accompaniment pattern, the I–V harmonic scheme and the regular 4/4 metre are the identifying elements of these fados and are basically fixed. All other elements are variable. *Fado corrido* and *mouraria*, in the major mode, are usually performed in a fast tempo and have similar accompaniment patterns. *Fado menor* is in the minor mode and is often performed in a slow tempo.[32]

---

[32]   Salwa El-Shawan Castelo-Branco, 'Fado', in L. Macy (ed.), *Grove Music Online*, http://www.grovemusic.com (1 June 2005). Three classic examples of the *castiço* styles that can be fairly easily sourced are : Lucília do Carmo, 'Maria Madalena' (*fado mouraria*); Carlos do Carmo, 'Por Morrer uma Andorinha' (*fado menor*); Maria Teresa de Noronha, 'Corrido em Cinco Estilos' (*fado corrido*).

Fado canção was a development of the late nineteenth century and evolved through theatrical *revistas* (shows). It is distinguished by a stanza-and-refrain song style and uses more complex harmonic structures. It is this style that came to be associated with Amália Rodrigues and those influenced by her, although both Amália and the 'new fadistas' continued to perform the more traditional styles.[33]

Saudade

One other quality which fado must possess, as all guidebooks will attest, is *saudade*. I wish to begin my investigation of this magical word with a curious fragment from September 1928, in which the Spanish poet Miguel de Unamuno nestles the word *saudade* among a selection of Spanish and Galician terms with which he wishes it to forge a poetic connection, before declaring: 'Lord, when will the day arrive?'; the question acts as a sort of translation for these supposed synonyms of yearning.[34] It was not the first time Unamuno had sought to find connections between Spanish and Portuguese terms of longing; a poem from earlier the same year, entitled 'Soidade + Saúde = Saudade', attempted a poetic etymology that made much of the relationship between the Portuguese words of the title and the Spanish words *soledad* (solitude) and *salud* (health). In doing so the poet was tapping into a debate that had long been underway in Portugal about the correspondence, or lack thereof, between *saudade* and words from other languages. Aniceto dos Reis Gonçalves Viana, writing a critique of Hugo Schuchardt's *Die Cantes Flamencos* in 1882, had the following to say on the relationship:

> The Spanish word *soledad* is given [by Schuchardt] as corresponding perfectly in its sense to the Portuguese *saudade* ... Looking at the soleá, the word *soledad* does not correspond to *saudade*, but rather to 'solitude', *solidão*.
>
> *Saudade* is nothing like this. *Saudade* is 'the sorrow of not having enjoyed that which was there to be enjoyed; it is the vehement but resigned desire to enjoy a thing we were deeply attached to; and also the yearning to see, or be in the company of, someone from whom we have reluctantly been parted'.[35]

Viana then goes on to liken *saudade* to the German *Sehnsucht*, the Icelandic *saknadr*, the Swedish *saknad* and the Danish *Savn*. As for an English equivalent, he can only settle for a phrase he finds in Fielding's *Tom Jones*: 'The remembrance

---

[33] Classic examples of *fado canção* include Alfredo Marceneiro's 'Há Festa na Mouraria' and Amália Rodrigues's 'Gaivota'.

[34] Miguel de Unamuno, untitled poem in *Escritos de Unamuno sobre Portugal*, ed. Ángel Marcos de Dios (Paris: Fundação Calouste Gulbenkian, 1985), p. 96.

[35] Quoted in Dalila L. Pereira da Costa & Pinharanda Gomes, *Introdução à Saudade: Antologia Teórica e Aproximação Crítica* (Porto, Lello & Irmão, 1976), p. 10.

of past pleasure affects us with a kind of *tender grief*, like what we suffer for departed friends; and the ideas of both may be said to haunt our imagination.'[36]

Aubrey Bell, writing some twenty years later, states that 'the word cannot be translated exactly, but corresponds to the Greek πόθος, Latin *desiderium*, Catalan *anyoranza*, Galician *morriña*, German *Sehnsucht*, Russian тоска (pron. *taská*). It is the "passion for which I can find no name"'.[37] Interestingly, Bell, like Viana before him, does not attempt a single English term for *saudade*, relying on a list of words in other languages and a quotation from George Gissing's *The Private Papers of Henry Ryecroft*.[38] The assumption by Bell seems to be that the foreign words are translatable amongst themselves (or are, at least, in 'correspondence' with each other) but not into English and that an allusion to a literary work about memory and meditation on loss is the nearest that we, as English speakers, might come to an understanding of *saudade*. A chain of references is set up through which a contemporary reader coming upon Bell's footnote of 1922 (probably via references to Bell in later works) is led to Gissing's fictional pastoralist Ryecroft and a whole set of methods of dealing with the past that in turn form a major defining aspect of modernity. Rodney Gallop provides us with yet more definitions:

> In a word *saudade* is yearning: yearning for something so indefinite as to be indefinable: an unrestrained indulgence in yearning. It is a blend of German *Sehnsucht*, French *nostalgie*, and something else besides. It couples the vague longing of the Celt for the unattainable with a Latin sense of reality which induces

---

[36]   Quoted in ibid., p. 11.

[37]   Aubrey F.G. Bell, *Portuguese Literature* (Oxford University Press, 1970), p. 135, fn. 1.

[38]   Actually a misquotation: the original reads 'a passion to which I can give no name'. The difference is immaterial yet it is worth remembering the original phrase within its context as it is most appropriate for a consideration of the relationship between loss and desire that *saudade* is supposed to evoke. The passage reads: 'I have been spending a week in Somerset. The right June weather put me in the mind for rambling, and my thoughts turned to the Severn Sea. I went to Glastonbury and Wells, and on to Cheddar, and so to the shore of the Channel at Clevedon, remembering my holiday of fifteen years ago, and too often losing myself in a contrast of the man I was then and what I am now. Beautiful beyond all words of description that nook of oldest England; but that I feared the moist and misty winter climate, I should have chosen some spot below the Mendips for my home and resting-place. Unspeakable the charm to my ear of those old names; exquisite the quiet of those little towns, lost amid tilth and pasture, untouched as yet by the fury of modern life, their ancient sanctuaries guarded, as it were, by noble trees and hedges overrun with flowers. In all England there is no sweeter and more varied prospect than that from the hill of the Holy Thorn at Glastonbury; in all England there is no lovelier musing place than the leafy walk beside the Palace Moat at Wells. As I think of the golden hours I spent there, a passion to which I can give no name takes hold upon me; my heart trembles with an indefinable ecstasy.' George Gissing, *The Private Papers of Henry Ryecroft* (London: Archibald Constable & Co., 1904), pp. 81–2.

realization that it is indeed unattainable, and with the resultant discouragement and resignation. All this is implied in the lilting measures of the *fado*, in its languid triplets and, as it were, drooping cadences.[39]

As these references increase, the need to negotiate a path through them – to find, perhaps, our own correspondence with the terms of reference – becomes ever more necessary; this is what Umberto Eco seems to drive at when he speaks of 'translation as negotiation'.[40] Svetlana Boym, for her part, likens *saudade* to the Czech *litost*, Russian *toska*, Polish *tesknota* and Romanian *dor*, and points out how each nation claims its term as untranslatable:

> While each term preserves the specific rhythms of the language, one is struck by the fact that all these untranslatable words are in fact synonyms; and all share the desire for untranslatability, the longing for uniqueness. While the details and flavors differ, the grammar of romantic nostalgias all over the world is quite similar. "I long therefore I am" became the romantic motto.[41]

One might well wonder given all this, especially after being informed that *saudade* is one of the essential ingredients of fado music, if there was a line of thought to be traversed whereby the 'untranslatability' of *saudade* would mean the impossibility of the conditions to describe an appreciation of fado by a non-Portuguese speaker (which would not necessarily entail going as far as to declare the impossibility of appreciating 'the music itself', though to do so would help to push at what we really mean by 'the music') – the logic being that, if fado must contain *saudade*, and *saudade* cannot be translated, then how do we translate, or negotiate, our appreciation of the music? Picking at this line of thought would inevitably lead us to further questions. Does, or can, *saudade* mean the same for all Portuguese (the implication, after all, in so many texts)?[42] Does it mean the same for other Portuguese speakers, for Brazilians, Angolans, Cape Verdeans? How might *saudade* be considered as another type of fencing-off? How, in the light of such reflections, do we understand loss and its expression as universal qualities?

---

[39] Gallop, 'The Fado': 211–2.

[40] See Umberto Eco, *Mouse or Rat?: Translation as Negotiation* (London: Weidenfield & Nicolson, 2003).

[41] Svetlana Boym, *The Future of Nostalgia* (New York: Basic Books, 2001)., p. 13.

[42] As for the association of *saudade* with Portuguese people *and* fado, Miguel Vale de Almeida notes 'the emic notion that the Portuguese are characterized by the sentiment of Saudade and that Fado is its artistic expression'. Vale de Almeida, 'Marialvismo', p. 12, fn.10.

Loss, Memory and Mourning

I wish to use this seeming clash between the local and the universal as the starting point for 'zooming out' of the world of fado and considering some of the debates and theories that inform my thinking about loss, memory and nostalgia. I intend to discuss these issues in a general way, by which I mean that I will not be focusing solely on fado but will be discussing theories that have arisen in other contexts. My justification for doing so is to give these ideas space to develop before applying them more rigorously to fado in later sections of the book. I wish to challenge the *doxa* that attempts to maintain the unique specificity of fado and Portuguese emotion, sentimentality, and so on, at the expense of allowing correspondence with other 'grammars of nostalgia'. While there *are* particularities that distinguish fado and Portuguese culture from other cultural forms, there are also qualities which it shares with them. It might be more accurate to suggest that fado presents a localized form of culturally widespread (which is not to say universal) cultural practices and represents a localized form of historically widespread events and situations. I will therefore be deliberately presenting my account of loss, memory and mourning with recourse to examples beyond the 'local knowledge' within which fadology so often dwells. I will, however, illustrate my discussion with examples drawn from Portuguese culture, to bring these elements into dialogue with each other. My first example is just such a hybrid and emanates from the Australian singer-songwriter Nick Cave. Addressing an audience in 1999 on the subject of 'the secret life of the love song', Cave made the following remarks:

> We all experience within us what the Portuguese call 'saudade', an inexplicable longing, an unnamed and enigmatic yearning of the soul, and it is this feeling that lives in the realms of imagination and inspiration, and is the breeding ground for the sad song, for the love song. Saudade is the desire to be transported from darkness into light, to be touched by the hand of that which is not of this world … [T]he love song is never simply happy. It must first embrace the potential for pain. Those songs that speak of love, without having within their lines an ache or a sigh, are not love songs at all, but rather hate songs disguised as love songs, and are not to be trusted. These songs deny us our human-ness and our God-given right to be sad, and the airwaves are littered with them. The love song must resonate with the whispers of sorrow and the echoes of grief. The writer who refuses to explore the darker reaches of the heart will never be able to write convincingly about the wonder, magic and joy of love, for just as goodness cannot be trusted unless it has breathed the same air as evil, so within the fabric of the love song, within its melody, its lyric, one must sense an acknowledgement of its capacity for suffering.[43]

---

[43] Nick Cave, 'The Secret Life of the Love Song', in *The Complete Lyrics 1978–2007* (London: Penguin, 2007), pp. 7–8.

Cave speaks also about *duende*, the Spanish word associated with the heightened emotional world of flamenco and bull-fighting. Cave quotes Federico García Lorca on the subject and claims that rock music, the field Cave operates in, generally lacks the qualities of *saudade* and *duende*: 'Excitement, often, anger, sometimes – but true sadness, rarely … [I]t would appear that the duende is too fragile to survive the compulsive modernity of the music industry.'[44]

My point here is not necessarily to invoke Cave as an expert on *saudade*, or to question the intricacies of a lack of distinction between *duende* and *saudade*. Rather, I wish to highlight the simultaneous locality and universality in this analysis of writing love songs. This tension is set up in the words 'we all have within us … saudade'; a universally recognizable feeling is presented via recourse to a very specific term from outside the language the speaker is using. This is, of course, a common rhetorical device and perhaps we should not take it for anything more than that. But I think it is provocative, especially coming in a discussion of the love song as something that must be happy and sad, partaking in a dialectic that is akin to the 'episode of the interval' that Pessoa used to define fado. Cave's love song seems to be precisely such an interval. It becomes even more provocative when one is asked to think of Nick Cave as a *fadista*. This is what had happened in 1994 when the controversial *novo fadista* Paulo Bragança recorded a version of Cave's song 'Sorrows Child' with the *guitarrista* Mário Pacheco. In an interview, Bragança maintained the validity of his choice: 'Throughout his life Nick Cave has been a *fadista* in the broadest sense of the word and the lyric of "Sorrow's Child" by itself is already a fado.'[45] Bragança and his 'transgressions' are more properly a subject for Chapter 4 and I will return to him there. For now, I hope I have started to show how a few associative steps can open the discourse out. This opening-out can also be found in Lorca's description of *duende*:

> This 'mysterious power that all may feel and no philosophy can explain,' is, in sum, the earth-force, the same *duende* that fired the heart of Nietzsche, who sought it in its external forms on the Rialto Bridge, or in the music of Bizet, without ever finding it, or understanding that the *duende* he pursued had rebounded from the mystery-minded Greeks to the Dancers of Cádiz or the gored, Dionysian cry of Silverio's *siguiriya*.[46]

This suggestion of a larger context in which to place *duende* is akin to both the 'longing for uniqueness' that Boym spoke of in when discussing the synonyms

---

44   Ibid., p. 8.

45   Paulo Bragança, interview with Catarina Portas, *Diário de Notícias* (30 July 1995), cited in Manuel Halpern, *O Futuro da Saudade: O Novo Fado e os Novos Fadistas* (Lisbon: Publicações Dom Quixote, 2004), p. 143. Bragança's version of Cave's 'Sorrows Child' can be found on *Amai* (Luaka Bop/Virgin 724384903725, 1996 [1994]).

46   Federico García Lorca, 'Play and Theory of the Duende', tr. Christopher Maurer, in *In Search of Duende* (New York: New Directions, 1998 [1955]), p. 49.

of yearning (all of the things Lorca mentions are unique, just as all grammars of nostalgia are) and a longing for negotiation. From here we can move on to consider that negotiation.

Loss

In historical studies a great deal of recent work has attempted to take account and make sense of the previous century. Much of this work has studied periods of great loss and trauma brought about by conflicts. History, trauma, loss and memory have arguably found their greatest focal point in the 'memory work' carried out around the Holocaust. Of more immediate influence in historiographical approaches to memory have been Pierre Nora's monumental work *Les Lieux de Mémoire* (1986–92), a collection of investigations into specific French 'memory places' (and the more general 'realm of memory') that paradoxically manages to be both highly selective and encyclopaedic; Raphael Samuel's two volumes entitled *Theatres of Memory* (1994 and 1998, the second volume published posthumously), accounts of the myths, memories and conservation culture of Britain; Andreas Huyssen's work, in particular *Twilight Memories* (1995) and *Present Pasts* (2003), both of which attend to the politics of remembering and forgetting in the late twentieth century and bring a historian's and a cultural critic's eye to issues relating to trauma, mourning and memorializing in post-war Germany, post-dictatorship Argentina and post-Twin Towers New York amongst other sites; and the continually engrossing and influential work of Michel de Certeau, which attempts to marry cultural theory, historiography, anthropology and a fascination with the causes and consequences of writing that links all of Certeau's profuse interests.[47]

Like Huyssen, a number of writers have dealt with the connections between urbanization, emigration, memory, loss and nostalgia: Christine Boyer's *The City of Collective Memory* (1994) deals with the consequences arising from the attempts by city planners and architects to entertain, discipline and instil memory in citizens; Svetlana Boym's *The Future of Nostalgia* (2001) offers a fascinating cultural history of that condition, a useful categorization of 'types' of nostalgia and a grounded study of the way 'nostalgia work' is carried out by Russian immigrants in the USA; Sylviane Agacinski's *Time Passing: Modernity and Nostalgia* (2000) provides a philosophical reflection on the obsession with memory and the necessity to forget and uses the figure of Walter Benjamin as an example of the urban walker, or stroller, who gets himself deliberately lost; Benjamin is also a point of reference for Rebecca Solnit, whose *A Field Guide to Getting Lost* (2005), like her earlier *Wanderlust* (2000), emphasizes the connections between loss and the situation of being lost.

In philosophy, Edward S. Casey's *Remembering: A Phenomenological Study* (a second edition of which was published in 2000) has been a useful resource both for thinking about the ways that memory denies some losses while straining

---

[47]   Details of these works and those that follow can be found in the Bibliography.

to retrieve others and for thinking about phenomenological method and the chronology of presentation and re-presentation. Casey also explores what he sees as the disappearance of memory in modern life and examines the connections between memory and place. With regard to the latter, his *Getting Back into Place: Toward a Renewed Understanding of the Place-World* (1993) has also been useful in highlighting the loss of place alongside that of memory. Paul Ricoeur's *Memory, History, Forgetting* (2004), as well as serving as a fitting monument to its late author, makes invaluable connections between these three subjects and offers readings of thinkers who have dealt with them, from the Greeks to the twentieth century.

A discussion of loss cannot very well ignore the work of Freud, fascinated as he was with memory, trauma, haunting and ways of dealing (or not) with the past. Yet if Freud was predominantly interested in the ways these issues played out in the individual psyche, a number of his contemporaries were equally fascinated by the capacity of humans to feel connected by collective losses, memories and nostalgias. Prominent amongst these were Freud's erstwhile colleague Carl Jung and Maurice Halbwachs, whose work on collective memory not only influenced the burgeoning discipline of sociology but also, more generally, stressed the importance of a collective imagination always influenced by the consciousness of its collectivity, a formulation that would be completed in the era of mass mediation by communications technology. In the century that Freud and Halbwachs helped inaugurate, a number of events have become attached to narratives of collective loss and memory.

How to begin to discuss all of this? We might start by recognizing the difficulties inherent in opening the floodgates of loss. Indeed, this is precisely how Michael Bywater begins his book *Lost Worlds*, pointing out that 'despite the obsession of our species with organizing, categorizing and making lists ... we have not managed to organize our thinking about loss. It still just ... happens.'[48] Accompanying this inevitability is a sense of infinitude – loss is never-ending: 'And the fact that the most difficult thing about writing on loss is knowing when to stop might also be the reason we have never managed to come up with a taxonomy of loss.'[49] Attempting to create any kind of definition of loss is always likely to result in both losing 'loss' itself and getting lost oneself. Indeed, one way into thinking about loss is to think about the related notion of *being* lost. Rebecca Solnit has explored the connections between loss, losing and getting lost in her *A Field Guide to Getting Lost*, and Sylviane Agacinski, to whom I will return below, has similarly explored the implications of allowing oneself to be lost. But it is also worth attending to various antonyms of loss: finding, regaining, recovering, recalling. For something to be lost is for it to not be (able to be) found. Bywater's first entry proper in his 'taxonomy' is, accordingly, derived from a very contemporary notion of not being

---

[48] Michael Bywater, *Lost Worlds: What Have We Lost and Where Did It Go?* (London: Granta, 2004), p. 3.

[49] Ibid., p. 4.

found: '404', the number shown when an internet browser attempts to open a page that no longer exists – '404. Page not found':

> For this most documented of ages, 404 is the Warhol number: the sign that your moment of fame (or at least of your existence's being made available to others outside your immediate circle) is over. You typed out your story, your thoughts … your tales of triumph or defeat, laboriously, perhaps. You scanned in your photographs. You checked your links. You worked out how the hell to get the stuff into … cyberspace. For a while, you were, if not known, knowable.
>
> Then something changed. Your account expired. You remarried, moved away, died; your Internet company went bust; a hyperlink broke; something. … So you became 404: Not found.[50]

This notion of loss coming about through an inability to make connections – to 'get through' – is arguably one of the defining metaphors of late modernity, as illustrated by so many of the absurd talking heads in the plays of Samuel Beckett. Beckett describes the setting of his short piece 'The Lost Ones' as: 'Abode where lost bodies roam each searching for its lost one. Vast enough for search to be in vain. Narrow enough for flight to be in vain.'[51] There is no escaping the search, in Beckett's formulation, but neither is there any hope for closure.

Yet, while these initial thoughts about the enormity of such an undertaking are invariably found in those who write about loss, these writers nevertheless, in true Sisyphean style, embark upon what the writer Jacques Roubard calls 'an endeavor of memory'.[52] The logs of these journeys through loss, not surprisingly, often consist of lists of lost objects. They may not necessarily be A–Z lists like Bywater's but the accumulated data result in a similarly elegiac, or 'litanistic', form. Roger Scruton's *England: An Elegy* (2000), for example, is a combination of memoir and litany of lost objects, of people and institutions one no longer finds but which were good identity-forming events for Scruton and, he would have us believe, the country. What is mostly mourned here, as in Peter Hitchens's *The Abolition of Britain* (1999), is a feeling of certainty in one's place and one's country's place. This is a factor present in numerous other cultural contexts, as evidenced by Lawrence Kritzman when he recognizes in the work undertaken by Pierre Nora 'the symptomology of a certain French *fin de siècle* melancholia'. Kritzman continues:

---

[50]   Ibid., p. 16.

[51]   Samuel Beckett, *Collected Shorter Prose 1945–1980* (London: John Calder, 1984), p. 159.

[52]   Jacques Roubard, *The Great Fire of London: A Story with Interpolations and Bifurcations*, tr. Dominic Di Bernardi (Elmwood Park, IL: Dalkey Archive Press, 1992 [1989]), p. 6.

for now, what remains of the idea of nationhood is engendered by a nostalgic reflection, articulated through the disjunctive remembrance of things past. In a way, one might argue that the quest for memory in the contemporary world is nothing more than an attempt to master the perceived loss of one's history.[53]

As we will see later in the distinction made by Svetlana Boym between 'restorative' and 'reflective' nostalgia and, to a certain extent, by Freud between mourning and melancholy, the ways of dealing with such lost objects can vary considerably.

Memory

If the impossibility of dealing with loss comprehensively has led to a sense of a 'task' to be achieved – as above, in my 'Sisyphean' metaphor and Roubard's 'endeavor' – then it is perhaps no surprise to find the term 'memory work' increasingly used in contemporary cultural theory. And if, as I have already suggested, one method of going about this work is to employ a ritualistic, or repetitive, process for 'listing' loss, then it is worthwhile beginning our account of remembering with an example of just such memory work, from what I am going to call the 'I remember' school of writers inspired by Joe Brainard's book of the same title. *I Remember* was first published in 1975 and consisted of a series of entries, all beginning with the words 'I remember', in which Brainard recollected moments from his past, some of them highly individual and others doubtless shared by an enormous number of his contemporaries. To take a typical trio of consecutive entries:

> I remember the first time I saw television. Lucille Ball was taking ballet lessons.
> I remember the day John Kennedy was shot.
> I remember that for my fifth birthday all I wanted was an off-one-shoulder black satin evening gown. I got it. And I wore it to my birthday party.[54]

The originality in Brainard's technique lies in the intermingling of personal and collective memories and in the recognition that the catalogue of human life as compiled by memory is made up equally of intense personal experiences, public events, fads, fashions and myths. Brainard's work shows how each person simultaneously carries within them official and unofficial histories, the contents of which are always at varying stages of being recalled or forgotten. The Kennedy assassination, for example, is an event unlikely to be forgotten in either official history or the unofficial history of a certain group of people alive at a particular time and in at least some level of connection via mass media with the rest of the

---

53   Lawrence D. Kritzman, 'Foreword: In Remembrance of Things French', in Pierre Nora (dir.), *Realms of Memory: Rethinking the French Past Vol. 1: Conflicts and Divisions*, ed. Lawrence D. Kritzman, tr. Arthur Goldhammer (New York: Columbia University Press, 1996), p. xiii.

54   Joe Brainard, *I Remember* (New York: Granary Books, 2001 [1975]), p. 9.

world (Brainard's generation, in other words). Indeed, for such a group, whose hegemony over these matters is only recently beginning to wane, this event has become *the* classic example of such individualized-yet-shared memory, with people being said to know exactly where they were when they heard the news of the president's murder. In the new millennium this event has been succeeded for many by the events of 11 September 2001. Yet if these events are subject to both official and unofficial memory, highly personal recollections such as those collated by Brainard still have within them a quality that is transferable to others who have experienced something comparable or who can connect to them simply through the fact that *they too have remembered (things)*. Indeed it might well be said that it is in the highly personal, idiosyncratic details (Brainard's evening gown) that the possibility for a universal recognition resides.

That is not to say, however, that such memory work is necessarily translatable to other cultural contexts. Although Brainard's book was translated into French by Marie Chaix, the French 'version' of *I Remember* which found most success and which has itself come to be regarded as a classic of the genre, is Georges Perec's *Je me souviens* (1978).[55] Perec reduces the autobiographical elements of Brainard's work to a certain extent, although these are still a prominent feature of his version alongside a higher proportion of memories likely to be shared with others. In producing a more pronounced cultural bias to the book, Perec is forced away from literal translation and towards the creation of a new work steeped in the resonance of the French imaginary. Perec's intention was to seek out, via his own recollection, moments of memory that could be 'deconsecrated' and returned to their 'collectivity'; speaking about the book he claimed, 'what came out most clearly for me was that I wasn't the only one to be remembering. It's a book I might call "sympathetic", I mean that it's in sympathy with its readers, that readers are perfectly at home in it.'[56] The fact that Perec's work increased the ratio of culturally shared to personal memories from Brainard's original was recognized in 1986 by the British writer Gilbert Adair when he decided to publish his own version of the 'I remember' template in his book *Myths and Memories*. The book was devised partly as a homage to two French writers he admired, Roland Barthes and Georges Perec, and partly as an attempt to apply the techniques of Barthes's *Mythologies* and Perec's *Je me souviens* to a British context. In Adair's opinion, Perec's version of Brainard's work was distinct enough to warrant its own 'translation' but a literal rendering of the French words would be pointless: 'the fact of its being anchored in a French experience has rendered [*Je me souviens*] definitively untranslatable; or, rather, translatable only by way of the metamorphosis, the kind

---

[55]   Georges Perec, *Je me souviens* (Paris: Hachette, 1978).
[56]   Georges Perec, *Species of Spaces and Other Pieces*, ed. & tr. John Sturrock, rev. edn (London: Penguin, 1999), p. 128.

of total Anglicizing, which it undergoes here.'[57] This observation has an obvious correlation with the earlier discussion of *saudade*.[58]

Adair's conflation of the work of Barthes and Perec serves as an intriguing invitation to think about the concept of mythology alongside that of memory. This has been a strategy taken up by a number of historians in recent years, especially those concerned with memory's associations with place. Prominent amongst these have been Raphael Samuel, whose thoughts on the tangled nature of myth and history I have already alluded to, and Pierre Nora, whose work on 'memory places' has also influenced my thoughts about fado. Samuel's 'theatres of memory' and Nora's *lieux de mémoire* are both influenced by the work of Frances Yates, whose exploration of 'the art of memory' relies crucially on notions of myth and place, yet there is an equally important role played by repetition – indeed, memory thought of as an art is born of the desire to be able to repeat. In this sense, it is interesting to note a connection between these historians and the work of the 'memorians' of the 'I remember' school. In the latter we find a recourse to a ritualistic process (anamnesis, recollection) grounded in the repeated act; this repetition is continued in the representation of memory as these writers follow the unchanging mantra of 'I remember...'. This is a device often used in popular songs, where memories are listed over various verses. Fado is no exception, containing a number of such songs. Katia Guerreiro's 'Romper Madrugadas', for example, provides a verse form built upon lines that begin with the word 'recordo' [I remember]:

> Recordo os segredos das noites da bruma   [I remember the secrets of the nights of mist
>
> Recordo os teus dedos bebidos de espuma   I remember your fingers dipped in foam
> Recordo o teu cheiro de amor perfumado[59]   I remember your smell of fragrant love].

From an earlier point in the twentieth century, we might look to Alfredo Marceneiro's 'Lembro-Me de Ti', each verse of which begins with the line 'I remember you' and carries with it another memory.[60] With seven verses and a running time of nearly six minutes the overall effect is one of extended ritual punctuated and regulated by the highly emotional lilt given to the title line by Marceneiro. Indeed the song is straining with emotion, Marceneiro's voice sounding as though it might break

---

[57] Gilbert Adair, *Myths and Memories* (London: Fontana, 1986), pp. xv–xvi.

[58] As for a Portuguese-language version of *I Remember*, the closest parallel would appear to be a Brazilian text entitled *Memorando*, by Geraldo Mayrink and Fernando Moreira Salles (Sao Paulo: Companhia das Letras, 1993). I have not been able to consult this text to see how it compares with the three versions discussed here.

[59] 'Romper Madrugadas', lyric by Paulo Valentim, music by Paulo Valentim & João Veiga, recorded by Katia Guerreiro, *Nas Mãos do Fado* (Ocarina OCA 007, 2003).

[60] 'Lembro-Me de Ti', lyric by João Linhares Barbosa, music by Alfredo Duarte, recorded by Alfredo Duarte ('Marceneiro'), *The Fabulous Marceneiro* (Valentim de Carvalho/EMI 724349526624, 1997 [1961]).

under the force of the memory and giving the song an emphatically nostalgic air. These seem to be the 'drooping cadences' that Rodney Gallop described.[61]

The notion of memory as ritual (and vice versa) is one I return to in Chapter 4 in a discussion of Mísia's album *Ritual*. The ritualized recitation of memory can also be found to account for irrevocable loss. Amália Rodrigues provides an excellent example in her self-written fado 'Gostava de Ser Quem Era':

Tinha uma louca esperança	[I had a crazy hope
Tinha fé no meu destino	Had faith in my destiny
Tinha sonhos de criança	Had childhood dreams
Tinha um mundo pequenino	Had a tiny world
Tinha toda a minha rua	I had all my street
Tinha as outras raparigas	Had the other girls
Tinha estrelas tinha a lua	Had stars had the moon
Tinha rodas de cantigas	Had song wheels [children's game]
Gostava de ser quem era	I would like to be who I used to be
Pois quando eu era menina	Because when I was a little girl
Tinha toda a Primavera	I had the entire Spring
Só numa flor pequenina[62]	Within just a tiny flower]

The 'tinha' ('I had') that begins each line of the first three verses of the song (the first is not quoted above) and that is multiplied in Amália's performance by the repetition of the last two lines of each verse, produces a litanistic quality that hints, even though it is not stated explicitly, that these things have been lost forever. The final verse seals this assumption with the confession that the singer used to like being who she was, with the concomitant suggestion that she no longer does.

The potential infinitude of memory work suggests that there is little that is not worth remembering. Noting the 'acceleration of history', Pierre Nora writes, 'Everything is historical, everything is worth remembering, and everything belongs to our memory.'[63] Accompanying history's acceleration we find an acceleration of chroniclers and rememberers, both amateur and professional, a

---

[61]   This is true for virtually all of Marceneiro's recorded performances. As the liner notes to *The Fabulous Marceneiro* boldly claim, with some justification: 'Here is ... his husky voice, plaintive to the point of near-disintegration, singing fados, tilting melodies that intoxicate like wine.'

[62]   'Gostava de Ser Quem Era', lyric by Amália Rodrigues, music by Carlos Gonçalves, recorded by Amália, *Gostava de Ser Quem Era* (Valentim de Carvalho/EMI 724383546527, 1995 [1980]).

[63]   Pierre Nora, 'General Introduction' (tr. Richard C. Holbrook), in *Rethinking France: Les Lieux de Mémoire*, tr. Mary Trouille (Chicago & London: The University of Chicago Press, 2001), p. xviii.

process that has been immeasurably widened by the invention and development of the internet. To take a couple of recent web-based developments in the growing ubiquity of chronicling and remembering, there has been an explosion in the amount of 'encyclopaedic' information available (most notable in the phenomenon of Wikipedia) and of personal archives (weblogs, or 'blogs'), many of which contain both autobiographical information and theoretical explication or discussion of wider issues. It was perhaps inevitable that the project initiated by Brainard and developed by Perec and Adair would find its modus operandi continued via the medium of the internet with 'I remember' blogs.[64]

But, as with endless loss, if we follow the logic of 'everything is worth remembering' to its extreme, we quickly realize the impossibility of such an undertaking. Hence, Jorge Luis Borges's hapless character 'Funes the Memorious', unable to forget the detail of anything he has perceived. Forgetting, as Borges reminds us, is essential to our ability to function in other spheres: 'With no effort, [Funes] had learned English, French, Portuguese and Latin. I suspect, however, that he was not very capable of thought. To think is to forget differences, generalize, make abstractions. In the teeming world of Funes, there were only details, almost immediate in their presence.'[65] And it is not only the potential for mental overload that too much remembering can bring; there is also the connected danger of being haunted or trapped by the past, as in much of Amália's work. Andreas Huyssen provides a critique of what he sees as the conservative aspects of memory obsession. He points out that the obsession with discourses of loss does no justice to the 'politics of memory'. In the introduction to *Present Pasts* he writes, 'At stake in the current history/memory debate is not only a disturbance of our notions of the past, but a fundamental crisis in our imagination of alternative futures.'[66] Huyssen recalls Nietzsche's call for 'creative forgetting' in the latter's *Untimely Meditations*, a text also discussed by Paul Ricoeur and Sylviane Agacinski. As Agacinski points out, Nietzsche and Freud are unusual in that 'they taught the value of oblivion', Freud in his insistence on working-through and Nietzsche with his creative forgetting: 'Life has always needed forgetfulness more than memory and even the desire for commemorative monuments satisfies the desire to entrust memory to material reminders – to better free us from the past.'[67]

64   See, for example, the following: *I remember/je me souviens*, http://i_remember. blogspot.com (28 May 2007); *I remember*, http://iremember.adetskas.net/ (28 May 2007); *I Remember*, http://www.writenet.org/iremember/iremembers/index.html (28 May 2007).

65   Jorge Luis Borges, 'Funes the Memorious' (tr. James E. Irby), in *Labyrinths*, ed. Donald A. Yates & James E. Irby (Penguin: Harmondsworth, 1985 [1964]), p. 94.

66   Andreas Huyssen, *Present Pasts: Urban Palimpsests and the Politics of Memory* (Stanford: Stanford University Press, 2003), p. 2.

67   Sylviane Agacinski, *Time Passing: Modernity and Nostalgia*, tr. Jody Gladding (New York: Columbia University Press, 2003 [2000]), p. 14. For Ricoeur's discussion of Freud and Nietzsche, see *Memory, History, Forgetting*, tr. Kathleen Blamey & David Pellauer (Chicago & London: University of Chicago Press, 2004), pp. 69–74, 287–92.

While it is necessary to recognize these points, they do not make the obsession with memory and loss disappear; in this sense, at least, loss cannot be lost, for forgetting, like remembering, is only ever partial (making it both partial and endless). This is what brings about haunting, the spectral permanence of the past in the present. Although the various thinkers I have mentioned have different notions of the politics of memory, they all share an obsession with remembering and all, we might add, have strong ideas about what *they* want memory work to be.

Yearning is a process that relies on the notion of *some* form of community in that it derives from prior experience. As Christine Boyer notes, drawing on the work of Maurice Halbwachs, 'memories [are] recalled by time periods, by recollecting places visited and by situating ideas or images in patterns of thought belonging to specific social groups'.[68] It follows from this that memory is always social. In Halbwachs's words, 'the individual remembers by placing himself in the perspective of the group, but one may also affirm that the memory of the group realizes and manifests itself in individual memories.' Furthermore:

> the collective frameworks of memory are not constructed after the fact by the combination of individual recollections; nor are they empty forms where recollections coming from elsewhere would insert themselves. Collective frameworks are, to the contrary, precisely the instruments used by the collective memory to reconstruct an image of the past which is in accord, in each epoch, with the predominant thoughts of the society.[69]

However, for Pierre Nora, whose work draws on Halbwachs, it is no longer clear that the collective memory knows what to do with itself. It may not even recognize its own existence:

> Things tumble with increasing rapidity into an irretrievable past. They vanish from sight, or so it is generally believed. The equilibrium between the present and the past is disrupted. What was left of experience, still lived in the warmth of tradition, in the silence of custom, in the repetition of the ancestral, has been swept away by a surge of deeply historical sensibility. Our consciousness is shaped by a sense that everything is over and done with, that something long since begun is now complete. Memory is constantly on our lips because it no longer exists.[70]

---

[68]   M. Christine Boyer, *The City of Collective Memory: Its Historical Legacy and Architectural Entertainments* (Cambridge, MA, & London: The MIT Press, 1996 [1994]), p. 26.

[69]   Maurice Halbwachs, *On Collective Memory*, ed. & tr. Lewis A. Coser (Chicago & London: The University of Chicago Press, 1992), p. 40.

[70]   Pierre Nora, 'General Introduction: Between Memory and History', in *Realms of Memory Vol. 1*, p. 1.

Because there are no longer *milieux de mémoire*, defined as 'settings in which memory is a real part of everyday experience', there has arisen a need for *lieux de mémoire*, 'sites ... in which a residual sense of continuity remains'.[71] As for the relationship between memory, often associated with individuals despite the work of Halbwachs and others, and the collective autobiography that goes by the name of 'history', Nora sees clear differences: 'Memory ... thrives on vague, telescoping reminiscences, on hazy general impressions or specific symbolic details. It is vulnerable to transferences, screen memories, censorings, and projections of all kinds.' History, on the other hand, 'calls for analysis and critical discourse'. In short, 'memory is an absolute, while history is always relative'. Due to its relativity, and of the multitude of ways of telling its stories, history requires its own history, bringing about the practice of historiography, which 'begins when history sets itself the task of uncovering that in itself which is not history, of showing itself to be the victim of memory and seeking to free itself from memory's grip'.[72] For Nora, there has been a renunciation of ritual, leading to an ignorance around what to make of the ever-increasing archives that have taken the place of memory: 'Museums, archives, cemeteries, collections, festivals, anniversaries, treaties, depositions, monuments, sanctuaries, private associations – these are relics of another era, illusions of eternity. That is what makes these pious undertakings seem like exercises in nostalgia, sad and lifeless.'[73]

Nora imagines a society so obsessed with the present that it spent all its time recording itself while postponing any self-analysis. He claims this is not the case with our society, which has become obsessed instead with history. But Agacinski offers a point of view more closely allied to the situation Nora denies. While agreeing that responsibility for remembering is handed over to the archive she claims that we *are* more interested in recording than analysing. Indeed the act of recording has become a part of the experience of the present – any significant present moment cannot go unrecorded. But, once recorded, it is seldom looked back on. For his part, Andreas Huyssen distinguishes memory from the archive precisely by the former's location in the present; 'it is this tenuous fissure between past and present that constitutes memory, making it powerfully alive and distinct from the archive or any other mere system of storage and retrieval.'[74]

Mourning

At this stage it is worth saying something about mourning, the standard account of which remains, for many, Freud's 'Mourning and Melancholia' (1917). The concept of loss that I sketched out above could well have come from Freud's essay,

---

[71] Ibid., p. 1.

[72] Ibid., pp. 3–4.

[73] Ibid., pp. 6–7.

[74] Andreas Huyssen, *Twilight Memories: Marking Time in a Culture of Amnesia* (New York & London: Routledge, 1995), p. 3.

for he immediately makes clear that mourning, as well as being associated with 'the loss of a loved person' can also be a reaction to 'the loss of some abstraction ... such as one's country, liberty, an ideal, and so on.'[75] As with the notion of memory work or 'endeavour' discussed above, Freud speaks of mourning as a kind of work. This work involves, of course, the painful coming to terms with the loss one has suffered, a process which can be seen as a working towards normality and away from inhibition: 'when the work of mourning is completed the ego becomes free and uninhibited again.'[76] Melancholia differs from mourning in that, while it too arises as a reaction to a loss, it is a 'loss of a more ideal kind'. Death may not be involved; it may be the loss of an 'object of love'. It may be that 'one cannot see clearly what it is that has been lost', or it is possible that 'the subject knows *whom* he has lost but not *what* he has lost in him', making the recovery process lengthier and more incomprehensible. There *is* work going on in the melancholic, Freud suggests, but the reason for the melancholia is unseen and therefore this 'work' remains puzzling. In a neat formula, Freud writes: 'In mourning it is the world which has become poor and empty; in melancholia it is the ego itself.'[77]

In a discussion of Freud's essay, Paul Ricoeur highlights this point of melancholy as work by comparing the essay to one Freud had published three years earlier, 'Remembering, Repeating, and Working-Through' (1914).[78] The main thrust of that essay had been the difference between remembering (*Erinnern*) and repeating (*Wiederholen*) and the notion of 'work' undertaken by both the analyst and the analysand in order to defeat the illness caused by repression. As Ricoeur puts it, 'Belonging to this work are both the patience of the analyst with respect to the repetition channeled by the transference and the courage required on the part of the analysand to recognize himself as ill, in search of a truthful relation to his past.'[79] Remembering, in this formulation, is a healthy, if sometimes painful, process (work, *Erinnerungsarbeit*), while repeating is a handing-over of remembering to an act of unhealthy compulsion. Ricoeur then bases his comparison of mourning/melancholia and remembering/repeating on this notion of healthy/unhealthy:

> If the work of melancholia occupies a strategic position in ['Mourning and Melancholia'] parallel to that occupied by the compulsion to repeat in ['Remembering, Repeating, and Working Through'], this suggests that it is as a work of remembering that the work of mourning proves to be liberating, although

[75] Sigmund Freud, 'Mourning and Melancholia', in *The Standard Edition of the Complete Psychological Works of Sigmund Freud*, Vol. 14, tr. & ed. James Strachey (London: The Hogarth Press, 1957), p. 243.

[76] Ibid., p. 245.

[77] Ibid., pp. 245, 246.

[78] Sigmund Freud, 'Remembering, Repeating and Working-Through', *The Standard Edition of the Complete Psychological Works of Sigmund Freud*, Vol. 12, tr. & ed. James Strachey (London: The Hogarth Press, 1958), pp. 145–56.

[79] Ricoeur, *Memory, History, Forgetting*, p. 71.

at a certain cost, and that this relation is reciprocal. The work of mourning is the cost of the work of remembering, but the work of remembering is the benefit of the work of mourning.[80]

It still remains to note what the 'work of mourning' might entail for our purposes. Two processes, at least, seem to be of importance to this project: firstly, what Jacques Derrida calls 'the ontologizing of remains', the process whereby some fixity is put on the loss of the object by attempting to fix a place for the object itself; and secondly, what is generally referred to after Freud as 'sublimation', here understood as a process by which investment in a lost object is converted into investment in creative acts. I will stay with the first of these processes briefly by quoting from Derrida's late work *Specters of Marx*:

> Mourning ... consists always in attempting to ontologize remains, to make them present, in the first place by *identifying* the bodily remains and by *localizing* the dead ... One has to know ... Now, to know is to know *who* and *where*, to know whose body it really is and what place it occupies – for it must stay in its place. In a safe place. Hamlet does not ask merely to whom the skull belonged ... He demands to know to whom the grave belongs ('Whose grave's this, sir?'). ... Nothing could be worse, for the work of mourning, than confusion or doubt: one *has to know* who is buried where – and *it is necessary* (to know – to make certain) that, in what remains of him, *he remains there*. Let him stay there and move no more![81]

We can see in Derrida's words, as we would expect, a continuation of Freud's definition of mourning as 'work' and we can remember that Freud contrasted the mourner and the melancholic by the former's knowledge of what was being mourned. In order to help that work, as Derrida points out, the knowledge that a specific object is fixed in a known and delineated place is vital. The idea of 'fixing' is taken up by Mark C. Taylor in his and Christian Lammerts's book *Grave Matters*, a pictorial account of graves of famous artists, writers and philosophers. Reading Taylor's accompanying essay we are reminded of the necessity to fix lives via writing and reciting (biographies, epitaphs, funeral services) and to fix bodies via some form of 'burial' (which may or may not include the placing of a body in the ground). Taylor traces the history of 'the privatization of the grave and individualization of death' that developed in nineteenth-century Europe and that marked (quite literally) a change in attitude from an earlier period of anonymous

---

[80] Ibid., p. 72.

[81] Jacques Derrida, *Specters of Marx: The State of the Debt, the Work of Mourning, and the New International*, tr. Peggy Kamuf (New York and London: Routledge, 1994), p. 9 (emphasis in original).

mass burial.[82] Taylor contrasts this process of individualization with his reflections on the seeming return to anonymity brought about by mass urbanization:

> What will happen to the eight million people in New York City when they die? Will they be cremated and their ashes scattered? Will they be buried and, if so, where? The cemeteries, which once were on the outskirts of the city, are, like the landfills, full. Where do remains now remain? Does it matter any longer?[83]

The second process I referred to above was that of sublimation and I would like to begin to think about its relevance to the current project by returning briefly to Georges Perec. In an issue of *Yale Language Studies* devoted to remembering Perec, Warren Motte presents the writer's oeuvre as a prolonged work of mourning. Via a reading of Freud's 'Mourning and Melancholia', Motte brings together the notions of remembering, repeating and working, reminding us of the ways writing itself is a process of 'working through', something that Perec was well aware of and foregrounded in his work. As Motte notes, Perec undertook analysis for significant periods with prominent French analysts and was well aware of the benefits of channelling and transferring anxieties. In his book *W, or, The Memory of Childhood* (1975), Perec writes, 'My mother has no grave', a line that brings us back to the point made above by Derrida. Perec lost both parents during the Second World War, his father to complications arising from shrapnel wounds and his mother to one of the Nazi camps, probably Auschwitz. It is both the ignorance over his mother's fate and the knowledge that, even were there records, she had escaped any kind of familial burial, that prompts both the line quoted and the book as a whole; as Motte suggests one of the projects of *W* is to provide the space denied Perec's mother in death.[84]

This notion of the use of art to provide a place for loved and lost objects and people via forms of representative framing, staging or fencing-off is one that I will pursue throughout this book. Here I will restrict myself to noting some observations made by Julia Kristeva which seem to apply to this form of sublimation, if such it is. In *Black Sun*, Kristeva discusses how loss and bereavement act as motors to the work of imagination and feed creative responses:

> Naming suffering, exalting it, dissecting it into its smallest components – that is doubtless a way to curb mourning. To revel in it at times, but also to go beyond it, moving on to another form, not so scorching, more perfunctory ... Nevertheless, art seems to point to a few devices that bypass complacency and, without

---

[82]   Mark C. Taylor & Dietrich Christian Lammerts, *Grave Matters* (London: Reaktion Books, 2002), p. 17.

[83]   Ibid., p. 19.

[84]   Warren Motte, 'The Work of Mourning', *Yale French Studies*, No. 105, Pereckonings: Reading Georges Perec (2004), pp. 56–71.

simply turning mourning into mania, secure for the artist and the connoisseur a sublimatory hold over the lost Thing.[85]

The 'Thing' posited by Kristeva is 'the real that does not lend itself to signification', meaning that the work of art, as a form of signification, can only ever be a working-towards any 'hold' over the Thing. She continues: 'Messengers of Thanatos, melancholy people are witnesses/accomplices of the signifier's flimsiness, the living being's precariousness.'[86] This notion of precariousness is one touched upon by Freud in his brief essay 'On Transience' (1916), where he describes taking a walk in the countryside 'in the company of a taciturn friend and of a young but already famous poet.' The latter is dejected because of his awareness of the transient beauty of the nature surrounding them. Freud notes:

> The proneness to decay of all that is beautiful and perfect can, as we know, give rise to two different impulses in the mind. The one leads to the aching despondency felt by the young poet, while the other leads to rebellion against the fact asserted. No! It is impossible that all this loveliness of Nature and Art, of the world of our sensations and of the world outside, will really fade away into nothing. It would be too senseless and too presumptuous to believe it. Somehow or other this loveliness must be able to persist and to escape all the powers of destruction.[87]

Freud attempts to dissuade the poet and the 'taciturn friend' from their pessimism by suggesting that there is an increase rather than a loss in the worth of things precisely because of their transience: 'Transience value is scarcity value in time. Limitation in the possibility of an enjoyment raises the value of enjoyment.' He also points out that nature, when measured against the length of a human life, is eternal even though the seasons wreak temporary changes. As his companions fail to see his version of events, Freud surmises that they were experiencing 'a foretaste of mourning', the pain of which has 'interfered' with 'their enjoyment of beauty'. As in 'Mourning and Melancholia' Freud admits that it is 'a great riddle' for psychologists to explain mourning but that it is possible to connect the pain felt in the mourning process to the pain associated with the transference of libido from the ego to objects and back again: 'We only see that libido clings to its objects and will not renounce those that are lost even when a substitute lies ready to hand. Such then is mourning.'[88]

[85] Julia Kristeva, *Black Sun: Depression and Melancholia* (New York: Columbia University Press, 1989), p. 97.
[86] Ibid., pp. 13, 20.
[87] Sigmund Freud, 'On Transience', in *The Standard Edition*, Vol. 14, p. 305.
[88] Ibid., pp. 305–7.

Sylviane Agacinski takes up Freud's observations of the pain of mourning and its foretaste in *Time Passing*, suggesting that loss is just something we have to put up with:

> There is nothing that can promise to eradicate the trial of loss, or its pain, except the assertion that it would be absurd to anticipate the time of mourning, to suffer in advance, and to deprive oneself of the pleasure of the present. Better to say goodbye to what no longer is, to resist the melancholy distaste that the ruin of things can inspire, and to ignore the – illusory – consolation found in the denial of death. Whether one abandons oneself to melancholy sadness and the foretaste of mourning or seeks refuge in the vain hope of eternity, in each case one turns from the real: what is there, in the process of (coming to pass and) passing. The anticipation of death, which we cannot help thinking about, has two possible effects: melancholy, which withdraws any present from us in advance and, conversely, love for finite things or beings, all the more intense since it is hopeless.[89]

Agacinski appears to be repeating the distinction made by Freud between a healthy and unhealthy attitude towards loss and, as we saw earlier, she wishes to stress the value of forgetting. Quite where we draw the distinction between forgetting and mourning-as-fixing is difficult to say. It does not seem appropriate to suggest that mourning is a process that is ever really over, at least in regard to the remembering part of mourning. Another way to put this is to say that, while mourning is, as Freud pointed out, the work of dealing with the immediate pain brought on by the lost person or object, there is an ongoing process for most people who have lost – one that is seemingly not only healthy but 'normal' and even expected – of remembering, commemorating and marking the loss: mourning, in this light, is an always unfinished process. This is not to deny that there are gradations to the work of lessening pain and gaining acceptance, but rather to suggest that the binary oppositions brought about by Freud's comparison of mourning and melancholia, and Agacinski's of 'melancholy sadness' and the 'vain hope of eternity', are perhaps overdrawn. This is a point raised, with regard to Freud, by Paul Ricoeur, who provides a reading of the book *Saturn and Melancholy* by Raymond Klibansky, Erwin Panofsky and Fritz Saxl that reminds us that melancholy has not always been associated with illness.[90] In the era of pre-Freudian humoral theory, melancholy as often connoted genius, or exceptionality of some 'positive' kind, as it did illness. Ricoeur then extends his analysis to consider 'poeticized figures of melancholia' such as Baudelaire, who 'restore[s] to melancholia its enigmatic profoundness, which no nosology could ever exhaust'.[91] Ricoeur also mentions Beethoven's final quartets as examples of what he finally brings himself to call 'sublimation', suggesting the latter

---

[89]   Agacinski, *Time Passing*, pp. 13–14.
[90]   Raymond Klibansky, Erwin Panofsky and Fritz Saxl, *Saturn and Melancholy: Studies in the History of Natural Philosophy, Religion, and Art* (London: Nelson, 1964).
[91]   Ricoeur, *Memory, History, Forgetting*, p. 77.

term as the 'missing piece in the panoply of Freud's Metapsychology [which] might perhaps have provided him with the secret of the reversal from complaisance toward sadness to sadness sublimated – into joy'.[92]

Melancholic Music

It does not take long to move from mourning and melancholy back into music. To help us on the journey, I would like to use some observations on music by Fernando Pessoa, the modernist poet whose work I will draw on at numerous points in this book. Pessoa is notable not only as a creator of poems but also of poets, writing under a variety of names that he called his 'heteronyms'. Each of these poets had a distinct biography and poetic characteristics, the main four being the Whitmanesque Álvaro de Campos, the 'sensationist' Alberto Caeiro, the classically minded poet-doctor Ricardo Reis and another called 'Fernando Pessoa' (often referred to by translators and scholars as 'Pessoa-Himself'). Another of Pessoa's heteronyms, Bernardo Soares, wrote prose and shared many of Pessoa's own characteristics – the poet referred to Soares as a 'semi-heteronym'. In recent years, many of Pessoa's poems have been adapted into fados.

The first feature worth mentioning in relation to this chapter is Pessoa's presentation of music as lull or unconsciousness. A short, one-sentence entry to Soares's main work, *The Book of Disquiet*, speaks of 'A breath of music or of a dream of something that would make me almost feel, something that would make me not think.'[93] Elsewhere, Soares wishes, 'To have no islands where those of us who are uncomfortable could go, no ancient garden paths reserved for those who've retreated into dreaming!' Could music be such an island? It seems likely, for Soares adds a further wish: 'not to be able to just dream it all, to express it without words, without so much as consciousness, through a construction of myself in music and diffuseness, such that tears would well in my eyes as soon as I felt like expressing myself ...'[94] He also speaks of 'daydreamers whose reveries are like the soul's music, lulling them and meaning nothing'.[95] Furthermore, 'In dreams I learned ... to gild, with the sun of artifice, the dark corners and forgotten furniture; and, whenever I write, to give music (as if lulling myself) to the fluid phrases of my fixation.'[96]

In many of these passages, music is an imagined or abstract quality, a way of thinking about non-thinking. Elsewhere in the book, and frequently in the poems of the various heteronyms, music features as a real presence, albeit one that

---

[92] Ibid., p. 77.

[93] Fernando Pessoa, *The Book of Disquiet*, tr. Richard Zenith (Harmondsworth: Penguin, 2001), p. 30.

[94] Ibid., p. 90.

[95] Ibid., p. 127.

[96] Ibid., p. 155.

quickly leads the poet to return to the association with non-consciousness. In one poem, Pessoa-Himself speaks of 'strains of music' that 'cut to the quick of one's heart!' and of a guitar that 'reaches the soul in its depths'. The poem ends with a command: 'Cease, O fluid consciousness! / be shadow, O heartfelt grief!'[97] Here, music is not a lull, but something that hurts.

When the music is real, and its appearance in the poet's sonic space unexpected, it is sometimes considered an unwanted guest, but more often it is simply associated with memory: 'Morning, spring, hope – they're linked in music by the same melodic intention; they're linked in the soul by the same memory of an identical intention';[98] 'How many things music suggests, and we're glad they can never be!'[99] The association between music and a mourned past is found in the reflective middle section of Álvaro de Campos's 'Maritime Ode', where the poet breaks off from singing his exultant hymn to the sea to dwell on his landlocked reality:

> My past resurfaces, as if that mariner's cry
> Were a scent, a voice, the echo of a song
> Calling up from my past
> That happiness I'll never again know.[100]

And, a little later:

> My old aunt used to sing me to sleep
> (Even though I was already too old for this).
> The memory makes tears fall on my heart, cleansing it of life[101]

This is precisely the kind of irrevocable loss hymned in the fado by Amália's 'Gostava de Ser Quem Era'. But music does not only bring one's own past back, it also evokes a far more general yearning, as in a poem by Pessoa-Himself in which the poet hears an 'old and uncertain tune' from a tavern across the street that 'makes / Me suddenly miss what I'd never missed'. He wonders whose past it is that the music is delivering, before deciding it is no one's; it is merely 'the past / All the things that have already died / To me and to everyone in the world … gone by'.[102] Pessoa hymns many ways in which music and loss are implicated in each other. Music is something transient that is no sooner experienced than it is lost; at the same time, it lasts just long enough to evoke sorrow and the past or

---

[97]   Fernando Pessoa, *A Little Larger Than the Entire Universe: Selected Poems*, ed. & tr. Richard Zenith (London: Penguin, 2006), p. 306.

[98]   Pessoa, *Book of Disquiet*, 328.

[99]   Ibid., p. 93.

[100] Pessoa, *A Little Larger*, p. 186.

[101] Ibid., p. 188.

[102] Fernando Pessoa, *Fernando Pessoa & Co.: Selected Poems*, ed. & tr. Richard Zenith (New York: Grove Press, 1998), p. 258.

to promise an alternative to the present. The desire to chase after the lost music becomes entwined in the desire to chase after the memories stirred by the music. And music is something itself to be lost in, to induce dreams and fantasies, to help forget as much as remember.

The nostalgia in much of Pessoa's work is all the more interesting for emanating from an imagined exile rather than a real one. Pessoa spent many of his formative years away from Portugal and, as Richard Zenith suggests, the English sensibility developed during his youth in Durban was as important to his work as his commitment to Portugal on his return.[103] Yet most of his work, and especially his nostalgic work, comes from the period in which he was settled back in Lisbon. Álvaro de Campos, as the heteronym who was most widely travelled (his biography included travels to the Orient and a period in Scotland), was able to embody the possibility of a more 'authentic' nostalgia than that which Pessoa might actually have lived.[104] Yet to make such a statement is to realize at least two things. Firstly, we have come to expect this kind of authenticity to narratives of exile and nostalgia; diasporic or exile communities must *really* have been forced to move and to settle in foreign lands, there to tell their stories of homelands and their children to tell stories of inherited, imagined homelands. The twentieth century has provided many opportunities for us to witness, through the arts and media if not at first hand, such legacies of displacement. Secondly, and more pertinently for a consideration of the work of Pessoa and other writers who have followed him (including the writers of fados), we must realize that, given nostalgia's birthplace in the imagination, it is as easily possible for artists prone to imaginative journeys to translate any sense of loss into an imagination of physical displacement. Nostalgia does not have to follow physical dislocation; any mind perceptive to the workings of memory and loss can produce work as strongly structured by nostalgia as the exile, for whom we might say that the nostalgic drive was a latent potential realized by the dislocation experienced. Pessoa's work, as Richard Zenith points out, thrived 'on ideas more than on actual experience'.[105]

To close this first encounter with Fernando Pessoa, it is worth noting the number of his poems which have been made into fados. To a certain extent, this might not seem surprising given the stature of the poet in Portuguese culture and the fado-esque quality of much of his work. However, it was by no means apparent during Pessoa's lifetime that his work would meet such a fate. At that time, fados were more strictly based on the traditional models and the tendency to adapt erudite poetry to fado compositions had yet to establish itself. This process would come to the fore during the career of Amália Rodrigues, which coincided with the period in which Salazar's Estado Novo demanded the professionalization of fado.

---

[103] Richard Zenith, 'Introduction: the Birth of a Nation', in Pessoa, *A Little Larger*, p. xiv.

[104] See, for example, Campos's two poems entitled 'Lisbon Revisited' in Pessoa, *A Little Larger*, pp. 216–20.

[105] Zenith, 'Introduction', *A Little Larger*, p. xvii.

For her part, Amália claimed that Pessoa's work, though she had great admiration for it, was unsingable.[106] She admitted, however, that the 'Quadras' – four-line verses in a popular style, of which Pessoa wrote or adapted hundreds throughout his life – might be set to music, as indeed they were. Although Pessoa never published a definitive version of the 'Quadras', he maintained that one in particular should go at the beginning:

Cantigas de Portugueses	[Songs of the Portuguese
São como barcos no mar –	Are like boats on the sea –
Vão de uma alma para outra	Going from one soul to another
Com riscos de naufragar.[107]	In danger of being shipwrecked.]

This verse is used as the final of five 'Quadras' set to a traditional fado style and recorded by Carlos do Carmo. A different set of 'Quadras' have also been recorded by Camané to music by the *guitarrista* Jaime Santos.[108] Camané, like many other contemporary *fadistas* has had none of the problems Amália found with setting Pessoa's other work to music, opening his 1998 album *Na Linha da Vida* with a version of the poet's 'Ah Quanta Melancolia' from 1924:

Ah quanta melancolia!	[Oh what melancholy!
Quanta, quanta solidão!	So much so much solitude!
Aquela alma, que vazia,	That soul, that emptiness,
Que sinto inútil e fria	That I feel useless and cold
Dentro do meu coração![109]	Within my heart!]

It is a little surprising that the great melancholic *fadista* Amália did not record work based on Pessoa, given how close such themes were to those she obsessively explored.

---

[106] Amália Rodrigues, in Vítor Pavão do Santos, *Amália: Uma Biografia*, 2nd edn (Lisbon: Editorial Presença, 2005), p. 142.

[107] Fernando Pessoa, *Obras Completas Vol. 9: Quadras ao Gosto Popular*, ed. Georg Rudolf Lind & Jacinto do Prado Coelho (Lisbon: Edições Ática, 1965), No. 1, p. 37.

[108] Carlos do Carmo, 'Quadras ao Gosta Popular', *Mais do que Amor é Amar* (Philips/Polygram 532340-2, 1996 [1986]); Camané, 'Quadras', *Esta Coisa de Alma* (EMI 7243525001 2, 2000); and *Ao Vivo* (Valentim de Carvalho/Capitol/EMI 724359648828, 2003).

[109] The full poem can be found in Fernando Pessoa, *Obras Completas Vol. 8: Poesias Inéditas de Fernando Pessoa (1919–1930)* (Lisbon: Edições Ática, 1963), p. 57. Camané's version, set to a *fado bailado*, is on *Na Linha da Vida* (EMI-Valentim de Carvalho 724349383227, 1998).

Amália

For the remainder of this chapter I will focus on Amália and her work. The connection between Amália and the themes outlined in this chapter is hopefully clear. On the one hand, there is her life and career, which can be quite easily presented in terms of melancholy and loss. This is not quite the path I take, but that is not because I have a particular problem with such an approach. On the contrary, while the conflation of life and art is often a problem in the discussion of popular music, I do not see how it is possible to avoid such a process when dealing with performers who have explicitly connected the two.[110] Some of this approach will certainly seep through my account of Amália, but I mainly want to use her career as a way to describe the fado world with which I am dealing in this book, a world constructed from the tangled relations between authenticity, innovation and the culture industry. I close my account of Amália with a reading of a fado written and performed by her which deals with many of the issues discussed in this chapter.

Amália Rodrigues remains the single most paradigmatic performer in modern Portuguese musical culture for a number of reasons. Her career spanned a crucial period of change in Portugal and in the recording industry worldwide. Filipe La Féria summarizes these connections as follows: 'Amália Rodrigues was born in the First Republic, lived with and for the Estado Novo and lived to see the 25 April Revolution. This can be seen as a very rich period and one that had a strong emotional effect on people.' La Féria, the creator of an enormously popular musical based on her life and times, attributes the success of the show to the combination of a celebrity with whom the audience are able to identify and her negotiation of a history they too have either lived through or recently inherited.[111] This identification is furthered in Amália's own work, which manages, from early on in her career, to define a star persona based on a number of fado mythemes. Her biographical details resound with references to poverty, to the Mouraria, to singing on the streets while selling fruit, to being discovered in the fado houses and wooed into the world of professional performance and recording, and, ultimately, to living her life in a fog of *saudade* and permanent unhappiness which no amount of success or fame could shift. The extent to which the development of this persona was deliberate or accidental seems to matter less than the place she came to occupy in the Portuguese imagination.

By the time Amália took on the role of Maria Severa in a 1955 Lisbon production of Júlio Dantas's play, she had already surpassed that early *fadista* in terms of myth and prominence, due mainly to the success she had achieved internationally. While fado had hardly been unknown outside Portugal previously, it had never

---

[110]   Edith Piaf, Nina Simone, Merle Haggard, Víctor Jara and Bob Dylan are just some of the artists from my own research where I have found this separation impossible for quite varied reasons.

[111]   Cláudia Rodrigues, 'Entrevista com Filipe La Féria', *Terranatal* website, http://www.terranatal.com/notic/entrev/e_filfer_10.htm (18 March 2005).

reached the level of exposure given it by Amália. Now an international star, she found herself being offered ever-increasing opportunities, from performances worldwide to cinema roles nationally and in France. She had also demonstrated a strong desire to explore beyond the limits of traditional fado. It had become increasingly popular for fado singers in the 1940s to move away from the rigidly structured verses of the earlier period towards a freer style based on the work of contemporary poets such as Frederico de Brito. In addition to these newer styles of *fado canção*, Amália recorded other non-fado and folk songs, as well as Spanish flamenco, Mexican rancheras, and French, English and Italian versions of Portuguese songs (most famously 'Coimbra', released in an Italian version under the same title and refashioned as 'Avril au Portugal' and 'April in Portugal' elsewhere). This explorative aspect of Amália's approach to her music encouraged musicians and songwriters to approach her with new ideas and led to collaborations that were to have an enormous impact on the direction fado would take.

On the musical side it is generally agreed – and was frequently admitted by Amália herself – that it was the collaboration with the pianist and composer Alain Oulman which caused the most far-reaching revolution in her fado style. What Oulman brought to Amália's work was an ability to break free of established fado styles through a sophisticated musical language, while maintaining a strong link with the essential elements that kept the music recognizable as fado. Amália would rehearse with Oulman at the piano and he would occasionally accompany her on her recordings alongside the time-honoured *guitarra* and *viola*. Oulman's arrangements allowed a greater variety of poetic styles to be utilized for fado lyrics, a development first brought to the public's attention on the 1962 album *Asas Fechadas*, popularly known as *Busto* after the bust of Amália which adorned the cover. Of the nine tracks on the album seven have music written by Oulman. The lyrics are provided by Rodrigues herself (the famous 'Estranha Forma de Vida') and by the poets Luís de Macedo, Pedro Homem de Melo and, mostly, David Mourão-Ferreira, whose 1960 collection *À Guitarra e à Viola* had been dedicated to Amália and contained the verses for 'Aves Agoirentas' 'Madrugada de Alfama', 'Maria Lisboa' and the political fado 'Abandono', all included on *Busto*.[112] Rodrigues and Oulman also collaborated on the work of less contemporary poets; 1965 saw the release of the EP 'Amália Canta Camões' and the album *Fado Português*, the former containing three adaptations of Portugal's national poet, the latter harbouring one of the Camões pieces, as well as a *cantiga de amigo* credited to the medieval troubadour Mendinho, and the title song based on José Régio's poem, alongside work by Mourão-Ferreira, Homem de Melo and Macedo.

---

[112] 'Abandono', also known by the title 'Fado Peniche', concerns a political activist locked up because of their 'free will' in the notorious Peniche fortress. Amália always maintained she sang it only as a love song, though it was significantly re-released as a single in 1974 following the overthrow of the Estado Novo bearing the title 'Fado Peniche' and a cover that clearly referenced the prison.

The third track on *Busto*, 'Estranha Forma de Vida' [Strange Way of Life], was notable for having a lyric by Amália herself:

Coração independente
Coração que não comando
Vive perdido entre a gente
Teimosamente sangrando
Coração independente[113]

[Independent heart
Heart that I don't command
Living lost among the people
Stubbornly bleeding
Independent heart]

The fatalism of fado is easily located in this song about an uncontrollable heart, along with a sense of estrangement or disquiet, most notable perhaps in the line about living lost among the people. The lyric was coupled with music by Alfredo Marceneiro, the leading *fadista* of the pre-Amália period and, as with most Marceneiro compositions, the melody is relatively simple. The significance of the track lies predominantly in the bringing together of these two major figures of twentieth-century fado, an event whose importance is underlined by the song's appearance on *Busto* alongside the work of Mourão-Ferreira and Oulman, and in the way that the song, together with Alberto Janes's 'Foi Deus', became an autobiographical marker – what Barthes might call a 'biographeme' – of Amália herself.

As mentioned previously, Amália's music can be read alongside not only her biography but also the history of Portugal. During the period of the Estado Novo (1933–74) both urban fado and rural folk music were appropriated by António Salazar's programme of nationalism, the former being strictly policed via the censorship of lyrics and the issuing of compulsory performance permits, the latter through the cultivation of *ranchos folclóricos* and the setting up of rural folklore competitions. Subsequently, fado came to be associated by many people with the authoritarian regime. For Joaquim Pais de Brito, however, Amália was able to elide such an association:

During the Estado Novo fado survived in a rather ambiguous position; as it became stationed – through successive laws prohibiting it from being sung in public houses – within the *casas típicas* which, through their nature, had the bourgeoisie and tourists as their public, fado lived alongside the regime, which, while not adopting or promoting fado, did not distance itself from it either. This did not matter overly since the problem was resolved by Amália. The quality of Amália's voice and the moment in which it appeared allowed, to a certain extent, the definitive stylisation of fado, exporting it and bringing to bear upon it major 'erudite' poets, all of them now writing for a single voice.[114]

---

[113] Amália Rodrigues, 'Estranha Forma de Vida', *Estranha Forma de Vida*.

[114] Joaquim Pais do Brito, 'Tudo Isto é Fado (II)', *Elo Associativo* No. 19 (June 2001), *Collectividades* website, http://www.colectividades.org/elo/019/p25.html (2 December 2004).

Leonor Lains makes a related point when she writes of Amália's broad appeal: 'She crossed all barriers and cultural prejudices. Amália had the gift of reconciling the urban with the rural, the cultured with the popular, through her unique quality of voice, full of sensual and musical emotion.'[115] Both de Brito's and Lains's points are relevant to another track from *Busto*, 'Povo Que Lavas no Rio' [You People Who Wash in the River]. The lyric, written by the poet Pedro Homem de Melo, works as both an evocation of rural values by a narrator who we assume to be a city dweller, or at least a person who has accepted a subject position that allows them to address the rural population with the familiar 'tu'. The first verse begins with the lines 'You people who wash in the river / Who cut with your axe / The planks of my coffin / There should be someone to defend you'. Subsequent verses speak of living among the people, of drinking from a cork cup and of the 'scents of heather and mud'.[116] Though there is an appeal to familiarity through a sense of belonging in the second and third verses, the distance maintained by the relationship described in the first is that which sets the underlying tone. Here the poet Homem de Melo and the singer Rodrigues take on the responsibility of hymning the people while also observing them at a geographical and temporal distance.[117] The combination of romanticism and identification is one that aims for quite distinct audiences. Whether it is possible to find in Amália's performance of the song the voice that de Brito tells us can resolve the problem of fado's relationship to the Estado Novo is harder to gauge.

Another way in which Amália was able to bridge the divide between urban and rural populations was her tendency to mix traditional folk songs of Portugal and the Lusophone world into her repertory of fados. In 1967 Valentim de Carvalho released three EPs of folk songs: 'Amália Canta Portugal', 'Malhão de Cinfães' and

---

[115] Leonor Lains, 'Amália Rodrigues', tr. John D. Godinho, *Vidas Lusofonos* website, http://www.vidaslusofonas.pt/amalia_rodrigues2.htm (30 March 2005).

[116] 'Povo Que Lavas no Rio', lyric by Pedro Homem de Melo, music by Joaquim Campos, recorded by Amália Rodrigues, *Estranha forma de vida*.

[117] 'People', used here as a translation of the Portuguese *povo*, does not adequately differentiate that term from the term *gente*, as used in the lyrics of 'Estranha Forma de Vida' quoted above, but is the best word to use in the context. Just as the word 'people' can imply all kinds of meanings in English, so 'povo' and 'gente' resist easy definition; *povo* can be translated as 'peasantry', 'race', 'common people' or just 'people', yet there is nothing to exclude any of these from the more general *gente*. There are strong rural connotations to *povo* but also political, class-conscious articulations such as that implied in the coalition between the Portuguese Communist Party and the Portuguese Democratic Movement, known as Aliança Povo Unido (United People's Alliance, 1979–87). Here I would want to understand the 'gente' used in the first song quoted as a very general 'people' among whom one shares a world – fellow human beings. The 'povo' of the second song signifies an identification with, in this case, a rural community viewed as a socio-economic class. For more on the 'povo', see Salwa El-Shawan Castelo-Branco and Jorge Freitas Branco (eds), *Vozes do Povo: A Folclorização em Portugal* (Oeiras: Celta Editora, 2003). The book also contains an article on Pedro Homem de Melo by João Vasconcellos, pp. 461–81.

'Folclore 3'. These were followed in 1971 by an LP, *Amália Canta Portugal 2*. The songs associated with this aspect of Amália's work, such as 'Caracóis' or 'Malhão de São Simão', often used fado instrumentation but the vocal tended to be rather different to that generally found in fado singing – a difference that would no doubt be even more noticeable had Amália not been a fado singer by vocation. What Timothy Mitchell says of flamenco singing in relation to Spanish folk singing is comparable to the different use of emotional expression in fado and Portuguese folk singing: 'the aesthetically differentiated moan of cante jondo can give the truth of the song style independent of the song lyrics, *which do not even need to be intelligible*; herein lies a crucial difference between deep song and Spanish folk song.'[118] It is worth remembering that lyrics are a crucial aspect of fado though it is also true, as in Mitchell's point, that emotional melisma does much of the expressive work. In addition, there are numerous examples of word fetishization in fado that shift the focus away from where it would be in a more narrative-style ballad.[119] Homem de Melo's poeticized account of life in the countryside is quite removed from the narrative ballad style, stressing as it does the cork cup, the heather and the mud over any conventional storyline.

It is interesting to speculate on the characteristic of the solo voice in *fado canção*, articulating as it often does a single highly poeticized viewpoint, and to ask what it says about the relationship between the individual and the collective. Certainly this type of song was considered by many fado aficionados to have little to do with the earlier fado, now coming to be known as *fado castiço*. Joaquim Pais de Brito stresses the links between fado's origins and ideas of collectivity when he says of the fado world of the late nineteenth century, '[I]t was an area where the excluded lived together: people from the street, immigrants, people without a past, people of mixed race, others who lived from the patronage of a decadent nobility.'[120] Music, and the venues in which it was created, brought people together in a way that, if less ritualized than in the villages, was nonetheless crucial in maintaining the social bond. For many, then, it was the subsequent journey fado took from the taverns to the theatre reviews that was responsible for erecting the wall between performer and audience, the fencing-off that – as in the museum and on the record – destroyed the possibility of a collectivized musical practice. It is at this same point that fado took on the responsibility of being the professional, 'official' Portuguese music of loss (or, as several fadologists would seem to prefer, the music of Portuguese loss, which is saying a rather different thing). Salazar's policies undoubtedly exacerbated this process of fencing-off but did not create it.

---

[118] Timothy Mitchell, *Flamenco Deep Song* (New Haven: Yale University Press, 1994), p. 128.

[119] I provide a few examples of Amália's melisma and word fetishization in my discussion of her song 'Lágrima' later in this chapter.

[120] Joaquim Pais de Brito, 'Tudo Isto é Fado (I)', *Elo Associativo*, No. 18 (April 2001), *Collectividades* website, http://www.colectividades.org/elo/018/index.htm (2 December 2004).

As with the emergence of rock 'n' roll in the United States, there are a number of issues to consider when determining why *fado canção* emerged when it did and why Amália Rodrigues became its paradigmatic performer, ranging from changes in the law (here, the Novo Estado policies were crucially determinant but previously extant copyright laws should not be forgotten, affecting as they do the role of the artist in the period of mass mediation); migration to the cities; changes in recording and media technology; shifts in the high/low divide in the arts.[121]

Whatever the purists thought, and despite (or because of?) the emphasis on the individual, Amália's music remained popular throughout the 1960s. For three years running, from 1967 to 1969, she received the MIDEM award for the artist selling the most records in their country, a feat only equalled by the Beatles.[122] The emerging protest song movement, the *canto de intervenção*, can be seen as a reaction to this dominance of the popular musical scene as much as to a perceived ideological impurity in fado. Many of the songwriters of *canto de intervenção* were also, in a way, more individualistic than the fado performers they sought to challenge. As with contemporaneous folk music movements in other countries there was, despite a strong desire to identify with the common man and woman, a tendency towards solo singer-songwriters keen to put *their* message across *their* way. The singer-songwriter, like the preacher, requires a charismatic individuality in order to be effective; at the same time they require a compliant congregation willing and able to take their message up and echo it with the power of choral unison. It was in his ability to do so that José Afonso took on the mantle of *the* musician of the revolutionary era in Portugal.

The bringing together of the worlds of the learned and the rustic, as exemplified by figures such as Pedro Homem de Melo, is mirrored in the evolution of those scholars who, in the years preceding the Revolution, became most associated with the burgeoning democracy movements. Their self-association with the working class came not from the simplified and prettified national populism of the Salazar regime but from an awareness that change should be driven from below and that the needs of the poorest members of Portuguese society, especially the rural poor, must be addressed if such change were to be possible. It is through this process that we find the most famous figure in Portuguese folk music, José Afonso, moving away from the Coimbra fado tradition of his university career towards a performing and writing space that allowed for the inclusion of material from the diverse musical regions of Portugal. Although Coimbra students had always maintained a group element to their performance style, there had also

---

[121]   It would be instructive to attempt a 'production of culture' account of the emergence of *fado canção* and the success of Amália along the lines of that provided by Richard Peterson for rock 'n' roll in his 'Why 1955? Explaining the Advent of Rock Music', *Popular Music*, 9/1 (1990): 97–116. Paul Vernon's work on fado history and practice gives some flavour of how the recording industry emerged as it did in Portugal but more work clearly needs to be done here. See Vernon, *A History*.

[122]   Vieira Nery, *Para uma História*, p. 245.

been a strong emphasis on the romantic individual, often hymned as the subject of unrequited love and unquenchable *saudade*.[123] Afonso, in moving away from this tradition and the contemporary Western tradition of the solo singer-songwriter, became a well-known exponent of collectivized performance, writing songs that encouraged group participation, and performing with large groups of singers in a style reminiscent of Alentejan polyphonic traditions.[124]

For Jorge Lima Barreto, the emerging democratic movement was echoed in the popular music of the late 1960s and early 1970s by a move away from notions of *música erudita* (art music) versus *música ligeira* (light music) to a new conception of democratic popular music as the site on which the challenge to the status quo should take place.[125] Comparing Afonso's 'Grândola Vila Morena' – the song that was broadcast as the signal for the armed forces to commence the coup that ended the Estado Novo – to Fernando Lopes-Graça's *Requiem pelos Vítimas do Fascismo* and Jorge Peixinho's *A Aurora do Socialismo*, Barreto writes, '"Grândola" places itself in another musical sphere; not only is it a reflection on the Revolution, it is a primary source of the Revolution itself – Portuguese Popular Music.'[126] He goes on to say:

> MPP [*Música Popular Portuguesa*] was immediately infectious; this infection was triggered by political conscience, inspired activity and, in the case of 'Grândola', drove us to march in the street and to construct a powerfully subversive imagination.
>
> 'Grândola' was not so much a place name as a set of topological references from commercial music wrapped in nostalgia and melodrama. 'Grândola' was a Portuguese cultural myth, yet a myth ... which triggered the most unshakeable humanistic and revolutionary conviction.
>
> In a political situation in which everyone claimed to represent themselves free of contradictions, whichever element increased those contradictions or their process of degradation was excommunicated (as in Santiago, as in Cape Town, as in East Timor, as in Tiananmen).
>
> 'Grândola' was primarily a synchronic and permanent reverification of the belief in democracy, so mixed up amongst the dross of bourgeois political ideology.[127]

---

[123] The song 'Saudades de Coimbra' on Afonso's *Fados de Coimbra* (Movieplay Portuguesa JA 8011, 1996 [1981]) provides a good example of the singer's 'Coimbran' repertoire.

[124] Polyphonic singing is particularly associated in Portugal with the southern region of Alentejo. Group singing here has traditionally accompanied agricultural work and, during the revolutionary period, the attraction of a collective 'voice of the people' was allied to issues of agrarian reform. To associate oneself with the region was to associate oneself with the progressive ideals of the Revolution.

[125] Jorge Lima Barreto, *Musa Lusa* (Lisbon: Hugin, 1997), p. 9.

[126] Ibid., p. 79.

[127] Ibid., p. 79.

In terms of breaking down boundaries, however, it must be recognized that Amália Rodrigues had already radically altered the musical soundscape in the two decades leading up to the Revolution. A glance through the part of her discography covering the latter half of this period reveals a bewildering array of material: fados (both *castiços* and *canções*), Portuguese folk songs, popular Lisbon marches, medieval poetry, French *chansons*, Italian and Spanish songs, Brazilian *bossa nova*, American show tunes, Christmas songs and more. Throughout this period Amália continued to be steadfastly apolitical, though a number of her collaborators did not remain so distant; David Mourão-Ferreira, José Carlos Ary Dos Santos, Alexandre O'Neill and Manuel Alegre were all leftist poets who wrote works either specifically for her or which were requested by her or Alain Oulman to be sung in concerts and on recordings. It was Oulman who approached the exiled Manuel Alegre for permission to include his 'Trova do Vento Que Passa' [Ballad of the Wind That Passes], a piece associated with the anti-fascist movement, on the 1970 album *Com Que Voz*. The recordings put out under her name in 1974 are perhaps the most telling: a reissue of Mourão-Ferreira's 'Abandono', now openly referred to by its alternative title 'Fado Peniche' in reference to the prison that had held many of the regime's political prisoners (the song had been banned during Salazar's rule); a single of Alegre's 'Meu Amor É Marinheiro' which, with its cover photo of a navy recruit, played on the popularity of the armed forces following their role in the Revolution; a single of 'Trova do Vento Que Passa' backed by Mourão-Ferreira's 'Libertação'; and a version of Afonso's 'Grândola Vila Morena'.

It was Amália's simultaneous ability to court these poets while remaining free from the persecutions of the Estado Novo that came to infuriate many people and that still divides opinion on the singer now. For her critics, Amália's political naivety smacked too much of the populism peddled by Salazar himself; this was hardly helped by the fact that fado and Amália had become synonymous and that, as fado now became tarred through association with the old regime, so, many felt, should its foremost proponent. This, allied to the sheer excitement of the new forms of music springing up in the wake of the *canto de intervenção* movement and imported Anglo-American rock music, helped to push fado out of the spotlight in the early days of democracy. Yet fado did not go away and neither did Amália, though her career took a definite downward turn within Portugal for a few years. It was during this period that Carlos do Carmo emerged as the new lantern bearer of fado. Less politically naive than Amália, Carmo brought a commitment to the ideas of the Revolution together with love, deep knowledge and experience of fado gained from his mother, the famous *fadista* Lucília do Carmo, and from the fado house he inherited from his father. Carmo worked frequently with the poet José Carlos Ary dos Santos and attempted, like Rodrigues and Afonso before him, to link the music of the city with that of the countryside. His most notable achievements in this respect were the albums *Um Homem na Cidade* (1977) and *Um Homem no País* (1983), built upon Santos's lyrics.

When Amália did return it was in triumph, performing to packed houses and initiating a new series of recordings which, though they would often veer towards the gimmicky, nonetheless paved the way for her powerful albums of self-written material at the beginning of the 1980s. It is perhaps worth considering Geoffrey O'Brien's discussion of the return of Burt Bacharach in the 1990s when considering both Amália's post-Revolution comeback and her audience's willingness to re-embrace her. The songwriting process that Bacharach and his colleagues symbolize is comparable to the creative process of *fado canção*, which can be seen as the driving force behind the musical period covered in this book. Like Rodrigues's 'classic' period, Bacharach's period was one of professionals – a Hollywood-style division of labour – as opposed to the singer-songwriter style that would come to dominate afterwards; O'Brien describes the process as 'a combination of perfectionism and commercialism'.[128] Eduardo Sucena's survey of songwriters, musicians and singers provides a good overview of how this relationship worked itself out in the fado world. As with the professional songwriters that O'Brien writes about, the creators of the *fados canções* produce a situation where there can be 'no assumption ... that the listeners could produce such a record themselves'.[129] This allows further for the adoption of star persona than would be the case with more amateur forms of music-making, leading to a situation where the performer's career becomes mythologized and lived through by the performer's public. It is the identification of the parallel existence of star and public that ensures the possibility of return:

> In such a process, the myth of the original career is amplified by the myth of the return. Each step of the comeback is charted as part of a legendary progression: years of glory, years in limbo, years of triumphant rebirth. The past is symbolically brought into the present, so that through the contemplation of Bacharach and his music ... latter-day devotees can gain access to a realm of lost bliss.[130]

Amália hardly endured 'years in limbo' but it was very much the case that the spectacular nature of her past ensured her a place in the public consciousness that not only outlasted the brief unpopularity she experienced in the mid-1970s but enabled her to be reborn in the 'latter-day devotees' who would pioneer the *novo fado* of the 1990s onwards. This is a process I will examine in more detail in Chapters 4 and 5; to start to bring the present chapter to a close, it would seem apt to consider a classic late Amália performance.

Performance: Lágrima

The song 'Lágrima' appeared on the 1983 album of the same name, which featured lyrics exclusively written by Amália and set to music by the *guitarrista* Carlos

---

[128] Geoffrey O'Brien, *Sonata for Jukebox: Pop Music, Memory, and the Imagined Life* (New York: Counterpoint, 2004), p. 20.

[129] Ibid., p. 21.

[130] Ibid., pp. 8–9.

Gonçalves. 'Lágrima' was the closing song on the album; its lyrics also appeared, alongside Amália's other poems, in her book *Versos* (1997). They are as follows:

Cheia de penas	[Full of suffering
Cheia de penas me deito	Full of suffering, I sleep
E com mais penas	And with more suffering
Com mais penas me levanto	With more suffering I awake
No meu peito	In my breast
Já me ficou no meu peito	Already lodged in my breast
Este jeito	Is this habit
O jeito de te querer tanto	The habit of wanting you so
Desespero	Despair
Tenho por meu desespero	I have my despair
Dentro de mim	Inside me
Dentro de mim um castigo	A punishment inside me
Não te quero	I don't want you
Eu digo que te não quero	I say that I don't want you
E de noite	And at night
De noite sonho contigo	At night I dream about you
Se considero	If I consider
Que um dia hei-de morrer	That one day I will die
No desespero	In the desperation
Que tenho de te não ver	That I have at not seeing you
Estendo o meu xaile	I lay out my shawl
Estendo o meu xaile no chão	I lay out my shawl on the floor
Estendo o meu xaile	I lay out my shawl
E deixo-me adormecer	And let myself fall asleep
Se eu soubesse	If I thought
Se eu soubesse que morrendo	If I thought that when I died
Tu me havias	You would have to
Tu me havias de chorar	You would have to cry
Uma lágrima	One tear
Por uma lágrima tua	For one of your tears
Que alegria	How happy
Me deixaria matar[131]	I would be to die]

---

[131] 'Lágrima', lyric by Amália Rodrigues, music by Carlos Gonçalves, recorded by Amália Rodrigues, *Lágrima* (Valentim de Carvalho/EMI 077778107729, 1995 [1983]), also on *Tudo Isto É Fado*.

In considering the song I am drawing upon ideas articulated by Jacques Lacan and Roland Barthes. I do so partly because these thinkers provide a useful vocabulary to attach to the expression of grief and partly because I wish to situate this exemplary instance of fado practice within the wider theories explored in this book. Lacan, in his commitment to Freud, provides a useful connection to the theories of mourning, remembering and working-through discussed earlier. Barthes, meanwhile, offers a vocabulary which is explicitly derived from the analysis of texts, whether written, visual or aural. Here, I find his theories of the visual field – as set out in his late work on photography, *Camera Lucida* (1980) – as relevant as his comments on music. Lacan and Barthes are quite different thinkers with divergent agendas, but their theories do overlap at important places. For Lacan, the 'Symbolic Order' is that represented by society's attempts to impose logic, structure and consistency upon the inconstant qualities of nature, a process carried out first and foremost through language. Against this is posited the 'Imaginary', those aspects of the subject's quest for a wholeness that is always unattainable but always desired, as in the 'Mirror Stage' of Lacanian theory. The third Order, the 'Real', is that which cannot be symbolized and which exists beyond our attempts to explain inconstant nature. It is inconstant nature itself, which yet, paradoxically, always 'comes back to the same place'.[132] The Real is that which irrupts into the Symbolic as trauma. Its connections with trauma, *jouissance* and death distinguish it from the more comforting Imaginary. The writings of Barthes that I invoke here are those in which we find a breaking-through of one (often ecstatic) mode of signifying into another, a rupture in the Symbolic Order that calls to mind the momentary glimpse of the Lacanian Real. The major examples of this type of Barthesian thinking are the concepts of *plaisir* and *jouissance*, of the *geno-* and *pheno-song*, and of the *studium* and *punctum* of the photographic image. What is notable about the lyric of 'Lágrima' is what it has to say about absence, how, for the vocal subject, the object of desire does not exist because of a refusal to recognize her. The subject posits a possibility for the object of desire to exist by hypothesizing a recognition – the recognition that the object of desire will mourn her after her passing – that will in turn betray a desire, the object's hitherto hidden desire for her. The price to be paid for this bringing-into-being of the object and the object's desire is, here, the subject's ceasing-to-be, her death.

What are the 'pleasures' suggested in the song? Or, rather, what are the signs of what Lacan calls 'the pleasure of desiring, or, more precisely, the pleasure of experiencing unpleasure'?[133] In short: despair, unrequited love, the dream-world and death. What is moving and pleasurable for the listener are the lengths to which this subject will go to achieve that *jouissance* which, Lacan reminds us, is in actuality suffering and pain. What is the significance, in Lacanian terms, of the

[132] Jacques Lacan, *The Seminar of Jacques Lacan, Book XI: The Four Fundamentals of Psychoanalysis*, tr. Alan Sheridan (New York and London: Norton, 1981 [1977]), p. 49.
[133] Jacques Lacan, *The Seminar, Book VII: The Ethics of Psychoanalysis, 1959–1960*, tr. Dennis Porter (London: Routledge, 1992 [1986]), p. 152.

subject's inability to perceive herself as fully constituted, or rather to see herself as constituted around a lack which she can only resolve by propelling herself from the Imaginary of fantasy to the Real of death? Or should one read the song less literally, as a song about the giving-up of oneself to the Other, an 'inevitable' love sacrifice or coming-into-symbolic-being?

We must also ask in what ways we can map musical meaning onto such a reading. One way might be to suggest that the lyrical structure of the poem has encouraged a musical arrangement which, in its simplicity, provides a drive towards emphasis on key lyrical moments. As Barthes notes of classical French *mélodie*:

> What is engaged in these works is, much more than a musical style, a practical reflection (if one may put it like that) on the language; there is a progressive movement from the language to the poem, from the poem to the song and from the song to its performance. Which means that the *mélodie* has little to do with the history of music and much with the theory of the text.[134]

Applying Barthes's notions of *studium* and *punctum* to 'Lágrima', we can attempt to sonorize these occularcentic figurations in an attempt to construct a theory of listening. For Barthes the *studium* is the cultural 'participat[ion] in the figures, the faces, the gestures, the settings, the actions', while the *punctum* is the 'element which rises from the scene, shoots out of it like an arrow, and pierces me'.[135] In a sonorized version the *studium* is the song text, the instrumental, vocal and lyrical setting which, within a few short bars, confirms this as a typical fado, albeit of the modernized *fado canção* style. Into this text are then studded a number of *puncta*, which can be identified as follows: the first syllable of 'penas' in the first line, echoed in the repetitions of the word in the subsequent three lines; the third syllable of 'desespero' in the first line of second verse, again echoed; the interplay between 'considero' and 'desespero' in the third verse. The fourth verse holds back from delivering its *punctum*, waiting, according to standard fado practice, for the repeat of the final phrase; when it comes (and we can detect in that word's double meaning an echo of Barthes's idea that the voice 'caresses, it grates, it cuts, it comes'[136]), it does so as the entire phrase 'que *alegria me deixaria matar*'. I interpret these as *puncta* mainly due to the vocal articulation audible at these points and with the repetitive pathos to be found in these over-emphasized words and phrases. While it would be possible to describe this process merely as a succession of emphases without resorting to Barthesian terms, I am keen to

---

[134] Roland Barthes, 'The Grain of the Voice', in *Image-Music-Text*, tr. Stephen Heath (London: Fontana, 1977), p. 186.

[135] Roland Barthes, *Camera Lucida: Reflections on Photography*, tr. Richard Howard (London: Vintage, 2000 [1980]), p. 26.

[136] Roland Barthes, *The Pleasure of the Text*, tr. Richard Miller (New York: Hill and Wang, 1975 [1973]), p. 67.

anticipate a connection established in subsequent chapters between photography and fado texts, as I believe that one of the things these texts do is to participate in an ongoing 'study' of Lisbon(ness), in which the oft-hymned city is both *studium* and stadium of memory. While 'Lágrima' makes no explicit mention of place, I would maintain that it inherits a sense of place due to the connections between text and context that I discuss later; the 'Lisbonness' of fado, here, is a state of mind which may be cognitively inaccurate but is mythologically and psychologically vital.

Barthes has saved us the effort, to some extent, of converting his theory of seeing to a theory of listening by speaking elsewhere about the interplay of the *pheno-song* and *geno-song* in vocal music. However, what is less stressed in 'The Grain of the Voice' than in 'The Pleasure of the Text' and *Camera Lucida* is the sense of the cut that the 'invasive' element (*punctum, jouissance*, grain) inflicts on culture.[137] Barthes writes of 'the deep laceration the text of bliss inflicts upon language itself'[138] and, in a sentence that might equally be a definition of the Lacanian Real, of 'the place where the death of language is glimpsed'.[139] This cut is also a cutting-off, or fencing-off, the creation of 'a site of bliss' that is simultaneously a site of loss. As Catherine Belsey puts it:

> The beautiful satisfies, Lacan argues, to the degree that it does, not by representing the real, nor by avoiding the drive, but instead by pointing to the lost real, while at the same time fencing-off any possibility that we might come too close to the Thing. Made objects offer a kind of satisfaction when the signifier encloses absence and at the same time offers pleasure.[140]

Lacan himself provides us with another metaphor of enclosure when he claims that 'it is obviously because truth is not pretty to look at that beauty is, if not its splendor, then at least its envelope'.[141] Going further, he says that the beautiful 'stops us, but it also points in the direction of the field of destruction' and, later, that 'the appearance of beauty intimidates and stops desire'.[142] Bearing this in mind, is it possible to think of fado as representing a safe (and beautiful) way of (re)encountering trauma, of encircling the Thing? As Nick Cave observes, 'the peculiar magic of the Love Song ... is that it *endures* where the object of the song does not.'[143] Fado provides a place (street, alleyway, museum, theatre, text, envelope) to (re)visit the traumatic. It is one of those musics that subscribes to the

---

[137] Although Barthes does use the metaphor of cutting when introducing a less formulated 'grain of the voice' in *The Pleasure of the Text*, as quoted above.

[138] Barthes, *Pleasure*, p. 12.

[139] Ibid., p. 6.

[140] Catherine Belsey, *Culture and the Real: Theorising Cultural Criticism* (London and New York: Routledge, 2005), p. 72.

[141] Lacan, *Ethics*, p. 217.

[142] Ibid., pp. 217, 238.

[143] Cave, *Complete Lyrics*, p. 3.

Aristotelian principle of catharsis, purgation and abreaction to which Lacan also refers. The single tear that the singer of 'Lágrima' desires is both the tear that will cleanse or purge and the tear (cut) that will rend.[144]

To return to Fernando Pessoa, *The Book of Disquiet* frequently includes displays of the kind of masochistic passion which I am here identifying with Amália's recognition of what fado makes possible. At one point Pessoa/Soares claims that he is 'grieved to the point of that old and familiar grief that likes to be felt, pitying itself with an indefinable, maternal compassion set to music.'[145] This grief is also fado's grief, as its pleasure is fado's pleasure. Elsewhere, however, Pessoa is not so sure. In *The Mariner*, a play all about looking back and trying not to look back, singing is proffered by one of the watchers as an alternative to the endless and meaningless talking the watchers are engaged in. But the suggestion is met with a negative response: 'When someone sings, I can no longer be with myself. I stop being able to remember myself. My entire past becomes someone else, and I weep over a dead life that I carry inside me and never lived. It's always too late to sing, just as it's always too late not to sing.'[146] Nostalgia is represented in many conflicting ways in Pessoa's work, appearing at certain times a revolutionary force and at others a passive retreat from engagement with the public world. So too in fado, a music which is often criticized for its seeming passivity and reversion to fate, but which might also be seen as a music of stubborn refusal, a music that, endlessly voicing its disquiet, provides a distinctive brand of nonconformity even as it conforms to its own inner forces.

---

[144] I cannot resist also pointing out the associations between the *guitarra* and the tear. Firstly, the body of the *guitarra* is tear-shaped and the model made in Coimbra is distinguished from its Lisboan counterpart by having the end of its tuning head shaped into a tear (Lisbon *guitarras* utilize a scroll design). Secondly, the notes plucked on the steel strings by the *unhas* resemble 'drops' and can fairly easily be imagined as the sound of tears falling between the words of the fado, the guitarist doing the 'crying' so that the singer can concentrate on the emotion of the lyrical message. Finally, to switch to the other use of 'tear' being offered above, these notes do seem to tear the unity of the song apart even as they hold it together; they irrupt into the symbolic structure of the fado text, cutting it into discrete moments of despair.

[145] Pessoa, *Book of Disquiet*, p. 122.

[146] Fernando Pessoa, *The Selected Prose*, ed. & tr. Richard Zenith (New York: Grove Press, 2001), p. 25.

Chapter 2
Taking Place: The Role of the City in Fado

For the city is a poem ... but not a classical poem, not a poem centered on a subject. It is a poem which deploys the signifier, and it is this deployment which the semiology of the city must ultimately attempt to grasp and to make sing.

– Roland Barthes[1]

We witness the advent of the number. It comes with democracy, the large city, administrations, cybernetics. It is a flexible and continuous mass, woven tight like a fabric with neither rips nor darned patches, a multitude of quantified heroes who lose names and faces as they become the ciphered river of the streets, a mobile language of computations and rationalities that belong to no one.

– Michel de Certeau[2]

Introduction

The previous chapter introduced a number of elements to be found in fado song texts. This chapter focuses more specifically on the centrality of the city of Lisbon. Fado, through the combination of word, music and gesture that has become solidified as the music's style, performs place in a very particular way, summoning up a mythology that attempts to trace the remembered and imagined city of the past via a poetics of haunting. At the same time certain locales of the physical city present themselves as exhibits in a 'museum of song', offering up haunted melodies of a Portuguese sonic past that serves to assert the city's identity. My account of this process makes use of literary sources such as Fernando Pessoa and Italo Calvino and considers the city as both historically specific and 'timeless'. In addition, as signalled by the epigraphs to this chapter, I wish to continue the dialogue between fado and theory, to bring together the ideas of the city expressed by *fadistas* such as Carlos do Carmo and José Carlos Ary dos Santos with those expressed by theorists such as Roland Barthes, Henri Lefebvre and Michel de Certeau.

The ubiquity of Lisbon's presence in fado lyrics is exemplified by the song 'Vielas de Alfama' [Alleyways of Alfama], created by Artur Ribeiro and

---

[1]   Roland Barthes, 'Semiology and Urbanism', in *The Semiotic Challenge*, tr. Richard Howard (Berkeley and Los Angeles: University of California Press, 1994), p. 201.

[2]   Michel de Certeau, *The Practice of Everyday Life*, tr. Steven Rendall (Berkeley & Los Angeles: University of California Press, 1984), p. v.

Maximiano de Sousa (commonly known as Max) in the middle of the twentieth century and revisited at the start of the twenty-first by Mariza on her album *Fado Curvo* (2003). The song hymns the eponymous alleyways of the ancient Alfama quarter and of 'old Lisbon', claiming 'Não há fado que não diga / Coisas do vosso passado' [There isn't a fado / That doesn't speak of your past]. At the close of the refrain, the singer wishes 'Quem me dera lá morar / P'ra viver junto do fado' [If only I could live there / To live close to the fado'].[3] A *fado menor* performed by Carlos do Carmo and his mother Lucília goes even further: 'Não há Lisboa sem fado, não há fado sem Lisboa' [There is no Lisbon without fado, no fado without Lisbon].[4] Whether referencing the city as a whole or one of the neighbourhoods most associated with the genre – Alfama, Mouraria, Bairro Alto and Madragoa – fado texts provide topographies of loss that place the city as either object of desire or lack, or as backdrop to another lost, remembered or desired object.

'Fado Lisboa' is a song that celebrates the city as a whole. It was originally performed by Ercília Costa (one of the great fado stars of the twentieth century) in a *revista* from 1939, *O Canto da Cigarra*. The song has also been performed by Lucília do Carmo under the title 'Sete Colinas', after the 'seven hills' of Lisbon. It has a distinctly royal tone and speaks of Lisbon as 'casta princesa' [chaste princess], going on to declare how beautiful the city must be 'Que tens de rastos aos pés / A majestade do Tejo' [That you have kneeing at your feet / The majesty of the Tejo].[5] As in many songs about Lisbon, the city is explicitly feminized. It also stresses Lisbon as a centre of empire, praising the discoverers who found 'so many deserted lands' and the heroes created in Madragoa, one of the historic quarters of Lisbon.

'É Noite na Mouraria' [It's Night in Mouraria], a fado performed by Amália Rodrigues and her sister Celeste, moves us toward a more particular location. Later recorded by Katia Guerreiro and Mísia, it is a typical 'atmosphere' song, listing a number of the mythemes we have come to expect from a fado narrative: the low sound of a *guitarra*, a fado being sung in a dark alleyway, the whistle of a boat on the Tejo, a passing ruffian.[6] This fado works as a companion piece to the classic song of fado's ontology quoted in Chapter 1, 'Tudo Isto É Fado';

---

[3]   'Vielas de Alfama', lyric by Artur Ribeiro, music by Maximiano de Sousa, recorded by Mariza, *Fado Curvo* (World Connection/Valentim de Carvalho/EMI 724358423723, 2003).

[4]   'Desgarrada com Carlos do Carmo', lyric by João Linhares Barbosa, recorded by Lucília and Carlos do Carmo, *Fado Lisboa: An Evening at the 'Faia'* (Polygram/Universal 066 933-2, 2003 [1974]).

[5]   'Fado Lisboa', lyric by Álvaro Leal, music by Raul Ferrão, recorded by Lucília do Carmo as 'Sete Colinas', on Lucília & Carlos do Carmo, *Fado Lisboa: An Evening at the 'Faia'*.

[6]   Lyric by José Maria Rodrigues, music by António Mestre, recorded by Katia Guerreiro on *Fado Maior* (Ocarina OCA 002, 2001) and by Mísia on *Ruas* (AZ/Universal France 5316562, 2009).

the delivery is not dissimilar, comparable mythemes are present, and there is a declaration in the song that 'all is fado / all is life'. Mouraria is also represented in fados that mention the Rua da Capelão, linked forever to the name of Maria Severa and to the birth of modern fado. The most famous, 'Rua do Capelão' (with words by Júlio Dantas and music by Frederico de Freitas), places the street at the centre of the Severa story. The site of Severa's house is now commemorated in a very Portuguese fashion, having its own dedicated pattern in the *calçada*, the white and black cobbled pavements found throughout Lisbon. At the entrance to the street there is also a monument to mark its place in history, consisting of a sculpture of a *guitarra* with the words 'Birthplace of fado' beside it. In this way, fado does not only reflect the city's presence, but asserts its own presence in the city. One can, if one desires, use the Rua do Capelão as the start of a walking tour of the city solely based on fadistic associations, from the labyrinth of Mouraria's streets up the slopes surrounding the Castelo de São Jorge to the neighbourhoods of Alfama, Graça and Madragoa.

Lucília do Carmo can again be our guide to Madragoa when she sings, in a fado named after the neighbourhood, of the Madragoa 'of the bakers and fish sellers / Of tradition'. This is the 'Lisbon that speaks to us / From another age'.[7] The verse of this fado utilizes an associative turn of phrase common to a number of 'city fados'; another associative fado, 'Ai Mouraria' speaks of 'the Mouraria of nightingales under the eaves', 'of pink dresses', and 'of Severa'.[8] These associations have a similar function to the texts written by the authors of the 'I remember' school discussed in Chapter 1, evoking both personal and collective memories. The 'Mouraria of processions' is also the Mouraria associated with the object of the singer's affections: both are now gone.

Zooming in still further, we encounter the alleyway, an unavoidable feature of the neighbourhoods surrounding the Castle. Alleyways are both places of intimacy (as in 'Vielas de Alfama' where they are 'kissed by the moonlight') and transgression (like the alleyway in Júlio Dantas's *A Severa*). In the fado 'A Viela' ('The Alleyway'), we meet a 'typical' character walking from alleyway to alleyway and encountering a 'lost woman' there.[9] The fado was recorded by Alfredo Duarte, better known as 'Marceneiro' after the name of his trade (joiner). Born in 1891, Marceneiro had a closer connection than many to fado's past by the time he was officially ordained the 'king of fado' in 1948. For many he was the living embodiment of the tradition, a *castiço* singer who, while born in

---

7   'Madragoa', lyric by José Galhardo, music by Raul Ferrão, recorded by Lucília do Carmo on *Lucília do Carmo & Carlos do Carmo, Fado Lisboa: An Evening at the 'Faia*.

8   'Ai Mouraria', lyric by Amadeu do Vale, music by Frederico Valério, recorded by Amália Rodrigues, on *Estranha Forma de Vida: O Melhor de Amália* (Valentim de Carvalho/EMI 724383444229, 1995).

9   'A Viela', lyric by Guilherme Pereira da Rosa, music by Alfredo Marceneiro, recorded by Alfredo Marceneiro, on *The Fabulous Marceneiro* (Valentim de Carvalho/EMI 724349526624, 1997 [1961]).

the phonographic era, did not seem part of it. Indeed, Marceneiro was deeply suspicious of recordings; his true home was in the fado houses of Lisbon, where, from the mid-century onwards, he was considered a living legend. If, as Rodney Gallop had suggested in the 1930s, one had to go a club such as the Luso to hold the fado 'surely in one's grasp', then one could look for no better guardian than Marceneiro. A regular at the Luso, he transcended the venue, connecting back to a time before the forced professionalization of fado performance. Marceneiro, then, is associated with the city not only because of fados like 'A Viela', but also in his very being, an authentic *fadista* who sang about the city, was mainly known in the city, and who represented the city (or a certain image of it) more than the cosmopolitan Amália. Much the same could be said for Fernando Farinha, with whom Marceneiro collaborated on occasion (most notably on the fado 'Antes e Depois'). Farinha, known as the 'Miúdo da Bica' [Kid from Bica] after the neighbourhood in which he lived, sang mainly of his life and the city he lived in. Farinha was not averse to recording, however, nor to appearing in films, such as the one that bears his nickname. His most famous recording, 'Belos Tempos', is rich with nostalgia and describes a desire to go back to the time of Maria Severa. Like Severa, Farinha's presence is marked in the city itself, on a plaque in Bica, the neighbourhood he helped to make famous.

We might say, then, that the discourse surrounding Marceneiro and Farinha is one rich with 'authenticity work'.[10] This work is done through ceaseless reminders of the connection between the performer and the neighbourhood/city; Farinha is 'do povo' but also 'da Bica', 'de Lisboa' and, ultimately, 'do fado'. From this position he could then make claims to the city and its music, as he did throughout his career. Marceneiro was a similarly 'ordained' commentator on the city, as can be heard on his version of Carlos Conde's 'Bairros de Lisboa', where the city's presence is introduced by the framing device of a walk through its streets. The verses, sung as a duet with Fernanda Maria, present a sort of competition between various neighbourhoods as to which is most relevant to fado: Campo de Ourique is the most elevated, Alfama is the most famous, the most *fadista* and maritime, Mouraria evokes the most nostalgia, Bairro Alto is praised for its inhabitants, Madragoa for its youthful optimism. In the end, there is a realization that the city should not be reduced to its parts: 'Why go any further / If Lisbon is all beautiful / And Lisbon is our neighbourhood!'[11] I will return to the notion of fado as a city tour later in this chapter. Now, however, I must go back to the Rua do Capelão and face reality. As is no doubt clear from many of the lyrics quoted above, the Lisbon being spoken about in many fados is a city of the past. If, having read

---

[10]   I am using this term following Richard Peterson's practice in his *Creating Country Music: Fabricating Authenticity* (Chicago and London: University of Chicago Press, 1997); I will return to Peterson's work in Chapter 5.

[11]   'Bairros de Lisboa', lyric by Carlos Conde, music by Alfredo Marceneiro, recorded by Fernanda Maria and Alfredo Marceneiro, *Biografias do Fado* (Valentim de Carvalho/ EMI 72438592822, 1997).

the inscription on the monument at the entrance to the Rua do Capelão, we turn around and face the opposite direction, this city of the past quickly vanishes.

Michael Colvin has narrated the story of the demolition of the lower Mouraria area undertaken by the city planners of the Estado Novo from the 1930s to the 1960s and the effect this had on fado and the *fadistas* who called this part of the city their home. Colvin begins *The Reconstruction of Lisbon* (2008) with a description of the void that was the lower Mouraria and is now the vast and soulless Martim Moniz Square. Having been lured to the area by the romance of fado song texts, he soon comes to realize the reality:

> The ideological tug of war between the Estado Novo's modernization of Lisbon and glorification of Portugal's past is palpable in the Baixa Mouraria. Tradition, as anything but an abstract notion, has lost! Street names tell the stories of inhabitants long gone: the palm tree on Rua da Palma; the plumbing on Rua dos Canos; the butchery on Rua do Açougue ... The Mouraria is rich in history and tradition archived in memory, however, in terms of architecture and urban planning, it is sad, decayed, abandoned, depressing.[12]

The tale Colvin proceeds to tell is both a sobering one, in terms of decisions taken and the possibilities ignored by the developers, and a hopeful one, in that he finds a song tradition that has maintained the hopes and alternative futures of the past in a critical nostalgia that stubbornly refuses to let go. Fados have become stand-ins for the vanished architectural delights as the remembered city is restored in the lines of songs and the resonance of *guitarras*. José Galhardo and Amadeu do Vale's 'Lisboa Antiga', recorded by Hermínia Silva in 1958, is a fado that once again feminizes the city, speaking of its beauty and declaring it a princess. An associative fado, it stakes its claim on nostalgia, asking its listeners to remember 'Esta Lisboa de outras eras ... das toiradas reais / Das festas, das seculares procissões / Dos populares pregões matinais / Que já não voltam mais' [This Lisbon of other times ... of the royal bullfights / Of the festivals, of the secular processions / Of the popular morning street cries / That will never come back].[13] Other songs, such as 'Mataram a Mouraria' [They Killed the Mouraria] were more explicitly political.

---

[12] Michael Colvin, *The Reconstruction of Lisbon: Severa's Legacy and the Fado's Rewriting of Urban History* (Lewisburg: Bucknell University Press, 2008), p. 11.

[13] 'Lisboa Antiga', lyric by José Galhardo & Amadeu do Vale, music by Raul Portela, recorded by Hermínia Silva, *O Melhor de* (iPlay/Edições Valentim de Carvalho IPV 12162, 2008).

Space and Place in the City

Fado provides topographies of loss in its hymning of the city, allowing a renegotiation undertaken by the citizens of the *fadista* world of what the names of the city's streets and neighbourhoods mean. What Michel de Certeau writes with other cities in mind might just as easily be said for Lisbon:

> *Saints-Pères, Corentin Celton, Red Square* ... these names ... detach themselves from the places they were supposed to define and serve as imaginary meeting-points on itineraries which, as metaphors, they determine for reasons that are foreign to their original value but may be recognized or not by passers-by ... They become liberated spaces that can be occupied. A rich indetermination gives them, by means of a semantic rarefaction, the function of articulating a second, poetic geography on top of the geography of the literal, forbidden or permitted meaning.[14]

Certeau is talking about words – names – but we should also note the relevance of this quotation to music itself, which also detaches itself from place to serve as metaphor, and which also becomes a liberated space to be occupied.

The occupation of which Certeau writes relies on memory as a spatial practice. Frances Yates tells the story of the ancient 'art of memory' known as 'mnemotechnics' that relied on the fixing of memories in particular places and how this art was later developed in the medieval 'memory theatre'.[15] The sense of memories occupying space depends on some notion of inscription. For Plato, memories were inscribed or imprinted in the mind, ready to be recalled and 'read' at a later date.[16] This also suggests that memory is a palimpsest, a notion that fits the idea of place as location of memory in the city.[17] As Yates notes with relation to the passing on of the art of memory from the Greeks and Romans to the European tradition, 'an art which uses contemporary architecture for its memory places and contemporary imagery for its images will have its classical, Gothic, and Renaissance periods, like the other arts'.[18]

---

[14] Certeau, *Practice*, pp. 104–5.
[15] Frances A. Yates, *The Art of Memory* (London: Routledge & Kegan Paul, 1966).
[16] Paul Ricoeur, *Memory, History, Forgetting*, tr. Kathleen Blamey & David Pellauer (Chicago & London: University of Chicago Press, 2004), pp. 7–15.
[17] Andreas Huyssen, *Present Pasts: Urban Palimpsests and the Politics of Memory* (Stanford: Stanford University Press, 2003). See also Pierre Nora (ed.), *Les Lieux de Mémoire*, 3 vols (Paris: Éditions Gallimard, 1997), and Raphael Samuel, *Theatres of Memory Volume 1: Past and Present in Contemporary Culture* (London & New York: Verso, 1996 [1994]).
[18] Yates, *Art*, p. xi.

In *The City of Collective Memory*, Christine Boyer notes the desire accompanying modernity for a disciplinarity in city planning that would double as a disciplinarity over the citizen:

> If the masses, housed and fed by meager allowances and expanding in number within the working-class districts of nineteenth-century industrial cities, presented a dangerous threat to social stability, then how better to discipline their behavior and instill democratic sentiments and a morality of self-control than through exemplary architectural expression and city planning improvements?[19]

Boyer also discusses Foucault's work on architecture as discipline. Foucault was fascinated with the ways in which space was used to exert power, whether through the surveillance allowed by the panopticon or by the disciplinary possibilities of modernist urban planning. Such disciplinarity is accompanied by, and largely a product of, capitalist accumulation, which, as many Marxist geographers have noted, has been the agent of continual change in the landscape. As David Harvey points out, the lip service paid to collective memory in the city is only one part of the equation:

> Capitalist development must negotiate a knife-edge between preserving the values of past commitments made at a particular place and time, or devaluing them to open up fresh room for accumulation. Capitalism perpetually strives, therefore, to create a social and physical landscape in its own image and requisite to its own needs at a particular point in time, only just as certainly to undermine, disrupt and even destroy that landscape at a later point in time.[20]

While for some writers the association between the Enlightenment project of 'totalizing' experience and the twentieth-century experiences of authoritarianism has been maintained, others have suggested that we have moved into a new 'post-disciplinary' era. Zygmunt Bauman, for example, in his account of globalization, has claimed that we have moved on from the panopticism described by Foucault to a 'synopticism' in which the many watch the few rather than vice versa. Globalization shows world affairs as indeterminate, unruly and self-propelled, in marked contrast to the Enlightenment project of universalization which contained the hope for order-making and was utopian. Capital has become 'emancipated from space', leading to a loosening of the spatial logic which previously bonded

---

[19]   M. Christine Boyer, *The City of Collective Memory: Its Historical Legacy and Architectural Entertainments* (Cambridge, MA, and London: The MIT Press, 1996 [1994]), p. 12.

[20]   David Harvey, cited in Edward W. Soja, *Postmodern Geographies: The Reassertion of Space in Critical Social Theory* (London and New York: Verso, 1989), p. 157.

industry, jobs and people.[21] Migratory flows create two classes of people that Bauman describes as 'tourists and vagabonds': tourists 'become wanderers and put the bitter-sweet dreams of homesickness above the comforts of home – because they want to', while vagabonds 'have been pushed from behind – having first been spiritually uprooted from the place that holds no promise, by a force of seduction or propulsion too powerful, and often too mysterious, to resist'.[22]

Mark C. Taylor describes the flows in terms of the changes wrought upon the metropolis:

> In the city, *place* is transformed into the *space* of anonymous flows. As technologies change first from steam and electricity and then to information, currents shift, but patterns tend to remain the same. Mobility, fluidity and speed intersect to effect repeated displacements in which everything becomes ephemeral, and nothing remains solid or stable.[23]

Charles Baudelaire's work holds a central place for Taylor and Harvey, as it does for many theorists of modernity, with its emphasis on the ephemeral with the permanent. Taylor notes how this fluidity in modernity is associated with the emphasis in philosophy on becoming over being:

> The infatuation with becoming issues in the cult of the new, which defines both modernity and modernism. The cultivation of the new simultaneously reflects and reinforces the economic imperative of planned obsolescence. In the modern world, what is not of the moment, up to date, *au courant* is as useless as yesterday's newspaper.[24]

The price of this, for Edward Casey, is 'the loss of places that can serve as lasting scenes of experience and reflection and memory'.[25] This in turn has led to the search for theories of belonging, dwelling and being-in-place, as can be found in the rather different projects of Martin Heidegger, Gaston Bachelard and Yi-Fu Tuan.

Place in contemporary thinking occupies many 'sites' that are the consequences of the rush to modernity, among them the postindustrial wasteland, the high-rises and 'concrete islands' described in the fictions of J.G. Ballard, the abandoned high street, the migratory routes of tourists and vagabonds, and the 'non-places' analysed

---

[21]   Zygmunt Bauman, *Globalization: The Human Consequences* (Cambridge: Polity Press, 1998), p. 93.

[22]   Ibid., p. 92.

[23]   Mark C. Taylor & Dietrich Christian Lammerts, *Grave Matters* (London: Reaktion Books, 2002), p. 19.

[24]   Ibid., p. 19.

[25]   Edward S. Casey, *Getting Back into Place: Toward a Renewed Understanding of the Place-World* (Bloomington and Indianapolis: Indiana University Press, 1993), p. xiii.

by Marc Augé.[26] These non-places are echoed in Beatriz Sarlo's discussion of the 'decentered city', in which she posits the out-of-town shopping mall as the quintessential example of a site for the contemporary consumer-subject to get lost. As Sarlo points out, displacement is happening here on more than just the physical level: 'the mall is part and parcel of an evacuation of urban memory.'[27] Zygmunt Bauman, meanwhile, points to the slipperiness of any sense of space within 'liquid modernity'.[28] In another kind of evacuation, we are also asked to consider the escape from 'real' place into the hyperreal space of simulation and the 'placeless places' of cyberculture described by Mark Taylor:

> The placeless place and timeless time of cyberculture form the shifty margin of neither/nor ... In this 'netherzone', 'reality' is neither living nor dead, material nor immaterial, here nor there, present nor absent, but somewhere in between. Understood in this way, cyberspace is undeniably spectral. The virtual realities with which we increasingly deal are ghostly shades that double but do not repeat the selves we are becoming.[29]

Before we lose sight of the actual citizen, however, we should think of how one responds to such developments in everyday life. Common to a number of the arguments presented above is an assumption that the city operates as an ideological pressure upon the subjected citizen, who is born into a time and place and must adapt to their situation. This immediately raises questions of negotiation between citizen and city, between dweller and dwelling place.

The geographer Yi-Fu Tuan begins his exploration of space and place with the body, describing a world which is made sense of spatially as a user moves through it. Tuan also presents space as a dialectic of freedom and constraint, shelter and venture, attachment and freedom. Place, meanwhile, is distinguished as 'enclosed and humanized space'.[30] Tuan makes the point that space can be both desirable in offering freedom and frightening in threatening loneliness. He is talking here about open space (against which the city might be built and defined) but the point also holds for certain city spaces. The inhabitation of space that produces place relies

---

26 Marc Augé, *Non-Places: Introduction to an Anthropology of Supermodernity*, tr. John Howe, 2nd edn (London: Verso, 2008).

27 Beatriz Sarlo, *Scenes from Postmodern Life*, tr. Jon Beasley-Murray (Minneapolis & London: University of Minnesota Press, 2001 [1994]), pp. 9, 13.

28 Zygmunt Bauman, *Liquid Modernity* (Cambridge: Polity, 2000).

29 Taylor & Lammerts, *Grave Matters*, p. 20. The notion of the 'netherzone' comes from the artist Eve André Laramée. On hyperreality and simulation, see Jean Baudrillard, *Simulacra and Simulation*, tr. Sheila Faria Glaser (Ann Arbor: The University of Michigan Press, 1994 [1981]), and William Gibson, *Neuromancer* (London: Harper Collins, 1995 [1984]).

30 Yi-Fu Tuan, *Space and Place: The Perspective of Experience* (Minneapolis & London: University of Minnesota Press, 2008 [1977]), p. 54.

on a certain amount of imaginary relationships with objects. There is a temporal as well as a spatial dimension to this process. Place is not just the taming of space but a pause in time. Objects, as well as familiarizing us with space, 'anchor time' and provide a relationship between person, space and time that is intimate:

> To strengthen our sense of self the past needs to be rescued and made accessible. Various devices exist to shore up the crumbling landscapes of the past. For example, we can visit the tavern: it provides an opportunity to talk and turn our small adventures into epics, and in some such fashion ordinary lives achieve recognition and even brief glory in the credulous minds of fellow inebriates. Friends depart, but their letters are tangible evidence of their continuing esteem. Relatives die and yet remain present and smiling in the family album. Our own past, then, consists of bits and pieces. It finds a home in the high school diploma, the wedding picture, and the stamped visas of a dogeared passport; in the stringless tennis racket and the much-traveled trunk; in the personal library and the old family home.[31]

There is an obvious correlation here with the process of remembering pioneered by Joe Brainard and discussed in Chapter 1. Tuan also reiterates the point that Georges Perec makes about the memorian's project, that it is meaningful even when (perhaps especially when) others do not share the specifics of the intimate moment; there is something about the process that is recognizable beyond the personal. It is worth positing, then, that what Brainard attempts for time, Tuan does for space. This relationship is even more notable in Bachelard's 'poetics of space', where the intimacy of the poetic line finds its mirror in the intimacy of the domestic sphere, itself a microcosm of the broader relationship between body and world.[32]

Nostalgia, for Tuan, is not simply a passive process to be opposed to agency; rather, the question of whether one feels nostalgic is intimately related to questions of power and control over one's destiny:

> In general, we may say that whenever a person (young or old) feels that the world is changing too rapidly, his characteristic response is to evoke an idealized and stable past. On the other hand, when a person feels that he himself is directing the change and in control of affairs of importance to him, then nostalgia has no place in his life: action rather than mementos of the past will support his sense of identity.[33]

---

[31]　Ibid., p. 187.

[32]　Gaston Bachelard, *The Poetics of Space*, tr. Maria Jolas (Boston: Beacon Press, 1994 [1958]).

[33]　Tuan, *Space and Place*, p. 188.

Mindful of theories of nostalgia and how they reflect or are challenged by supposedly nostalgic practices, I am not sure whether we can import this suggestion of Tuan's wholesale into an analysis of fado. On the one hand it seems like common sense, but on the other, as my discussion of Carlos do Carmo below will suggest, it is conceivable to imagine a progressive, agency-oriented programme that deliberately and explicitly uses nostalgia as its base.

Another way of dealing with the relationship between citizen and city can be found in Kevin Lynch's book *The Image of the City* (1960). Although dated in many ways, the book describes a way of thinking about this relationship which is still of interest. Lynch and his fellow researchers were interested in the 'cognitive maps' which people carry of the cities in which they live. Wanting to find out what the relationship was between these cognitive maps and official maps of the city, they asked people to draw their own maps of the city and of particular routes through it, supplementing this information with questions regarding how their respondents dealt with particular negotiations when using the city, what they thought of different neighbourhoods and features, and so on. The results of this research showed that there were quite different imaginations of the city and that these, perhaps not surprisingly, were dependent on particular subject positions. While this data, as Edward Soja suggests, ultimately had the effect of reproducing certain dominant discourses of the city and of social relationships, it nevertheless provided a valuable 'tilting' of the normally-designated representation of space from an 'official' to an 'unofficial', or at least 'semi-official' discourse.[34]

Lynch identified five main elements of the city from his respondents' representations:

- Paths – 'channels along which the observer customarily, occasionally, or potentially moves ... streets, walkways, transit lines, canals, railroads'. Lynch found that these were the predominant way of imagining the city.
- Edges – 'linear elements not used or considered as paths', such as 'shores, railroad cuts, edges of developments, walls'. These features help people organize and make sense of space.
- Districts – 'medium-to-large sections of the city' which can be mentally entered and have some distinguishing feature.
- Nodes – 'strategic points in a city into which an observer can enter', such as junctions, crossings, squares or other concentrations or condensations of space.
- Landmarks – external point references whose 'use involves the singling out of one element from a host of possibilities'.[35]

---

[34] Edward W. Soja, *Thirdspace: Journeys to Los Angeles and Other Real-and-Imagined Places* (Cambridge, MA, & Oxford: Blackwell, 1996), pp. 79–80.

[35] Kevin Lynch, *The Image of the City* (Cambridge, MA, & London: The MIT Press, 1996 [1960]), pp. 47–8.

To take some examples from the city of Lisbon, we might consider the following: Rua Augusta, Avenida da Liberdade, the Avenida 24 de Julho, or the tram and Metro lines, paths along which one might customarily move; the Tejo, Monsanto park, or the train lines at Alcântara, edges which help to organize space; Alfama, Bica, or Chiado, districts with distinguishing features; Rossio, Praça da Figueira or Martim Moniz, nodes which act as points of concentration; the Castelo de São Jorge, the Ponte 25 Abril or the Elevador da Santa Justa, landmarks that can be singled out. Fado hymns such elements while also overlaying them with a wealth of less obvious cognitive mappings such as alleyways, windows and rooftops.

Another way of negotiating the city is that utilized in artistic practice, which may present itself as critique of the place in which one finds oneself, as an attempt to tame the chaos of space, or as a mixture of the two. Fernando Pessoa is an interesting example of such practices in that he provided a variety of different ways of mapping the city of Lisbon. The most obvious, and arguably the least interesting, is a tourist guide to the city which he wrote in the 1920s but which remained unpublished until after his death. *Lisbon: What the Tourist Should See* was written in English and presented a conventional description of the city, detailing the various monuments, parks, museums, churches and other historic buildings. It is an interesting exercise to compare this Lisbon with the city of the present and the book's historical detail is useful, but there is little sense of the lived city. Citizens make only an occasional appearance, such as in this revealing snapshot of Alfama:

> The tourist who can spend a few days in Lisbon should not omit to visit this quarter; he will get a notion no other place can give him of what Lisbon was like in the past. Everything will evoke the past here – the architecture, the type of streets, the arches and stairways, the wooden balconies, the very habits of the people who live there a life full of noise, of talk, of songs, of poverty and dirt.[36]

Apart from this, the people are mainly absent from Pessoa's account of Lisbon, perhaps not surprisingly for a writer who often displayed an ambivalent attitude to his fellow citizens in his work. However, Pessoa's literary work conveys a mentality that is lacking in his guidebook. Even when describing his own kind of 'non-place' in the form of an imaginary journey, Pessoa is able to lay claim to the importance of place and journeying in mental life:

> I didn't set out from any port I knew. Even today I don't know what port it was, for I've still never been there. And besides, the ritual purpose of my journey was to go in search of non-existent ports – ports that would be merely a putting-in at ports; forgotten inlets of rivers, straits running through irreproachably unreal cities ... I found myself in other lands, in other ports, and I passed through cities

36   Fernando Pessoa, *Lisbon: What the Tourist Should See* (Exeter: Shearsman Books, 2008), p. 31.

that were not the one I started from, which, like all the others, was no city at all
... My voyage took place on the other side of time, where it cannot be counted
or measured but where it nevertheless flows, and it would seem to be faster than
the time that has lived us.[37]

This fantastical voyage relates the importance of the process of arriving and departing while maintaining a stubborn remove from any 'real' city, a remove, however, that is more provocative than the official presentation of the city and its real places given in Pessoa's guidebook. More often, however, Pessoa steered a course between this city of the imagination and the real city. *The Book of Disquiet* is both a meditation on consciousness and recognizably a book about Lisbon, where its narrator Soares is able to claim that 'the street is all of life'.[38] At another point, Soares makes the observation that '[t]here is no difference between me and these streets', suggesting a relationship between citizen and city that one finds given visual representation in M.C. Escher's *Metamorphosis I* (1937).[39] There is an indeterminacy to the life he witnesses in the streets: 'The people passing by on the street are always the same ones who passed by a while ago, always a group of floating figures, patches of motion, uncertain voices, things that pass by and never quite happen.'[40] This impressionistic portrayal of city life suggests that citizens are much like the city itself, always coming into being and never completed.

Jonathan Raban's *Soft City* (1974) attempts a similar idea by presenting the city as something which becomes gradually 'legible' to the citizen. For Raban, the city is an 'emporium of styles' from which the initially confused 'greenhorn' (the newcomer to the city) learns to select. This notion of choice is expanded to include the playing of roles – city life for Raban is always performative and the city is as much a collection of stages as an emporium.[41] If the city does impose its ideology, it has to be recognized in this formulation that, while the city is always at work on us we are always at work on the city too: this 'work' involving both the constant rebuilding of the city and the effort put into the performance of identity. This involves a physical and a mental building, the latter represented by Raban's suggestion that, as we reinvent ourselves, the city rebuilds itself around us.

A more critical version of this has been that associated with so-called 'psychogeographers', from figures related to surrealism and situationism such as André Breton, Louis Aragon and Guy Debord to more recent writers like J.G. Ballard, Iain Sinclair and Paul Auster. Of these, Iain Sinclair's work has perhaps come closest to the exploration of the city as museum, with various books

---

[37]   Fernando Pessoa, 'A Voyage I Never Made (I)', in *The Book of Disquiet*, tr. Richard Zenith (Harmondsworth: Penguin, 2001), p. 461.

[38]   Pessoa, *Book of Disquiet*, p. 313.

[39]   Ibid., p. 14. Escher's cityscapes from this period manage to represent the 'impossibility' of labyrinthine historical quarters such as Alfama.

[40]   Ibid., p. 127.

[41]   Jonathan Raban, *Soft City* (London: Collins Harvill, 1988 [1974]), p. 67.

dedicated to physical and psychical explorations of forgotten areas of London.[42] Psychogeography has come to be associated with taking control of one's place and agency in the controlling city, a project in which the act of walking is crucial, as Merlin Coverley highlights:

> The wanderer, the stroller, the flâneur and the stalker – the names may change but, from the nocturnal expeditions of De Quincey to the surrealist wanderings of Breton and Aragon, from the situationist *dérive* to the heroic treks of Iain Sinclair, the act of walking is ever present in this account. This act of walking is an urban affair and, in cities that are increasingly hostile to the pedestrian, it inevitably becomes an act of subversion. Walking is seen as contrary to the spirit of the modern city with its promotion of swift circulation and the street-level gaze that walking requires allows one to challenge the official representation of the city by cutting across established routes and exploring those marginal and forgotten areas often overlooked by the city's inhabitants. In this way the act of walking becomes bound up with psychogeography's characteristic political opposition to authority, a radicalism that is confined not only to the protests of 1960s Paris but also to the spirit of dissent that animated both Defoe and Blake as well as the vocal criticism of London governance to be found in the work of contemporary London psychogeographers such as Stewart Home and Iain Sinclair.[43]

Psychogeographers attempt to utilize the lost elements of city as the basis for a kind of militant remembering. The connection between a textual, 'readable' city and the processes of change inaugurated by the demands of capitalism brings us back to David Harvey's work. As Edward Soja writes, with Harvey in mind, capital is 'a crude and restless auteur' when it inscribes its narrative upon the city streets.[44]

Harvey opens *The Condition of Postmodernity* (1990) with a discussion of Raban's *Soft City* and suggests that we should read it 'not as an anti-modernist argument but as a vital affirmation that the postmodernist moment has arrived'.[45]

---

[42]   See Iain Sinclair, *Lud Heat and Suicide Bridge* (London: Granta, 1998), *White Chappell, Scarlet Tracings* (London: Paladin, 1988), *Lights out for the Territory* (London: Granta, 1997), and Sinclair (ed.), *London: City of Disappearances* (London: Hamish Hamilton, 2006).

[43]   Merlin Coverley, *Psychogeography* (Harpenden: Pocket Essentials, 2006), p. 12.

[44]   Soja, *Postmodern Geographies*, p. 157. This applies equally to the ceaseless dance of colonialism. The work of António Lobo Antunes is ideal for a psychogeographical reading of Lisbon which also deals with issues of memory, mourning and witnessing in relation to Portugal's bloody history in Africa. See Richard Zenith, 'The Geographer's Manual: The Place of Place in António Lobo Antunes', *Portuguese Literary & Cultural Studies*, 15/16 (2008), University of Massachusetts Dartmouth website, http://www.plcs.umassd.edu (1 June 2009).

[45]   David Harvey, *The Condition of Postmodernity* (Cambridge, MA, & Oxford: Blackwell, 1990), p. 6.

The play that Harvey finds in postmodern art and architecture is linked, in his mind to a lack of any sense of historical continuity:

> Given the evaporation of any sense of historical continuity and memory, and the rejection of meta-narratives, the only role left for the historian, for example, is to become, as Foucault insisted, an archaeologist of the past, digging up its remnants as Borges does in his fiction, and assembling them side by side, in the museum of modern knowledge.[46]

It is precisely as a 'museum of modern knowledge' that many of those concerned with the loss of the city of the past have come to treat it. For Iain Sinclair this means putting together a 'book of disappearances' that attempts to discover the 'missing pieces' of London. For Maria Tavares Dias it involves the publication, over two decades, of a nine-volume set of books on 'disappeared Lisbon'.[47] The motivations for such projects will be varied and will not necessarily coincide with Harvey's view of such work as simple 'lining up' in the present. As many writers on memory have noted, we go to our past not only for trophies to place in a cabinet of curiosities but with questions that may help to deal with impasses in the present. Sinclair suggests one such motivation in compiling his book on London: 'By soliciting contributions to an anthology of absence, I hoped that the city would begin to write itself (punningly, in both senses).'[48] By collectivizing the authorial voice, there is a possibility for an 'anonymous' documentary of the city that may also help to 'right' some of the wrongs inflicted on it. And there is another sense in which 'right' can be attached to the city, as Tuan suggests:

> An old run-down neighborhood should be saved from urban renewal because it seems to satisfy the needs of the local residents, or because, despite a decaying physical environment, it promotes certain human virtues and a colorful style of life. The appeal is to qualities inherent in established ways and to the people's moral right to maintain their distinctive customs against the forces of change.[49]

It is this 'moral right' that seems to be voiced in the fados identified by Colvin that cry out against the urban renewal inflicted on the Mouraria. Henri Lefebvre, meanwhile, speaks of a 'right to the city' that is 'a cry and a demand' and that 'slowly meanders through the surprising detours of nostalgia and tourism, the return to the heart of the traditional city, and the call of existent or recently developed

---

[46] Ibid., pp. 54, 55–6.
[47] Sinclair (ed.), *London*; Maria Tavares Dias, *Lisboa Desaparecida*, 9 vols (Lisbon: Quimera, 1987–2007).
[48] Iain Sinclair, 'Preface: Smoke and Mirrors', in Sinclair, *London*, p. 2.
[49] Tuan, *Space and Place*, p. 197.

centralities'.[50] Lefebvre contrasts this with the encouragement by the dominant powers to focus on the right to nature and to locate leisure outside the city. Rather than renovate the deteriorated sites of the city, citizens are encouraged to avoid them for the pleasures of the countryside or of some form of 'nature' brought into the city. The right to the city, however, should not be a simple visiting right but 'a transformed and renewed right to urban life'.[51]

The Real-and-Imagined City

For the psychogeographers mentioned above, the city becomes both a mental space and a physical problem. This interlinking is something that is taken up in the work of cultural geographers such as Edward Soja and Derek Gregory.[52] Both thinkers are influenced by the work of Lefebvre, who attends to both the real problem of capitalism's devastating restructuring of the landscape and to the everyday negotiations of citizens in their responses to the situation in which they find themselves. Lefebvre defines three ways of thinking about space: spatial practice, representations of space and representational spaces (or spaces of representation). The first relates to perceived space, the way that socio-spatial relationships are experienced and deciphered materially. Spatial practice is the basic functioning of social space, both the ground on which social space is produced and the means of producing and reproducing itself: 'The spatial practice of a society secretes that society's space; it propounds and presupposes it, in a dialectical interaction.' Representations of space are those conceptions of space that tend toward the abstract (geometry, for example) or a certain kind of artistic vision or imagination. It is 'conceptualized space, the space of scientists, planners, urbanists, technocratic subdividers and social engineers'. Lefebvre sees this space as the dominant form of spatial thinking in any given society, one that relies on verbal signs to assert its power. Representational spaces refer to 'space as directly *lived* through its associated images and symbols, and hence the space of "inhabitants" and "users"'. This lived space is also the space appropriated by imagination and of art that seeks to 'describe and do no more than describe'.[53] Lefebvre posits a theory of the 'production of space' in which all of these features come into play. Social space is the outcome of all three practices, though, as Edward Soja notes, Lefebvre's presentation is largely a critique of the representation of space and a consideration

---

[50] Henri Lefebvre, 'The Right to the City', in Lefebvre, *Writings On Cities*, ed. & tr. Eleonore Kofman & Elizabeth Lebas (Oxford and Cambridge, MA: Blackwell, 1996), p. 158.

[51] Ibid., p. 158.

[52] Soja, *Thirdspace*; Derek Gregory, *Geographical Imaginations* (Cambridge, MA, & Oxford: Blackwell, 1994).

[53] Henri Lefebvre, *The Production of Space*, tr. D. Nicholson-Smith (Oxford and Cambridge, MA: Blackwell, 1991), pp. 38–9.

of the possibilities of representational spaces: 'It is political choice, the impetus of an explicit political project, that gives special attention and particular contemporary relevance to the spaces of representation, to *lived space as a strategic location* from which to encompass, understand, and potentially transform all spaces simultaneously.'[54] I will return to the implications for this favouring of what Soja calls Thirdspace later on. For now, I want to briefly mention Lefebvre's thoughts on cities as 'works', 'products' and 'works of art'.

Lefebvre begins to discuss this issue by pointing out that nature does not produce, because the way we think of production in a Hegelian or Marxian manner is as something that deliberately creates products. Nature creates but its creations are not products; they are all differentiated and, while they have use value, they are not designed for a reproducibility based on exchange. A city begins as a work, an operation of spatial practice in which initially it becomes, for various reasons, what it is destined to become. But at a certain point its work (the work of becoming a city) has been done and it starts to more closely resemble a product. This is notable in the fact that cities are made up of reproducible parts, which is one reason why they tend to look alike. The tools with which they are built are designed to reproduce certain templates and to themselves be reproducible. But with this realization comes another, that the city was always a product, having been built for particular reasons and developed according to particular motivations. A city, especially a beautiful or unique one, may look like a work (of art) but it was not built to look like one; its workliness came about as a side effect of its productliness. This is related to economics because the tools have been paid for, designed and built and the labour force trained to serve the purpose of a reproducible product. It is no wonder, Lefebvre says, that all cities begin to look alike, for the economic patterns that guide them are all alike. Venice may appear as a unique and unrepeatable work, but it is no more a work of art than those cities which flaunt their reproducibility – it too was the product of capitalist desires and needs and endlessly repeated actions. But it still revels in diversity. There must therefore be a connection between city as work and city as product.

Is it perhaps the case that art provides the space that the city as product needs? In doing so, does it remove the politics of the situation by paying more attention to the aesthetic beauty of the city than to the toil and capitalist ruthlessness that produced it? If fado hymns an aestheticized, imagined city, does it highlight a blindness in the music as to 'real life'? Lefebvre seems to suggest that we need not go this far. By introducing Tuscany into his discussion, he shows how the creators of cities and the artists who represent those cities have existed in a dialectical relationship to each other. Perspectivism develops in Italian painting as a response to the new social spaces but social spaces come to rely on perspectivism in turn. I think we can allow fado a similar role. It comes about doubtless as a 'production of space' but is able to offer a dialectical response in the shape of a music that both hymns the aestheticized city and provides fuel for changes in the social space of the city.

---

[54] Soja, *Thirdspace*, p. 68.

Fado is a superlative art form for bringing together the representational spaces of the city with the representation of space, arguably doing so more effectively and more persistently (stubbornly even) than the other arts in Portugal.

With the issue of perspective in mind, I wish to return to Michel de Certeau and his text 'Walking in the City', from *The Practice of Everyday Life*. Like Raban, Certeau presents the city as a text, suggesting there is legibility to it. However, this legibility changes with perspective. Certeau famously opens his essay with a meditation on New York City as seen from the 110th floor of the World Trade Center (a view which is, of course, now lost). But, he suggests, this perspective was always a false one; while the 'God's eye' view of the high-rise, the aerial or satellite photo or the map may present the city as a kind of 'printed' text, this is not the way that citizens encounter the city on a day-to-day basis, even if they can access such views with increasing ease. The citizen as 'walker' writes the text without being able to see what they have written:

> These practitioners make use of spaces that cannot be seen; their knowledge of them is as blind as that of lovers in each other's arms. The paths that correspond in this intertwining, unrecognized poems in which each body is an element signed by many others, elude legibility. It is as though the practices organizing a bustling city were characterized by their blindness.[55]

Yet there is a process somewhere between writing and reading, a negotiation with the text that they are producing, that enables the citizens to use the city productively, and not only passively. Though caught in a story which has 'neither author nor spectator', a way of mastering space is nevertheless fashioned via 'another spatiality', with the result that 'a *migrational*, or metaphorical, city ... slips into the clear text of the planned and readable city'.[56] The names given to these places inherit a magical quality in this process of migration, as can be heard in the countless fado songs that take Lisbon as their subject matter.

I wish to proceed, then, with a continuation of theories of place and space that starts to more explicitly include examples relevant to the Portuguese situation and to Lisbon and fado specifically. I am going to do so by following one of the most suggestive elements of psychogeography, the interlinking of the imaginary and the real city. In my discussion of real-and-imagined cities, I have attempted to find a place for Lisbon, for I believe that fado invites such a theorization. Yet, in attempting to make this connection, one cannot help but notice the absence of Lisbon, Portugal or the Iberian Peninsula from the discussion of much cultural geography, where the literature has shown an overwhelming obsession with Paris and the modern cities of the USA – Los Angeles especially. Areas such as the Algarve are seemingly in Lefebvre's mind when he speaks of 'the current [early 1970s] transformation of the Mediterranean into a leisure-oriented space for industrialized Europe' and of

---

[55]   Certeau, *Practice*, p. 93.
[56]   Ibid., p. 93.

'the consumption of space, sun and sea, and of spontaneous or induced eroticism, in a great "vacationland festival"', but industrial centres of the Iberian Peninsula have not generally received the attention given to other European cities.[57] It could be argued that this is due to a fairly late industrialization of this area but such an argument would neglect the importance of Iberia as a world centre in the past; it is Venice's past, after all, rather than its present that made it exemplary for Lefebvre in his description of the city as work and product.

Prior to the obsession with American cities, the models had often been 'literary' European capitals such as London, Paris, Rome or Vienna. The Iberian Peninsula was less frequently brought into the discussion despite the presence of its cities in literature. As Joan Ramon Resina writes: 'For the Lisbon of Pessoa, the Madrid of Galdós, the Barcelona of Oller, Pla, or Rodoreda, there has been nothing on the scale of the attention brought to Paris by readers of Balzac or Zola or to Vienna by the great novels of Roth and Musil.'[58] Resina's own response to this absence comes in the form of an edited book entitled *Iberian Cities*. While this endeavour is a laudable attempt to reassert the 'place' of these metropolises, the reader interested in the Portuguese city cannot help but notice two things: firstly, there is the country's continued marginalization via the inclusion of only one city (Lisbon) alongside eight Spanish cities (one of which, Madrid, gets two essays devoted to it); secondly, it is hard to know what to make of the air of melancholy with which that one chapter is delivered by its author, Miguel Tamen. Tamen chooses to emphasize the lack of anything to see in Lisbon, the difficulty entailed in getting around due to the steep hills and uneven pavements, and the confusion produced by the different names given to places by official maps and everyday local usage.[59] It is certainly the case that, outside the flat grid of the Baixa, the city provides certain challenges for navigation. It is also true that Lisbon does not offer up a host of 'obvious' monuments from which to fashion a tourist itinerary (although this did not stop Pessoa from doing so). But what those who have been drawn to the city have invariably reported on is the pleasure to be found in this lack of obviousness. This has particularly been the case for those coming from outside the country. Ángel Crespo's tour of Lisbon dwells on the pleasures of the stroll, the literary and mythical connections encountered in the city, and the numerous opportunities to gain different perspectives on the city from a variety of vantage points.[60] Similarly, Paul Buck, in his 'cultural and literary companion' to Lisbon, is struck by the city's potential for narcissism:

> It is a beautiful city, for it is built on a series of hills and valleys whose steepness give rise to a multitude of viewing points, such that the city can become almost

---

[57]   Lefebvre, *Production of Space*, p. 58.

[58]   Joan Ramon Resina, introduction to Joan Ramon Resina (ed.), *Iberian Cities* (New York & London: Routledge, 2001), p. x.

[59]   Miguel Tamen, 'A Walk about Lisbon', in Resina (ed.), *Iberian Cities*, pp. 33–40.

[60]   Ángel Crespo, *Lisboa Mítica e Literária* (Lisbon: Livros Horizonte, 1990 [1987]).

narcissistic, encouraging one to re-viewing it, akin to stepping inside a house choked by mirrors, continually catching the reflections, sucked into the space of admiration.[61]

There are, of course, a profusion of guidebooks and websites devoted to Lisbon, all of which maintain that there is plenty to see. All have their own agendas and may be more or less implicated in the representation of space that Lefebvre identified as the dominant mode of spatial thinking. It is less likely (though perhaps not for those who can afford to do so) that one would take the car tour suggested by Pessoa, not least because the streets are nowhere near as painlessly negotiable as in his day. It is quite likely that one might pay for a bus tour or take the 'tourist tram' that combines authentic travelling with ease of transit. But equally, one might choose to walk and, if not content to follow one's footsteps, to take one of the walking guides on offer. One company that implicitly challenges Tamen's assertion that Lisbon is 'a town with no *flâneurs*' offers a range of walks tailored to specific ways of seeing the city. One of these, entitled 'Lisbon Old Town', promises 'Maze-like streets, 'Hidden vantage points', 'Migration and dockers' and 'Fado as the soundtrack of Lisbon' among its features.[62] Each of these is related to one aspect or another of the theories discussed in this chapter. The maze-like streets are the embodiment of Certeau's point about the blindness of the city, yet vantage points emerge from the confusion to allow a sudden switch back to the controlling gaze. The history of comings and goings that have created the riverside neighbourhoods of Lisbon (of which Alfama is just one) is one in which the precursors and contemporaries of Bauman's postmodern vagabonds have plied their trades. As for fado as a soundtrack, I will have more to say in the next chapter but it is worth noting that, due to the difficulty (perhaps impossibility) of accurately mapping Alfama in any conventional manner, music may be as believable a map of this area as any.

References to the city occur even in highly metaphorical fados; here, the intention seems not so much to describe or represent the city as to ground otherwise 'universal' material. An example can be found in a lyric written by Amália Rodrigues, in which she speaks of an 'icy sea' that enters her when her lover is absent and of being 'um barco naufragado / Mesmo sem sair do Tejo' [a boat shipwrecked / without even leaving the Tejo].[63] In another fado associated with Amália, Alexandre O'Neill's 'Gaivota' [Seagull], we hear of a seagull that might

---

[61]   Paul Buck, *Lisbon: A Cultural and Literary Companion* (Oxford: Signal Books, 2002), p. 2.

[62]   Promotional material from the *Lisbon Walker* website, http://www.lisbonwalker. com (accessed 1 June 2009).

[63]   'Se Deixas de Ser Quem És', lyric by Amália Rodrigues, music by Carlos Gonçalves, recorded by Amália Rodrigues, *Gostava de Ser Quem Era* (Valentim de Carvalho/EMI 724383546527, 1995 [1980]).

come 'trazer-me o céu de Lisboa' [to bring me the Lisbon sky].[64] The success of this song, which has been recorded by a number of performers, has arguably strengthened the possibility of a metonymy utilized in many fados whereby the image of the 'gaivota' comes to stand in for Lisbon itself. The same can be said for the 'Varinas' mentioned in many older fados; these are female fish sellers famed for carrying their baskets of fish on their heads as they walked through the streets. Now more prevalent in songs than in reality, they are also hymned by mythologists such as Ángel Crespo.[65]

'Gaivota' also highlights the desire to move to a space where one can look down on the city. It is not, after all, accurate to say that we dismiss the 'God's eye' view of the city, for it is a desirable perspective. It is what allows us to read the city and try to get a sense of what the city might mean. While it is true that the view from above is one which has power and authority attached to it, it is also a view that the city – in the form of the polis, the citizens – requests. There is a pleasure to viewpoints that allow a looking-back on the city text, which is why they are frequently included on tourist itineraries and prominently signposted from the 'depths' of the city itself. Fado's association with Alfama has allowed its songwriters not only to negotiate the dark alleyways and labyrinths of the quarter, but also to look down on the city and the river below. Hermínia Silva can thus sing of the 'Telhados de Lisboa' [Rooftops of Lisbon] and Tristão da Silva of the view 'Da Janela do Meu Quarto' [From the Window of My Room], from where he sees Alfama, the seven hills of Lisbon, the *varinas*, the cathedral and the Tejo.[66]

A Man in the City: Carlos do Carmo with Michel de Certeau

I wish to revisit some of the theories explored in this chapter through a consideration of the album *Um Homem na Cidade* [A Man in the City], recorded by Carlos do Carmo in 1977.[67] In 1976 Carmo had represented Portugal in the Eurovision song contest and had recorded what would become one of his signature tunes, 'Lisboa, Menina e Moça', a popular song which feminizes the city as a 'young girl'. It was the 1977 album, however, which really showcased what Carmo meant for the future direction of fado. Described by Rui Vieira Nery as 'one of the most significant albums in the whole fado discography', it consisted of a series of specially written poems about Lisbon by José Carlos Ary dos Santos and set to music by a variety of composers from the worlds of Portuguese pop,

---

[64] 'Gaivota', lyric by Alexandre O'Neill, music by Alain Oulman, recorded by Amália Rodrigues, *Estranha Forma de Vida*.

[65] Crespo, *Lisboa*, pp. 7–9. Also, see David Cohen, *Fado Português: Songs from the Soul of Portugal* (London: Wise Publications, 2003), p. 40.

[66] Tristão da Silva, 'Da Janela do Meu Quarto', *Patrimônio* (Companhia Nacional de Música NM218CD, 2009).

[67] Carlos do Carmo, *Um Homem na Cidade* (Philips 5189182, 1995 [1977]).

jazz and fado.[68] It was a concept album and one which clearly was aimed at the post-revolutionary metropolis, showcasing new possibilities of being in the city alongside recognition of longstanding customs that pre-dated (and could therefore escape the taint of co-optation by) the recently overthrown dictatorship. The album came with liner notes by Carmo, Ary dos Santos and two of the composers, António Vitorino D'Almeida and Martinho D'Assunção, all of which stated a commitment to creativity, modernity, Lisbon and the people. 'With love we leave you this disc', wrote Carmo at the end of his note. The 'man in the city' is also to be found in the dedication at the beginning of Certeau's *The Practice of Everyday Life*:

> To the ordinary man.
> To a common hero, an ubiquitous character, walking in countless thousands on the streets. In invoking here at the outset of my narratives the absent figure who provides both their beginning and their necessity, I inquire into the desire whose impossible object he represents. What are we asking this oracle whose voice is almost indistinguishable from the rumble of history to license us, to authorize us to say, when we dedicate to him the writing that one formerly offered in praise of the gods or the inspiring muses?[69]

Certeau's words bear an echo of the commitment shown by Lefebvre to the lived experience of those connected to representational spaces. It bears a challenge to authority and the 'view from above', while also acknowledging the modest endeavour of a description of the everyday. So, too, with Carmo's album, which mixes quotidian description with an imagination that recognizes the potential for transformation. Almost all of the tracks included in the album make reference to the city of Lisbon. The title track records the Tejo and the Rossio area, 'Fado do Campo Grande' refers to the area of the same name, and 'O Homem das Castanhas' uses Praça da Figueira and the Jardim da Estrela as backdrops to the chestnut vendor's song. Two songs celebrate the public transport systems that connect Lisbon's neighbourhoods to each other and to the world beyond. 'O Cacilheiro' describes the ferries that criss-cross the Tejo, connecting the quays of Cacilhas, Seixal, Montijo and Barreiro and carrying 'lovers, sailors, soldiers and workers' to their destinations, while the tram system is the subject of 'O Amarelo da Carris' (Carris is the company that operates the buses and trams in Lisbon, easily recognized by their distinctive yellow colour).

'O Amarelo da Carris' provides a good example in its lyrics of the theories outlined above regarding agency, passivity, consciousness and the unconscious in the city. The first verse describes the tram which runs from runs from Alfama to Mouraria, from Baixa to Bairro Alto and 'climbs shuddering to Graça / without

---

[68]   Rui Vieira Nery, *Para uma História do Fado* (Lisbon: Corda Seca & Público, 2004), p. 258.

[69]   Certeau, *Practice*, p. v.

knowing geography'.[70] On one hand, the tram serves a purpose similar to the train in many popular song texts, providing a potent metaphor for the workings of fate as it faithfully follows its preordained course. Its passengers are passive citizens unable to alter the text of the city, etched as it is in the steel rails. Like the tram itself, which does not require knowledge of geography, the passengers can put their trust in the hands of the network and its operatives (which include, of course, the tram driver). On the other hand, they have chosen to be carried thus and are actively using the tram for their own purposes. They have a starting point and an ultimate destination; the tram and its driver are merely the means to achieve this destiny.

Similarly, the lovers described in 'Namorados da Cidade' are like Certeau's 'lovers in each other's arms', blind to anything beyond themselves while simultaneously creating that 'beyond' by going about their business. The protagonist of the title track, the man in the city, is the equivalent of the walkers found in Certeau, Aragon and Sinclair, going through the street under a 'moon / that brings my Tejo into season / I walk through Lisbon, naked tide / that flows into Rossio'.[71] Another song, 'Rosa da Noite', also hymns the incorporation of the city into the body and vice versa, claiming that 'each street is an intense vein / where the song flows / from my huge voice'.[72] The city is both body (a theme employed by other fados such as David Mourão-Ferreira's 'Maria Lisboa') and a channel through which other bodies (human, non-human, mechanical) flow. *Um Homem na Cidade* celebrates all these corporeal manifestations. It is, importantly, an *album*, and therefore, like a photograph album, something to be taken as a whole; its songs are snapshots of the city and its citizens, a collective creating a collection, a thing. This sense of the album as a thing-in-itself was highlighted by the release, in 2004, of an album entitled *Novo Homem na Cidade* which re-created the original album with versions of its songs, in the same running order, recorded by twelve different artists, a number of them associated with the *novo fado* of the early 2000s.[73] In addition to showcasing these younger performers, the album serves two other purposes, commemorating Carlos do Carmo's original album as a thing-in-itself (without which the new album would not exist) and highlighting the continued relevance of the city of Lisbon as a thing-in-itself to be celebrated (without which neither album would exist).

I have suggested that fado texts provide a tour of the city of Lisbon by incorporating various names associated with the city and, in Certeau's terms, 'liberating' them into a new poetic and metaphoric language. Yet, given that we

---

[70]   'O Amarelo da Carris', lyric by José Carlos Ary dos Santos, music by José Luís Tinoco, recorded by Carlos do Carmo, *Homem na Cidade*.

[71]   'Um Homem na Cidade'.

[72]   'Rosa da Noite', lyric by José Carlos Ary dos Santos, music by Joaquim Luís Gomes, recorded by Carlos do Carmo, *Homem na Cidade*.

[73]   Various Artists, *Novo Homem na Cidade* (Mercury/Universal Portugal 9868409, 2004).

are dealing with a musical form, it is also necessary to remember the role played by sound in this process. If fado texts take us on a tour of the city, part of that tour involves the hearing of fado music itself. The sound of fado, its instruments and cries, are both representations of space and representational spaces, products of and responses to space itself. In *Um Homem na Cidade*, there are additional sounds of the city referenced, such as the sound of the tram bell emulated by the *guitarra* in 'O Amarelo da Carris' or the use of the chestnut vendor's cry in the refrain of 'O Homem das Castanhas'.[74] This practice develops in sonic form a process earlier undertaken by numerous European and American modernist writers and artists to provide a representation of the noise of the city, albeit witnessed in silence (in the space of writing). For example, we find the following in Fernando Pessoa's *Book of Disquiet*:

> Future married couples pass by, chatting seamstresses pass by, young men in a hurry for pleasure pass by, those who have retired from everything smoke on their habitual stroll, and at one or another doorway a shopkeeper stands like an idle vagabond, hardly noticing a thing. Army recruits ... slowly drift along in noisy and worse-than-noisy clusters. Occasionally someone quite ordinary goes by. Cars at that time of the day are rare, and their noise is musical. In my heart there's a peaceful anguish, and my calm is made of resignation.
>
> All of this passes, and none of it means anything to me. It's all foreign to my fate, and even to fate as a whole. It's just unconsciousness, curses of protest when chance hurls stones, echoes of unknown voices – a collective mishmash of life.[75]

This 'collective mishmash of life' is wonderfully transformed in 'Fado Varina', from *Um Homem na Cidade*, into a noisy and salty metaphor suggested by the cries of a woman selling fish in the market: 'Os teus pregões / são iguais à claridade / caldeirada de canções / que se entorna na cidade' [Your cries / are like brightness / a fish stew of songs / spilling over the city].[76]

Carlos Saura's use of 'Um Homem na Cidade' in his film *Fados* (2007) is rather more postmodern but maintains the idea of a tour through the city. Saura's visualization of the song opens with Carmo standing in front of three musicians (*guitarra*, *viola*, *viola baixo*), who in turn are seated in front of a screen showing

---

[74] Mariza's version of 'O Amarelo da Carris' on *Novo Homem na Cidade* takes this emulation a step further by incorporating sampled tram sounds into the recording. This process foregrounds the reality of contemporary popular music song texts as palimpsests, the 'final' version having been made up from various layers of sound. Such practices inevitably issue challenges to the supposed 'purity' of 'traditional' instrumentation.

[75] Pessoa, *Book of Disquiet*, p. 14.

[76] 'Fado Varina', lyric by José Carlos Ary dos Santos, music by Moniz Pereira, recorded by Carlos do Carmo (*Um Homem na Cidade*), Ana Moura (*Novo Homem na Cidade*) and Carla Pires (on *Ilha do Meu Fado* (Ocarina OCA 011, 2005)).

filmed footage of Lisbon street life. As the song progresses, Carmo walks forward until he is flanked by two large screens with photographs of Lisbon on them. He walks between these screens, advancing towards the camera, between further pairs of screens all depicting the city until he comes to a halt during the closing of the song in front of what is now a collage of images made up of the photographs he has passed. In a sense he is touring through the city but it is a city of mostly static images and the focus remains on the singer throughout, zooming in on him as he delivers the final line of the song.

Saura has arguably missed something in the song by singling out Carmo and superimposing him on both the musicians and the city. To see what he is missing, let us return to Certeau's rousing dedication:

> The floodlights have moved away from the actors who possess proper names and social blazons, turning first toward the chorus of secondary characters, then settling on the mass of the audience ... Slowly the representatives that formerly symbolized families, groups, and orders disappear from the stage they dominated during the epoch of the name. We witness the advent of the number.[77]

Saura, then, has returned the floodlight to the individual, as have I. There is a seeming paradox here. How do we reconcile an insistence on the number, the everyday, the move away from the proper name, with an account such as that presented in this book, which emphasizes biographies and recordings of prominent fado stars? Would it not be more apposite to Certeau's vision to take the route more usually frequented by the ethnomusicologist and attend to the everyday practice of fado by less well-known amateurs ('users', in Lefebvre's and Certeau's formulation)? This is a topic I have touched on in the Introduction and will return to again in Chapter 5; but I want to foreground it briefly here in order to connect it to the theories of spatiality outlined above and to the practice of theory itself.

The key is in Certeau's mention of metonymy, the part taken for the whole. It is time, he says, for the floodlights to move from the actors representing the people to the people themselves. But what this does not take into consideration is the audience's desire, the fact that they came to the theatre in the first place wishing to see themselves represented by those privileged, highlighted and floodlit actors. The same is true for the godlike view of the city, a view that is actively desired. People want to get out of the city and look back or down on it, to look back, as it were, on 'themselves' in the place where they normally are. It should be remembered that the request for representation of the community – be it visual, sonic, theoretical or academic – comes from within the community itself. There is no privileged 'theorist' forever in a position on the 'outside'. Which is not to say that there is not power, and abuse of power and misrepresentation and non-reflexive categorization. All this exists but it cannot all be laid at the feet of those with proper names. Celebrity culture is something that feeds on a desire that emerges from the

---

[77] Certeau, *Practice*, p. v.

everyday. This paradox is also encountered in those artists who are simultaneously feted as 'one of the people' and as celebrities. Even the celebrant of anonymity and the practice of everyday life still attaches to his celebration a proper name: Michel de Certeau.[78]

The Sounded City

As we have seen, Certeau was keen to present the negotiation of the city as both writing and reading, an in-between process where one is constantly aware of shifting perspectives and of alternations between activity and passivity. However, in moving towards the themes of the next chapter, it is necessary to consider the potential problems of this association between street and page. In his book *Species of Spaces* – a work that has influenced my own thinking about the possibilities of building relationships between different spatial categories – Georges Perec begins with the space of the page upon which the letters he writes are displayed, before zooming out to the book in which he is writing, the desk upon which the book sits and so on until we have left the room, the house, the street, the city and even the world far behind. The 'problem', however, is that we reach the end of his adventure without having really left the space of the page.[79]

Derek Gregory highlights a similar issue in the work of geographer Alan Pred, who explicitly uses wordplay and textual strategies (like Perec, Pred utilizes white space, unconventional line breaks and vertical text) to introduce a spatial element into his writing and to let it perform what it is writing about. Pred describes this as an exploitation of 'the landscape of the page' and, while it is true that his reader is forced to be aware, like Derrida's, that a point is being made about the performative power of writing, his account of the landscapes he describes remains a description and not the landscape itself.[80] Gregory finds more success in Pred's inventive visual mappings of the itinerary of workers' everyday lives, where the routes traced by workers are superimposed in a temporal-spatial representation onto the terrain of

---

[78]   When Certeau opens his essay with a description of the view from the World Trade Center, is he standing there as a theorist or a tourist? It is tempting to say 'both and neither': both, because he can occupy both positions at once; neither, because he is not 'there' anyway. He is an example of the anthropologist discussed by Clifford Geertz who has to bring the 'being there' of field work to the 'being here' of writing and dissemination, and whose readers have to take the reverse journey from the 'being here' of reading to the 'being there' of identification with the object of the text. See Clifford Geertz, *Works and Lives: The Anthropologist as Author* (Stanford: Stanford University Press, 1988).

[79]   Georges Perec, 'Species of Spaces / Espèces d'espaces', in *Species of Spaces and Other Pieces*, ed. & tr. John Sturrock, rev. edn (London: Penguin, 1999), pp. 1–96.

[80]   Alan Pred, *Lost Words and Lost Worlds: Modernity and the Language of Everyday Life in Late Nineteenth-Century Stockholm* (Cambridge: Cambridge University Press, 1990), p. xvi. See Gregory's discussion of Pred in *Geographical Imaginations*, pp. 241–56.

the city. But, like Certeau and Perec, description is still anchored to the page no matter how much it drifts.

Certeau seems aware of these issues in his comparison between walking and speech acts. Just as a written text cannot represent for us what the speaking (or singing) voice can do in the process of enunciation, neither can the tracing of an itinerary on a map give us a clue as to the processes involved in traversing territory:

> Walking affirms, suspects, tries out, transgresses, respects, etc., the trajectories it "speaks." All the modalities sing a part in this chorus, changing from step to step, stepping in through proportions, sequences, and intensities which vary according to the time, the path taken and the walker. These enunciatory operations are of an unlimited diversity. They therefore cannot be reduced to their graphic trail.[81]

Certeau's reliance on a musical vocabulary is particularly telling. Henri Lefebvre, meanwhile, is interested throughout his later work with a theory that begins with the body. Indeed, Lefebvre's insistence on the centrality of the body and on others' bodies, constantly encountered in the production of social space, is one of the areas in which representations of space and representational spaces are seen to come into close relationship with each other. As we have seen, Lefebvre finds the representation of space connected to the dominant order (what Jacques Lacan would call the Symbolic Order[82]) to be one that relies on illusory symbols:

> Perhaps it would be true to say that the place of social space as a whole has been usurped by a part of that space endowed with an illusory special status – namely, the part which is concerned with writing and imagery, underpinned by the written text (journalism, literature), and broadcast by the media; a part, in short, that amounts to abstraction wielding awesome reductionist force vis-à-vis 'lived' experience.[83]

In contrast to this, Lefebvre suggests that music and other 'non-verbal signifying sets' (painting, sculpture, architecture, theatre) that rely to a greater extent on space than do 'verbal sets' are more likely to keep a sense of space alive, thus challenging the reductionist abstraction of the verbal.

For Alain Badiou, theatre is distinct from the other arts because of its reliance on being acted out in space; the fact that it cannot come together until the time and the space of performance gives it an 'eventual' quality that makes each performance singular:

---

[81]   Certeau, *Practice*, p. 99.

[82]   Lefebvre was deeply critical of Lacan, but this should not deter us from the centrality of the role of symbolic language in the work of the two theorists.

[83]   Lefebvre, *Production of Space*, p. 52.

theater is the assemblage of extremely disparate components, both material and ideal, whose only existence lies in the performance, in the act of theatrical representation. These components (a text, a place, some bodies, voices, costumes, lights, a public ...) are gathered together in an event, the performance, whose repetition, night after night, does not in any sense hinder the fact that, each and every time, the performance is evental, that is, singular.[84]

Musicologists reading such a passage will no doubt be struck not only by the fact that musical performance could be spoken of in much the same way, but also that it has already been done, most notably in the work of Christopher Small.[85] I wish to stay with Badiou, however, in order to maintain the idea of the theatre event and what he calls 'theatre-ideas', the ideas created at the point of performance which could not have been created prior to it or in any other space. This has relevance for the importance we place on the text in a theatrical event (and I am thinking of a musical practice such as fado singing as precisely such an event), for '[i]n the text or the poem, the theatre-idea is *incomplete*'. Until the moment of performance the theatre-idea is in an 'eternal form' and 'not yet itself'.[86]

While this seems evident in terms of a play we might go to see in the theatre, it is equally true of the theatre of everyday life that Lefebvre recognizes in the street: 'here everyday life and its functions are coextensive with, and utterly transformed by, a theatricality as sophisticated as it is unsought, a sort of involuntary *mise-en-scène*.'[87] Here, the 'external' text would be the symbolic law of the representation of space, the legal script that underwrites how we perform in social space. Lefebvre would later develop these ideas in his essays on 'rhythmanalysis', where patterns are discerned in everyday life.[88] The practice of everyday life exceeds the dominant script of symbolic law but it does not get rid of the script. Lefebvre speaks of a 'spatial economy' whereby users of a city space have an unspoken 'non-aggression pact' that determines their rules of engagement with each other.[89]

---

[84]   Alain Badiou, *Handbook of Inaesthetics*, tr. Alberto Toscano (Stanford: Stanford University Press, 2005 [1998]), p. 72.

[85]   Christopher Small, *Musicking: The Meanings of Performing and Listening* (Middletown: Wesleyan University Press, 1998).

[86]   Badiou, *Handbook*, p. 73.

[87]   Lefebvre, *Production of Space*, p. 74.

[88]   Henri Lefebvre, *Rhythmanalysis: Space, Time and Everyday Life*, tr. Stuart Elden & Gerald Moore (London & New York: Continuum, 2004). There are two potential connections to Lisbon and fado here. Firstly, Lefebvre based his essays on work by Gaston Bachelard, who in turn claimed to have been influenced by philosopher Lúcio Alberto Pinheiro dos Santos. Santos had developed his thoughts on rhythmanalysis in Brazil or Portugal (accounts differ). Secondly, there is a section in Lefebvre's book where he describes the view from his balcony; the rhythms of the street he observes are directly comparable to those described in Tristão da Silva's 'Da Janela do Meu Quarto' (see above).

[89]   Lefebvre, *Production of Space*, p. 56.

It is this spatial economy that determines what Peter Stallybrass and Allon White call the 'politics and poetics of transgression', those moments when the rules of engagement are ignored but whose ignorance relies on the economy both for its beginning and its end (the return to normality).[90]

With this in mind it is worth paying attention to the role of music and festivals in the city as forms of both divergence from and reassertion of social norms. In Lisbon, this is particularly notable during the period known as the *Festas de Lisboa*, a series of festivals held in celebration of the 'popular saints' and in which there is an interesting mixture of official and semi-official events. The former comprise concerts, marches, exhibitions, screenings and so on. The semi-official include the taking over of public spaces by stalls serving drinks and stages where music is played. The fact that the predominant music at this point is *pimba* and that the food served is grilled sardines reflects the sense of tradition and of the country in the city (*pimba* is generally more associated with the countryside).[91] *Pimba* is explicitly rude, does not attempt any of the erudite airs and graces of fado (although there is a rude undercurrent to fado too), and, as a music that cannot be cleaned up or made cool, lurks as the obscene underbelly of popular culture in Portugal.

Such events allow power to continue, as Slavoj Žižek explores in much of his work. Using the example of the mutiny against Captain Bligh on *The Bounty*, Žižek focuses on the uses of unofficial power and the relationship between power and enjoyment. The enjoyment, or *jouissance*, associated with unofficial power – the power that operates 'below decks' – must be recognized and allowed to operate by the forces of official power 'above'. Should the official power attempt to curtail the unofficial, the latter will most likely rise up against the former: 'The mutiny – violence – broke out when Bligh interfered with this murky world of obscene rituals that served as the phantasmatic background of power.'[92]

The connection between official and underground power tends to be more prevalent in the case of authoritarian regimes. It is interesting to note the use of music and festivities in films from the era of the Estado Novo to see how this connection is played out. In *Canção de Lisboa* (1933), there are various moments when impromptu moments of transgression break out, such as an improvised fado in the street and a drunken rant by the main protagonist against fado and *fadistas*, during which he proposes an 'anti-fado' week to cure the nation's social ills. As commentators on the film have noted, however, these are moments of mild transgression which allow for the presence on screen of police officers or other

---

[90] Peter Stallybrass and Allon White, *The Politics and Poetics of Transgression* (London: Methuen, 1986).

[91] A brief description of *pimba* is provided at the start of Chapter 4.

[92] Slavoj Žižek, '"I Hear You With My Eyes"; or, The Invisible Master', in Renata Salecl & Slavoj Žižek (eds.), *Gaze and Voice as Love Objects* (Durham, NC, & London: Duke University Press, 1996), p. 100. See also Žižek's 'Superego by Default', in *Metastases of Enjoyment: On Women and Causality* (London & New York: Verso, 2005 [1994]), pp. 54–85, for a similar discussion of the hidden workings of power.

patriarchal figures associated with the state to reassert the law.[93] In this film, as in others such as *O Costa do Castelo* (1943), *Fado, História D'uma Cantadeira* (1948) and *O Grande Elias* (1950), fado is cast as both hero and villain. A common theme is commitment to the social group, often epitomized by the family, with a typical plot involving deception or abandonment of certain family members, resolved by a conversion in which the transgressor sees the error of their ways. In *Fado, História D'uma Cantadeira*, the fado singer (played by Amália Rodrigues) abandons her family to become a famous performer. She transgresses to such an extent that she even abandons fado. At the point where she enacts the ultimate betrayal – not reading a note that has been sent to her regarding a family illness – she is seen singing flamenco.

This dialectic between transgression and the law is visible also in the mass fencing-off that is the result of what Lefebvre calls 'vacationland festival', those areas marked off for rest and relaxation that promise utopia but rely on careful staging and investment by capitalists.[94] It is visible too in the spaces allotted to fado, from the *taberna* to the large-scale shows put on for the *Festas*. In these events, fado fills the streets and lays claim to the city, to the people and to an escape from its boundaries. What we can determine from the festival and other negotiations of power in the social space is a reliance on a script which may be exceeded but cannot be done away with.

In 'The Right to the City', Lefebvre provides us with an excellent way to move from de Certeau's 'written' city to a sonic one when he observes that 'The city is heard as much as music as it is read as a discursive writing'.[95] For Ángel Crespo, too, it is necessary to encounter the city via its flavours, smells and music.[96] And while it is not at all surprising to us to think of the city as a site of noise, we need to consider the differences between seeing from a distance and hearing from a distance. Sonic knowledge can only be a local knowledge in that, moving away from the site of the sound, we lose earshot. We cannot have the extensive zooming-out of the visual realm, though on the other hand we can hear around corners and through walls. We can also distinguish between background noise and differentiated noise, and it is possible to imagine a sound that would zoom in and out between the dull roar, the resonance and the zoned, and we can still think of music as organizing the chaotic space of sound. As Diane Ackerman writes: 'Sounds have to be located in space, identified by type, intensity, and other features. There is a geographical quality to listening.'[97] This is true for both our perception

---

[93] See Lisa Shaw, 'A Canção de Lisboa / Song of Lisbon', in Alberto Mira (ed.), *The Cinema of Spain and Portugal* (London & New York: Wallflower Press, 2005), p. 27.

[94] Lefebvre, *Production of Space*, pp. 58–9.

[95] Lefebvre, 'The Right to the City', p. 109.

[96] Crespo, *Lisboa*, p. 12.

[97] Diane Ackerman, *A Natural History of the Senses* (London: Phoenix, 1996 [1990]), p. 178.

of the world 'outside' and for the more intimate place of private listening where music can act as a taming of space.

In closing this chapter, we have not been unburdened of the recording 'problem'. When Badiou speaks of the theatre-idea as a possibility that only emerges from the theatrical event, he puts in mind the absolute precedence of this event. If anything can come after it to recall it and keep it within knowledge, it can only be a transcription. As Certeau and Lefebvre point out, this scriptural process can only be a reduction of lived experience. And yet we cannot deny the desirability of such transcriptions, a desirability born from a need to revisit these evental sites. We need, therefore, to distinguish between the event and the knowledge of the event which can only come after. This realm of knowledge is where recording resides, a thing we can go back to, a sonic space we can tame and revisit and a fantasy we can enter.

Recording may reduce the complexity of the sonic space just as knowledge is always a reduction of what just *is*. The danger, for Lefebvre, is that this knowledge can become the basis for a dominant ideology. The solution is not to get rid of the representation of space (Lefebvre knows this is not possible) but to recognize how it works in conjunction with spatial practice and spaces of representation. As Victor Burgin suggests, 'The city in our actual experience is *at the same time* an actually existing physical environment, *and* a city in a novel, a film, a photograph, a city seen on television, a city in a comic strip, a city in a pie chart, and so on'.[98] This 'and so on' must include music, for the city is also a city in a song. Our knowledge is gained both from lived experience and from the representations of our and others' experience. Sylviane Agacinski recognizes this in her account of Walter Benjamin, the archetypal *flâneur*, pointing out that he is never innocent of the city through which he strolls:

> What Francis Bacon called 'lettered experience' (experience transmitted through books) interferes here with a reading of the city that comes about through walking. Thus the walker's *lived* experience is traversed by a 'second existence,' the result of books, in such a way that the different types of experience merge and fade into one another.[99]

It is with this notion of a lack of innocence that I wish to move on to the next chapter, where I will suggest that we need to add the notion of 'sounded experience' into the mix. For now, hopefully I have been able to highlight the prevalence of the city of Lisbon in fado songs and to locate it alongside a range of theories concerning the role of the city in modernity. While many of these debates have taken place in contexts far removed from vernacular music practice, the bringing

---

[98] Victor Burgin, *In/Different Spaces: Place and Memory in Visual Culture* (Berkeley & London: University of California Press, 1996), p. 28 (emphasis in original).

[99] Sylviane Agacinski, *Time Passing: Modernity and Nostalgia*, tr. Jody Gladding (New York: Columbia University Press, 2003 [2000]), p. 56.

of these worlds together reminds us that the issues of modernity and postmodernity that shape critical debate are also negotiated in practices of everyday life. Music has an important role to play in these processes, as George Lipsitz notes:

> Through music we learn about place and about displacement. Laments for lost places and narratives of exile and return often inform, inspire, and incite the production of popular music. Songs build engagement among audiences at least in part through references that tap memories and hopes about particular places. Intentionally and unintentionally, musicians use lyrics, musical forms, and specific styles of performance that evoke attachment to or alienation from particular places.[100]

This mention of intentionality brings us back to the uses of memory described in Chapter 1, where memory was both the unexpected and the desired revisiting of the past. As described in the next chapter, the narrator of Marcel Proust's *A la recherche du temps perdu* is thrust suddenly into his past by the tasting of a *petite madeleine*, which subsequently sends him on a mission to recapture and recount this past. As we will see, Proust's character Swann, having been taken unaware by the sound of a particular piano sonata, finds himself wishing to 'own' the music in some manner. As for Swann, so for us: we can choose to (re)visit places via deliberate musical choices, or we can be taken unaware by musical madeleines.

---

[100] George Lipsitz, *Dangerous Crossroads: Popular Music, Postmodernism and the Poetics of Place* (London and New York: Verso, 1994), p. 4.

Chapter 3

'Trago Fado nos Sentidos':
Memory, Witnessing and Testimony in Fado

My consciousness of the city is, at its core, my consciousness of myself.
— Fernando Pessoa[1]

Introduction: Witnessing and Fixing

This chapter continues the work on the city begun in Chapter 2 while placing a greater emphasis on temporal issues. I do not neglect the spatial, as it is important to keep both space and time in play. The focus here, though, is on witnessing and on the fixing of the temporal flow. I think of the city of Lisbon and fado songs as bearing witness to each other. As the fado singer Beatriz de Conceição sings, 'Lisboa é testemunha' [Lisbon is witness] to the life of its citizens and the history of change in its streets.[2] By asserting this in song, Conceição also proves fado itself to be a kind of testimony, presenting evidence of the everyday life of those same citizens and streets. The questions that interest me in this area concern the desire to bear witness, the methods by which subjects do so, and the 'use' that can be made of both witnesses and their testimony.

Memory and forgetting are intricately connected to our sense of place, as a number of late twentieth century works have shown.[3] Many of these works draw

---

[1]   Fernando Pessoa, *The Book of Disquiet*, tr. Richard Zenith (Harmondsworth: Penguin, 2001), p. 329.

[2]   Beatriz da Conceição, 'Lisboa É Testemunha', *Clássicos da Renascença* (Movieplay MOV 31.021, 2000).

[3]   Sylviane Agacinski, *Time Passing: Modernity and Nostalgia*, tr. Jody Gladding (New York: Columbia University Press, 2003 [2000]); M. Christine Boyer, *The City of Collective Memory: Its Historical Legacy and Architectural Entertainments* (Cambridge, MA, & London: The MIT Press, 1996 [1994]); Svetlana Boym, *The Future of Nostalgia* (New York: Basic Books, 2001); Andreas Huyssen, *Twilight Memories: Marking Time in a Culture of Amnesia* (New York & London: Routledge, 1995), and *Present Pasts: Urban Palimpsests and the Politics of Memory* (Stanford: Stanford University Press, 2003); Paul Ricoeur, *Memory, History, Forgetting*, tr. Kathleen Blamey & David Pellauer (Chicago & London: University of Chicago Press, 2004); Raphael Samuel, *Theatres of Memory Volume 1: Past and Present in Contemporary Culture* (London & New York: Verso, 1996 [1994]), and *Island Stories: Unravelling Britain (Theatres of Memory, Volume II)*, ed. Alison Light, Sally Alexander & Gareth Stedman Jones (London & New York: Verso, 1998).

on ideas from the classical period relating to the use of place in the perfecting of memory. The history of mnemotechnics has been well described by Francis Yates, but here I wish to draw a fictional example from a writer whose work I will be returning to later. Italo Calvino's *Invisible Cities* presents itself as a series of tales told by Marco Polo to Kublai Khan about the cities he has visited on his travels. All these cities are grouped according to a range of features: memory, desire, signs and meanings, continuity and discontinuity, and so on. Zora, a city associated with memory, is presented as the exemplification of mnemotechnics:

> Zora's secret lies in the way your gaze runs over patterns following one another as in a musical score where not a note can be altered or displaced. The man who knows by heart how Zora is made, if he is unable to sleep at night, can imagine he is walking along the streets and he remembers the order by which the copper clock follows the barber's striped awning, then the fountain with the nine jets, the astronomer's glass tower, the melon vendor's kiosk ...[4]

To a certain extent, then, we are back to the idea presented in Chapter 2 of the city as a text which can be read, although there is already a suggestion in the associative nature of the series of memory places that this is not a text that can be taken in at a glance but one which has to be negotiated 'point by point'. Like the memory theatres described by Yates, it is the bringing together of the spatial and the temporal that aids recollection. But Calvino/Polo finds a paradox: in order to be an effective memory theatre, Zora cannot change. By remaining static, the city 'has languished, disintegrated, disappeared. The earth has forgotten her.'[5]

A related idea comes in the form of the danger presented by repetition, as in another invisible city, Zirma, where the narrator is forced to claim that 'The city is redundant: it repeats itself so that something will stick in the mind'. But memory is equally redundant: 'it repeats signs so that the city can begin to exist.'[6] The desire to fix something that is in danger of being lost leads to often paradoxical ends. As Paul Ricoeur recounts, the tool which would come to be seen as the ultimate solution to such a problem – writing – was the very thing that, for Socrates, would be the end of true memory, demoting recollection to recitation.[7] And, as Jacques Derrida showed, the philosophical problems raised by the interaction between memory, speech and writing would continue to resound well into our

---

[4]   Italo Calvino, *Invisible Cities*, tr. William Weaver (London: Secker & Warburg, 1974), p. 15.

[5]   Ibid., p. 16.

[6]   Ibid., p. 19.

[7]   Paul Ricoeur, *Memory, History, Forgetting*, tr. Kathleen Blamey & David Pellauer (Chicago & London: University of Chicago Press, 2004) pp. 7–21.

own era.[8] Similar problems emerge with the onset of recording technology in the phonographic era, as I will discuss below.

In mentioning this material, my primary interest is with writing (in its broadest sense) as a form of fixing, for, in order to do the work of remembering, be it a melancholy or a militant elegizing or a post-traumatic 'working-through', there is generally a clear desire to 'get it down' somehow. I wish to stay with this theme by thinking of the ways that writing functions as a form of witnessing. The following extract from a short piece by Jorge Luis Borges entitled 'The Witness' gets to the heart of the matter:

> He is awakened by the bells tolling the Angelus. In the kingdoms of England the ringing of bells is now one of the customs of the evening, but this man, as a child, has seen the face of Woden, the divine horror and exultation, the crude wooden idol hung with Roman coins and heavy clothing, the sacrificing of horses, dogs and prisoners. Before dawn he will die and with him will die, and never return, the last immediate images of these pagan rites; the world will be a little poorer when this Saxon has died.[9]

Borges is here exploring one of his favourite themes, oblivion. He goes on to note that with every death 'one thing, or an infinite number of things, dies'. And he finishes, not surprisingly, by reflecting on his own transient world: 'What will die with me when I die, what pathetic or fragile form will the world lose? The voice of Macedonio Fernández, the image of a red horse in the vacant lot at Serrano and Charcas, a bar of sulphur in the drawer of a mahogany desk?'[10]

What is notable here is the recourse to the 'pathetic or fragile form', the suggestion that history and biography be thought of as fragments, seemingly unimportant details that have stubbornly persisted in memory. In this sense they resemble the memories of the 'I remember' school discussed in Chapter 1, those random fragments, personal or shared, that are placed together to form a life. In terms of biography they accord with Roland Barthes's use of the 'biographeme', the detail that escapes the remembering of an individual in terms of chronology. As Seán Burke notes of Barthes's use of the device in the latter's *Sade, Fourier, Loyola*:

> These details – Fourier's cats and flowers, Sade's dislike of the sea – are crystalline moments in lives whose motion and totality are necessarily irrecoverable. While the conventional biographer will seek to mimic the impetus of a life, to register it according to certain representative proportions, the biographeme breaks with the teleology implicit in this lambent narrative movement. Events are not

---

8   Jacques Derrida, *Dissemination*, tr. Barbara Johnson (London & New York: Continuum, 2004 [1972]), pp. 67–186.

9   Jorge Luis Borges, 'The Witness' (tr. James E. Irby), in *Labyrinths*, ed. Donald A. Yates & James E. Irby (Penguin: Harmondsworth, 1985 [1964]), p. 279.

10   Ibid., p. 279.

connected to imply any destiny or purpose in the course of a life, rather the biographemes are the shards of any such forward movement, those velleities that are passed over in the more frenetic, directed movement of the footprint-following biographer.[11]

In doing so, the biographeme partakes of a process similar to the 'flash' of history that Walter Benjamin proposes.[12] This notion of history is similar to the kind of collective memory that Gilbert Adair evokes when he describes his versioning of Roland Barthes and Georges Perec as 'tiny shards of a common nostalgia'.[13] The shards suggest a series of broken-off memories that, while difficult to locate, may prick the conscience at any given time. As Burke says:

> The biographeme suspends narrative time and the *telos* that only such time can insure. Its ethos has affinities with the Proustian concept of 'involuntary memory' as it has too with the repertoires of ordinary memory. Those who have lost their nearest and dearest do not recall their departed in the manner of the monumental biographer, but through discrete images, a love of cats and flowers, a liking for particular cakes, watery eyes like Ignatius of Loyola.[14]

Lost shards become found through this involuntary process, bringing the past to the present: 'For Barthes, never far from Proust, the biographeme reverberates with the pathos of lost time, and yet participates in its recovery.'[15]

There is still no certainty of any kind of permanence to these shards. Yet Borges and Barthes are already attempting a solution to the problem by writing it down. As Barthes struggles with the dilemma of whether or not to keep a diary, he records the following:

> Death, real death, is when the witness himself dies. Chateaubriand says of his grandmother and his great-aunt: 'I may be the only man in the world who knows that such persons have existed': yes, but since he has written this, and written it well, we know it too, insofar, at least, as we still read Chateaubriand.[16]

---

[11]   Seán Burke, *The Death and Return of the Author: Criticism and Subjectivity in Barthes, Foucault and Derrida*, 2nd edn (Edinburgh: Edinburgh University Press, 1998), pp. 38–9.

[12]   'The past can be seized only as an image which flashes up at the instant when it can be recognized and is never seen again.' Walter Benjamin, 'Theses on the Philosophy of History', in *Illuminations*, ed. Hannah Arendt, tr. Harry Zorn (London: Pimlico, 1999), p. 247.

[13]   Gilbert Adair, *Myths & Memories* (London: Fontana, 1986), p. xiv.

[14]   Burke, *Death and Return*, p. 39.

[15]   Ibid., p. 39.

[16]   Barthes, *The Rustle of Language*, tr. Richard Howard (Berkeley & Los Angeles: University of California Press, 1989), pp. 362–3.

Fernando Pessoa had earlier discussed a similar process and its implications:

> We say 'Cromwell *did*' but 'Milton *says*.' And in the distant future when there is no more England ... Cromwell will be remembered only because Milton mentioned him in a sonnet. The end of England will signify the end of what we may call the work of Cromwell, or the work in which he collaborated. But the poetry of Milton will end only with the end of all civilization or of man's presence on earth, and perhaps even then it won't have ended.[17]

There is clearly an importance being placed here on biography, for biography is strongly associated with the types of remembering associated with death rites (the witness, the epitaph, the obituary, the gravestone). Furthermore, biography serves both to distinguish individuals from each other and to bring them together in community through similarity and shared qualities, intimately connecting personal and collective memory and identity while attempting to fix the messy fluidity of lived life. Mark C. Taylor, in his fascinating survey of final resting places, discusses the rise of biography following Augustine (whose *Confessions* may remind us that autobiography is not so much telling the truth of oneself as deciding what, how much and to whom to confess). Taylor suggests that the rise of cemeteries and marked graves 'invented' death, a point that relates to the notion that writing invents speech and that scores, transcriptions, instruments and ultimately recording invent (or at least reinvent) music.[18] It may initially be hard to see popular song in similar terms given its apparently transient nature, but the contention throughout this book is that popular song, as much as any other part of popular culture, has, in the modern era, become subject to the kind of desire for perpetuation that has long been literature's domain. This has happened via the technology of recording and storing but also by the desire that drives the development of such technology, the desire to ward off loss, to archive, to remember even if it is by means of a relegated memory. There are important differences, of course. Recorded music has not had nearly the erasing effect on live performance that writing brought about and it has never been convincing that preservation is recording's *raison d'être* in the way that it is arguably writing's. But even these differences, in the work of a thinker such as Jacques Derrida, can be seen to be constructions.

From Transcribing to Writing

When talking about witnessing we must be clear what we are describing. In his poem 'Elegy', Borges lists some of the many 'things that men see' but notes a time when all that he could see was 'the face of a girl from Buenos Aires / a face that

---

[17]   Fernando Pessoa, *The Selected Prose*, ed. & tr. Richard Zenith (New York: Grove Press, 2001), p. 166.

[18]   Mark C. Taylor & Dietrich Christian Lammerts, *Grave Matters* (London: Reaktion Books, 2002), p. 17.

does not want you to remember it'.[19] The conflict between what the witness cannot forget and what the witnessed wants to be forgotten highlights three basic processes of witnessing: firstly, a reception of something (an image, a sound, a smell) that has left some form of imprint in the mind; secondly, a presentation (a making-present) to the self of the impression (memory); and finally, a re-presentation of that memory to an other (here, the reader). Of these, only the last might be said to be voluntary; Borges has not only remembered the face that did not want to be remembered but he has told his readers about it. Or has he? We still know nothing about that face, only his remembering it. We might compare this 'witness report' with that of Borges's fellow Argentine, the novelist Juan José Saer, whose novel *The Witness* (1983) plays with the standard accounts of the colonization of the New World by having a sixteenth-century Spaniard caught and kept prisoner by an Indian tribe solely so that he can be released and act as witness to the tribe's existence and destruction, to tell their story to the world.[20]

This allows us to reduce the main aspects of witnessing to two: seeing and saying. In this sense we might call to mind the witness as used in law courts, where a witness who has seen but will not say what they have seen is of little use. The witness is carrying something that is wanted by the other; we might define the 'active' witness by saying that it is the desirability of their information that makes of them a witness. For our purposes we also need to expand the notion of witnessing from merely 'seeing' to include the other senses. Borges has already provided guidance for this in his use of fragments that go beyond the visual in 'The Witness': the tolling of bells, the voice of Macedonio Fernández, the smell of sulphur. Listening, here, can be thought of as a carrying which may be borne but which may also be unburdened by passing on. In the latter process this carrying becomes a carrying-out – the completion of a task – and witnessing moves from a passive to an active role, as in the witness before the Law.

Witnessing, then, can be a *productive* force in that it results in the transference of a thing presented to a thing re-presented (this use of the word 'transference' serves to remind us that psychoanalysis is a form of witnessing: a kind of double witnessing, where the analyst witnesses the analysand witnessing themselves). Writing is an example of this, the transference from the witnessed to the represented. Something is inevitably lost in the process, as Roland Barthes observes in 'From Speech to Writing', an essay prefacing a series of interviews with him that have been transcribed: 'This inscription, what does it cost us? What do we lose? What do we win?'[21] Jacques Roubard, in trying to weigh the benefits and dangers of writing, also stresses the notion of transference from one place or state to another:

---

[19]   Jorge Luis Borges, 'Elegy' (tr. Donald A. Yates), in *Labyrinths*, p. 287.

[20]   Juan José Saer, *The Witness*, tr. Margaret Jull Costa (London: Serpent's Tail, 1990 [1983]).

[21]   Roland Barthes, *The Grain of the Voice: Interviews 1962–1980*, tr. Linda Coverdale (Berkeley & Los Angeles: University of California Press, 1985), p. 3.

Once set down on paper, each *fragment of memory* ... becomes, in fact, inaccessible to me. This probably doesn't mean that the record of memory, located under my skull, in the neurons, has disappeared, but everything happens as if a transference had occurred, something in the nature of a translation, with the result that ever since, the words composing the black lines of my transcription interpose themselves between the record of memory and myself, and in the long run completely supplant it.[22]

Roubard's friend Georges Perec concurs: 'The work of writing is always done in relation to something that no longer exists, which may be fixed for a moment in writing, like a trace, but which has vanished.'[23] We are back to the notion of forgetting and we can see here how writing, along with other methods of recording, is a vital tool in allowing us the possibility to forget.[24] Let us move now towards a notion of recording closer to our desired goal of dealing with sound.

Phonography

Borges provides us with the written report of his Saxon's witnessing but, in doing so, he reminds us that we have neither the Saxon's *own* written account nor the sonic record of those bells (nor, presumably, of Macedonio Fernández's voice): those sounds are lost. Recording is intimately connected with the notion of destruction, both the destruction of the past and of the self, for there is a sense in which autobiography and the work of remembering can be seen as a self-witnessing and a destruction of the self's past. Self-witnessing is dramatically exemplified in Edgar Allan Poe's story 'MS. Found in a Bottle' (1833, rev. 1845), where the narrator attempts to record his fate on a 'doomed' ship: 'I shall from time to time continue this journal ... At the last moment I will enclose the MS. in a bottle, and cast it within the sea.'[25] The close of the tale, which we assume to be the found manuscript itself, attempts to stay true to this promise as the ship goes down in a whirlpool:

> But little time will be left me to ponder upon my destiny – the circles rapidly grow small – we are plunging madly within the grasp of the whirlpool – and

---

[22] Jacques Roubard, *The Great Fire of London: A Story with Interpolations and Bifurcations*, tr. Dominic Di Bernardi (Elmwood Park, IL: Dalkey Archive Press, 1992 [1989]), pp. 197–8 (emphasis in original).

[23] Georges Perec, *Species of Spaces and Other Pieces*, ed. & tr. John Sturrock, rev. edn (London: Penguin, 1999), p. 133.

[24] The story of remembering, reciting, forgetting and writing is told evocatively in Geoffrey O'Brien, *The Browser's Ecstasy: A Meditation on Reading* (Washington: Counterpoint, 2000).

[25] Edgar Allan Poe, 'MS. Found in a Bottle', in *The Fall of the House of Usher and Other Writings*, ed. David Galloway (Harmondsworth: Penguin, 1986), pp. 105–6.

amid a roaring, and bellowing, and thundering of ocean and of tempest, the ship is quivering, oh God! And – going down.[26]

If Poe's tale still bears a sense of horror nearly two centuries after its first publication, it is surely because we recognize that, even in an era where the black boxes of aeroplanes provide records of doomed journeys far more accurate than the writing and dispatching of the manuscript allowed Poe's narrator, there is still a point beyond which nothing more can be recorded that would be of relevance to the person marked for death. As Poe's epigraph to the tale translates: 'He who has but a moment to live / No longer has anything to dissimulate.'[27] But what has been dissimulated up to that moment lives on, in a manner of speaking. This sense of being too short of time to communicate what is necessary is captured nicely in a fado performed by Ana Laíns and entitled 'Pouco Tempo' [Little Time]. The song describes a situation in which there is not enough time to 'keep everything I carry / in thought / to write everything I feel'; everything disappears in the wind.[28]

What are the limits to witnessing? Can we be witnesses to our own destruction? In the sense of Poe's narrator, the answer must be no: we are always stuck in a 'working-towards' such a witnessing via a process of 'getting down' what we can get down before we 'go down'. From another viewpoint, however, we might say that remembering is about witnessing our own destruction. Both of these possibilities are played out quite literally in Samuel Beckett's monologue *Krapp's Last Tape* (1958), in which we witness a man, Krapp, witnessing his own life as he records memories onto his tape recorder in 'celebration' of his birthday and plays back old recordings from previous similar occasions. The 39-year-old Krapp – the 'middle voice' of the three (re)presented – is 'played' by the actor manipulating a tape machine on which is heard his 'younger' voice; the 'actual' Krapp being played by the actor is thirty years older. 'Middle Krapp' recounts his thoughts on listening to an earlier tape (which we do not get to hear) made when he was younger. He is furious with the romantic idealist he used to be and mocks his younger self, allowing 'Old Krapp' to join in as he listens. But the 39-year-old still holds to certain ideals, the recording of which is now treated with contempt by the old man, who then records his own critique. The process we catch Krapp in, then, is similar to the perfecting process, or 'working-toward' mentioned above. Each successive attempt to fix life and thought somehow gets it wrong and must be updated, though for how much longer we cannot be sure due to Old Krapp's admonishments to himself to cease this endless torture and to the 'last tape' alluded to in the title. Do we *know* this is the last (final) tape that we are witnessing being

---

[26] Poe, 'MS.', p. 109. See also Mark C. Taylor's use of this same quotation in *Grave Matters*, pp. 18–19.

[27] 'Qui n'a plus qu'un moment à vivre / N'a plus rien à dissimuler – Quinault, *Atys*', Poe, 'MS', p. 99.

[28] 'Pouco Tempo', lyric by Lídia Oliveira, music by Diogo Clemente, recorded by Ana Laíns on *Sentidos* (Different World DW50018CD, 2006).

made in the same way that we know we are reading the message in the bottle in Poe's tale? Or is 'last' only supposed to refer to 'preceding', as in the way Krapp continues to listen to preceding attempts to come to terms with his life?

Krapp's Last Tape provides a good example of how nostalgia and loss interlock with technological attempts to prevent loss, and how those attempts are both a damming of the reservoir of memories and the means by which that reservoir can be tapped. Krapp is caught in a cyclical process of remembering and memorializing, of recapturing the past and planning for the future (a future where the importance of remembering the past now being recaptured *and* the moment of recapturing it will prove both fascinating and repellent). In other words *the past of the now* and *the now* are the raw materials to be mined in *the future of the now*. The *now*, at the same time, is the repository of the sum of experience of *the past of the now* – the latter has no substance outside of the former – just as *the now* will become a part of the repository that constructs *the future of the now*. In the words of film director Atom Egoyan, who filmed Beckett's monologue in 2001 (thus providing another kind of 'last tape' in the form of a videotape), 'With [the play], a man listening to his younger self commenting on his even younger self – Beckett is able to express the central paradox of personal archiving technology; its ability simultaneously to enhance and trivialize experience.'[29] David Toop, who discusses Egoyan's work, has his own 'take' on this: 'a strip of tape passing through the playback head of a tape recorder, threatening to unspool as it comes to the end of its reel, is analogous to the memory of a life threading through the space and time of the world, then unspooling into nothingness.'[30]

It is possible to bring together the Beckett of *Krapp's Last Tape*, the Barthes of *Camera Lucida* and the Walter Benjamin of 'The Work of Art in the Era of Mechanical Reproduction' in considering the implications that mechanical reproduction has for the process of witnessing. In all there seems to be a division between the faithful witnessing offered by the mechanical process of recording and that element that breaks through (punctures) the 'merely' mechanical. This element is the fetishized object, the aura regained. It is this regaining of the aura that is connected to Egoyan's point about technology enhancing even as it trivializes. It is useful here to consider the ways in which recording has followed writing in embracing a dialectic of transcription and creation. Just as writing is both a creative and transcriptive act in that it not only records but invents (is inventive), so mechanical reproduction is, as is already apparent in its name, a form of production as much as mimesis. As has often been noted, composition in Western classical music developed to such a degree that it reached a point where music no longer preceded text – the complexity of the orchestral score was such that the realization of it in music was inconceivable without the finished 'text'. In considering *Krapp's Last Tape*, we must not only dwell on the use of recording

---

[29]   Quoted in David Toop, *Haunted Weather: Music, Silence and Memory* (London: Serpent's Tail, 2004), p. 99.

[30]   Ibid., p. 99.

technology to 'memorize' the protagonist's life and experiences but must bear in mind the use of the same technology to allow Beckett to create his dramatic monologue.[31] In this sense, recording has a creative as well as transcriptive role 'to play'. This is a point that Toop takes up in connection with his own work as a musician and composer. Refusing the 'pessimism' of Jean Luc Godard – who has one of his characters suggest that 'technology has replaced memory' – Toop claims:

> Other than those times when I'm sorting back through boxes of tape, like wearish old man Krapp, delving into the archives for the purpose of resuscitating past music for a new audience, I record on minidisk, onto CD, or directly onto the hard disk of my computer. Then I work on the sound files, burrowing into their imaginary space microscopically, transforming them from raw material into a sketch, a fragment moving towards a composition, even a finished composition.
>
> In one sense this is comparable to the practice of composing music by writing notation on staves, building a composition by remembering or imagining sounds and their organisation, then documenting by purely visual method the information needed to bring that remarkable feat of imagination to life at some time in the future.[32]

The use of recorded sound to reconfigure the sonic past has been central to sample-based musics such as hip hop and its numerous offshoots, leading to a revolution in the way popular music is produced, performed and heard (albeit one that has numerous precursors in twentieth-century avant-garde music).

There are spatial as well as temporal implications arising from these processes, all of which contribute towards the production of social space. Beckett's stage instructions and Egoyan's filmic interpretation are important in this regard; in both we find that a space of intimacy is produced. The use of microphones, tape recorders, cameras and broadcasting technologies creates a totally reconfigured sonic space in the twentieth century. The implications for fado practice, as for other popular music genres, are numerous. Not least among these is the fact that there is no longer a necessity for projection, or rather that there are possibilities for new kinds of projection. What defines many modern fado singers such as Carlos do Carmo and Camané is their 'microphone voices', a point to which I will return. These technologies also have implications for the process of bearing witness,

---

[31]   I have used the term 'monologue' a couple of times now (as Toop does). But *is* it a monologue? Certainly, it is a dramatic work voiced by one actor/character but he possesses numerous voices – the voices of his three ages compounded by the 'voices' of the recording and playback devices and the inevitable 'voice' of decay that is constantly at work on them.

[32]   Toop, *Haunted Weather*, pp. 99–100. However, Toop does go on to say that 'in another sense, it's completely different' as his music is all stored in the computer and the computer can play it (no need for an ensemble).

bringing with them new possibilities of surveillance, bugging, and listening-in. This allows a removal from the 'primal scene', a putting-off and making-distant of the act of witnessing, notable in the experience of the contemporary listener of music. The fact that witnessing can involve removing oneself from the action via technologies of surveillance is often forgotten in the literature on witnessing, no doubt due to the emphasis placed in that literature on 'first hand' witnessing, of *having been there*.

Krapp's Last Tape suggests an updating of relationships between The Proustian 'involuntary memory' and Proust's project of refinding time and place via the act of consciously recording memory; the evocative power of the *petite madeleine* and the conscious act of recollection of time and place become one in *A la recherche du temps perdu*. Proust often plays out these different kinds of memory via references to music, such as the episode of Vinteuil's sonata. Proust's character M. Swann is initially affected by the music a year before the events being narrated but does not recognize it and has no way of finding out what it is. The following year, at a *soirée*, Swann rediscovers the music and is this time affected not by the immediate perception of it, but by the memory of it. Yet, even on the first listen, memory was at work. As Proust describes the impossibility of capturing music due to its fleetingness, he describes memory, in a manner that utilizes an understanding of memory as place, as 'a labourer working to put down lasting foundations in the midst of the waves, by fabricating for us facsimiles of these fleeting phrases'.[33] On Swann's rediscovery of the music, however, he is furnished with a better way of keeping hold of it: 'now he could ask the name of his stranger ... he possessed it, he could have it in his house as often as he liked, try to learn its language and its secret.'[34] Proust here combines music, place and memory in a number of ways: firstly, Swann's initial exposure to the music is described in terms of the fleetingness of spatial perception; secondly, his mind attempts to hold onto the music via the swift erection of memory places; thirdly, he is now able have the music 'in his house' where he can guard it and visit it as often as he likes.

An example of this process from the world of fado is provided in the figure of Alfredo Marceneiro. As reported in Chapter 2, Marceneiro did not record extensively, preferring to sing live in the *casas de fado* in which he was a legendary figure. The contrast between this 'authentic' but undocumented world of fado performance and the promise of reproducibility are hymned in the liner notes to the 1960 album *The Fabulous Marceneiro*:

> Here is, at last in high-fidelity, his husky voice, plaintive to the point of near-disintegration, singing fados, tilting melodies that intoxicate like wine. All this we can hear on record for the first time; and those who had the privilege of actually seeing him (a privilege he is jealous of granting) will recall the small

---

[33] Marcel Proust, *In Search of Lost Time Vol. 1: The Way by Swann's*, ed. Christopher Prendergast, tr. Lydia Davis (London: Penguin, 2002), p. 212.

[34] Ibid., pp. 214–15.

figure, the wrinkled face contrasting with the surprisingly black, wavy hair, the swaying body accompanying the inflections of the voice, the silk neckerchief significantly protecting his throat from the outrages of time and weather: the true 'fadista', the living legend ... For years and years we had been trying to get him to grant us a recording session in high-fidelity. When at last he bowed to our entreaties and could bring himself to come to our studio he was disgusted. He hates machines and things to 'interfere' with his fado (he hates 'progress' anyway). So he tried to sing with closed eyes not to see the outrage. And when that proved insufficient he grabbed his neckerchief, tied it round his eyes and started to sing all over again in complete darkness. Yet, it is to high-fidelity that we owe this rare joy: the fabulous, reluctant Marceneiro singing for us, in our homes, as many times as we please.[35]

There is much to note here. Most of the points are based around the opposition between Marceneiro as an authentic, and somehow primitive, *fadista*, and the producers and consumers involved in the recording process, who, while perhaps inauthentic, at least have 'progress' on their side. The 'disintegration' associated with Marceneiro's voice is not only an aesthetic statement (although as an aesthetic statement it works quite well at pinning down the unsettling nature of his vocal style) but also a comment on a kind of loss that is extra to the loss of *saudade* being hymned by the singer: the fact that we might lose this voice to the 'outrages of time and weather'. Without 'high-fidelity' recording we would have to rely on memory, just as those who 'had the privilege of actually seeing him' have had to do until now. But the recording promises to do more than just fix the voice; on hearing it, we will be able to recall the man himself. Writing is as important as audio recording here in at least two ways that may not immediately be obvious and which are not stated explicitly. Those behind the recording, along with its consumers, are associated with writing while Marceneiro is associated with speech and the oral tradition. Those of us who have not been fortunate enough to witness Marceneiro in the flesh have been able to read a description of him penned by C.B. Carvalho, meaning that we now possess an image to accompany our listening. Marceneiro, meanwhile, can sing in complete darkness and without the help of a lyric sheet, summoning up the verses from somewhere deep inside him (no mean feat with a lengthy song like 'Lembro-Me de Ti)'. In this sense he is, as Paul Ricoeur says of musicians, an 'athlete of memory', set apart from the everyday person even as he lives his authenticity.[36] Finally, of course, there is the resonant echo of Proust in the closing declaration that we may now possess this elusive moment and relive it 'as many times as we please'.

---

[35]   C.B. de Carvalho, liner notes to *The Fabulous Marceneiro* (Valentim de Carvalho/ EMI 724349526624, 1997 [1961]). These notes are from the original LP and were provided in both Portuguese and English.

[36]   Ricoeur, *Memory, History, Forgetting*, p. 61.

Witnessing Place: Fado's Invisible Cities

I wish to connect this discussion of witnessing, recording and fixing back to the account initiated in the previous chapter of fado's connection with the city. In that chapter we saw that some thinkers have wished to place greater emphasis on the spaces of representation than on the dominant symbolic logic of the representation of space. Svetlana Boym would seem to follow such a line of thinking when she writes: 'Places are *contexts* for remembrances and debates about the future, not *symbols* of memory or nostalgia. Thus places in the city are not merely architectural metaphors; they are also screen memories for urban dwellers, projections of contested remembrances.'[37] However, we also saw that it was necessary to keep in play the relationship between these types of space. I believe that fado song texts allow us to think of the city as both context *and* symbol. Taking on the dual roles of character and stage, the city acts very much as it might in a photograph or film; the same shift of focus from the cityscape to the human life within the cityscape occurs in fados, photographs and films. With the numerous references to the old city – the lost city that was the victim of demolition and renovation – the fado text becomes a snapshot of the past, rendered in sepia and always in danger of fading from view, of failing to be fixed for posterity.

Italo Calvino uses the imagery of the postcard to illustrate the role of the remembered city and the problems it forces upon both visitors and inhabitants, who find themselves contemplating it from the location of the remoulded city. Calvino describes Maurilia, one of his 'invisible cities', thus:

> In Maurilia, the traveler is invited to visit the city and, at the same time, to examine some old post cards that show it as it used to be: the same identical square with a hen in the place of the bus station, a bandstand in the place of the overpass, two young ladies with white parasols in the place of the munitions factory. If the traveler does not wish to disappoint the inhabitants, he must praise the postcard city and prefer it to the present one, though he must be careful to contain his regret at the changes within definite limits: admitting that the magnificence and prosperity of the metropolis Maurilia, when compared to the old, provincial Maurilia, cannot compensate for a certain lost grace, which, however, can be appreciated only now in the old post cards, whereas before, when that provincial Maurilia was before one's eyes, one saw absolutely nothing graceful and would see it even less today, if Maurilia had remained unchanged; and in any case the metropolis has the added attraction that, through what it has become, one can look back with nostalgia at what it was.[38]

One reason the city can be a source of nostalgia is that, despite the history of appeals to a rural Arcadia, the city of the past only ever survives as a fragment of

---

[37] Boym, *Future of Nostalgia*, p. 77.
[38] Calvino, *Invisible Cities*, p. 30.

the city of the present and loss is always referenced. The city is never static but is always rebuilding itself; the longing for stasis that has so often been connected to the (falsely remembered, idealized) countryside can as easily be transferred to the (falsely remembered, idealized) city of the past. The longing that is felt is the desire to see through the palimpsest that is the modern city.

As Michael Colvin suggests, fados that bemoan the destruction and mourn the loss of the old Mouraria also come to stand as witnesses of the lost city, not only in recordings but also in forming the points of reference and even source materials for scholarly works on fado, such as Colvin's own discussion of the neighbourhoods 'condemned to progress' by the Estado Novo.[39] The parts of the lower Mouraria that were left, such as the sixteenth-century hermitage of Nossa Senhora da Saude, become fetishized as remainders of the past: 'The hermitage's anomolic condition, perched unscathed among unsophisticated shopping centres and cement fountains … has made it a symbol of tradition in a Lisbon compelled to modernization.'[40] Fado, meanwhile, can act as a subversive text when highlighting not only the lost past but the wrong decisions made about the future: 'Gabriel de Oliveira's "Há Festa na Mouraria" has inspired a subversive trend in the *fado novo*: the idealization of a pre-Republican Mouraria … as an alternative to the Estado Novo's notion of progress.'[41] If we compare the Maurilia of Calvino's work with the Mouraria of fado songwriters we find a similar obsession with the city of the past, albeit articulated rather differently. Where Calvino's narrator warns against praising the old at the expense of the new, many of the fados discussed by Michael Colvin have taken the opposite view.

Here, the city becomes both 'theatre of memory' *and* museum. It is not a museum that demands the silent contemplation of a preserved site but a modern, interactive museum, more akin to a performance space, where, as Kimberly DaCosta Holton points out, the 'occularcentrism' of traditional anthropology has been converted into an appeal to all the senses.[42] Yet, while museums have developed methodologies to bring the object ever closer to a point of virtual reality, the Baudrillardian conquest of the signifier over the signified has yet to come about.[43] This is in large part due to the act of 'roping off' that provides the necessary borderline between viewer and viewed; this may entail literal ropes, or it may involve a border of another sort, be it the walls of the museum or the entrance gate to the theme park, or the recorded boundaries of a song.

---

[39]   Michael Colvin, 'Gabriel de Oliveira's "Há Festa na Mouraria" and the *Fado Novo*'s Criticism of the Estado Novo's Demolition of the Baixa Mouraria', *Portuguese Studies*, 20 (2004): 134.

[40]   Ibid.: 135.

[41]   Ibid.: 135.

[42]   Kimberly DaCosta Holton, 'Bearing Material Witness to Musical Sound: Fado's L94 Museum Debut', *Luso-Brazilian Review*, 39/2 (2002): 108.

[43]   Jean Baudrillard, *Simulacra and Simulation*, tr. Sheila Faria Glaser (Ann Arbor: The University of Michigan Press, 1994).

DaCosta Holton describes the exhibition 'Fado: Vozes e Sombras', which took place in Lisbon in 1994 and which subsequently travelled to Brazil and France. The exhibition marked an effective break with the silent gaze of traditional museology by attempting a successful fusion of sight and sound within a museum space that could allow an 'embodied spectatorship'.[44] Furthermore, with reference to the long decadence of the Portuguese empire, DaCosta Holton notes how the exhibition worked as an attempt both to break with the past by embracing its recently acquired position within a modern European Union *and* to lay claim to a national history; '"becoming closer" to other European nations meant roping off and showcasing a *national* cultural heritage worthy of *international* celebration.'[45] She also notes the role played by visual and aural representations of the city in the exhibition: 'by combining the photographic images of Lisbon with auditory samples of its social life, the museumgoer is instructed that Lisbon is not only a space of sights but a space of sounds, and that the two sensory faculties must be combined to understand fado.'[46]

As discussed earlier, a set of processes also occur in which photographs and recordings perform a creative role. As Roland Barthes pointed out, 'Photography, in order to surprise, photographs the notable; but soon, by a familiar reversal, it decrees notable whatever it photographs.'[47] Similarly, comparing writing to oral storytelling, Michel de Certeau claims: 'In combining the power to keep the past (while the primitive "fable" forgets and loses its origin) with that of indefinitely conquering distance (while the primitive "voice" is limited to the vanishing circle of its auditors), writing *produces history*.'[48] Fernando Pessoa makes a similar observation in *The Book of Disquiet*:

> To express something is to conserve its virtue and take away its terror. Fields are greener in their description than in their actual greenness. Flowers, if described with phrases that define them in the air of the imagination, will have colours with a durability not found in cellular life.
>
> What moves lives. What is said endures. There's nothing in life that's less real for having been well described. Small-minded critics point out that such-and-such poem, with its protracted cadences, in the end says merely that it's a nice day. But to say it's a nice day is difficult, and the nice day itself passes on. It's up to us to conserve the nice day in a wordy, florid memory, sprinkling new flowers and new stars over the fields and skies of the empty, fleeting outer world.

---

[44] Holton, 'Bearing Material Witness': 108.

[45] Ibid.: 112 (emphasis in original).

[46] Ibid.: 109.

[47] Roland Barthes, *Camera Lucida: Reflections on Photography*, tr. Richard Howard (London: Vintage, 2000 [1980]), p. 84.

[48] Michel de Certeau, *The Writing of History*, tr. Tom Conley (New York: Columbia University Press, 1988), p. 215.

... The grand, tarnished panorama of History amounts, as I see it, to a flow of interpretations, a confused consensus of unreliable eyewitness accounts. The novelist is all of us, and we narrate whenever we see, because seeing is complex like everything.[49]

In summoning *The Book of Disquiet* to provide more examples for this book, I want to connect fado to the Pessoan project of estranging the world, of locating its disquiet. This line of thinking stresses the links to modernity that one finds in both Pessoa and fado while also opening a dialogue with existentialism and phenomenology, highlighting fado's links to perception and to lived experience, space and place. It is also worth commenting on the fragmented nature of Pessoa's most famous prose work. These fragments seem crucial to the growth in the twentieth century of archived knowledge, written texts, museum exhibits and recorded sounds: at once parts of a whole they can never fully catalogue and desperate attempts to salvage the present as it slips from view and earshot. They anticipate a whole range of fragmented experiences of the twentieth century: the 'fragments I have shored against my ruin' in T.S. Eliot's *The Waste Land*; the wealth of ethnomusicological collections made possible by advances in recording technology; the broadcast media and its love of the soundbite; David Harvey's 'museum of modern knowledge' (see Chapter 2); the internet and its hyperlinked web of information.

The *Book of Disquiet* is also a book about Lisbon and about the ways of living made possible by city life. The role of the observer and chronicler is crucial and Pessoa creates a special character, Bernardo Soares, to achieve this task for him. Soares interweaves his own existential confusions into his descriptions of other city dwellers who walk past his place of work, his rooms or the cafés in which he spends much of his free time. A self-described dweller on the fringe of society, Soares represents what had by this time become a defining trope in Western literature, from Poe's 'The Man of the Crowd' (1840, rev. 1845) through Baudelaire's 'The Painter of Modern Life' (1863) to Rilke's *The Notebooks of Malte Laurids Brigge* (1910). A strong sense of alienation amongst the crowd comes into play in Pessoa's work, leading to yearning for a past in which individuals were more noticeable. In this way, Pessoa's book speaks to earlier modern works on the city. The excitement that Walter Benjamin finds in the Baudelairean city, for example, is present in Pessoa yet it is an excitement that mixes uneasily with a sense of estrangement.[50]

From where does this disquiet emerge? Perhaps it is from what Italo Calvino, writing on Balzac, calls the 'intuition of the city as language, as ideology, as the conditioning factor of every thought and word and gesture ... as monstrous as a

---

[49]   Pessoa, *Book of Disquiet*, p. 30.

[50]   Walter Benjamin, 'On Some Motifs in Baudelaire', in *Illuminations*, pp. 152–96. It is worth noting that Pessoa was a keen reader of Baudelaire and Poe: see George Monteiro, 'Poe/Pessoa', *Comparative Literature*, 40/2 (Spring 1988): 134–49.

giant crustacean, whose inhabitants are no more than motor articulations'.[51] The imposition of (the idea of) the city upon the citizen is alluded to by Svetlana Boym when she identifies the prevalence in the modern world of an urban identity which, while not vanquishing national identity, has taken over some of nationalism's most pertinent features, yet which 'appeals to common memory and a common past but is rooted in a man-made place, not in the soil: in urban coexistence at once alienating and exhilarating, not in the exclusivity of blood'.[52] This mixture of communal and alienating aspects is crucial to fado, where the modern disquiet of the city dweller so well captured by Pessoa is always already entangled in the responsibilities of communal living that urban society demands. If this disquiet is to be seen as one symptom of late modernity, it is possible to link the longing for freedom from the trappings of the past as another, something Boym seems to have in mind when she writes that the city is 'an ideal crossroads between longing and estrangement, memory and freedom, nostalgia and modernity'.[53]

Furthermore, there is a sense in *The Book of Disquiet* of the attempt of the individual to overcome the monstrous in the city, to imprint his or her own trace upon the structured, symbolic city plan. It is surely no coincidence that in José Saramago's *The Year of the Death of Ricardo Reis*, a magical realist tale of the dead Pessoa returning to visit one of his surviving heteronyms, the figure of Ricardo Reis is constantly encountered walking the streets of Lisbon in a recurrent pattern that, spelled out (on the sidewalks and in Saramago's wandering prose), symbolizes his brief presence in the city as a kind of psychogeographer.[54] This, along with the fact that – in Saramago as in Pessoa – the city is as much a living, breathing character as its human inhabitants, is reminiscent of Certeau's observations about the migrational or metaphorical city that coexists with the planned city. Citizens, as we have seen, are able to take partial ownership of the city. Yet that partiality only leads to a new type of symbolic ownership and, though the culturally scripted city has been challenged by this new symbolic city, the new symbolic city becomes both familiar and fantastic. With its always-threatened loss it becomes an object of nostalgic desire, forever in danger of obliteration by the real city, which cannot be symbolized or familiarized. Into what we might term, following Barthes, the *studium* of the Symbolic irrupts the *punctum* of the Real, penetrating the studied and reliable, ostensibly 'known' city and lending an aura of disquiet to what was supposedly familiar. This disquiet, in turn, nags at any comfortable sense of nostalgia that contemplation of the familiar, familial, home might otherwise suggest, for there is a danger present: that the object of nostalgia might not, after all, be lost. This is dangerous because the object of nostalgia seeks to find its

---

[51]   Italo Calvino, *The Literature Machine: Essays*, tr. Patrick Creagh (London: Secker & Warburg, 1987), p. 185.

[52]   Boym, *Future of Nostalgia*, p. 76.

[53]   Ibid., p. 76.

[54]   José Saramago, *The Year of the Death of Ricardo Reis*, tr. Giovanni Pontiero (London: Harvill, 1992 [1984]).

greatest effect in the safety promised by its inability to return and contradict the nostalgic subject. The lost and mourned object does not reply and this is part of what comforts the loser and the mourner. Yet at the same time that the mourner takes comfort in this stable situation, the danger is never altogether absent that the tranquillity so longed for will not be pierced by a *punctum*, a reminder of the reason for mourning.[55]

Above all, *The Book of Disquiet* is a book of witnessing. Pessoa introduces Soares in his preface as someone who was looking for a witness, someone who would carry his story to the world. Soares himself describes the book as 'a factless autobiography', suggesting that it will be a biography without biographemes.[56] It is arguably more like biography as a process of writing, a life *produced by writing*:

> For a long time … I haven't recorded any impressions; I don't think, therefore I don't exist. I've forgotten who I am. I'm unable to write because I'm unable to be. Through an oblique slumber, I've been someone else. To realize I don't remember myself means that I've woken up.[57]

But, if writing is presented by Soares as an affirmation of existence, he is not always convinced that the message can be transmitted to another:

> What is there to confess that's worthwhile or useful? What has happened to us has happened to everyone or only to us; if to everyone, then it's no novelty, and if only to us, then it won't be understood. If I write what I feel, it's to reduce the fever of feeling.[58]

It would be unfair of us to expect a work as fragmentary and unstructured as *The Book of Disquiet* to provide a consistent viewpoint about the processes of witnessing as both seeing and saying. Rather, it is a book plagued by doubts such as those just cited, an internal conflict between the desire to record and an uncertainty as to whether the record should be passed on. Bernardo Soares realizes (as does the Pessoa who, having written as Soares, then stores the writings in an enormous case destined to some kind of future revelation) that between the extremes of 'everyone' and 'I', there is a community of like-minded people to whom he is speaking: 'It sometimes occurs to me, with sad delight, that if one day (in a future to which I won't belong) the sentences I write are read and admired, then at last I'll have my own kin, people who "understand" me, my true family in which to be born and loved.' And shortly after: 'It seems that civilizations exist

---

55   This danger is beautifully visualized in Andrei Tarkovsky's film *Solaris* (USSR, 1972). Steven Soderbergh's remake of the film (USA, 2002) provides a useful contribution to the debate about translating loss.

56   Pessoa, *Book of Disquiet*, p. 21.

57   Ibid., p. 314.

58   Ibid., p. 21.

only to produce art and literature; words are what speak for them and remain.'[59] Soares is writing for a community that will come later, which is no doubt why he wants his manuscript to be taken by Pessoa and disseminated.

Fate

Of all Pessoa's creations, Ricardo Reis is both the most classically-minded and the one who dwells closest to the classical sense of fate that fado seems to echo. 'Each man fulfils the destiny he must fulfil', he writes:

> Like stones that border flower beds
> We are arranged by Fate, and there remain,
> Our lot having placed us
> Where we had to be placed.
> Let's have no better knowledge of what
> Was our due than that it was our due.[60]

The images of collapse, resignation and decay in fado – homologically registered in falling vocal lines (what Rodney Gallop called fado's 'drooping cadences') – cannot help but associate fado with an absence of agency, the mirror image of a 'collapsed' and fatalistic people. But in placing fado against political ideology it is never altogether clear how the music 'sizes up'. In hymning decay/decadence, could the music in fact have been a retort to an Estado Novo whose very *raison d'être* was to *arrest* further decay? What is the significance in the fact that the State was unable to completely adopt and assimilate fado, that it was unable to paper over the cracks that fado revealed? Is it conceivable that fado could be what Roland Barthes called an *acratic* language in its refusal to be assimilated?[61]

   António Osório, the author of *A Mitologia Fadista*, would vehemently deny such a claim. For Osório fado, in addition to idealizing poverty and objectifying women, hymned a defeatism bound up in '*saudosismo*, "the fumes of India", *Sebastianismo*, the "spectres of the past", the petulance of Marialva, a lachrymose predisposition, … narrow-mindedness … [and] a distaste for life'.[62] Going on to parody the famous Amália Rodrigues song 'Tudo Isto É Fado', Osório wrote:

> Misery, prostitution, sickness, dishonour, debasement, all this is 'fado'. It explains and, indirectly, absolves all ills. Before the 'laws of destiny', willpower shows itself to be non-existent; the 'philosophy' of fado condenses into an inexorable

---

[59] Ibid., pp. 167, 171.

[60] Fernando Pessoa, *A Little Larger Than the Entire Universe: Selected Poems*, ed. & tr. Richard Zenith (London: Penguin, 2006), p. 106.

[61] Roland Barthes, 'The War of Languages', in *The Rustle of Language*, pp. 106–10.

[62] António Osório, *A Mitologia Fadista* (Lisbon: Livros Horizonte, 1974), p. 11.

fatalism, ultimately nothing more than the *fatum mahumetanum* defined by Leibniz: free will can never be because men and events are automatically governed by the 'force of things'. The corollary can be instantly deduced – no one is responsible for anything.[63]

Such an opinion was undoubtedly persuasive in 1974, when Osório was writing. Apathy in the face of authoritarianism had festered for too long and change was needed. Fado was discouraged but refused to crawl away and die in a pool of its own tears. Why? One suggestion is that the power of fado's mythemes and the ease with which it can be connected to ideas of Portugueseness – however problematic such a concept remains – enforce its appropriateness and effectiveness as a staging of a traumatic *jouissance* that has meaning far beyond the world of fado music. It could be argued that Osório overstated his case and, effectively, centred fado and the '*fadista* mythology' as a cause rather than a reflection, as a constitutive element in the formation of subjectivity rather than the recognition of a subjectivity already constituted around a radical loss. He does seem to recognize this possibility at certain points, such as his consideration of how a similar experience is to be found in modern literature:

> man's impotence in the face of circumstance, the central experience of fado, does not only permeate the work of contemporary Portuguese writers, because it is at the heart of Kafka, of Beckett, of all the representative writers of our time. The seeds of dejection proliferate in these times of oppression and individual paralysis.[64]

Locating ideology within a framework suggested by Jacques Lacan and Slavoj Žižek may help us here. In doing so, we can posit the Symbolic as the realm of language, or discourse, that attempts to 'explain' the Real but which never can, for the Real remains that which cannot be symbolized. Yet that very lack in the Symbolic Order constitutes a gap and it is because of this gap, if we follow Žižek, that ideology is needed.[65] To use a metaphor not entirely inappropriate with Lisbon in mind, if the Symbolic acts as a wall to obscure the Real, a wall that has, however, seen better days and which threatens to allow the chill of the Real in through its cracked tiles and holed plaster (to be punctured, as it were, by the Real), then ideology is the sheen of new plaster needed to fill those fissures. A music more concerned with crumbling, decay, collapse and the wounds that rupture the sheen of everyday 'bearing up', a music, moreover, which dwells on melancholy and which actively seeks to remain unreconciled to the world can perhaps be a music closer to challenging ideology than might at first be imagined.

---

[63]   Ibid., p. 103.

[64]   Ibid., p. 117.

[65]   See Slavoj Žižek, *The Sublime Object of Ideology* (London & New York: Verso, 1989).

Can it be that fado operates as a sublimation of the forces operating on the modern subject, that, furthermore, it occupies the place of what Catherine Belsey calls an 'abolished particularity'? Belsey suggests that 'the abolished particularity returns as resistance, marking the speaking being's loss of the unnameable real, which is still there, but no longer there-for-a-subject. This resistance makes itself felt not only in individual experience, but also as incoherences in the apparent homogeneity of culture itself.'[66] The stubbornness of fado's mythemes, the persistence with which the same elements of Lisbonness, shame, jealousy, collapse, flight, the seasons and *saudade* are endlessly and imaginatively recombined, suggests an unwillingness to move on from the objectification of loss, a process akin to Freud's definition of melancholy. But what does it mean to be 'cured' of this stubbornness except to be taken once more into the Symbolic realm, a realm one might be unwilling to recognize as one's own?

It is important to note that both António Osório and Ricardo Reis are standing outside of such a situation, granting themselves a privileged position. Reis's 'no better knowledge' is presumably a kind of consciousness of one's lot, a consciousness that can be found in much of Pessoa's work. Pessoa, perhaps not unusually for an artist of his time, often applies a somewhat patronizing tone to the 'normal people' he writes about. The poet is always the suffering artist, whom no one else can understand and whose sufferings they, in the simplicity of their everyday lives, cannot imagine. This is true even of the Whitmanesque Álvaro de Campos, in whose celebrations of collectivity there can always be sensed an obverse impossibility for the poet himself to fully participate in the collective. The reflective middle section of Campos's 'Maritime Ode' demonstrates this, as does the concluding section of the poem when the possibilities opened up by the opening hymn are left unrealized. The sense of removal from the world he is describing is more explicit in the later poetry. In the poem that begins 'At the wheel of the Chevrolet on the road to Sintra', Campos describes passing a 'humble' cabin in the countryside and thinking 'Life there must be happy, just because it isn't mine'. In a poem from 1934, he writes of the people in the building across the street from him, 'They're happy, because they're not me'.[67]

Sometimes Pessoa does attempt to place himself among the people: 'How many, under their de rigueur jackets, / Feel, like me the horror of existence!'[68] But often people he observes labour under a false consciousness, or, in Pessoan terms, a permanent 'unconsciousness'. In 'Almost' we read of a:

Peddler crying out her wares like an unconscious hymn,
Tiny cogwheel in the clockwork of political economy,

---

[66]   Catherine Belsey, *Culture and the Real: Theorising Cultural Criticism* (London & New York: Routledge, 2005), p. 37.

[67]   Pessoa, *A Little Larger*, pp. 226, 251.

[68]   Ibid., p. 151.

Present or future mother of those who die when Empires crumble,
Your voice reaches me like a summons to nowhere, like the silence of life ...[69]

Under Pessoa's own name, hearing a woman reaper sing:

Ah, to be you while being I!
To have your glad unconsciousness
And be conscious of it![70]

Or he might try to project his feelings of difference on to others. In 'Sintra', he imagines a child gazing back from the window of the cabin at him driving by: 'Perhaps ... I looked (with my borrowed car) like a dream, a magical being come to life'. But he is still the centre of this, 'the prince of every girl's heart'.[71] To a certain extent, we might recognize an echo of the tension between Pessoa the poet and the people who populate his poetry in the distinction often drawn between the erudite and the vernacular in fado, and between the *fado castiço* and the *fado canção*. We glimpsed something of this tension in Chapter 1 when we considered the 'povo' of 'Povo Que Lavas no Rio', with Amália voicing Homem de Melo's imagination of the people. We might recognize in Homem de Melo's lyric something of the man in a Ricardo Reis poem who 'enjoys, uncertainly, / The unreflected life'.[72] How might a version of witnessing that considers the everyday help to resolve some of this tension?

Witnessing / Carrying / Bringing

I want to return to my earlier presentation of witnessing in which I suggested a focus on the carrying or bearing that the process involved. The kind of carrying I am thinking of can be heard in a fado written by Amália Rodrigues and recorded on one of her late albums. It is entitled 'Trago Fados nos Sentidos' [I Carry Fados in My Senses]:

Trago fados nos sentidos	[I carry fados in my senses
Tristezas no coração	Sadness in my heart
Trago os meus sonhos perdidos	I bear my lost dreams
Em noites de solidão.	In nights of loneliness

---

[69] Ibid., p. 237.
[70] Ibid., p. 285.
[71] Ibid., p. 226.
[72] Ibid., p. 113.

Trago versos trago sons	I bear verses, I bear sounds
D'uma grande sinfonia	Of a grand symphony
Tocada em todos os tons	Played in all the tones
Da tristeza e d'agonia.[73]	From sadness to agony]

This is the form of witnessing which I believe is most important to fado, this sense of carrying and unburdening, of passing on. Interestingly, in other versions of this song such as that recorded by Cristina Branco, the word 'fados' is changed in the title and the verse to 'fado'.[74] The change is slight but helps us to make the claim for fado not only as a series of witnessed symbols but also as *a process* of witnessing. The verb 'trazer', from which 'trago' comes is very popular in fado texts. It can be translated variously as 'to bring', 'to wear', 'to bear' and 'to carry'. Among contemporary fado lyricists, Helder Moutinho seems particularly fond of the verb. In 'Ai do Vento', he sings 'Sao as saudades que nos trazem as tristezas' [It's *saudades* that bring us sadness]; in 'Ao Velho Cantor', he addresses an 'old singer of the past' whose eyes 'trazem imagens de fados' [bear images of fados]; in 'Não Guardo Saudade a Vida' he claims 'Trago a saudade esquecida' [I carry a forgotten *saudade*]. One of Moutinho's albums even bears the title *Que Fado É Este Que Trago?* [What Fado/Fate Is This That I Bear?]. Even when this verb is not used we find many lyrics which deal with what is borne or held inside by the singer, such as the 'fado no peito' [fado in my breast] in Moutinho's 'Lisboa das Mil Janelas'.[75]

A vital correlative, and one which connects with the sense of fate, is the sense of being carried too, as in Ana Laíns's 'O Fado Que Me Traga' [The Fado/Fate That Carries Me]. A crucial metaphor in bringing together these senses of carrying and being carried is the air, and especially the wind, that carries our testimony to others and delivers theirs to us. Helder Moutinho's 'Fado Refugio' speaks of carrying 'in my voice / the life that has been offered me' and each verse contains the line 'Eu trago na voz o vento' [I carry the wind in my voice].[76] Many fados talk about the wind and things which are carried on the wind, not only the seagulls that populate numerous songs but also the uncertainties and hopes of the future.

---

[73]   'Trago Fados nos Sentidos', lyric by Amália Rodrigues, music by José Fontes Rocha, recorded by Amália, on *Gostava de Ser Quem Era* (Valentim de Carvalho/EMI 724383546527, 1995 [1980]).

[74]   Cristina Branco, 'Trago Fado nos Sentidos', *Live* (EmArcy/Universal France 9843206, 2006). Gonçalo Salgueiro's version, on *...No Tempo das Cerejas* (Companhia Nacional de Música CNM116CD, 2004 [2002], retains the word 'fados' in the song but changes the title to the singular.

[75]   The lyrics to all these fados are by Helder Moutinho and can be found on his album *Luz de Lisboa* (Ocarina OCA 010, 2004).

[76]   'Fado Refugio', lyric by Helder Moutinho, music by Alfredo Duarte, recorded by Helder Moutinho, *Luz de Lisboa*. Celeste Rodrigues recorded this fado as 'Trago na Voz o Vento' on her album *Fado Celeste* (Coast Compnay CTC-2990490, 2007).

The wind is also a force against which things are fixed, so as not to blow away or be turned: the wind of change, or of destiny. The wind is both something that carries, upon which one can be passive, and something that threatens loss: words disappear into the wind. To return to an example used earlier in relation to Poe's shipwrecked diarist, Ana Laíns's 'Pouco Tempo' is an attempt to preserve what is being lost to the wind. This is the message the written text (a poem by Lídia Oliveira) tells us and to a certain extent it is the message that the song enacts; by being a song it is a song dispersed in the air and lost. Like the poem, though, the CD on which we find Laíns's performance tells us something else: the concept has been fixed in rhyme, set to music ('set' promises permanence) and recorded.

'Ai Mouraria', recorded by a number of *fadistas*, speaks of:

Amor que o vento, como um lamento	[Love that the wind, like a lament
Levou consigo	Carried with it
Mas que ainda agora	But that still now
A toda a hora	All the time
Trago comigo[77]	I carry with me].

In this song, the love that the singer remembers and that disappeared with the wind, is connected to the winds of change and destiny that would affect Mouraria itself, making it both an example of the kind of mourning work described by Michael Colvin and an example of the bringing together of personal and public memories. The numerous recordings of the song by Amália at different points in her career helped to ensure that this relationship remained in people's minds.

By the 1960s, when Amália came to record this song once more, the trope of the wind was prevalent in many popular songs. Bob Dylan used it in a number of songs that looked back to the folk, blues and country traditions of singing about travelling and being 'in the wind'. Most famous, however, would be his use of the trope as a political metaphor in 'Blowin' in the Wind'. The lyric of that song finds an interesting parallel in a song entitled 'Trova do Vento Que Passa' [Ballad of the Wind That Passes], written by the Portuguese poet Manuel Alegre and roughly contemporaneous with Dylan's anthem. Alegre had been imprisoned by the PIDE, the special police force of the Estado Novo, for his political views. Following his release he spent half a year in Angola, returning to Portugal in 1963 where he wrote 'Trova do Vento Que Passa'. The words were set to music by António Portugal and performed by Adriano Correia de Oliveira, a singer associated with the Coimbra fado. 'Trova' made an instant impression with listeners and became a popular staple of the student resistance against the Salazar regime much as Dylan's 'Blowin' in the Wind' would in the US Civil Rights Movement.

---

[77] 'Ai Mouraria', lyric by Amadeu do Vale, music by Frederico Valério, recorded by Amália Rodrigues, *Estranha Forma de Vida: O Melhor de Amália* (Valentim de Carvalho/ EMI 724383444229, 1995).

Adriano's version had three verses, which describe the poet asking the wind for news of his country but hearing nothing. The second verse claims that 'There is always someone that sows / Songs on the wind that passes', while the third affirms that 'Even on the saddest night / During time of servitude / There is always someone who resists / There is always someone who says no'.[78] The verses provide a number of issues familiar to the other songs mentioned above, including the unanswering wind, a voice lost in the wind and a sense of futility. But the message changes and the crucial final lines get their full enunciatory power as the repeated words that resolve the song, becoming the 'answer' that had been missing. Manuel Alegre himself emphasized the importance of music in the creation of poems and poetry; music allowed the poem 'to be a vehicle of history and memory, to sing of love or to give the signal of past or future epics, to inform and to form, to witness and to bear witness'.[79]

Amália recorded Alegre's poem in 1970 on *Com Que Voz*, her album of adaptations of great Portuguese poets, with different music composed by Alain Oulman. The version adds a verse that highlights the carrying nature of fate, describing rivers that 'take dreams and leave sorrows'.[80] Amália recorded two more verses of the poem, making her version more wordy than Oliveira's. She did not, however, include the outspoken final verse and, unusually for a fado, the final lines of her version are not stressed; instead the voice disappears and the guitars bring the piece to a restrained close. It could be argued that these two versions present opposing qualities of activity and passivity. Although Amália's version is sometimes cited as an example of her alliance with committed leftists poets (see Chapter 1), the use of different music and the removal of the 'call to arms' could be said to severely lessen the impact, making it a universal song about love, exile and loss, as Amália was to also say of the song 'Abandono' which she recorded around the same time.

Voice

The voice, above all, is that which is lost to the wind. Mafalda Arnauth recorded a song entitled 'Esta Voz Que Me Atravessa' [This Voice That Crosses Me], which speaks of a voice that does not live inside the singer but in a shadow beside her. In the second verse she sings:

[78] 'Trova do Vento Que Passa', lyric by Manuel Alegre, music by António Portugal, recorded by Adriano Correia de Oliveira, *Trova do Vento Que Passa: Adriano Canta Manuel Alegre* (Movieplay MOV 35.006, 1994).
[79] Cited in Eduardo M. Raposo, *Canto de Intervenção 1960–1974* (Lisbon: Público, 2007), pp. 67–8.
[80] 'Trova do Vento Que Passa', lyric by Manuel Alegre, music by Alain Oulman, recorded by Amália Rodrigues, *Estranha Forma de Vida: O Melhor de Amália*.

Trago cravado no peito	[I bear, embedded in my chest,
Um resto de amor desfeito	A shard of broken love
Que quando eu canto me dói	That hurts me when I sing
Que me deixa a voz em ferida	That leaves my voice wounded].

The final verse reveals that the voice that has possessed the singer is in fact that of Maria Severa and did not die with the *fadista*.[81] The singer is encountering a voice older than she. Here, the voice itself is the site for an acting out of the memory work supposedly undertaken by all *fadistas* who show fidelity to the originary figure of Severa. The voice becomes an object, like the shawl worn by female fadistas as a sign of mourning for Severa. This object bears none of the claims to originality familiar to so many commentaries on the individuality of the voice; rather, it is collectively owned, something to be taken up, borne and passed on.

There is a responsibility to fado singing, then, one that permits Mariza to name her first album *Fado em Mim* [Fado in Me] and to include on it a song explicitly about responsibility, 'Ó Gente da Minha Terra' [O People of My Land]. It might be more accurate to say that there is a responsibility to singing in general which fado recognizes. This allows the *fadista* António Zambujo, for example, to sing 'Trago Alentejo na Voz' [I Carry Alentejo in My Voice], in which the carrying of a place and style quite other to that of Lisbon fado can be voiced. Zambujo signals recognition of the polyphonic singing tradition common to the area of Alentejo in the south of Portugal both in the lyrical message he delivers and in the addition of a male choir to his recording of the song.[82] Another example of this carrying of a responsibility can be found in the work of the *fadista* Gonçalo Salgueiro, especially his debut album *...No Tempo das Cerejas* (2002). I will be returning to this disc in Chapter 4 when I discuss the 'Amálian' legacy among the recent generation of *fadistas*. For now, I wish to focus on the album as an example of a number of issues relating to this chapter's themes.

The album opens with a song entitled 'Grito' [Shout/Cry], a verse written by Amália and set to music by her former guitarist Carlos Gonçalves. *Guitarra* and *viola* set the musical scene for around half a minute before falling fall silent. The word 'silêncio' is voiced, stretching over ten otherwise silent seconds with the majority of work being engaged on the middle vowel as Salgueiro introduces us immediately to his, at first subtle, vocal ornamentation. An audible intake of breath is then followed with the following section of the verse, still unaccompanied by the guitarists and with increasing ornamentation on each word:

---

[81]   'Esta Voz Que Me Atravessa', lyric by Hélia Correia, music by Amélia Muge, recorded by Mafalda Arnauth, *Esta Voz Que Me Atravessa* (Virgin/EMI-Valentim de Carvalho 724353155728, 2001).

[82]   António Zambujo, 'Trago Alentejo na Voz', *O Mesmo Fado* (Música Alternativa/ Valentim de Carvalho/EMI MA035CD, 2002).

Do silêncio faço um grito	[From the silence I make a cry
E o corpo todo me dói	And my whole body hurts
Deixai-me chorar um pouco[83]	Leave me to weep a little]

Over the course of the first four lines, and occupying a significant section of the song in terms of duration, we experience what Simon Frith calls 'the sheer physical pleasure of singing itself ... the enjoyment a singer takes in particular movements of muscles'.[84] Furthermore, a message is communicated directly: voice will be central to this recording project. And so it turns out. Following a fairly strident rendition of 'Meia Noite e uma Guitarra', a different enjoyment of the voice that complements the subtle intricacy of the album's opener, the third track comes in the form of a poem written by Maria de Lourdes DeCarvalho with Amália in mind and entitled 'Tenho em Mim a Voz dum Povo' [I Have in Me Voice of a People]. The poem sings of a 'Voz com que canto e me encanto / Em cada canto do meu pranto / Uma estranha lágrima de fogo' [Voice with which I sing and which enchants me / in each song of my lament / A strange tear of fire].[85] Responsibility is key here. Salgueiro is carrying a responsibility, as the liner notes to the CD make clear. He is in the tradition of Amália and veers, according to Rui Vieira Nery's version of the singing-as-enjoyment phenomenon, between 'the joy of risk-taking and a liking for conservatism'.[86] As the accompanying biography alerts us, Salgueiro was invited by João Braga to be part of a show that accompanied the moving of Amália's body to the National Pantheon in 2001. There is a layering of responsibility here as Salgueiro is given the task of 'carrying' Amália in his voice and Amália is given the posthumous responsibility of eternal national recognition. In her third verse, DeCarvalho has Salgueiro speak on behalf of Amália of the latter's new home alongside the poets Camões and Pessoa, a home that is both the Pantheon itself (the home of mortal remains) and the Infinite in which her 'eternal soul' will sing a song in the presence of God.

This appeal to God should not surprise us. While I am not focusing on the religious world of fado texts in this book, it cannot be completely ignored. Fado, like other cultural products and processes in Portugal, has deep connections with Catholicism and many of its key tropes (fate, sin, guilt, redemption) could be traced back to religious practices. For my part, I wish to maintain the focus on the voice and we can find a fine example of the divine implications of the fado voice in a song written for Amália by Alberto Janes and entitled 'Foi Deus' [It Was God]. The song begins, not unlike 'Tudo Isto É Fado', with the singer claiming ignorance; in

---

[83] 'Grito', lyric by Amália Rodrigues, music by Carlos Gonçalves, recorded by Gonçalo Salgueiro, ...No Tempo das Cerejas.

[84] Simon Frith, *Performing Rites: On the Value of Popular Music* (Oxford: Oxford University Press, 1996), p. 193.

[85] 'Tenho em Mim a Voz do Povo', lyric by Maria de Lourdes DeCarvalho, music by Carlos Gonçalves, recorded by Gonçalo Salgueiro, ...No Tempo das Cerejas.

[86] Rui Vieira Nery, liner notes to Salgueiro, ...No Tempo das Cerejas.

this case it is the reason for the sorrowful tone with which she sings fado of which she is ignorant. But this ignorance is superseded by this declaration:

> It was God
> That placed in my chest
> A rosary of pain
> For me to speak
> And to cry while singing
> He made the nightingale a poet
> Put rosemary in the fields
> Gave flowers to the Spring
> Ah, and gave this voice to me.[87]

In one rather simplistic sense, this provides us with an 'answer' to a question posed in Chapter 1 as to the magical power attributed by so many commentators to Amália's voice. How did that voice allow her to transcend the politics and traditions of her time and become so 'universally' acknowledged? The answer appears that to be that it was not her voice after all but part of God's plan. In Mafalda Arnauth's 'A Voz Que Me Atravessa' the voice that passed through the singer, while capable of travelling across time and space, had mortal origins in the figure of Maria Severa. Here, the origins are explicitly divine. In one song, we hear the voice of the people; in the other, the voice of God. This relationship is an important one for understanding any modern politics of the popular, as Richard Middleton has shown.[88]

Manuela Cook suggests that the fatalism of fado is generally connected to an earlier fatalism found in the Romans and Greeks and is in fact in tension with Catholic faith in which 'a Christian healing power defies a non-Christian merciless destiny.' But it is the latter, the 'omnipotent but merciful God', that Cook recognizes in Amália's 'Foi Deus' rather than 'ancient inexorable deities'.[89] Cook's discussion of the role of women in fado singing covers the witnessing of the Fátima miracle in 1917, offering a useful reminder of the role of witnessing in religious lore. Many different religions place emphasis on witnessing, testifying, performative preaching, ritual and what Simon Frith calls 'the collective voice of religious submission'.[90] Notions of submission and possession are frequently given voice in fados such as Maria da Fé's 'Cantarei Até Que a Voz Me Doa'

---

[87]   'Foi Deus', lyric and music by Alberto Janes, recorded by Amália Rodrigues, *Estranha Forma de Vida*.

[88]   See the introduction to Richard Middleton, *Voicing the Popular: On the Subjects of Popular Music* (New York & London: Routledge, 2006), pp. 1–36.

[89]   Manuela Cook, 'The Woman in Portuguese Fado-singing', *International Journal of Iberian Studies*, 16/1 (2003): 27, 26.

[90]   Frith, *Performing Rites*, p. 196. The relationship between music and religious ritual is epitomized in the title of Frith's book.

[I Will Sing Until My Voice Hurts].[91] This song is a speaking-out, or singing-out, a stubborn persistence to make oneself heard and to not have one's voice lost to the ether. Like 'A Voz Que Me Atravessa' and 'Foi Deus', it represents a giving of oneself over to the voice and the song. But the reliance on another figure is lessened; neither God nor the mythological *fadista* are required. The witness here, like the witness in court, is someone who takes the stand and who is given their moment to speak out, licensed by the people to speak for the people. In this sense, it is a very public song and immediately brings to mind visions of its performance in a *casa de fado* such as the one Maria da Fé herself operates.

This emphasis on speaking out and on public voices should not distract us from the privacies and intimacies of speaking and listening allowed by sound recording. Aldina Duarte, no stranger to the *casa de fado*, nonetheless fashioned an intimate form of communication on her first album *Apenas o Amor* (2004) that could only have come about through the medium of recording.[92] The album is notable for having a sense of sonic intimacy that is attained by the unhurried nature of the arrangements and the way the voice and guitars have been miked and recorded, with a slight echo that serves to emphasize the clean silence surrounding the words and notes. This is further highlighted by songs which reference the affect of voice. The first song begins with the evocation of a 'voice in the silence', while the second opens with 'the memory of a sad voice'; another speaks of 'an unconscious voice / that deep down is always fado'. On the slower tracks, José Manuel Neto's *guitarra* is a model of minimal accompaniment, allowing the voice room to materialize in the sonic field. It is no surprise that fellow musicians Carlos do Carmo and Jorge Palma, who both provide liner notes to the album, speak of silence in their comments.

As Simon Frith writes, 'The microphone made it possible for singers to make musical sounds – soft sounds, close sounds – that had not really been heard before in terms of public performance ... [it] allowed us to hear people in ways that normally implied intimacy – the whisper, the caress, the murmur'.[93] This intimacy is hymned in Alexandre O'Neil's 'Há Palavras Que Nos Beijam' [There Are Words That Kiss Us], a poem that has been performed as a fado by Mariza and Cristina Branco.[94] Meanwhile, the 'memória duma voz triste' [memory of a sad voice] that Aldina Duarte sings about also suggests a carrying on the part of the listener too, a reminder that in listening something is placed in the mind, becoming a part of consciousness itself.

---

[91]   'Até Que a Voz Me Doa', lyric by José Luis Gordo, music by José Fontes Rocha, recorded by Maria da Fé on *Clássicos da Renascença* (Movieplay 31.009, 2000).

[92]   Aldina Duarte, *Apenas o Amor* (Valentim de Carvalho/Virgin/EMI 724359828329, 2004).

[93]   Frith, *Performing Rites*, p. 187.

[94]   'Há Palavras Que Nos Beijam', lyric by Alexandre O'Neil, music by Mário Pacheco, recorded by Mariza, on *Transparente* (World Connection/Valentim de Carvalho/ Capitol/EMI 724347764622, 2005). Cristina Branco recorded the lyric to different music on her album *Murmúrios* (CD, Music & Words, MWCD4023,1999).

Sounded Experience

Strolling

This positing of listening as the allowing of something into the consciousness brings us back to the dialectic between agency and passivity. Listening, as Mladen Dolar suggests, 'is "always-already" incipient obedience; the moment one listens one has already started to obey'.[95] The form this obedience takes is inherently spatial, as we saw in Chapter 2, but this should not blind us to the obvious temporal implications of listening. Listening to music, for example, offers us a possibility to pass time and, as Simon Frith points out, an experience of time passing: 'In the most general terms, music shapes memory, defines nostalgia, programs the way we age (changing and staying the same).'[96] For Sylviane Agacinski, who presents a similar discussion of passing time (focusing on both senses of the term), Walter Benjamin remains a key figure, one for whom the act of strolling through a city street was akin to strolling through a series of memory places, stumbling upon evidence of one's own past and that of one's society. Here, then, a giving of oneself over to happenstance is presented in distinction to the strict control of the searcher who is on a quest. Comparisons with forms of reading, viewing and listening are immediately apparent: the browser flicking through the pages of a book, the television viewer cruising the various stations, the radio listener trusting to the dial, or the iPod listener setting their collection to 'Shuffle'. Agacinski sets up this apparent distinction between agency and passivity by opposing the figure of the historian to that of the stroller:

> The historian takes possession of the past by interpreting traces, whereas the trace of the past happens to the stroller and takes possession of him. Let us not claim, however, that nothing happens to the historian; undoubtedly his desire also involves an anticipation, a curiosity with regard to what will come to him from the past, what he will discover in the shadows and encounter. There is often a stroller at the heart of each historian, a part of him that is trying to let himself be touched by the traces.[97]

Agacinski admits in a footnote that she is thinking of Michel de Certeau when she writes the foregoing, and it is no coincidence that this stroller-historian should also become the author of a discussion of walking that, as we saw in Chapter 2, wishes to problematize the distinction between active and passive ways of being in the city. As with the historian, so too with the browser, the cruiser and the shuffler, who may well be enjoying the 'ecstasy' of discoveries made by accident or by

---

[95]   Mladen Dolar, *A Voice and Nothing More* (Cambridge, MA, & London: The MIT Press, 2006), p. 76.

[96]   Frith, *Performing Rites*, p. 149.

[97]   Agacinski, *Time Passing*, p. 52.

the equally pleasurable activities of browsing among bookshops, record stores or other collections.[98] Continuing the idea of browsing-as-activity, Agacinski writes:

> For Benjamin, the possibility of experiencing the past requires certain conditions. In particular, the frame of mind for letting oneself be touched, for letting oneself be taken by the aura, requires a true idleness. The stroller cannot want to arrange time himself, for example, by undertaking some project or by precisely scheduling his course of action; rather, he must be available to time, to let time pass, to spend it without keeping count, to know how to waste it.[99]

This is not a simple form of passivity; to make oneself available is still to make something, to do something. We should also remember that the stroller strolls with a prior knowledge of certain features which they are going to encounter, a point to which I will return shortly.

The City Sounded

A number of themes covered in this chapter and its predecessor are explored in Wim Wenders's film *Lisbon Story* (1994): the city as museum, tourist destination and object of navigation by its citizens; the importance of recording; stylization and the city's style; the sound of the city; fate and deliberation. The film also allows us to focus on the role of technology in the processes of recollection, witnessing and representation, playing out the double nature of technology as recording and creative tool. Wenders's film itself contains a film-within-the-film in which one of the characters, Friedrich Monroe, is attempting to document the city and to record the notable. *Lisbon Story* began life as a commission from the city of Lisbon for Wenders to produce a promotional film in the year that the city was European Capital of Culture (1994). At some point Wenders decided to add a fictitious narrative to give the film more dynamism. The storyline allows his protagonist, Phillip Winter (a character Wenders would use in other films), to embark on various quests: for his friend Monroe, for a sense of identity, for love and for perfect sounds (Winter is a sound recordist). Monroe has contacted Winter to ask him to join him in Lisbon, where he has been shooting film of the city and to add sounds to his footage that will bring his visual images to life. From the outset, sound is the medium through which the technological era is explored. The opening scene in Winter's car as he drives from Germany to Portugal is accompanied by an ever-shifting radio soundtrack that acts as both travelogue and as an example of the web of broadcast sound which had come to dominance in the twentieth century. Winter carries with him the tools of his trade, a variety of recording devices and objects

---

[98] Geoffrey O'Brien, from whom I borrow this usage of 'ecstasy', writes beautifully on this topic in *The Browser's Ecstasy*; see also his *Sonata for Jukebox: Pop Music, Memory, and the Imagined Life* (New York: Counterpoint, 2004).

[99] Agacinski, *Time Passing*, p. 55.

with which to emulate natural sounds. As we discover on his first meeting with the children who follow him around recording him on video, Winter is an illusionist, conjuring sound from the simplest of objects via the magic of technology. Monroe, meanwhile, is revealed as a psychogeographer, wandering the city reciting lines from Fernando Pessoa between ruminations on the cityscape; a figure resembling Pessoa is also spotted on a couple of occasions in the street. In the time between Monroe's original invitation and Winters's arrival, the filmmaker has become disillusioned; at one point he declares, 'Images are no longer what they used to be. They can't be trusted anymore.'

Music is a central component in the film, especially that provided by the group Madredeus, who had already had a prominent recording career prior to the film but gained even greater exposure after soundtracking it and appearing in it. Outside of Portugal, the group became one of the first Portuguese acts – and certainly the first 'non-traditional' act – to be included in the newly formed 'world music' category, gaining them further exposure via the emerging world music media. Although there are elements of fado practice and style in the group's music, theirs is not fado music. It does, however, provide a good example of the ways in which recording technology would be used in the subsequent promotion of 'new fado' artists of the 1990s and 2000s. A notable aspect would be the use of what we might think of as the 'sacred silence' of world music recording. By this, I mean the use of recording technology to attain a crisp, digital silence around the voice and instruments and to single out individual sounds (Teresa Salgueiro's voice, Pedro Ayres Magalhães's guitar, or the accordion of Gabriel Gomes in the recordings leading up to *Lisbon Story*). This stylization of the group's sound is extended into a visual stylization in Wenders's film in what seems, at times, to be a promotional video for Madredeus. The group are seen first playing the song 'Guitarra', bathed in light in a heavily stylized setting which Winter stumbles upon as an 'accidental' witness. The sound attains the clarity we have come to expect from modern studio recordings. These isolated sounds and visuals are contrasted with the 'mishmash of life' and 'sea stew' of background noises Winter witnesses as he wanders around the city with his microphone. These field recordings are opposed to the clarity of the rehearsal and studio spaces in a manner analogous to the contrast between 'ethnomusicological' and 'world music' recordings, as I will discuss in Chapter 5.

Another way in which *Lisbon Story* is related to late twentieth-century musical aesthetics is in its deliberate (some might say 'postmodern') use of glitch. Just as his character Monroe wishes to recreate the early days of cinema by becoming like Buster Keaton's cameraman, so Wenders pays homage to early film by including deliberate glitches in some of his footage of Lisbon. Early film and early sound recording, of course, achieved their aesthetic due to the limits of the technology; what is notable about much film and music recorded at the turn of the millennium is that the loss of these limits evokes the desire to recreate them, not because it is necessary but because it is possible. Moreover, Monroe knows (because Wenders knows) that there is no one way to approach or capture the city; it must be 'taken' from as many angles as possible. Monroe realized the destructive force that can come with the representation of space: 'pointing a camera is like pointing a gun. And each time I pointed it, it felt like life was drained out of things ... With each turn of the handle, the city was fading further and further.' Monroe's radical solution is to assemble an archive of unseen footage, filmed automatically and not viewed but stored away for future viewings. His goal is to record the city 'as it is, not as how we want it to be'. He here enacts a commitment, like Henri Lefebvre, to a politics connected to representational spaces and lived experience. He seeks restrictions that will allow him to remove himself from the controlling centre of representation, believing that an escape from perfection and a moving toward randomness and luck will help to bring the human back into the city.

Ó Gente da Minha Terra

My focus on the processes of witnessing and re-presenting is intended to highlight the importance of the technologies of memory for both transcriptive and creative means. Fado, like other popular musics, is irreversibly implicated in such technologies, a matrix of stylistic and stylized sounds, words and gestures forced to negotiate the necessities of mediation just as the citizen navigates the mediated city. Contemporary recording technology, as magically invisible as any invisible city, promises proximity while also maintaining a distance from the site of witnessing. Fado recordings witness the city by unburdening seeing into saying, producing, with ever greater technological flourishes, the 'surprise' of history they once sought merely to record. Fado, we might say, having once *found* the city notable, now *makes* the city notable.

The process, as we have seen, is a dialectical one, where the desire to record leads to the development of technologies of memory that in turn shape subsequent recollections. Sylviane Agacinski describes the stroller as 'the witness of the world *in the process of passing*, just as a colour fades; he is witnessing the very event of the city's aging'.[100] What is important here is the emphasis on process. There is not a static past and a static present but a continuum of movement between the one and the other. Agacinski recalls Francis Bacon's description of 'lettered experience', the experience gained from reading, and suggests that this experience interacts fluidly with lived experience, each being transformed by the other.[101] To this she adds a suggestion of an 'imaged experience' shared by the spectator in the city, to which I would propose a further addition, 'sounded experience', that gained by the listener in the city.

What experience has this listener gained? He or she has learned, no doubt, how to zone and direct their hearing, how to control the geography of listening. They have learned, in the case of fado, the toponymic nature of a music that has mapped out the city before they have even set foot in it. They can wander the streets of Mouraria, Alfama and Graça, should they wish, to a soundtrack of fado.

[100] Ibid., p. 58.
[101] Ibid., pp. 56–7.

They can compare, eventually, the recorded presence of the city in song with the living presence of the city underfoot. They can scan the streets for landmarks mentioned in songs and find, as Michael Colvin did, a catalogue of absence. They can remove their headphones and feel the rushing inward of the real sonic tide, the collective mish-mash of noise freed from the imprisoning silence of modern record production. In making such comparisons, they may realize, as Friedrich Monroe did, that such recording can never do justice to the reality of the city. They may feel that, while it is highly likely that Lisbon will continue to play a starring role in new fados, the 'world sound' will ensure that the real city is silenced. Equally, they may take the more optimistic view of Phillip Winter, who brings his illusory art to the rescue of Monroe's stricken images and who responds to his friend's disillusionment by quoting Pessoa: 'in broad daylight even the sounds shine'.

This pleasure in the technical construction of sonorous moments is part and parcel of contemporary sound recording and is particularly notable in what I have just termed the 'world sound'. This sound is epitomized by a dialectic in which the fetishization of the local is achieved by the cleaning out of all sound that does not pertain to the delivery of the local. Mariza's recordings are excellent examples of this process and I wish to close this chapter by considering one of them, 'Ó Gente da Minha Terra', which also has relevance to other issues raised in this chapter. The song, from the singer's first album *Fado em Mim*, is the result of a composer, Tiago Machado, setting an unrecorded lyric by Amália to music. The song begins by declaring that singer and audience are connected by fado/fate and goes on to declare that it is impossible to hear a guitar 'singing' a lament without being overcome by the desire to weep. The verse that began Amália's original poem is moved in the song to become the refrain:

Ó gente da minha terra	[O people of my land
Agora é que eu percebi	Now I understand
Esta tristeza que trago	This sadness which I bear
Foi de vós que recebi[102]	Was received from you.]

The aching melancholy and drama of the lyric seems to license Mariza to utilize her considerable vocal talent, strategically placing emotional hooks at various points in the narrative. Amália has written the script and Mariza has taken on the role, both voicing the lost *fadista*'s paean to fate and responsibility and 'versioning' it to make it her own. The scriptor suggests the giving over of oneself to destiny; the singer to the pleasure of singing and of being carried by the music. With other singers in mind, Simon Frith suggests something similar:

> One effect of such pleasure is that for many singers what they are singing, a word, is valued for its physical possibilities, what it allows the mouth or throat

---

[102] 'Ó Gente da Minha Terra', lyric by Amália Rodrigues, music by Tiago Machado, recorded by Mariza, *Fado em Mim* (World Connection 43038, 2002 [2001]).

to do. The singer finds herself driven by the physical logic of the sound of the words rather than by the semantic meaning of the verse, and so creates a sense of spontaneity: the singing feels real rather than rehearsed; the singer is responding (like the listener) to the musical event of which they are part, being possessed by the music rather than possessing it.[103]

This is exactly what Mariza does with 'Ó Gente da Minha Terra'. On the first recorded version, from her first album, the singer employs a steadily increasing vocal attack in the delivery of the verses, the first half of the song marked by a reflective mode, the second half, from the first sounding of the chorus ('Ó gente da minha terra ...') onwards, by a mixture of anger, bewilderment and resignation. Such a delivery is in keeping with the lyrical development of the song and with conventional performance of this kind of fado. The emotional pivot of the performance comes, as we might expect, at the end, though it is not via the conventional repetition of a couplet. Firstly, Mariza plays with the final phoneme of the second line (the 'i' of 'percebi'), twisting it over three syllables into quite a different sound altogether: 'ee-ee-ay'. Next, she repeats the penultimate line of the chorus only – 'Esta tristeza que trago' – and places vocal emphasis on 'tristeza [sadness]' and 'trago [bear]'; both words are stretched, the latter in particular. Finally, the closing line is centred on the word 'vôs' [you], the vowel presented as a series of descending tones. It is a dramatic delivery, thoroughly suited to such a melodramatic lyric and Mariza has generally sought to capitalize on this drama in concert performances by inserting a dramatic pause before the final line and extemporizing on the sonorities available in its words.[104]

If this is defeat, it is clearly a very pleasurable one. Perhaps we should put it another way and say that there is actually an indeterminacy of possession going on here. The sheer fact of singing and of standing outside the situation being portrayed in the lyrics means that what is really being performed is a kind of victory. In the midst of this defeat, it is paradoxically the very act of giving oneself over to the song that allows for the staging of victory. This becomes even more obvious in a recorded performance of the song given by Mariza at Lisbon's Torre de Belém in 2005, a massive open air concert that was both a spilling over of fado into the

---

[103] Frith, *Performing Rites*, p. 193.

[104] There is a slightly different emotional arc deployed in the second version of 'Ó Gente da Minha Terra' included as a 'hidden' track on the CD of *Fado em Mim*. This version, which features Mariza accompanied only by Tiago Machado's piano, adds additional drama at certain points through the volume of the piano, features a fully repeated chorus at the end and closes with a gentle repeat of the opening line, a reassertion that 'this fado/fate is both yours and mine'. This arrangement of the piece was also used for Mariza's concert at the Union Chapel in London in 2003, where the guitarists left the stage and Machado came on to play piano. This concert was filmed and released as a DVD, *Mariza Live in London* (EMI 724359962795, 2004).

city and a carefully managed official 'event', much like the annual concerts put on throughout the city during the summer to celebrate the *Festas de Lisboa*.

Mariza chose 'Ó Gente da Minha Terra' as the final song of the evening, a move no doubt designed to capitalize on the emotional power of the lyrics and her performance of it. Witnessing the recording of the song (the concert was released as both a CD and DVD and was also broadcast on national television), one can see that it is as emotionally resonant as ever for the greater part before reaching an even higher emotional plateau towards the finale. When the time comes for Mariza to deliver the final refrain, she sings the first line – 'Ó gente da minha terra ...' – and then the music takes over, accompanied by the applause of the audience. The film of the concert allows us to see what would have been evident to many present at the event and which we might have already implied from listening to the audio recording. The emotional import of the song has overcome the singer and she has been brought to tears. An unforgiving camera follows her, zooming in on her face, allowing no privacy, as though she really were the property of the people after all. The musicians fill in until she has brought herself back to a point where she can sing. Then, with the musicians silent, and to the sound of continued applause, Mariza launches the first line of the chorus again. The musicians join her and this time we hear the whole chorus with its now familiar extemporizations over the key words 'minha', 'terra', 'percebi', 'tristeza', 'trago', 'vós' and, finally and victoriously, 'recebi'.

For those who attended the concert, for those who listened to the recording of it on CD, and perhaps even more for those who watched it on television or DVD, it is clear that something, or several things, have been witnessed. A fado audience has witnessed the elevation of fado onto the national stage again. Mariza's audience has witnessed the victory of a 'homecoming' concert. Fans of Amália have witnessed her life, work and voice passing through one of her heirs, seeing her words made flesh. Above all, perhaps, an audience has witnessed itself. Here sound has served to 'interpellate' an audience, allowing that audience the chance to glimpse itself as a faithful subject.[105] The interpellative work that Mariza and her musicians perform is central to this process. But I would go further and suggest that it serves also to place fado at the centre of interpellation. For while it may be true that what Mariza does with the words of this and other songs could be (and is) done by numerous skilled performers working with other genres and other languages (Simon Frith, after all, is thinking of Otis Redding in the passage I quoted above), it is nevertheless true that the placing of *this vocal work* in the midst of a narrative dense with fado imagery and sonority produces a singularity. In the case of the Belém concert, it is the recognition of this on the part of all involved that leads to

---

[105] I am using the concept of interpellation, or 'hailing', that Louis Althusser proposes, in which the subject (or addressee) of the hail recognizes, via their obedience to it, their subjectivity. As Althusser stresses, this is a power relationship. See Louis Althusser, 'Ideology and Ideological State Apparatuses (Notes towards an Investigation)', tr. Ben Brewster, in *On Ideology* (London & New York: Verso, 1988 [1971]), pp. 1–60.

the emotional climax near the end. We know that Mariza could have become a soul singer, that she considered it as an early career choice, that she is influenced by a wide range of singing practices beyond fado. And yet she has made the choice to perform fado. The concert at Belém, then, is a homecoming in more ways than one: back to Lisbon, back to fado. What could be a more appropriate acknowledgement of this than to close with 'Ó Gente da Minha Terra?'

Perhaps to say this to be taken in too obviously by what, after all, was a performance. As well as all the things we know above, we know that Mariza has played this song countless times in concert venues around the world and that she is prone in interviews and in the speeches she gives between songs in concerts to dwell on the sentimental. She is, to a detached observer, overly emotional about fado, about Portugal and about the message of her music. But this is precisely what such a performance is about: the melting of such doubts so that the presentation of the performer to 'her' public (and the possessive pronoun is important to note), no matter what the size or the complexity of the machinery involved to get her there in the first place, takes on a magical transparency. This is something recognized by Simon Frith when he strategically places this quotation from Erving Goffman at the start of a chapter on performance – which I strategically place at the close of a chapter on witnessing:

> At one extreme, one finds that the performer can be fully taken in by his own act; he can be sincerely convinced that the impression of reality which he stages is the real reality. When his audience is also convinced in this way about the show he puts on … then for the moment at least, only the sociologist or the socially disgruntled will have any doubts about the 'realness' of what is presented.[106]

---

[106] Cited in Frith, *Performing Rites*, p. 203.

Chapter 4
New Citizens of the *Fadista* World

Introduction

Having addressed some of the ways in which place is inscribed into fado, I want to make a partial return to the earlier presentation of the genre as a music of Portugal. While fado is a music inextricably connected with Portugal, it is by no means the dominant form of music in the country. To say this is not just to recognize the huge popularity of international genres such as Anglo-American pop (and all its attendant subgenres), or even the popularity of more linguistically specific genres such as those from Brazil and, increasingly, Africa. It is also to register the popularity of very specifically Portuguese musical forms such as *pimba*. *Pimba* is the name given to a form of light music that is often associated with rural areas of Portugal but which in fact has an audience throughout the country. The music is generally uptempo, featuring electronic beats and keyboards mixed with 'rural' textures such as the accordion or brass instruments. Although it can include sentimental numbers, *pimba* is more generally characterized by the use of wordplay and innuendo, often utilizing 'earthy' imagery associated with farm animals, countryside festivities, food and drink. It is a deliberately 'low' form of music and shuns most forms of sophistication; this quality as much as its musical style distinguishes it from contemporary fado. Both musics have associations with *revistas*, and fado has often been associated with low humour, but in general it has abandoned this approach for a more sombre existentialism; one learns to understand and appreciate fado over time, whereas *pimba* is designed to be instantly catchy. *Pimba* is the dominant form of music in many village festivals and also has a vibrant presence on the streets of Lisbon, often becoming the soundtrack to the *festas populares* during the summer in a far more obvious way than fado. Despite a notable presence on national television, *pimba* has often functioned in a semi-official manner in terms of recordings. In 2000, it was estimated that *pimba* could account for nearly half of the national sales of music, circulating via cassettes and CDs sold in restaurants, at roadside service stations and at village concerts.[1]

I do not intend to discuss *pimba* further, but it is useful to note its place in the Portuguese popular musical field, not least because it can be contrasted strongly with fado in terms of its potential appeal outside Portugal. While *pimba* has an audience in the Portuguese diaspora, it is not the kind of music that could be marketed as 'world music' to non-Portuguese speakers. Fado, on the other hand, has always been marketable to other cultures and makes it a prime candidate for

---

[1]   Terry Berne, 'Portugal's Year of Transition', *Billboard* (11 November 2000): 76.

the world music treatment, as I will discuss later in this chapter and in Chapter 5. Before doing so, however, I wish to consider the role of rock and pop music in Portugal and of Portugal in the history of rock and pop. This second issue is one that is directly related to the world music phenomenon, for, while it would be inconceivable to imagine an English-language reference book on world music omitting Portugal and its folk and fado traditions, it is seemingly the norm to ignore the country's involvement in any other popular music making. In the introduction to *The Virgin Encyclopedia of Popular Music*, for example, Colin Larkin writes, 'Historically, more commercially marketed popular music comes from the USA (they invented it) and the UK (we stole it, and do a pretty good job at copying it). We have, however, attempted to fully represent other geographical areas of music that have not been covered in reference books.'[2] One searches in vain for representatives of Portuguese popular music. There are numerous references to 'Latin' artists, a common label for music that is sung in Spanish or Portuguese but which generally refers to Latin American artists. One can therefore find the Cuban singer-songwriter Silvio Rodríguez but not the *fadista* Amália Rodrigues or the globally popular band Madredeus. France fares better, however, with entries on singers such as Edith Piaf and Charles Aznavour. More surprisingly, the volume of *The Continuum Encyclopedia of Popular Music of the World* devoted to Europe (Vol. 7) has no entry on Portugal, meaning that Portuguese popular music beyond fado and folk (covered in encyclopaedias published by Garland and Grove) is seriously lacking in English language reference works.[3] I cannot hope to fill that gap in the present book given my focus on fado, but I do wish to give a brief overview of pop and rock music in Portugal in order to fill out the various 'scapes' of the Portuguese popular music field.

The emergence of rock 'n' roll in the 1950s initiated a major change in popular musics far beyond the initial 'homeland' of the music. Thanks to recording technology, the broadcast media and a pattern of socio-economic conditions, those with a thirst for the new sounds coming out of the USA – and the scope of such a constituency was quickly revealed – were able to get some kind of access to the latest developments in the new music. In this sense, at least, rock 'n' roll was a major cultural event of the twentieth century. But it is possible to take this notion of the rock 'n' roll event further. In my own work I have found it useful to adopt some of the vocabulary utilized by Alain Badiou in his theory of the event, notably 'situation', 'eventual site', 'truth' and 'fidelity'.[4] For Badiou, an event is something

---

[2]   Colin Larkin, introduction to Larkin (ed.), *The Virgin Encyclopedia of Popular Music: Concise Fourth Edition* (London: Virgin & Brentwood: Muze, 2002), p. v.

[3]   The forthcoming *Enciclopédia da Música em Portugal no Século XX* (Encyclopedia of Music in 20th Century Portugal) will go a long way towards filling a similar gap in Portuguese-language reference works.

[4]   Richard Elliott, 'Popular Music and/as Event: Subjectivity, Love and Fidelity in the Aftermath of Rock 'n' Roll', *Radical Musicology*, 3 (2008), http://www.radical-musicology. org.uk, 60 pars.

that occurs as a complete break with the continuum of being; for this reason he distinguishes between the terms 'being' and 'event'. For Badiou the fields of human interaction where events can emerge are those of science, art, politics and love. An event is a creative, assertive act that breaks with what has gone before and sets in motion a new truth that in turn creates subjects who show fidelity to it. Examples used by Badiou include the French Revolution, Galilean physics, Schoenberg's twelve-note serialism and the event of any amorous encounter that entails a change for the subjects constituted by that encounter. The event itself cannot be verified, but fidelity to its truth can be maintained after it has been recognized. For Badiou, fidelity to the event is a process that exceeds the event itself, a truth process by which subjects are created. A revolution thus consists both of the *event* of the Revolution (an irruption into the established order of a completely new situation) and a *fidelity* to this event (an ongoing commitment to the revolutionary project). An event adds something to knowledge but does so by splitting, or subtracting itself, from what is already known. This realm of the already known, referred to by Badiou as the veridical or as encyclopaedic knowledge, is what is always around us, the steady accumulation of the results of analysing, categorizing and narrating the world in which we live. This does not mean that, away from the glamour and dazzle of the event, veridical knowledge is to be deemed undesirable; it is always, as Badiou says, 'appropriate to be knowledgeable'.[5]

It is this appropriateness that has justified, for me, the bringing together of Badiou's account of event with the process inaugurated by rock 'n' roll in the middle of the twentieth century. I am interested in the processes of fidelity to the rock 'n' roll event that contribute to the shaping of popular musics globally over the course of subsequent decades. Fidelity to the event of rock 'n' roll allowed 'believers' such as the British beat groups to take on what for them was a quite foreign sound and, spurred on by the thrill of otherness and newness, to follow the pathways it opened and become proselytizers for the new cause, the result of which led to a reignition of faith in the USA in the wake of the 'British invasion' of the 1960s. It was arguably at this point that the templates for the subsequent Anglo-American pop and rock styles were fixed, though such templates were clearly built on earlier prototypes. The sound that was subsequently developed in Anglo-American popular music has been described as a 'universal' one.[6] From an ethnographic perspective, such an assertion can seem worrying and I will rehearse at least some of the debates that emerge from this topic in the final chapter. For now, however, I wish to consider the consequences of the Anglo-American

---

[5]   Alain Badiou, *Being and Event*, tr. Oliver Feltham (London & New York: Continuum, 2005 [1988]), p. 294.

[6]   As Simon Frith writes, 'No country in the world is unaffected by the way in which the twentieth-century mass media ... have created a universal pop aesthetic'. Simon Frith, 'Introduction', in Frith (ed.), *World Music, Politics and Social Change: Papers from the International Association for the Study of Popular Music* (Manchester & New York: Manchester University Press, 1991 [1989]), p. 2.

popular music revolution for Portugal, for it cannot be denied that, like many other countries, Portugal responded to the call of the new music with its own versions of the templates.

I wish to retain some Badiouian terminology, especially the notion of fidelity. To begin with, I am referring to fidelity in the sense just described – as a faithfulness to the new pop and rock sound; later, however, I wish to think of other fidelities such as that shown by a generation of *fadistas* to the 'event' of Amália Rodrigues, also to the more general notion of subjectivity ushered in by what Richard Middleton has called, after Badiou, the 'phonographic event'.[7] I am fully aware that I may be in danger of diluting the power of Badiou's notion of the event by wishing to utilize his lexicon for so many purposes. However, I feel the risk is worth taking not only because Badiou furnishes us with a vocabulary that fits well with popular music discourse, but also because one of the challenges that his theory has to face up to is its applicability to everyday life. As I have argued before, and as I have also argued in this book by presenting a tension between exceptional witnessing and everyday witnessing, the popular sphere provides a unique testing point for just such tensions as it inaugurates and rehearses so many of the processes of identification upon which evental sites rely.

One obvious difference between identification with rock 'n' roll taking place in Portugal and a similar process in Britain is the language in which the music was performed. However, we should be careful to avoid over-simplifying this. Rock 'n' roll was, as already suggested, a 'foreign' sound to British ears when it first crossed the Atlantic and this accounted for a great deal of its appeal. But by claiming the privileged title of 'event' for the music we have already gone further than this; rock 'n' roll was a foreign sound to *everyone* upon its emergence, including those involved in first disseminating it. It was its very otherness that made it new, even if it helped to have an expert 'translator' in the figure of Elvis Presley. It is nonetheless the case that a certain kind of English became the norm for performing the music and for furnishing the discourse surrounding the music with neologisms. The Rolling Stones may have been putting on foreign accents (both vocally and instrumentally) in their music but, for those who cared about such things and who spoke English, the words coming out of Mick Jagger's mouth could be largely understood by a constituency extending beyond Britain.

The situation for Portuguese performers was more complex. While 'international' stars such as Amália were not necessarily expected to sing in any language other than their own (although many, including Amália, did), it was generally understood that what was attractively international about them in the first place was a talent that defied the boundaries of language. As a number of

---

[7]   See Richard Middleton, '*Vox Populi, Vox Dei*. Or, Imagine, I'm Losing My Religion (Hallelujah!): Musical Politics after God', in *Musical Belongings: Selected Essays* (Farnham: Ashgate, 2009), pp. 329–52. While I do not go into the specific details of this third reading of event in this chapter, it should be understood to underlie many of my arguments throughout the book, guided as it is by the idea of fado as a recorded practice.

reviews of fado recordings in the 1950s and 1960s asserted, it was not necessary to understand the words to find pleasure in the music; while trade magazines such as *Billboard* would assure retailers that 'language is no barrier'.[8] There was a recognition that music coming from specific sources had its true form in an unaltered form. This logic of authenticity may have been one of the reasons for the perception that the new Anglo-American pop and rock styles should be performed in English. If this is the case, a paradox emerges: the very forces that would lead to the 'universalization' of the Anglo-American pop sound might have been based on a desire to keep it sonically localized. More likely, however, is the suggestion made by a number of scholars that, emerging from centres of advanced industrialization and capital accumulation, the new pop sound was heard as the sound of modernity and progress.[9] As Simon Frith summarizes, 'Anglo-American pop is always present [in accounts of non-Anglophone popular music] anyway – it is the way of music-making to which all other musical changes [since the 1950s] must be referred'.[10]

For a variety of reasons, performers in many non-Anglophone countries began either performing in English or performing music that was very closely based on that of Anglo-American performers. Some acts, such as the pioneer *roqueiro* Zeca do Rock and beat group Os Ekos, performed in Portuguese from the outset of their careers. Others, such as Os Claves, would sing in English (often versions of tracks already performed by British or American acts) or, as in the case of Conjunto Mistério, a mixture of Portuguese and English versions of acts such as The Beatles, The Kinks and The Searchers, as well as instrumental rock influenced by The Shadows. The Sheiks sang in English and did covers of British and American hits; the group included Paulo de Carvalho and Fernando Tordo, who would go on to be major Portuguese pop stars and to have an active involvement in commercial fado (I will return to Carvalho later on).

If one of the attractions of post-rock 'n' roll styles of music was their oppositional element, it is interesting to note their contemporaneous existence alongside other music of conscience. In the Anglophone world, this played itself out in the battle between folk and rock music. A similar dynamic occurred in Latin America, where highly politicized *nueva canción* movements relying on traditional musics and folk aesthetics came into conflict with groups of rock fans who saw in their music a practice that was inherently oppositional and which did not require additional allegiance to the politics of the various New Song movements. In Argentina and Chile rock musicians from the late 1960s through to the 1990s bemoaned the

---

8   'The Billboard Buying Guide for Packaged Records', *Billboard* (30 March 1959): 34. See also the regular reviews of fado in the 'Continental Records' section of *Gramophone* in the 1950s and 1960s.

9   See Peter Manuel's discussion of acculturation in his *Popular Musics of the Non-Western World: An Introductory Survey* (New York & Oxford: Oxford University Press, 1988), pp. 19–23.

10   Frith, 'Introduction', *World Music*, p. 5.

demands made on them for their political opinions when what they really wanted was to maintain fidelity to a quite different form of liberation ushered in by the event of rock 'n' roll and its attendant countercultural possibilities. This is an argument with which many musicians and fans in areas associated with the source of this event (mainly Britain and the USA) have not had to grapple.[11]

In the case of Portugal, the emergence of the *canto de intervenção* was contemporaneous with the 1960s Anglo-American pop and rock boom; both offered oppositional spaces. Some groups attempted to occupy both spaces. Quarteto 1111, for example were a group who formed in 1967, influenced by The Beatles, but who also went on to perform notably Portuguese material. The group featured José Cid, whose own epic story in the history of Portuguese pop – from beat group through psychedelia, prog rock, pop, Eurovision, folk and fado to his position as an Elton John-like figure – is best told elsewhere.[12] Of main interest in the light of the points raised here are songs such as Quarteto 1111's 'Ode to The Beatles' (sung in English), which incorporates Beatles tunes into its structure and turns the British group's own melancholic nostalgia back on to its originators. Coming on the heels of Quarteto's hit single, 'A Lenda de El-Rei D. Sebastião' [The Legend of King Sebastian], it is hard not to assign a certain *Sebastianismo* to the line 'maybe they'll return one day'. The group also recorded 'Trova do Vento Que Passa', the anti-Salazar student anthem discussed in Chapter 3. Their album *Quarteto 1111* (1970) was seized by the PIDE (Portuguese secret police), proof that the combination of musical styles they were offering was indeed oppositional.

If Portuguese pop and rock music in the 1960s had shown a particular fidelity to both the pleasurable and oppositional elements of the Anglo-American style, the following decade saw the emergence of a number of bands who wished to add to the formula a more explicit political attachment. Notable among such groups was Trovante, formed in 1976 in Sagres. From the outset, the group displayed a strong political thrust and collaborated with artists associated with *canto de intervenção* such as José Afonso and Fausto. They emphasized elements of traditional Portuguese music mixed with rock, with certain sonic features being used to support the sense of solidarity with new political programmes, such as the collective voice used to great effect on the title track of *Chão Nosso* (1977). 'Cantemos Victor Jara' on *Em Nome Da Vida* (1978), evokes the sound world of Latin American *nueva canción* as well as articulating solidarity with the anti-dictatorship movements in

---

[11]   The Latin American case is explored more fully in Richard Elliott, 'Loss, Memory and Nostalgia in Popular Song: Thematic Aspects and Theoretical Approaches', PhD thesis (Newcastle University, 2008), pp. 186–207. See also Sergio Pujol, *Rock y Dictadura: Crónica de una Generación (1976–1983)* (Buenos Aires: Emecé Editores, 2005), for an analysis of the Argentinian situation.

[12]   At the time of writing, two websites provide the best account of Cid's life and work. The official site (http://www.josecid.com) gives an amusing year-by-year autobiography; the blog *José Cid D. Camaleão* (http://josecidcamaleao.blogspot.com) provides a detailed discography.

that continent through lyrics which remember the murdered Chilean singer Víctor Jara. Luís Represas, a key member of Trovante, had gained a lasting interest in Latin America, its politics and music. He was particularly interested in Cuba, making numerous trips to the country and collaborating with musicians such as Pablo Milanés. Represas would later translate Cuban singer-songwriter Silvio Rodríguez's signature song 'Unicornio' into Portuguese for the *fadista* Mísia.[13] Jara, meanwhile, provided inspiration for the name of another folk-based group which formed in the 1970s, Brigada Victor Jara. These groups, along with Banda do Casaco, Fausto, Janita Salomé and Né Ladeiras, brought folk music into the commercial popular music.

Portuguese rock in the 1970s also responded to the rise of progressive forms in other countries, notably progressive rock. Like many musicians moving from the 1960s into the new decade, José Cid transferred from psychedelia to progressive rock, releasing albums such as the space-rock epic *10.000 Anos Depois Entre Vénus e Marte* (1978). Another group, Ananga Ranga, utilized elements of progressive rock, jazz rock and (Anglo-American) country rock during the late 1970s and early 1980s, singing in English. Tantra, a progressive rock act who performed in Portuguese, used symphonic forms to good effect on albums such as *Mistérios e Maravilhas* (1977) and *Holocausto* (1978). Listening to albums such as *Mistérios e Maravilhas* and Cid's *10.000 Anos...*, it is easy to forget issues of language because, even though the lyrics are sung in Portuguese, they are minimized by extended instrumental passages. It is not so much that they sound 'English' (so much progressive music was made in other countries that this cannot be the case) as that progressive rock was somehow beyond any specific language, or rather that it was a language of its own based on particular arrangements, rhythms, changes and instrumentation.

The real 'boom' in Portuguese rock came with the 1980s. By this point a number of groups were pledging more explicit allegiance to Anglo-American forms. It could be argued that the punk 'revolution' made more of an effect in Portugal than rock 'n' roll had in the 1950s and 1960s and this may well have been due to a sense of liberation following the Revolution in 1974. Certainly, a host of Portuguese acts responded enthusiastically to the stylistic innovations inaugurated by punk, post-punk and New Wave. A good example of this would be Grupo Novo Rock (GNR), formed at the start of the 1980s in Porto. The group's name made was both a play on the acronym of the Portuguese National Republican Guard (*Guarda Nacional Republicana*) and a claim to newness (Grupo Novo Rock = New Rock Group). The group started with a strong tendency towards experimental and improvised music. Their singer Rui Reininho had been involved in Jorge Lima Barreto's Anar Band, an electroacoustic free-improvisation project that released an album (*Anar Band*) in 1977. If the first side of GNR's debut album *Independança*

---

[13] Ary dos Santos provided a similar service for Carlos do Carmo in 1980, creating a Portuguese version of Rodríguez's 'Pequeña Serenata Diurna'. See Carlos do Carmo, *Álbum* (Polygram/Universal 066934-2, 2003 [1980]).

(1982) seemed to follow a reasonably conventional rock template, the second side, comprising just one track, presented a far more avant-garde direction. At around 27 minutes long, 'Avarias' is an extended workout mixing improvised elements, a strong drumbeat, sampled and distorted vocals, guitar and bass that manages to create its own sound world as it progresses. 'Avarias' renders discussion of imitation redundant, bearing witness instead to the pleasure of sonic invention. Over the course of subsequent releases for EMI (*Defeitos Especiais*, 1984; *Os Homens Não se Querem Bonitos*, 1985; *Psicópatria*, 1986; *Valsa dos Detectives*, 1989), the group settled into a smoother pop-rock sound and became a popular mainstay of *Música Popular Portuguesa* (MPP).

Over the course of the 1980s a number of bands emerged who would become dominant names on the Portuguese popular music scene. These included Da Vinci, formed in 1982, whose early work emphasized bass and synthesizer and was 'futuristic' in the manner of early Depeche Mode; Xutos & Pontapés (who marked their thirtieth anniversary in 2009), whose early style relied on spiky post-punk guitar and vocal styles and foregrounded percussion, later moving towards a more conventional rock format; UHF (another long-running group), who played a form of hard rock and whose lyrics focused on everyday life in Portugal; The Delfins, informed by new wave sounds, who produced bass heavy tunes with 'dancey' electric guitars and synthesizers (heard to good effect on 'Estrelas do Rock'n'Roll'); Mão Morta, who opted for a darker sound that incorporated elements of industrial music and heavy metal.

Another big name from the 1980s was Rui Veloso, who began his career influenced by BB King and Eric Clapton. His work follows a template similar to Clapton's, though Veloso displayed a commitment to singing in Portuguese from the outset, earning him a reputation as one of the founding figures of 'authentic' Portuguese rock.[14] It is interesting to note how a complex sense of place works itself out in Veloso's work, reflecting a fidelity both to Portuguese regionalism (in particular the north of the country) and the mythical landscape of American blues. This complexity is often marked by the simultaneity of real and imagined spaces, as in 'Sayago Blues', which opens with a classic blues progression over which Veloso sings about travelling up and down the river 'from Miranda to Araínho'. He dreams that the river he is travelling on (the Douro) is the Mississippi 'and that Memphis was in Pinhão / Harvesting grapes to the sound of *adufe* / *Bandolim* and accordion'.[15] Sayago is an area of Spain near that borders Portugal to the north. Miranda, Araínho and Pinhão are all places around the Douro, the river here transposed to the land of the blues. The references to wine and harvesting are due to the Port wine trade which dominates this part of Portugal. The *adufe* is a square drum of Moorish origin found in Portugal and associated, along with the *bandolim*

---

[14]   Veloso's music is tied to Portugal far more than that of the contemporaneous Go Graal Blues Band who sang in English and adopted American accents.

[15]   Rui Veloso, 'Sayago Blues', *Fora de Moda* (Valentim de Carvalho/EMI 724382846420, 1993 [1982]).

and the accordion, with the folk music of this area. Mention of these instruments adds to the tension already inherent in the overlaying of Portuguese and North American landscapes by suggesting an equally compromised soundscape; we do not hear the *adufe*, *bandolim* or accordion, only the guitars and drums of a musical style which shows utmost fidelity to the blues of the southern USA. In this sense, Veloso has followed Clapton in the adoption of an imagined, yearned-for and ultimately subjectivating sonic space: both, we might say, are blues subjects. Veloso would go on to author a number of fados for 'new fadistas'.

The importance of regionalism, often expressed by a reliance on toponyms, can be found in a number of Portuguese rock groups from the era. While it may have seemed fairly common for fado and Portuguese folk musics to mention place names, to do so in rock music could be seen more as a territorializing practice. No matter whether the dominant musical forms were coming from elsewhere, to listen to Heróis do Mar's 'Portugal', or, less nationalistically, to hear Rádio Macau emphasize the word 'Lisboa' in 'Bom Dia Lisboa' and sing about the Elevador da Glória that leads up to Lisbon's Bairro Alto (both one of its historic quarters and one of the places that would become a central location for the new rock- and pop-based bars and clubs), or to hear UHF celebrate place names like Rua do Carmo, Chiado and Bairro Alto was to hear the ways a 'universal' language could be localized.

By the end of the 1980s, then, Portuguese rock music had created its own field, allowing for a situation where fans could choose between the dominant Anglo-American pop and rock acts and homegrown talent that relied to a greater or lesser extent on Anglo-American models. By this point, music fans also had a dedicated music press, most notably the magazine *Blitz*, which had been launched in 1984 and was itself a product of the 'boom'. *Blitz* eventually settled on a formula that fairly well reflected the musical balance in the country, featuring stories on predominantly British and American artists while ensuring coverage for Portuguese bands and a small but significant amount of coverage for fado music, especially following the emergence of the 'new fadistas' of the 2000s. The magazine remains the premier source of pop information in the country and now hosts an online archive giving access to stories, interviews and reviews. Other websites have been set up devoted exclusively to 1980s Portuguese rock acts, reflecting the importance of the era in creating what is still the main reference point when speaking of Portuguese popular music.[16]

One of the reasons for the boom in rock and pop music during the 1980s, as has been suggested, was the sense of a fresh start following the move to democracy and the end of the colonial wars in the former Portuguese colonies in Africa. Connected to this, as Rui Vieira Nery points out, was a growing sense of economic security as Portugal started to move towards EEC membership. Younger people, the obvious target for most rock and pop music, had more spending power and were able to use it on the growing number of imported products available

---

[16]   See, for example, the *Música Portuguesa – Anos 80* website, http://anos80.no.sapo.pt.

in the country. Fado, meanwhile, was suffering a 'crisis of identity' partly but not exclusively arising from the negative image it had gained during the Salazar period. A number of artists did not record during this period (although there were notable exceptions such as the self-written albums released by Amália and the continued success of Carlos do Carmo) and attendance at *casas do fado* dropped (again with notable exceptions, such as Maria da Fé's Senhor Vinho house, which remained popular).[17]

A number of artists who were identified with the rock boom made a connection with fado, no doubt as a strategy to localize the otherwise 'placeless place' of Anglo-American pop and rock. Mler Ife Dada, a group formed in 1984 in Cascais, provide a good example of this strategy. In 1986, the group were joined by singer Anabela Duarte, who participated on two seminal albums, *Coisas Que Fascinam* (1987) and *Espírito Invisível* (1989). The latter contained a song called 'Dance Music' which set up the complexities of the Portuguese popular musical field simply but effectively: over a funk arrangement of bass, horns and guitar, an angry male voice asks in a semi-rap (in English), 'Why do you have to hear dance music on your radio / if you're not dancing, you're listening to the radio?' and then 'Why do you have to hear this song in English language / If you're not English and this ain't no English song?'[18] The first album contained a number of varied elements, from experimental pop-rock with dada-ist overtones to music informed by an explicit internationalism. 'À Sombra Desta Pirâmide' includes Arabic sonorities; 'Siô Djuzé', a brief duet between Duarte and Rui Reininho, uses the style of Cape Verdean *coladeira*; 'Passarella' mixes English lyrics with Portuguese; and 'Desastre de Automóvel em Varão de Escadas' uses random lines of German alongside wordless singing and a musical accompaniment that evokes the honking of car horns. 'Alfama' is clearly a gesture towards fado, performed not by a particular instrumental style but via the sense of place evoked in the lyrics and by Duarte's voicing of the words. Against a minimal electric guitar, an associative style not dissimilar to that of the city fados discussed in Chapter 2 is used: the Alfama of painted shards, of paint, of winds on the river, knife tips, alpaca, famous people, the flea market, and 'knife-like winds / that slice Alfama / into doors painted / with the fame of fado'.[19] The lyrics involve a series of plays on words and heavy use of alliteration so that the ultimate number of associations is multiplied, the portrait becoming more than the sum of its parts, an intricate word labyrinth that echoes the tumbling streets of its subject.

Duarte went on to release a series of solo albums, including *Lishbunah* (1988), which included traditional fado instrumentation (Martinho de Assunção on *viola*

---

[17] Rui Vieira Nery, *Para uma História do Fado* (Lisbon: Corda Seca & Público, 2004), pp. 260–65.

[18] Mler Ife Dada, 'Dance Music', *Espírito Invisível* (Polydor 841272-2, 1998 [1989]).

[19] Mler Ife Dada, 'Alfama', *Coisas Que Fascinam* (Polygram Portugal 831 984-2, 1987). This is a very rough translation as the lyric relies on alliteration and double meaning.

and Manuel Mendes on *guitarra portuguesa*), opening it with José Régio's poem of fadontology, 'Fado Português'. Over a decade later, Duarte produced a more ghostly and futuristic fado on the album *Delito* (1999), which reprised her Mler Ife Dada song 'Alfama' and introduced a new piece called 'Planeta Phado'. The album did not utilize fado instrumentation but relied on a variety of sounds and recording and post-production techniques to lend the music a fractured, fragile quality. 'Planeta Phado' presents itself as a sort of palimpsest, a new song sung (or recorded) over the distant trace of a traditional lament. Speaking about her ideas for the album, Duarte said:

> We need to take the fado further. Cut its corsets, let it breathe. There have been some bold attempts, but a cyber-fado would be something completely new. In Planeta Phado, I tried to mix *Blade Runner* with fado. The cloning and the mechanisms of fiction and the multiple directions, or simultaneous directions, the matrix, cyberpunk, is something that has not been attempted yet in fado. Phado Planet is there.[20]

Duarte did not specify who had been responsible for the previous 'bold attempts' to ally fado with other sonic possibilities but she might have been thinking of António Variações. Variações (a pseudonym taken from the Portuguese word for 'variations') was responsible for 'queering' both fado and Portuguese pop by fusing elements of folk, fado, new wave and other contemporary pop forms in his music and by applying an openly homosexual appropriation of Portuguese musical tradition. Prior to his premature death in 1984, Variações released two revolutionary albums *Anjo de Guarda* (1983) and *Dar & Receber* (1984), the former containing a version of 'Povo Que Lavas no Rio' which removed the song from traditional fado accompaniment by adding synthesizer, drums and electric bass. Vocally, the song is not so far removed from Amália's version, with Variações's vocals often operating on a high, 'feminine' register, and this was something the singer seemed to recognize in another song on the album, 'Voz-Amália-de-Nós', where he sings 'We all have Amália in our voice'. At the same time, this register alternates with a deeper 'blank croon' (more noticeable on the album's third track 'Visões-Ficções (Nostradamus)'), suggesting a hitherto unexplored connection between Rodrigues, Nico and Brian Ferry, another of the singer's influences.[21] Variações's albums were popular in Portugal, suggesting the ways that the 1980s might sound

---

20   Anabela Duarte, cited in Manuel Halpern, *O Futuro da Saudade: O Novo Fado e os Novos Fadistas* (Lisbon: Publicações Dom Quixote, 2004), p. 80. Full interview available at http://rayso.weblog.com.pt/arquivo/cat_musica.html (29 May 2009). It is worth noting that Lula Pena had already used the word 'Phados' to describe her own ghostly take on the genre the year before: Lula Pena, *[phados]* (Carbon 7 C7-032, 1998).

21   António Variações, 'Povo Que Lavas no Rio', 'Voz-Amália-de-Nós' and 'Visões-Ficções (Nostradamus)', all on *Anjo da Guarda* (EMI/Valentim de Carvalho 724382373223, 1998 [1983]).

and playing a dominant role in interpellating young people into the pop world, including those musicians (the *fadista* Camané among them) who came together in 2004 as the group Humanos to record a highly successful album of songs recorded by Variações but unreleased at the time of the singer's death.[22]

Paulo Bragança is an interesting figure to mention in this context. Like Variações, he had a sacrilegious approach to fado that was nonetheless rooted in a serious consideration of fado's possibilities. Declaring himself an enemy of the genteel tradition of the *puristas*, Bragança took upon himself the role of a 'true *fadista*' by drawing comparisons between the original *fadistas* and the punks. He would perform on the fado circuit barefoot, dressed in jeans, T-shirts and leather jackets and making declarations such as 'Fado for Portugal is like a sacred altar covered in dust. And if someone dares to clear the dust, he'll be shot.'[23] Bragança's first album *Notas Sobre a Alma* (1992), which featured the *guitarra* of Mário Pacheco and the *viola* and production of Jorge Fernando (a major figure in what was to become *novo fado*), was restricted to mostly traditional fado, apparently at the request of his record company. His second, *Amai* (1994), was a different affair, featuring a wide range of instruments (synthesizers, samplers, organ, *guitarra*, accordion, and strings) and styles (fado, flamenco, rock, pop and Brazilian music), and containing a number of self-written songs and cover versions of non-fado material, such as Nick Cave's 'Sorrow's Child' (in English) and Heróis do Mar's 'Adeus'. The bringing together of Cave's lyric and Pacheco's *guitarra*, as mentioned in Chapter 1, was designed as a way of showing how *saudade* and a *fadista* worldview could reside in musics outside the Portuguese world. In 1996 Luaka Bop, the label created by David Byrne and Yale Evelev to promote progressive world music, reissued *Amai* for an international market; Bragança and Carlos Maria Trindade of Madredeus also contributed a track to *Red Hot & Lisbon* (1999), a compilation released by Luaka Bop as a snapshot of Lusophone music at the time of Expo 98 in Lisbon. Bragança released a third solo album in 1996 containing traditional fados and a fourth (*Lua Semi-Nua*) in 2001 which reprised the large instrumental palette of *Amai* and contained a number of songs written by pop legend José Cid, who also produced the album.

The Road to *Novo Fado*

During the 1990s there was a notable trend back towards a commercially popular form of fado music, centred on a group of mostly young musicians from the post-revolutionary generation. A brief summary of the key artists involved in this regeneration of fado would probably need to start with the emergence in the late 1980s of the group Madredeus. Though far removed from fado proper, their

---

[22]   Humanos, *Humanos* (EMI/Valentim de Carvalho 724356065222, 2004).

[23]   Paulo Bragança's artist page on Luaka Bop website, http://www.luakabop.com (20 May 2009).

combination of musical styles (described in *Billboard* as 'an amalgam of fado, classical string quartets, Parisian chanson, and a strong hint of the melodramatic harmonium and vocal solo albums of the late Nico, of the Velvet Underground'[24]) established a sound quite unlike that being performed by other groups within or outside Portugal and moved them away from their own roots in rock music (the group was formed by Pedro Ayres Magalhães and Rodrigo Leão of rock group Sétima Legião; Leão left the group in 1994 and was replaced by Carlos Maria Trindade) toward an arena where the possibility of a new native music could be played out. The hint of fado was never far away in this, hardly surprising given singer Teresa Salgueiro's background as a performer of *fado vadio* (amateur fado, as practised in local neighbourhood *tabernas* or cafes rather than professional fado houses). The group became the most popular Portuguese group outside the country and their music was used to great effect in Wim Wenders's film *Lisbon Story*, providing a link between music and place as crucial as that forged in the director's other work. Another boundary-crossing artist from this period was Dulce Pontes, who first came to national attention as a television star before going on to represent Portugal in the 1991 Eurovision Song Contest. The song she performed, and which subsequently became a hit in both Portuguese and English versions, was entitled 'Lusitano Paixão' and was essentially a hymn to the time-honoured emotions of sadness, grief and *saudade*. It was not, however, fado.[25] Her second album, discussed in more detail below, *was* a landmark fado album, combining famous fados of the past with folk songs and pop instrumentation to forge an album with genuine crossover appeal. Its 'Canção do Mar' became known internationally when used in the film *Primal Fear* (1996).

Also in 1991 also came the release of the first album by Mísia, a more 'authentic'-sounding *fadista* than Dulce Pontes if only in the sense that she was backed up by the traditional arrangement of *guitarra* and *viola*. The material she included on the album was more eclectic than traditional, however, and included a song by pop singer Carlos Paião ('Ai Que Pena'), a version of Rui Veloso's 'Porto Sentido' and a gesture towards Brazilian popular music in the form of 'Samba em Prelúdio' by Vinicius de Moraes and Baden Powell. Other songs on the album were more obviously fados. Her second album, *Fado* (1993), initially given a limited release in Japan but later distributed in Portugal, Spain and South Korea, continued this eclectic mix of fado and other popular musics, including lyrics sung in Spanish ('De Alguna Manera'), Catalan ('La Gavina') and English ('As Time

---

[24]   Philip Sweeney, 'The Billboard Report', *Billboard* (8 January 1994): 2.

[25]   It is interesting to note how, since entering the competition for the first time in 1964, Portugal has tended to favour music that does not carry a sense of Portugueseness much beyond its lyrical content. The nearest fado has come to being represented was probably Carlos do Carmo's entry in 1976. Liana, who performed as the young Amália Rodrigues in Filipe La Féria's musical and who produced the ambitious crossover album *Fado.pt* in 2004, won the 2000 *Festival RTP da Canção*, the national song festival that is used to select the Eurovision entry (Portugal did not enter in 2000), but her song was not a fado-style song.

Goes By') and a translation into Portuguese of Jacques Brel's 'La Chanson des Vieux Amants' ('Os Velhos Amantes'). The album opened with a song written by Sérgio Godinho and entitled 'Liberdades Poéticas', which seemed to offer directions as to where Mísia was hoping to take fado. The song began with the lines 'Perdoai-me se este fado é feito com / Liberdades poéticas' [Forgive me if this fado is made with / Poetic liberties], a claim it then confirmed lyrically and sonically by the use of self-confessed 'asymmetric', 'non-fado' rhyme schemes and the 'small flame' it offered in place of 'the violent jealousy / that fado so often sings of'.[26]

Mísia brought to the genre a sense of visual style that had been absent for some time, appearing in concert and on her CD covers dressed in *haute couture* outfits that referenced both fado's past (its shawls, dark colours and poses) and its present in a world of high definition photography, light shows and contemporary fashion. Of great importance also was her choice of material, bringing to new life the work of some of Portugal's most notable poets – including, increasingly, many female poets who had been given far less attention than their male counterparts.[27] By the middle of the 1990s Mísia had become a success outside of Portugal, touring Europe, Japan, Australia and the Middle East. She became, along with the other young female *fadistas* whom her success helped bring to the public's attention, a substitute for the ailing Amália Rodrigues, whose passing in 1999 once more brought fado to the attention of the nation and of the international community where Amália had made such an impact.[28] Mísia's 2001 album *Ritual* was a homage to Rodrigues, containing versions of songs associated with her, a track written in her memory and a new arrangement of Rodrigues's unrecorded poem 'Vivendo Sem Mim' [Living Without Me]. Mísia's voice, like Teresa Salgueiro's and Dulce Pontes's, was also heard in the cinema when her songs 'Paixões Diagonais' and 'Triste Sina' provided the fados performed by the female lead in the film *Passionada* (2002). In 2003, Mísia was involved in another homage when she invited the poet Vasco Graça Moura to write lyrics to be sung to the instrumental compositions of the *guitarrista* Carlos Paredes. This was an unusual request as it was far more common for those performers inspired by Amália to compose music for existing poems. Indeed, one way of distinguishing the modern form of fado would be via this tendency, earlier more traditional fados often involving new or improvised words set to existing tunes. What Moura had to accomplish, then,

---

[26]   'Liberdades Poéticas', lyric and music by Sérgio Godinho, recorded by Mísia, *Fado* (Ariola/BMG 74321165622, 1993).

[27]   This is particularly notable on the fourth album *Garras dos Sentidos* (1998), where poems by Agustina Bessa-Luis, Lídia Jorge and Natália Correia are set to conventional fado arrangements.

[28]   In Portugal three days of national mourning were announced following Rodrigues's death and countless newspaper and magazine articles started to emerge about the late 'queen of fado'. Internationally, there were numerous obituaries and feature articles, followed by the inevitable rush releasing of compilation albums.

was to replace the 'voice' of Paredes's *guitarra* with words for Mísia to sing. The resulting album, *Canto* (2003), was dedicated to the ailing Paredes, who passed away the following year.

Ritual and *Canto* reintroduced to fado the notion of the concept album, a practice that had been undertaken in earlier decades by Amália and Carlos do Carmo. These albums were clearly demarcated as 'projects' and were part of a larger package including styling, CD design and live performances. Mísia continued this practice with her next two albums *Drama Box* (2005) and *Ruas* (2009), the latter of which I will return to in the next chapter. *Drama Box* is an oddity even in the discography of the eclectic Mísia, a mixture of fados, Mexican boleros, Argentinian tangos and spoken intervals. The album opens with two songs by the Mexican songwriter Armando Manzanero, which Mísia performs in Spanish. These are followed by a reading by Ute Lemper, in German, of a poem by Vasco Graça Moura ('Fogo Preso'/'Feuerwerk'). Mísia then performs the same poem as a fado, in Portuguese, to music written by the *guitarrista* José Fontes Rocha. There follow a number of 'regular' fados, setting lyrics by Moura, Natália Correia, Rosa Lobato Faria and José Saramago to music by *guitarristas*. The album closes with three tangos by Virgilio and Homero Expósito, Juan Carlos Cobián and Enrique Cadícamo, and Horácio Ferrer and Astor Piazzolla. The final piece is a reprise of 'Fogo Preso' spoken by four actresses in four languages: Maria de Medeiros (Portuguese), Fanny Ardant (French), Carmen Maura (Spanish) and Miranda Richardson (English). Such deliberately cosmopolitan and postmodern strategies have helped to situate Mísia more within an international art world than within fado: as a *fadista*, she remains perhaps the most complex.

The spectacular appearance of Mariza on the Portuguese and world music scenes was the real success for fado in the new century. More extravagantly outfitted and hairstyled than Mísia, and with a powerful voice and dramatic stage presence, she became an instant television celebrity following her appearance on the popular *Herman SIC* show.[29] With the release of her debut album, *Fado em Mim* (2001), Mariza went on to enjoy sales and chart positions only previously achieved in Portugal by Amália and to international success on the world music circuit, where she made appearances at the major world music festivals and was the recipient of numerous awards. The major influence on *Fado em Mim* was, once again, Amália; half of the album's songs were fados previously performed by Amália, another being an arrangement of one of the *fadista*'s unrecorded poems.

---

[29] It is sometimes mistakenly reported that Mariza only gained popularity in Portugal after finding success abroad. It is true that she was unable to secure a recording contract initially in Portugal and ended up signing with the Dutch label World Connection. However, Mariza was a regular guest and performer on the *Herman SIC* in 2000 and 2001. A very early appearance found her, somewhat strangely, participating in a rendition of the fado 'Nem às Paredes Confesso' with Anjos, a pop duo who were highly successful in Portugal at the time. This moment, as much as any, can signal both Mariza's journey from the world of pop singing to fado and her arrival on the national musical scene.

Mariza's voice, not surprisingly, is foregrounded in the production and has an exceptional clarity and resonance (enhanced by an occasional hint of echo). There is an equal clarity and separation in the recording of the guitars. On the opening track, 'Loucura', it is the guitars that introduce us to the soundworld of the album and provide the momentum against which the scene-setting declamation of the verse can be sounded:

Sou do fado	[I am of the fado
Como sei	How do I know
Vivo um poema cantado	I live a poem sung
De um fado que eu inventei.[30]	From a fado that I invented].

This approach contrasts with that of Mísia, who recorded the song a decade earlier on her debut album, by leading with the voice and extending the first word ('sou') to provide a dramatic launching pad for the lyric. Both artists seem to be presenting declarations of intent: I represent fado, I am fado, and this is how fado sounds now. For me, there is more drama in Mariza's version for two reasons. Firstly, it comes as the opening to her album, whereas it is near the end of Mísia's. Secondly, there seems to be a greater tension between Mariza's voice and the guitars that gives the song an edge. The guitars proceed at a steady but leisurely pace, while the voice is clipped in places, suggesting an impatience and brevity that lends great urgency to the lyrics. The song's refrain is marked off from the strophic verses by a change in melodic line and a change of vocal emphasis: 'Chorai, chorai / Poetas do meu país' ['Cry, cry / Poets of my country']. For listeners versed in fado lore, this immediately evokes the oft-repeated lines 'Chorai fadistas, chorai', which can be found in numerous fados relating the story of Maria Severa and in Júlio Dantas's play. The poet/fadista connection is emphasized in the second half of the chorus:

E se vocês	[And if all of you
Não estivessem a meu lado	Were not at my side
Então não havia fado	Then there would be no fado
Nem fadistas como eu sou	Nor fadistas such as I].

Lyrically, the blame is placed on the poets but vocally, the singer takes all the responsibility, revelling in the distinctively Portuguese nasal sound of 'então' before delivering the chorus's resolution.[31] At the close of the song this strophe is

---

[30]   'Loucura', lyric by Júlio Campos Sousa, music by Joaquim Frederico de Brito, recorded by Mariza, *Fado em Mim* (CD, World Connection 43038, 2002 [2001]). Also recorded by Mísia, *Mísia* (Valentim de Carvalho/EMI 077779655823, 1991) and by Carlos do Carmo, *Clássicos da Renascença* (Movieplay MOV 31.004, 2000).

[31]   There are other versions of 'Loucura' (somtimes 'Fado da Loucura' or 'É Loucura') which have different lyrics (also by Frederico de Brito) and in which the refrain is 'Chorai, Chorai / Guitarras da minha terra', thus placing the blame on the music rather than the

repeated and, as has become customary in many fado performances, the words are stretched out to create a time outside of that set by the guitars' rhythm, allowing the voice to attain its full presence before reigning itself in and leaving the guitars to deliver the two-note sign-off.

Following this declaration of intent, *Fado em Mim* delivers a challenge with its second song. 'Poetas', another song devoted to poets, opens with piano, shortly followed by a bowed double bass. Mariza sings the first two verses of the lyric (adapted from the work of Portuguese poet Florbela Espanca) over this instrumentation. There is a pause around one minute in, after the second verse, and then the fado instruments join in. With these first two songs, then, the musical template for Mariza's project has been largely determined. The rest of the album continues the process of instrumental clarity, thanks to the production and to the inventiveness and cleanliness of Custódio Castelo's *guitarra*. The pacing of the album is carefully managed too, with the uptempo 'Maria Lisboa' breaking the melancholy spell of the first three tracks as well as providing Mariza with a further vehicle for vocal prowess, notably at the song's resolution where the word 'Maria' is expanded to set up a contrast with the swiftly delivered final line. This song is one Mariza would continue to use in concert performance to pick the momentum up at critical moments in the set. Here, it clears the ground beautifully for 'Ó Gente da Minha Terra' (discussed in the previous chapter), in many ways the emotional centrepiece of the album.

Mariza's second album, *Fado Curvo* (2003), experimented with the musical style by adding trumpet and piano and by utilizing song structures that, even allowing for the now longstanding tendency toward *fado canção*, were still quite different from those of other fados. The production came this time from Carlos Maria Trindade of Madredeus and the almost sacred silence that seems to surround the music is reminiscent in places of Madredeus's own hallowed sound. Mariza's voice is allowed to assert its dominion over this silence as in the first album. The opening song, 'O Silêncio da Guitarra' alternates moments of *guitarra* and voice, before bringing them together to deliver the lyric over a 'traditional' fado style. Mariza's vocal picks out key tropes from the lyric: 'guitarra', 'Tejo', 'Lisboa', 'saudade', 'tristeza' [sadness]. The second track, 'Cavaleiro Monge', provides an excellent example of the collaborative work between poet, composer/musician and singer. The song is an adaptation of a poem by Fernando Pessoa, which, even prior to being set to music, carries a strong sense of rhythm and musicality:

Do vale a montanha,	[From the valley to the mountain,
Da montanha ao monte,	From the mountain to the hill,
Cavalo de sombra, cavaleiro monge,	Horse of shadow, monk rider,
Por casas, por prados,	Through houses, through meadows,

---

words. Fernando Mauricio and Lenita Gentil have both recorded this version of the fado; the lyrics can be found in Eduardo Sucena, *Lisboa, o Fado e os Fadistas*, 2nd edn (Lisbon: Vega, 2002), pp. 328–9.

| Por quintais, por fontes, | Through gardens, through fountains, |
| Caminhais aliados.[32] | In alliance you walk.] |

Each verse of the poem follows the same structure, repeating the first three lines and varying the last three. Repetition is a dominant theme at both a structural and an enunciative level, the alliterated words following close on the hooves of the rhythmic progression. Mariza stresses these relationships by her pronunciation of the 'm's, 'c's and 'p's, and by allowing the word sounds to escape narrative progression and become, as Pessoa seems to have intended, ingredients in a ritualistic litany, a summons sent out to the 'monk rider' of the title. If anything, it is Mário Pacheco's melody, picked out on the *guitarra* at the song's introduction, which provides the most narrative, moving the song forward on its inexorable journey. As with her first album, where she worked with Custódio Castelo, Mariza chose in Pacheco a *guitarrista* associated as much with composition as with accompaniment; Pacheco clearly owns 'Cavaleiro Monge' as much as the singer.[33] In addition to these tracks, *Fado Curvo* featured songs associated with Amália ('Primavera') and José Afonso ('Menino do Bairro Negro'), two written by Carlos Maria Trindade and others by Gil do Carmo (Carlos's son) and Rui Veloso. While the latter is a figure associated with blues and rock music, the song he and Paulo Abreu Lima composed for Mariza ('Feira de Castro') does not sound like a departure from the world of fado; the most sonically wide-ranging track is Trindade's 'O Deserto', with its evocation of desert wind at the introduction, its leading piano, occasional whispered lyrics and a trumpet solo.

Mariza released her third album, *Transparente*, in 2005. In terms of the material chosen for the album, there were strong similarities to the previous projects: another adaptation of Pessoa by Mário Pacheco ('Há uma Música do Povo'); a lyric by Artur Ribeiro ('Quando Me Sinto Só' – Mariza had performed Ribeiro's 'Vielas de Alfama' on *Fado Curvo*); a poem by Florbela Espanca ('Desejos Vãos' – there had been an Espanca poem on each of the previous albums) and a song by Paulo Abreu Lima and Rui Veloso ('Transparente'). The main difference on this occasion was the additional instrumentation. The album was produced and arranged by the Brazilian Jaques Morelenbaum, who brought a very different soundworld to Mariza's work. The songs were backed up by a string ensemble and additionally featured, alongside the classic configuration of *guitarra* and *viola*, accordion, *cavaquinho*

---

[32] Fernando Pessoa, *Obras Completas Vol. 1: Poesias de Fernando Pessoa*, 12th edn (Lisbon: Edições Ática, 1987), p. 148. Set to music as 'Cavaleiro Monge' by Mário Pacheco, recorded by Mariza, *Fado Curvo* (World Connection/Virgin/EMI-Valentim de Carvalho 724358423723, 2003). I have used the (uncredited) translation provided in the CD liner.

[33] Pacheco, one of the leading *guitarristas* of his generation and the owner of the highly successful Clube de Fado in Alfama, would go on to release his own album featuring guests Camané, Mariza, Ana Sofia Varela and Rodrigo Costa Félix. Mário Pacheco, *Clube de Fado* (World Connection WC 43062, 2006).

(a four-stringed guitar-like instrument used in some Portuguese traditional musical styles), flutes, clarinet, French horn and percussion. As with Amália and Carlos do Carmo, who had also used orchestral arrangements in previous decades, the music alternated between being led by the fado instrumentation and by the strings (or, in the case of 'Transparente', the percussion and flute.)

For the most part, Mariza continued to tour with a minimal group of musicians (with Luís Guerreiro rather than Mário Pacheco providing *guitarra*), although she also put on concerts such as that discussed in Chapter 3 with Morelenbaum and a string orchestra. In 2008, Mariza released her fourth studio album, *Terra*. The CD cover was strange, more akin to the kind of fantasy art normally found on heavy metal albums than those containing fado. Mariza sat perched in front of a fiery orange sky, the skirt of her black dress melding into the terrain of what looked like a dark fantasy city. On closer inspection, it became clear that the objects lying in the folds of the dress were musical instruments (a *guitarra*, a piano keyboard) and that the buildings and monuments behind the singer were those associated with Lisbon (The Torre de Belém, the monument to the Discoveries, the Castelo São Jorge). The apocalyptic look of this reconfigured Lisbon, along with the inclusion of Big Ben and the Eiffel Tower in the far background, suggested that this 'terra' [land] might be rather different to that which had featured so centrally in Mariza's first album. On playing the album, such suspicions were quickly affirmed.

The album leads off with some beautifully recorded *guitarra*, backed up by the steady rhythm of a *viola*. Mariza's voice enters and among the first words we hear are the fado staples 'saudade', 'fado', 'antigo', 'lamentos' and 'cidade'. The song is 'Já Me Deixou' by Artur Ribeiro and Maximiano de Sousa (Max), the team behind an earlier success by Mariza, 'Vielas de Alfama'. All the signifiers of fado tradition seem to be in place. But at the start of the chorus, about a minute into the song, percussion enters that is clearly derived from accompaniment to flamenco rather than fado. Turning to the album credits, one finds that percussion has been provided by Piraña, a musician normally to be heard accompanying flamenco artists such as Paco de Lucia. Furthermore, the album was produced by Javier Limón, associated with *nuevo flamenco* as producer, writer and musician, and it was recorded in his studio in Spain. Just as Mariza's previous producers had been musicians who also played on her recordings, so Limón provides flamenco guitar to some of the songs on *Terra*. The second song on the album, Paulo de Carvalho's 'Minh'Alma', is closer to flamenco-pop than fado. The third track, 'Rosa Branca', keeps the percussion but ensures its *portugalidade* via the 'fadistic' practice of repeating each couplet. *Guitarra* leads on David Mourão-Ferreira's 'Recurso' and the sound is closer to Mariza's previous soundworld. 'Beijo de Saudade' is a duet with the Cape Verdean singer Tito Paris. The song itself is written by Cape Verdean musician and composer B. Leza and the lyric is about the 'kiss of yearning' sent out from the Tejo across the sea to the singer's homeland. The listener is reminded of the *morna* style popularized by Cesaria Evora and its associative links with Portuguese fado (both are musics of melancholic yearning and are frequently toponymic). Paris's voice brings the distinctive Cape Verdean accent familiar to listeners of Evora and the musical accompaniment is also close to the styles utilized by Evora. This is the song that places the word 'terra' at the centre of its refrain, clarifying further that the land hymned in the album's title is Portuguese only in an associative manner; the music, the musicians and the lyrical references journey far beyond the city most associated with fado. This is perhaps the closest any *novo fadista* has yet come to a truly globalized fado. Furthermore, the colonizing associations cannot be ignored; in 'Vozes do Mar' ('Voices from the Sea'), the following refrain is repeated to the sound of a yearning trumpet: 'Donde vem essa voz, ó mar amigo? ... / ... Talvez a voz de um Portugal antigo / Chamado por Camões numa saudade' [Whence comes this voice oh friendly sea? / Perhaps the voice of an ancient Portugal / Summoned by Camões in an act of yearning].[34]

Terra, ultimately, presents a fado that wishes to expand its horizons while also holding on to an idea of Lisbon. The former tendency is present in those tracks already mentioned and in others, such as that written by Limón, on which Mariza duets with the flamenco singer Concha Buika. It is also notable on 'Guitarras' written by the Brazilian jazz pianist Ivan Lins, and 'Frontier', which, while containing a lyric by Pedro Homem de Melo and music by Mário Pacheco, is driven by the Cuban pianist Chucho Valdés. 'Home' is represented by the tracks 'Recurso', 'Alfama' (the closest to the kind of fado Mariza had previously performed) and 'Tasco da Mouraria' (by Lima and Veloso). It was clear, with the release of *Terra*, that Mariza had positioned herself in the strangely placeless terrain of the world music circuit, with all its promises and disappointments.

Katia Guerreiro is a *fadista* who emerged at the same time as Mariza and who quickly built a strong national and international audience. Her albums *Fado Maior* (2001), *Nas Mãos do Fado* (2003), *Tudo ou Nada* (2005) and *Fado* (2008) have consistently set her voice against the traditional instrumental line-up (notwithstanding the use of Bernardo Sassetti's piano on one track of the third album), though her choice of material has sometimes been far from traditional. As Pedro Baptista-Bastos writes:

> more than the arrangements, more than the addition of strange instrumentation to traditional fado, it is the poems that colour contemporary fado. The themes are no longer the Rua da Mariquinhas, the *fadistas gingões*, *tascas* and the *guitarradas*. But they continue to be the great human themes: love, solitude, jealousy, death. They are about divorces, drugs, social problems and personal dramas.[35]

---

[34] 'Vozes do Mar', lyric by Florbela Espanca, music by Diogo Clemente, recorded by Mariza, *Terra* (Capitol/World Connection/EMI Portugal 5099922942326, 2008).

[35] Pedro Baptista-Bastos, 'O "Novo Fado" Não Existe', liner notes to *O Fado do Público* CD, vol. 5 (Lisbon: Corda Seca & Público, 2004), pp. 6–7. The Portuguese terms refer to a street (Rua da Maraquinhas) associated with local fado lore from the time of Maria Severa onwards, the 'swaying *fadistas*' of fado legend, the cheap eating places (*tascas*), and the guitar 'duels' or improvisations set up between fado instrumentalists.

In Guerreiro's case this has meant making fados from the work of António Lobo Antunes, Maria Luísa Baptista and Ana Vidal, alongside established (if not quite *castiço*) work by Pessoa, Camões and Florbela Espanca. Guerreiro's work is interesting in the ways it points toward the difficulties and contradictions of maintaining a position in a musical world imbued with tradition yet which has always, in its most spectacular forms, resisted tradition. In early interviews, Guerreiro often spoke of the need to avoid excessive experimentation and to keep fado 'authentic', while at the same time acknowledging that fado's most famous exponent, Amália Rodrigues, was never one to do so.[36]

The link to tradition is something that many commentators have highlighted when speaking about Guerreiro. Her first album came with a liner note by fado historian Rui Vieira Nery, in which he notes the emergence over the previous decade of a generation of young talented fado performers who have brought a new vitality to the genre. Vieira Nery notes two streams, one of which opts for fusion with other musical practices and another which looks to continuity. Both have contributed to a change in the perception of fado amongst young people, who had largely avoided fado during the 1970s and 1980s. Having established the historical situation, Vieira Nery introduces Guerreiro's ability to represent this changed perception and to contribute to bringing fado into the new century. Central to this is her voice, an instrument which, for Vieira Nery, has 'a warm, thick timbre, loaded with authentic emotion and capable of murmuring in a confessional tone one minute and crying with passionate grief the next and in which one feels no pretence but rather a powerful capacity for dramatic communication'.[37]

Given the consistency of the soundworld created by Guerreiro and her musicians over the course of her first four albums, it may come as something of a surprise to learn that she was previously the singer for a rock group. That she, like many other artists, has made the career choice to turn to fado highlights not only the process of generic migration common to popular music practice but also, given the consistency of her performance, the commitment with which she has shown in this choice. Indeed, Guerreiro has generally shown fidelity to the fado style of singing even when working outside its boundaries, as can be witnessed on a series of duets she has recorded with Brazilian singers. The verse she provides to 'Dar e Receber' on samba artist Martinho da Vila's album

---

[36] When questioned on this apparent contradiction by *fRoots* magazine, Guerreiro responded: 'Amália was the only person in this world that could do it. She was the queen. It's [a] very strong expression but she was the owner of fado and she could do whatever she wanted with fado because it would always be fado.' Again, as with the earlier quotations of Joaquim Pais de Brito and Leonor Lains, there is this sense of this Voice seeming to banish all contradictions through some magic power it carries. Guerreiro's comments can be found alongside interviews with other 'new fadistas' in Jon Lusk, 'Fado Figures', *fRoots* website, http://www.frootsmag.com/content/features/mariza/page04.html (18 March 2005).

[37] Rui Vieira Nery, liner notes to Katia Guerreiro, *Fado Maior* (Ocarina OCA 002, 2001).

Brasilatinidade (2005) is sung in a style markedly different from Vila's own contributions and one which is recognizably 'fado' despite the 'foreign' musical backdrop. Guerreiro's third album *Tudo ou Nada* was re-released in 2006 with the addition of two songs on which she duetted with Ney Matogrosso; again her style is noticeably that of a *fadista* and acts as a greater contrast to the male vocal than the relative pitch of the singers (Matogrosso is famed for his high singing voice). Another contrast can obviously be found in the quite different tonalities of Brazilian and Iberian Portuguese, a fact made clear on two duets Guerreiro has performed with Maria Bethânia, one a reprise of the Pessoa poem 'Ave Maria' that Guerreiro had originally performed on her first album.

The use of fado as a base from which to explore other musical avenues has also been present in the work of Cristina Branco. Her albums have set work by Camões, Pessoa, Homem de Melo and Mourão-Ferreira to music by the *guitarrista* Custódio Castelo. Yet she has also featured songs such as 'Molinera', a traditional dialect song from northern Portugal, and work by the Dutch poet Jan Jacob Slauerhoff. Branco, who began her career in the Netherlands, has produced an entire album based on Slauerhoff's work, emphasizing the intercultural dialogue between the two nations and the popularity of fado in the Netherlands.[38] More recently she has produced a collection of songs based on erotic poetry that includes fados derived from the work of Maria Teresa Horta, one of the so-called 'Three Marias' who achieved notoriety in 1972 when they were arrested for obscenity following the publication of their book *Novas Cartas Portuguesas*, a landmark feminist text whose subsequent republication in 1974 became one of the major successes of that revolutionary year. On her album *Ulisses* (2005), Branco includes a cover of Joni Mitchell's 'A Case of You', a nod to another model of female writing from the early 1970s. Like Mísia, Branco likes to base albums around particular concepts. In addition to the Slauerhoff album she has devoted albums to the major themes of love (*Sensus*, 2003), space (*Ulisses*, 2005) and time (*Kronos*, 2009). In 2007 she released an album to mark the twentieth anniversary of José Afonso's death. Named after the month of the 1974 Revolution, *Abril* featured sixteen songs by or associated with Afonso. Branco was accompanied by a jazz group featuring Ricardo Dias (keyboards), Mário Delgado (guitars), Bernardo Moreira (bass) and Alexandre Frazão (drums). The line-up subtly reinvents Afonso's work, which had also been influenced by jazz and which was often marked by an experimentalism and lyrical surrealism that fits well with the new arrangements. There is no gesture towards fado, but neither is there towards folk (Afonso's signature song 'Grândola Vila Morena' is notably omitted); instead the songs are presented as the modern musical works they always were. Another way in which Branco's work resembles

---

[38] This popularity can be asserted by witnessing the number of tours of the Netherlands by Portuguese artists such as Mariza, Cristina Branco and Ana Moura; the existence of home-grown fado clubs in Amsterdam and Utrecht; the easy availability of fado recordings by both established and less-famous performers in the record stores; and the fact that Mariza signed to a Dutch record label (World Connection) rather than a Portuguese one.

Mísia's is the use of musical arrangements by musicians from outside the world of fado. This has been notable on a number of her albums, particularly *Ulisses* and *Kronos*. For the more recent album, she invited songwriters to compose fados based on the theme of time, but many returned songs that were not remotely fado-like. The result is a mixture of fado instrumentation and other popular styles, dominated by the arrangements of Ricardo Dias (a member of Brigada Victor Jara), whose piano has been a constant presence in Branco's group in recent years.[39]

Branco is one example of a 'new generation' *fadista* whose career has followed a slower, perhaps more 'normal', growth pattern than was the case for Mariza. This is also true of Mafalda Arnauth, whose career as a *fadista* began in the 1990s but who has gained greater recognition since the turn of the century. In Paul Vernon's survey of the fado scene in the late 1990s, Arnauth was mentioned as someone who had already performed in London, at a fado concert with Argentina Santos and Carlos Zel. In 1999 she released her debut self-titled album, a disc notable for her involvement in its songwriting. Challenging the established distribution of work between lyricists, composers and singers, Arnauth wrote lyrics to nine of the eleven songs and music to five of them. Her second album *Esta Voz Que Me Atravessa* (2001) continued the practice, while also featuring a number of songs written or co-written by Amélia Muge, a Portuguese artist who had been releasing solo records since the start of the 1990s and whose own work is based on an experimental mixture of rural folk, jazz, world music and classical styles. *Encantamento* (2003), Arnauth's third album, contained songs mostly written by the singer in collaboration with the guitarist Luis Oliveira. Her fourth album *Diário* (2005) is presented as a journey across time and space, a reflection on the journey the *fadista* has taken. This presentation begins for the listener who has bought the CD with the booklet, which is full of pictures of mementoes and travel items. Dates written next to the songs for which Arnauth has provided the lyric or music indicate that there is a history to this music, the earliest lyric ('Para Maria') being dated 1992, the latest 2004. This presentation stretches Arnauth's career beyond its 'mere' six years of recorded presence, providing a connection between singer and vocation and an authentication that is reinforced by the note Arnauth provides to the booklet. Geographically, the album ranges not only in its visual depictions of foreign visits and tours undertaken, but also by the inclusion of two songs in foreign languages, one of which is 'La Bohème', sung in French to music by Charles Aznavour. Aznavour already had a connection to fado, having written 'Ay Mourir pour Toi' for Amália in the 1950s and a song entitled 'Lisboa', which Katia Guerreiro recorded on her album *Fado*. Guerreiro, like Rodrigues and Arnauth before her, sings the lyric in French.

If these songs, like Carlos do Carmo's renditions of the work of Jacques Brel, help to reinforce the connection between fado and the French *chanson* and to underline the huge popularity of fado in France, another song on *Diário* links fado

---

[39] Cristina Branco speaks about *Kronos* in an interview with Lia Pereira in *Blitz* (April 2009), p. 30.

to another urban folk music, the tango of Buenos Aires. 'Milonga do Chiado', with lyrics in Spanish and Portuguese, is co-written by Nestor Muñiz and Arnauth and is set to music by the tango guitarist Ramón Maschio. Ricardo Dias provides accordion to the track, moving it closer to a tango style. Maschio would go on to become a regular accompanist for Arnauth, touring with her and collaborating closely on her next album, *Flor de Fado* (2008). Classical guitars are more prominent than Portuguese guitars on many of the songs on this album, with some songs containing no *guitarra* at all. In addition to a number of lyrics by Arnauth herself, there are four by Tiago Torres da Silva, a Portuguese poet and playwright who has connections to both fado and Brazilian popular music, having written a play about Amália Rodrigues and lyrics for artists such as Ney Matogrosso, Maria Bethânia and Olivia Bylington. Bylington, the Brazilian singer, provides the music and a duet vocal to one of the tracks on *Diário* ('Entre a Voz e o Oceano'). The overall sound of the album is quite removed from the world of fado, although there are strong reminders of Arnauth's influences such as a version of Amália's 'Povo Que Lavas no Rio' and one of 'Flor de Verde Pinho', a song strongly associated with Carlos do Carmo.

Some artists cast as *novos fadistas* had a recorded presence prior to the new century but benefitted from the increased exposure granted fado since 2000. One example is Joana Amendoeira, whose first album was released in 1997, when the singer was only fifteen years old. Amendoeira had started singing much younger and had participated in the junior stream of the Grande Noite de Fado competition in Lisbon when she was twelve; the following year she won the Porto version of the junior competition. She became professional shortly afterwards under the guidance of the veteran *fadista* Carlos Zel, later securing a residency at Mário Pacheco's Clube de Fado while she attended university in Lisbon. It is interesting to note Zel's involvement in Amendoeira's career as he went on record declaring that fado can only be sung once one has reached thirty years of age.[40] He doubtless made this point not to deny the need to start young (he was a guiding force in the careers of other young singers too) but to highlight the fact that a vital part of fado's ontology is its recourse to experience. The paradox is that there is something both inauthentic and authentic about a *fadista* starting so young. As Amendoeira admitted to Manuel Halpern, at nine years of age she could sing Amália's signature tune 'Estranha Forma de Vida' as though her life depended on it without understanding what she was singing.[41] Yet, the very longevity of her commitment also authenticates her, arguably more than those who have turned to

---

[40]   'At 30, we have finally experienced much happiness, sadness, life and death; we have witnessed births, burials, loved and been unloved in turn.' Carlos Zel, cited in Maria Luísa Guerra, *Fado: Alma de um Povo* (Lisbon: Imprensa Nacional-Casa da Moeda, 2003), p. 110.

[41]   Halpern, *O Futuro da Saudade*, p. 239.

singing fado after trying other forms of music-making. When she sings 'Entrei na Vida a Cantar' [I Entered Life Singing], there is a stamp of truth to it.[42]

Amendoeira released her second album *Aquela Rua* in 2000 and a third in 2003 bearing only her name and presenting itself as her first mature work. Since then she has released a fourth studio album (*À Flor da Pele*, 2006) and two live albums. The first of these presents a set rooted in a fado tradition that owes much to the work of Amália; the second is based on a show entitled 'Poetas do Meu País' [Poets of My Country] and finds the singer accompanied by a string ensemble. While the show that was recorded was one of those put on for the festival of fado during June 2008, it journeys beyond fado both in terms of material and instrumentation.

Another singer who turned professional after winning the junior Grande Noite de Fado in Lisbon is Raquel Tavares, who was twelve when she came first in 1997. Her first (self-titled) album did not come out for another nine years, allowing her time and space for development. It was produced by Jorge Fernando, who also contributed a number of songs and played *viola*; the other notable presence was Diogo Clemente. Clemente acts as co-producer on the first album and producer on its successor *Bairro* (2008); he also provides *viola* to both albums. The instrumentation on both discs is kept to *guitarra*, *viola* and *baixo*, maintaining a sense of tradition that is supported by the photography that graces both albums and the participation of veteran *fadista* Fátima Fernandes on one track on *Bairro*. This duet ('Tia Dolores') is also provided as a video accompanying the album. Tavares is an example of the interconnecting worlds of popular music, fashion and television. She became as well-known in Portugal for her participation in the television show *Dança Comigo* (the Portuguese equivalent of *Strictly Come Dancing*) and subsequent representation of Portugal at the Eurovision Dance Contest in Glasgow in 2008.

Ana Moura is an artist who, like Tavares, has been guided by Jorge Fernando and presented in a highly stylized way. Like Tavares, she is also possessed of a powerful voice that can escape such trappings. 'Sou do Fado', by Fernando, is structurally quite far from fado yet it also insistently lays claim to the genre. The lyrics to the verses are too long for regular fado lines and the song contains both pre-chorus and chorus, the latter far closer to a pop song than a fado. The words are unavoidable, however: 'Sou do fado / Sou do fado / Sou fadista' [I am of/from fado … I'm a *fadista*]. Moura's first three albums all contain a mixture of pop-oriented or *fado canção* material (much of it by Fernando) and more traditional work. *Aconteceu* (2004), her second album and a double CD, highlights the split by placing songs that derive from pop songwriters such as Tozé Brito and writers of *fado canção* such as Fernando and Alberto Janes (author of Amália's 'Foi Deus') on the first disc and a

---

[42]   We might compare this to the way a picture of the eleven-year-old Mariza singing fado in the Adega Machado club is used in Simon Broughton's fado documentary and in an accompanying magazine article to authenticate Mariza's connection to the genre. See *Mariza and the Story of Fado*, dir. Simon Broughton (UK/Portugal, 2006) and Simon Broughton, 'On the Tiles with Mariza', *Songlines* 47 (November 2007): 32.

series of *fado castiço* melodies on the second. Even though contemporary lyricists are used on the second disc, the various styles (*corrido, meia-noite, Franklin, margaridas* and others) mean that the lyrics must adhere to rigid structures. By the time of her third album *Para Além da Saudade* (2007), constructed via a similar mixture of traditional and contemporary elements, Moura had perfected a style of singing as clear and direct as Katia Guerreiro while also developing the look and outlook of a successful pop artist. As related in Chapter 5, this combination would earn her the notice of major international rock and pop stars.

It will be clear from the above that the most successful *novo fado* artists have been female, a fact that cannot help but contribute to the association of fado with Amália Rodrigues. This association, which is also based on the repertoire the new singers share with Rodrigues and on the ability their position in the international music scene gives them to work outside the traditional structures of the genre, leads to an even greater generalization that is always in danger of asserting itself: that, just as female *guitarristas* are not to be expected, so the quintessential fado singer must be female.[43] In fact, this split allows for the continuing feminization of the *guitarra* itself, highlighted by António Chainho's album *A Guitarra e Outras Mulheres* [The Guitar and Other Women] (1998), on which the *guitarrista* is accompanied by a number of female guest singers including Teresa Salgueiro, Elba Ramalho, Marta Dias, Ana Sofia Varela and Filipa Pais. The process of feminization is extended, as we saw in Chapter 2, to the city of Lisbon itself. Connecting this practice to female fado singers, Manuela Cook writes:

> The woman who has fado in her life also has the makings of a good citizen and mother. Indeed, she is the staple of the nation and an inspiration to all. Her sons are the true heroes who honour Portugal. Furthermore, personified as a woman, Lisbon itself is perceived by some as the womb and cradle of both Portugal's Christian vocation and glorious history, as well as being the womb and cradle of fado as we know it today.[44]

Woven into the mythology of fado is the complex relationship between mother and prostitute, most notable in the figure of Maria Severa, both fallen woman and mother of fado. In the moralistic films of the Salazar era, such as *História D'uma Cantadeira*, fado is presented as a career choice with the potential to lead to sin; such associations were also part and parcel of the reasons for the forced professionalization of the genre after the establishment of the Estado Novo. Whatever the image of the woman, fado has been given a strong feminine image which is no doubt due to the lingering influence of Maria Severa and the

---

[43]   Marta Pereira da Costa is a notable example of a female *guitarrista* whose work has been recorded. She can be heard on Mário Pacheco's *Clube de Fado* album and seen on the accompanying DVD.

[44]   Manuela Cook, 'The Woman in Portuguese Fado-singing', *International Journal of Iberian Studies*, 16/1 (2003): 32.

more recent domination of the scene by Amália Rodrigues. As Cook notes, 'If nineteenth-century Severa had lived a hundred years later, she would probably have entered the history of fado with a different aura. In the twentieth century, Amália became a national icon. She was judged by canons forged in the days of the Estado Novo, which to some extent were still influential in 1999, at [the] end of the century and her life.'[45]

The history of fado bears witness to an enormous number of male *fadistas* but there have been relatively few male artists as visible or successful as the women mentioned above in the period under discussion. A notable exception is Camané, who has built a solid reputation in Portugal since his emergence in the 1980s. Camané's approach, based on that of Carlos do Carmo (who also continued to be very popular within Portugal during this time), stresses links with the 1960s and 1970s via his renditions of work by David Mourão-Ferreira and Ary dos Santos and via his association with José Mário Branco.[46] These figures represent a continuing link with the revolutionary period and allow for a dialogue between fado and more explicitly committed material. Other notable male figures are Jorge Fernando and António Zambujo, who has attempted his own style of crossover by bringing fado together with Alentejan polyphonic singing, suggesting an updating of José Afonso's project; although it could be argued that, in the absence of a political context equivalent to that in which Afonso operated, the 'collectivity' made resonant in Zambujo's work is a marker of what was once revolt turned into style.

The presence of much of this 'new fado' (Teresa Salgueiro's voice in *Lisbon Story*, Dulce Pontes's in *Primal Fear*, Mísia's in *Passionada*, Mariza's at Euro 2004) brought a level of international awareness of fado and the fado voice that had not been matched since the heyday of Amália Rodrigues – and perhaps not even then, given the frequent perception of Amália as an 'international' star rather than as a singer of fados. *Novo fado* has also found itself placed alongside other less traditional musical endeavours due to its inclusion in the series of Atlantic Waves concerts inaugurated in 2001. These annual events, subtitled 'Exploratory Music from Portugal', take place in London and are accompanied by extensive media coverage and by CDs compiling the featured artists. The first series of concerts featured Jorge Lima Barreto and Vítor Rua's group Telectu; jazz duo Maria João and Mário Laginha; improvisers Carlos Zíngaro, Emídio Buchinho, Nuno Rebelo and Marco Franco; former Madredeus member Rodrigo Leão; Lisbon DJs; and performances of classical music by Portuguese composers. Fado was represented by Mísia (performing on the second anniversary of the death of Amália Rodrigues) and Lula Pena. Subsequent years were no less eclectic; among the fado acts who

---

[45]   Ibid.: 32.

[46]   Branco, a contemporary of and collaborator with José Afonso, was exiled during the Estado Novo period before returning to be a major contributor to the post-revolutionary Portuguese popular music. His albums *Mudam-se os Tempos, Mudam-Se as Vontades* (Valentim de Carvalho/EMI 724383565528, 1998 [1971]) and *Margem de Certa Maneira* (Valentim de Carvalho 724383565627, 1996 [1972]) are considered classics of the period.

performed were Mariza, Katia Guerreiro, Ana Sofia Varela, António Zambujo, Carla Pires, Cristina Branco, Joana Amendoeira, Helder Moutinho and Carlos do Carmo. Carmo, appearing in 2006, was the first *fadista* from the older generation to perform, although he was billed as the 'special guest' of Mariza, thus keeping the emphasis on the figures of new fado. In 2007, an evening dedicated to 'Grand Divas of Fado' rebalanced the emphasis somewhat with Beatriz de Conceição and Maria da Fé appearing alongside younger artists such as Aldina Duarte, Mafalda Arnauth, Joana Amendoeira and Raquel Tavares. It might be argued that the 'glamorous' elements of *novo fado* had created a space for more traditional performers to be welcomed. Interestingly, the same year saw an evening dedicated to 'Portuguese Guitar Masters' (António Chainho, Custódio Castelo and Ricardo Parreira), thus reinforcing the split between female singers and male guitarists.

There are a number of factors which seem to point to the emergence in this period of what has come to be termed *novo fado*. Among these we must list the following:

1. The depolarization of ideological positions surrounding the music following a time period that had allowed for a mellowing of cultural opinion and that reflected the gradual political softening, during the two decades following the Revolution, of the pro-Salazar right and pro-Warsaw Pact left into an increasingly stabilized political democracy.

2. The emergence of a potential conflict, as membership of the EEC finally became a reality for Portugal (as it did for Spain) in 1986, between national and European identity, a conflict whose possibility had been denied by the isolationist policies of the Estado Novo. As Kimberly DaCosta Holton notes,[47] the process of becoming more European was simultaneously a process of roping off what was most Portuguese.

3. The emergence in the 1980s of the increasingly popular genre of world music, to which fado, as the music most associated with Portugal, was soon added, providing fado once again with an international audience. While fado had enjoyed international exposure during the previous half-century due to the phenomenal success of Amália Rodrigues, the newly coined 'world music' category gave a fresh image to any musics associated with it, as Timothy D. Taylor points out: 'In one gesture the old but not quite gone "international" label ... [was] supplanted by a trendier, less musty, less your-grandparents'-music category.'[48] Interestingly, there has been an important role played by record labels from outside of Portugal

[47]   Kimberly DaCosta Holton, 'Bearing Material Witness to Musical Sound: Fado's L94 Museum Debut', *Luso-Brazilian Review*, 39/2 (2002): 107–23.

[48]   Timothy D. Taylor, *Global Pop: World Music, World Markets* (London & New York: Routledge, 1997), p. 3.

in the distribution and popularization of contemporary fado, especially in France and the Netherlands where labels such as L'Empreinte Digitale and World Connection have been the driving forces behind CDs by the likes of Cristina Branco and Mariza.

4. Developments in recording, playback and performance technology which have been used in very specific ways in world music. In Chapter 3 I discussed the change from the transcriptive role of technology (recording as the first part of witnessing, the 'seeing') to a more creative role in producing atmosphere. I also suggested that what was found visually and sonically notable in Lisbon in the past has become what is made notable by visual and sonic recording equipment. But in the process of being made notable in as clear a way as possible, much of the original detail (the background noise, as it were) disappears. To use the analogy of the witness, we might say that the witness's second task – 'saying' what they saw – is one in which the original complexity of the situation must be stripped down to the essential message (which is why, in the court room, the witness will be thrown 'yes or no' questions or asked to focus only on 'relevant' details). I will return to this issue in Chapter 5.

Bearing all these points in mind it is worth briefly surveying some responses to the existence (or not, as some would have it) of *novo fado* before going on to discuss the contemporary scene.

Writing under the title 'O Novo Fado Não Existe', Pedro Baptista-Bastos makes the point that fado has never gone away and that its current practitioners are part of a tradition of adaptation that places them in a continuum rather than a vanguard. Although he does not use the words 'renovado' or 'renovar', Baptista-Bastos's contention seems to lie in an emphasis on renewal rather than on newness *per se*. Some of his observations, which formed the introductory notes to a CD of fados by young singers entitled *Novas Vozes, Novos Fados* (2006), are worth bearing in mind when discussing the state of the music as it found itself at the turn of the century. Baptista-Bastos goes on to say:

> The passing of time – the thirty years from 25 April, the European Union, the Internet, the coming of the twenty-first century – has forced us to stop identifying fado as a spent, reactionary and senile song style, and made us connect it, today, with the voices presented on this CD, which provide us with a picture of a different Portugal.[49]

Numerous signs of continuation could be posited, such as the recurrent versions of songs connected to Amália, tribute albums featuring young singers performing material from predecessors like Amália (*Amália Revisited*, 2004) and Carlos

---

[49] Baptista-Bastos, 'Novo Fado', p. 6.

do Carmo (*Novo Homem na Cidade*, 2004), the involvement of 'old school' arrangers such as Jorge Fernando (who worked with Amália) with the new generation and the emergence of new *fadistas* from the Grande Noite de Fado, an annual song contest that has been running for many years. Yet, while it is true that fado has never disappeared from the Portuguese music scene since it first became consolidated as a popular music form, it nevertheless remains the case that the song form enjoyed a distinct boost at the turn of the millennium due to a number of young performers who were able to adapt the form to contemporary tastes and market it to a new audience both nationally and internationally. These producers of what I will continue to call, for want of a better term, *novo fado* were distinguished by the sheer fact of having come into musical maturity at a time when the polarization that followed the Revolution had eased into a less strictly policed arena of democratic choice.[50] Interest in national identity was far from slacking but now it was tempered with a desire to work that identity into the context of a modern Europe. Fado was arguably the most recognizably Portuguese of musics in the international community.

As for the response of the music audience to *novo fado*, it may well be worth bearing in mind the possibility that a certain staleness had befallen the once vital project of *Música Popular Portuguesa*. As a *Billboard* report on the state of the Portuguese music industry noted in 1994, the reliance on Anglo-American models of popular music tended to mean that sales for domestic bands were not terribly high, with only a couple of bands cited who had achieved success through stamping a Portuguese identity on the rock music they produced.[51] This can be linked to the point made earlier about the need, on entering the EEC (and later the EU), to adopt a Europeanness that simultaneously allowed for a sense of Portugueseness – a desire, in this case, to produce popular music that would not be lost among all the competing popular musics from Europe and beyond. A return to a music that was identifiably Portuguese could serve as a resistance to the Anglo-American popular music models that had become hegemonic over the previous few decades, a point that could subsume any worries that such a return might also be a return to the 'bad old days' of Salazarian corporatism. Many of the new generation of singers had grown up listening to Anglo-American pop music and were deeply influenced by it, yet could still appreciate the thrill of rediscovering a native treasure that made up for the absence the other music inevitably brought into play. With this in mind, it may be worth considering what Geoffrey O'Brien, writing on the return of lounge music in the 1990s, has to say about identification with the Other:

---

[50]   There is much to be said here, no doubt, about market choice too but I do not have space to discuss the political economy of fado in this chapter. See Chapter 5's discussion of the world music network for more on this.

[51]   Sweeney, 'Billboard Report'.

Permissiveness is of the essence here. The listener is encouraged to surrender to music that not so long ago he might have defined as the Other, the enemy, the counter-counterculture. At the same time, however, he is left free to distort or reimagine it any way he pleases. History in this context amounts to little more than a crowded closet from which, with a bit of scrounging, useable bits of fabric or costume jewelry can be salvaged for an extended game of dress-up.[52]

O'Brien's point here seems to be to reference the kind of knowing, ironic use of history that we have grown accustomed to reading and hearing about in descriptions of postmodernism. What listeners could appropriate from music that had hitherto seemed opposed to their sense of self-distinction (to use Pierre Bourdieu's terminology) – a music that was old-fashioned, corny, 'cheesy', terminally un-hip – was that which, through conscious reference and redeployment, could come to determine a new paradigm of distinction, coolness or suavity. In addition to lounge music, where the original object is redeployed in an unaltered form that nevertheless comes to mean something entirely different in its new surroundings, there is the ubiquitous sampling of the past in numerous music genres. For fado, the appearance in 2004 of the CDs *Chillfado V.01* and *Amália Revisited*, both containing techno-influenced reworkings of classic fado tracks and with numerous samples from the original source material, showcased certain ways in which it might be possible to (re)visit an older, more parochial Portuguese musical identity while still maintaining a subscription to a youth-oriented Portugal of the twenty-first century. At the same time, the 'revisiting' of the Amália tribute was not just a reminder of the artist herself, but also a reminder of her project to work outside the bounds of traditional fado; in this sense, perhaps, it was more faithful than might at first be thought.[53] Where the original objects – the fado recordings of Amália Rodrigues, Carlos Paredes, Fernando Farinha and others – were also sought out in their 'unaltered' state, it is entirely possible that this was done in a highly selective, revisionist, knowing or ironic way.[54] However, as Manuel Halpern's survey of the *novos fadistas* of the new millennium maintains, the sense of seriousness and responsibility which a new generation of fado performers has shown in engaging with the genre's history suggests a project that entails far more than 'an extended

---

[52] Geoffrey O'Brien, *Sonata for Jukebox: Pop Music, Memory, and the Imagined Life* (New York: Counterpoint, 2004), p. 10.

[53] This is confirmed by the comments of one of the participants, Miguel Cardona of Lisbon City Rockers: 'Not being an expert on Fado and much less someone with a deep knowledge [of] the work of Amália, I decided that producing this song in the closest possible way to my own language would be the most honest tribute that I, as an artist, could make.' Liner notes to *Amália Revisited* (CD, Different World DW50009CD, 2004). This is not unrelated to the notion of 'critical fidelity' which I discuss in Elliott, 'Loss, Memory and Nostalgia', pp. 198–207.

[54] Quite how 'original' these recordings can remain in their journey through transference to new media, remastering and restoring is a highly debatable issue.

game of dress-up'.[55] There seems to be enough new about these artists to justify the focus on them as a distinct generation. At the same time, the lines of continuity are vitally important. As has already been shown, these lines of continuity can be determined both in the involvement of a whole 'popular music world' in the production of *novo fado* and in the importance of tribute and homage.

Career Choices

In this section, I wish to consider the role of a few particular individuals who began their careers outside the world of fado but have had an important role in shaping the current configuration of the genre. The advantage of this type of reflection, hopefully, is that it challenges the perception of fado as a closed-off world. As I have had recourse to suggest at numerous points in this book, it is often necessary to fence off and focus on certain elements of a genre in order to give an account of what makes that genre worthy of comment in the first place. Nevertheless, I also wish to emphasize that fado, like any other popular music genre, has a place in the larger musical field and the borders of that place are far from impermeable, fixed or non-negotiable. A clear way to see this is by thinking of fado as a career choice. A common theme in most descriptions of the *novos fadistas* is the fact of turning to fado singing after having considered, and even practised, other musical styles (generally pop, rhythm and blues, rock or jazz, but also occasionally classical).[56] But it is also interesting to look at the movement between styles observable by more veteran practitioners in the field of Portuguese popular music. Three such figures are Paulo de Carvalho, Pedro Ayres Magalhães and Carlos Maria Trindade.

Paulo de Carvalho is an intriguing figure whose career has bridged the worlds of pop, rock, jazz and fado. He began his career with Os Sheiks, a 1960s beat group modelled on the British formula. After becoming a solo artist, Carvalho recorded a number of mainstream pop songs and ballads. Throughout the 1970s he appeared regularly in the national RTP Song Contest, winning it in 1974 and going on to represent Portugal in the Eurovision Song Contest. His winning song, 'E Depois do Adeus' was used (along with José Afonso's 'Grândola Vila Morena') as a signal during the Carnation Revolution. Carvalho was responsible for a number of songs that other fado performers have recorded, notably Carlos do Carmo on *Um Homem na Cidade* (Mariza has recorded a few of his songs, for example the pop-like 'Meu Fado Meu'), and he gradually started to show his interest in

---

[55]   Halpern, *O Futuro da Saudade.*

[56]   Information about similar choices made by guitarists is scarcer, especially in English, as it is far more common for singers to be interviewed than their accompanists. A rare exception can be found in an interview in *Songlines* magazine with Luís Guerreiro, a *guitarrista* who has accompanied Mariza. See Simon Broughton, 'Tools of the Trade: Portuguese Guitar', *Songlines*, 47 (November 2007): 48–51.

fado in his own work. The double disc *Antologia 71/85* gives some indication of the change in Carvalho's style over this fourteen-year period, with the first disc mainly comprising songs performed in various pop styles and the material on the second much closer to fado.[57] In 1986, he released an album entitled *Um Homem Português*, on which he was accompanied by *guitarra*.

Subsequent years find a continued mixture of styles. *Terras da Lua Cheia* (1987) sounds, in many places, like a pop record drenched in *guitarra*. Listening to it, however, one is reminded that the same could be said for much work by Carlos do Carmo, who duets with Carvalho on 'Coração Vagabundo'. A *fado corrido* entitled 'Sem Pés nem Cabeça' sounds as traditional as one would expect such a fado to be, albeit supercharged (a *supercorrido* perhaps). The final track is pure pop, with elements of *pimba* even. This aesthetic is continued on *Gostar de Ti* (1990), where the keyboards are as prevalent as the *guitarra*. Indeed, the fetishization of the electronic sound stretches to the liner notes, where the various different keyboards and drum machines used are detailed in a manner not uncommon to this era. The album contains a medley of three songs ('Homem das Castanhas', 'Os Putos' and 'Lisboa Menina e Moça') that were co-written with José Carlos Ary dos Santos and were memorably recorded by Carlos do Carmo in the 1970s. Again, one is reminded that Carmo is a figure who has often moved from fado towards pop and that Carvalho is very much Carmo's complement, having made the opposite journey. The 2004 album *Cores do Fado* contains jazz piano on some tracks ('O Cacilheiro', 'A Voz') and Carvalho's voice at times suggests flamenco styles rather than fado. The album also contains a version of a song by Argentinian *nueva canción* singer Atahualpa Yupanqui. Carvalho reworks 'Uma Canção' from *Gostar de Ti* but makes it more like a *fado canção* than before. This fits into another 'tradition', of making non-fados into fados by the appliance of voice and instrumentation, as Mísia does with Rui Veloso's 'Porto Sentido' and as Zé Perdigão does at greater length on *Fados de Rock* (2008), an album containing versions of songs originally written and performed by rock groups such as Heróis do Mar, the Delfins and Rádio Macau and converted into fados.[58]

Carvalho's songwriting could be said to follow its own, essentially pop, aesthetic, with the subsequent application of music lending it whatever qualities of fado it attains. This would be in contrast to the idea that the fado style drives the composition of the song from the start. This is one major difference between *fado castiço* and *fado canção*, but it is one explored decades earlier by Amália so that it could now be seen to be part of the tradition. Tradition in fado could arguably be defined as a moving back and forwards between *castiço* and *canção* styles. This idea is close to Richard Peterson's analysis of US country music, which he sees as moving in a dialectic of 'hard core' and 'soft shell' styles; certainly, parallels could

---

[57]   Paulo de Carvalho, *Antologia 71/85* (Universal Portugal 172339-4, 2007).

[58]   Paulo de Carvalho, *Terras da Lua Cheia* (CBS Portugal 4604272, 1987); *Gostar de Ti* (CBS Portugal 4674382, 1990); *Cores do Fado* (Som Livre SL06602, 2004).

usefully be made between these genres.[59] Like some of the 'crossover' figures considered by Peterson, Paulo de Carvalho is a bridging figure between the worlds of pop and fado as well as between the Amália era and the *novo fado* era. Like his contemporary Fernando Tordo (another member of Os Sheiks), he has been an important figure in the careers of Carlos do Carmo and, more recently, Mariza. Mariza included two songs by Carvalho ('Meu Fado Meu' and 'Fado Português de Nós') on *Transparente* and another ('Minh'Alma') on *Terra*; each album also contained a song by Tordo. Mariza, in turn, sang a duet with Carvalho on his 2008 album *Do Amor*; the song, 'O Mundo Inteiro', was a pop ballad, casting Mariza in a role closer to that of a soul singer. In acting as bridges such figures also help bolster the case for a dialectic approach to fado and pop, showcasing the fact that these competing aesthetics have been reacting to each other for a long time.

A similar constellation of stylistic migration can be found in two of the key members of Madredeus. The guitarist Pedro Ayres Magalhães began his career as a bassist in the punk group Faísca, followed by Corpo Diplomático, who released one album (*Música Moderna*) in 1979. With other members of Corpo Diplomático he formed Heróis do Mar, whose pop-rock sound was very different from the post-punk of Corpo Diplomático. In 1982, he founded the record label Fundação Atlântica along with writer Miguel Esteves Cardoso and Ricardo Camacho. The label released records by Portuguese artists Anamar, the Delfins, Sétima Legião, Xutos & Pontapés and Magalhães himself, as well as by British acts Durutti Column, Virginia Astley, Young Marble Giants and The Raincoats.[60] In 1986 Magalhães co-founded Madredeus with the keyboard player Rodrigo Leão and has remained the centre of that group since. He has also been involved in the group Resistência, an occasional 'supergroup' made up of members of Xutos & Pontapés, Santos & Pecadores and the Delfins, who perform cover versions of tracks by acts from the 1980s Portuguese rock boom. Songs written by Magalhães have been performed by *fadistas* such as Mísia, Carla Pires and Ana Moura. His colleague, the keyboard player Carlos Maria Trindade, has had a long career as both musician and producer. He was a founding member of Corpo Diplomático and subsequently Heróis do Mar. Trindade released a solo single in 1982 while continuing to be a member of the band and turning to production. During the 1980s he produced albums by Rádio Macau, Xutos e Pontapés and the Delfins. In

---

[59]   Richard A. Peterson, *Creating Country Music: Fabricating Authenticity* (Chicago & London: University of Chicago Press, 1997). I will return to Peterson's categorization in the next chapter.

[60]   Ana da Silva of The Raincoats is Portuguese, though she formed the group in Britain and continued her career there. The album released by Vini Reilly's The Durutti Column on Fundação Atlântica was recorded in Portugal and entitled *Amigos em Portugal* (1983). While the music of these acts was not in any way obviously 'Portuguese', it is interesting to note that twenty years later both Silva and Reilly would perform in the Atlantic Waves concerts held in London to celebrate Lusophone music (Silva with The Raincoats in 2003 and solo in 2005; Reilly with The Durutti Column in 2008).

the mid-1990s he produced Paulo Bragança and became a member of Madredeus. He was involved in various world music projects in the 1990s, including the *Red, Hot & Lisbon* project on which he collaborated again with Bragança. In 2003, Trindade produced Mariza's second album *Fado Curvo* and contributed two songs for it. Looking at the career trajectories of Trindade and Magalhães, there are a number of striking features. It is difficult to believe, for example, that the same musicians at the centre of Corpo Diplomático are at the core of Heróis do Mar, and even more so that the same musicians are involved in Madredeus.

Considering the careers of particular artists allows us to see how career choice can often inevitably lead to a blurring of generic boundaries. In societies where access to many styles of music is so easily available, this should not be surprising. It is additionally not at all uncommon for performers to furiously deny categorization, a practice which is arguably inherited, via the rock tradition, from a sense of the music as art. What it does mean, however, is that in talking about a musical genre such as fado, one is always already involved in creating boundaries. In 1988, Peter Manuel was able to write the following in his introduction to *Popular Musics of the Non-Western World*:

> This volume concerns itself only with popular musics that are stylistically distinct from mainstream Western styles (rock, disco, slow ballad, etc.) ... Here, we are not concerned, for example, with the music of the Greek pop singer Nana Mouskouri, since her music conforms to a standard Western sentimental popular style; however, this text does treat Greek *rebetika* and *bouzouki* music, which, although incorporating elements of Western music, are stylistically quite distinct.[61]

Manuel's text also treats fado, providing a useful English-language account of the music as it appeared before the 'boom' of *novo fado*, albeit one tempered by the fear that commercial recordings of *fado canção* had led to a situation in which the *fado castiço* of the *casas de fado* was in danger of becoming extinct. I will return to this issue in Chapter 5. For now, I would merely suggest that the examination of a career such as Paulo de Carvalho's (whose music often 'conforms to a standard Western sentimental popular style') shows that it is possible to be both 'in' and 'out' of fado. My point is not to criticize Manuel, who to a certain extent is both proved 'correct' by figures such as Carvalho, and who additionally had to draw strict boundaries on his ambitious project, but to suggest that there are only so many degrees of separation from one style to another and that they are frequently traversed. To maintain the separation not only requires constant policing but also threatens the possibility, as in Italo Calvino's mnemonic city Zora, of languishment and destruction.

Another issue that the consideration of career paths and genre-crossing suggests is the extent to which a community of Portuguese popular musicians has

---

[61] Manuel, *Popular Musics*, p. vi.

formed itself over recent decades. One phenomenon of this is the recording of tribute albums. In addition to numerous tribute albums to icons such as Amália, José Afonso and Carlos Paredes, there have been others which show the rock and pop community reflecting on itself. These include tributes to António Variações (*As Canções de António*, 1993, featuring Madredeus, the Delfins and Mão Morta among others); Xutos & Pontapés (*XX Anos XX Bandas*, 1999, featuring GNR, Mão Morta, Rui Veloso and seventeen other artists); Rui Veloso (*20 Anos Depois*, 2000, with Ala dos Namorados, Xutos & Pontapés, Mão Morta, and others); GNR (*Revisitados*, 2006); and Mão Morta (*E Se Depois*, 2007).

An Eternal Farewell: The Shadow of Amália

I have already mentioned a number of ways that Amália shaped the course of fado at the turn of the millennium. In Manuel Halpern's words, 'Amália is the paradigm, the hinge and the epicentre of fado. She reinvented it and reinvented herself through successive revolutions. To a certain extent, *novo fado* began with Amália over forty years ago, with the release of *Asas Fechadas*.'[62] No doubt due to the fact that Amália's passing coincided with the emergence of a new generation of *fadistas*, there was a strong desire on the part of many commentators to speak of the 'new Amália'. As has been noted, this desire was aided by the singers themselves, many of whom felt compelled to show their attachment to the late 'Queen of Fado'. In this sense, they proved themselves to be faithful subjects to what we might think of as the 'Amália event'. Sometimes, this would take the form of a critical fidelity, in which the best way to be faithful was to change the template (António Variações being a good example). Often, however, a more conventional faith was kept, as in the case of Katia Guerreiro. At the outset of her career, Guerreiro was frequently compared to Amália both physically and vocally, as in the following press review of a concert held to mark the anniversary of Amália's death at which Guerreiro sang:

> Katia Guerreiro is physically a double of Amália …The face, the curl of the eyebrows, the mouth, the expression, the closed eyes, the tilt of the head. It's Amália in her youth … Her voice took on the same register as Amália at her deepest [*mais grave*]. Katia sang 'Barco Negro' and 'Amor de Mel, Amor de Fel'. A ghost appeared in the Coliseu.[63]

Guerreiro is also compared to Amália in terms of gesture and voice in Rui Vieira Nery's notes to *Fado Maior*. But, as Vieira Nery says, the point is not that she is a

---

[62]   Halpern, *O Futuro da Saudade*, p. 47.

[63]   Fernando Magalhães, 'Uma Voz na Voz dos Outros', *Público*, Cultura (8 October 2000): 34.

mere replica (a 'double' or a 'ghost' as the press review had it) but that she brings something of herself to the role and adds to the Amálian legacy.

A model of the kind of post-Amália memory work that was to become the norm can be found in Gonçalo Salgueiro's album ...*No Tempo das Cerejas* (2002). Salgueiro had previously had a part in Filipe La Féria's musical *Amália* and was also involved in the homage to Amália when her body was moved to the Pantheon. Salgueiro's album takes its title from a poem written by Maria de Lourdes DeCarvalho from the point of view of the absent Amália. The poem was set to music by José Fontes Rocha, one of Amália's former *guitarristas*, and sung by Salgueiro. One of the lines of the fado speaks of 'an eternal farewell', an appropriate description of the way in which Amália would be treated over the ensuing decade. The rest of the album, which also includes DeCarvalho's 'Tenho em Mim a Voz do Povo' (discussed in Chapter 3), comprises fados about Amália or which are associated with or written by her. There is an emphasis on the late work, which João Braga highlights as being unusual in his liner notes but which would prove to be quite common for a number of the new *fadistas* for whom Amália's self-penned material (whether from her two late studio albums or from her book *Versos*) was a touchstone. Rui Vieira Nery, who also provides a liner note, emphasizes the androgynous nature of Salgueiro's performance style and gestures, and it is certainly the case that the *fadista* possesses an almost genderless voice at times. This quality would be even more prevalent on his subsequent album *Segue a Minha Voz* [Follow My Voice] (2006), on which the exquisite 'Voz do Escuro' [Voice from the Dark] sets the scene, Salgueiro's voice floating in its highest register above the clear crystal *guitarra* of Custódio Castelo. At one point, the refrain of the song – a *fado canção* by Jorge Fernando, who also produces – gives way to the *guitarra*, the latter taking on the vocal melody as if the voice has disappeared into the ether. The ethereal quality is continued on the second track, a more *castiço* treatment of a David Mourão-Ferreira lyric, utilizing a vibrato that evokes a female *fadista* of the past.[64]

In connection with this notion of an androgynous voice, it is worth considering the work of Nuno Guerreiro, vocalist with the group Ala dos Namorados. The group was formed by Manuel Paulo, João Gil and João Monge, who came from a range of backgrounds (Gil from Trovante, Paulo from Rui Veloso's band, Monge as a songwriter for Trovante). With the addition of Guerreiro, they attained one of their unique features, a vocalist with an astonishingly high and clear vocal register. The group's albums all contained one or two songs that gestured towards fado, such as 'Fado da Rádio', 'Mistérios do Fado' (a song also covered by Paulo Bragança and Mísia), 'Fado Siciliano' and 'Fado de Amor e Pecado' (an unusual fado-flamenco hybrid). Most relevant for a consideration of Amália's legacy, however, was their version of 'Fado de Cada Um' on the album *Por Minha Dama* (1995), a

---

[64] Intriguingly, Goncalo Salgueiro later took the part of Jesus in Filipe la Féria's *Jesus Cristo Superstar*, an adaptation of the Lloyd Webber/Rice musical, thus increasing his otherworldliness.

song performed by Amália in 1947 for the film *Fado, História D'uma Cantadeira*. Nuno Guerreiro's uncannily high voice seems to take on a register which, while not that of Amália herself, suggests a possession by the feminine. The connection is strengthened on António Zambujo's album *Outro Sentido* (2007) when, among a collection of songs rich with associations to Amália, Zambujo includes a version of 'Ao Sul' by Ala dos Namorados, one of Nuno Guerreiro's vocal masterpieces (and now one of Zambujo's too).

In Chapter 1, I presented an interpretation of Amália's 'Lágrima' based on a move from what I called the *studium* of the song text to the *punctum* of the anguished performance. In a more recent version of 'Lágrima' by Jorge Fernando and Argentina Santos there is an even clearer example of such a move.[65] Following a verse sung movingly but not dramatically by Fernando, a *studium* is set up of melancholic meditation on hurt and loss (fado's bedrock, we might say). The entry of Argentina Santos's vocal into this *studium* shatters (cuts) the 'stillness' of the preceding moments. Through her vocalizing, from the anguished cry of 'se considero' to the almost whispered final 'uma lágrima', Santos creates these *puncta* via stark contrasts with the surrounding song text. Fernando's verse and the oboe/cello part create a 'safe' space of sadness. Santos's voice, in its urgency and extremity, destroys this place and reminds us of the 'real' pain at the heart of the lyric. This echoes the contrast implicit in the verse structure where a fragmented line is offset against a developed line, the former containing the fetishized object (the immediate thought, the attempt, however doomed, at freedom from language), the latter the interpreted (Symbolic) meaning of the thought.

The fact that Fernando and Santos take ownership of 'Lágrima' in the way they do is important in terms of thinking about the fado 'family tree', a term which can be understood to relate both to the varieties of fado derived from the basic core of *fado corrido*, *fado mouraria* and *fado menor*, and to the symbolic lineage of fado performers through the years. In this case there is the association of Argentina Santos with a school of singers contemporaneous with Amália Rodrigues – though it should be noted that Santos, like many of her contemporaries, did not tend to be as adventurous as Rodrigues with the material she chose to sing, sticking to a far more 'traditional' repertoire.[66] Jorge Fernando was a guitarist for Amália Rodrigues during the final part of her career before going on to release albums made up of his own material alongside work by other fadistas and to produce and play on Mariza's first album, also contributing three songs to it ('Chuva' 'Terra d'Água' and 'Oxalá'). Fernando, who also had a career as a pop singer-songwriter, played a major role in Ana Moura's career as arranger, producer and

---

[65] Jorge Fernando & Argentina Santos, 'Lágrima', *Velho Fado* (CD, Times Square/World Connection TSQD 9017, 2001).

[66] At the same time, it could be argued that Rodrigues was in large part able to pursue the exploratory paths she did due to the relative luxury afforded her by her recording and film career and by her international success. There is an obvious disparity between an artist-centred and a 'production of culture' account here.

songwriter. Like Paulo de Carvalho, Fernando acts as a bridge both between the old generation and the new and between pop and fado.

Prior to the Fernando/Santos recording of 'Lágrima', the song had appeared on other fado albums of the 1990s. Dulce Pontes recorded a version on *Lágrimas* (1993), an album that highlighted the sense of fusion that would come to determine much of *novo fado*. Emphasizing the notion of a 'family tree', Pontes prominently placed a genealogy on the album cover that stated: 'Father – Zeca [José] Afonso; Mother – Amália Rodrigues; Grandparent – Portuguese folklore; Cousins – Bulgarian folklore, Arabic music'.[67] The instrumentation on the album consisted of the classic fado accompaniment (*viola, guitarra*) but, with the addition of vocoder, Fairlight synthesizer, electric guitar, piano and orchestra, this was a clear departure from fado norms. The song selection was evidence that, with the passing of time, the strands of folk and fado that had seemed so antithetical to each other in the post-revolutionary era could now be brought together in a useful synthesis: half the songs on the album were ones associated with Amália Rodrigues, the other half with José Afonso. The mixture proved successful and the album has remained a constant seller nationally and internationally since its release in late 1993, judging by its perennial availability in European record shops such as Fnac, Valentim de Carvalho and HMV. The appeal of Pontes's voice seems to lie in its clarity and consistency and she has adopted a register that sits easily within a range of western popular musical styles, as is noticeable on her 2003 collaboration with Ennio Morricone, *Focus*, where she provides vocals in Portuguese, English, Spanish and Italian to the familiar tunes of various Morricone soundtracks. As a consequence, her music is arguably less subcultural than that of, say, Argentina Santos, a difference that can be read into Pontes's rendition of 'Lágrima' on the 1993 album. This track, along with a version of Amália's 'Estranha Forma de Vida', were recorded live in the studio, presumably to catch the feel of an 'authentic' fado performance. Yet, without the 'grain' and anguish that Amália and Santos bring to their renditions, the song emerges as 'merely' beautiful, somehow missing the cathartic elements of the older *fadistas'* versions. In Lacanian terms, there is less a fencing-off of the Thing than an unwillingness to go anywhere close to it; in Barthesian terms, there is an excess of *pheno-song* and a lack of *geno-song*, a *studium* with no *punctum*. The traumatic potential of 'Lágrima' is here elided in a move that maintains the performance firmly within the Symbolic Order, a kind of sanitized mourning that is also to be found ten years later in the song 'Amália por Amor' on *Focus*.

Mísia, for her part, chose to revisit the song on her 2001 album *Ritual*, having already recorded a version for her second album in 1993. Where the earlier version, like Pontes's from the same year, was fairly understated, the second presentation of the song utilized a style not dissimilar to that of Argentina Santos, stressing extremities of vocalization and putting particular emphasis on the key lyrical points discussed earlier. Mário Jorge Torres, in his liner notes to the CD,

---

[67]   CD liner to Dulce Pontes, *Lágrimas* (Movieplay Portuguesa PE 51.003, 1993).

suggested this 'new intensity and intentionality' was due to the song's inclusion in what was clearly a project inspired by the recent death of Amália.[68] The musical arrangements and *guitarra* accompaniment are provided by Carlos Gonçalves, who had been Amália's composer and accompanist during the last stage of her career and had composed the music to 'Lágrima'. Like Jorge Fernando, Gonçalves here becomes a bridge between the old and new worlds of fado, providing new compositions for Mísia, such as that for 'Xaile de Silêncio', a poem sent to Mísia on the occasion of Amália's death. In addition to these tracks, Amália is referenced by the inclusion of two songs that seek to extend the late singer's legacy through the addition of new elements. 'Mistério Lunar' is a modern poem put to music written by the famous *guitarrista* Armandinho that Amália had sung with different words as 'Fado Mayer' in the 1950s. 'Vivendo sem Mim' is a poem written by Rodrigues, published in *Versos* but not recorded by her; here, it is put to music by Mário Pacheco and performed by Mísia and the pianist Christian Boissel in a move designed to evoke the way Amália rehearsed with Alain Oulman at the piano. By thus adding words to an 'Amália' tune and music to Amália's words, Mísia suggests the ways in which this dialogic 'ritual' might proceed. The ritual extended beyond the song texts to the recording process too, with the use of valve microphones and single takes to emulate recording practices of the 1940s and 1950s.

A similar project to Mísia's *Ritual* can be found on Mariza's *Fado em Mim*, from the same year. As mentioned previously, many of the songs included on the album are ones associated with Amália Rodrigues. A video for 'Ó Gente da Minha Terra' highlights the ways Mariza has taken on a dramatic presence that echoes Amália's influence in bringing vocalists out from behind the guitarists – where they had been 'imprisoned' in traditional fado performance – and creating a performative style that could be used to great effect on stage, on the cinema screen and on television (the emergence of which was contemporaneous with Amália's initial rise to fame). As we saw in Chapter 3, Mariza has been able to set herself apart quite dramatically from Amália's legacy while still attaching herself to the Amália event.

Amália continued to cast a shadow onto the contemporary Portuguese popular music field well into the first decade of the new century she did not live to see. Cristina Branco performed a series of concerts in Portugal that consisted of a tribute to Amália in the first half and a tribute to José Afonso in the second, using a different configuration of musicians for each set: the Afonso tribute was performed by the group who would play on *Abril*, the Amália songs were given the appropriate fado instrumentation, but with the addition of Ricardo Dias's piano.[69] Branco took her tribute to Amália to Belgium and the Netherlands in 2008 and in the same year appeared at Institut de Recherche et Coordination

---

[68]   Mário Jorge Torres, liner notes to *Ritual* by Mísia (CD, Erato 8573-85818-2, 2001).

[69]   The results can be heard on Branco's album *Live* (EmArcy/Universal France 9843206, 2006).

Acoustique/Musique in Paris in *Com Que Voz*, a classical piece by Stefano Gervasoni based on sonnets by Camões and fados by Amália. 2008 also saw the release of the film *Amália*, a biopic that leaned heavily on the singer's romantic life. In 2009, members of pop group The Gift, a group known for singing mainly in English, were involved in a project entitled *Amália Hoje*, ('Amália Today'), the purpose of which was to present songs associated with the singer as pop songs. The album they released was very popular, going platinum within months of being released, no doubt aided by the heavily-circulated videoclip produced for their version of 'Gaivota', which showed the singer – as stand-in for Amália – at the head of a procession taking ownership of the Lisbon streets.

If, as has already been suggested, to tell the story of fado is also to tell the story of the myths of fado, then to tell the story of Amália is to enter a world no less mythological. Many of the new *fadistas* choose to stage their encounter with this world via explicit reference to Amália, as has been noted. Yet, there have been other important influences on fado as it is performed at the turn of the millennium. One major factor, observed already in discussing Dulce Pontes's work, has been the mixing of fado with the folk music associated with performers of *cantos de intervenção* such as José Afonso. Another has been the popularity of covering Brazilian songs by writers such as Caetano Veloso, Chico Buarque and Vinicius de Moraes; Lula Pena's *[phados]* (1998) and Maria Teresa's *O Mar...* (2002) both contain a mixture of fados, Portuguese folk songs and Brazilian songs, while Mariza collaborated with the Brazilian musician and arranger Jaques Morelenbaum for her third album *Transparente*. Brazil has always been important in shaping fado, the debate over possible Brazilian origins of the music being just one often-cited example. Amália Rodrigues spent a formative part of her early career in Brazil, made her first recordings there, released a collaborative album with Vinicius de Moraes in 1970, and maintained links with the country through numerous tours. In turn, many Brazilians have been influenced by fado; Caetano Veloso has described the music as a formative part of his early listening and has often performed material associated with Amália Rodrigues – such as 'Coimbra', 'Foi Deus' and 'Estranha Forma de Vida' – in his concerts. Strong links were formed in the 1970s between politically committed Portuguese musicians and their counterparts in various parts of Latin America – Hispanic and Lusophone – and the musical expression of an 'Iberian Atlantic' was a notable feature of the period.

Chapter 5

Tudo Isto Ainda É Fado?
Fado as Local and Global Practice

Tradition never ends.   – Alfredo Marceneiro[1]

Much invention is needed to safeguard what deserves to last.   – Sylviane Agacinski[2]

I don't want to put fado in a museum.   – Mariza[3]

Introduction

It is tempting to argue that fado has always been a global practice. If we go back to the (admittedly contested) accounts of its origins, we find references to Arabic, African, Brazilian and European sources all coming together (whether in harmony, spontaneity or agonism) in the hybridizing waterfront areas of Lisbon to create a music that would become inextricably linked to Portugal. Another way of putting this is to describe fado as a product of Portuguese globalizing processes, to say that it comes about due to the massive and various Portuguese colonial experiments; such a definition also allows room for those who wish to place fado's origins among the sailors involved in these expeditions. It is not without some difficulties, however, that we bring together the globalizing projects of the sixteenth to eighteenth centuries with the more recent ones of the twentieth. Rather than add to that debate, I propose in this chapter to focus on the more recent era of globalization, in which it could be argued Portugal has been more of a recipient than a protagonist. That said, Portuguese people and music have continued to travel and fado is globally present. Fado performers have become stars on the world music network and have become ambassadors for their culture. The presentation of fado as 'world music' has led to notable developments in live and recorded performance, where a balance is sought between the presentation of fado's specificity as a music associated with Portugal and the felt necessity

---

[1]   'Bairros de Lisboa', lyric by Carlos Conde, music by Alfredo Marceneiro, recorded by Fernanda Maria and Alfredo Marceneiro, *Biografias do Fado* (Valentim de Carvalho/EMI 72438592822, 1997).

[2]   Sylviane Agacinski, *Time Passing: Modernity and Nostalgia*, tr. Jody Gladding (New York: Columbia University Press, 2003 [2000]), p. 9.

[3]   Reported in *Billboard* (24 May 2003), p. 45.

for a technologically-enhanced 'universal' acoustic world. This chapter intersects with the others by asking what is gained and lost through this process in terms of fado's locality, its place in the world. This locality needs to be understood as both a physical one (fado as a cultural product of Portugal) and as a generic one (fado as a form of contemporary popular music); in other words, fado needs to be located in 'real' and discursive space – the real space of Portugal and the discursive space of the popular. To do this work of locating fado, it is necessary to consider features of globalization such as flows, technology, mass mediation, time/space compression, and the global/local dynamic.

The flows I am considering include those of capital, people, politics, mass-mediated ideas and ideologies and, above all, culture. As we saw in Chapter 2, there is a sense for many that we live in a world of 'placeless places' and 'timeless times' and where 'all that is solid melts into air' just as Marx and Engels had foreseen. International trading and transnational companies may have been with us for centuries but the scale, speed and ease with which international exchange can now occur, along with the lack of necessity for many traders of material (and non-material) goods, means that flow is unrestricted (or de-stricted, un-policeable, invisible). Meanwhile, one of the human costs is an increased flow in workers, migrants and refugees, for whom the world is unstable rather than placeless. Or rather, the notion of placelessness is significantly different for families uprooted, made homeless and forced to move on than it is for those who are able to take advantage of blurred boundaries, 'soft cities' and identity games. This is the distinction drawn by Zygmunt Bauman between 'vagabonds' and 'tourists'.[4]

Another cost is the loss of tradition. Paul Heelas notes the existence of two tendencies in describing 'detraditionalization': on the one hand, there is a radical thesis which claims that tradition is eroded and the past; on the other, a 'coexistence thesis' states that reality is more complex and that detraditionalization takes place alongside other strategies such as reconstruction and retraditionalization. The radical thesis posits a past that was closed and ritualized and that staked a lot on fate and a self under control; contrasting with this past is a present that is open and experimental and values choice and a self in control. Similarly, necessity is contrasted with contingency, certainty with uncertainty, the communal with the individualistic, the other-informed with the self-informed. Against such rigid polarization, the coexistence thesis holds that individuals always live in the conflict zone between the 'other-informed' and the 'self-informed', that traditions are traces, and that, as anthropologists have long pointed out, there is internal pluralism in so-called 'traditional' societies. But people are never simply autonomous either; they are still controlled by rules, customs, languages and ideologies. This thesis

---

[4]   Zygmunt Bauman, *Globalization: The Human Consequences* (Cambridge: Polity Press, 1998), p. 92.

makes much of Eric Hobsbawm's formulation of tradition as something that is invented.[5]

The upshot of these processes, for many, is that we have come to live in an era where the standardization of products (including cultural practices such as music) has become globally normative. When presented as 'McDonaldization' or 'Nike-ification', there is a clear reflection of American or Western cultural norms becoming hegemonic. This is far from being an unproblematic position, as Arjun Appadurai has argued: 'it is worth noting that for the people of Irian Java, Indonesianization may be more worrisome than Americanization, as Japanization may be for Koreans, Indianization for Sri Lankans, Vietnamization for the Cambodians, and Russianization for the people of Soviet Armenia and the Baltic republics'.[6] Nevertheless, it cannot be denied that the accusations of Americanization in certain cultural fields – popular music being one – are often very near the mark. Flow has not only been the subject of criticism, however, and it is the less publicized cultural practices that may point toward more celebratory narratives, as we will see below.

If homogeneity in the form of such standardization has been a concern for many, for others the more significant issue is that of heterogeneity, of difference. This heterogeneity is seen as the result of a constant fragmentation taking place across the globe. Again, celebratory and critical positions manifest themselves. For the celebrants, the fragmentation of a hegemonic conception of the human subject is a vital part of recognizing neglected and often brutalized minorities and of establishing alternate identities. This line of thinking often connects itself to the celebratory postmodernism that hails the 'decentred subject'. It should be remembered, however, that such a fractured subject is also a central concept for many of those who are highly critical of postmodernism. Accompanying this debate are others concerning essentialism, anti-essentialism and 'strategic essentialism'. As indicated above, issues of postcolonialism are always in some way implicated in those of globalization. It is thus useful to consider Portuguese culture as something that has both accompanied and been altered by the country's colonizing project, but also as something that has had to respond to other colonizing cultural processes such as those described in Chapter 4. This entails thinking about the role of Portuguese, Angolans, Mozambicans, Brazilians and others, affected in different ways but changed all the same by the colonial project.

Technology has a central role to play in these issues. If we must fix a time frame to a process such as globalization which, after all, is as old as the human desire to migrate, then one reason for choosing the second half of the twentieth century is the unprecedented and all-pervading role of technology (particularly mass communication) in connecting the world, both physically and virtually,

[5]   Paul Heelas, Scott Lash & Paul Morris (eds), *Detraditionalization: Critical Reflections on Authority and Identity* (Cambridge, MA, & Oxford: Blackwell, 1996).

[6]   Arjun Appadurai, *Modernity at Large: Cultural Dimensions of Globalization* (Minneapolis: University of Minnesota Press, 1996), p. 32.

during this period. While we must be careful not to overemphasize technological determinism, two aspects of determinism are central to the globalization of music: techno-utopianism and techno-dystopianism. The utopian aspects of technology are often allied to the celebratory possibilities of music, the idea of a world connected via telephone and broadcasting technologies finding a resonance with those musico-utopianists who see music as some form of connecting principle – a universal language, even. Such an ideology is common in many world music promoters – the name of Mariza's record label, World Connection, sums it up well. Techno-dystopianism is that branch of thinking that criticizes the role machines have come to hold in our lives and wonders, as in the ultimate techno-dystopian film *The Matrix* (1999), where humans are slaves to the technologies they brought into being.

Capital also plays a vital role, as discussed to a certain extent in Chapter 2. As Marx repeatedly made clear, capital both needs to expand to survive and is very capable of fitting into new spaces of potential accumulation. In the twentieth century, both Marxist and non-Marxist economists have shown many different strategies for this expansion and occupation to take place (quite literally). One major strategy has been the rise of the multinational or transnational companies, the object of attention of the anti-globalization movement and of those in popular music studies who wish to criticize or defend the culture industry. Debates around so-called musical piracy in the twenty-first century have solidified existing relationships between mass-produced music and capital while also highlighting the emergence of previously unthought-of synergies, strategies and counterstrategies. As with tradition and technology, we need to be careful not to lean too far towards economic determinism but one does not have to be a regular reader of *Billboard* to see the seemingly unbreakable bond between music and capital.

While I have not (yet) dealt with all of them, it should be clear that much of the above corresponds to Appadurai's 'scape' system. Appadurai identifies five '-scapes' – Ethnoscape, Technoscape, Financescape, Mediascape and Ideoscape – which designate the field of possibilities regarding people, technology, capital, communication and ideology at any one time and for any one group. Like landscapes, these 'scapes' are made up of interlocking elements which will not be seen from the same angle by everyone, being 'deeply perspectival constructs, inflected by the historical, linguistic, and political situatedness of different sorts of actors: nation-states, multinationals, diasporic communities'.[7] In a sense, then, what I am attempting to do throughout this book – and particularly in this closing chapter – is offer some reflections on the 'fadoscape'. I use this term not to add to the plethora of neologisms that theory invariably brings with it, but to reinforce the fact that everything that is said here for fado is said very much with the idea of a perspective and a 'scape' in mind. I have emphasized the nature of the popular music field and fado's place in it. This is 'scape-thinking', but so is tackling fado from the perspective of its highly mediated appearance in this and other fields.

---

[7]   Ibid., p. 33.

I have already begun to suggest some of the ways in which these general theories of globalization can be applied to music. The most obvious narrative to remind ourselves of here is that accompanying world music. As a number of commentators have noted, the music now labelled 'world music' had a history in commerce as much as in the academy. Earlier labels included 'folk', 'ethnic' and 'international'. 'World' evolved due to the need for a marketing term, but also because some of the earlier labels were deemed archaic. A notable feature of the new 'world music' was its accompanying media, which came in the form of targeted magazines, radio shows and a desire to sell a lifestyle. Steven Feld has reported on these developments, noting the celebratory and anxious narratives that accompany them. Timothy Taylor deals with the role of record companies and marketing strategies in his exploration of 'global pop', giving a perspective of the world music network that owes much to Appadurai's Financescape while not losing sight of the importance of the Mediascape and Ideoscape in disseminating cultural stereotypes.[8] Feld and Taylor both focus on the role of collaboration and curation in world music, from The Beatles and Ravi Shankar in the 1960s, through Paul Simon's albums *Graceland* (1986) and *The Rhythm of the Saints* (1990), to Ry Cooder's numerous projects with African, Hawaiian, Caribbean, Latino and Cuban musicians. The setting up of record labels by Anglo-American pop stars has raised issues around their curatorial role and the subsequent tendency to museology in collecting and re-presenting musicians under distinctive brand names: examples include Peter Gabriel's involvement in WOMAD and the Real World label, David Byrne's Luaka Bop label and Mickey Hart's World Series for Rykodisc.[9] Also connected to the curatorial and collector mentalities is the emergence of directories, such as *The Virgin Directory of World Music* (1991), *World Beat* (1992) and *World Music: The Rough Guide* (1994), and branded compilations such as those produced by or for Putamayo, Starbucks, the *Rough Guides* and HEMIsphere. As with the processes of globalization mentioned above, there has been an emphasis on the ways in which difference is represented and there have been, perhaps inevitably, what Feld refers to as 'anxious' and 'celebratory' narratives. The former stress the dangers of capitalist concentration, the threat that 'world music' poses to authentic musics of the world, the erasure of difference and individual identity, the drive for larger financial returns, the commoditization of ethnicity and the essentialization of the other. Celebratory narratives instead focus on the reappropriation of Western pop by non-Westerners, the creative potential of fusion forms which reject bounded, fixed, or essentialized identities and the value of conversation, dialogue, exploration and development.

---

[8]   Steven Feld, 'A Sweet Lullaby for World Music' in Arjun Appadurai (ed.), *Globalization* (Durham, NC, & London: Duke University Press, 2001), pp. 189–216; Timothy Taylor, *Global Pop: World Music, World Markets* (New York & London: Routledge, 1997).

[9]   David Byrne, who had earlier signed Paulo Bragança to his label, appears at the beginning of the documentary *The Art of Amália* (Bruno de Almeida, Portugal/USA, 2000) to speak about the effect the singer had on him.

Technologies of *Saudade*

If one consults the second edition of the *Rough Guide* to World Music (1999) to find out about Portuguese fado, one is presented with the lyrics to the song 'Tudo Isto É Fado', made famous by the genre's biggest star Amália Rodrigues. As I indicated in Chapter 1, by using it for a similar purpose, the song provides a poetic description of fado's ontology: defeated souls, lost nights, bizarre shadows in the Mouraria, love, jealousy, ashes, fire, sorrow and sin. The second edition of the *Guide* dates from what would be the final year of Amália's life (the *Guide* reports her as being 'in semi-retirement') and the eve of the recent fado 'boom'; Paul Vernon, writing the entry for fado, was able to reflect on the current state of fado in the following manner:

> the need for a new fado icon has been obvious for some time. Perhaps it's a shade early to begin drawing conclusions as to who that might be, but Mísia is a clear front runner in the current stakes ... She looks set to be the first major fado star of the twenty-first century and, along with others like Mafalda Arnauth – a fine and underrated singer who deserves wider recognition – should ensure that the fado has a future in the new millennium.[10]

I have tried to suggest in Chapter 4 the sort of future fado would have in this period and also given a general overview of the debates about innovation and tradition that the emergence of a number of highly visible younger singers brought about. There are many others who I have not had space to discuss but who are helping to ensure the vitality of the genre. These figures represent, for now, what Manuel Halpern calls 'the future of *saudade*'.[11]

One aspect of fadology which seems destined to remain constant is the necessity to make reference to *saudade*, a word which, according to the *Rough Guide*, 'has no direct translation in English'.[12] As I outlined in Chapter 1, there is a long established history around attempting to define this word, which can be partially summarized in a list of suggested synonyms: *Sehnsucht, saknadr, saknad, Sawn, πόθος, nostalgie, anyoranza, morriña, Тоска, litost, tesknota, dor* and *yearning* are just some of them. I suggested, following Svetlana Boym's line

---

[10]   Paul Vernon, 'Fado', in Simon Broughton et al. (eds), *World Music: The Rough Guide*, 2nd edn, *Vol. 1: Africa, Europe and the Middle East* (London: Rough Guides Ltd, 1999), p. 231. At the time of writing, the third edition of the *Rough Guide* was imminent. It will no doubt contain a quite different account of fado's place, given the popularity of the genre in the decade since the second edition. I felt it was still pertinent to record the findings of the second edition, however, as they remained one of the guiding English language resources on fado during the time period covered in this book.

[11]   Manuel Halpern, *O Futuro da Saudade: O Novo Fado e os Novos Fadistas* (Lisbon: Publicações Dom Quixote, 2004).

[12]   Vernon, 'Fado', *Rough Guide*, p. 229.

of thinking, that the proliferation of these terms centred on notions of yearning, longing and nostalgia, and the possibility to suggest some kind of synonymity seems at odds with their untranslatability. Or rather, the untranslatability may be seen as a willed one rather than a 'purely' linguistic one. But, in focusing here on issues of globalization, there are other factors to acknowledge too. For example, a search on the word 'saudade' in the twenty-first century is more likely to return Brazilian uses of the word, especially when connected to music. If, in Chapter 1, I asked how *saudade* might be considered as a fencing-off of a protected national imaginary, one of the most obvious challenges to this would be the Brazilian case. Another would be the Cape Verdean case, where *saudade* (or *sodade* in the Cape Verdean dialect Kriolu) as a central theme in music has become familiar to international listeners of artists such as Cesaria Evora, Mayra Andrade, Lura, Tito Paris and B. Leza.

In Chapter 3, I referred to the 'sacred silence of world music', the magical sheen of sound against non-sound that marks out the high-fidelity recording from the fuzzy resonance of music situated in spaces of everyday background noise. An example of this silence can be found in the song 'O Silêncio da Guitarra' which opens Mariza's album *Fado Curvo*. The sound that breaks the silence of the album is ten seconds of *guitarra*, not playing a melody but setting a scene, preparing us for something. That something turns out to be Mariza's voice, isolated for a couple of seconds as she sings the words 'o silêncio da guitarra', then joined by a simple strum on the *guitarra* as she reaches the final syllable of the last word. For the rest of the first verse, the *guitarra* provides a subtle backdrop to allow the voice to dominate. The tempo picks up for the second and third verses, with the voice soaring above the accompaniment of *guitarra* and *viola*. The song ends with an isolated voice singing the words from the title again before the *guitarra* adds a final brief signature. There is an attempt, as with Camané's live recording of Frederico de Brito's 'Acordam as Guitarras', to illustrate a song about guitars by using the instrument to announce itself alongside its linguistic signifier. But, more than this, there is a clear isolation of the sound elements to send another non-verbal message: this is fado and this is what it sounds like in high definition.[13]

The technological 'silence' I refer to could be seen as an elaboration of the silence demanded at the outset of a fado performance ('Silêncio, que se vai cantar!' – 'Silence for the one about to sing!') but it goes much further, possibly even to the point where it removes atmosphere. This is not always a bad thing, as for example when it allows for the fetishization of a sound: not only the singer's voice, but her breath, her body, her gesture, her silence; not only the guitarist's notes but the 'silence of the guitar', the sound of *unhas* on strings, the resonances that announce silence and its end. When we are listening to such recordings, we are ever more aware of the act of listening as a resonance. It is the singling out of what was

---

[13] Mariza, 'O Silêncio da Guitarra', *Fado Curvo* (World Connection/Valentim de Carvalho/EMI 724358423723, 2003); Camané, 'Acordam as Guitarras', *Uma Noite de Fados* (Valentim de Carvalho/EMI 72438329052, 1995).

always precious in fado performance, but, as Friedrich Monroe and Phillip Winter might well remind us, high definition comes at the expense of grain.

Developments in recording, playback and performance technology play a crucial role here, especially in the *novo fado* that has been courted in recent years by the world music network. As with Roland Barthes's discussion of photography, we can detect a change, first in notation and later in recording, from a transcriptive response to music – 'getting it down' – to a more productive role in creating music. I have suggested that what was found visually and sonically notable in Lisbon in the past has become what is made notable by visual and sonic recording equipment. But in the process of being made notable in as clear a way as possible, much of the original detail (the background noise, as it were) disappears. There is a need to 'frame' the complexity of the situation and excerpt the most telling details. What is notable in the production techniques of much contemporary world music is the way in which background noise is eliminated to emphasize the fact that these are artistic recordings *by* professionals rather than field recordings *of* amateurs (the prepositional difference is crucial). *Novo fado*, then, like many other popular musics, might be defined as music that could only be made in a studio or performed live with state-of-the-art equipment.

This difference is well illustrated by comparing concerts featuring professional performers with amateur fado nights. The ideal way to do this remains firsthand experience. The former practice can be witnessed in any major concert hall where fado performers appear; the latter is more restricted to the fado houses of Portugal or other areas in which there is a sufficiently large Portuguese community to sustain amateur fado practice. However, we may also witness the differences on film. For my purposes, I wish to compare the performance of fado as it is presented in a variety of films, beginning with a focus on the live performance but ending in a seemingly quite different performative space.

The documentary *Fado: Ombre et Lumière* (1989) was produced prior to the fado boom and focuses mainly on the localized fado scene in Lisbon, although it also narrates the story of Amália's international stardom. One section of the film focuses on the Guitarra da Bica, a *casa de fado* run by Milú Ferreira in the Bica neighbourhood. One of the songs performed there concerns famous *fadistas* of the past and the footage of the performance is intercut with images of these figures. The lyrics of the song, known as 'Figuras do Passado' or 'Vozes do Passado' [Figures (or Voices) of the Past], ask the listener to consider the past and the theme of Lisbon fado which 'time does not forget'. Over subsequent verses, the 'vozes do passado' are listed, among them Fernando Farinha, Alfredo Marceneiro ('the embodiment of fado'), and Hermínia Silva (remembered for playing in *revistas* and films). At the close of the song we are asked to recall all '*fadistas* and *guitarristas* / And other great figures / In this Lisbon of artists / Their names will never die'.[14] The lyrics are notable for their use of Marceneiro and Farinha as markers of authenticity.

---

[14]   'Figuras do Passado', lyric by João Alberto, set to Fado Mouraria, sung by Luís Costa in *Fado: Ombre et Lumière*, dir. Yves Billon (France, 1989). A version of the song by

As we saw in Chapter 2, both *fadistas* have very strong ties to place and history and the evocation of Farinha would be particularly resonant in Milú Ferreira's venue, so close to where the 'Miúdo da Bica' used to live. As Manuel Halpern points out, the figures mentioned in this song are all representatives of the people [*povo*] rather than singers associated with the more aristocratic strand of fado.[15] Watching the performance, one is more struck by the style of singing and the locale in which it takes place. Luís Costa, seemingly always on the verge of forgetting the words, and even in danger of losing his balance, offers a throaty, gasping rendition that can only just be heard over the noise of crockery being moved around and people talking. The venue itself is on the small side and performer and audience are thrust together in the minimal space between the tables. While Costa may be no Marceneiro on this evidence, there are strong affinities of style between the two *fadistas*, a fact underlined in the film by the subsequent footage of Marceneiro performing in a similar venue.

The second filmed 'evidence' I wish to consider is far closer to what we have come to expect from footage of live music performance. In March 2003, Mariza put on a concert at the Union Chapel in London. She had already made a name for herself on the world music circuit and the concert was filmed by the BBC, who produced a DVD in association with Mariza's record company, World Connection. This DVD, clearly aimed at an international market, presents the concert exactly as we would expect. There is a professional stage set, strong lighting and excellent sound recording. Mariza performs the songs from her first and second albums that have made her name known and the package as a whole has a clearly defined place in her discography. The first track on the DVD is the aforementioned 'O Silêncio da Guitarra' here allowed even more dynamism between singer and musicians due to the additional aspect of Mariza's stage presence. It seems a world away from Milú's *casa* in Bica. How can this music go under the same name?

We appear to be left with a local fado scene that has continued unabated and a globalized scene attached to a world music network. Mísia, speaking about her album *Ritual*, appears keen to affirm such a distinction:

> I dedicated a disc to the small world of fado, because, no matter what people might think, it is those zealous amateurs who maintain the ritual and perpetuate the tradition. Fado with a capital 'F' is not Amália, Mísia or Mariza; it is this river of anonymous souls who play and sing in the *tabernas*. It's the mechanics, lawyers, seamstresses, merchants, fishmongers, primary school teachers, nurses and office workers who get up in the semi-darkness of the vaulted basements and sing for friends, onlookers and lost tourists. For me, it's they who keep fado alive, not the commercial enterprise of 'novo fado', which like all trends is

António Paiva, with slightly different lyrics, is available on the CD *Ó Vadio: Fado na Tasca do Chico* (Transformadores 5600304510073, 2005).

[15] Halpern quotes a set of lyrics slightly different again from the two versions mentioned in the previous note. Halpern, *O Futuro da Saudade*, pp. 59–60.

bound to die. Fado of the street has this immortal quality: being new every day
rather than being fashionable![16]

The ritual that Mísia wishes to emphasize, then, in her album of that name, is
the everyday practice of fado, a practice which renews itself so does not need
'newness' foisted on it. But I am suspicious of this segregating of an artistic world
(Mísia et al.) and an everyday world of real, authentic people and the reasons for
my suspicion lie in the very ubiquity of representations of fado, not least because
Mísia's album is also very clearly about Amália. It is important that we bear in
mind the role such public figures have in the popular memory. In *Fado: Ombre
et Lumière*, for example, we can witness a singer performing a set of lyrics about
famous *fadistas*. This footage was then edited by the filmmakers to include vintage
footage of these *fadistas* appearing in films and on television; in other words,
the reference to these precursors was allied immediately to their mass-mediated
images, suggesting that the archive of public memory relies as much on mass
mediation as on the more localized phenomenon of inclusion in fado lyrics. Of
course, the audience in the *casa de fado* was not witnessing this edited footage
but the people there *were* hearing lyrics relating these *fadistas*' experiences of
performing in *revistas* and films and could just as easily make connections to the
corresponding imagery as the film's editors did. Here we find the famous figures
of fado, those who moved from the *tabernas* and *casas* to the stages and screens of
the nation, returning as mythologized characters in local repertoire, simultaneously
present in the local and the national imaginary. And while Luís Costa is busy
framing these mythologized figures, he is himself becoming the subject of another
framing, as the French film team use him to economically express three core points
of their film: a sense of *locality* – footage of the *casa*; a sense of *history* – footage
of famous fadistas; and the conflation of these two points – a sense of *continuity*.
The footage of Alfredo Marceneiro in the past that completes this sequence is not
so different from the footage of Luís Costa in the present.

Similarly, we find in the case of mass-mediated *novo fado* a desire to stage
localness. Throughout Mariza's Union Chapel show, the production quality is of
the high quality we have come to expect from a world music recording. The final
track, however, finds singer and guitarists venturing out into the audience to perform
'Povo Que Lavas no Rio' without amplification. At this stage the recording of the
concert begins to resemble a field recording with noticeably directed microphones,
made explicit when Mariza turns away from them and her voice is lost from the
soundtrack. This strategy, common to a number of young fadistas who have made
the move to the stages of larger concert venues, seems to be an attempt to remove
the barrier that has been built between performer and audience as a result of this
move. This can be interpreted as a recognition on the part of the performers of
the loss of the local in the shift to mass mediation. The local they wish to refer

---

[16]   Mísia, interview in Hervé Pons, *Os Fados de Mísia: Conversas com Hervé Pons*,
tr. António Carlos Carvalho (Lisbon: Oceanos, 2007), pp. 72–3.

back to, meanwhile, is never as untainted by mass mediation as they might think. The tradition is constantly being changed and no pure origin can be referenced. Rather, as the musicians attempt to evoke the pre-amplification days of fado in a process that entails a considerable reintroduction of background noise, we realize the desirability of amplification to keep the rest of the set 'silent' and 'clean'.

This sense of the local and global blurring together is highlighted in a more recent film featuring Mariza, Simon Broughton's documentary *Mariza and the Story of Fado* (2006). The film provides a historical account of the genre while also giving a snapshot of contemporary Lisbon. Mariza acts as a tour guide to some of the fado nightspots in the city and at one point she is shown performing in the Tasca do Chico, a tiny venue in the Bairro Alto famed for its regular evenings of *fado vadio*. The film, like *Fado, Ombre et Lumière*, suggests a moving between the worlds of the amateur and professional. A more cynical ('anxious') narrative might suggest that Broughton's film is really about authenticating Mariza by showing she can cut it in the local *tasca*. This would then be connected to the larger project of what the *Rough Guide* mentality is 'really all about', selling us authentic travel experiences. The accompanying *Songlines* feature, 'On the Tiles with Mariza', could equally be seen as both promotion for the film and a tourist guide to Lisbon's fado houses. I do not wish to go that far, mainly because I wish to suggest that there is a productive tension between the packaged and the unpackaged (which is really not all that unpackaged anyway) and that such an anxious narrative would suggest the 'users' of this film were no more than dupes of the culture industry.

I will have more to say below about the association between fado and tourism. Before doing so, I wish to mention two more filmic representations of fado. The first is the film *Passionada*, mentioned in passing in Chapter 4 due to the film's use of Mísia's singing. I do not wish to discuss the film at any length here but just to note its use of fado. The film is set in the town of New Bedford, home to a large Portuguese-American community, and one of the main protagonists is a fado singer who performs in a local seafood restaurant. As many observers have noted, the fidelity to Portuguese (or Portuguese-American) customs is minimal, from the use of names (and actors) that are not Portuguese to the depiction of 'typical' foods and festivities that actually have more to do with other cultural groups.[17] This in itself is of interest in the way it allows a blurring of boundaries (and doubtless a lack of research on the part of the filmmakers) to create a mythologized and hybridized space for Portuguese culture on the international stage. It is also of interest in the placing of fado in a restaurant setting, in which, as in the more upmarket venues of Lisbon, a distance is created between the singer and the diners. Fado, like the Portuguese-American setting of the story, becomes the differential for the film, marking it in contrast to other films of its type. What it fails to achieve in an accurate framing of a diasporic group it attempts to balance with its differentiation within the market.

---

[17] A list of the errors in the film can be found at *The Internet Movie Database*, http://www.imdb.com/title/tt0285879 (14 December 2005).

The most recent of the films I wish to consider is Carlos Saura's *Fados* (2007), a project which seems both determined to rile *puristas* and keen to present an accurate representation of the genre's tangled roots and trajectories.[18] *Fados*, which is completely shot on a huge indoor soundstage, opens to the sound of Carlos do Carmo singing 'Fado Saudade', a song that speaks of 'old Lisbon', the *tabernas* of Alfama, and of Bica and Madragoa. As the city is brought into being once again by this act of naming, the singer warns that 'whoever lives only in the past / stays trapped in destiny'. Fado, however, is always alive and, as 'crystal song', escapes this entrapment. The film then quickly changes rhythm, cutting to a multiracial crowd of drummers and dancers choreographed by a whistle blower in a scene that evokes the encounters between Portugal and Africa. From here we move to 'Mozambique' via a performance of 'Transparente' by Mariza accompanied by a dancer and a selection of musicians including a bouzouki player, a percussionist playing the *cajón* and Rui Veloso on electric guitar. After another brief detour from fado and *fadistas*, Camané appears, singing lines by Fernando Pessoa to a *fado menor do Porto*. Two songs follow based on the Severa legend, the second being Júlio Dantas's 'Rua de Capelão', performed by Cuca Roseta and Mário Pacheco; while this song is playing, footage from José Leitão de Barros's *A Severa* is shown. More archive footage is used in the next section, which consists of a homage to Alfredo Marceneiro. Two dancers perform in front of a massive screen on which Marceneiro is seen singing 'Tricana', his face and voice a ghostly presence in the otherwise ultra-high definition audiovisual world of Saura's studio. To complete the Marceneiro homage, hip hop artists NBC, SP & Wilson perform a 'Marceneiro rap' in which the *fadista* is praised as a 'poet of the streets' over beats and samples of his voice. Carlos do Carmo provides a move partly back towards tradition with a performance of 'Homem na Cidade' against a backdrop of Lisbon (discussed in Chapter 2) and then there is a homage to his mother, Lucília do Carmo, featuring a recording of her singing Gabriel Oliveira's 'Foi na Travessa da Palha' followed by a performance of the same song by Mexican singer Lila Downs. Argentina Santos sings dressed in black with her eyes closed and a microphone prominently positioned in front of her. There is a return to Africa in the form of a *lundum* performed by members of Brigada Victor Jara, succeeded by a *morna* by Cape Verdean singer Lura. Camané returns to sing more Pessoa ('Quadras') prior to a homage to Amália that begins with archive footage of her practising with Alain Oulman at the piano and continues with a version of 'Estranha Forma de Vida' by Brazilian singer-songwriter Caetano Veloso, here singing at his highest register and evoking the highly pitched male versions of Amália songs by the likes of Gonçalo Salgueiro and Nuno Guerreiro. The next part of the film is devoted to revolution and features José Afonso's 'Grândola Vila Morena' played over footage of the 25 April 1974 Revolution and Brazilian singer-songwriter Chico Buarque singing his 'Fado Tropical', a song written about Portugal the year before the Revolution.

---

[18] Carlos do Carmo and Rui Vieira Nery acted as 'musical consultant' and 'musicological consultant' respectively.

Perhaps not surprisingly for a Saura film, there follows a section entitled 'Fado Flamenco', consisting of a dance sequence and a duet between Mariza and flamenco singer Miguel Poveda of Paulo de Carvalho's 'Meu Fado Meu', Poveda singing in Spanish and Mariza responding with Portuguese. The finale to the film involves the recreation of a *casa de fado*, with customers sat at long tables and posters of famous *fadistas* on the 'walls'. In turn, Vicente da Câmara, Maria da Nazaré, Ana Sofia Varela and Carminho (the first two representing the 'old guard' and the second two the new generation) each sing a few verses while the *guitarristas* improvise around them. There follows a brief *guitarrada* before a song dual between Ricardo Ribeiro and Pedro Moutinho. Between this scene and the credits, one more process is set in motion. To a recording of Mariza singing 'Ó Gente da Minha Terra', Saura has his camera make a long crane shot across the studio in which the scenes have been filmed. This works as a deconstruction of the whole film, allowing us to see that everything has been happening in the same place while also taking in the various screens that have been operating as backdrops and the filmmakers and technicians reviewing the process at one end of the studio, finally zooming slowly and impossibly into the camera lens itself.

Even without further analysis, it should be clear from the foregoing that *Fados* brings together many of the narratives explored in this book, uniting disparate historical moments, cultural groups and practices into one 'global', yet concentrated, space. It playfully hints at processes of construction, deconstruction and reconstruction that are central to the practice of fadology, moving dialectically between the illusory and the real. Yet, while Saura's tactic usefully highlights the polyglot roots of fado and the problematics of its place in the contemporary music world, it is not difficult to see why some Portuguese viewers were upset. At the very moment that fado was regaining its visibility and audibility on the global stage, its Portugueseness was repeatedly removed by the inclusion of actors who were, according to some, just 'not fado'. Of all the films considered here, *Fados* has arguably moved us furthest from the place of traditional fadology. A more positive way to view the film might be to consider it as a 'spatial history' of the kind discussed in my Introduction, wherein a metaphorical language allows for the creation of a horizon of possibilities within which one can then begin to make decisions about which stories to tell and which memories to stake a commitment to.

Migrating Musics

With Saura's *Fados* still in mind, I wish to briefly consider the interaction of fado with other popular musics. I began this process in the previous chapter by suggesting that it was necessary to view fado alongside other forms of popular music – mostly rock and pop – in Portugal and to consider its interaction with the broader popular music field. In continuing this discussion, I also want to briefly mention some other musical forms not discussed previously and to consider the role of fusion musics.

As we have seen, Carlos Saura, in wishing to present the story of fado's origins, in fact created new fusions by staging a series of encounters between fado and the contemporary performance of other Lusophone and Hispanic musics. That we are witnessing contemporary performers in his film should remind us of the popularity of such musics in Portugal. A walk around a large Portuguese record shop is instructive here, especially for anyone who is accustomed to finding non-Anglophone music in one section called 'World'. CD retailers such as Fnac are generally divided up as follows: a promotional section, often dominated by Anglo-American acts but also containing major Portuguese releases of all kinds; a large rock and pop section, almost exclusively Anglo-American; sections for various genres, such as Metal, Alternative, and Dance; Classical and Jazz (on which more below); Portuguese rock, pop and folk; Fado; World Music and other international genres such as Celtic folk and US country; Brazilian; and 'PALOPs'. This last section refers to the 'Países Africanos de Língua Oficial Portuguesa', the group of African countries where Portuguese is the official language: Angola, Mozambique, Cape Verde, Guinea Bissau and São Tomé and Príncipe. Here, one can find a wide range of musical genres, among the most popular of which are *kizomba* (Angola), *morna* (Cape Verde) and *marrabenta* (Mozambique). While these are reasonably established genres, with a listenership outside the Lusophone community, other popular genres, especially those involving hybrids, are also popular. The kind of global flows discussed above might best be sampled by listening to the group Buraka Som Sistema, who specialize in a twenty-first-century take on *kiduro* music from Angola. Their album *Black Diamond* (2008), which presents a 'global' sound rooted in the suburbs of Lisbon, saw them achieve widespread visibility beyond the Lusophone community. No attempt at any kind of 'African' authenticity is attempted; rather the point is to show how modern cities are made up of exactly the kind of polyglot culture that Buraka put into sonic form. This is the background noise of the city and, while emanating from a quite specific geo-political situation, escapes that situation in a global shout-out (Buraka's 'Luanda-Lisboa' is a good example).[19]

If PALOPs music has been a more recent taste acquisition for non-African Portuguese people, Brazilian music has long been popular in the country. Indeed, Latin American music generally has globalized more successfully in the twentieth century than Iberian music. 'Latin' instrumentation, rhythms and dance have influenced musical styles across the world and have contributed to the field of global popular music in ways that cannot be ignored. While there is reasonable general knowledge about many of these styles across the world, there is a particular familiarity in the Iberian Peninsula due to shared language and culture and the flows that inevitably follow Hispanic and Lusophone diasporic groups. These flows, of course, are not unidirectional, though it has not gone unnoticed by

---

[19]   Buraka Som Sistema, *Black Diamond* (Fabric B001XNL97Q, 2009 [2008]).

the culture industry that Latin American music tends to have a greater impact on the Iberian Peninsula than Iberian music has in Latin America.[20] This dominance is also reflected in the English-language coverage of the music by journalists, broadcasters and academics and, for this reason, I do not intend to discuss Brazilian music here.[21] It is, however, worth noting the influence of Brazilian music on the *novos fadistas*, a number of whom have included Brazilian songs in their recordings and live performances. Again, Amália is a prime example, having begun her recording career in Brazil and recorded with Brazilian artists.

Jazz represents another music that has emerged from the Americas to spread around the world and, while its North American performers may remain the most famous, the South American variants have also had an equally global effect. This can be heard in the wealth of US jazz flavoured with bossa nova, samba and 'Latin' rhythms and tonalities. If jazz 'in Portuguese' is most commonly thought to be that associated with the musicians who made 'Girl from Ipanema' a global hit, this should not detract from the lower-key but interesting story of jazz in Portugal.

The Portuguese jazz musician Luís Villas-Boas set up the Hot Clube de Portugal in Lisbon in 1948, providing a venue for jazz that has remained constant ever since. Villas-Boas was also responsible, alongside the *fadista* João Braga, for creating the Cascais Jazz Festival. The first festival took place in 1971 – the same year as the Vilar de Mouros rock festival – and was a stellar event, featuring Miles Davis, Ornette Coleman and Dexter Gordon. Beyond its stature as the inauguration of a major ongoing jazz event, the first festival has become famous for an incident which occurred during Ornette Coleman's set. Charlie Haden, who was playing bass in Coleman's group, dedicated his composition 'Song for Che' to the 'the black people's liberation movements of Mozambique, Guinea and Angola'. The dedication drew huge applause from the crowd and caused Haden to be subsequently arrested by the PIDE. Haden would continue to have connections with Portugal. In 1976, he composed a piece entitled 'For a Free Portugal' which sampled a recording of his 1971 dedication and also edited in recordings of Angolan music and the voice of an MPLA freedom fighter. Haden's 1983 album *The Ballad of the Fallen* featured a version of José Afonso's 'Grândola Vila Morena'. Then, in

---

[20]   See the 'Billboard Spotlight' on 'Latin America and markets in Spain, Portugal and the US', *Billboard* (24 October 1981), special supplement, and 'Spain and Portugal: An International Expanded Section', *Billboard* (11 November 2000): 75–8.

[21]   See, for example, Chris McGowan & Ricardo Pessanha, *The Brazilian Sound: Samba, Bossa Nova, and the Popular Music of Brazil* (Philadelphia: Temple University Press, 1998); Hermano Vianna, *The Mystery of Samba: Popular Music & National Identity in Brazil*, ed. & tr. John Charles Chasteen (Chapel Hill: University of North Carolina Press, 1999); Charles A. Perrone & Christopher Dunn (eds), *Brazilian Music & Globalization* (New York & London: Routledge, 2001); Carlos Basualdo (ed.) *Tropicália: A Revolution in Brazilian Culture (1967–1972)* (São Paulo: Cosac Naify, 2005); John P. Murphy, *Music in Brazil: Experiencing Music, Expressing Culture* (New York: Oxford University Press, 2006).

1990, Haden collaborated with the *guitarrista* Carlos Paredes on a set of concerts, the pair releasing an album of their improvisations.[22]

Since Cascais, Portuguese jazz artists have become more noticeable, from the saxophonist and flautist Rão Kyao in the 1970s to more recent artists such as saxophonist Carlos Martins (and his group the Sexteto de Jazz de Lisboa), singer Maria João, pianists Mário Laginha and Bernardo Sassetti, and bassists Carlos Bica and Bernardo Moreira. These and other musicians have ensured that jazz has a strong presence on the Portuguese musical scene. Through international collaborations, they have also helped to export Portuguese jazz to numerous other locations. There have been a number of fusions of jazz and fado, such as those by Rão Kyao. *Fado Bailado* (1983) utilizes fado instrumentation (António Chainho's *guitarra*) with Kyao's saxophone providing the 'voice' on a set of staple fados such as 'Canção do Mar', 'Fado Dois Tons' and 'Fado Vitória'. *Viva ao Fado* (1996) presents a fuller *conjunto* of guitars and Kyao using flute to voice the fados, many reprised from the earlier album alongside renditions of other pieces such as Amália's 'Lágrima'. *Fado Virado a Nascente*, again with Kyao's flute as its starting point, is a more ambitious concept which attempts to draw connections between fado and Arabic music, adding additional instrumentation to get the necessary tonalities. This recording also features the singing of Deolinda Bernardo and Teresa Salgueiro.

Joel Xavier is another artist who has used an instrument to voice fados. Xavier is a virtuoso guitarist who has recorded a number of solo albums as well as a disc of improvisation with the American jazz bassist Ron Carter. In 1996, Xavier released an album entitled 'Sr Fado', which featured him performing electric guitar versions of fados such as 'Povo Que Lavas no Rio' which relied heavily on vibrato and tremolo effects. Although some jazz-style keyboards could be discerned behind the tremolo attack, much of the backing music was rather insipid, only making the guitar stand out more prominently. If little else, the result raised questions about the use of hysterical voice in fado and the over-performance of emotion. More successful was Xavier's collaboration with Carlos do Carmo on Alexandre O'Neill's 'Gaivota', a genuine collective improvisation which highlighted some of the common characteristics of jazz and fado and underlined the extent to which Carmo's singing had always veered as much towards jazz as towards traditional fado styles. This point was also made apparent by Carmo's collaboration with Dutch saxophonist Henk van Twillert and with Portuguese saxophonist Carlos Martins (who has also collaborated with Camané).[23]

---

[22] Charlie Haden, *'Closeness': Duets* (A&M/Polygram 397 000-2, 1989 [1976]); *The Ballad of the Fallen* (ECM 1248, 1983); Charlie Haden & Carlos Paredes, *Dialogues* (Polydor France 843445-2, 1990).

[23] Joel Xavier, *Sr Fado* (Ariola/BMG 74321425632, 1996); *Lisboa* (Zona Música ZM00094, 2002); Henk van Twillert, *Fado Saudades* (Numérica NUM1094, 2001); Carlos Martins com Orquestra, *Do Outro Lado* (Som Livre SL 8802, 2006).

Also of interest in relation to Carmo's work is the partnership of Bernardo Moreira and Paula Oliveira, who have released two quietly impressive albums, *Lisboa Que Adormece* (2005) and *Fado Roubado* (2007). Moreira had earlier paid homage to the *guitarrista* Carlos Paredes on his album *Ao Paredes Confesso*. With Oliveira, he explored a range of songs from the Portuguese popular music repertoire, many of them fados or associated with fado singers. The first album focuses mostly on songs from the revolutionary 1970s, providing luminous versions of work by José Luis Tinoco, Sérgio Godinho and José Carlos Ary dos Santos. Songs include 'No Teu Poema', 'Um Homem na Cidade' and 'Uma Flor de Verde Pinho', all previously recorded by Carlos do Carmo. Although associated with Carmo, these songs were not strictly fados and there is as much space devoted to Portuguese pop of the period such as versions of two Paulo de Carvalho hits, 'E Depois do Adeus' and 'Maria, Vida Fria'. The instrumentation throughout is strictly jazz: Moreira's bass, Leo Tardin's piano, Bruno Pedroso's drums and João Moreira's trumpet. This set-up is maintained on *Fado Roubado*, which features more songs associated with popular poets of the 1960s and 1970s but with a slightly stronger emphasis on fado, as signalled by the title. Oliveira sings 'Há uma Música do Povo', a Fernando Pessoa poem set to music by Mário Pacheco and previously recorded by Mariza, as well as 'Estrela da Tarde' and 'Gaivota', both strongly associated with Carmo.[24]

The Quinteto de Jazz Lisboa have provided more chapters in the fusion of jazz and fado on their albums *Viragens* (1999) and *Coisas do Fado* (2001). The quintet comprises vocals, saxophone, keyboards, drums and bass. The first album contains versions of 'Gaivota', 'A Rosinha dos Limões' and 'Bairro Alto' alongside other songs such as Max's novelty record 'A Mula da Cooperativa'. The second album contains versions of eleven classic fados, including 'Ai Mouraria', 'Estranha Forma de Vida' and 'Rua da Capelão'. Whereas some of the tracks on the first album had utilized scat vocals, here the lyrics of all the fados are sung, bringing them a little closer to the originals while still maintaining a 'jazz distance', providing useful deconstructive takes on these well-known songs.[25]

Jazz has a long history of collaboration with world music. In recent years the Lebanese oud player and flautist Rabih Abou Khalil has been a notable figure in this process, combining the soundworlds of Arabic music and Western jazz. His numerous albums have seen him collaborating with musicians from all over the world, among them a number of leading contemporary American jazz musicians. In 2008, he launched a new project entitled *Em Português*, in which he collaborated with the Lisbon fado singer Ricardo Ribeiro.[26] Ribeiro is among

---

[24] Bernardo Moreira, *Ao Paredes Confesso* (EmArcy/Universal Portugal 066890-2, 2003); Paula Oliveira & Bernardo Moreira, *Lisboa que Adormece* (Universal Portugal 9870260, 2005); *Fado Roubado* (Polydor/Universal Portugal 1748860, 2007).

[25] Quinteto de Jazz Lisboa, *Viragens* (Ovação, 1998); *Coisas do Fado* (Ovação, 2006).

[26] Rabih Abou-Khalil, *Em Português* (Enja ENJ-95202, 2008).

the more traditional of the new *fadistas* and has been compared to Alfredo Marceneiro and other *castiço* Lisbon singers. It is certainly possible to tell that the songs – especially a version of a Marceneiro song – are sung by a *fadista* but overall the music is not fado, as most responses to the album were quick to point out. The review in *Songlines* magazine even went as far as declaring it not 'remotely Portuguese in character', while also noting that 'Abou-Khalil's music is rarely Arabic in any traditional sense'. Clearly, the music exists in some liminal space, which the review suggests is the 'common ground between the melancholic passion of Andalusian *muwashshahat* and Portuguese *saudade*, the wistful longing that suffuses fado'.[27] Is this where global fusion music leads us, to the 'placeless place and timeless time' of the 'netherzone' described by Mark C. Taylor earlier in this book, a soundtrack perhaps to one of Marc Augé's 'non-places'?

Tourists and Vagabonds

Abou-Khalil's Portuguese project may put us in mind of another exploratory jazz album from fifty years earlier. Miles Davis's *Sketches of Spain* (1960) bucked what was already becoming a trend in 'Latinized' jazz by recording music associated with the Iberian Peninsula rather than Latin America. The album was dominated by Gil Evans's arrangement of Joaquín Rodrigo's *Concierto de Aranjuez* and also contained a brief piece by Manuel de Falla and some compositions by Evans based on Spanish folk and flamenco forms. The *Concierto* (1939) is arguably the most famous piece of Spanish classical music of the twentieth century and has been used to signify many different things. In films and on television, the use of Rodrigo's music can often be found to signify Spain, but it has had other uses too. The work was designed to foreground the guitar and it has become something of a guitarists' favourite. In Richard Linklater's film *School of Rock* (2003), the students of an exclusive private school are shown performing the piece, allowing the viewers and the film's protagonist (Jack Black) to witness the prowess of the young guitarist Zack. The music is used here primarily to denote the 'classical', against which the power, authenticity and excitement of rock music and the electric guitar can be counterpoised. In the film *Brassed Off* (1996), about a Yorkshire colliery band entering a brass competition while the government is attempting to close down their colliery, Rodrigo's music is used both as a narrative device to heighten the emotional pace at which events are unfolding at the pit and as a way of bringing together the worlds of the middle-class female Coal Board worker and the male working-class miners (she calls it 'Concierto de Aranjuez'; they call it 'Orange Juice'). Meanwhile, Amália Rodrigues's version of 'Aranjuez Mon Amour'

---

[27]   Bill Badley, review of Abou-Khalil, *Songlines*, 54 (August/September 2008): 77.

(an adaptation of Rodrigo's music with lyrics by Guy Bontempelli) serves as a reminder of her involvement in both the *chanson* and flamenco traditions.[28]

These different uses of a single piece of music illustrate an interesting tension between global and local meanings. Accompanying this tension are questions of authenticity. In his liner notes to *Sketches of Spain*, the jazz critic Nat Hentoff was keen to emphasize Miles Davis's authenticity as a jazz player *and* a flamenco musician:

> What is most remarkable is the surprising authenticity of phrasing and timbre with which he plays. It is as if Miles had been born of Andalusian gypsies but, instead of picking up the guitar, had decided to make a trumpet the expression of his *cante hondo* ("deep song"). And Evans also indicates a thorough absorption of the Spanish musical temper which he has transmuted into his own uncompromisingly personal style.[29]

Of course, there is an element of exaggeration here. But what is interesting is the staging of authenticity as ability to convincingly take on characteristics of the Other. This corresponds to one of two main authenticating processes that can be identified with popular music, both concerned with issues of truth: on the one hand, a being true to oneself as an individual and an artist – this manifests itself in the artistic propensity towards originality and reinvention; on the other, a being true to some kind of template, such as when one speaks of an authentic blues artist or *fadista*. These two authenticities are by no means exclusive (and are far from exhaustive – authenticity is too complex for that) and, in fact, Hentoff would like to apply both to Miles Davis, who as well as having the authenticity of an 'Andalusian gypsy' is also presented as a restless sonic adventurer. However, there is often a tendency to focus on one or other of the pair.

Is Miles Davis a native or a tourist? I do not intend to answer that question here, but I do want to bring the issue of tourism into the discussion, both as a physical process of journeying accompanied by music and as a musical process accompanied by (at least virtual) journeying. With regard to fado, the most obvious example of the former is the case of 'typical' fado houses in Lisbon and elsewhere geared towards the tourist. These are the places where the visitor can go to experience both local food and examples of Portuguese music, not only fado but also sometimes rural folk music and dancing, followed by the chance to take a sonic souvenir of the evening away in the form of a recording. This association of fado with tourism has undoubtedly cast a stigma on the music as strong as

---

28 Amália Rodrigues, 'Aranjuez Mon Amour', *Ses Plus Belles Chansons* (EMI France 1994 CD EMI France 8290842, 1994). The fact that Amália could be brought in at almost any part of the discussions in this chapter only goes to highlight the extent to which she showed the possibilities for a globalized fado.

29 Nat Hentoff, liner notes to Miles Davis, *Sketches of Spain* (Columbia/Legacy CK 65142, 1997 [1960]).

the genre's co-optation by the Salazar regime, from which period the association largely derives. This is true both for local people and for visitors who would like to explore areas such as the Bairro Alto of Lisbon without being ushered towards gaudy *casas de fado* by jacketed doormen. Indeed, many of the nightspots of Bairro Alto and Bica seem to present themselves in marked opposition to such establishments; the bars and clubs are almost painfully cool and happening while the tourist fado houses are stuffily unhip.

In 1970, Mascarenhas Barreto complained about the 'lucrative trail of tourist policy' that mixed fado and folk song in the *casas* and declared, 'it is necessary to discern clearly where the *Fado* starts and ends!'[30] In 1997, Jorge Lima Barreto associated contemporary developments in commercial popular music with a slickness that was itself connected to tourism. Barreto suggested that light music especially had become typified by an absence of experimentalism and complexity and an emphasis on 'meticulously measured out choral, vocal and instrumental elements ... syncopated rhythms, up-to-date studio technology ... and scene-setting'.[31] His comments were about *música ligeira* in general and not specifically about fado, but he clearly had fado in mind, not least through his mention of poets such as Pedro Homem de Melo, Ary dos Santos and David Mourão-Ferreira, and *fadistas* such as Amália, and his subsequent observation that fado 'has a touristic connotation' when its music is combined with entertainment.[32] One way in which this scene-setting is transferred to the world of recording is via the compilation, of which there are countless dedicated solely to fado. These compilations are marketed to a domestic audience as convenient ways to get hold of favourites and to a tourist audience as a flavour of Portugal, a souvenir of their visit. I wish to consider this relationship between tourism and compilations by considering not only this kind of souvenir disc, but also the more paradoxical idea of a souvenir of a foreign place available even to those who have not physically travelled.

Souvenirs of Unvisited Places

It has become quite common in the UK to find world music compilations marketed at audio tourists, people with an interest in the sounds from elsewhere but who are content to witness them via a trip to the local music shop or by online ordering. To choose a recent example, *Bar Lisbon: Classic and New Portuguese Flavours* is a compilation from Nascente's 'Bar 2CD Range', described by the parent company Demon as 'attractively packaged titles compiled by world music specialists aimed

---

[30] Mascarenhas Barreto, *Fado: Origens Líricas e Motivação Poética/Fado: Lyrical Origins and Poetic Motivation*, il. José Pedro Sobreiro, parallel English text by George Dykes (Frankfurt am Main: TFM, 1994), p. 185.

[31] Jorge Lima Barreto, *Musa Lusa* (Lisbon: Hugin, 1997), p. 189.

[32] Ibid., p. 191.

to appeal to fans of lounge-style compilations'.[33] The description on the back of the CD is as follows:

> Portugal's capital city is an ancient and vibrant hotbed of Latin temperament. Of all the musical forms that permeate the city's steamy nightlife the sound of Fado is the most addictive. Dating back to the early eighteen hundreds its haunting sound embodies the Portuguese spirit. This exciting selection features classic Fado from the likes of Gonçalo Salgueiro and Maria da Fé, plus contemporary world sounds from Sara Tavares, and cool, cutting edge chill out flavours from the likes of Cool Hipnoise and Deeper Sense.[34]

The use of the word 'flavours' in the CD subtitle may put us in mind of another area where we are presented with regional culture 'out of bounds'. Cafés, restaurants, bars and clubs provide specialized forums for the partaking of other cultures, and the connection between food, drink and world music has provided sustenance for a number of scholars.[35]

One aspect of this is the way compilation CDs are used to provide 'atmosphere' in public spaces. From my own experience, I recall the use of a compilation called *Café Portugal* (a compilation I own and therefore recognized) in a 'Mediterranean' restaurant in York. Hearing this disc being used, I was struck by a distinction between what might be called the 'transcriptive' and 'prescriptive' modes of such compilations. The transcriptive mode would be the attempt to 'get down' the authentic experience of, in this case, a Portuguese café so that it could be recreated on a future occasion – an aural souvenir, in other words, relying on memory. A transcriptive mode would be an attempt to create such an experience from scratch so that a listener with no experience of a Lisbon café could imagine (not remember) what it might be like. In his liner notes to *Café Portugal*, Jon Lusk suggests that it is the former process that is being aimed for; the desire is to provide an 'authentic' sample of the fado music of Lisbon. But there is also a strong prescriptive element at work, resulting from the conceit of the series of discs based on 'imaginary' cafés in which this title appears (others in the set include *Café Parisien, Café Argentina, Café Bombay,* all conveniently advertised in the CD liner). The conceit is that these cafés would provide the music contained in the CDs as background music for their listeners, as Lusk's evocation of the fictional Portuguese café makes clear: 'Paulo's ... dream of recreating the shady intimacy of one of Portugal's small fado restaurants in the middle of London had taken shape ... For the final touch, he'd

---

[33]   Demon Music group website, http://www.demonmusicgroup.co.uk/nascente (21 June 2009).

[34]   Liner notes to *Bar Lisbon: Classic & New Portuguese Flavours* (Nascente NSBARCD 020, 2008).

[35]   See David Clarke, 'Beyond the Global Imaginary: Decoding BBC Radio 3's *Late Junction*', *Radical Musicology*, 2 (2007), http://www.radical-musicology.org.uk (20 December 2007), 96 pars.

compiled a selection of his favourite fados to play while the customers tucked into their enormous meals.'[36] This is a self-aware compilation, its potential use already inscribed into its design. Hearing it played in a restaurant merely 'completes' a process that was fully intended from its inception. These are not tourist souvenirs, the 'everyday' version of ethnography for the modern middle-class holidaymaker; rather, they are blueprints for virtual journeys to imaginary destinations. They *precede* the encounter with the Other instead of providing a post-experience memento. The cities represented in the 'Café' series are 'invisible cities', akin to the reports Marco Polo brings back to Kublai Khan in Italo Calvino's book.

The notion of 'holiday records' for armchair travellers or café diners has a history. A review in a 1965 edition of *Gramophone* for a record entitled *Holiday in Portugal* relates it to the 'holiday madness' of that year, suggesting it will be popular with returning holidaymakers but deserves attention 'in its own right'.[37] The same reviewer was not so impressed four years earlier by a record by Bert Kaempfert entitled *Portugal: Fado, Wine and Sunshine*:

> I have great admiration for Bert Kaempfert's work as musician and band leader, but I always feel that any connection between his arrangement of a given song and the original version of the same song is purely coincidental. This is particularly true on the above disc. Some of the titles on the label are famous Portuguese songs such as: Tudo Isto E Fado [*sic*], Fado de Vila Franca, Rosa Engeitada and Sempre Que Lisboa Canta. Others, like Petticoats Of Portugal, and Les Lavandieres Du Portugal, are not Portuguese songs at all. However, I found great difficulty in recognizing these songs after the Kaempfert treatment, and most of them I happen to know very well indeed.[38]

This appears to be a reissue of Kaempfert's 1959 album *April in Portugal*, the liner notes of which proclaimed:

> This album comprises a collection of some of the most popular and delightful music of and about Portugal ... authentically interpreted in the lush orchestral style of Bert Kaempfert and his orchestra.
>
> To the encyclopedist Portugal is a republic in the south-west part of the Iberian peninsula – the world's largest producer of cork; according to the travel bureaus, it's a tourist mecca; to the Portuguese themselves, it's home sweet home.
>
> Songwriters, on the other hand, like to expound on the traffic-stopping appeal of The Petticoats of Portugal. They find special appeal in Les Lavandieres Du

---

[36] Jon Lusk, liner notes to *Café Portugal: Fado & Football, Ceramics & Sun* (CD, Metro METRCD126, 2004).

[37] William Gilman, 'Continental Records', *The Gramophone*, 507 (August 1965), p. 126.

[38] William Gilman, 'Continental Records', *The Gramophone*, 453 (February 1961), p. 460.

Portugal (Washerwomen of Portugal), and the elegant Fadistas (men-about-town). In essence this sparkling collection magnificently captures the flavor of April in Portugal.[39]

What is the authenticity of which these notes speak? The easy answer would seem to be that this can't be authentic fado given that it has been adapted to an orchestra (the *Gramophone* reviewer William Gilman's argument along these lines is repeated in his 1965 review of *Holiday in Portugal* when he criticizes the inclusion on that record of an orchestral version of 'Fado Hilário'). Yet, given the tendency to release orchestral versions of fados and other popular songs in Portugal, Kaempfert's recording might at least be faithful to those releases. It is also tempting to ask whether this is the same authenticity that Nat Hentoff found in the contemporaneous *Sketches of Spain*. Again, the answer seems a simple 'no'; Miles Davis had the authenticity of an 'Andalusian gypsy' and presumably no one would claim the mantle of *fadista* for Kaempfert. But Davis was also presented as a sonic innovator, as someone who added something to the tradition, and it could be argued that Kaempfert is doing the same. Perhaps what keeps the two musicians from easy comparison is Davis's role as an icon of cool and Kaempfert's as an example of what would come to be known as 'cheese' (at least until the unexpected resurgence of lounge music in the 1990s).

There is more to be mined from the liner notes to *April in Portugal*. They read as though they have been written by someone with little or no experience of Portugal; the recourse to the encyclopaedist's knowledge may be a rhetorical device, but equally sounds as though the writer has gone to an encyclopaedia for something to say about the country; this would certainly fit well with the idea of lounge music (listeners are invited at the end of the notes to 'close your eyes and listen' – the journey to be taken is one that does not require physical movement). Furthermore, there is the use of the word 'flavor' again; April in Portugal (the experience, the recording) is something to be consumed like a fine wine (it's a 'sparkling collection'). As for the music itself, two of the dominant sounds are Spanish guitar and castanets, again making the album closer to *Sketches of Spain* than might be expected. The tunes bear some resemblance to the fados on which they are based but, given the 'Spanish' resonance it is tempting to find as little knowledge about Portugal in the music as in the notes. The album takes its title from the smash hit 'April in Portugal', which started out as a song called 'Coimbra' and was recorded by Amália Rodrigues. As recounted in Chapter 1, Amália subsequently recorded the song in Italian, French and English versions. In addition to Kaempfert, Perez Prado and Liberace also recorded the tune. This song more than any other suggested the possibility of fado as exotica – a 'magic music from a far away place' to paraphrase the title of another Kaempfert album.

---

[39]   Uncredited liner notes to Bert Kaempfert & his Orchestra, *April in Portugal* (LP, Decca DL881, 1959). The album was later issued on CD by Polydor.

Authenticity

The *Gramophone* examples also serve as reminders of the attempt on the part of the critic/expert to counteract any unwanted inauthenticity with genuine knowledge, a topic with which all commentators on music must be familiar. As Simon Frith writes, 'To understand the social and discursive practices through which people respond to music as good or bad necessarily involves paying attention to what they perceive to be *in* the music.' There exist 'everyday processes of musical judgement ... in which people just know (within genres) that one artist or recording is better than another'.[40] In addition to this everyday practice, of course, the discourse is shaped by the professionalized practice of music journalism. Consumers of music look to critics for guidance in choosing which records to purchase, borrow or download. If one detects a somewhat paternalistic tone in the expert opinions printed in the mid-twentieth century reviews of *The Gramophone* and its like, it is as well to note that this is down to the inevitably shifting nuances of language over time and to the ease with which consumers are now able to become experts themselves. Many of the processes highlighted in these old magazines and newspapers are ongoing, as are the musical issues they explore. With this in mind I wish to quote from Rodney Gallop's review 'Some Records of the Portuguese Fado', which appeared in *The Gramophone* in 1931. Gallop begins his review in the following manner:

> 'I ... look to the gramophone,' wrote Constant Lambert recently in the *New Statesman*, 'to give me works which I cannot hear every week in the concert hall; in particular native music of different types which, but for the gramophone I should never hear at all. One's exasperation with the excessively drab catalogues issued recently by the gramophone companies is increased by the knowledge that the very same factory ... is at the same time producing records of the greatest interest which are destined to be immediately sent abroad, whence they can only be obtained at the expenditure of time, trouble and money... '
>
> I do not know whether Mr. Lambert had in mind, among others, the Columbia records of the Portuguese *fado*, which are all manufactured in England, but if he can prevail upon the company to sell him one or two he will be well rewarded. The services which the gramophone companies have rendered the cause of music in recording the folksongs of many and divers nations is increased when, as in this case, it is the original singers whose voices are recorded with all the subtle inflections and mannerisms of performance without which folksong loses so much of its value and charm.[41]

---

[40] Simon Frith, 'Introduction', in Frith, *Taking Popular Music Seriously: Selected Essays* (Aldershot: Ashgate, 2007), p. xi.

[41] Rodney Gallop, 'Some Records of the Portuguese Fado', *The Gramophone*, 101 (October 1931), p. 173.

It is worth noting the contemporary feel to Constant Lambert's 'problem' and Gallop's 'solution': the problem is that most of the music being released is too familiar and dull; the solution is to hear music from elsewhere. Gallop goes on to describe the Lisbon and Coimbra fado styles. What continues to be striking is the extent to which the overall thrust of this review article, if not its now dated language, might be found in a similar magazine today. Gallop closes the review with some advice that serves both as a recommendation for the reader and as a tool to distinguish Gallop's own expert opinion:

> Dr. Menano's *fados* are a bone of contention in Portugal. He composes many of them himself, and some say that he has departed too far from the genuine tradition. Others maintain that he sings *fados* as no other has ever sung them before. His are certainly the élite among *fados* (and his records are proportionately expensive), and the *Fado da Sé Velha* is one of the loveliest that I know. But the ordinary person who is ready to spend 6s. and wants representatives of both the Lisbon and Coimbra types would be best advised to buy Columbia 8102 and LL30.

Once again we witness the tension between tradition and modernity, here played out in the recordings of the Coimbran *fadista* António Menano. What I wish to highlight is the long-running nature of this process and to relate it to another motivating force in fado's evolution. This is the tension, already described in a number of the examples above, between 'commercial' and 'authentic' forms of music, which I would like to think of, following Richard Peterson's work on US country music, as a dialectic of 'hard core' and 'soft shell' styles.

In country music, the traditional and the 'commercial' are often presented as quite different entities. However, as Peterson has shown, such polarization obscures the extent to which seemingly opposing elements in country music play off each other, the fact that tradition can be (re)invented and also the fact that the 'commercial' is not necessarily inauthentic. To overcome this problem Peterson has categorized country music according to 'hard-core' and 'soft-shell' elements. These terms are used to differentiate music that remains insular in both origin and outlook from that which blends more easily with other styles of music. Peterson thus makes a distinction between the hard-core performer and audience for whom country is the music of choice (a self-contained lifestyle), and their soft-core counterparts for whom country is a choice among many others (part of a lifestyle). He contrasts numerous factors to do with appearance, song styles, vocal and instrumental techniques, public personae and audience lifestyle.

Hard-core performers tend to deliver their material in noticeably strong regional accents and ground the songs in identifiable geographic locations. Vocally, the untrained voice is foregrounded to the extent that the singer appears to be 'speaking' with rather than singing to his or her audience. In a particularly hard-core performer, the vocal is often nasal, implying rusticity, though a 'close microphone' or 'crooning' style might also be employed to increase the conversational nature of singer and listener. Soft-shell performers tend to sing in a relatively accent-free manner (quite possibly having a marked difference between their speech and singing), to foreground a trained voice and professional microphone technique and to employ studied interpretations of songs.[42]

Many performers have had a foot in each camp, straying closer to one style or another depending on the target audience. Peterson allows that an artist may well be soft-shell in some aspects of their work while being hard-core in others. The categories, as he uses them, are not supposed to be pigeonholes in which to place performers but rather tools to use in explaining a dialectic in country music involving the interplay between hard core and soft shell. For, as he points out, the commonly accepted idea of a trend in country from traditional roots to pop crossover is an inaccurate depiction of the music's history. Not only did country music become properly institutionalized as a genre only in the mid-1950s, but the thirty years prior to this – the period of Peterson's study – saw the emergent music frequently drift between styles, from 'pop' to 'traditional'. It is Peterson's contention that country music reinvents itself constantly in a cycle that sees one 'roots' style become popularized and commercialized only to be reacted against by another 'return to roots'. What these roots are is never entirely clear, for authenticity in this matter reflects the time, place and arbiters involved. It is also a 'socially agreed-upon construct in which the past is to a degree misremembered'.[43] What is vital in the 'fabrication' of authenticity is for performers to engage in 'authenticity work', the effort made to fit in with fans' expectations of authenticity.[44]

As I suggested earlier, authenticity can be further problematized by considering whether one is speaking of being true to a template or to an original vision. When I quoted Mísia's views on *novo fado*, we could see that she was also thinking in these dualistic terms; the 'anonymous river' of people were those who kept the tradition (the template) alive, while the artists (Mísia, Mariza, Amália) could range much further, stopping off to visit the 'small world' of fado when it suited their broader artistic vision. If we were to take this proposition too literally, we would be forced towards a logic that said that such artists cannot make fado. Given Mísia's descriptions of the battles she has had to fight with record companies on the one side and fado purists on the other, such logic would seem to be a misrepresentation of her position. Rather, we need to think about the possibility that the fadoscape can accommodate such contradictions providing it is peopled with performers and audiences who are committed to some form of authenticity work.

---

[42]   Richard A. Peterson, *Creating Country Music: Fabricating Authenticity* (Chicago & London: University of Chicago Press, 1997), pp. 137–55; see also Richard A. Peterson, 'The Dialectic of Hard-Core and Soft-Shell Country Music' in Cecilia Tichi (ed.), *Reading Country Music: Steel Guitars, Opry Stars and Honky-Tonk Bars* (Durham, NC, & London: Duke University Press, 1998), pp. 234–55.

[43]   Peterson, *Creating Country*, p. 5.

[44]   Ibid., pp. 211–25.

Tourists and Guests

In 2009, Mísia released a double CD entitled *Ruas* ('Streets'). The album was a concept album, or rather a two-concept album; the first disc bore the title 'Lisboarium' and the second, 'Tourists'. Mísia described the concepts in the following manner on her website (I am quoting from the English language version of the site):

LISBOARIUM (CD1)

Lisboarium was born in the Bouffes du Nord theatre in Paris, a city where I came to settle in 2005. Waiting for the Saudade to attack, I dream of Lisbon from a distance ... Lisboarium is an oniric [*sic*] and imaginary voyage through the streets of Lisbon, its neighbourhoods and its music, not only 'Fado' but also the 'Marchas de Lisboa' and the 'Morna'. The sounds of Lisbon with the richness of its mixture of cultures and its peripheral European perch. Lisboarium is a dream where everything is possible, even a French fado written by one of the greatest living poets in Portugal, Vasco Graça Moura. The ships, the seagulls, the church bells of Lisbon. Lisbon and its poets, Lisbon and its music, Lisbon and its special luminosity ...

TOURISTS (CD2)

The Tourists are artists from other streets in the world, other cultures, but I think they have a 'fado' soul. Some of them would certainly have sung the Fado if they had been born in Portugal. Through their tragic relationship with life, present in their music and in their work, through an existential exhaustion made of extreme emotion, of artistic licence and solitude. Some met with a tragic end but all are and remain alive within us. My guests belong to this tribe of artists who, like me, stare alone right into the eyes of Fate.[45]

The imaginary city is sounded at the outset of the first disc via a recording of water, boats and seagulls. Immediately after this comes Mísia's unaccompanied voice singing about Lisbon, and then the *guitarra*, *viola* and *baixo* are introduced. The commitment to Lisbon and fado is immediate, even as the lyric takes on the theme of departure. The second track is a version of Vitorino Salomé's 'Joana Rosa', a song about a Cape Verdean migrant in Lisbon. Vitorino had released a single of the song in 1986 backed by a version in Cape Verdean Kriolu and it is this version that Mísia performs. The song has notable references to the city in it, as does the next track, 'Conjugar Lisboa', a heavily toponymic lyric that aims at naming rather than narrating. The sounds of names such as Cais do Sodré, Madragoa,

---

[45] From *Misia: the Official Site*, http://www.misia-online.com/official/uk/discography. html (21 June 2009).

Graça and Amoreiras provide the main focus of the vocal. The disc continues on this journey through contemporary Lisbon, offering lyrics by Rosa Lobato Faria e Botto, Mario de Sa-Carneiro, Ary dos Santos and Fernando Pessoa. The second disc, as Mísia suggests, is a departure. The 'tourists' she encounters include the legendary flamenco singer Camarón de la Isla, Mexican singer Cuco Sanchez, Egyptian-born *chanteuse* Dalila, and rock bands Nine Inch Nails and Joy Division. The Nine Inch Nails song she covers is 'Hurt', inspired by Johnny Cash's genre-crossing recording. Mísia's version is far heavier than Cash's, veering from jagged electric guitar during the verses to full-on riffing and rock drums in the refrain, bringing the result closer to something Nico might have produced in the 1970s.

Mísia's 2009 album was international in every respect, from the scope of the material recorded on it to the promotion of it via the artist's website, where, along with multiple language versions of the site, one could also read press reports from numerous countries about Mísia. As with other music genres, websites have become powerful tools for the virtualization and globalization of fado. Considering the number of events advertised on these sites that occur outside Portugal, they arguably represent not 'Lisbon' or 'Portugal', but a deterritorialized area existing somewhere in the netherzone. For example, Cristina Branco's site (www.cristinabranco.com), when accessed in 2008, appeared to be Dutch given the contact details provided. By 2009, following a redesign coinciding with the release of *Kronos*, all contact addresses provided, including those of the designers responsible for the site, were Portuguese (though Branco's CDs continued to be released by the French branch of the appropriately named Universal company). It did not really matter from where this information was coming as long as it was there on the site.

Another phenomenon of recent years for musicians in many countries has been MySpace. Researching fado's place at the beginning of the twenty-first century, it can be a fascinating exercise to visit a number of *fadistas'* MySpace pages, not so much to find out about them (these pages remain, at the time of writing, strangely unsophisticated compared to artists' websites and blogs), but more to see their extended network of friends. Searching for information on a young singer like Raquel Tavares, it is not surprising to be directed towards her MySpace page. More unexpected, perhaps, is to find Amália's sister Celeste Rodrigues (b. 1923) among Tavares's 'friends'. A little extra research provides the most likely clue to this seemingly atypical octogenarian internet use in that Tavares and Celeste Rodrigues share the same artist management company, who have their own MySpace site and are doubtless responsible for creating those of the artists they represent. However, this does not detract from the fact that it is possible to follow a chain of links from Tavares to Rodrigues and on to Gonçalo Salgueiro, then to Ana Moura, and then to be able to choose between Beatriz da Conceição, Sérgio Godinho, Antony and The Johnsons, and the Rolling Stones.

With this mention of the Rolling Stones, we might consider the probable reason for this connection, an encounter between the group and Moura that was widely reported in the Portuguese press and also featured in the international media.

The following passage, from the travel (web)pages of *The New York Times*, is worth quoting at length as it showcases a number of the themes discussed in this chapter while also moving the discussion of 'friends' to one of collaborations and guest appearances:

> Ana Moura is in a trance. Eyes closed, head tilted back, the black-clad 28-year-old Portuguese diva lets her long, dark hair fall over half of her face as she fills the air with a soaring nocturnal lament.
>
> Next to her, two guitarists pluck the minor-key accompaniment as the singer's voice echoes through the 16th-century stone walls of Casa de Linhares ... perhaps the most atmospheric old music club in the medieval Alfama district in Lisbon.
>
> ...
>
> When night settles over the hilltop castle of São Jorge and darkness fills the cobbled streets below, the neighborhood's venerable fado houses come alive, reverberating with nocturnal music until the wee hours of the morning. Crowds fill the vaulted stone cellars. Servers deliver plates of blood sausage, traditional bacalhau (salt cod) and bottles of Portuguese red wine. And singers of all ages, mostly female, take turns distilling stories of gut-wrenching loss into glimmering crystalline melodies.
>
> Last year, Mick Jagger, Keith Richards and other members of the Rolling Stones dropped in to Casa de Linhares to witness Ms. Moura perform. (She wound up collaborating on adapted versions of Stones classics 'Brown Sugar' and 'No Expectations' for a coming album of Stones songs.)
>
> And while the origins of fado are somewhat nebulous ... its powerful emotions are clearly universal. Like midnight itself, the music is dark, mysterious and utterly enveloping.
>
> 'I once heard a lady say – she had been crying – "I cannot understand the lyrics, but I can feel it inside,"' Ms. Moura said. 'That's the thing with fado.'[46]

A number of familiar features are present in this story: the spectacular nature of the fado performance; a sense of history and tradition; the packaging and selling of an experience of which the paper's readers can partake (web addresses and phone numbers are provided); the conflation of authentic 'other' music with authentic 'other' cuisine; the romance and mystery of fado; its universal qualities that transcend language; and the stamp of importance placed on this music and this performer by a group of VIP tourists.

This latter point can also be found in a more recent story reported in the French and Portuguese press and featuring the same *fadista*. Following a concert by Ana Moura at La Cigalle in Paris, it was reported that pop star Prince had flown across the Atlantic in order to meet her and see her perform and that the two singers had

---

[46] Seth Sherwood, 'Lisbon: A House of Soulful Songs', *The New York Times*, online edn (April 20 2008), http://travel.nytimes.com/2008/04/20/travel/20lisbonnight.html (21 June 2009).

made plans to record together.[47] At the time of writing, it was unclear whether these plans would come to anything, but the earlier Stones-related project was released in 2008. It appeared as a recording led by Tim Ries, a saxophonist who had been playing with the group since 1999. Ries had released an earlier album called *The Rolling Stones Project* (2005), on which he and members of the band performed well-known Stones songs with guest musicians. For the sequel, Ries opted to reflect the sounds of some of the places the Stones passed through on their world tours. *Stones World* featured a massive list of musicians from around the world, including Ana Moura, Custódio Castelo and Jorge Fernando.[48]

In a review of the album on the *All About Jazz* website, Mark Turner wrote:

> These re-Stoned gems are truly eclectic. The Stones's [*sic*] essence is faithfully retained within the varied cultural signature – the balmy Puerto Rican clave in 'Under My Thumb,' African dialect and instruments in 'Hey Negrita,' or Manhattan swing in 'You Can't Always Get What You Want.' ... We'd love to hear Jagger belt out the old favorite 'Brown Sugar' yet fado singer, Anna Moura [*sic*] delivers quite nicely in a unique version that combines honky-tonk and Portuguese folk music.[49]

Turner describes the project in terms of its authenticity to the original versions. This is a fairly normal reaction to hearing new versions of songs with which we are already familiar. What is perhaps unusual here is that, when discussing world music, authenticity is so often directed at the 'world' musicians. Ana Moura is not to be considered as an authentic or inauthentic singer of fado but as an interpreter of 'Brown Sugar'. Whether the 'quite nicely' is meant to damn with faint praise is not clear, but the actual success of the hybrid certainly deserves questioning. What actually happens in the version of 'Brown Sugar' is an introduction played on the *guitarra* by Custódio Castelo, which is then drowned out by the saxophone and piano ushering in the familiar riff. Guitars enter then Ana Moura sings the lyric 'quite nicely' as a Rolling Stones cover song. For the next two and a half minutes, the version is entirely conventional (though with more saxophone than normal). The *guitarra* re-enters in what could be an introduction to a fado or a *guitarrada* and Moura starts to sing the lyric in Portuguese; there follows a reprise of the English language cover and the song closes with a meditative return to the *guitarra*. There is no real fusion because the various elements are presented as

---

[47]   Daniel Ribeiro, 'Prince entusiasma-se com Ana Moura em Paris', *Espresso*, online edn (15 May 2009), http://aeiou.expresso.pt/prince-entusiasma-se-com-ana-moura-em-paris=f514858 (22 June 2009).

[48]   Tim Ries, *Stones World: The Rolling Stones Project II* (2CD, Sunnyside Records SSC4104, 2008).

[49]   Mark F. Turner, review of Tim Ries, *Stones World: The Rolling Stones Project II*, *All About Jazz* website (14 October 2008), http://www.allaboutjazz.com/php/article.php?id=30593 (22 June 2009).

separate sections, none of which really gels with the other. Far more successful is the version of 'No Expectations' which Moura and Castelo also guest on. This version was the outcome of the original meeting with the Rolling Stones in Lisbon, when Moura was invited to participate in the song during the band's concert there. Moura begins the song in English, sounding much less forced than on 'Brown Sugar', possibly due to the slower tempo of this country-style song. Midway through she switches to a Portuguese lyric; Castelo's guitar, meanwhile, meshes with the other instrumentation, suggesting that a country/fado comparison might be more apt than the overused description of fado as the 'Portuguese blues'.

Mariza is another fado artist who has been involved in crossover collaborations. In addition to those on her own albums, she has recorded duets with Sting, Paulo de Carvalho and Tim, the lead singer from Xutos & Pontapés; all have been pop songs. A more 'fado-sounding' collaboration can be found, rather unexpectedly, on an album by Portuguese hip hop artist Boss AC, who has released a number of increasingly acclaimed and popular solo recordings (*Manchuka*, 1999; *Rimar Contra a Maré*, 2002; *Ritmo, Amor e Palavras*, 2005) since emerging from the mid-1990s collective Rapública.[50] His second album sampled Portuguese and Luso-African musics (Boss AC was born in Cape Verde and his mother, Ana Firmino, was a *morna* singer). 'Que Deus', on the third album, had music by Pedro Ayres Magalhães of Madredeus, featured *guitarra* and sampled excerpts of Madredeus's song 'O Pastor'. The collaboration with Mariza came on Boss AC's fourth album, *Preto no Branco* (2009), on a track called 'Alguém Me Ouviu (Mantém-Te Firme)'. It opens with Boss AC rapping over a background of solo piano (played by Tiago Machado, the artist responsible for putting 'Ó Gente da Minha Terra' to music for Mariza and for the arrangements on Liana's *fado.pt*, among numerous other projects). In hip hop conventions, this signifies the likelihood of a 'sensitive' track and this is confirmed when, forty seconds in, we hear the sound of *guitarra*, immediately followed by Mariza singing the word 'Chorei', the preterit form of the verb 'chorar' ('to cry') so loved by fado lyricists. Something in the texture of the singer's voice suggests fado even as she is accompanied by the hip hop beats which, interestingly, only appear as she begins to sing, in contrast with the beatless first verse of the rap. Mariza here performs the role so often given to female singers by male rappers, delivering the emotional centre of an otherwise 'controlled' narrative. The use of a well-known fado singer in this case serves to highlight the use of highly gendered roles in both hip hop and fado.[51]

---

[50]   I have decided not to give an account of rap and hip hop in Portugal alongside my brief overviews of other musics. This is not because there is not an interesting story to tell, but rather because, of all the musics considered here, hip hop seems the least prone to overlapping with fado. The exceptions tend to prove the rule: the use of rap in Saura's *Fados*, the *Chillfado* and *Amália Revisited* projects.

[51]   Boss AC feat. Mariza, 'Alguém Me Ouviu (Mantém-te Firme)', *Preto no Branco* (CD, Farol FAR91769, 2009).

Sam the Kid, another Portuguese hip hop artist who has used samples of fado in his work, has been reported as saying that he does so because he can be confident that no foreign musician has used them before.[52] We can detect in his claim a tactic similar to that highlighted earlier in relation to the film *Passionada*, an awareness that fado can be used as a differential when working in an overpopulated field; it fences off something that can be claimed as one's own. If the Boss AC/Mariza collaboration suggests the way in which a 'texture' of fado can be utilized without fado itself happening, it is worth mentioning a few other popular music projects not discussed in Chapter 4 which also make reference to fado 'from a distance'. The groups I briefly discuss here are also notable for bringing a number of themes covered in this chapter to the foreground, not least the question of fado's place in the contemporary popular music field.

The group A Naifa were formed by the late João Aguardela (founder of the folk-rock band the Sitiados, and of the groups Megafone and Linha da Frente and a collaborator with Paulo Bragança), Luís Varatojo (also of Linha da Frente and formerly of Peste & Sida), amateur fado singer Maria Antónia Mendes and drummer Vasco Vaz. The group released their first album, *Canções Subterrâneas*, in 2004, its soundworld a mixture of fado, rock and trip-hop textures. It opens to the sound of chatter and *guitarra*, sounding a carnivalesque note that is undermined by increasingly dissonant notes which lead the brief 'Intro' to a grinding halt. The first song proper, 'Skipping', introduces an industrial beat, over which Mendes's voice delivers a lyric about the badly surfaced streets of the suburbs to the accompaniment of Varatojo's *guitarra* and Aguardela's bass guitar. The effect is akin to the ethereal sound of Madredeus, the slightly removed female voice floating above a soundworld that references fado while being quite other. The rest of the album continues in a similar vein. Towards the end, a song entitled 'Bairro Velho' [Old Neighbourhood] provides a connection back to the city of the past. Musically, it is closer to rock but, again, the texture of the *guitarra* sounds through the 'noise' to provide a companion to a short repeated lyric that evokes 'tradition' with its mention of fishmongers' cries echoing behind the 'new avenue'.[53] A second album, *3 Minutos Antes de a Maré Encher* (2006), continued the project along similar lines, albeit with a different drummer and a slightly more ominous tone to Aguardela's bass at times. It became clear that this was very much a 'project' – encompassing a distinct soundworld, a commitment to erudite culture (the songs on the first album came with 'recommended reading' for each track), graphic design, a stage show and a website setting out the group's agenda (in both senses of the term: their aims and their touring and recording schedule). Photographs and videos of the band illustrate the odd fusion at their centre: on one side of the stage, a seated *guitarrista* as might be found in any fado performance, on the other a drum kit and roaming bass player adopting 'rock' poses. A third album followed in 2008, *Uma Inocente Inclinação Para o Mal*, but the death

---

[52] Cited in Halpern, *O Futuro da Saudade*, p. 262.
[53] A Naifa, *Canções Subterraneas* (CD, Columbia COL 517186 9, 2004).

in January 2009 of João Aguardela brought the A Naifa project to an uncertain future; the website continued as a forum for messages of condolence and plans to commemorate the late musician's achievements.

A Naifa proudly placed the following tongue-in-cheek comment from writer Miguel Esteves Cardoso on their website: 'They can't play their classical Fado guitars very well; they have a punky drummer and the Fado singer not only smiles pouts and shakes her hips, but actually seems to enjoy herself! What's become of this country?'[54] The same question might have been asked of Donna Maria, another group who have mixed *guitarra portuguesa* with rock and hip hop styles to produce a hybrid style. I do not wish to claim, in speaking about these groups, that *guitarra* is somehow 'enough' to justify a claim to fado; the instrument is obviously used in other musical forms and the fact that Donna Maria make much use of accordion shows that they are influenced by traditions other than fado. However, just as A Naifa had a 'fadistic' element to their music, so Donna Maria have made explicit connections with fado. The group, whose core is Marisa Pinto (voice), Ricardo Santos (keyboards, bass) and Miguel Ângelo Majer (percussion, samples, drum programming), appeared on the *Amália Revisited* tribute album, contributing a version of 'Foi Deus', the religiously inflected song of fate/fado/voice discussed in Chapter 3. Their sound was augmented for this track by accordion but no *guitarra*. This version, which might initially invite accusations of dubious fusion, actually yields some interesting suggestions in that it makes thinkable the notions of the sounded city and the sonic palimpsest in ways that go beyond the kind of lyrical representation I discussed in Chapter 2 – indeed, the lyric is not one that references the city. It is a modern beat-governed version of a long-established and much-covered song, setting up the notion of a text superimposed upon another. At one point the voice falls to the background (a notable factor given that it is supposed to be delivering a lyric about the power of the voice) and attains the sound that we might associate with an amplified but unclear voice heard across the cityscape. In fact, in Lisbon this sound might well be recorded fado music, heard from afar, or emanating from a stall selling fado recordings in the flea market or the Rua do Carmo (notable for the regular fixture that is the 'fado van' parked halfway up the street), or the snatched 'glimpses' of *fado vadio* emanating from the open door of a venue such as the Tasca do Chico in Bairro Alto. In this channelled voice, there seems to be an accurate representation of the sounded city. Also of interest in the recording is the way that the first time the word 'Deus' is voiced, it is broken up into electronic 'bleeps' so as to render it less powerful, a stammering impossibility of naming God; the voice subsequently falls away entirely only to return later as perhaps a vindication of the divine intervention described in the lyric.

---

[54] Miguel Esteves Cardoso, 'A Star is Born', on A Naifa's website (English version), http://www.anaifa.com/en_anaifa.html (31 January 2009).

'Foi Deus' also appeared on Donna Maria's first album *Tudo É Para Sempre...* (2004), which presented the musical template of the main core of the group augmented with *guitarra*, accordion, 'electric Indian guitar' and 'banjolim'. The songs were mostly pop-folk-fado hybrids, with a strong emphasis on beats and sampled sounds. Carlos do Carmo contributed a liner note, as did Pedro Abrunhosa and Vitorino, indicating the worlds of progressive fado, pop and folk that the group seemed to be embracing. The pop-fado-folk template is followed on the group's second album *Música Para Ser Humano* (2007), which opens with a song written by Rui Veloso and Paulo Abreu Lima, the team behind Mariza's 'Feira de Castro' (though this track contains no *guitarra* and does not attain the 'fado-ness' of 'Feira'). Raquel Tavares guests on one track, her voice containing something of the timbre of fado-singing but fado seems a more distant memory on this dance-oriented album; Tavares is accompanied by rapping and, while there are flashes of Ricardo Parreira's *guitarra*, the overall soundworld is one of beats, accordion and strings (a string quartet is used very effectively on four tracks on the album; as with Boss AC's *Preto no Branco*, there seems to be a desire to reverse the longstanding hip hop practice of sampling strings by having an actual quartet play on recordings). The album closes with a version of Max's 'Pomba Branca' a song also recorded by Max himself, Beatriz da Conceição and Cristina Branco.

A more recent project to emerge from Lisbon is the group Deolinda, named after the fictitious young woman whose stories about city life form the basis of their concept-based concerts and their album *Canção ao Lado* (2008). The majority of their songs are made using two guitars, a double bass and a singer named Ana Bacalhau. They do not use fado instrumentation, but fado appears as one of the themes in their concept and the album contains songs with titles such as 'Fado Toninho', 'O Fado Não É Mau' [Fado's Not Bad] and 'Garçonete de Casa de Fado' [Waitress from the Fado House]. Like A Naifa, the band employ a variety of media to establish their conceit, including illustration, costume, stage sets, videos and a website that contains separate Portuguese and English descriptions of the group. The English text, by Sue Steward, is not a translation of the Portuguese but a separate narrative that explains the jokes and ironical references employed by Deolinda, as well as other felicities, such as the fact that Ana Bacalhau's surname is the Portuguese word for 'salted cod' (*the* national dish) and that double bass player Zé Pedro Leitão's name translates as 'suckling pig'. The Portuguese text, meanwhile, decides to lead with the polemics of the group's relationship to fado:

> There is a long list of clichés associated with fado. For example, fado requires *guitarra portuguesa*. Deolinda do not use *guitarra portuguesa*. Fado has to be sober, serious, convincing, fatalistic and sad. Deolinda are none of these things. Fado cannot be danced to. It can be danced to with Deolinda. Finally, the *fadista* has to dress in black as if she were at her own funeral. Ana Bacalhau ... dresses in lively, happy, colourful clothes. But Deolinda are ... fado despite all this, and

￲se of what their music holds. Music that visits Portuguese popular
￲a universe that comprises José Afonso and António Variações, Sérgio
￲ho, Madredeus and the 'most *fadista* of all', Amália Rodrigues and Alfredo
￲rceneiro – and visits Greek rembetika, Mexican ranchera, samba, Hawaiian
￲nusic, jazz and pop …[55]

If this description suggests a tension between the local and the global, the group seemed keen to exploit a sense of liminality in other aspects of their marketing. The video for 'Fado Toninho' places the group in a series of liminal Lisbon spaces, areas of wasteland against backdrops of the city's office and apartment blocks.[56]

Another group who use a concept-based, ironically detached take on Portuguese music (including fado) is OqueStrada, who released an album titled *Tasca Beat: O Sonho Português* in 2009. The CD cover features the group's singer sat in a deliberately kitsch-looking *tasca* playing a *guitarra*, an ironic twenty-first-century Severa in a flowery dress and a flower in her hair. The opening song referenced Marceneiro and other *fadistas*, and the music contained *guitarra* while being other than fado. The group's website claims that the group 'is not fado' but 'celebrates fado and its fadistas' and 'is not world music' but 'celebrates the Portuguese world', and their record company's website suggests that they be thought of as a 'fado of the suburbs'.[57] While such claims can easily be dismissed as the hype of a new band marking themselves apart from their peers, they still pose the theoretically interesting question as to what a 'fado of the suburbs' might be. One thing it suggests is that, like Deolinda's 'Fado Toninho' video, there could be an appeal to both a universality (European city suburbs have a tendency to look rather similar, stripped as they are of the singular landmarks of the city centre) and local (Deolinda and OqueStrada are working in a recognizably Lisbon-centred space). At the same time, as proven by groups like Buraka Som Sistema (whose music has also been successfully exported), the sound of the suburbs (the group are named after Buraca, a suburb of Lisbon) is drawn from many sources.

---

[55]   http://www.deolinda.com.pt (22 June 2009).

[56]   Deolinda's album *Canção ao Lado* proved to be a massive success in Portugal and in 2009 World Connection began to market the album internationally, gaining exposure both in the world music media and international press.

[57]   OqueStrada website, http://www.oquestrada.com (5 May 2009); OqueStrada page, Sony BMG Portugal website, http://www.sonybmg.pt/Artista.php?IdArtista=179&Sid=de df15eb2c1c2efaa2ca39a36e664680 (5 May 2009).

Conclusion

> And Polo said: 'Every time I describe a city I am saying something about Venice.'
>
> — Italo Calvino[58]

I have been speaking throughout this book of perspectives. What happens when we take a single song and hear it presented from a number of perspectives? Let us consider the case of 'Gaivota', a fine example of *fado canção*. Written by Alexandre O'Neill, set to music by Alain Oulman and recorded by Amália Rodrigues, the song became a twentieth-century fado classic. Central to its appeal are the dense metaphorical language, the references to Lisbon, a maritime flavour, an aching longing at the heart of the refrain and Amália's deep *saudade*-drenched voice. The song was both a culmination of all those seagulls that had provided part of the poetic language of fado and an inspiration to subsequent fados. In the 1970s, Carlos do Carmo lent his jazz-influenced phrasing to the song and it was reinvented, arguably becoming as much his as it was Amália's. In 1990, Carmo's occasional collaborator Paulo de Carvalho included the song on his album *Gostar de Ti*, a pop-fado project that mixed state-of-the-art keyboard sounds with *guitarra*. In 1998, it became one of Lula Pena's 'phados', a stark, almost-not-there exercise for husky voice and guitar haunted by the ghostly presence of Amália. In 2002, Gonçalo Salgueiro used the song to show his dedication to the Amálian event and to highlight his vocal ornamentation, while Carlos do Carmo sang a more unusual version than normal to the accompaniment of Joel Xavier's inspired acoustic guitar improvisation. Margarida Bessa's version from 1995, complete with tenor saxophone, turned up on Metro's *Café Portugal* in 2004, one part of a jigsaw of songs making up that invisible city. Cristina Branco used 'Gaivota' as a homecoming at the close of her far-ranging album *Ulisses*. For the Quinteto Jazz de Lisboa and for Paula Oliveira and Bernardo Moreira it became once more an exercise in jazz singing, Oliveira providing an achingly fragile reading over Leo Tardin's minimal piano that aimed for the song's lonely heart. Then in 2009 'Gaivota' was suddenly the focal point for a Number One album by Hoje, the project featuring members of pop band The Gift, whose Nuno Gonçalves wished to prove that 'Amália is more than fado – Amália is pop'.[59]

What to make of the forty-five-year flight of this seagull? Does it tell us a story about fado or 'only' about Amália? Can the two be separated at this stage? Can 'Gaivota' tell us any more about what fado 'is'? Does its arrangement determine its fado-ness? If so, does Carlos do Carmo stop being a *fadista* when accompanied by Joel Xavier? How does fado differ from other song genres? How does the commissioning of lyrics and arrangements affect authenticity in comparison to

---

[58] Italo Calvino, *Invisible Cities*, tr. William Weaver (London: Secker & Warburg, 1974), p. 86.

[59] Amália Hoje MySpace page, http://www.myspace.com/amaliahoje (25 April 2009).

pop and rock? Was 'Gaivota' always a pop song, as Nuno Gonçalves claims? And what does it mean to claim, as Gonçalves does, that 'pop' is something bigger than 'fado'? Hoje's version soars and swoops, aiming for that place on high from where the lyric speaks and proving itself to be a song about singing, about fado and pop music: a self-aware object that escapes the drooping cadence. But which version can be said to be truer to the word and spirit of fado? The fact is that groups such as A Naifa, Donna Maria, OqueStrada and Hoje seem to climb to a place outside of fado. But this would suggest a music that 'just is' and a music that 'gets outside', which seems too neat. What are the elements within fado itself that make it seem 'natural', 'transparent'?

The answers to some of these questions can be found in the growing literature on fado that attempts to deal with issues of origins, categorization, place, paths and trajectories. Answers to a few of them can hopefully be found in this book. I am aware that my narrative has moved increasingly towards what might be called 'limit cases', examples where the point may seem to be to say what challenges fado rather than what is fado. Certainly, a lot of my examples from Chapters 4 and 5 have been accompanied by qualifiers along the lines of 'this was not (strictly) fado' and I may well be accused of writing an account of non-fado rather than fado. However, just as I suggested in the Introduction that we needed to focus on the 'is' in 'what fado is', so I believe it is necessary to focus on the 'is not'. Both terms were used by Mísia to distinguish herself and her fellow stars from the lesser-known citizens of the *fadista* world. But in doing so she was always in danger of setting up a false opposition between a tradition which has no vision other than its own self-prolongation and a series of artists who somehow 'transcend' the restrictions of the style. I would rather say that it is these very restrictions, rules, norms and reference points which allow the successful articulation of the vision and that fado is a musical practice that allows the articulation of particular artistic visions. Like a haiku artist who uses restriction to posit a singular (yet universal) vision, so a concept-minded *fadista* can use the apparatus of fado as the vehicle to drive her vision. Fado is not an accessory here; the end result would simply not work without fado. Furthermore, to discuss border-crossing is always already to discuss borders. In Chapter 4, I quoted Pedro Baptista-Bastos claiming that '*novo fado* does not exist' but it is precisely its exceptionality that marks '*novo fado*' (whatever it might be) as a symptom of 'fado'.[60]

I have made numerous references throughout the preceding chapter to a variety of media whose purpose is not primarily to deliver music (films, television, internet). My reason for doing so was not only to furnish examples for my discussion, but also to highlight the multimedia world within which any

---

[60] For a comparable discussion, see Richard Middleton's comparison of Jacques Lacan's claim '(The) Woman does not exist' with his own version, '(The) Popular music does not exist'. Richard Middleton, '*Vox Populi, Vox Dei*. Or, Imagine, I'm Losing My Religion (Hallelujah!): Musical Politics after God', in *Musical Belongings: Selected Essays* (Ashgate, 2009), pp 330–31.

discussion of contemporary culture needs to be situated. Fado is no exception. For all the literature exploring and reinforcing its historical dimension and its links with tradition, national soul and so on, there is no getting away from the fact that fado, like every other form of mass-mediated culture, exists within and is partially responsible for producing a globalized discursive space. All the musical examples provided in the preceding chapters also strengthen the argument that the mass mediation of fado has produced what fado now is. All of *this* is fado now. Fado is not now, if it ever was, the product of a nostalgic mariner. What romantic narratives fail to take account of is the production of the contemporary entity that is fado. Indeed we could go as far as to say that fado is not only an invented tradition, but is musically an invention of the phonographic era as so many other modern popular music genres are.[61]

Fado is as much the result of the various mythologies that have grown up around it in oral tradition, literature, film and sound recording as it is the cause of these mediated versions. Earlier we saw how films and sound recordings are stitched into subsequent accounts of fado and become historical documents. They contribute both to the 'imaged experience' that Agacinski discusses and the sounded experience which I have suggested as its complement. But these mediations also require considerable replenishing, with the result that a great amount of cultural work, authenticity work and fencing-off is required to feed the representational spaces back into the representation of space, not least given the latter's propensity to becoming the dominant form of experiencing space. If we consider the phenomenon of videos made by the new fado stars, for example, we become aware of the kind of effort put in to 'fabricating authenticity'. Many of these videos fetishize the city, as might be expected, but it is often a city deserted save for the singer. Camané's video for 'Sei de um Rio' (2008) shows the singer alone at night near a staircase which we assume is in a neighbourhood of Lisbon. No one else is there, which seems strange until we remember that the scene has been fenced off by a video production team, a practice with which many occupants of picturesque cities have become familiar. The city now must double as a film set, must simulate itself. Related to this need to 'manage' the recording process is the comfort and ease with which contemporary fado singers have adapted to the demands of recording. If we compare the pictures in contemporary CD liners of headphone-wearing musicians preparing and recording their parts and lyrics with the projection of Alfredo Marceneiro on his 1961 album as someone who hated the recording environment, we witness a world of difference. There, recording was associated with interference; now the machinery of recording is so visible as to become invisible. The 'sacred silence' of the world sound is as dominant as the 'invisibility' of the real city within the filmed city. The romance of the represented spares us the noise and ugliness of the real. But perhaps that is what we want

---

[61]   Tellingly, there is no discussion of a music industry in Maria Luísa Guerra's book *Fado: Alma de um Povo* (Lisbon: Imprensa Nacional-Casa da Moeda, 2003) beyond a discussion of string-makers.

from such experiences, an escape from noise, a happy giving-in to any necessary fencing-off that other professionals can do for us so that we may experience a pleasure only intimate musics can bring. The gaze of spectatorship, this view from nowhere, blanks out the possibility of recording engineers, camera crews and displaced citizens. There, for now, and for as many times as we please, is Camané, alone with the night, the city and fado, lost in memory and *saudade*.

Bibliography

Ackerman, Diane, *A Natural History of the Senses* (London: Phoenix, 1996 [1990]).

Adair, Gilbert, *Myths & Memories* (London: Fontana, 1986).

Agacinski, Sylviane, *Time Passing: Modernity and Nostalgia*, tr. Jody Gladding (New York: Columbia University Press, 2003 [2000]).

Althusser, Louis, *On Ideology* (London and New York: Verso, 1988 [1971]).

Appadurai, Arjun, *Modernity at Large: Cultural Dimensions of Globalization* (Minneapolis: University of Minnesota Press, 1996).

Appadurai, Arjun (ed.), *Globalization* (Durham, NC, and London: Duke University Press, 2001).

Augé, Marc, *Non-Places: Introduction to an Anthropology of Supermodernity*, tr. John Howe, 2nd edn (London: Verso, 2008).

Bachelard, Gaston, *The Poetics of Space*, tr. Maria Jolas (Boston: Beacon Press, 1994 [1958]).

Badiou, Alain, *Being and Event*, tr. Oliver Feltham (London and New York: Continuum, 2005 [1988]).

———, *Handbook of Inaesthetics*, tr. Alberto Toscano (Stanford: Stanford University Press, 2005 [1998]).

Baptista-Bastos, Pedro, 'O "Novo Fado" Não Existe', liner notes to *O Fado do Público* CD, vol. 5 (Lisbon: Corda Seca & Público, 2004).

Barreno, Maria Isabel, Maria Teresa Horta and Maria Velho da Costa, *New Portuguese Letters*, tr. Helen R. Lane, Faith Gillespie and Suzette Macedo (London: Victor Gollancz, 1975 [1973].

Barreto, Jorge Lima, *Musa Lusa* (Lisbon: Hugin, 1997).

Barreto, Mascarenhas, *Fado: Origens Líricas e Motivação Poética/Fado: Lyrical Origins and Poetic Motivation*, illus. José Pedro Sobreiro, parallel English text by George Dykes (Frankfurt am Main: TFM, 1994).

Barthes, Roland, *The Pleasure of the Text*, tr. Richard Miller (New York: Hill & Wang, 1975 [1973]).

———, *Image-Music-Text*, tr. Stephen Heath (London: Fontana, 1977).

———, *Camera Lucida: Reflections on Photography*, tr. Richard Howard (London: Vintage, 2000 [1980]).

———, *The Grain of the Voice: Interviews 1962–1980*, tr. Linda Coverdale (Berkeley and Los Angeles: University of California Press, 1985).

———, *The Rustle of Language*, tr. Richard Howard (Berkeley and Los Angeles: University of California Press, 1989).

———, *The Semiotic Challenge*, tr. Richard Howard (Berkeley and Los Angeles: University of California Press, 1994).

————, *Sade, Fourier, Loyola*, tr. Richard Miller (Baltimore: Johns Hopkins University Press, 1997 [1971]).

Basualdo, Carlos (ed.), *Tropicália: A Revolution in Brazilian Culture (1967–1972)* (São Paulo: Cosac Naify, 2005).

Baudelaire, Charles, *Selected Writings on Art and Artists*, tr. P.E. Charvet (Cambridge: Cambridge University Press, 1981).

Baudrillard, Jean, *Simulacra and Simulation*, tr. Sheila Faria Glaser (Ann Arbor: The University of Michigan Press, 1994).

Bauman, Zygmunt, *Globalization: The Human Consequences* (Cambridge: Polity Press, 1998).

————, *Liquid Modernity* (Cambridge: Polity, 2000).

Beckett, Samuel, *Collected Shorter Prose 1945–1980* (London: John Calder, 1984).

Bell, Aubrey F.G., *Portuguese Literature* (Oxford University Press, 1970).

Belsey, Catherine, *Culture and the Real: Theorising Cultural Criticism* (London and New York: Routledge, 2005).

Benjamin, Walter, *Illuminations*, ed. Hannah Arendt, tr. Harry Zorn (London: Pimlico, 1999).

Berne, Terry, 'Portugal's Year of Transition', *Billboard* (11 November 2000): 76.

Borges, Jorge Luis, *Labyrinths*, ed. Donald A. Yates and James E. Irby (Penguin: Harmondsworth, 1985 [1964]).

Born, Georgina and David Hesmondhalgh (eds), *Western Music and Its Others: Difference, Representation, and Appropriation in Music* (Berkeley: University of California Press, 2000).

Boyer, M. Christine, *The City of Collective Memory: Its Historical Legacy and Architectural Entertainments* (Cambridge, MA, and London: The MIT Press, 1996 [1994]).

Boym, Svetlana, *The Future of Nostalgia* (New York: Basic Books, 2001).

Brainard, Joe, *I Remember* (New York: Granary Books, 2001 [1975]).

Brito, Joaquim Pais de, (ed.), *Fado: Vozes e Sombras* (Milan/Lisbon: Electa/Museu Nacional de Etnologia, 1994).

————, 'Tudo Isto é Fado (I)', *Elo Associativo*, No. 18 (April 2001), *Collectividades* website, http://www.colectividades.org/elo/018/index.htm (accessed 2 December 2004).

————, 'Tudo Isto é Fado (II)', *Elo Associativo*, No. 19 (June 2001), *Collectividades* website, http://www.colectividades.org/elo/019/p25.html (accessed 2 December 2004).

Broughton, Simon, 'On the Tiles with Mariza', *Songlines* 47 (November 2007): 32.

————, 'Tools of the Trade: Portuguese Guitar', *Songlines*, 47 (November 2007): 48–51.

Broughton, Simon et al. (eds), *World Music: The Rough Guide,* 2nd edn, *Vol. 1: Africa, Europe and the Middle East* (London: Rough Guides Ltd, 1999).

Buck, Paul, *Lisbon: A Cultural and Literary Companion* (Oxford: Signal Books, 2002).

Burgin, Victor, *In/Different Spaces: Place and Memory in Visual Culture* (Berkeley and London: University of California Press, 1996).

Burke, Seán, *The Death and Return of the Author: Criticism and Subjectivity in Barthes, Foucault and Derrida*, 2nd edn (Edinburgh: Edinburgh University Press, 1998).

Bywater, Michael, *Lost Worlds: What Have We Lost and Where Did It Go?* (London: Granta, 2004).

Calvino, Italo, *Invisible Cities*, tr. William Weaver (London: Secker & Warburg, 1974).

————, *The Literature Machine: Essays*, tr. Patrick Creagh (London: Secker & Warburg, 1987).

Carter, Paul, *The Road to Botany Bay: An Exploration of Landscape and History* (New York: Alfred A. Knopf, 1988).

Carvalho, José Pinto de, *História do Fado* (Lisbon: Publicações Dom Quixote, 2003 [1903]).

Casey, Edward S., *Getting Back into Place: Toward a Renewed Understanding of the Place-World* (Bloomington and Indianapolis: Indiana University Press, 1993).

————, *Remembering: A Phenomenological Study*, 2nd edn (Bloomington and Indianapolis: Indiana University Press, 2000 [1987]).

Castelo-Branco, Salwa El-Shawan, '"In Search of a Lost World": An Overview of Documentation and Research on the Traditional Music of Portugal', *Yearbook for Traditional Music*, 20 (1988): 158–192.

————, *Voces de Portugal*, tr. Ana Isabel Moya and María José Morales (Madrid: Akal, 2000 [1997]).

————, 'Portugal' in *The Garland Encyclopedia of World Music*, Vol. 8, Europe, ed. T. Rice, J. Porter and C. Goertzer (London and New York: Garland, 2000), pp. 576–587.

————, '"Músicos Ocultos": Percursos dos Instrumentistas do fado', paper presented at the conference 'Fado: Percursos e Perspectivas', Lisbon, 18–21 June 2008.

————, 'Fado', in L. Macy (ed.), *Grove Music Online*, http://www.grovemusic.com.

Castelo-Branco, Salwa El-Shawan and Jorge Freitas Branco (eds), *Vozes do Povo: A Folclorização em Portugal* (Oeiras: Celta Editora, 2003).

Cave, Nick, *The Complete Lyrics 1978–2007* (London: Penguin, 2007).

Certeau, Michel de, *The Practice of Everyday Life*, tr. Steven Rendall (Berkeley and Los Angeles: University of California Press, 1984).

————, *The Writing Of History*, tr. Tom Conley (New York: Columbia University Press, 1988).

Clarke, David, 'Beyond the Global Imaginary: Decoding BBC Radio 3's *Late Junction*', *Radical Musicology*, 2 (2007), http://www.radical-musicology.org.uk, 96 pars.

Cohen, David, *Fado Português: Songs from the Soul of Portugal* (London: Wise Publications, 2003).

Colvin, Michael, 'Gabriel de Oliveira's "Há Festa na Mouraria" and the *Fado Novo*'s Criticism of the Estado Novo's Demolition of the Baixa Mouraria', *Portuguese Studies*, 20 (2004): 134–51.

———, *The Reconstruction of Lisbon: Severa's Legacy and the Fado's Rewriting of Urban History* (Lewisburg: Bucknell University Press, 2008).

Contador, António Concorda and Emanuel Lemos Ferreira, *Ritmo & Poesia: Os Caminhos do Rap* (Lisbon: Assírio & Alvim, 1997).

Cook, Manuela, 'The Woman in Portuguese Fado-singing', *International Journal of Iberian Studies*, 16/1 (2003): 19–32.

Costa, Dalila L. Pereira da and Pinharanda Gomes, *Introdução à Saudade: Antologia Teórica e Aproximação Crítica* (Porto: Lello & Irmão, 1976).

Coverley, Merlin, *Psychogeography* (Harpenden: Pocket Essentials, 2006).

Crespo, Ángel, *Lisboa Mítica e Literária* (Lisbon: Livros Horizonte, 1990 [1987]).

Dantas, Júlio, *A Severa (Peça em Quatro Actos)*, 4th edn (Lisbon: Sociedade Editora Portugal-Brasil, c. 1920).

Derrida, Jacques, *Dissemination*, tr. Barbara Johnson (London and New York: Continuum, 2004 [1972]).

———, *Specters of Marx: The State of the Debt, the Work of Mourning, and the New International*, tr. Peggy Kamuf (New York and London: Routledge, 1994).

Dias, Maria Tavares, *Lisboa Desaparecida*, 9 vols (Lisbon: Quimera, 1987–2007).

Dolar, Mladen, *A Voice and Nothing More* (Cambridge, MA, and London: The MIT Press, 2006).

Eco, Umberto, *Mouse or Rat?: Translation as Negotiation* (London: Weidenfield & Nicolson, 2003).

Eisenberg, Evan, *The Recording Angel: Music, Records and Culture from Aristotle to Zappa* (London: Picador, 1988 [1987]).

Elliott, Richard, 'Loss, Memory and Nostalgia in Popular Song: Thematic Aspects and Theoretical Approaches', PhD thesis (Newcastle University, 2008).

———, 'Popular Music and/as Event: Subjectivity, Love and Fidelity in the Aftermath of Rock 'n' Roll', *Radical Musicology*, 3 (2008), http://www.radical-musicology.org.uk, 60 pars.

Feld, Steven, 'A Sweet Lullaby for World Music', in Arjun Appadurai (ed.), *Globalization* (Durham and London: Duke University Press, 2001), pp. 189–216.

Fradique, Teresa, *Fixar o Movimento: Representações da Música Rap em Portugal* (Lisbon: Dom Quixote, 2003).

Freitas, Frederico de, 'O Fado, Canção da Cidade de Lisboa: Suas Origens e Evolução', *Língua e Cultura*, 3/3 (1973): 325–337.

Freud, Sigmund, *The Standard Edition of the Complete Psychological Works of Sigmund Freud*, Vol. 14, tr. and ed. James Strachey (London: The Hogarth Press, 1957).

————, *The Standard Edition of the Complete Psychological Works of Sigmund Freud*, Vol. 12, tr. and ed. James Strachey (London: The Hogarth Press, 1958).

Frith, Simon (ed.), *World Music, Politics and Social Change: Papers from the International Association for the Study of Popular Music* (Manchester and New York: Manchester University Press, 1991 [1989]).

Frith, Simon, *Performing Rites: On the Value of Popular Music* (Oxford: Oxford University Press, 1996).

————, *Taking Popular Music Seriously: Selected Essays* (Aldershot: Ashgate, 2007).

Gallop, Rodney, 'Some Records of the Portuguese Fado', *The Gramophone* (October 1931), 173.

————, 'The Fado: The Portuguese Song of Fate', *The Musical Quarterly*, 19/2 (1933): 199–213.

————, *Portugal: A Book of Folk-Ways* (Cambridge University Press, 1961 [1936]).

Geertz, Clifford, *Works and Lives: The Anthropologist as Author* (Stanford: Stanford University Press, 1988).

Gibson, William, *Neuromancer* (London: Harper Collins, 1995 [1984]).

Gissing, George, *The Private Papers of Henry Ryecroft* (London: Archibald Constable & Co., 1904).

Gregory, Derek, *Geographical Imaginations* (Cambridge, MA, and Oxford: Blackwell, 1994).

Guerra, Maria Luísa, *Fado: Alma de um Povo* (Lisbon: Imprensa Nacional-Casa da Moeda, 2003).

Halbwachs, Maurice, *On Collective Memory*, ed. and tr. Lewis A. Coser (Chicago and London: The University of Chicago Press, 1992).

Halpern, Manuel, *O Futuro da Saudade: O Novo Fado e os Novos Fadistas* (Lisbon: Publicações Dom Quixote, 2004).

Harvey, David, *The Condition of Postmodernity* (Cambridge, MA, and Oxford: Blackwell, 1990).

Heelas, Paul, Scott Lash and Paul Morris (eds), *Detraditionalization: Critical Reflections on Authority and Identity* (Cambridge, MA, and Oxford: Blackwell, 1996).

Hitchens, Peter, *The Abolition of Britain: The British Cultural Revolution from Lady Chatterly to Tony Blair* (London: Quartet, 1999).

Holton, Kimberly DaCosta, 'Bearing Material Witness to Musical Sound: Fado's L94 Museum Debut', *Luso-Brazilian Review*, 39/2 (2002): 107–23.

Huyssen, Andreas, *Twilight Memories: Marking Time in a Culture of Amnesia* (New York and London: Routledge, 1995.

————, *Present Pasts: Urban Palimpsests and the Politics of Memory* (Stanford: Stanford University Press, 2003).

Klibansky, Raymond, Erwin Panofsky and Fritx Saxl, *Saturn and Melancholy: Studies in the History of Natural Philospohy, Religion, and Art* (London: Nelson, 1964).

Kristeva, Julia, *Black Sun: Depression and Melancholia* (New York: Columbia University Press, 1989).

Kritzman, Lawrence D., 'Foreword: In Remembrance of Things French', in Pierre Nora, *Realms of Memory: Rethinking the French Past Vol. 1: Conflicts and Divisions*, ed. Lawrence D. Kritzman, tr. Arthur Goldhammer (New York: Columbia University Press, 1996), pp. ix–xiv.

Lacan, Jacques. *The Seminar of Jacques Lacan, Book XI: The Four Fundamentals of Psychoanalysis*, tr. Alan Sheridan (New York and London: Norton, 1981 [1977]).

———, *The Seminar, Book VII: The Ethics of Psychoanalysis, 1959–1960*, tr. Dennis Porter (London: Routledge, 1992 [1986]).

Lains, Leonor, 'Amália Rodrigues', tr. John D. Godinho, *Vidas Lusofonos* website, http://www.vidaslusofonas.pt/amalia_rodrigues2.htm (accessed 30 March 2005).

Larkin, Colin (ed.), *The Virgin Encyclopedia of Popular Music: Concise Fourth Edition* (London: Virgin / Brentwood: Muze, 2002).

Lefebvre, Henri, *The Production of Space*, tr. D. Nicholson-Smith (Oxford and Cambridge, MA: Blackwell, 1991).

———, *Writings On Cities*, ed. and tr. Eleonore Kofman and Elizabeth Lebas (Oxford and Cambridge, MA: Blackwell, 1996).

———, *Rhythmanalysis: Space, Time and Everyday Life*, tr. Stuart Elden and Gerald Moore (London and New York: Continuum, 2004).

Lévi-Strauss, Claude, *Structural Anthropology*, tr. Claire Jacobson and Brooke Grundfest Schoepf (New York: Basic Books, 1963).

Lipsitz, George, *Dangerous Crossroads: Popular Music, Postmodernism and the Poetics of Place* (London and New York: Verso, 1994).

Lopes-Graça, Fernando, *Disto e Daquilo* (Lisbon: Cosmos, 1973).

Lorca, Federico García, *In Search of Duende*, tr. Norman Thomas di Giovanni et al. (New York: New Directions, 1998 [1955]).

Lusk, Jon, 'Fado Figures', *fRoots* website, http://www.frootsmag.com/content/features/mariza/page04.html (accessed 18 March 2005).

Lynch, Kevin, *The Image of the City* (Cambridge, MA, and London: The MIT Press, 1996 [1960]).

Magalhães, Fernando, 'Uma Voz na Voz dos Outros', *Público*, Cultura (8 October 2000): 34.

Manuel, Peter, *Popular Musics of the Non-Western World: An Introductory Survey* (New York and Oxford: Oxford University Press, 1988).

McGowan, Chris and Ricardo Pessanha, *The Brazilian Sound: Samba, Bossa Nova, and the Popular Music of Brazil* (Philadelphia: Temple University Press, 1998).

Middleton, Richard, *Voicing the Popular: On the Subjects of Popular Music* (New York and London: Routledge, 2006).

———— '*Vox Populi, Vox Dei*. Or, Imagine, I'm Losing My Religion (Hallelujah!): Musical Politics after God', in *Musical Belongings: Selected Essays* (Ashgate, 2009), pp. 329–52.

Mira, Alberto (ed.), *The Cinema of Spain and Portugal* (London and New York: Wallflower Press, 2005).

Mitchell, Timothy, *Flamenco Deep Song* (New Haven: Yale University Press, 1994).

Monteiro, George, 'Poe/Pessoa', *Comparative Literature*, 40/2 (Spring 1988): 134–49.

Motte, Warren, 'The Work of Mourning', *Yale French Studies*, 105, *Pereckonings: Reading Georges Perec* (2004): 56–71.

Moura, Vasco Graça, *Mais Fados & Companhia* (Lisbon: Corda Seca & Público, n.d.).

Murphy, John P. *Music in Brazil: Experiencing Music, Expressing Culture* (New York: Oxford University Press, 2006).

Nagel, Thomas, *The View from Nowhere* (New York and Oxford: Oxford University Press, 1986).

Nora, Pierre (ed.), *Les Lieux de Mémoire*, 3 vols. (Paris: Éditions Gallimard, 1997).

———— (dir.), *Realms of Memory: Rethinking the French Past Vol. 1: Conflicts and Divisions*, ed. Lawrence D. Kritzman, tr. Arthur Goldhammer (New York: Columbia University Press, 1996).

———— (ed.), *Rethinking France: Les Lieux de Mémoire Vol. 1 : The State*, tr. Mary Trouille (Chicago and London: The Univerisity of Chicago Press, 2001).

O'Brien, Geoffrey, *The Browser's Ecstasy: A Meditation on Reading* (Washington: Counterpoint, 2000).

————, *Sonata for Jukebox: Pop Music, Memory, and the Imagined Life* (New York: Counterpoint, 2004).

Osório, António, *A Mitologia Fadista* (Lisbon: Livros Horizonte, 1974).

Perec, Georges, *Je me souviens* (Paris: Hachette, 1978).

————, *Species of Spaces and Other Pieces*, ed. and tr. John Sturrock, rev. edn (London: Penguin, 1999).

Perrone, Charles A. and Christopher Dunn (eds), *Brazilian Music & Globalization* (New York and London: Routledge, 2001).

Pessoa, Fernando, *Obras Completas Vol. 8: Poesias Inéditas de Fernando Pessoa (1919–1930)* (Lisbon: Edições Ática, 1963).

————, *Obras Completas Vol. 9: Quadras ao Gosto Popular*, ed. Georg Rudolf Lind and Jacinto do Prado Coelho (Lisbon: Edições Ática, 1965).

————, *Obras Completas Vol. 1: Poesias de Fernando Pessoa*, 12th edn (Lisbon: Edições Ática, 1987).

————, *Fernando Pessoa & Co.: Selected Poems*, ed. and tr. Richard Zenith (New York: Grove Press, 1998).

————, *The Book of Disquiet*, tr. Richard Zenith (Harmondsworth: Penguin, 2001).

————, *The Selected Prose*, ed. and tr. Richard Zenith (New York: Grove Press, 2001).

————, *A Little Larger Than the Entire Universe: Selected Poems*, ed. and tr. Richard Zenith (London: Penguin, 2006).

————, *Lisbon: What the Tourist Should See* (Exeter: Shearsman Books, 2008).

Peterson, Richard A., 'Why 1955? Explaining the Advent of Rock Music', *Popular Music*, 9/1 (1990): 97–116.

————, *Creating Country Music: Fabricating Authenticity* (Chicago and London: University of Chicago Press, 1997).

————, 'The Dialectic of Hard-Core and Soft-Shell Country Music', in Cecilia Tichi (ed.), *Reading Country Music: Steel Guitars, Opry Stars and Honky-Tonk Bars* (Durham and London: Duke University Press, 1998), pp. 234–55.

Pimentel, Alberto, *A Triste Canção do Sul: Subsídios para a História do Fado* (Lisbon: Livraria Central de Gomes de Carvalho, n.d. [1904]).

Poe, Edgar Allan, *The Fall of the House of Usher and Other Writings*, ed. David Galloway (Harmondsworth: Penguin, 1986).

Pons, Hervé, *Os Fados de Mísia: Conversas com Hervé Pons*, tr. António Carlos Carvalho (Lisbon: Oceanos, 2007).

Pred, Alan, *Lost Words and Lost Worlds: Modernity and the Language of Everyday Life in Late Nineteenth-Century Stockholm* (Cambridge: Cambridge University Press, 1990).

Proust, Marcel, *In Search of Lost Time*, ed. Christopher Prendergast, tr. Lydia Davis et al., 6 vols (London: Penguin, 2002).

Pujol, Sergio, *Rock y Dictadura: Crónica de una Generación (1976–1983)* (Buenos Aires: Emecé Editores, 2005).

Raban, Jonathan, *Soft City* (London: Collins Harvill, 1988 [1974]).

Raposo, Edurado M., *Canto de Intervenção 1960–1974* (Lisbon: Público, 2007).

Régio, José, *Fado* (Lisbon: Portugal Editora, 1969 [1941]).

Resina, Joan Ramon (ed.), *Iberian Cities* (New York and London: Routledge, 2001).

Ricoeur, Paul, *Memory, History, Forgetting*, tr. Kathleen Blamey and David Pellauer (Chicago and London: University of Chicago Press, 2004).

Rilke, Rainer Maria, *The Notebooks of Malte Laurids Brigge*, tr. Stephen Mitchell (London: Picador, 1988).

Robinson, Richard, *Contemporary Portugal: A History* (London: George Allen & Unwin, 1979).

Rodrigues, Amália, *Versos* (Lisbon: Cotovia 2003 [1997]).

Rodrigues, Cláudia, 'Entrevista com Filipe La Féria', *Terranatal* website, http://www.terranatal.com/notic/entrev/e_filfer_10.htm (accessed 18 March 2005).

Roubard, Jacques, *The Great Fire of London: A Story with Interpolations and Bifurcations*, tr. Dominic Di Bernardi (Elmwood Park, IL: Dalkey Archive Press, 1992 [1989]).

Saer, Juan José, *The Witness*, tr. Margaret Jull Costa (London: Serpent's Tail, 1990 [1983]).

Salecl, Renata and Slavoj Žižek (eds), *Gaze and Voice as Love Objects* (Durham and London: Duke University Press, 1996).

Samuel, Raphael, *Theatres of Memory Volume 1: Past and Present in Contemporary Culture*. (London and New York: Verso, 1996 [1994]).

———, *Island Stories: Unravelling Britain (Theatres of Memory, Volume II)*, ed. Alison Light, Sally Alexander and Gareth Stedman Jones (London and New York: Verso, 1998).

Santos, Vítor Pavão dos, *Amália: Uma Biografia*, 2nd edn (Lisbon: Editorial Presença, 2005).

Saraiva, José Hermano, *Portugal: A Companion History*, ed. Ian Robertson and L.C. Taylor (Manchester: Carcanet, 1997).

Saramago, José, *The Year of the Death of Ricardo Reis*, tr. Giovanni Pontiero (London: Harvill, 1992 [1984]).

Sarlo, Beatriz, *Scenes from Postmodern Life*, tr. Jon Beasley-Murray (Minneapolis and London: University of Minnesota Press, 2001 [1994]).

Scruton, Roger, *England: An Elegy* (London: Chatto & Windus, 2000).

Shaw, Lisa, 'A Canção de Lisboa / Song of Lisbon', in Alberto Mira (ed.), *The Cinema of Spain and Portugal* (London and New York: Wallflower Press, 2005), pp. 23–9.

Sherwood, Seth, 'Lisbon: A House of Soulful Songs', *The New York Times*, online edn (April 20 2008), http://travel.nytimes.com/2008/04/20/travel/20lisbonnight.html (accessed 21 June 2009).

Sinclair, Iain, *White Chappell, Scarlet Tracings* (London: Paladin, 1988).

———, *Lights out for the Territory* (London: Granta, 1997).

———, *Lud Heat and Suicide Bridge* (London: Granta, 1998).

——— (ed.), *London: City of Disappearances* (London: Hamish Hamilton, 2006).

Small, Christopher, *Musicking: The Meanings of Performing and Listening* (Middletown: Wesleyan University Press, 1998).

Soja, Edward W., *Postmodern Geographies: The Reassertion of Space in Critical Social Theory* (London and New York: Verso, 1989).

———, *Thirdspace: Journeys to Los Angeles and Other Real-and-Imagined Places* (Cambridge, MA, and Oxford: Blackwell, 1996).

———, *Postmetropolis: Critical Studies of Cities and Regions* (Malden, MA, and Oxford: Blackwell, 2000).

Solnit, Rebecca, *Wanderlust: A History of Walking* (London: Verso, 2002 [2000]).

———, *A Field Guide to Getting Lost* (Edinburgh: Canongate, 2006 [2005].

Sontag, Susan, *Regarding the Pain of Others* (New York: Farrar, Strauss & Giroux, 2003).

Sousa, Avelino de, *O Fado e os Seus Censores* (Lisbon: self-published, 1912).

Stallybrass, Peter and Allon White, *The Politics and Poetics of Transgression* (London: Methuen, 1986).

Sucena, Eduardo, *Lisboa, o Fado e os Fadistas*, 2nd edn (Lisbon: Vega, 2002).

Sweeney, Philip, 'The Billboard Report', *Billboard* (8 January 1994): 2.

Tamen, Miguel, 'A Walk about Lisbon', in Joan Ramon Resina (ed.), *Iberian Cities* (New York and London: Routledge, 2001), 33–40.

Taylor, Mark C. and Dietrich Christian Lammerts, *Grave Matters* (London: Reaktion Books, 2002).

Taylor, Timothy D., *Global Pop: World Music, World Markets* (New York and London: Routledge, 1997).

Teles, Viriato, *Carlos do Carmo: Do Fado e do Mundo* (Lisbon: Garrido Editores, 2003).

Tinhorão, José Ramos, *Fado: Dança do Brasil, Cantar de Lisboa* (Lisbon: Caminho, 1994).

Toop, David, *Haunted Weather: Music, Silence and Memory* (London: Serpent's Tail, 2004).

Tuan, Yi-Fu, *Space and Place: The Perspective of Experience* (Minneapolis and London: University of Minnesota Press, 2008 [1977]).

Turner, Mark F., review of Tim Ries, *Stones World: The Rolling Stones project II*, All About Jazz website (14 October 2008), http://www.allaboutjazz.com/php/ article.php?id=30593 (accessed 22 June 2009).

Unamuno, Miguel de, *Escritos de Unamuno sobre Portugal*, ed. Ángel Marcos de Dios (Paris: Fundação Calouste Gulbenkian, 1985).

Vale de Almeida, Miguel, 'Marialvismo: A Portuguese Moral Discourse on Masculinity, Social Hierarchy and Nationhood in the Transition to Modernity' (1995), Série Antropologia, No. 184, Departamento de Antropologia, Universidade de Brasília, http://www.unb.br/ics/dan/Serie184empdf.pdf.

Vernon, Paul, *A History of the Portuguese Fado* (Aldershot: Ashgate, 1998).

Vianna, Hermano, *The Mystery of Samba: Popular Music & National Identity in Brazil*, ed. and tr. John Charles Chasteen (Chapel Hill: University of North Carolina Press, 1999).

Vieira, Nelson H. (ed.), *Roads to Today's Portugal: Essays on Contemporary Portuguese Literature, Art and Culture* (Providence: Gávea-Brown, 1983).

Vieira Nery, Rui, *Para uma História do Fado* (Lisbon: Corda Seca & Público, 2004).

Yates, Frances A., *The Art of Memory* (London: Routledge and Kegan Paul, 1966).

Zenith, Richard, 'The Geographer's Manual: The Place of Place in António Lobo Antunes', *Portuguese Literary & Cultural Studies*, Vol. 15/16 (2008), University of Massachusetts Dartmouth website, http://www.plcs.umassd.edu (accessed 1 June 2009).

Žižek, Slavoj, *The Sublime Object of Ideology* (London and New York: Verso, 1989).

————, 'Superego by Default', in *Metastases of Enjoyment: On Women and Causality* (London and New York: Verso, 2005 [1994]), pp. 54–85.

————, '"I Hear You With My Eyes"; or, The Invisible Master', in Renata Salecl & Slavoj Žižek (eds), *Gaze and Voice as Love Objects* (Durham, NC, and London: Duke University Press, 1996), pp. 54–85.

Discography

All items listed are CDs unless otherwise indicated. Dates in square brackets indicate original release date if different to the edition listed. Various Artist compilations are listed separately following the A-Z artist list.

Abou-Khalil, Rabih, *Em Português* (Enja ENJ-95202, 2008).
Afonso, José, *Baladas e Canções* (Valentim de Carvalho/EMI 724383661725, 1996 [1967]).
———, *Cantigas do Maio* (Movieplay Portuguesa JA 8004, 1996 [1971]).
———, *Fados de Coimbra* (Movieplay Portuguesa JA 8011, 1996 [1981]).
Ala dos Namorados, *Por Minha Dama* (EMI 724383341122, 1995).
Amendoeira, Joana, *Olhos Garotos* (Espacial 3200224, 1998).
———, *Joana Amendoeira.* (Companhia Nacional de Música CNM103, 2003).
———, *Ao Vivo em Lisboa* (Companhia Nacional de Música CNM 158, 2005).
———, *Magia do Fado* (Espacial 3200783, 2006). Note: This disc resissues the album *Aquela Rua* (2000) and adds seven songs from *Olhos Garotos*.
———, *À Flor da Pele* (HM Música HM001CD, 2006).
Arnauth, Mafalda, *Esta Voz Que Me Atravessa* (Virgin/EMI-Valentim de Carvalho 724353155728, 2001).
———, *Encantamento* (Virgin/EMI-Valentim de Carvalho 724358460827, 2003).
———, *Diário* (Polydor/Universal 9874943, 2005).
———, *Flor de Fado* (Polydor/Universal 602517836044, 2008).
Bobone, Maria Ana, *Senhora da Lapa* (MA Recordings M046A, 1998).
———, *Nome do Mar* (Vachier & Associados/Farol FAR51650, 2006).
Boss AC, *Preto no Branco* (Farol FAR 91769, 2009).
Bragança, Paulo, *Amai* (Luaka Bop/Virgin 724384903725, 1996 [1994]).
———, *Lua Semi-Nua* (Membran/Ovação 222297-207, 2004).
Branco, Cristina, *Murmúrios* (CD, Music & Words, MWCD4023,1999).
———, *Post-Scriptum* (L'Empreinte Digital/Nocturne ED 13131, 2000).
———, *Corpo Iluminado* (EmArcy/Universal France 014 151-2, 2001).
———, *O Descobridor: Cristina Branco Canta Slauerhoff* (EmArcy/Universal France 472 281-2, 2002).
———, *Sensus* (Universal Classics France 067 168-2, 2003).
———, *Ulisses* (EmArcy/Universal France 0602498208984, 2005).
———, *Live* (EmArcy/Universal France 9843206, 2006).
———, *Abril* (EmArcy/Universal France 0600753022436, 2007).
———, *Kronos* (EmArcy/Universal France 00289480199-60, 2009).
Branco, José Mário, *Margem de Certa Maneira* (Valentim de Carvalho 724383565627, 1996 [1972]).

————, *Mudam-se as Vontades* (Valentim de Carvalho/EMI 724383565528, 1998 [1971]).

Brigada Victor Jara, *Marcha dos Foliões* (Valentim de Carvalho/EMI 724349593329, 1983).

————, *Contraluz* (Columbia/Sony Portugal COL 4779112, 1984).

Buraka Som Sistema, *Black Diamond* (Fabric B001XNL97Q, 2009 [2008]).

Camané, *Uma Noite de Fados* (Valentim de Carvalho/EMI 72438329052, 1995).

————, *Na Linha da Vida* (Valentim de Carvalho/EMI 724349383227, 1998).

————, *Esta Coisa de Alma* (EMI 7243525001 2, 2000).

————, *Pelo Dia Dentro* (EMI7243536798 2, 2001).

————, *Ao Vivo* (Valentim de Carvalho/Capitol/EMI 724359648828, 2003).

————, *The Art of Camané: The Prince of Fado* (Hemisphere/EMI 724359434520, 2004).

————, *Sempre de Mim* (EMI Portugal 5099 9 214675 2 3, 2008).

Carmo, Carlos do, *Um Homem na Cidade* (Philips 5189182, 1995 [1977]).

————, *Álbum* (Universal 066934-2, 2003 [1980]).

————, *Um Homem no País* (Philips/Polygram 8146582, 1983).

————, *Mais do que Amor é Amar* (Philips/Polygram 532340-2, 1996 [1986]).

————, *Clássicos da Renascença* (Movieplay MOV 31.004, 2000).

Carmo, Lucília do, *Recordações* (EMI/Valentim de Carvalho 724349528529, nd [1971]).

Carmo, Lucília do and Carlos do Carmo, *Fado Lisboa: An Evening at the 'Faia'* (Polygram/Universal 066 933-2, 2003 [1974]).

Carvalho, Paulo de, *Terras da Lua Cheia* (CBS Portugal 4604272, 1987).

————, *Gostar de Ti* (CBS Portugal 4674382, 1990).

————, *Cores do Fado* (Som Livre SL06602, 2004).

————, *Antologia 71/85* (Universal Portugal 172339-4, 2007).

————, *Do Amor* (Farol FAR 81738, 2008).

Conceição, Beatriz da, *Clássicos da Renascença* (Movieplay MOV 31.021, 2000).

Davis, Miles, *Sketches of Spain* (Columbia/Legacy CK 65142, 1997 [1960]).

Deolinda, *Canção ao Lado* (iPlay 12892, 2008; subsequently released internationally by World Connection WC43084, 2009).

Donna Maria, *Tudo é para Sempre.* (Different World/EMI Portugal DW50006CDDVD, 2004).

————, *Música para ser Humano* (Capitol/EMI 5099951592820, 2007).

Duarte, Aldina, *Apenas o Amor* (Valentim de Carvalho/Virgin/EMI 724359828329, 2004).

————, *Crua* (Capitol/EMI Portugal 094635348729, 2006).

————, *Mulheres ao Espelho* (Roda-La Music RLM0001, 2008).

Duarte, Anabela, *Lishbunah* (Polygram, 1988).

Fé, Maria da, *Clássicos da Renascença* (Movieplay 31.009, 2000).

————, *Memórias do Fado* (Ovação 375CD1, 2003).

Fernando, Jorge, *Velho Fado* (Times Square/World Connection TSQD 9017, 2001).

Godinho, Sérgio, *Pré-Histórias* (Universal Portugal 2001 848103-2, 2001 [1972]).

Guerreiro, Katia, *Fado Maior* (Ocarina OCA 002, 2001).

———, *Nas Mãos do Fado* (Ocarina OCA 007, 2003).

———, *Tudo ou Nada* (Som Livre SL 8402, 2005).

———, *Fado* (KG Produções/Sony 88697434422, 2008).

Haden, Charlie, *'Closeness': Duets* (A&M/Polygram 397 000-2, 1989 [1976]).

———, *The Ballad of the Fallen* (ECM 1248, 1983).

Haden, Charlie and Carlos Paredes, *Dialogues* (Polydor France 843445-2, 1990).

Humanos, *Humanos* (EMI/Valentim de Carvalho 724356065222, 2004).

Kaempfert and his Orchestra, Bert, *April in Portugal* (LP, Decca DL881, 1959).

Kyao, Rão, *Fado Bailado* (Vertigo/Polygram 810457-2, 1983).

———, *Viva ao Fado* (Polygram, 1996).

———, *Fado Virado a Nascente* (Universal Portugal 016 354-2, 2001).

Laíns, Ana, *Sentidos* (Different World DW50018CD, 2006).

Liana, *fado.pt* (Different World/Valentim de Carvalho/EMI DW50003CD, 2004).

Madredeus, *Existir* (Valentim de Carvalho/EMI 7946472, 1990).

———, *Ainda: Original Motion Picture Soundtrack from the Film 'Lisbon Story'* (EMI/Valentim de Carvalho 724383263622, 1995).

———, *Antologia* (EMI/Valentim de Carvalho 724352594528, 2000).

Marceneiro, Alfredo [Alfredo Duarte], *The Fabulous Marceneiro* (Valentim de Carvalho/EMI 724349526624, 1997 [1961]).

———, *O Melhor de Alfredo Marceneiro* (Valentim de Carvalho/EMI 077779176823, 1988).

———, *Biografias do Fado* (Valentim de Carvalho/EMI 72438592822, 1997).

Maria Teresa, *O Mar ...* (Le Chant du Monde 2741144, 2003 [2002]).

Mário & Lundum, *(H)á Fado!* (Valentim de Carvalho/EMI 724386075123, 2005).

Mariza, *Fado em Mim* [bonus disc version] (World Connection 43038, 2002 [2001]).

———, *Fado Curvo* (World Connection/Valentim de Carvalho/EMI 724358423723, 2003).

———, *Transparente* (World Connection/Valentim de Carvalho/Capitol/EMI 724347764622, 2005).

———, *Concerto em Lisboa* (Capitol/World Connection/EMI Portugal 094637788622, 2006).

———, *Terra* (Capitol/World Connection/EMI Portugal 5099922942326, 2008).

Martins, Carlos com Orquestra, *Do Outro Lado* (Som Livre SL 8802, 2006).

Mísia, *Mísia* (Valentim de Carvalho/EMI 077779655823, 1991).

———, *Fado*, (Ariola/BMG 74321165622, 1993).

———, *Tanto Menos Tanto Mais* (Ariola/BMG 74321307872, 1995).

———, *Garras dos Sentidos* (Erato/Warner 3984227312, 1998).

———, *Ritual* (Erato/Warner 8573858182, 2001).

———, *Canto* (Warner Jazz France 2564608952, 2003).

————, *Drama Box* (Tropical Music 68.850, 2005).

————, *Ruas* (AZ/Universal France 5316562, 2009).

Mler Ife Dada, *Coisas Que Fascinam* (Polygram Portugal 831 984-2, 1987).

————, *Espírito Invisível* (Polydor 841272-2, 1998 [1989]).

Moreira, Bernardo, *Ao Paredes Confesso* (EmArcy/Universal Portugal 066890-2, 2003).

Morricone, Ennio and Dulce Pontes, *Focus* (Universal Netherlands 980 829-1, 2003).

Moura, Ana, *Guarda-me a Vida na Mão* (Mercury/Universal Portugal 067 923-2, 2003).

————, *Aconteceu* (Mercury/Universal Portugal 9868877, 2004).

————, *Para Além da Saudade* (Mercury/Universal Portugal 060251733975, 2007).

Moutinho, Helder, *Luz de Lisboa* (Ocarina OCA 010, 2004).

————, *Que Fado É Este Que Trago?* (HM Música/Farol FAR81762, 2008).

Naifa, A, *Canções Subterraneas* (Columbia COL 517186 9, 2004).

————, *3 Minutos Antes de a Maré Encher* (Zona Música ZM00179, 2006).

————, *Uma Inocente Inclinação para o Mal* (Lisboa Records LX003, 2008).

Oliveira, Adriano Correia de, *Trova do Vento Que Passa: Adriano Canta Manuel Alegre* (Movieplay MOV 35.006, 1994).

Oliveira, Paula and Bernardo Moreira, *Lisboa que Adormece* (Universal Portugal 9870260, 2005).

————, *Fado Roubado* (Polydor/Universal Portugal 1748860, 2007).

OqueStrada, *Tasca Beat: O Sonho Português* (Sony Portugal 88697522282, 2009).

Pacheco, Mário, *Clube de Fado* (World Connection WC 43062, 2006).

Paredes, Carlos, *Movimento Perpétuo* (Valentim de Carvalho/EMI 724359357621, 2003 [1971]).

Pena, Lula, *[phados]* (Carbon 7 C7-032, 1998).

Pires, Carla, *Ilha do Meu Fado* (Ocarina OCA 011, 2005).

Pontes, Dulce, *Lágrimas* (Movieplay Portuguesa PE 51.003, 1993).

Quinteto de Jazz Lisboa, *Viragens* (Ovação, 1998).

————, *Coisas do Fado* (Ovação, 2006).

Ries, Tim, *Stones World: The Rolling Stones Project II* (2CD, Sunnyside Records SSC4104, 2008).

Rodrigues, Amália, *Amália Canta Portugal 2* (LP, Columbia/EMI 8E062-40112, 1971).

————, *Gostava de Ser Quem Era* (Valentim de Carvalho/EMI 724383546527, 1995 [1980]).

————, *Lágrima* (Valentim de Carvalho/EMI 077778107729, 1995 [1983]).

————, *No Olympia* (Valentim de Carvalho/EMI 077779125920, 1988).

————, *Estranha Forma de Vida: O Melhor de Amália* (Valentim de Carvalho/ EMI 724383444229, 1995).

―――, *Tudo Isto é Fado: O Melhor de Amália Volume II* (Valentim de Carvalho/ EMI 724353007829, 2000).

Rodrigues, Amália and Don Byas, *Encontro* (Valentim de Carvalho/EMI 077779087426, 1988 [1973]).

Rodrigues, Celeste, *Fado Celeste* (Coast Company CTC-2990490, 2007).

Rodrigues, Marco, *Fados da Tristeza Alegre* (Ocarina OCA015, 2006).

Salgueiro, Gonçalo, *...No Tempo das Cerejas* (Companhia Nacional de Música CNM116CD, 2004 [2002]).

―――, *Segue a Minha Voz* (Movieplay Portuguesa MOV 30.578, 2006).

Santos, Argentina, *Clássicos da Renascença* (Movieplay Portuguesa MOV 31.005, 2000).

Silva, Hermínia, *O Melhor de* (iPlay/Edições Valentim de Carvalho IPV 12162, 2008).

Silva, Tristão da, *Patrimônio* (Companhia Nacional de Música CNM218CD, 2009).

Tavares, Raquel, *Raquel Tavares* (Movieplay Portuguesa MOV 30.579, 2006).

―――, *Bairro* (Movieplay Portuguesa MOV 30.606, 2008).

Trovante, *Chão Nosso* (LP, Sassetti, 1977).

―――, *Em Nome Da Vida* (LP, Mundo Novo, 1978).

Twillert, Henk van, *Fado Saudades* (Numérica NUM1094, 2001).

UHF, *À Flor da Pele* (EMI, 724382841128, 1993 [1981]).

Variações, António, *Anjo da Guarda* (Valentim de Carvalho/EMI 724382373223, 1998 [1983]).

―――, *Dar & Receber* (Valentim de Carvalho/EMI 724382373322, 1998 [1984]).

Veloso, Rui, *Fora de Moda* (Valentim de Carvalho/EMI 724382846420, 1993 [1982]).

Xavier, Joel, *Sr Fado* (Ariola/BMG 74321425632, 1996).

―――, *Lisboa* (Zona Música ZM00094, 2002).

Zambujo, António, *O Mesmo Fado* (Musica Alternativa/Valentim de Carvalho/ EMI MA035CD, 2002).

―――, *Outro Sentido* (Ocarina OCA024, 2007.

Various Artist Compilations

Amália Revisited (Different World DW50009CD, 2004).

Bar Lisbon: Classic & New Portuguese Flavours (Nascente NSBARCD 020, 2008).

Café Portugal: Fado & Football, Ceramics & Sun (Metro METRCD126, 2004).

Chillfado V.01 (M247/2Dance 64001, 2004).

E Depois de Adeus (FAROL FAR72754, 2007).

O Fado do Público, (20 vols, Lisbon: Corda Seca & Público, 2004).

Musiques Traditionnelles de l'Alentejo/Traditional Musics of the Alentejo (Playasound 65017, 1987).

Novo Homem na Cidade (Mercury/Universal Portugal 9868409, 2004).

Ó Vadio: Fado na Tasca do Chico (Transformadores 5600304510073, 2005).

Variações: As Canções de António (EMI Portugal 0946 3 72489 2 8, 2006 [1993]).

Videography

Films

Amália – O Filme (Carlos Coelho da Silva, Portugal, 2008).
The Art of Amália (Bruno de Almeida, Portugal/USA, 2000).
Canção de Lisboa (José Cottinelli Telmo, Portugal, 1933).
O Costa do Castelo (Arthur Duarte, Portugal, 1943).
Fado, História d'uma Cantadeira (Perdigão Queiroga, Portugal, 1948).
Fado: Ombre et Lumière (Yves Billon, France, 1989), available on DVD as *Music from Portugal: Fado, Lights and Shadows* (Universal Music France, 2004).
Fados (Carlos Saura, Portugal/Spain, 2007).
O Grande Elias (Arthur Duarte, Portugal, 1950).
'Krapp's Last Tape' (Atom Egoyan, Ireland, 2001), part of the *Beckett on Film* season screened on RTÉ (Ireland), Channel Four (UK) and at the Barbican Centre in London in September 2001.
Lisbon Story (Wim Wenders, Germany/Portugal, 1994).
Mariza and the Story of Fado (Simon Broughton, UK/Portugal, 2006).
Passionada (Dan Ireland, USA, 2002).
School of Rock (Richard Linklater, USA/Germany, 2003).
A Severa (José Leitão de Barros, Portugal/France, 1931).

Music videos

Mariza, *Live in London* (DVD, EMI 724359962795, 2004).

Index

Adair, Gilbert, 36–7, 39, 100
Afonso, José, 56–8, 140, 152, 156, 161,
        166, 170, 173, 174, 175, 188, 191,
        211
Africa, 19, 23, 78, 177, 188, 190
    Angola, 120, 190, 191
    Cape Verde, 153, 183, 188, 190, 203,
        207
    Mozambique, 188, 190, 191
    PALOPs, 190
Agacinski, Sylviane, 32, 33, 39, 41, 46, 95,
        97, 126–7, 129, 177, 214
agency, 3, 74–5, 78, 86, 115–16, 126
'Ah Quanta Melancolia', 50
'Ai Mouraria', 67, 120, 193
Ala dos Namorados, 170, 171–2
Alegre, Manuel, 58, 120–21
Alfama, 2, 14, 15, 24, 52, 65–6, 67, 68,
        76, 77, 84, 85, 86, 129, 144, 152,
        188, 205
'Alfama' (song), 144, 145
alleyways, 14, 16, 17, 63, 66, 67, 76, 85
Amália (film), 175
Amália (musical), 51, 147, 171
Amália Hoje, 175, 212–13
Amália Revisited, 163, 165, 207, 209
'Amarelo da Carris, O', 86–7, 88
Amendoeira, Joana, 20, 158–9, 162
Antunes, António Lobo, 78, 155
Appadurai, Arjun, 179, 180, 181
April in Portugal, 198–9
'April in Portugal', 52, 199
Aragon, Louis, 77, 78, 87
architecture, 69, 70–71, 76, 79, 91
archive, 5, 6, 39, 41, 101, 105–6, 112, 129,
        186, *see also* museum
Arnauth, Mafalda, 121–2, 124, 157–8, 162,
        182
Art of Amália, The, 17, 181

Ary dos Santos, José Carlos, 58, 65, 85–9,
        141, 161, 167, 168, 196, 204
Asas Fechadas, see *Busto*
Atlantic Waves, 161, 168
Augé, Marc, 73, 194
authenticity, 6, 25, 49, 51, 68, 107–8, 139,
        155, 157, 158, 173, 181, 184–5,
        186, 187, 190, 195, 197, 198–9,
        200–202, 205–6, 212, 214
Aznavour, Charles, 136, 157

Bachelard, Gaston, 7, 72, 74, 92
Badiou, Alain, 91–2, 85, 136–7, 138
Bairro Alto, 2, 66, 68, 86, 143, 187, 196,
        209
Baptista-Bastos, Pedro, 154, 163, 213
Bar Lisbon, 196–7
Barreto, Jorge Lima, 5, 57, 141, 161, 196
Barreto, Mascarenhas, 19, 24, 196
Barthes, Roland, 15–16, 36, 37, 53, 61–3,
        65, 99–100, 102, 105, 111, 113,
        115, 173, 184
Baudelaire, Charles, 46, 72, 112
Baudrillard, Jean, 73, 110
Bauman, Zygmunt, 71–2, 73, 84, 178
bearing witness, 4, 98, 106–7, 118, 142,
        see also carrying
Beckett, Samuel, 34, 104–6, 116
Belsey, Catherine, 63, 117
Benjamin, Walter, 32, 95, 100, 105, 112,
        126–7
Bethânia, Maria, 156, 158
Bica, 68, 76, 184, 185, 188, 196
biographeme, 15–16, 53, 99–100, 114
Blitz, 143, 157
Book of Disquiet, The, 47, 48, 64, 77, 88,
        98, 111–14
Borges, Jorge Luis, 39, 79, 99, 100, 101–2,
        103
Boss AC, 207, 208, 210

Bourdieu, Pierre, 165
Boyer, M. Christine, 3, 32, 40, 71, 97
Boym, Svetlana, 3, 29, 31–2, 35, 97, 109, 113, 182
Braga, João, 123, 171, 191
Bragança, Paulo, 31, 146, 169, 171, 181, 208
Brainard, Joe, 35–6, 39, 74
Branco, Cristina, 119, 125, 156–7, 162, 163, 174, 204, 210, 212
Branco, José Mário, 161
Brel, Jacques, 148, 157
Brito, Frederico de, 52, 150, 183
Brito, Joaquim Pais do, 17, 21–2, 53–4, 55, 155
Broughton, Simon, 1, 159, 166, 187
Buarque, Chico, 175, 188
Buck, Paul, 83–4
Buraka Som Sistema, 190, 211
Burke, Seán, 99–100
Busto, 52–3, 54, 170
Byrne, David, 146, 181
Bywater, Michael, 33–4

Café Portugal, 197–8, 212
Calvino, Italo, 65, 98, 109, 110, 112–13, 169, 198, 212
Camané, 50, 106, 146, 152, 161, 183, 188, 192, 214, 215
Camões, Luís Vaz de, 52, 123, 154, 155, 156 ,175
Canção de Lisboa, 14, 93–4
canto de intervenção, 56, 58, 140
capital and capitalism, 71–2, 78, 80–81, 94, 139, 178, 180, 181
Carminho, 189
Carmo, Carlos do, 6, 26, 50, 58, 65, 66, 75, 85–90, 106, 125, 141, 144, 147, 148, 150, 152, 153, 157, 158, 161, 162, 163–4, 166, 167, 168, 188, 192, 193, 210, 212
Carmo, Lucília do, 26, 66, 67, 188
carrying, 4, 19, 102, 114, 118–23, 125
Carter, Paul, 7–8, 10
Carvalho, José Pinto de, 13, 20, 21
Carvalho, Paulo de, 139, 153, 166–8, 169, 173, 189, 193, 207, 212

casa de fado, 4, 53, 107, 125, 144, 169, 184, 185–6, 189, 196
Casey, Edward S., 32–3, 72
Castelo-Branco, Salwa, 11, 26, 54
Castelo, Custódio, 151, 152, 156, 162, 171, 206
'Cavaleiro Monge', 151–2
Cave, Nick, 30–31, 63, 146
Certeau, Michel de, 7, 32, 65, 70, 82, 84, 86–7, 89–90, 91, 94, 95, 111, 113, 126
Chainho, António, 160, 162, 192
Chiado, 76, 143, 158
Cid, José, 140, 141, 146
citizens, 32, 71, 73, 75–6, 77, 80, 82, 85, 87, 97, 113, 127, 215
city, the, 1–3, 14–15, 32, 65–96, 97–8, 109–14, 126–30, 214–15
   imagined, 66, 81, 82, 203, 214
   real, 77, 82, 113, 130, 214
   real-and-imagined, 80–85
   sounded city, the, 90–96, 209
   see also Lisbon, psychogeography
Clemente, Diogo, 104, 154, 159
Cohen, David, 17, 85
Coimbra, 25, 56, 57, 64, 120, 201
'Coimbra', 52, 175, 199
collectivity, 33, 36, 55, 117, 161, *see also* individuality
colonialism and postcolonialism, 19, 78, 143, 177, 179
Colvin, Michael, 69, 79, 110, 120, 130
Conceição, Beatriz de, 97, 162, 204, 210
Cook, Manuela, 124, 160–61
Corpo Diplomático, 168, 169
Correia de Oliveira, Adriano, 120–21
Costa do Castelo, O, 94
Costa, Ercília, 9, 66
Costa, Luís, 184–5, 186
country music (US), 167, 201–2, 207
Crespo, Ángel, 83, 85, 94
critical fidelity, 165, 170
critical nostalgia, 69
cultural theory, 10, 61, 89–90
cyberspace, 34, 73

Dantas, Júlio, 13, 14, 16, 17, 51, 67, 150, 188

Davis, Miles, 191, 194–5, 199
death, 17, 19, 42, 43–4, 46, 61–2, 99, 100, 101, 104
DeCarvalho, Maria de Lourdes, 123, 171
Delfins, 142, 167, 168, 170
Deolinda, 210–11
Derrida, Jacques, 43, 44, 90, 98–9, 101
destiny, 19, 74, 87, 100, 103–4, 115, 120, 124, 130, 188, *see also* fate
destruction, 45, 63, 103–4, 110, 169
detraditionalization, 5, 178
Dias, Ricardo, 156, 157, 158, 174
disquiet, 3, 53, 64, 112–13
Dolar, Mladen, 126
Donna Maria, 209–10, 213
Duarte, Aldina, 125, 162
Duarte, Alfredo, *see* Marceneiro, Alfredo
Duarte, Anabela, 144–5
duende, 31
Dylan, Bob, 51, 120

'É Noite na Mouraria', 66–7
Eco, Umberto, 29
EEC/EU, *see* Europe
Eisenberg, Evan, 9
Espanca, Florbela, 151, 152, 154, 155
Estado Novo, 15, 22, 49, 51, 52, 53, 54, 57, 58, 69, 93, 110, 115, 120, 160, 161, 162
'Estranha Forma de Vida', 18, 52, 53, 54, 158, 173, 175, 188, 193
ethnomusicology, 5, 6, 21, 89, 112, 128
Europe, 2, 16, 111, 162, 163, 164
    EEC/EU, 111, 144, 162, 164
    France, 2, 14, 24, 52, 111, 136, 157, 163
    Netherlands, 2, 149, 155, 156, 163, 174, 192, 204
    Spain, 27, 31, 55, 83, 147, 153, 162, 194
    see also Portugal
Eurovision Song Contest, 85, 140, 147, 159, 166
event, 91–2, 95, 136–7, 138, 170, 174
Evora, Cesaria, 153–4, 183

Fabulous Marceneiro, The, 37, 38, 67, 107–8

fado canção, 26, 27, 52, 55, 56, 59, 62, 118, 151, 159, 167, 169, 171, 212
fado castiço, 26, 55, 58, 118, 160, 167, 169
fado corrido, 26, 160, 167, 172
Fado Curvo, 66, 151–2, 169, 183
Fado em Mim, 122, 130–31, 149–51, 174
Fado, História D'uma Cantadeira, 24, 94, 160, 172
'Fado Lisboa', 66
fado menor, 26, 66, 172, 188
fado mouraria, 26, 172, 184
Fado: Ombre et Lumière, 17, 20, 184–5, 186, 187
fadology, 18, 20, 21–5, 30, 182, 189
Fados (film), 1, 88–9, 188–9, 207
Farinha, Fernando, 68, 165, 183, 185
fate, 10, 19–20, 23, 44, 64, 87, 88, 103–4, 115–18, 119, 121, 123, 127, 130–31, 178, 203
Fausto, 140, 141
Fé, Maria da, 124–5, 144, 162, 197
Feld, Steven, 181
fencing-off, 2, 3, 6, 29, 44, 55, 63, 94, 166, 173, 183, 208, 214–15, *see also* framing, roping-off, staging
Fernando, Jorge, 146, 159, 161, 164, 171, 172–3, 174, 206
Ferreira, Milú, 184–5
festivals, 41, 69, 83, 93–4, 132, 135, 149, 159, 191
fidelity, 122, 136–7, 138, 140, 142, 143, 155, 187
    critical fidelity, 165, 170
    high-fidelity, 107–8, 183
field work, 9, 20, 21, 90, 128, 184, 186
fixing, 43, 46, 70, 97, 99–101, 109, *see also* recording
flamenco, 17, 27, 31, 52, 55, 94, 146, 153, 154, 167, 171, 189, 194, 195, 204
flows, 71–2, 97, 178–9, 191–91
'Foi Deus', 53, 123–4, 125, 159, 175, 209–10
folk music, 1, 5, 25, 139, 181, 200
    Portuguese, 5, 24–5, 53, 54–5, 56, 58, 136, 141, 143, 147, 156, 157, 173, 175, 190, 195, 196, 210
forgetting, 2, 9, 19, 32, 39–40, 46, 49, 97, 102, 103, 111, 184

framing, 2, 4, 44, 68, 184, 186, 187,
    see also fencing-off, roping-off,
    staging
Freitas, Frederico de, 14, 20, 23, 24, 67
Freud, Sigmund, 33, 35, 39, 41–3, 44,
    45–7, 61, 117
Frith, Simon, 123, 124, 125, 126, 130–31,
    132, 133, 137, 139, 200
fRoots, 1, 155

'Gaivota', 27, 84–5, 175, 192, 193, 212–13
Galhardo, José, 17, 67, 69
Gallop, Rodney, 14–15, 21, 22–3, 24, 25,
    28, 38, 68, 115, 200–201
gente, see people, the
Gift, The, 175, 212
Gilroy, Paul, 23
glitch, 128
globalization, 2–3, 4–5, 6–7, 71, 137, 154,
    177–81, 183, 185, 187, 189–91,
    194–5, 204, 211, 214
GNR (Grupo Novo Rock), 141–2, 170
Godinho, Sérgio, 148, 193, 204, 211
Gonçalves, Carlos, 38, 59–60, 84, 122,
    123, 174
Gonçalves, Nuno, 212, 213
'Gostava de Ser Quem Era', 38, 48
Graça, 67, 86, 129, 204
Gramophone, 139, 198–9, 200
'Grândola Vila Morena', 57, 58, 156, 166,
    188, 191
Gregory, Derek, 80, 90
'Grito', 122–3
Guerra, Maria Luísa, 17, 19, 20, 158, 214
Guerreiro, Katia, 1, 25, 37, 66, 154–6, 157,
    160, 162, 170–71
Guerreiro, Luís, 153, 166
Guerreiro, Nuno, 171–2, 188
guitarists, 11, 17, 26, 64, 162, 166, 192
guitarra portuguesa, 17, 18, 19, 25–6, 64,
    67, 88, 149, 150, 151, 160, 167,
    183, 192, 209, 210, 211

Haden, Charlie, 191–2
Halbwachs, Maurice, 33, 40, 41
Halpern, Manuel, 4, 30, 145, 158, 165,
    170, 182, 185, 208
hard core and soft shell, 167, 201–2

Harvey, David, 71, 72, 78–9, 112
Heróis do Mar, 143, 146, 167, 168
hip hop, 6, 106, 188, 207, 208, 209, 210
history, 1, 4, 6, 7–8, 18, 21, 86, 97, 111,
    112, 129, 165, 185, 186, 189, 205
    and memory, 32–3, 35–7, 38–9, 40–41,
        99–100, 121
    and myth, 13, 15, 20
holiday records, 198–9
Holton, Kimberly, 110–11, 162
homage, 36, 128, 148, 163–4, 165, 166,
    170, 171, 174, 188, 203, 209
Homem de Melo, Pedro, 52, 54, 55, 56,
    118, 154, 156, 196
Horta, Maria Teresa, 156
Huyssen, Andreas, 32, 39, 41, 70, 107

I Remember, 35–7
ideology, 3, 17, 21–3, 56, 57, 69, 73, 77,
    95, 112–13, 115–17, 132, 162, 178,
    180
individuality, 33, 35–6, 40, 41, 43–4, 55,
    56–7, 89, 99, 101, 112–13, 116,
    122, 178, 195, see also collectivity
interpellation, 132, 146
intimacy, 7, 67, 74, 95, 106, 125, 197, 215,
    see also listening
Invisible Cities, 98, 109–10, 198

Janes, Alberto, 53, 123, 124, 159
Jara, Víctor, 51, 140, 141
jazz, 86, 141, 154, 156, 157, 161, 166, 190,
    195, 201, 211, 212
    Portuguese, 191–4
João, Maria, 161, 192

Kaempfert, Bert, 198–9
Khalil, Rabih Abou, 193–4
kiduro, 190
Krapp's Last Tape, 104–7
Kristeva, Julia, 44–5
Kritzman, Lawrence, 34–5
Kyao, Rão, 192

La Féria, Filipe, 51, 147, 171
Lacan, Jacques, 61, 63–4, 91, 116, 173,
    213
Laginha, Mário, 161, 192

'Lágrima', 59–64, 172–4, 192
Laíns, Ana, 104, 119, 120
language, 10, 29, 31, 61, 62, 63, 87, 91,
        112, 115, 116, 138–9, 141, 143,
        144, 165, 172, 178, 180, 183, 189,
        208, *see also* translation
Latin America, 136, 139–40, 141, 175,
        190–91, 194
    Argentina, 32, 139–40
    Brazil, 19, 23, 29, 37, 58, 92, 111, 135,
        146, 147, 152, 154, 155, 156, 158,
        175, 177, 179, 183, 188, 190–91
    Chile, 139–40, 141
    Cuba, 136, 141, 154, 181
    Mexico, 52, 149, 188, 204, 211
Leão, Rodrigo, 147, 161, 168
Lefebvre, Henri, 7, 65, 79–81, 82–3, 84,
        86, 89, 91, 92–3, 94, 95, 129
'Lembro-Me de Ti', 37–8, 108
Lévi-Strauss, Claude, 14
Leza, B., 153, 183
Lima, Paulo Abreu, 152, 210
Lipsitz, George, 96
Lisbon Story, 127–9, 147, 161
Lisbon, 6, 10, 13, 14, 15, 16, 19, 23, 24,
        25, 26, 49, 58, 63, 65–9, 76–7, 78,
        79, 82–9, 92, 93, 95, 97, 110–13,
        116, 117, 122–9, 130, 131, 133,
        135, 143, 146, 153, 154, 158,
        159, 160, 163, 175, 177, 184, 187,
        188, 190, 191, 193, 194, 195, 196,
        197, 201, 203, 204, 205, 207,
        209, 210, 211, 212, 214, *see also*
        Alfama, Bairro Alto, Bica, Graça,
        Madragoa, Mouraria
listening, 62–3, 94–5, 102, 104, 105, 107,
        108, 125, 126, 129–30, 183–4, *see*
        also intimacy
local, *see* globalization
longing, 3, 27–9, 31–2, 40, 48, 110, 112,
        113, 153, 182–3, 194, 212
Lopes-Graça, Fernando, 24–5, 57
Lorca, Federico, García, 31–2
loss, 1, 3, 6, 28, 29, 32–5, 38–9, 40, 41–6,
        48–9, 51, 55, 63, 66, 70, 72, 79,
        101, 105, 108, 110, 113, 114,
        116–17, 120, 121, 172, 178, 186,
        205

Lynch, Kevin, 75–6
lyrics, 4, 9, 10, 26, 52, 53, 55, 65, 96,
        148–9, 160

Machado, Tiago, 130, 131, 207
Madragoa, 66, 67, 68, 188, 203
Madredeus, 128, 136, 146–7, 151, 161,
        168, 169, 170, 207, 208, 211
Magalhães, Pedro Ayres, 128, 147, 168–9,
        207
Malhoa, José, 17
Manuel, Peter, 139, 169
Mão Morta, 142, 170
maps and mapping, 62, 75–6, 82, 83, 84,
        90–91, 129
Marceneiro, Alfredo, 9, 27, 37–8, 53, 67–8,
        107–8, 177, 184, 185, 186, 188,
        194, 211, 214
Marialvismo, 16
Mariza, 1, 5, 66, 88, 122, 125, 130–33,
        149–54, 156, 157, 159, 161, 162,
        163, 166, 168, 169, 172, 174, 175,
        177, 180, 183, 185, 186–7, 188,
        189, 193, 202, 207, 208, 210
Mariza and the Story of Fado, 1, 159, 187
Marx, Karl, 71, 81, 178, 180
Matogrosso, Ney, 156, 158
Max (Maximiano de Sousa), 66, 153, 193,
        210
melancholy, 34–5, 41–3, 44–50, 51, 83,
        99, 116–17, 130, 140, 151, 153–4,
        172, 194
memory, 3, 32, 33, 35–41, 97–114, 126,
        129, 171–5, 186, 197–8
    memory places, 32, 37, 70, 98, 107,
        126
    memory theatre, 4, 32, 37, 63, 70, 98,
        110
    memory work, 32, 35–6, 38–9, 40, 42,
        122, 171
    mnemotechnics, 70, 98, 169
microphone, 106, 125, 128, 188, 201–2
Middleton, Richard, 124, 138, 213
Mísia, 5–6, 66, 141, 147–9, 150, 156, 161,
        167, 168, 171, 173–4, 182, 185–6,
        202, 203–4, 213
Mitchell, Timothy, 55
Mitologia Fadista, A, 20, 22, 115–16

Mler Ife Dada, 144, 145
Moita, Luís, 22
Monge, João, 171
Moraes, Vinicius de, 147, 175
Moreira, Bernardo, 156, 192, 193, 212
Morelenbaum, Jaques, 152, 153, 175
morna, 153, 188, 190, 203, 207
Moura, Ana, 1, 156, 159–60, 168, 172, 204–7
Moura, Vasco Graça, 148–9, 203
Mourão-Ferreira, David, 52, 53, 58, 87, 153, 156, 161, 171, 196
Mouraria, 2, 13, 14–15, 16, 18, 26, 51, 66–7, 68–9, 79, 86, 110, 120, 129, 182
mourning, 30, 32, 35, 41–7, 48, 61, 78, 110, 114, 120, 122, 148, 173
Moutinho, Helder, 119, 162
Moutinho, Pedro, 162
MPP (Música Popular Portuguesa), see pop
Muge, Amélia, 122, 157
museum, 41, 55, 63, 65, 77, 79, 110–11, 112, 127, 177
mytheme, 14, 15–16, 20, 21, 25, 51, 66, 67, 116, 117
mythology, 1, 2, 13–17, 18–19, 20, 21, 25, 35, 36–7, 51, 57, 59, 63, 65, 83–4, 116, 125, 160, 175, 186, 187, 214

Nagel, Thomas, 7
Naifa, A, 208–9, 210, 213
national identity, 2, 16, 21, 22, 34, 111, 113, 162, 164, 186
nationalism, 6, 8, 19, 21–5, 53, 113, 143
No Tempo das Cerejas, 119, 122–3, 171
noise, 76, 88, 94, 128, 130, 184–5, 190, 208, 214–15
Nora, Pierre, 32, 34–5, 37, 38, 40–41, 70
Noronha, Maria Teresa de, 9, 26
Novo Estado (New State), 15, 22, 49, 51, 52, 53, 54, 57, 58, 69, 93, 110, 115, 120, 160, 161, 162
nostalgia, 1, 3, 7, 8, 10, 29, 30, 32, 33, 35, 41, 49, 57, 64, 68, 69, 74–5, 79, 100, 105, 109, 113–14, 126, 140, 183, *see also* critical nostalgia, longing, *saudade*

novo fado, 2, 4, 5, 59, 87, 146–66, 168, 169, 170, 173, 184, 185–6, 202, 213
nueva cancion, 139, 140, 167

'Ó Gente da Minha Terra', 122, 130–33, 151, 174, 189, 207
oblivion, *see* destruction, forgetting
O'Brien, Geoffrey, 59, 103, 127, 164–5
Oliveira, Paula, 193, 212
O'Neill, Alexandre, 58, 84–5, 192, 212
OqueStrada, 211, 213
Osório, António, 20, 22, 115–16, 117
Oulman, Alain, 18, 52, 53, 58, 85, 121, 174, 188, 212

Pacheco, Mário, 31, 125, 146, 152, 153, 154, 158, 160, 174, 188, 193
palimpsest, 70, 88, 110, 145, 209
Paredes, Carlos, 148–9, 165, 170, 192, 193
Paris, Tito, 153, 183
Parreira, Ricardo, 162, 210
Passionada, 148, 161, 187, 208
passivity, 64, 74, 82, 86–7, 90, 102, 120, 121, 126–7
Pena, Lula, 14, 145, 161, 175, 212
people, the, 7, 18, 53, 54, 57, 68, 76, 77, 86, 89–90, 94, 117–18, 123, 124–5, 132, 185
Perec, Georges, 36, 37, 39, 44, 74, 90, 91, 100, 103
perspective, 7, 40, 81–2, 83, 85, 90, 180, 212, *see also* scapes
Pessoa, Fernando, 20, 31, 47–50, 64, 65, 76–7, 83, 84, 88, 97, 101, 111–15, 117–18, 123, 128, 130, 151–2, 155, 156, 188, 193, 204
Peterson, Richard A., 56, 68, 167–8, 201–2
phonography, 9, 21, 68, 99, 103–8, 138, 214
photography, 61, 63, 87, 89, 95, 109, 111, 184
pimba, 93, 135, 167
Pires, Carla, 88, 162, 168
place, 1–2, 3, 4, 8, 14, 17, 33, 37, 43, 61, 63, 65–96, 97–9, 107, 112, 122, 142–3, 144, 178, 180, 185, 194, 196–9, 213
non-places, 72–3, 76–7, 194

Poe, Edgar Allan, 103–4, 105, 112, 120
poetics, 7, 10, 19, 65, 74, 93
polyphonic singing, 57, 122, 161
Pontes, Dulce, 14, 147, 148, 161, 173, 175
pop, 159, 160, 173, 181, 189–90, 202, 213
    Anglo-American, 6, 58, 137–40, 141,
       143, 144, 164, 181, 190
      Portuguese, 57, 85, 136–46, 147, 149,
        164, 166–9, 170, 175, 193, 207,
        210, 211, 212
Portugal, 1, 2, 5, 15, 16, 18–19, 22, 25, 27,
    53–5, 56–7, 82, 93, 122, 123, 133,
    135, 136–7, 138–46
Portugueseness, 3, 16, 21–5, 116, 147, 164,
    189
'Povo Que Lavas no Rio', 54, 118, 145,
    158, 186, 192
povo, see people, the
Proust, Marcel, 96, 100, 107, 108
psychogeography, 77–8, 80, 82, 113, 128
punctum and *studium*, 61–3, 113–14, 172,
    173

Quarteto IIII, 140

Raban, Jonathan, 77, 78, 82
Rádio Macau, 143, 167, 168
recording, 5–6, 9, 41, 56, 95–6, 100–115,
    127–9, 130, 132, 136, 145, 150,
    163, 174, 183–9, 195–8, 214
    prescriptive, 197
    transcriptive, 104–6, 129, 163, 184,
      197
    see also technology, phonography,
      photography
Red, Hot & Lisbon, 146, 169
Régio, José, 18, 52, 145
religion, 123–4, 209
Represas, Luís, 141
revolution, 57, 137–8
    Portuguese Revolution (1974), 22, 51,
      56, 57, 58–9, 86, 141, 146, 156,
      162, 164, 166, 188
Ribeiro, Álvaro, 32
Ribeiro, Artur, 19, 65, 152, 153
Ribeiro, Ricardo, 189, 193–4
Ricoeur, Paul, 33, 39, 42–3, 46–7, 70, 97,
    98, 108

ritual, 35, 37, 38, 41, 55, 93, 124, 152, 178,
    186
Ritual (album), 38, 148, 149, 173–4, 185–6
Rocha, José Fontes, 119, 125, 149, 171
Rodrigo, Joaquín, 194–5
Rodrigues, Amália, 1, 3, 5, 9, 13, 14, 15,
    17, 18, 24, 25, 27, 38, 39, 48,
    49–50, 51–63, 66, 68, 84–5, 94,
    115, 118–19, 120, 121, 122, 123–4,
    130, 132, 136, 144, 145, 147, 148,
    149, 152, 153, 155, 157, 158, 159,
    160, 161, 163, 164, 165, 167, 168,
    170–75, 182, 184, 185, 186, 188,
    191, 192, 194–5, 196, 199, 202,
    204, 211, 212
Rodrigues, Celeste, 66, 119, 204
Rodríguez, Silvio, 136, 141
Rolling Stones, The, 138, 204–7
'Romper Madrugadas', 37
roping-off, 110, 111, 162, *see also* fencing-
    off, framing, staging
Roubard, Jacques, 34, 35, 102–3
Rough Guide to World Music, The, 181,
    182, 187
Ruas, 66, 149, 203–4

Salazar, António, 15, 22, 24, 49, 53, 55,
    56, 58, 120, 140, 144, 160, 162,
    164, 196
Salgueiro, Gonçalo, 119, 122–3, 171, 188,
    197, 204, 212
Salgueiro, Teresa, 128, 147, 148, 160, 161,
    192
Samuel, Raphael, 20, 32, 37, 70, 97
Santos, Argentina, 157, 172, 173, 188
Santos, Jaime, 17, 50
Saramago, José, 113, 149
Sarlo, Beatriz, 73
Sassetti, Bernardo, 154, 192
saudade, 3, 19, 27–31, 37, 51, 57, 108,
    117, 119, 146, 147, 151, 153, 154,
    182–3, 212, 215, *see also* longing
saudosismo, 22, 115
Saura, Carlos, 1, 88–9, 188–9, 190, 207
scapes, 77, 109, 136, 180, 181, 202, *see*
    also perspectives
Sebastianismo, 26, 115, 140
Severa, A (film), 13–14, 24, 188

Severa, A (play), 13–17, 67
Severa, Maria, 13, 14, 51, 67, 68, 122, 124,
    150, 154, 160
shadows, 17, 18, 182
Sheiks, Os, 139, 166, 168
silence, 88, 118, 122, 123, 125, 128, 130,
    151, 183, 214
Silva, Hermínia, 9, 69, 85, 184
Silva, Tristão da, 85, 92
Sinclair, Iain, 77–8, 87
singing, 10–11, 55, 57, 64, 91, 92, 122,
    123, 124–5, 130–31, 133, 201–2,
    213, *see also* voice
Small, Christopher, 92
Soja, Edward W., 71, 75, 78, 80–81
Solnit, Rebecca, 32, 33
Songlines, 1, 159, 166, 187, 194
sound, *see* noise, silence
sounded experience, 9, 95, 126–30, 214
Sousa, Avelino de, 20, 21–2
souvenirs, 195–9
space, 7–8, 44, 70–96, 97, 105, 106–7,
    109–11, 129, 142–3, 156, 157, 172,
    178, 180, 183, 194, 211, 214
    production of, 7, 80–82, 91, 92–3, 94
    see also place
spatiality, 2, 4, 7–8, 10, 70, 71–2, 73, 74,
    80–82, 84, 89–93, 95, 97, 98, 106,
    107, 126, 189
staging, 2, 5, 23, 44, 94, 109, 116, 133,
    186, 195, 214–15, *see also* fencing-
    off, framing, roping-off
Stones World, 206–7
studium, see *punctum*
sublimation, 43, 44–5, 46–7, 117
Sucena, Eduardo, 20, 23–4, 59, 151

tasca, 6, 154, 187, 209, 211
Tavares, Raquel, 159, 162, 204, 210
Taylor, Mark C., 43–4, 72, 73, 101, 104,
    194
Taylor, Timothy D., 162, 181
technology, 5, 33, 56, 72, 99, 101, 105–8,
    112, 127–9, 136, 163, 178, 179–80,
    182–5, 196, *see also* recording
Terra, 153–4, 168
testimony, *see* witnessing
Tinhorão, José Ramos, 20, 23

Tinoco, José Luís, 87, 193
Toop, David, 105–6
topography, 66, 70, *see also* maps and
    mapping
toponyms, 4, 10, 129, 143, 153, 203
Tordo, Fernando, 139, 168
tourism and tourists, 21, 53, 72, 76, 79, 83–
    5, 90, 127, 178, 185, 187, 194–9,
    203–4, 205
'Trago Fados nos Sentidos', 118–19
transience, 45–6, 48, 99, 101
translation, 27, 29, 36, 103, 182, *see also*
    language
Transparente, 125, 152–3, 168, 175
trauma, 32, 33, 61, 63, 99, 116, 173
tribute, *see* homage
Trindade, Carlos Maria, 146, 147, 151,
    152, 168–9
Trovante, 140–41, 171
truth, 20, 55, 63, 101, 136–7, 195
Tuan, Yi-Fu, 72, 73–4, 75, 79
'Tudo Isto É Fado', 18, 66, 115, 182, 198

UHF, 142, 143
Um Homem na Cidade (album), 58, 85–90
'Um Homem na Cidade' (song), 87, 88–9,
    188, 193
Unamuno, Miguel de, 27
universal and particular, the, 10, 29, 30–31,
    36, 71, 84, 91–2, 117, 121, 132,
    137, 139, 143, 178, 180, 204, 205,
    211, 213

vagabonds, 72, 84, 178, 194
Vale de Almeida, Miguel, 16, 29
Vale, Amadeu do, 67, 69, 120
Valério, Frederico, 67, 120
Varela, Ana Sofia, 152, 160, 162, 189
Variações, António, 145–6, 170, 211
Veloso, Caetano, 175, 188
Veloso, Rui, 142–3, 147, 152, 154, 167,
    170, 171, 188, 210
Vernon, Paul, 1, 21, 56, 157, 182
Vieira Nery, Rui, 4, 20, 22, 23, 25, 56, 85,
    123, 143, 155, 170, 171, 188
viola (Spanish guitar), 18, 26, 52, 88, 122,
    144, 146, 147, 152, 153, 159, 203
viola baixo, 26, 88

voice, 26, 37–8, 53–4, 55, 57, 62, 63, 79, 86, 87–8, 91, 99, 106, 108, 111, 121–5, 128, 132, 140, 155, 167, 171, 172–3, 183, 192, 201–2, 209, *see also* singing
'Voz Que Me Atravessa, A', 121–2, 124, 125

walking, 67, 78, 82, 84, 86, 91, 95, 98, 126
websites, 84, 143, 203, 204, 208, 209, 210, 211
    MySpace, 204
Wenders, Wim, 127, 128, 147
wind, the, 104, 119–21
witnessing, 2, 3, 5, 19, 77, 78, 88, 89, 97–133, 138, 158, 163, 186, *see also* carrying

world music, 1, 2, 5, 128, 135–6, 146, 149, 157, 162, 163, 169, 177, 180, 181, 183–90, 193, 196–8, 206, 211
    world music network, 1, 4, 7, 154, 177, 181, 184
writing, 101–3

Xavier, Joel, 192, 212
Xutos & Pantapés, 142, 168, 170, 207

Yates, Frances, 37, 70, 98
yearning, *see* longing, *saudade*

Zambujo, António, 122, 161, 162, 172
Zel, Carlos, 157, 158
Zenith, Richard, 49, 78
Žižek, Slavoj, 8, 93, 116

....

THE EX-WIVES

Russell Buffery is a superannuated old actor with a wonderful voice, 'his most reliable organ where women are concerned'. Thrown out by his third wife he lives in spectacular squalor in Maida Vale, companioned only by his small, matted dog. One day his life changes when he meets Celeste, a dewy young girl who works in the local chemist's shop. Dazzled by love, Buffy little suspects that Celeste is systematically searching out his ex-wives— Penny, a magazine journalist; Jacquetta, a neurotic painter; and Popsi, a brassy actress who now runs an antiques stall on the south coast—discovering along the way a bewildering medley of lovers, children and step-children. While Buffy bitterly mulls over the women in his past Celeste is busy infiltrating herself into their lives. Why she does so is revealed in a wonderful, witty and startling climax.

THE EX-WIVES

Deborah Moggach

CHIVERS PRESS
BATH

First published 1993
by
Willian Heinemann
This Large Print edition published by
Chivers Press
by arrangement with
Random House UK Ltd
2001

ISBN 0 7540 1555 6

British Library Cataloguing in Publication Data available

Printed and bound in Great Britain by
REDWOOD BOOKS, Trowbridge, Wiltshire

'I don't think I'll get married again. I'll just find a woman I don't like and give her a house.'

Lewis Grizzard

For Max Eilenberg, Mike Shaw and Rochelle Stevens

CHAPTER ONE

Buffy was sitting in what he still insisted on calling the saloon bar of his local, The Three Fiddlers. The racing commentary was drowned by the noise of a drill. Outside, as usual, they were digging up the road. This time, according to one of those self-congratulatory *Bringing It To Your Community* placards, they were laying down cable TV. The noise of the drilling was joined by the hooting of cars, stuck in the inevitable traffic jam this caused at the junction with the Edgware Road. He was feeling mulish and dyspeptic. Despite his post-breakfast sachet of Fybogel his bowels had failed to move that morning; nor had his first Senior Service, inhaled vigorously into his lungs, had its usual, prompt effect.

He gazed into his foam-laced, empty glass. He was feeling his age, whatever that meant. Depending on his mood, *sixty-one* shifted both ways—*only sixty-one* and *my God, sixty-one.* Today it was *my God.* Events had conspired to irritate him, an elderly reaction he knew, but still. First there was the bowel business, or non-business. Then, when he had gone out on this glorious summer's day he had had another undeniably elderly reaction: how did young girls manage to wear such indescribably hideous clothes? Once he had looked forward

1

to hot weather, revealing, as it did, achingly tender shoulders, slim legs and promising hints of cleavage. Now girls cropped their hair and wore those awful, awful boots. Those with the most monumental buttocks wore luminous shorts; the slim ones, on the other hand, enveloped themselves in drooping layers of black, like Greek grannies. And he himself, of course, was entirely invisible. Not a flicker from them. Nothing.

It was then, when he was looking at the only recognizably female woman, that he had tripped up on an upturned paving stone, outside his block of flats, and almost taken a header. Blasted TV cables. Testily, he reflected upon choice. Nowadays, choice had been removed in the things that mattered, like saloon and public bars. Once harmlessly divided into two sections, two pungent little microcosms of society which one could visit at will, depending upon one's finances and the presence of a female companion, pubs had now been knocked-through and neutered— Tony Blackburned into a mid-Atlantic no man's land of bleeping machines and androgynous creatures probably working in PR. On the other hand, there seemed to be a proliferation of choice in what one already had too much of anyway. Take lager. Nowadays there were about a million different brands, the more obscure the better—he should know, he'd done the voice-over for one from East

Senegal or somewhere—who needed them? Though of course the repeat fees were welcome.

And then there were all these TV channels, cable and things, popping up when it was flustering enough keeping up with the four one already had, especially now they had a video and Penny kept recording *The Clothes Show* over his *Palm Beach Story*. And then self-righteously blaming *him* because he apparently hadn't labelled it.

'I don't see why you make such a fuss,' she said, 'you never get around to watching all those boring old films anyway. It's so anal, darling, to hoard.'

'I just like to know they're there. It's like church.'

'But you never go to church.'

'Exactly. But I know I could, if I wanted. It's *there*.'

She had tossed her shiny hair and clipped shut her briefcase. Then paused. She had stood still, like a fox, scenting a rabbit a long way off, through the undergrowth. Her nostrils flared. *Maybe she could write a piece on it.* That's what she was thinking. He knew her so well. Maybe one of her cuddly, tabloid *Aren't Men the End?* pieces, with blush-making references to himself; maybe something for a woman's glossy, *Cosmopolitan* or something, *Ten New Grounds for Divorce.* An amused, middle-class think-piece for *The Times.* She

3

spread her talents widely. My God, she even wrote for *High Life*—one of the ten grounds for divorce, in his opinion.

But Penny was in Positano, writing a travel piece for somebody or other. She was writing a lot of travel pieces lately. This, of course, was the real reason for his irritability. It was lonely, shuffling along to Marks and Sparks to buy a *Serves One* meal. By now he knew them by heart. *Cumberland Fish Pie*—disappointing, too much potato; *Lasagne*—a bit ersatz but okay. They reminded him of periods in his life he preferred to forget. Besides, there was never quite enough in a *Serves One* so he usually bought a *Serves Two,* which was just too much, of course, but being greedy he always ate the lot, scraping out the foil dish, and then fell heavily asleep, waking in the middle of the night with heartburn. Then there was the wine problem. A half-bottle wasn't nearly enough, of course, not nearly. But a whole bottle was marginally too much, with the same results except when he woke it was with a flaming throat and palpitations. When Penny was there it was fine; she was a light drinker which meant he could polish off practically the whole bottle but not quite.

Besides, he liked to chat. He liked her breezing in from the outside world, tut-tutting at the mess and half-listening to the events of his afternoon. She was invigorating, in a vaguely abstracted way. She had breeding—

4

her father was a brigadier—and a Home Counties gloss to her, she sorted things out and got things done. She could be good company—amusing, full of gossip—especially when there were other people present; when they were alone she was inclined to boss him about. She was at her best with workmen—good-natured but firm and authoritative; rather the way she handled him, in fact. Otherwise she treated him the way she treated the dog—with brisk testiness, especially when he got under her feet or stood in front of the fridge.

He wasn't good at being alone. He got bored. He missed the bickering, the sulks, even the hours she spent on the phone when he was trying to watch the TV. Scents in the bathroom—perfumes she got as promotional freebies—lingered for days after her departures. Actually, they didn't exactly remind him of her; they reminded him of some idealized female presence, the sort of woman he had never met, and certainly never married. The sort of woman who cooked him dinner unresentfully and laughed at his anecdotes even though she had heard them before; who didn't record over his videos. Who didn't call him 'darling' with an edge to it; why did women only use endearments when they were particularly irritated, or trying to make some sort of point?

He got to his feet. George's tail thumped;

5

he got up, with difficulty, and gazed up at Buffy, his eyes moist with devotion. Why had no woman, in all these years, ever looked at him quite like that?

Buffy bought another pint from the landlord. He was new, an impossibly tanned, athletic type. God knew why he had decided to run a pub. The world was becoming filled with handsome, vigorous young men. They sprang up from nowhere, or sometimes from Australia, and ran the sort of enterprises that seemed vaguely beneath them; the sort of businesses which used to be run by boring old geezers you could rely on to be there year in year out, for ever. These new ones all looked as if they had just dropped in to do you a favour. This particular one was called Curtis, he had heard the name, but the moment had passed when he could have called him Curtis, casually, and now it was too late.

Buffy sat down; George sank to the floor. Penny seemed to have been away for ages; in fact she had only been gone for two days. The trouble with these absences was that you had to be particularly nice to the person before they departed, and particularly nice to them for quite a while after they returned; it gave a marriage an unnatural glaze, a stagey feel. Also, because they had been abroad it made everything you had done seem even more petty and trivial than usual. If that was possible. She always returned tanned and

6

somehow taller—he forgot how tall she was until he saw her again. Radiant, too, but full of complaints to make him feel better. 'Christ, the hotel . . . more like a building site . . . bulldozers, mud . . . We had to watch a fashion display, three hours, would you believe it they all wore *flares* . . . almost as bad as folk dancing, no, not quite, nothing's as bad as that . . . then we had this nightmarish rum'n'rhumba evening . . . Shirley got totally paralytic, you know, she's the one from *Family Circle* . . . and everyone had the most appalling hangovers the next day . . .'

She brought him back things to eat—obscure Greek sweetmeats wrapped in foil, Sicilian anchovies, things that leaked in her suitcase. He was touched by this, of course, but it made him feel like a housewife whose husband was returning home. This in turn led to the inevitable operational hitches once they had gone to bed. The longer she had been away, the more honour-bound he felt to attempt some sort of sexual congress on her return. After some dampish fiddling around they both knew they would never get any sleep this way, it could go on for hours. 'Don't worry,' she'd whisper, 'I'm totally zonked, anyway.'

7

CHAPTER TWO

Celeste. Charming name, charming girl. Celeste, handing round chicken sandwiches. It was a hot day in July; the day of her mother's funeral.

Celeste lived in Melton Mowbray. She was twenty-three, an only child, now orphaned by her mother's final shuddering breath. She had an only child's tended look, and indeed had been dearly loved. She smelt of soap. Her hair was cropped short, and there were small gold studs in her ears. Her fragile grace and inky eyes gave her the look of an antelope, startled by an intruder, but like all impressions this was partially misleading. In fact she had a stubborn streak, and was very good at maths. Her nimble fingers had made her Cats Cradle Champion at her primary school. She was logical. Columns of figures were to be one of her few reassurances in the tumultuous year that lay ahead. Buffy was deeply impressed, when he first saw her, by the way she cupped a phone to her ear, wedging it with her shoulder, whilst with her free hands she wrapped his numerous pharmaceutical purchases in plastic bags and rang them up at the till. He was hopeless at that sort of thing.

In those days Celeste wore angora sweaters in pastel colours. Sometimes, when she cycled, she wore a track suit. Fashion, that collusion of narcissists, did not engage her interest for she was a solitary person and her pleasures were solitary ones—swimming in the local baths, her stinging eyes blind to the gaze of the lifeguard; bicycling; biting the bits of skin around each of her fingernails, one by one. If she had neuroses she was unaware of them, for her family had no words for stuff like that, nor sought them because they were nothing but trouble. They led a quiet life. She wore a gold crucifix around her neck but the reason for this, the fathoms of faith it crystalized, were so far largely unexamined too. She was an innocent, something still possible in Leicestershire.

The lounge was crowded with mourners. *Mourners.* She had to fit this unfamiliar word to the faces. Some of them were relatives she had never seen before, and would never see again. Amongst the people there were several large men from Ray-Bees Plumbing Services. They fingered the mantelpiece ornaments that from now onwards, for ever, it would be her job to dust. Though chronically unreliable— 'Don't get rabies!' was a cry that had once confused her—they had turned up *en masse* for the funeral, probably as a skive. Her Mum used to clean their offices.

Celeste went into the kitchen to fetch the stuffed eggs. She unpeeled the cling film; it shrivelled, and stuck to the down on her arm.

9

She wanted to ask her mother the names of the relatives in the other room, but simultaneously she knew this was impossible. Post still arrived for her mother, wasn't this strange? Envelopes addressed to Mrs Constance Smith, one of them offering her the exciting chance of winning a Vauxhall Astra. There was a burst of laughter from the next room; funerals can be surprisingly jovial affairs. She longed for them all to go, and yet she dreaded the moment when they would leave.

She carried the stuffed eggs into the lounge. The noise changed; under the voices she could hear the low murmur of condolence, like another instrument, a cello, being added to an orchestra. 'Let me take those.' 'Why don't you sit down?' 'Budge up, Dennis!' She was Connie's little girl and what was she going to do with herself now? *Orphan* was like mourner, a new word she had to fit to herself. A word she had to be fitted up with, like a surgical implant, for life.

The air thickened with cigarette smoke. 'Little mole on his cheek,' she heard. 'Brand new candelabra.' There was a stirring. 'What time did you order that minicab, Irene?' Upstairs, in the wardrobe, hung her mother's clothes. They would remain there, hanging. Each time she visited they would remain in exactly the same order. If, that is, she could bring herself to open the door. She had no idea it would be like this; that death would change all her mother's possessions—transform each one of them into something charged and motionless. Objects that were meaningless and yet impossible to touch, as if a spell had been put on them.

In the end, of course, she had to do something about it all. She took a week off work, to sort things out. Shoes were the saddest, with their dear, empty bunion bumps. Scrawled recipe cards were the worst, in her mother's handwriting. So was anything her mother had repaired doggedly, with bits of Sellotape. So was everything. Celeste felt frail and elderly; she did it slowly, and had to sit down a lot. Outside there was the blast from a radio as Stan next door repaired his car; she didn't even know what day of the week it was. She emerged like an invalid, blinking in the sunshine. She was numb but surprisingly enough she still noticed things, as if she had a secretary beside her, taking notes. What was this new cereal called Cinnamon Toasts? Why did the scratchy beat of Walkmen always sound the same, as if everyone was listening to exactly the same pop song, all over Britain? Who could answer her questions now?

She was basically a cheerful sort of person and grief was like a foreign and alarming country, visited by other people but never by herself. The death of her father didn't really count because she was only six at the time. She

11

must be in that country now, though it didn't affect her as she had imagined, the landscape didn't look like the brochures, and she couldn't recollect the exact moment when she had crossed the frontier. In some ways she felt exactly the same, though Wanda, who lived opposite, said she looked awful and how about coming over for a spot of supper, they were having Turkey Thighs Honolulu? Douggie was cooking it, with tinned pineapples not fresh, but what else could you expect in a dump like this?

Celeste ate heartily. She had always had a good appetite and it seemed to persist through everything, like traffic lights still working when a city has been evacuated. Wanda wore a purple leotard; below her freckled cleavage her breasts looked as tight and glossy as plums. She was a bit of a goer; her husband Douggie had had a vasectomy.

'Why don't you go to London?' she asked.

'Why?' asked Celeste.

'Why not? Want to be stuck *here* all your life? God, I'd do anything to get away.' She sighed. People confided in Celeste nowadays, more than they used to do. Her bereavement had made them readier to pour out their own complaints, maybe to keep her company. She had learnt a lot about other people's troubles these past few weeks. 'Sub-let the maisonette,' said Wanda.

Celeste felt nauseous. 'I can't decide things

12

like that.' She couldn't decide what *clothes* to wear in the mornings. Such an effort. Tonight she felt stupid and sluggish, like an amoeba; like some lowly, spongey form of life that only flinched when prodded. She felt sleepy all the time. Was this grief?

She walked home, across the street. Behind her it darkened; the porch light was switched off, in Wanda and Douggie's house. She let herself into the empty hallway. Silence. This was the worst part; coming home. If she had switched on the radio she would have heard Buffy's voice reading the Book at Bedtime ('Ivanhoe') but she never listened to Radio 4. She went upstairs, past the closed door of her mother's bedroom, and brushed her teeth. Wanda was right; she was alone in the world now, she could do anything. She could give in her notice at Kwik-Fit Exhausts. The overall'd men there, joshing around, seemed big and oily and threatening now; the word 'fuck' made her flinch.

Suddenly she felt dizzy. She sat down, abruptly, on the lavatory seat. This panic, it had struck her several times in the past few days. It resembled the panic she felt when she repeated the same word—'basin', say, or 'sausages'—over and over until it became meaningless, except it applied to every word in her head. It was as if knitting had been unravelled and she couldn't work out how to bundle it together again and push it back into some kind of shape. Oh, for those safe days of cats' cradles! She gazed at the tiles her Dad had plastered around the bath. Every third, and sometimes fifth, tile had a shell printed on it. As a child she had tried to work out the inexplicable, adult reason for this but she had never asked him; the minute she had left the bathroom she had forgotten all about it and now it was too late. Her own name, Celeste, seemed strange to her. *Celeste.* So utterly unlikely.

*   *   *

It was a stifling night. Across England, people slept fitfully. Buffy grunted, exhaling a rubbery snore. He was dreaming of toppling columns. Children had kicked off their duvets; they lay, breathing hoarsely, their damp hair painted onto their foreheads. Dogs lay on downstairs rugs, their legs twitching with the voltage of their hunts. Celeste lay, dewy between her chaste white sheets, unaware of the clock that was already ticking, that would transform both her past and her future, and take the decision about going to London out of her hands.

*   *   *

The next morning, two days after the funeral, she knew she could put it off no longer. She had to tackle the stuff in the sideboard drawer.

14

Shoeboxes and envelopes and tins full of paperwork. She lifted them out and spread them over the floor—old bills and letters, yellowing guarantees for long-vanished appliances. Careful, biro'd sums in her mother's writing. Now she knew why she had been so reluctant to start this. It made her mother so completely dead.

She opened a biscuit tin—Crawford's Teatime Assortment. Inside it were some old post office books, Spanish pesetas, odds and ends. And an envelope. *Celeste.*

Later, she would remember the moment when she picked up the envelope. The ache in her thighs from kneeling on the floor; the sunlight on the carpet. The thud, thud of a ball in the street outside; it was a Saturday, she was only aware of it then. The different, ringing thud when the football bounced on a car.

She opened the envelope. Inside it was a letter in her mother's handwriting. And a small gold fish.

CHAPTER THREE

None of the usual doddery old regulars was in the pub that day—the four or five men who made even Buffy feel sprightly. He drained his glass and walked out, blinking, into the sunshine. Penny was due back from Positano

15

the next day, flying into Heathrow at some time or other. Eight years ago, that was how they met. They had both been what was coyly called 'between relationships' at the time—i.e., in his case, bloody lonely. He had been in L.A., the loneliest place on earth, working on a pilot for a TV series that in fact never got made.

He noticed her on the plane: shiny chestnut hair, cut in a bob; it swung when she moved. Silk blouse. Her head bent over one of those portable computer things hardly anybody had then. A look of high-powered, total absorption in what she was doing that posed a challenge to a chap. Very attractive.

After the meal he had made his way to the loo, and got pinioned against her seat by the duty-free trolley; even in those days he was by no means slim enough to squeeze past. He had bent down to her and whispered: 'Why is it, when the duty-free trolley comes round, it is pushed by a steward you've *never seen before*. And *never see again*? During the entire flight?' She had laughed and whispered, 'They keep them in a special storage compartment.'

The plane landed and they bumped into each other in the terminal. He was trying to smuggle in some particularly fine bottles of Napa Valley claret and, approaching the *Nothing to Declare* part of customs with his clanking carrier bags, he had tapped her on the shoulder. 'Be a sport, and bring these through.' She was a sport, she did. For all she

16

knew the bags could have been full of IRA guns. Full marks to her; she carried them through with that upper-class confidence, that stop-me-if-you-dare, little man look which he had always found impressive in a woman, especially when directed at someone else.

Once safely through he had introduced himself. 'Russell Buffery,' he said, shaking her hand.

Her face lit up. 'I thought I recognized the voice! Golly, you don't look like I expected.'

People were always saying that. What did they mean? What on earth were they expecting? He had never liked to ask.

'You were such a marvellous Mr Pickwick,' she said. 'I was in bed with glandular fever, I heard all the episodes. Glandular fever takes that long.'

So they shared a cab into London. She said she was a journalist and she wanted to do him for one of those *My Room* things in one of the colour supplements. He gave her his address: a mansion block in Little Venice. Well, Maida Vale.

On the appointed day she turned up, with a photographer. She wore a white linen suit; she looked as brisk and businesslike as a staff nurse. He adored nurses. On the threshold of the living room she stopped and stared. 'My God, what a pigsty!' She wandered around the room, stepping over the various items strewn on the carpet. Her eyes were wide with wonder—admiration, almost. 'People usually clean up for days before we arrive.'

It looked perfectly all right to him—in fact, he *had* tidied it up a bit—but he sensed he was onto something here. Something powerful. *Pity*. It was here to be tapped.

'My ex-wife threw me out, you see. I ended up in this place. Blomfield Mansions is full of redundant husbands, a human scrap heap.' His voice rose, his rich brown voice. Molasses, tawny port, liqueur chocolate dripped through honeycomb—all these comparisons had been made. His voice-box had brought pleasure to thousands, seen and unseen—millions, maybe. It was without a doubt his most reliable organ, where women were concerned. 'They fester here, crippled by alimony,' he throbbed. 'They sit alone in the pub, gazing at polaroid photographs of their childrens' birthday parties they've been banished from attending. They sit in the launderama watching, through the cyclops eye of the washing machine, their single, bachelor bedsheet turning, entwined with their pair of Y-fronts, a parody of the embraces they had once known . . .' He stopped. Maybe this was a bit over the top. But no; her face had become softer, blunter somehow. Even the photographer had sat down heavily in the one good armchair and was fumbling for his cigarettes.

'At night they wander the streets, watching young men buying bunches of flowers at the

18

Top Price Late Nite Store; young men, clutching a bottle of wine, eagerly springing up front steps and pressing the bell of their beloved. They pass pubs whose windows, nowadays tactlessly unfrosted, display tableaux of loving couples who, between kisses, argue playfully about what film they're going to see that night, ringing their choices with biro in their outspread copies of *Time Out*.'

Her eyes were moist; so were his. When she switched on her tape recorder, her fingers trembled. 'Tell me about your little room,' she said.

It wasn't little, actually; it was quite large. But she was obviously deeply affected. He had her now; he was an actor, after all. George Kaufman had said: if you hook your audience in the first ten minutes, you've got them for the play. And dammit, this story was true. He himself was quite overwhelmed.

'Of course, she kept most of the furniture,' he said, kicking aside some takeaway containers as he crossed the room. 'Except one or two family heirlooms even *she* didn't have the gall to nick, mostly because they're so hideous.' He pointed to the sideboard. 'That was my granny's. The door's broken, where she kicked it in.'

'Your granny?'

'No no. Jacquetta. My ex-wife. We were having a row.' He pointed to the wall. 'This is the only picture she let me keep. An incredibly dull lithograph of my old Oxford college.'

Penny nodded. 'It is dull, isn't it.' She picked up a piece of pizza crust. 'Shall I throw this away?'

He nodded. 'I always leave the edge, don't you?' He pointed out the curious china object that the cast had given him when he had played *Lear* in Hartlepool; could she make out what it was? She couldn't.

He went to the mantelpiece, moved aside a bottle of Bells, and pointed to a photo. 'These are my sons, Bruno and Tobias.'

'Aren't they sweet!'

'I've got some more, somewhere.'

'More what?'

'Children. Older than this, though.'

She looked at the two smiling faces in the tarnished frame. 'When do you see them?'

'Weekends. When she lets me.'

She pointed to a glass tank. 'What's this?'

'Their stick insects.'

She peered into the wilting foliage. 'Where are they?'

'Difficult to spot them. You see, they keep quite still and they look just like sticks. Sometimes I look in there and think: maybe that's the way to go through life—in camouflage, not moving. The only way to avoid the pain.'

That did it. She was his. And within a month she had moved in.

20

Pulling George behind him, Buffy made his way along the parade of shops. Eight years had passed since then. Abercorn Hardware had become the Video Palace. There were Arabic newspapers at the newsagents, and kiwi fruit, each with a little 50p sticker on it, outside what was once a proper greengrocers but was now Europa Food and Wine. 50p each! Schoolboys sauntered, sucking ice lollies; they seemed to be let out at all hours of the day, now. One of them said: 'It was him what stole it. I was well gutted.'

What did he mean by that? *Well gutted.* Buffy had to keep in the swim, for the sake of his sons. Bruno and Tobias were teenagers now; they had put stick insects behind them. They mustn't think of him as an old fuddy-duddy. He had a suspicion they found him vaguely dated and irrelevant, like an ionizer.

It was hot. The workmen had gone, leaving paving stones stacked like dominoes and treacherous pits of sand. George suddenly stopped, pulling Buffy back; he lifted his leg and relieved himself against a length of plastic piping. The sign above him said: *Sorry for Any Inconvenience.*

Buffy chuckled. He must remember to tell Penny that. She would be home soon, and everything would be all right. He was hopeless at being alone. Without her invigorating

21

company he felt rudderless and bereft . . . Had any of his wives ever felt the same way about him?

For some reason this made him feel irritable again. He glared at a car, double-parked outside the dry cleaners. It was empty; its engine was running, filling the air with exhaust fumes. There was a baby seat inside. On the back window was a sticker saying: *Keep Your Distance! Give My Child a Chance!*

Buffy stood, transfixed. He read it again. Car stickers in general irritated him, of course—from the leery *Honk If You Had It Last Night* to the prissy *I'm Lead-Free, Are You?* But this one, for some reason, filled him with an almost apoplectic rage. It was so bloody self-righteous, that was why.

A woman came out of the dry cleaners, carrying a plastic bag. She stopped, and stared at him. 'Can I help you?' She looked him up and down. He looked down. It was only then that he realized he was still wearing his bedroom slippers.

CHAPTER FOUR

Penny wasn't in Positano. She was in a flat in Soho, three miles up the road, lying spreadeagled over a man called Colin. He was asleep. Sun glowed through the blinds; the room was bathed in that soupy twilight known only to invalids and adulterers. She wasn't the sort of person who usually went to bed in the afternoon. The street sounds below—a car door slamming, the idling mutter of a taxi cab, waiting for somebody—they had a sharp, tinny echo. Guilt did that. The sounds could come from another country. In fact, she was supposed to *be* in another country. She had spread out her guide books, fanwise, on the rush matting of Colin's floor. Berlitz, Baedeker, Penguin. Glancing at them, she wrote in her notebook.

Positano, the haunt of sybarites and sun-worshippers, is still the Med's best-kept secret. Its winding, cobbled streets offer breathtaking vistas of the wine-dark ocean . . . Down below a car alarm sounded, *hee-haw* . . . *Braying donkeys tippety-tap down the lanes, carrying picturesque panniers of local produce* . . . Lazily, she ran her finger over Colin's hard, broad shoulder. *Towering, majestic cliffs* . . . she wrote, *terraced with vineyards and olive groves, and charming pink dwellings* . . . She ran her finger down his back . . . *dropping to a rocky shore far below* . . . She slid her hand between his legs . . . . *where boulders nestle between the luxuriant foliage of the bougainvillaea* . . .

Colin grunted, and shifted. She moved, her skin unsticking from his. It was very hot; the Pentel was slippery in her hand. She had arrived at Naples now, *bustling and*

23

cosmopolitan, home to superb museums and 499 churches, a city that bestows its favours generously but that only opens its heart to the cognoscenti . . . She sipped her tea; it was stewed. *Sitting at a bustling pavement café in the Palazzo Reale I treated myself to a welcome glass of their refreshing local wine, Lacryma Christi del Vesuvio* . . .

She thought: *Penny Warren took a mid-week bargain break, departing Gatwick and flying to Soho, still London's best-kept secret, where she travelled from the bedroom to the bathroom, returning from the bathroom to the bedroom courtesy of Sunspot Holidays Ltd* . . .

Colin mumbled into the pillow: 'Your elbow's digging.'

'Sorry.' She removed her arm. She was so apologetic with him; despite her hard elbows she felt softer, more yielding.

'Where've you got to?'

'Sorrento.'

She lay slumped across his hard buttocks, her Pentel poised. The sheer *thisness* of what was happening made her stomach contract. Until she met Colin she hadn't committed adultery; she hadn't had time. She had written lots of pieces about it, of course: *Infidelity, Do's and Don'ts. Lipstick on his Collar,* God, how corny. *It's Your Affair—the Cosmo Guide to Extra-Marital Manners.* But then she had written pieces about everything. She mostly wrote for women's magazines and the women's

24

pages of newspapers, cunningly disguised as *You* or *Living* though everyone knew that only women read them. She had been doing it for twenty years now. She was brisk and reliable, or she had been until recently. She knew where to lunch, and what sort of mineral water to order. She knew the difference between collagen and silicone. She thought she knew everything. She ruthlessly plundered her friends' lives for copy and cross-questioned their adolescent children about the latest trends. Despite her Sloaney shoes and Conran suits she knew what 'well gutted' meant. She knew all the fashion designers by their first names and went to the memorial services for their boyfriends. She held the fort in editorial offices when somebody took time off briefly— very briefly—to have a baby, or when they took a bit longer off to write a sex-and-shopping novel they got their colleagues to plug. This was what she was like, this Penny who took the tube to work and taxis at lunchtime, who breezed through London unaware, who juggled a demanding husband and a busy freelance career, who thought she knew everything.

Until now. She didn't know about this. She had no idea it would feel like this. The simple fact of another man's hands on her skin, the smell of him. The pole-axing body of him. His breath in her ear. His damp balls beneath her tenderly kneading fingers. All this. The other

25

Penny he awakened, who was always there but she didn't know it, who surrendered herself up to him—softer, more yielding, nicer. Who charted his moles between her outstretched forefinger and thumb, wondering at anything so humdrum, but not humdrum to her. Who rubbed her chin against his stubble. What was this, pheremones? Had she written a piece about them yet? It was exhilarating to be so lost, and yet discovered. It was terrifying.

*   *   *

This simply wouldn't do, she knew that. Her mother would be appalled; she would advance on Colin with her secateurs. Buffy would be— she mustn't think of Buffy. Even calling him a demanding husband made her feel guilty. Demanding was much too simple a word, even she knew that; marriage was more complicated than that. But you tried to make your husband simple, the equation an understandable one. When Colin called Buffy a boozy old fraud she bristled with hastily-assembled loyalty, but she was grateful, too. It made her position clearer, as if it were printed in one of her magazines. *P. W.—let us call her that—is a successful career woman and has been married eight years to a man fifteen years her senior. Once a well-known Shakespearean actor, his career had suffered a decline, due to domestic complications and a reputation for drink, and he was now known*

26

mainly for his mellow tones extolling the benefits of Rot-Away Damp Proof Courses. Was his a huge talent tragically squandered or a very small talent ruthlessly exploited? Time alone will tell. All P. W. discovered was that as her career prospered, his stagnated, that while she changed and grew, becoming a strong, independent woman in charge of her own life, etc etc, how many times had she written this, *he needed more from her than she was prepared to give. Like many men, a seemingly strong exterior* (in his case, pretty fat) *concealed inner insecurities and a man out of touch with his feelings. As the years passed she realized that instead of marrying a father figure she had in fact married a child.*

Oh, God, this made her feel even more guilty. It was a wholly new sensation, like the first twinges of shingles. She wasn't used to having a conscience. She was a *journalist.* Journalists are born without a conscience, like certain car engines are constructed without a fan belt. She was tough, wasn't she? From strangers, she had extracted humiliating personal confessions; from public figures she had dug out revelations of bisexual encounters. One of her best friends hadn't spoken to her since being featured in one of her most successful series, *Me and My Depression.* That's what journalists *did.* They fiddled their expenses; they never paid for a holiday in their lives. It was part of their job description. She had had the country cottage

27

totally redecorated, and a large Victorian conservatory added, for a feature that she had never got round to writing at all.

Poor Buffy. She was really very fond of him. Like communism in Eastern Europe, her marriage was suddenly crumbling so fast that she couldn't keep up with it. She was betraying her husband with chilling efficiency. She had been away on six trips now, packing her suitcase with suitable clothes for the South of France or the Norwegian fjords, ostentatiously—probably too ostentatiously—hunting for her passport, casually dropping the names of the imaginary hacks whose drunken exploits she would catalogue upon her return. Kissing Buffy goodbye, with Judas lips, and hailing a cab in the Edgware Road.

She travelled straight here, of course, to her other life. If it was an early morning flight Colin would still be in bed. Dumping her luggage on the floor she would tear off the clothes she had just put on and joyfully join him on his futon. For the three or four days of her trip she didn't dare leave the flat, in case somebody saw her. It was Colin who went out for supplies, and to buy the relevant guide books for her to crib. She had once written a piece about a man with two families, neither of which knew about the other's existence. She had called it *The Man who Ate Two Christmas Dinners*. In fact, he had to eat so many meals twice that he put on three stone and both

28

women finally fell out of love with him and ran away with other men. But she had learnt some valuable tips about the mechanics of the whole operation. The alibis. Well, lies. The construction, in her head, of a whole scenario she came to half-believe in herself, with its own cast of colourful characters. She felt like Trollope, or someone. There was Shirley from *Family Circle,* and Coral from *Chat* who always went down with migraine. Then there was Hamish Dimchurch—God knows how she had thought up the name but she felt she knew him quite well by now. Hamish Dimchurch was a sozzled old freeloader who worked for *Catering Today* and who cropped up in all her stories simply because Buffy always asked about him—maybe he recognized a kindred spirit. 'Was that old rogue Hamish there?' he would ask eagerly.

Something wet was running down her face. It was tears. Surprised, she wiped her nose and sat up. She hardly ever cried. She looked at Colin's prone, naked body, the new pattern of hairs she was only just getting used to—thick on his legs and a little trail down his lower back. He was still asleep. Her husband liked chatting but Colin hardly talked at all; that was one of the things that had attracted her to him in the first place. Buffy was like the dog; he followed her around the flat, telling her the plot of some old movie he had been watching that afternoon on the TV—Gene Tierney in

29

The Razor's Edge, stuff like that. He adored old films and knew the names of everybody; he had even worked with some of them. She should never have married an actor, everybody said they were impossible—egocentric, childish.

She was crying properly now; loud, dry sobs. She got up and took her tea mug into the kitchen. Her legs were bendy from lovemaking; her hipbones felt sore from Colin's incredibly hard futon. He was too young to mind about things like comfort. Buffy, on the other hand, was a martyr to his back. When he had tried to seduce her, that first time, he had said: 'You've just got to try out my new orthopaedic mattress.'

She pulled off a piece of kitchen roll and blew her nose. She mustn't wonder what he was doing, and how he was managing without her. That way madness lay. After all, she had slipped from him and he hadn't even noticed. What sort of marriage was that? It was the most peculiar sensation, falling in love with somebody else. She felt nauseous all the time. Her rib-cage ached. She felt as if her spirit had moved out of Blomfield Mansions and only a husk remained there, like a pupa whose butterfly had flown. She probably looked all right to Buffy, from the outside. But if he prodded her, she would collapse.

In the next room, Colin got up. Hurriedly she wiped her eyes. He wandered in and levered open a bottle of lager. His body looked damp; his cock hung red and raw. He looked well-used.

'Why are photographers so hairy?' she asked. 'I've often wondered.'

'Hey, how many've you seen like this?'

'None, I told you. But they all wear Paul Smith jackets with the sleeves rolled up, and you can tell by their wrists.'

He crooked his arm around her neck. 'Come and live with me, or I'll do my karate chop.'

'Oh, what's going to happen to us?'

He didn't reply. She looked at her watch; the adulterer's reflex gesture.

*   *   *

It was convenient, Colin living in Soho. Despite the ravages of redevelopment there were still some of the old speciality shops left. On the last day of her trip she would go out and buy stuff to bring home—*kephtédés* and *hummus* if she had been to Greece; salt cod, from a place near Brewer Street, if she had been to Portugal. It was risky, of course, because she might be spotted by somebody coming out of the Groucho Club, but she couldn't bear to let Colin do it—not this. Making love to him was bad enough, but sending him out to buy food for Buffy seemed in even poorer taste.

31

On Thursday she went out to Camisas and bought some Neapolitan specialities—buffalo mozzarella, *prosciutto* and tiny, ethnic-looking olives. She packed them in her suitcase. Then she rubbed some Sudden Tan cream onto her face, and typed up her copy on her portable 'Tosh. She didn't feel guilty about this—who cared if she actually went to Italy or not? Most of her fellow hacks spent their entire time in the hotel bar anyway, and cribbed it up on the flight home. Besides, her copy would probably be subbed down to 300 words, or maybe cut altogether if there was a last-minute ad. No, this part of the operation just gave her the pleasant, prickly sensation of petty lawlessness, like feeding foreign coins into a parking meter. Nothing more than that.

She closed her laptop with a click. She was dressed in her travelling outfit, ready to leave. In the other room, Colin was watching TV. There was an advertising jingle, then Buffy's voice boomed out, loud and clear: 'Baileys Babywipes. Big absorbency, for little bottoms.'

'Turn it off!' she yelled.

She dragged her luggage down the stairs. Colin kissed her goodbye, in the hallway. She nuzzled the gold hoop in his ear.

'Come on, Pen,' he said, 'make up your mind.'

'How'll he manage without me? He'd be lost.'

'Don't listen to that helpless crap. He's a

ruthless old bugger. He'll survive.'

She held him, tightly. It still surprised her, to embrace such a slim man. She was forty-six. Was it fashionable, at her age, to have a toy boy? She had written pieces about it. On the other hand she had written just as many pieces on the advantages of an older man. He ran his lips over her face.

'Don't!' she said. 'My tan'll come off.'

She sat in the cab as it crawled up Regent Street. When did *having an affair* become *leaving your husband*? They were two such different things. She hadn't realized this until now. It was like sexual intercourse and childbirth; one might lead to the other but need they? The prospect of moving from the first experience to the second felt utterly terrifying, like stepping out of an open window into thin air. Could she really make it happen? Did she dare?

In fact, it happened without any decision on her part at all. And sooner than she thought.

CHAPTER FIVE

Blomfield Mansions wasn't full of ex-husbands. Years earlier Buffy had told Penny that it was full of lonely men crippled by alimony but that was just a sob story. In fact, the residents of the grimy old Edwardian

33

building consisted of the usual mix found in this part of London: Arabs—though not really wealthy ones or they wouldn't be living there—whose wives hid their faces from Buffy when they found themselves squashed next to him in the lift but whose children stared up at him with the usual candid interest. Old couples who had lived in the place all their lives. A pallid doctor called Lever who Buffy was convinced was an abortionist. Some bland and pleasant Americans who never stayed long. And a large proportion of what Penny called Anita Brookner women—spinsterly or widowed, of an indeterminate age and usually engaged in some dowdy job, probably of a clerical nature. Buffy had lived in the building for ten years and knew a lot of the inmates; he was also a loud and active member of the Residents' Committee—a sure sign of his own lack of outside employment, but still, he enjoyed the cut and thrust of the meetings.

His long-term enemy was an elderly Hungarian called Mrs Zamiski. She lived in the next flat and for many years had waged a war against his dog—one of those rumbling campaigns that have gone on for so long that everyone has forgotten about them, like events in Namibia. Her windows faced the front. They overlooked the main road and the so-called gardens. These consisted of a strip of balding lawn and a dense, dusty shrubbery. Several times a day Buffy took George out, and it was amongst these bushes that he (the dog) relieved himself—or, as one American child shrilly pointed out, w*ent to the bathroom.* Mrs Zamiski, who seemed to keep a perpetual vigil behind her net curtains, always timed it perfectly. She waited until George was in a squatting position, then she flung open her window and yelled, 'Feelthy animal—I call the porter!' So Buffy had devised an ingenious plan, whereby he and George crept along the edge of the lawn, close to the building and out of her line of vision. From there it was a brisk trot straight into the middle of the shrubbery, where nobody could see them at all.

It was a shame, really, that he couldn't just let George off the lead and disclaim responsibility, sauntering past the bushes and letting the dog get on with it. But George had become unpredictable in his old age. Most of the time he was as lazy as Buffy—even lazier, if that was possible—and needed to be dragged along on his walks, sometimes in a sitting position. Lately, however, he had been seized with sudden and unprovoked rages. Off he would dash, barking wildly, and fling himself at the person who had unknowingly offended him. This was usually a cyclist. Seeing some pleasant, Friends of the Earth type pedalling along sent him into paroxysms of fury. But then sometimes so did a perfectly normal person walking along the pavement. This mostly happened, embarrassingly, when the person was black. 'He's turning into the most awful old fascist,' said Penny. 'It'll be homosexuals next.' She had always loathed the dog.

This particular afternoon Buffy left the flat to buy his *Evening Standard*. It was one of his rituals. He didn't like the paper much, but on the other hand he couldn't bear not to read it in case he missed something. He felt like this about a lot of things. He was looking forward to seeing Penny; she was due back at any time now, and she always took a cab straight home from the airport. She had promised to bring back something nice for supper; he adored Italian food.

He shared the lift with an unknown businessman, possibly Lebanese. George growled at him. Powerful aftershave filled the air as they descended wordlessly together. Not for the first time, Buffy speculated whether one of the Anita Brookner women was in fact a high-class call girl. He often encountered strange men in the lift, who never said hello, and Miss Bevins two floors up wore surprisingly high heels. It was a fun thought, anyway.

Buffy walked out into the sunshine. It was one of those blazing July days that made even the Edgware Road look picturesque. Shiny red buses trundled by. A nanny pushed a pram; above it floated a silver balloon. Passers-by had a shiny, hometown innocence, like extras in a Frank Capra film. His spirits lifted. It reminded him of the old days when he had emerged from the Colony Room, blinking, into the middle of a staggeringly normal weekday afternoon.

He edged along the side of the building and pulled George into the shrubbery. It was just then that a taxi arrived, though he didn't hear it, the traffic was too loud. Penny stepped out of the cab and unloaded her luggage.

At the same moment a courier, wearing arousingly shiny cycling shorts, came out of the front door. Chattering into his walkie-talkie, he mounted his bike and sped away.

George's lead jerked from Buffy's hand. The dog shot out of the bushes, barking hoarsely, and raced after the departing cyclist. Penny saw him. 'George!' she yelled, and ran after him.

Buffy emerged from the bushes and stared at Penny's departing figure, running down the pavement. She always caught the dog, in the end; she ran much faster than he did.

He walked to the taxi. Its engine was throbbing; the driver was obviously waiting. Later, Buffy remembered what he was thinking, just at that moment. That in the old, Colony Room days the driver would have unloaded her bloody suitcases himself and probably chased the dog too. Buffy also tried to remember if he had done the washing up for the past few days and collected Penny's clothes from the cleaners, as per instructions. He remembered thinking all this, the moment before he spoke.

'She paid you?' he asked the driver.

The man shook his head. Buffy looked down the road. Penny had disappeared. He took out his wallet; after all, she could pay him back from her expenses. He drew out a couple of twenty pound notes.

'So what's the damage?' he asked.

The driver flicked his cigarette out of the window and pointed to the fare, illuminated in its little box.

'Three pounds fifty,' he said.

CHAPTER SIX

Autumn, in London. The wind whipped the leaves off the trees and slewed them into the gutters. Black plastic sacks fattened in the public parks; it looked as if somebody had dropped them there from a great height. City brokers—even city brokers—were caught off-guard by a brooding melancholy they didn't have time to name. Restaurateurs dragged in their pavement tables; assistants in Selfridges discussed their Christmas plans, though they had been discussing them since the spring. Swallows departed; the first frost arrived, by stealth, one night. People sat in their cars, warming up their engines. Women searched for their one lost glove.

Celeste, who had lost her mother, moved to London in October. She rented a flat just off the Kilburn High Road. It was two rooms above a mental health charity shop. She tried to keep herself safe but oh, the noise, the fumes, the jostling crowds! The drilling in the streets, the skips full of rubble! Buses roared past her windows; beneath her, tubes rumbled along the Jubilee Line, making her house plants shiver. In the streets people bumped into her; they threw back their heads, draining Pepsi from cans. They stuffed their faces with handfuls of crisps. London assaulted her; she had been tenderly nurtured in the sleepy provinces, she wasn't used to this. Her London was picture postcards and Monopoly. Where was Vine Street, with its big red hotel? She was lost; she had lost everything. When she stepped out, in the mornings, she had to look down quickly to make sure she was dressed.

She had always been a slip of a thing but now she looked transparent. Shock had done that. The shock of the death was disorientating enough, but then she had been companioned in her grief. Not entirely, because grief removes the grief-stricken, nobody can reach them in their separate exiles where they have to suffer it out alone. But at least other people have been there too; they can describe the location and some of its features are familiar.

This was different; she was totally alone in this. Nobody knew about the contents of the envelope, she had kept it a secret. And starting a new life, in a new city, sent her spinning into the bright October air, lost in space.

She knew where to go, and she often walked there. The streets were deafening, how did people bear it? On either side, houses were being gutted and refurbished. In Melton Mowbray everything stayed the same but here lives were being dismantled, nothing was certain. Rooms collapsed while workmen whistled; empty windows, like dragons' nostrils, breathed out smoke. From upper storeys long, jointed tubes of buckets dangled into skips; they looked like elephants' trunks. As she walked past they vomited noisily, disgorging dust. Nobody else seemed to notice. She passed a bakery; its buns were split open, like mouths, frothing cream at her. She flinched at everything, she felt so raw. The high street was jammed with traffic. How could there be so much, and where was it going? It was never-ending, like scarves pulled from a conjuror's pocket. Even the bicyclists were alarming, bumping on and off the pavement, glaring at people over their gas masks.

She went there and she stayed for a while, just looking, just telling herself she had come to the right place. She hid in a bus shelter on the opposite side of the road. She looked up at the windows of the building. Her heart thumped. Which windows were the right ones? Soon, somehow, she would find out. She would find a way.

She walked back in the dusk, down Kilburn High Road, the street of shoes. So many shoe shops, Saxone, Dolcis, their racks on the pavement, their wire baskets filled with ladies shoes, the sort her mother used to wear, *Final Clearance Sale!* Rows of single shoes, unbunioned as yet. She stood there, trying to cry, but she was beyond tears now. *To the best Mum in the world!* she used to write. She made her Mum birthday cards, they used to take hours. She remembered the weight of her mother's hand in hers. Grown-ups were baffling, but you thought you could rely on them. They worried about stupid things but that was what they were supposed to do. It made you feel superior. Adults never realize how superior children feel, how much of the time.

Celeste went back to her flat. She felt both very old, wearily so, and at the same time infantile and bereft. Somewhere in the middle should be herself, bringing home a Birds Eye Fisherman's Pie for supper, just arrived in London and looking for a job. She must learn to be this woman, a step at a time. And she must learn how to lie.

Beside the doorbell was a note. *Waxie, I'm at Lynns.* Who was Waxie? She didn't know any of the people in the flats yet, they were just thumps and muffled music. Opposite was a building with barred windows called Reliance House. It always looked closed, but today some men were going in and out, unloading cardboard boxes. What was everyone up to? The key to it all had been taken away from her. One letter, in a biscuit tin, had done it.

Celeste went upstairs and unloaded her shopping. Her skull ached; her insides felt heated and swollen. But it wasn't the beginnings of flu. It was anger.

CHAPTER SEVEN

'Madam, I would like a shampoo and set!'

'Hang on.' Archie fiddled with the volume controls. 'Okay. Once more, from the top. A bit louder.'

'Madam,' boomed Buffy, *'I would like a shampoo and set!'*

Archie rewound the tape— *tesdnaoopmahsaekildluowi, gabble gabble*— listened and nodded. 'Carry on.'

'Fill her up please, top grade,' said Buffy, into the mike. *'Show me to a table where I can see the pianist's hands.'*

'A bit more feeling on the *hands*,' said Archie.

'What is this, the blooming Old Vic?'

It was suffocating in the little booth. The air was thick with smoke from Archie's cheroot, and the walls were scribbled with multi-lingual graffiti, probably of an obscene or homesick nature.

'This wine is corked!' said Buffy. *'Take it back to the cellar!'*

The St Reginald College of English was situated above a massage parlour in Balham. Archie ran it, together with a couple of seedy ex-teachers who looked as if they had been sacked for paedophilia. The embossed crest above the door fooled nobody except foreigners; Archie had copied it from a jar of marmalade. Reginald was the name of his uncle.

'I am a stranger to this town. Please direct me to your nearest building society!'

The tape they were recording was compiled for East Europeans, newly-liberated fodder for Archie's language school. He called them 'the Great Stonewashed' after he had seen newsreels of them clambering over the Berlin Wall—clambering not to freedom but to enrolment at his establishment. These tapes were a bona fide money-spinner, that was what he thought—think of the market openings!—and were peppered with queries about mortgage rates and venture capitalism.

'May I make a down-payment on this appliance?' asked Buffy, choking in the smoke. 'For God's sake, Archie, put that thing out!'

43

He squinted at his sheet of paper and leant towards the mike. *'Does this cellphone come with a written guarantee?'*

Why am I here? he wondered. To what depths have I sunk? I, who like Tiresias, have seen it all. What am I doing, stuck in a suffocating booth in Balham, teaching a lot of Lithuanians how to order shares in British Telecom? The chair was hard; his backside ached. No wonder his haemorrhoids were playing up again.

'Madam, kindly sell me a suppository!'

'What?' Archie squinted at him through the smoke.

He was doing it for the money, of course. The fee was really quite decent. Archie must be making a bomb from this place, in addition to—as he felicitously put it—dipping his wick into some fairly acceptable Commie crumpet. Ex-Commie crumpet.

But then Archie had always been a bit of a spiv. They had met during National Service when they had both been stationed in an arctic base camp near Kettering. Even then Archie had been involved in some complex manoeuvres involving petrol and bulk-order baked beans; no fool, he had been in cahoots with Warrant Officer Pickering, a key figure at the time and the springboard to a lifetime's racketeering. Bored and freezing, Buffy had loathed the entire two years and spent his time being as inconspicuous as possible, listening to

44

Fats Waller records on his bunk and creeping out at night to meet girls from the local chicken-gutting factory. Despite his public school education he had failed to rise above the rank of sergeant, a tribute to the good sense of those in charge. Whilst he languished, Archie thrived and left the Army a fully-fledged entrepreneur. First it was reconditioned fridges, then snooker halls and the leisure industry. 'I got into gravel pits,' he said. 'The genesis of the theme park should, by rights, be credited to yours truly.' Buffy hadn't seen him for decades; they had happened to bump into each other recently in the Charing Cross Road, where Buffy had been browsing in a second-hand bookshop—another sure sign of his excess leisure, like knowing the names of all the waitresses at his local patisserie.

'It's a wrap!' said Archie in an irritating American accent. He disconnected the mike and they went into a small, leprous office. On the wall hung a framed certificate, testifying to Archie's qualifications as a senior EFL instructor. The Tippex beneath the name *Archibald Bingham* was clearly visible. Archie scratched his balls, coughed, and unlocked a drawer. From it he produced a wad of soiled banknotes and counted them out, one by one.

'Know how to say *You're a horny tomato* in Japanese?' he asked.

'No,' said Buffy. He took the notes. 'Shouldn't there be another ten?'

'My mistake, squire.' Archie reopened the drawer and passed it over.

It was lunchtime. Now he had no wife to go home to, Buffy had an impulse to ask Archie— even Archie—out for a drink. He felt this about the most unlikely people. But Archie shook his head and squirted some breath freshener into his mouth.

'Got a date with a promising little Czech.' He grinned. 'Play my cards right and it'll soon be Czech-mate.'

A wave of desolation swept over Buffy. Not that he was excluded from this twosome, but that he was desperate enough to have issued such an invitation to Archie in the first place. He had noticed this before, with a sinking sense of recognition. Once divorced, your standards plummeted. You rang up acquaintances you hadn't seen for years; you endured whole evenings in Dollis Hill with your accountant and his wife, drinking microscopic scotches and watching videos of their Kenyan safari. You sat in a pub for hours while some near-stranger told you about all the amazing things you could do with computer graphics. It was like suddenly having no money and going back to eating tinned macaroni. Anything to delay the return to that darkened flat.

He took the bus home. In the seat behind him an inebriated Irishman sang 'Loveboat, loveboat' all the way to Victoria, until the word lost all meaning—if, that is, it had any in the first place. Buffy didn't have the energy to shut him up. Was this all there was? Was this all he could expect, now? He thought of Prospero. His maturity fitted him for this role, he had grown into it—the noble forehead, the experience. My God, the experience. Why, now he had arrived at this bus-stop in life's journey, did nobody recognize it? Surely his past should lend him gravitas, but nowadays it was all producers half his age, drinking mineral water and getting phone-calls from their children.

All his old mates, the real characters, had gone; they had died from cirrhosis of the liver or retired to cottages in France. This young lot was sort of odourless, no patina to them. Even in its heyday the BBC didn't lend itself to dissipation but there was a certain style to things then, a Fitzrovian camaraderie, men with no discernible home life, women producers called Muriel, gruff and reckless, who were built like shire-horses and who could drink you under the table, and who knew who you might discover the next morning, snoring peacefully on your floor while the gas fire still blazed?

Buffy got off the bus at Maida Vale. The wind whipped his face; it was November and already freezing—why did November always seem colder than any other month? An illegally-parked car was being towed away;

47

weeee-weeee wailed its alarm. How helpless it looked. He felt just like that himself. What a humiliating morning!

He tried to cheer himself up. At least there was no Penny waiting, with her hoots of mirth. *Honestly, Buffy, how could you?* It was undeniably lonely, that she wasn't there to listen to his exploits at the language school, which by now he would have worked up into one of his anecdotes. On the other hand it was a relief, that she wasn't there to be all superior about it. He must remember that. She had been insufferably superior. Her greatest feat, her most awesomely mind-boggling one, was that she managed to be superior *even when it was revealed she had been double-crossing him. For months.* He, Russell Buffery, had been the totally innocent party. She had been lying and cheating, packing and unpacking, and all the time shagging herself senseless with some under-aged photographer in Soho. *And yet she had managed to still be hoity-toity about it.* The whole thing was breathtaking.

Looking back over those final explosive weeks, he couldn't remember how she did it, probably some sort of conjuring trick. But she had managed, in some appallingly female way, to make *him* feel to blame. It was all, obviously, his fault . . . 'Your infantile egocentricity . . . your drinking . . . your hypochondria . . . And another thing . . .' All his ex-wives said that, *and another thing.* You

48

never helped with the children, you never helped with the washing up . . . you were never supportive with my career . . . *and another thing* . . . you dropped ash on the duvet . . . you laughed at your own jokes . . . at that dinner party at the Robinsons', remember, you fell asleep in the soup, *the soup,* remember, we hadn't even started the main course, I could've *died* . . . a blizzard of *another things*, a smokescreen of them . . .

He remembered that mockingly sunny day, three months earlier. How he had unzipped her suitcase with feverish hands.

'I told you, I changed taxis!' she had cried. 'The cabbie from the airport, he was going on about darkies and what's the country coming to and I simply couldn't stand it. Racism is so repellent, especially when one's paying for it. So I got into another one!'

The self-righteousness of her voice, barely faltering even when she saw him taking out the bottle of Sudden Tan!

'That's for my legs. They always take the longest to get brown, not that *you'd* notice.'

See! She had managed to put him in the wrong, even then. 'Where's your plane ticket?' he had demanded. 'Where's your lira?'

'Don't be so paranoid, darling. It's bad for your blood pressure.'

Just then she stopped. He had pulled out a newspaper—*La Stampa.* It still had its sticker on: *Pat's News and Smokes, Wardour St.* W.1.

49

'Oh shit,' she said.

*   *   *

Buffy paused outside Blomfield Mansions and looked up at the porch. Two cupids, carved in stone, were entwined above the doorway. They were portly and sooty; the private parts of one of them had chipped off. He knew how they felt. With what hopes, years before, had he once carried Penny across the threshold—well, not carried, because of his bad back, but he had lifted her, with a little hop, over the rubber doormat. How those cupids mocked him now! My God he was feeling maudlin, and he hadn't even had a drink.

He let himself into the flat, stumbling first over the dog and then over a plastic bag of empties. There was a funny smell coming from somewhere. Once he had been in the place for a bit he got used to it, but it always hit him on entering. The answerphone showed '1'. Briefly, but unconvincingly, he had an image of Penny, sobbing on the other end of the line and begging to come home. Asking him to forgive her. Grovellingly telling him that for once it was her mistake and she would always love him.

He replayed the message.

'Granada TV here, could you call back as soon as possible and ask for Gwenda.'

Granada TV! His spirits rose. He dialled

50

the number. Maybe it was a cameo role—a fatherly family doctor, say, or a charismatic local MP. About time he was on the TV again. Maybe it was a major costume drama set in the Caribbean! They wanted him to play a plantation owner with a doting young native mistress.

By the time Gwenda's voice answered he was already making his acceptance speech at the BAFTA awards. 'Mr Buffery?' she said. 'Just to remind you, we don't seem to have received last month's rental on your video recorder. Would you like to pop in, or pop a cheque in the post?'

It was that sort of day. Well, year. Gloomily, he put George on his lead and left the flat. He stopped at The Three Fiddlers for a pint. His piles were so painful that he didn't sit down; he stood at the bar. In this position the weight on his feet made his corns throb but this was marginally preferable to the other thing. He had wedged cotton wool as well as corn plasters against his toes but they still pressed against the sides of his espadrilles, the thinking man's bedroom slippers.

None of his ex-wives had understood a simple fact: he didn't want to be a hypochondriac—nobody did—he just happened to have a lot of things wrong with him, mostly of a vaguely undignified but not life-threatening nature. He didn't seek the bloody things out. He didn't *want* them.

51

Bitterly, he remembered Penny's shrill giggle when she first opened his bathroom cabinet. 'What're they all for? No, don't tell me!' Strong and vigorous, she had no patience with any sort of infirmity, and less so as their marriage progressed. Erotic back-rubs became brisk ones; brisk ones became progressively brusquer until they ceased altogether. 'Well they don't do much good, darling, do they? Why don't you go to your funny little osteopath?' When he was bedridden, the approaching rattle of the supper-tray took on an accusatory clatter, a *still-in-bed?* clatter, and she started forgetting the pepper mill.

It was a shame she wasn't ill herself more often because he was wonderful with ill women. Like many so-called hypochondriacs he was as interested in other people's symptoms as his own. In fact some of the most tender moments of his previous marriage to Jacquetta had come each month when she suffered her crippling period pains. She had had migraines too, an affliction Penny had airily dismissed as neurotic. 'Christ,' she'd said, 'you must've been a right couple of crocks.' That was long ago, when she was still interested enough in his past to be jealous.

It was late. The pub was empty except for Buffy, the bitter aftertaste of his various marriages and a couple of old girls called Una and Kitty, who always bagged the seats near the fire. They had men's voices and the compacted, pressed-meat complexions of serious boozers. Buffy was fond of them, but their wrecked faces always made him uneasy— did he look like that, or would he soon? Besides, he didn't feel like any sort of conversation today, even the amiable but minimal kind he would have with them.

He walked up the street, pausing briefly to enter the smoky inferno of Ladbrokes to see if his horse, Genie Boy, had won. It hadn't.

*   *   *

In the months to come he tried to recollect his state of mind that Friday afternoon. Bitter and gloomy, oh, yes. Vaguely cosmic too. His company had been spurned by Archie Bingham, and you couldn't get lower than that. His exes were living with other men, more harmoniously than they had ever lived with him, they made that perfectly plain, and his children were growing up without the benefits of his jovial good nature and panoramic breadth of experience. Did none of them realize what they were missing? He nearly tripped; the blithering pavement had been dug up, yet again. This time it was something to do with British Telecom. A pit was revealed; within it hung a knotted tangle of wires. You opened up somebody, and look at the mess inside! Divorce did that; surely it was a better idea to keep the lid on? Women were always prodding around inside him, tut-tutting like workmen, shaking their heads sorrowfully, sucking through their teeth and occasionally bursting into hysterical giggles. What was so bloody funny?

That was how he was feeling towards women in general, towards life itself, when he stopped outside the chemist's. He was, of course, a regular and valued customer at this shop. The same with Victoria Wine, opposite. He sometimes wondered what might happen if he ever moved away; how either establishment could possibly carry on.

He went in; *ping*. A blast of warm air caressed his face; perfume filled his nostrils. He paused on the threshold. A mysterious sense of well-being flooded through him.

Did it? Did it already? Even before he saw her? Yes!

Or was he just a corny old romantic, a silly old fool?

He felt it—warmth, happiness. He crossed the shop, past the racks of flowery spongebags and the cards of sparkling hairclips. Mr Singh, the pharmacist, didn't seem to be around, and the usual assistant was busy with a customer.

'It has its own tingle scrub,' she was saying, 'to tighten the pores.'

Then he heard a voice. 'Can I help you?'

He turned. A young woman got to her feet. She had been kneeling on the floor, stocking some shelves, that was why he hadn't seen her.

54

'Hello!' His voice sounded ridiculously hearty. He felt himself blushing. At his age! 'You're new,' he said stupidly, just for something to say.

She nodded. She was enchanting. Utterly, entirely enchanting. Slender, shy, beautiful; halo'ed, somehow, in innocence. She wore the usual pink overalls; above it her face was delicate and translucent. Limpid brown eyes, pointed chin, achingly stem-like neck. My God! She was like a sapling, a silver birch. She was like a single daffodil, surrounded by coarse plastic blooms. How on earth was he going to ask her for a packet of suppositories?

'Er, is Mr Singh around?'

She shook her head. 'He's just popped out to the post office.'

How could he discuss his piles with this radiant creature? If only it were the other assistant, the big motherly one, but she was still busy. It was the old French letters syndrome: why, when one wanted to buy something embarrassing, was one faced with the prettiest salesgirl? If only he could ask for something impressive—special pills, say, to curb his incredibly powerful sexual drive.

'Anusol Suppositories, please,' he said. 'Oh, what a bag of infirmities is man!'

'Anusol? What's it for?'

'Haemorrhoids. Humiliating, I know.'

'It's all right, I won't tell anybody.' She smiled at him. 'Where are they?'

55

He paused. 'Er. The usual place.'

'No—I mean do you know where they're kept? The suppositories?'

'Ah. Up there.' He pointed to the cabinet behind her. She reached up. Her sleeve fell back, exposing a slim bare arm and a shadowy armpit.

'I'm going to the cinema tonight' he said, suddenly reckless, 'and it's agony sitting down.' *Come with me. Come out tonight. Like all ruins, I look best by moonlight.*

'What's on?'

'About six different films. Have you noticed how lovely, big things like cinemas have been divided into little cupboards, yet lovely little cupboards, like grocery shops, have been made into enormous big Waitroses? All the wrong way round, in my opinion. Still, you're too young to remember.'

'We only had a tiny cinema anyway, where I come from.'

'Where's that?'

'Melton Mowbray. Me and pork pies.' She fetched down a packet. 'Twelve or twenty-four?'

'Twenty-four. And I need some Algipan and some Multivite . . .' He fished in his pocket. 'And I've got some repeat prescriptions here . . .'

'Mr Singh will be back in a tick.' She took the bits of paper. 'Simvastatin,' she read.

'That's for my heart.'

'Fybogel,' she read.

'That's for my bowels.'

She gazed at him. He felt her tender curiosity bathing his internal organs. His embarrassment disappeared; he surrendered to her. He was all hers—his body, and all it was still capable of.

'What I really need is a complete set of new parts,' he said. 'Trouble is, the guarantee's expired.'

She laughed. 'I know about Algipan,' she said, fetching the bottle. 'My Mum was prescribed it.'

'Did it work?'

'Well, she's dead now.' Suddenly, her eyes filled with tears.

'Oh, Lord.' He fumbled in his pocket but all he brought out was a sort of compost—a sediment of disintegrated bus tickets and so on.

'I'm sorry,' she sniffed. 'Don't know why I said that.'

'Are you all right?'

She nodded. She wiped her nose, like a child, on the back of her hand, and bent her head to look at the prescriptions.

There was silence. Something had happened. When she looked up, her face was drained.

'Russell Buffery,' she whispered.

'That's me.' He gazed at her. 'What's the matter?'

She didn't reply. At that moment the other

assistant strolled over, smiling.

'Hello.' She turned to the girl. 'This is one of my favourite customers. Isn't he nice? Remember Uncle Buffy, on *Children's Hour?*'

The girl stared at him. Then she slowly nodded.

'Uncle Buffy and his Talking Hamster.'

'Hammy,' said the girl.

'I didn't make up the name,' said Buffy. 'They did.'

The girl said: 'I used to listen to you, with my milk. That was *you?*'

Buffy nodded. 'Both of me.'

'Go on,' said the other assistant, 'do Hammy for her!'

'Why not Buffy?' He had always felt hurt, that Hammy used to get more fan mail than he did. He had grown to loathe his little sidekick. 'I can do other animals, you know. Hens. Grasshoppers.' He made a small, scraping sound with his teeth. 'I can do a marvellous W C Fields.'

'Do Hammy!'

He sighed. Oh, well, at least he was famous for *something.* And it was delightful, that he had spoken to this girl when she was little, even if it had been through a radio. He raised his voice to a squeak. *'Well bless my cotton socks! Who's that coming through the dell? That rough little fellow with the twinkle in his eye?'*

'That was Voley,' said the girl. 'The rough little fellow with the twinkle in his eye.'

'You remember?'

She nodded. 'The vole. He was a burglar. He stole all the squirrels' nuts. Once I tried to open the radio, to see if you were all inside.'

'Never a good idea,' said Buffy, thinking of the knotted British Telecom wires.

'You were famous,' she said.

'Except all my fans were under five.'

'I used to wonder what you looked like.' Tilting her head, she inspected him. 'You're not like I thought.'

'Why? My ears aren't all furry?'

'Oh, I don't know,' she said, and sighed. When she looked up her eyes were glistening with tears again. Why? 'What happened, anyway?'

'The writer had a nervous breakdown. Couldn't handle all the sex and violence in the stories. So they got rid of us and brought in—'

'Timmy McTingle and his Little Red Choo-Choo Train.'

'Bit Freudian, I always thought.'

'I never liked him as much.' Her face cleared; she smiled again. It was extraordinary, watching the weather-changes on her face. Suddenly the shop was flooded with sunlight. *Ping.* Some customers came in. Just then the music started and they all broke into song, *Pennies from Heaven,* the bottles dancing on their shelves, lights chasing around *L'Oreal* and *Dispensary.* The spongebags, bellows-like, grunted the rhythm; on their display cards, the

59

golden hairclips clattered their applause.

They did, in his middle-aged, susceptible heart. She had stepped into him, like a deer into a thicket, turning round and round until she had made herself the warmest of nests. He felt her there, lodged in him, even as she answered the phone, cupping it against her shoulder, and another customer came in and asked for something or other. It was the strangest sensation.

He walked down the street. There was a lift in the air, a quickening of London's pulse. Cars hooted, buses were crammed, the sodium lights flickered on, one by one, down the Edgware Road. For the first time in months he didn't feel excluded; he felt he had rejoined the bright, sliding stream of the city. She probably thought he was a boring old fart. Maybe she was a dream. Next time she wouldn't be there. But just now he was so utterly undone he had even forgotten to buy the *Standard*.

CHAPTER EIGHT

Things aren't as they appear. Celeste was learning this. Take Kilburn High Road; the shops in it. You thought they were selling one thing and they turned out to be selling something totally different as well. The florist's shop sold discount videos. The window of the post office was heaped with porcelain shepherdesses and packets of chamois leathers. She was surrounded by tricks and illusions. Some of the shops lied outright. Matthews Greengrocers was full of office equipment; a shop that said it sold office equipment was full of saris and canteens of cutlery. She walked past them on her way to work, past men holding cans of lager in front of them like votive offerings, at 8.30 in the morning! When she came home the shops had mysteriously been replaced, like stage props; windows were barred and new stalls had appeared on the pavement selling bin liners and Irish leprechauns. She couldn't get a grip on the place. The neighbourhood seemed like a pack of cards being shuffled behind her back. *Got you!* it sniggered.

She didn't like the way men looked at her, either. In the evenings they still carried cans of lager, but they were more pressing. It didn't do, to dawdle. She walked briskly even when she had nowhere to go. Sometimes she had to dodge into shops, the hot breath of them blowing onto her face, the *can I help you*'s. She felt sickly and bewildered. Even her body was something she had to re-learn. Men fixed their eyes on it but it was not quite her own, not yet. Her arms hung from her shoulders, her toenails were there, okay, but she felt she had been taken apart and reassembled. She had to check that everything was in place.

Nesta helped her; Nesta at work. 'It's one thing to be pale and interesting,' she said, 'but honestly, Celly, you look as if you've seen a ghost.' She sat her down. 'You've got a bone structure to die for,' she said. 'Build on it.' Nesta had worked in the shop for a year and she was familiar with all the new products. 'I'd give my right arm for your eyes,' she sighed. In the mid-afternoons, when the place was quiet, she held a mirror up to Celeste's face and gave her make-up lessons. It was soothing. At work, Celeste became reacquainted with her skin and dusted powder onto it. 'Cleanse, tone, nourish,' chanted Nesta, like a prayer. 'They'll be around you like bees round a honeypot.' Her voice was wistful; she herself was plain and plump, though she had a devoted boyfriend who arrived each day at six o'clock prompt and loaded her onto his Honda.

Celeste had been working in the shop for a week before Buffy came in. It had been so simple; she had walked by, seen a *Salesperson Wanted* sign in the window, gone in and got the job. By the second day she had felt part of the fixtures and fittings. There was a lot to learn but it was only bottles and packets and things you could grasp. She was a whizz at the till; after all, she had done the accounts at Kwik-Fit, she was over-qualified for this. She liked stocking the shelves and pricing things, *pzzz, pzzz*, with her pricing gun. She liked the photos of lustrous women on the display cases, their pouting beauty invited her to accompany them to a place of which she was only dimly aware. She wasn't ready, yet. The outside world confused her but Mr Singh ran a tight ship and his shop was an oasis of perfumed confidentiality.

Alpha Pharmacy was in a parade of shops just off the Edgware Road. Blocks of mansion flats rose up behind it; down the road stretched the creamy crescents of what she discovered was Little Venice. She could walk to work each day; it was only a mile from the chaos of Kilburn but it was like stepping into another world. She felt stabilized; a hand steadied her on the playground swing. The shops sold exactly what they said they did, and she was working in one of them. She was in a middle-class neighbourhood where people knew what they wanted. She hadn't met Buffy yet, and she didn't know what he wanted, but she sensed a certain thrust and confidence in the air. Things didn't shift, and disappear overnight. The wine merchants opposite said *Est. 1953* on its sign and there they were every day, the same bottles in the window. Buffy, she was to discover, bemoaned the changes in their locality but she only noticed the reassuring continuity; such is the seeking magnet of our needs. Even the drilling in the street outside didn't impinge, not while she was punching the numbers on her bleeping till. She liked it when

63

the shop was busy and she didn't have time to think.

That day. What was special about that day? A Friday, and by lunchtime the city was quickening. She had felt this each week since she had arrived. In schoolrooms, unknown children fidgeted at their desks. Out in the hinterlands, in the factories, people listened restlessly for the hooter. Down the road, still unknown to her, Buffy was sipping his late scotch in The Three Fiddlers.

'Malcolm's taking me bowling,' said Nesta, 'after we've had a snack. You ever been bowling?'

Celeste shook her head.

'Got to find you a boyfriend, preferably with wheels,' said Nesta.

Celeste was standing on a chair, stocking a shelf with nasal sprays. She was remembering her dream, from the night before. She had pricked her mother with a pin, *hsssss* . . . The body deflated into a folded packet of plastic. She mustn't think of these things. Dreams were like those shops in Kilburn; their displays were so jumbled up it gave you a jolt, to look.

'Be good, girls,' said Mr Singh, 'I'm popping out to the post office.'

He left. An elderly lady called Mrs Klein came in. Celeste was becoming familiar with customers' bodily disorders. When people passed by the window she felt intimate with their hidden organs, like a plumber looking at

64

a bathroom he had worked on and knowing the layout of the pipes. She was getting to know the regulars. Underneath Mrs Klein's musquash-clad exterior there lurked an irritable colon. The man in the wine merchants opposite had, beneath his polished brogues, a chronic attack of athlete's foot. In this city full of strangers women were emerging whose contraceptive methods were to become more familiar to Celeste than to their own nearest and dearest. Already she knew that the check-out girl at Cullens was on the Pill, and that the big, disordered-looking blonde at the framer's shop used an Ortho-Diaphragm size 75, plus jelly.

'You going out tonight?' asked Nesta.

Celeste shook her head; she always seemed to be shaking her head. She never went out; she didn't know anybody, she only knew what ointments they used. She wrapped Mrs Klein's purchases, then she sank to her knees and started to refill a shelf with Clairol Hair Tones. Another customer had arrived; she was talking to Nesta about rejuvenating face packs.

'My problem's a greasy panel,' said the woman, 'so I need two types in combination.'

Ping. Someone else came in.

'. . . it has its own tingle scrub . . .' Nesta was saying.

Celeste climbed to her feet. 'Can I help you?'

He was a large, florid, bearded man, well muffled up in a checkered scarf. He wore a beret. The first things she noticed were his eyebrows: thick black caterpillars with a life of their own. He was accompanied by a small dog. It was flat and matted, as if it had been run over at some point in the past.

She thought, at first, he might be an artist. Some local character, anyway. Bit of an eccentric. He had twinkly eyes and, when he spoke, a really beautiful voice—deep and resonant.

'Anusol Suppositories, please.'

For a moment she thought he was talking in some foreign language—he did look vaguely continental. Then he explained himself.

Looking back, she tried to remember what they said. He made her laugh, she remembered that. *Uncle Buffy*. It was him, how incredible! The voice inside her radio, inside her head. He had told her so many stories already. The musty scent of the armchair where she had curled up, picking at the bits of skin around her fingernails . . . The faint pop-pop of the gas fire. Her hands, smudgy from school. Hammy's squeaky falsetto, *' 'pon my soul!*, as she fiddled with her plaits, pulling at the elastic bands. He was a whole company of furry creatures, her friends; squeaks and grunts from her lost past.

66

Her throat closed. She felt dizzy, momentarily. But she was chatting quite normally, though there was a roaring in her ears. She wrapped up his parcels; she told him her name, Celeste. And now there was another man standing in front of her.

'Got any disclosing fluid?' he asked.

'Disclosing?'

'For these.' He opened his mouth and tapped his teeth.

CHAPTER NINE

Love, ah love. Warm sap rising through his wintry branches. What a miracle! Who would believe, at sixty-one, that such a miracle was possible? An old has-been like him, a discontinued model consigned to the scrap-heap. A man, spurned and cuckolded. A man who had seen his ex-wives, wearing their familiar clothes, in the company of unfamiliar men. He was an old pit pony, put out to grass. A noble monument, vandalized and corroded, fallen to ruin. All these, and more, if he could think of them.

Celeste had flung open the doors to his heart, dazzling him with her sunlight. A slip of a thing in a pink nylon overall. Looking back over his life, he wondered if he had ever felt like this before and decided he hadn't. Not like this, for love makes amnesiacs of us all. Besides, the break-ups of his marriages had spreadingly infected the past, like poisonous chemicals leaking from a shattered container, and even his early months with the various women he thought he had loved, when things should have been all right, were already tainted with something he should have recognized spelt danger ahead.

Take Jacquetta's moody, I'm-so-spiritual behaviour in Venice, on their honeymoon. The way she had stood for hours in front of that Titian painting, oblivious to his fidgety glances at his watch and longings for lunch. At the time he had been impressed by her rapt stillness, by the way other people washed over her but she remained, like a rock each time the waves receded. She had also looked very fetching in her velvet cape. But already there was something ostentatious in her solitude; she was making him feel lowly and coarse, preoccupied with his stomach and excluded from the higher plane inhabited only by the Venetian painters and herself. She had a knack of doing this, a knack which developed as the years passed. When she started sleeping with her shrink she actually managed to make him feel excluded from a twosome too sensitive for him, a twosome which alone breathed the rarefied air of her psyche. It was Titian all over again. Worse, of course, but the same sort of thing.

Then there was Popsi's behaviour in John Lewis, when they were buying curtains. Popsi, his first wife. Years and years ago, this was, back in the sixties. They were both hopelessly undomesticated but they had just moved into two rooms in Bloomsbury and were making an effort. Popsi was a cheerful, accommodating girl; she was usually cast in walk-on parts as a country wench, bursting out of her bodice. That day she had failed an audition and had sunk a few on the way to the store. First she had stilled the department with her rendering of 'There was a young lady from Bristol.' Then, in an abrupt mood-switch, tears streaming down her cheeks, she had told the elderly salesman about her abortion, how his cutting scissors reminded her, how she was only sixteen at the time and how it would have been a strapping boy by now. Taking her arm and steering her towards the fabric rolls, Buffy had realized that even if there wasn't going to be trouble ahead, there was bound to be a fair amount of embarrassment.

Celeste wasn't like any of them. In fact, she wasn't like any girl he had ever met. She was fresh and unused. She was like a shiny new exercise book in which he would begin writing his most entertaining thoughts in his best italics. Her youth made him feel wise and experienced, and about time too. Where women were concerned he had always been susceptible; well, foolish sometimes. But she

69

really was enchanting, the way she gazed at him in her forthright way and asked him questions. It was the next day and he had brought in a roll of film to be developed. She really seemed pleased to see him.

'What are these then?' she asked. 'Holiday snaps?'

'Photos of the pavement.'

'The pavement?'

'The dug-up bits,' he said.

'Why've you taken photos of the pavement?'

'I'm going to send them off with a letter of complaint. Nearly broke my neck again this morning.' He handed her the film. 'It was already in my camera. Must've been there for ages, God knows what else is on it.'

'What do you think is?' She looked at him, frowning.

'Something embarrassing, probably. Something that's better left there undeveloped, like a thought you don't put into words.'

Yesterday she had been some blurred vision, as radiant and featureless as an angel. Today he saw her more clearly. Cropped hair, brown eyes, thick eyebrows—a delicate face but also a face of character and determination. There was a small pimple on her chin; her forehead was shiny, it was hot and stuffy in the shop. These minor imperfections made her human—more intimate and dear to him. He felt ridiculously familiar with her already.

'The past is mostly embarrassing,' he said. 'You haven't had enough of it yet to find out. It's there, ready to put out its foot and trip you up from behind.'

She paused. 'You're right, actually,' she said. 'I didn't realize that till lately. You think you know everything, that it's all what you think it is, then—whoosh!'

'What do you mean?'

She didn't reply. She looked at the order form in her hand. 'Matt or glossy?'

'I don't know. My wife was the camera expert.'

'Wife?'

'Ex-wife.'

They weren't divorced yet but to all extents and purposes she was an ex. Soon would be, anyway.

'What's happened to her?'

'She ran away last summer. With a photographer, appropriately enough. A gorilla called Colin. Christ knows what they find to talk about. Exposures or something.'

'Where do they live?'

'Above a pasta restaurant in Soho.' He snorted. 'Hope she's putting on weight.'

'You look terrible,' said Celeste. 'Here, sit down.' She indicated the chair which was set aside for old dears waiting for their prescriptions.

'When's your tea break?'

71

They sat in the patisserie down the road. From time to time she bent down and fed George pieces of buttered bun. 'He's the most slobbery dog I've ever met,' she said, fascinated. She wiped her hand on the tablecloth.

'What I don't understand about dogs,' he said, 'is why, when they only eat meat, does their breath smell of fish?'

'I know. Funny, isn't it. How're the piles?'

'Better.'

'Did you go to the pictures?'

He nodded. 'Have you noticed something? How, when they show a huge list of songs at the end of a film, Brahms and Diana Ross and the Beatles, there's always much more of them than you actually heard in the film itself?'

She paused, considering. There was a crumb on her lip. He leant across and wiped it off with his napkin, as if she were one of his children. How many times—hundreds, thousands—had he sat with his children in teashops, through marriage and separation, wiping their faces and trying to answer those totally unanswerable yet vaguely cosmic questions children ask, like *How many people in the world have the same birthday as me?* Now some of them shaved, his children and his step-children, and had driving licences, and still their questions hadn't been answered.

'Tell me things,' she said. 'I don't know

anything.'

'Ask me a question.'

'Tell me about your wife.'

'Ex-wife.' He paused. He didn't really want to talk about Penny. She was like a room full of disgusting clutter one kept from the visitors. Nor did he want to do that throbbing, poor-me number that had once, all those years before, proved so effective with Penny herself. Celeste deserved better. He looked at her, fondly. Extraordinary thing, love. A miracle, after all he had been through, that he could feel the first stirrings of it, like the first stirrings of hunger after an appalling attack of food poisoning.

'What does she look like?'

'Not like you,' he said. 'Glossy and thoroughbred, in an impervious sort of way. As if water would run off her. She's a journalist, you see.'

'I've never met a journalist. Never met an actor, either. Back home, the high spot of the week was having our meter read.'

He laughed. Under her coat she wore a white fluffy jumper. There was a tiny gold crucifix around her neck. She was soft and feminine—the way girls should look, but never did anymore. Sort of absorbent. The opposite of Penny. He pictured a working-class home, factory hooters, a headscarved mother. Celeste, fragrant and solitary amongst the back-to-backs. She was too young to have seen

73

A Kind of Loving. Oh, there was so much to tell her!

'Do you still see her?'

'Who?'

'Your ex-wife.'

'Not if I can help it. She has breakfast at Bertaux's every morning, I bumped into her there once, so now *that's* out of bounds. One of my favourite places too.' Bitterly, he lit a cigarette. 'They don't just steal your money and your furniture and your house, oh, no. They even steal your favourite tea shop, that *you* introduced them to in the first place.' He started coughing; his eyes watered.

Actually, Penny hadn't been so rapacious as some people he could mention. They had put the country cottage on the market but when it was sold she was only going to claim half. So decent of her, considering he had bought it in the first place. The Blomfield Mansions flat was rented so she couldn't get her claws on that. No, she had simply moved out, taking her designer clothes and her cookery books. Not even all of those. This was even more of a snub, of course. She was obviously far too preoccupied, too blithely happy, to bother about mere possessions. Too sexually sated to argue. Once the rows were over and the decision taken she had been rather kind, actually—more considerate and generous than she had ever been before. Nauseatingly condescending, in fact. Once she had actually

74

asked: 'You sure you're going to be all right?' Like a torturer bringing you a cup of tea after they had just been pulling out your toenails.

He couldn't involve Celeste in all this; it was far too sordid for her. Look at her now, munching her second Viennese slice! The resilience, the appetite! The miraculous possibility of renewal! His past was a ditch clogged with half-submerged debris and broken prams. She was a lotus flower, rising out of it, unfolding her petals one by one.

'Have I got cream on my chin?' she asked anxiously.

He shook his head; he couldn't speak.

'What're you looking at?' she asked.

'Just you.'

CHAPTER TEN

The next day, her day off, Celeste took the bus down to Soho. In their woollen gloves, her hands were clammy. *She lives above a pasta restaurant.* She felt nauseous yet excited, as if she were about to step onto a stage. She also felt furtive—a new sensation, this; one of the many new sensations that were assaulting her nowadays. This one wasn't unpleasant, however; it was like a feather duster stroking her insides, heating her face and tingling her eardrums. As she neared her destination the buildings changed. They became pregnant with meaning; they almost bulged with it. *She*, Penny, had seen them. Maybe *she* walked past them each day.

Celeste got off in the Charing Cross Road. Thank goodness Buffy couldn't see her. He would think it really odd. They hardly knew each other and yet here she was, tracking down his ex-wife! Somebody pointed her in the right direction. Soho. She pictured strip clubs and scantily-clad women lounging in doorways. *Want a good time?* For a mad moment she pictured Buffy's ex-wife in a suspender belt and patent leather boots, blowing cigarette smoke at passing men. Soho was such a wicked word that her parents would only have spoken of it in lowered voices. If, that is, it had ever come up. The naughtiest thing in their street was Wanda's lurex leggings.

It was ten in the morning and a light drizzle was falling. Celeste stood, undecided, in Old Compton Street. Men approached her, one by one. They didn't want her body, however, they wanted her money. 'Got fifty pence?' A hand stretched out. 'Got some change for a cup of tea?' A purple face loomed close. 'A quid, God bless you, miss?' She couldn't see any women at all; maybe they emerged at dusk, like slugs. The only person she could see in a doorway was so bundled up she couldn't tell what sex it was; it sat there, surrounded by carrier bags.

She walked past boutiques selling clothes so

76

unwearable-looking they must be fashionable. A lot of shops were closed, with *To Let* signs on them. On a corner, some Japanese tourists were standing around looking pinched. It was a chilly day. In the doorway of the Prince Edward theatre there was a large cardboard box with *Sony* on it; inside it, somebody was stirring. Soho wasn't how she imagined, but then none of London was how she imagined. There weren't any strip clubs, as far as she could see. None at all. Only pasta restaurants.

Lots and lots of pasta restaurants. *Pasta Fina. Fasta Pasta. Pasta'N'Pizza. Fatso's Pasta Palace.* Above them were rooms, she could see that all right. Lots of rooms, lots of flats. Windows with blinds on them, windows with curtains.

Which one was Penny's? How on earth could she hope to spot her? She couldn't possibly hang around outside every pasta restaurant in Soho waiting for somebody to emerge from the flat above. She didn't even know what this Penny looked like. She was probably out at work anyway.

Celeste walked into Soho Square. She sat down heavily on a bench. A one-legged pigeon hopped away. It was hopeless. She should have realized that.

*   *   *

Back home there was another note to Waxie,

77

Sellotaped to the door. *'See you at Bim's at 5.'* In this huge city, so huge she could never glimpse the edge of it, people were connecting up. Unknown people called Waxie and Bim, even with names like that they were finding each other. In the flat upstairs, music was playing. Footsteps thudded across the ceiling. Through the walls they laughed their loud Waxie laughs and left notes for each other.

She wasn't lost; she mustn't panic. She had stepped out of the past into this windy city, she had woken up from the long, false sleep of her youth. She had sub-let the maisonette back in Willow Drive, she had finished with all that, and finally she had found Buffy. He had embraced her outside the patisserie, holding her in a bear hug. His girth, his warm tobacco breath . . . He seemed to need her. He had mumbled into her hair, 'I want to dissolve you in water and drink you up.' At least that's what it had sounded like. Did he really say that? Was it possible?

It was all so confusing. She had never felt like this before. Oh, she had felt desire—the flush and moistness of it, the dryness and the dizzy spells, the whooping clarity of the streets. She had kissed men in cars and she had even been to bed with one or two of them, but nobody had really entered her. With Buffy it was different. She didn't know what she was feeling, she didn't dare to think, but the next day, at work, there she was watching the door and waiting for him to come in. She borrowed a tester and rubbed blusher into her cheeks; she applied more lipstick. Still he didn't come. She stayed in at lunchtime; she just ate a sandwich in the back room, pausing when she heard the *ping* of the door and casually leaning forward to look into the shop.

No time passes more slowly than an afternoon in an empty shop. Nesta didn't notice anything, but then Nesta never did. Her friend from Nautilus Fitness down the road came in—business was slow there too—and took out her wedding photos. Nesta spent a long time over each one, sighing. It was four o'clock now. Celeste made up little ploys. If she went out to the lavatory he would come in . . . If she closed her eyes and counted to ten . . . Suddenly, ridiculously, she needed him. Maybe he had forgotten all about her. Maybe that tea had meant nothing.

'Shame his little face is out of focus,' said Nesta. Celeste turned. For the first time, she looked at what they held in their hands. Photos.

The package from the photographic lab was delivered at 4.30. It was her job to take out the individual wallets of photos and put them into the desk drawer, ready to be collected by the customers.

At six o'clock Nesta cashed up. Mr Singh opened the door to let the last customer out. In the street, the Honda puttered to a halt.

Celeste slipped behind the counter, opened the big beige envelope and took something out.

*　　　*　　　*

She walked home along Kilburn High Road, past closed shops with their ghostly displays of shoes, past the illuminated pavement stalls selling jewellery. The bracelets winked at her confidingly. She felt like a criminal with a bomb in her pocket. She felt guilty, and deeply embarrassed, that she had borrowed Buffy's photos. It seemed such an intrusion into his life. She hadn't looked at them yet; she was putting it off, almost luxuriously, until she got into her flat. She passed *Afro-Caribbean Hair Beauty,* a big, busy place advertising *100% Human Hair Sold Here.* It was still open; within the shop, veils of hair hung from the ceiling like seaweed. She crossed the road, clutching her coat to her chest. In her pocket lay pieces of Buffy's life. It was amazing that nobody guessed what she had in there. Not amazing really, but *she* felt that. She paused at her doorway, fumbling for her keys. The charity shop was dark. Behind the window the mannequin leant towards her; today it was wearing a pillbox hat, set crooked on its bald head.

Upstairs she took out the wallet of photos and spread them over the table. The photos of the pavement hadn't been developed. He was either such a hopeless photographer that they hadn't come out or the lab had presumed they were a mistake, and too boring to print. She leant on her elbows, staring at the others. A train passed, way below. The table shook, as if there was a séance going on.

There were several photos of a country cottage; it had a conservatory, with a blurred figure inside it. In other photos various people lay around on rugs in the garden; Buffy was amongst them, fast asleep. He wore a red shirt and baggy blue trousers. Her throat tightened; looking at old snapshots always made her want to cry. Buffy, on some golden afternoon, raising his wine glass at the camera. Probably his wife was taking the photo. He looked younger, but then people in photos always did. Some teenagers, looking sullen. She couldn't spot a family resemblance but maybe they weren't his, she didn't even know if he had any children.

And one photo of Buffy, standing in a vegetable garden holding up a bunch of carrots. A bunch of carrots! How unlikely. He wore a panama hat and a floppy cravat; there was a broad smile on his face. His arm around a woman with shiny chestnut hair.

Celeste sat there for a long time, looking at the photo. The sun on the two faces; the woman's half in shadow, but distinct enough. His wife; you could tell, by the way they stood

81

together. Chestnut hair, cut in a bob; jeans, white blouse.

Celeste sat there for a long time, gazing at this lost summer's afternoon, fixed forever. A whole life she knew nothing about. Buffy, holding up the carrots like a trophy. His hand on his wife's shoulder. The woman's lips were parted. What was she saying? Something even they had long ago forgotten. A moment between them, frozen. From time to time a tube train passed beneath the house; Celeste shook, the table shook, her teeth chattered. She gazed at Penny. Now she knew what she looked like. She could memorize the face, now. And she was going to find her.

CHAPTER ELEVEN

The hour before dawn, damp and dark outside, blackness pressing at the windows. In homes all over Britain nothing stirred except the glowing flip of digital clocks, keeping vigil in slumbering rooms. Couples slept back to back, dreaming their separate dreams whose wacky stories would dissolve in the morning like Alka-Seltzer in water. Children's noses were cold. A click, in a bedroom, as a light was switched on. A click, in a kitchen, as a boiler hummed into life. Lorna was getting ready for work. The floorboards creaked as she crossed the room; behind the plasterwork, pipes hissed as she turned on the taps in the bathroom.

She lived alone, deep in the countryside. As the sky lightened her cottage grew solid, detaching itself from its surroundings as if it were stepping forward. Behind it rose the shoulder of a hill. This was dotted with grey rocks which, as the light grew, revealed themselves as sheep. Below it lay a wood; tangled trees and the inkier clots of conifers. A fox slipped from it and crossed the lawn. Birds pecked at the swinging gibbets of bacon rind; they flew off when she emerged and reappeared when she left. She had lived here for years but she had always felt like a transient, tolerated by the animals who were the real inhabitants of the place. She didn't mind this; in fact she found it reassuring.

She bundled herself into her overcoat and scarf, pulled on her gumboots and set off through the wood. She was only middle-aged but from a distance she looked like an ancient crone in a fairy story. An old tramp, even. Who cared? She didn't.

Spiders' webs wreathed the bushes. She knew every inch of this path—the bleached, flattened grass; the rotting plank over the ditch. Above her the bare branches rose imploringly to the sky. It wasn't a large wood; she was familiar with most of the trees, as a teacher might be with her pupils. Some more than others, of course, one couldn't help having favourites. They had grown older, just as she had, but in their case they had grown taller too. Brambles choked their ankles and some had fallen, slantingly, and come to rest against their neighbours. She passed the dark, hushed fir trees; between their trunks the silence was thick enough to touch. The air there held its breath; nothing stirred.

She emerged from the wood and walked along the edge of a ploughed field. Peewits rose and wheeled around her, crying. They did this every morning; you'd think they would have got used to her by now. A few rosehips still clung to the hedge. The earth in the field was so freshly-turned, so sharply-cut that it gleamed like flesh. The sun was still low. Why, she wondered, did the clouds lie motionless on the horizon yet race at the top of the sky? There was nobody to reply to this but she didn't mind. Usually she didn't. She had always been a solitary person and was accustomed to making up conversations in her head. It was like cooking for one—at least you knew what you were going to get.

She wriggled through the barbed wire and crossed the next field: a sheep meadow with a puddled, rushy pond in the middle. In the spring she found frogspawn in it. Each year, when she discovered the grey tapioca knobbling the surface, she felt the same electric jolt she had felt as a child; it was one of the few surprises that never wore off. The low sun cast a pearly pink light on the trunk of an ash tree. Below her lay the valley, sunk in mist. It was a lost, secret valley. Nothing disturbed it, not even the hum of the main road beyond the gate. Far away, a dog barked.

She crossed the next field and climbed over the gate—she preferred climbing gates to opening them. A container lorry thundered past. She had emerged onto the A2 dual carriageway. Each morning she felt shy, suddenly coming into the public like this. She smoothed down her coat, and walked along the verge.

The Happy Eater stood a hundred yards up the road: a brightly-lit cube against the brightening sky. It stood alone on the windy ridge—it, and its large plastic elephant slide. The sun shone on the dome of the elephant's head. A few cars were already parked outside. She made her way round them, and pushed open the *Staff Only* door. Inside, dazzling strip light; the Forest Pine fragrance of the rest rooms. She unwound her scarf and pulled off her gumboots.

*   *   *

Sixty miles away, in London, Celeste was nibbling a croissant. She was sitting in Maison Bertaux. *Penny has breakfast there each morning.* Each time the door opened, with a rush of cold air, Celeste's heart thumped. She looked up—not at the door but at the mirrored wall that reflected it. Each time she saw a mirrored stranger. Nobody she recognized, anyway, from the photo. She saw her own face—blank, peaky, glistening with sweat.

She fingered the chain around her neck. She had removed the crucifix, now; in its place she had threaded the tiny, gold fish. The fish she had found in the envelope.

*　　　*　　　*

'Two portions of toast, one Farmhouse Breakfast, one Yankie Do . . .'

Lorna carried the plates through the steamy kitchen. She spoke to Klaus, his face glistening under his paper cap. She worked automatically; her hands had a life of their own. She could do this in her sleep.

'One sausage and french fries, one hash browns . . .'

She was a dreamer; she dreamed up stories about people. They were like the birds in her veranda, flying in, swinging on the string as they pecked at the bacon rind, flying off. Each day it awed her, that there were so many unknown people in the world. For half an hour they warmed their plastic seat and then they were off again. Fuelled by a fry-up they disappeared from her life for ever, on their way to London one direction or Dover the

86

other, to points beyond, to points anywhere, leaving a scraping of ketchup and a scrumpled paper napkin. Some of them were foreigners. She had to explain the menu to them; they counted out the strange coins, laboriously, for her tip. There were men in business suits who wolfed down the sort of breakfasts nobody's wives made anymore. Where were they driving, in their company cars? They left behind book matches from the Orion Hotel, Bridlington, and copies of the *Daily Express* with pencilled sums in the margin. They called her 'love' but this time tomorrow they'd be in Humberside. How many times, between then and now, would she have wiped this table clean? Even the waitresses came and went, girls called Peg and Gwen; they drifted through, their faces vague above their black bow ties. She was forever getting new name badges printed.

Meanwhile the rising sun was warming her garden; the mist was dispersing in the frogspawn meadow. She had worked here for two years but it never failed to surprise her, that she could step out of the countryside into this seasonless box whose Muzak played the same tunes all the year round, tunes she almost recognized but never quite.

She squirted a table and wiped it down; she laid out the cutlery. It was half past eleven but breakfast and lunch were all the same here. Customers ate the Traditional English

Breakfast at two in the afternoon and the Gammon Steak at teatime. When people stepped in here time was suspended, as if they were in a plane. In fact a burly businessman was sitting down right now and ordering Scampi Tails. He had a sheaf of papers with him. Outside, his Ford Granada was spattered with mud, though she couldn't see that. He was muttering into a portable phone but she didn't catch the words. In fact she didn't notice because she was ringing up the till and it was Audrey who was serving him.

Besides, she was day-dreaming. As she re-stocked the lollipop jar she was thinking *it's only a matter of time.* As she tidied the courtesy newspapers she was thinking *someone I recognize, they'll come through the door.* A blast of cold air, a face puzzlingly familiar, like the familiar chords in the Muzak. Surely, if you stayed in one place long enough, by the law of averages it must occur? There must have been countless people already who had touched her life at some point, if only she knew it, somewhere along the way. In fact, only the day before a man who had buggered Buffy at public school had stopped here for a Danish pastry but she wasn't to know that.

All her life things had slipped through her fingers. Men; other things. Things she thought about in the middle of the night. Jobs, too. At her age she should be doing something more demanding than this but she had never got the hang of how people did it—the planning, the known destination. When she was younger she hadn't listened to anybody's advice, she was wild and wayward, and now she was in her forties nobody gave her any advice at all. People didn't, at her age.

Business was slow. The scampi eater had long since gone, unnoticed by her. She re-stocked the wall holders with leaflets. They listed Happy Eater Restaurants. All of them seemed to be situated on roundabouts and motorways—*Ripley By-Pass. M50 Junction 5 (Northbound). A55 Interchange, Clwyd.* Bit like her, really. People thundering past, knowing exactly where they were going, nobody stopping for long. *Got to get back to the wife.*

She went off-duty at three, clomping away in her gumboots. Outside the sun cast a golden light on the Happy Eater logo: a fat red face pointing to its open mouth. A man and a woman were arriving in separate cars; rural trysts took place here because there was bound to be nobody local around. At weekends other couples converged here; divorced couples who sat in the smoking section, they always smoked, while their child played listlessly with the complimentary Lego. At the end of the meal the child would be passed from one to the other, like a baton in a relay race; on the Sunday they would reappear and the child would be passed back.

Don't think of it.

89

She walked along the verge. Traffic rushed past. She was heading for some farm buildings half a mile away, to do some photocopying.

*　　　*　　　*

Sprockett's Farm had been converted into retail units. It was called The Sprockett's Farm Country Mall. Conveniently sited on the A2, within easy access of the M2, it was in a prime position to draw in customers from a fifty-mile radius. The canny farmer had realized this, when he sold the land to the developers, and he had now retired to the Canary Islands. The orchard had been tarmacked over to provide parking for four hundred cars. Various outbuildings, picturesquely lopsided, housed various business concerns—the Threshing Barn Travel Agency, the Old Piggeries Video Rental. There was even a food store, of sorts. In the local village the shop had long since disappeared, killed by the megastores, so when Lorna needed some marmalade she had to walk here, to Quality Country Fayre, and buy a ludicrously expensive pot topped with a gingham mob cap and really made in a factory in Southall.

The Rank Xerox Copy Shop was housed in the old hen house. Beneath the ancient beams machines hummed—fax, photocopiers, printers. On the wall were clocks displaying the time in Tokyo and New York. Lorna went

90

in. When she had first lived here there had been real chickens pecking around but now the floor was covered with beige carpet tiles.

Keith, the manager, was on the phone; he was always on the phone. His family had once owned a smallholding, across the valley, but it had been turned into a dry-ski slope and he had become a wheeler-dealer. He nodded at the photocopier and Lorna opened it. She had some staff documents to copy.

The last piece of paper, from the preceding customer, was still under the lid. She took it out. The scampi-eater had been the last customer but she didn't know this. She just glanced at the sheet of paper, automatically, as one glances at a postcard on someone else's doormat.

She read it once. Then she read it again. Keith was still on the phone. 'Bring Barry along on Tuesday,' he muttered, 'we'll have that pow-wow about the hot-dog franchise.' He had seen nothing.

She stared at the piece of paper. It was the last page of a memo concerning a planning application. She stared at it, her heart knocking against her ribs. Then she bundled the piece of paper into her pocket.

CHAPTER TWELVE

The flat was so damned small; that was the trouble. As a love-nest in Soho it had been deliciously romantic, how did that John Donne thing go, *and make our little room an everywhere* . . . Penny had to admit it; she had been hoist with her own petard. It was fine when she and Colin were grappling on the bed, but once they started walking about and doing normal things they kept bumping into each other. It was a trendy conversion, all uplighters and granite worktops, but it was far too trendy to have any storage space and she and Colin kept tripping over each other's stuff. That was why she had jettisoned most of her possessions back in Blomfield Mansions. The bathroom here was so tiny that whoever was sitting on the lavatory found themselves jammed into a foetal position. Colin had suggested cutting two cat flaps in the door, so the person's knees could poke through, but he hadn't got a saw to do it with because there was nowhere to keep it.

At least Colin didn't read, so there were no books cluttering up the place. Maybe he couldn't read. She realized, with surprise, that despite their intimacy she had never seen what his handwriting looked like. He did everything on the phone, or else he punched in messages on his personal organizer. He was a child of the microchip era, and entirely visual. This, however, brought problems. His kitchen was a style statement and he didn't like Nescafé jars and things cluttering it up and blocking the view of his Phillipe Starck lemon-squeezer, which stood alone, spotlit like a museum specimen. Sometimes, when she wanted a laugh, she tried to imagine what this flat would be like if Buffy lived in it.

How weird, how totally absorbing it was, stepping from one life into another, from one man's arms to another's! The difference between their bodies was the big shock at first, the big, guilty thrill, but she had got used to this by now. She had surrendered herself entirely to Colin—his stubble, the scent of his breath, his limbs slippery with sweat during their vigorous and ever-more-inventive lovemaking. He was such a stylist in this, too. An animal and a stylist. He had changed her, she became different creatures for him. Sometimes she was an eel, sliding all over him insinuatingly, her own boneless gymnastics astonishing and impressing her. Sometimes she became a boy for him, juddering and perverse. Oh, and more, more. Their bodies went on such adventures together in the dark; the next morning she blushed to think of it. Of course, she remembered Buffy but she felt disloyal to compare them—Buffy's frequently fruitless huffings and puffings, the things he said that suddenly made her giggle, the companionability and occasional joint success. The sudden freeze when he got a twinge in his back. She was a different woman now, drugged with sex, smiling at shopkeepers. Maybe she was like this during the early years of her marriage but she could no longer remember that, she didn't want to. Life with Buffy in the big, peeling flat was in the past, and she was slowly getting used to another man. His domestic habits and routines were becoming familiar to her. She readjusted to him without thinking now, as if she had gone to France and had learnt to drive on the right side of the road.

But the flat stayed small. That was why she liked to go out for breakfast. Besides, it made her feel continental. Buffy had introduced her to Bertaux's. He had gone on about Soho being a village, the good old days, Bohemia and all that, actors and their floozies. However, she herself hardly ever met anyone she knew; the only salutations she received were the Triple X cans waved at her from the doorway of a defunct boutique. A row of men sat there and whooped at her when she passed.

She usually breakfasted alone. Colin either got up early to go out on a shoot or else he slept late, obliterated like a teenager, his face buried in the pillow and his shoulders crisscrossed with the marks of her fingernails. She bought her usual pile of newspapers, went into Bertaux's and sat down. Like most journalists she speed-read all the papers and never remembered a word of them afterwards.

She was just dipping her croissant into her coffee when she heard a voice.

'Excuse me, are you Penny Buffery?'

'Penny Warren, actually.' Buffy had recently asked her, sourly, why all his exes, the moment they left him, dropped his name with such unseemly haste and reverted to their old ones. She had told him she had always worked, as a journalist, under her maiden name. Besides, who wouldn't drop *Buffery* if they had the chance. 'It's ancient Huguenot!' he had said. 'It's terribly distinguished.' A lie, of course.

'Do you mind me butting in?'

'Of course not. Sit down.'

It was a pale young woman with a pointed chin and thick, surprised eyebrows that needed plucking. Pretty enough but, oh, Lord the clothes! So terribly anodyne. She was wearing a fluffy pastel sweater, the type of thing somebody would wear if they sang in a provincial choir. That complexion cried out for strong colours.

'How amazing, seeing you here!' said the girl. 'You're the journalist, aren't you?'

Penny nodded modestly.

'Gosh! How wonderful. You see, I've read a lot of your things. Articles and things.'

Later, Penny would wonder how she knew she was a journalist if she had got her name

95

wrong. Later, much later, she realized that the whole meeting had been engineered. At the time, however, she just felt ridiculously flattered.

'They're really great,' said the girl.

'How nice.' She laughed. 'You probably remember them better than I do.'

'Have you got any tips?'

Penny looked at her. Boxy shoulders would set off the neck; emphasise the *gamine*.

'You know, tips on writing,' said the girl.

'Don't tell me you want to be a journalist.'

The girl nodded. She didn't seem more than a girl, though she was probably in her twenties. There was a dateless, fashionless air about her that made her look young and . . . Penny searched for the word. *Innocent.* It took her a moment to find it because it had been so long since she had met anybody to whom it could be applied. How sweet! She felt a warm rush of motherliness—a new sensation.

'You sure?' she asked. 'Karl Kraus said *journalists write because they have nothing to say, and they have nothing to say because they write.*'

'Is that true?'

'I've never had time to work it out.' She laughed. 'The thing is, do you believe what you read in the papers?'

'I used to. I don't know what I believe in now.'

'Ah! The first qualification for a journalist.

That's a good start.'

'What do you mean?'

'What you have to do is believe in it while you're writing it. Like a man murmuring nonsense to a woman while he's in bed with her. Each piece you write, it's a little seduction.'

The girl looked shocked. 'That's ever so cynical.'

'I find it rather bracing,' said Penny. 'Still want to do it?'

The girl nodded. She was looking at her with a fixed intensity that Penny found gratifying. She seemed to be devouring every detail of her. In her Kenzo jacket Penny felt chiselled and experienced, a woman of the world with this young Candide.

They talked for a while. Penny told her how she herself had started. The girl seemed refreshingly eager to learn about the business. She also looked biddable. What a stroke of luck, to have bumped into her! Or was it the other way round?

Beckoning for the bill, she asked: 'Want to start right now? Want to do a job for me?'

*   *   *

She took Celeste back to the flat; she had learnt her name by now. Celeste wore track-suit bottoms and pink trainers, dear oh dear. The sort of thing a children's TV presenter

97

would wear on a Fun Run. Penny would have to sort her out. She felt like a mother, taking her daughter in hand. Motherhood was another thing she had been too busy writing about to ever get round to doing herself.

'It all started with my column *Penny for Them.* Ever read it? It's in *Mine.*'

'*Mine?*'

'The magazine. You read it?'

'Oh, yes,' said Celeste. 'Yes, of course.'

She certainly looked like a typical *Mine* reader. C/D Socio-economic group. *Mine* was a reasonably downmarket women's weekly, created to rival *Best* and *Chat.* Recipes, showbiz gossip and for God's sake nothing longer than 1.5 column inches. *Mine* readers had the attention-span of gnats. *Penny for Them* was a nice little earner because all Penny had to do was to reply to readers' tips. These were suggestions like: *To make that casserole stretch, mix the stewing steak with tinned macaroni for a family supper Italian style!* Or Buffy's favourite, *To make wet concrete more workable, add a little washing up liquid when mixing it.* For this, readers received a £5 postal order and all Penny had to do was write: *Great idea, Mrs B of Bolton!* or *I agree, but for a low-cal treat try substituting yoghurt.* Buffy, of course, had found the whole thing hysterical and made up his own, like: 'Wondering what to do with those worn-out diaphragms? Try using them as handy kneeling pads when gardening!'

98

They walked up the stairs and Penny unlocked the front door. 'I thought I'd tap my readers' ingenuity. Recycling's the thing nowadays but it's so terribly dowdy, isn't it? So I thought that they could send in suggestions and Colin and I would do a book on it. *Recycle with Style*, something like that. Colin's going to take the pics. He's a super photographer.'

'Recycling what?'

'Anything.'

'What sort of things?'

'Things you don't need anymore.' Penny laughed. 'Like old husbands. I know! *100 Uses for an Ex-Husband*. Lay him on the floor, he makes a great draught excluder! Put him on all fours, to create a super bedside table!'

Celeste was staring at her. 'Really?'

'Only joking.' Penny laughed. 'No, it's things like how to grow avocados in your old Ford Escort.' She led her into the bedroom. The door wouldn't open properly. 'You see, I asked readers to send in their ideas and they did. We're being absolutely inundated.' The door was blocked by a large pile of packages. 'We can't move. Colin's kicking up such a stink. Have you got somewhere with a bit of room?'

Celeste nodded. 'I live in Kilburn.'

'Well somebody has to, I suppose.' She paused, and looked at her. 'Do you want to do a job for me?'

'What?'

'Take the stuff home and sort it into

categories. I'll pay you, of course.'

Celeste stared at her. Slowly, she nodded.

'Done.' Penny shook her hand; it was small and surprisingly cold. What a relief! She needed to get this book finished quickly. A lot of her freelance work had dried up since the discovery of last summer's bogus travel pieces and she needed the money. Besides, it was supposed to be a fun thing to do with Colin. But what had started out as a sure fire money-spinner, and a bit of a hoot to boot, was rapidly turning into a source of friction between them because of those damn parcels cluttering up the place.

'I'll call you a cab. Could you take them right now?'

She was just lifting the phone when Celeste cleared her throat and asked: 'What was your ex-husband like?'

How did she know she had an ex? Maybe from the inventive nature of her uses for one. Penny sat down. 'I'm rather fond of him, actually. He's called Russell. Colin calls him a boozy old fraud but Colin can talk. He makes his living squirting washing up liquid into beer so it all froths up for the photograph.'

'What's he like?'

'Colin?'

'Your ex.'

'Why on earth are you interested?' asked Penny.

'I just am.'

The girl had a flat, Midlands accent. *I just um*. Despite the delicate appearance there was something forthright about her. Perhaps they were all like that up there, in the wilds of wherever—forthright, curious. Her colleagues weren't curious about anything unless they were going to write a piece about it. This candid interest was rather flattering.

'I'll tell you his all-time favourite scene in a film. It's a Truffaut film, you know Truffaut?'

Celeste shook her head.

'A babysitter arrives at an apartment one evening. She's a young girl, very pretty. A middle-aged man opens the door and welcomes her in. He shows no sign of leaving, nor does he show her the child she's supposed to be looking after. Finally she asks him, *Where's the baby?* He smiles and replies: *L'enfant, c'est moi.* That's Buffy for you.'

Celeste had sat down on the Eames chair. She was listening intently. What an odd little thing she was, with that direct gaze! Penny was starting to enjoy this. Colin never asked about Buffy. He was either too painfully jealous of her past, or else totally uninterested. She hoped it was the former, of course, but she had her suspicions. It was nice to talk to such an eager listener. She missed the rambling, chatty conversations of her previous life.

She settled into the sofa, remembering the first time she had met Buffy. It had been on that flight from L.A. She had been

101

interviewing a particularly moronic film starlet and was feeling homesick for England. Californians, she had decided, all had irony bypasses. Then along came this big, twinkly man who had made her laugh.

'He's older than me,' she said. 'Our first date was going to the opticians to get a new prescription for his glasses.' She remembered the dinner afterwards, followed by the invitation to try out his Rest Assured Support Mattress—such an unusual seduction line that she had gone along with it. The experience had been quite erotic actually, in a cosy sort of way. 'I thought older meant wiser, ho ho. Just because he'd seen the original production of *French Without Tears*. Probably *been* in it, for all I know. He moved in a different world to me, that was part of the attraction I suppose. He had a Past.'

'What sort of past?'

'The usual sort. In other words, lots of mess. He lived in the most indescribable pigsty, till I came along. The first time I got into bed with him, I found a whole piece of toast in it.'

'In the bed?'

She nodded. 'With marmalade on it. The lazy slob. Terribly unfit—all that smoking and drinking, he comes from the generation when everybody did, only he kept on at it. He once acted out Erich Von Stroheim being the butler in that Greta Garbo film, *As You Desire Me*, you ever seen it?'

'No.'

'I hadn't, then. Well, he was showing me how Erich Thingy did it, with hardly any movements—just a flick of the wrist, a flicker of the eyes. And afterwards he was panting away as if he'd run in the Olympics.'

'Did you love him?'

Penny paused. 'I suppose so.' She smiled. 'Women like him because he's interested in the same sort of things they are. Gossiping. Sitting around talking about people.' Buffy had said that his ideal life would be to live in a brothel as a sort of mascot, like Toulouse Lautrec but bigger, watching the girls dressing up and hearing them nattering about their clients. Or else to be a salesman in the Harvey Nichols lingerie department. He loved making up scenarios for himself.

Her mother had adored him. She still did. Her mother thought Penny was mad, leaving him, but then she didn't have to live with him did she? Hauling him out of the boozer at four in the afternoon, making excuses on the phone to furious producers, having his horrible dog tripping her up and weeing on the carpet.

'He had this revolting little dog which looked like a hairpiece—an incontinent hairpiece. He was a terrible driver too. Weaving all over the road. When it was dusk he'd start flashing his lights at the other drivers, the belligerent bugger, and then he'd find he hadn't put his own lights on in the first

103

place. Typical Buffy. Or he'd try to flash them and squirt his own windscreen instead.'

'You left him because he was a bad driver?'

'No, no. I left him because I fell in love with Colin.'

'What happened?'

Penny looked at her. She was leaning forward, her face pale against the black leather of the chair. 'Now I see why you want to be a journalist. Funny, you didn't look the curious type.'

'Oh dear, I'm sorry. Do you mind?'

Penny shook her head. 'We had this cottage in Suffolk. Still have, though it's up for sale now. Anyway, I got a conservatory built onto it, for a feature actually. Always a danger sign, building a conservatory.'

'Why?'

'It's a displacement activity. I've always thought divorce lawyers and conservatory architects should go into partnership together, save a lot of bother.' She paused. Had she thought of this herself or read it somewhere? Either way, was there a piece in it? Could she stretch it out to 800 words? 'Anyway, I had it built—classy job, carpenter called Piers, that's how classy. And Colin came to photograph it. It was lust at first sight.'

'Did you grow carrots?'

Penny hesitated. Was this some sort of sexual euphemism? Celeste said: 'I mean—I just meant—did you have a vegetable garden?'

Penny nodded. 'I did all the digging, of course. Buffy said he couldn't because of his back.' She smiled. 'When the film *Batman* came out he called himself Backman. Just about to do some daring feat, music playing da-da-da-da, then he'd groan and stop. *"Backman!"'* She was laughing, now. 'Anyway, I did all the work and he took all the credit, of course. I think he believed he actually did it. He has a bottomless capacity for self-deception.'

'Has he?'

'Bottomless. He can make himself believe anything. He's an actor, you see. I forgot to tell you that. They're even worse than journalists. They have to tell lies, and believe them. That's how they make their living. Then—poof!—it's all gone. In their case, into thin air. Not even wrapping up fish and chips.'

'You mean he's a liar?' Celeste paused. 'Can I have a glass of water?'

'You do look pale.' Penny jumped up and went into the kitchen. She opened the fridge and inspected the bottles of mineral water. 'Carbonated, decarbonated, double decarbonated, double-double decarbonated with a twist of lemon?' she called.

'Pardon?'

'Or just tap water?'

She gave Celeste the glass of water. The girl's hand was trembling. Maybe she was going through some traumatic affair, too. Must send myself a memo to ask her, Penny thought. She was in that sort of mood—skittish.

The cab arrived and they carried the parcels downstairs. Celeste was driven off. Penny returned to the flat.

Talking about Buffy had done it. On the one hand she was deeply relieved to have left him—not since she was a child had she offered up such fervent prayers of thanks. On the other hand she missed him too. Perverse, wasn't it?

She sat on the bed—they had got rid of the futon now. Gazing at the now-empty expanse of carpet she remembered one afternoon last summer, when she had still been married. She and Colin were making love in a field and she had suddenly burst out laughing. 'What's the matter?' Colin had asked, put off his stride. She was remembering something Buffy had said when they were discussing those yellow fields of oilseed rape. 'They smell like ovulating gerbils,' he had said. She couldn't tell Colin this, of course. She had simply replied: 'I'm so happy.' Which was true. It was just that two men happened to be making her happy at the same time: one in her head and one in her body.

Adultery: The Positive Aspect. She could write a piece about it. Soon, maybe. Just now it was too painful.

CHAPTER THIRTEEN

'Wasn't it you I heard on the TV last night?' asked Mr Woolley. 'I recognized the voice.'

Buffy was lying in a flat in Hans Crescent. He was having his prostate probed. Hunched on his side, staring at the moquette wallpaper, he felt Mr Woolley's warm finger goosing him. This was far from dignified, but not entirely unpleasant either.

'I said to my wife: that's him. Advertising something or other . . . relax . . . that's better. What were you extolling the virtues of this time?'

'Barbecued Niblets,' said Buffy.

'I never remember what it is, do you? Wonder anyone remembers what to buy.' His finger slid deeper.

'What's it like?' asked Buffy.

'Enlarged, yes. Feel that?'

Buffy nodded.

'Enlarged, but not inordinately so.'

Buffy had explained to him in detail his difficulties when passing water—a vaguely Biblical phrase he liked using with medical men. How the whole process, the scattered grapeshot nature of it, took so long nowadays that by the time he was finished it was practically time to start all over again. Mae West said *I like a man who takes his time.* But

107

this was ridiculous.

'And then there's the dry rot.'

'What?' Buffy froze.

'Dry rot, isn't it? Rising damp, that sort of thing.'

'What? Where?'

'Always a problem, in old buildings. Dry rot, wet rot.'

For a moment Buffy thought he was being addressed in some hideous metaphor. Was the fellow trying to tell him something? Then he realized.

'Ah,' he said. 'The advertisements, you mean. Rot-Away Damp Proof Courses.'

'Must keep the wolf from the door. I said to my wife, I said with that voice our Mr Buffery could sell diet pills to the Somalians.'

Buffy's breathing had returned to normal. Not for the first time, he wondered why private consultants made such terrible jokes. The more expensive they were, the more tasteless their sense of humour. They looked so pleased with themselves, too, with their shiny faces and bow ties. Not surprisingly, really. How could one answer back if one's mouth was stuffed with cotton wool or one's spine was being ruthlessly pummelled? How could one interrupt the unfunny patter for which one was paying, as it were, an arm and a leg? He had had a wide experience with consultants—his heart, his teeth, his gums, his waterworks. Just when you thought everything

108

was all right another bit of the old body packed up. He was familiar with all the properties for sale in *Country Life*, read tensely in waiting rooms from Knightsbridge to Wigmore Street. He even knew which Right Honourable was marrying which.

'No need for any further action at this point,' said Mr Woolley, 'but see me again in six months.'

'What further action had you in mind?'

'You really want me to describe it?'

'No, no!' said Buffy hastily.

Mr Woolley's finger was withdrawn; the glove crackled as it was peeled off.

'Haemorrhoids okay?' asked Buffy.

'Fine. Nothing much the matter with you, really, old chap. Only the things one would expect . . .'

'. . . at my age. I know, I know.'

Buffy paid a large cheque to the receptionist and emerged into the sunshine. Outside Jaguars waited, their engines throbbing. He felt both relieved and obscurely disappointed that there was nothing really wrong with him. Just the ordinary depredations of age.

He walked down the street. One didn't exactly grow old; it wasn't as simple as that. One just felt a growing irritation with a whole lot of things which nowadays seemed designed to baffle and frustrate, like the impossibly-sealed plastic around a Marks and Spencer sandwich. The way that books seemed to be

109

published with smaller and smaller print. The way that when he switched on Radio 3 and got settled into something it promptly changed to organ music. It probably had in the past, but not with such growing regularity. Did other people feel any of this, or was he entirely alone? Why, when he paid for something with a £20 note, did the sales assistant hold it up to the light and give it such a hostile and lengthy examination? Was there something wrong with him? There seemed no end to the small indignities of the modern world; each day another popped up, like the paving stones, to trip him over. Only yesterday he had gone to his local bottle-bank—he was a late but enthusiastic convert to this—and while he was flinging in his empties, glaring at the man next to him who was putting his green bottles into the clear receptacle, he had suddenly felt a trickle of cold wine travelling down his sleeve. He had ended up soaked; who would have thought bottles had so much left in them? Especially *his* bottles.

Even without meeting Celeste he would have felt this, but she threw the whole business into sharper focus. The thing was, she made him feel both incredibly young and yet incredibly old. Both at the same time. There was that leaping, breathless possibility of renewal which was so rejuvenating. The world reborn through her fresh young eyes, the miraculous prospect of the old engine

110

coughing into life, as if he were a dusty Hispano-Suiza mouldering away in some garage; she had pulled off the wraps, polished him up and lo and behold! He roared into life. There was all this—the way she listened, wide-eyed, to the anecdotes that everybody else had got bored of by now. All this. Yet her very youth taunted him. He had taken her to Covent Garden, the week before, to hear *Cosi*, and the way she had bounded up the stairs, as lithe and thoughtless as a colt . . . How elderly he felt as she waited for him to dodderingly join her. And when she asked what the Home Service was he suddenly felt utterly alone.

He was aware of the sugar-daddy aspect of all this; of people either thinking he was a lucky old pervert or else simply out on the town with a doting niece. The plain fact was: nothing had really happened yet. He had known her for two weeks now. They kissed; she stroked his beard; he ran his hands over her firm young body—oh, her skin! So smooth, so elastic! But then she slithered like a fish from his embrace and said she must be getting home. Though inflamed by her—he was only flesh and blood, after all—he was also secretly relieved. How could he compare with the young men she must have known? (He couldn't bring himself to ask about them.) Of course he had a wealth of experience behind him, marriages and liaisons galore, but he suspected that this didn't count anymore. The old body wasn't what it was; besides, maybe they did things differently now. Through Penny, and through his many hours spent in doctors' waiting rooms, he was thoroughly *au courant* with what went on in women's magazines, and he was only too aware that nowadays the sexual demands of young women were, well, demanding. The vigour of them, the shrill and taunting battle-cries! The strident right to multiple orgasms achieved by ever-more-gymnastic methods. Hadn't they heard of a hernia?

Celeste wasn't like this, of course. She didn't read *Cosmopolitan*. This was one of her attractions. But he still felt there was something to be said for a Dante-and-Beatrice-type relationship of unfulfilled yearnings. Possibilities, after all, were as infinite as the solar system; they had no boundaries and there was nothing to bring you down to earth. With no destination there need be no endings, and he had had a bellyful of those. By golly he had. Botched, ugly, drunken, keeping you up all night on the endless carousel of recriminations and home truths; neither participants possessing the energy to halt the mechanism and get off. There was a lot to be said for a soft-focus kind of celibacy, and a nice mug of Horlicks. He knew a turning-point had been reached the year before, actually, when he had taken Penny to a musical called *Blues in the Night*. When a delicious black girl had come on stage dressed in peachy silk underwear he had whispered to his wife: 'Couldn't we have stuff like that for the living-room curtains?'

He walked along Knightsbridge. Upper-class, rosy girls loped past. Shoppers were accompanied by tiny dogs. In this area you could even glimpse that endangered species, a woman in a fur coat. Sometimes he felt that this street was his spiritual home. He too could have been a man of leisure, living in Montague Square and buying *objets d'art* at lunchtime, if he hadn't been crippled by alimony. Prosperous-looking continental couples paused to look in the windows of Jaeger; the men wore leather trench-coats and the women looked pampered and ruthless, with burnished hair and Gucci boots. They were bound to have lovers. Why were the French so efficient in matters of the heart? They dealt with it as efficiently as they dealt with their digestive systems. Compared to theirs, his life seemed such a muddle—a Flodden Field compared to their Garden of Versailles.

On the other hand, what a rich full life he had had, the lucky bugger. One could look at it that way, the Chimes at Midnight way. That a marriage ends, does that make it a failure? After all, life itself ends, at some point or another. Does this make life a failure too?

It was in this reflective mood, always brought on by a visit to a doctor, that he

113

downed a malt whisky in a mock-mahogany pub somewhere off Beauchamp Place. Two solicitors sat nearby. '. . . not a lot of legroom, but that's the Nips for you,' said one of them. Buffy could spot a solicitor a mile off; he had known so many. These two were only about twelve years old, of course, but that was par for the course now. During their divorce proceedings, Jacquetta's solicitor was so young that Buffy had suggested he went to the lavatory before they started. Neither of them had laughed, but then Jacquetta had never been blessed with a sense of humour.

Solicitors, flat-rental agencies and removal men—how well he had got to know them over the years, what a good and trusty client he had been! Pickford's Head Office even sent him a Christmas card.

He downed another Glenfiddich. He would buy Celeste a present—something wildly extravagant, at Harrods. A nice repeat fee had come through that morning and he was feeling flush. It was funny; every now and then he earned quite a lot of money, usually for something he couldn't remember doing, but it didn't last long. All his wives had complained about his sojourns in the betting shop. 'It's so stupid!' they said. 'It's not betting that's stupid,' he had replied, 'it's losing.'

He emerged from the pub. It was already dusk. How quickly darkness fell, in the winter! He passed a Boots and thought fondly of

Celeste, toiling away in her nylon overall. When he got to know her better he would take her away from all this, if she would let him. The whole strategy was rather vague so far because he didn't really know what she wanted. She spoke very little about herself. In fact he hadn't told her much about his own life, either, though she had asked him rather a lot about Penny. This seemed more encouraging than any amount of endearments.

What an adventure, to start again! A new woman, a new life. He felt optimistic and energized now. So energized, in fact, that he had another little drink to celebrate, in a hostelry across the street. He could hear about her past. Once again he would memorize the names of relatives, and hear about a childhood he painfully wished he had witnessed from a fly-on-the-wall position. He would learn that her father had never shown her enough affection—every woman he had ever known said that. He would become acquainted, through her upbringing, with a corner of England he had never known existed, but which would become a warm, glowing spot on the map—even when his relationships collapsed these places retained a tarnished sort of significance. First bikes; first bras. He loved hearing about all that. He would learn, agonizingly, of early crushes on the boy-next-door, and even more agonizingly of first affairs with men he might have sat next to, unknowingly, on the bus.

How mysterious they were, these forays into the past! Through women he had entered into a gambolling-over-the-hills childhood in the Brecon Beacons, into a fraught and chilly household in Leamington Spa. It was the most tender sort of history lesson. The cumulative effect was like *Old Macdonald Had a Farm;* one story added to another, a *quack-quack* here and a *bow-wow* there, more and more as time went on, wife after wife, until the song was so long it was quite a strain to memorize it. Especially after a few peerlessly unblended malts.

Buffy made his way across the street. He would become young again, he would get his mojo working, whatever that meant. He would even go dancing, if that was what she wanted, and make a complete prat of himself. And in return he would initiate her into the bliss of opera, in his experience totally unappreciated by the young—not that all the women he had loved had been as dewy as Celeste but none of them had understood the joys of Verdi, they had that in common. Thanks to him, there were at least seven women currently at large who could hum whole chunks of *Rigoletto*. That was an achievement of sorts, wasn't it?

He approached Harrods and stopped dead. Behind one of the windows a young man was busy working on the Christmas display; he adjusted a ball gown over the cleavage of a mannequin and stood back to look at the effect. It took Buffy a moment to recognize him.

Then he realized. It was Quentin, his son.

*   *   *

How tall he was! Tall and lithe. Neither Buffy nor Popsi had been slim, even then; how miraculous that this willowy creature had sprung from their loins. Quentin was dressed in black, like a modern dancer. His mouth glinted with pins.

Buffy hadn't seen him for some months now. Well, years. For a moment, the weirdness of his own son's name struck him anew. Popsi had insisted on it. At the birth—from which Buffy was of course absent but all chaps were in those days, they went to the pub—at the moment of birth Popsi had apparently said 'That's Quentin.' Not in general a stubborn woman, she hadn't budged on this one. 'He just is.'

Buffy waved, but his son didn't see him through the glass. He was about to shout *Quentin* but suddenly felt self-conscious. A couple, arm-in-arm, stopped to stare. Maybe they thought he was some pathetic old poofter, trying to attract the attention of this comely window-dresser.

Quentin knelt to fix a piece of fabric with some sort of staple gun. He looked graceful, and totally absorbed. The window was a tableau of family Christmases past—a handsome pair of mannequin parents, plus three offspring in velvet knickerbockers, flanked by reproduction furniture. Fake candlelight shone on their shiny, sightless faces. The smallest hint of a smile seemed to play around their lips as they gazed past Buffy. How superior they looked! Standing in the dark, he tried to collect his thoughts: last time he had seen Quentin he had been at St Martin's Art School, hadn't he? Was it really that long ago?

Buffy waved again but his son didn't look up. He tapped on the glass, but no response. Quentin was pinning up some ribbon, his head cocked sideways, his back to the window. He was totally sealed off in his aquarium. *Remember me?* Buffy wanted to shout. *Look, it's your father!*

Some more people stopped and stared. He hadn't really shouted it, had he? The traffic rumbled past. He tapped on the glass again but his son was speaking, wordlessly, to another young man who had just appeared, carrying a length of red ribbon. They nodded to each other, laughed, and just as Buffy was about to tap again, louder this time, Quentin slipped away behind a partition and was gone.

Buffy was in Harrods now, pushing through the shoppers. A woman stepped out, pointed something at him and sprayed him with perfume. How could he get to the window, inside the shop? All he could see were scarves and handbags and solid walls filled with shelves full of scent bottles. 'Can I help you?' somebody asked. He knocked over a stand of leather gloves, they fell like leaves around him. Maybe he wasn't even on the right *side* of the shop; he had lost his sense of direction. It was never that reliable, even at the best of times. He found himself squeezing behind a counter.

'Excuse me, sir.' A man in uniform took his arm.

Buffy laughed. 'Just looking for the exit.'

Now he seemed to be out in the street, hailing a taxi. He sat in the back, utterly exhausted, as it drove him home. Anyway, he could see Quentin anytime. He could pop round one evening for a glass of wine. Quentin lived in Leytonstone, didn't he? Or was that Maxine, Popsi's daughter by what's-his-name, the man she married after him, Terry? Buffy's head span; just for the moment he couldn't quite work it out. How many children had he actually got? There was Nyange, of course, his daughter Nyange. He hadn't seen her for quite a while, either. She lived somewhere awful too, almost as bad as Leytonstone. Where was it? Carmella, her mother, had told him when he had bumped into her in Shaftesbury Avenue, he was sure he had written down the address on a piece of paper . . .

He stopped the cab on the corner of his

119

street. Suddenly, desperately, he wanted to see Celeste. Just to see her, even if he didn't talk to her. Just to see her face.

He hurried across the road to the chemist's shop. It was closed, of course; he had already realized that. He looked at his watch: 6.20. He stared into the shadowy interior of the shop. Nothing stirred. Women's faces stared at him, from the rows of packets. He tapped on the glass. No point in doing that, of course, but he had to do something. He seemed to have been tapping on windows a lot today.

'Left something in there?' Paddy, one of the regulars at The Three Fiddlers, had stopped to look in the window too.

'Yes!'

'By Jesus, the stink on you! You smell like a whorehouse!' said Paddy, flinching back. 'Coming for a drink?'

CHAPTER FOURTEEN

While Buffy was sitting in the pub that evening Celeste was in Frith Street, ringing Penny's doorbell. She didn't know her phone number, that was her excuse for coming round like this. Thank goodness Penny was at home. She opened the door; her face was plastered with yellow stuff.

'It's all right. It's mud from the Nile. Don't

120

make me laugh or cry, else it'll all flake off.'
She took Celeste upstairs. 'How nice to see
your pure young face. It's been a perfectly
ghastly day.' She opened the fridge and got out
a bottle of wine. She was wearing a towelling
robe with *Hotel Cipriani* embossed on the
pocket. 'Everything's broken down. The
espresso machine, the fax machine.'

'Perhaps you could grow mustard and cress
in them.'

She laughed; her hand flew to her cheeks.
'Don't!'

'I opened all the parcels last night,' said
Celeste.

'Already? How marvellous.'

'Some of them are ever so ingenious.
There's a shower cap made out of a baby's
plastic pants, stapled together. But it's going to
take a bit of time. A lot of them are rather
complicated. There's something made out of a
colander and old hoover bags that I haven't
got the hang of at all.'

'You're an angel. I can see you're going to
be quite indispensible.'

It was easier somehow, talking to this
masked woman. She looked so impervious.
Celeste decided to plunge straight in.

'Talking of growing things, did you and your
ex-husband, what was his name?'

'Buffy.'

'Did you and Buffy have any children?'

'God, no! He was a terrible father!'

121

Celeste paused. 'What do you mean? Was he married before?'

'Was he married? Taking over Buffy was like taking over a house full of sitting tenants.' She poured out two glasses of wine. 'All of them wanting rate rebates.'

'Who was he married to?'

'A ghastly, neurotic woman called Jacquetta. They had two delinquent sons who used to come round every weekend and wreck the place. I had to be nice to them, of course. Wicked stepmother and all that. All good copy, I suppose. Got a lot of pieces out of it.'

'What were they like?'

'Lounging in front of the TV all day watching *Neighbours*, amazing they haven't grown up with Australian accents. Crisp wrappers everywhere, horrible sticky things under the cushions. Table manners like baboons, of course. When they were little it was toys scattered all over the place with endless dead batteries, Buffy used to buy them terribly complicated things, guilt of course, but he never put them together, he was hopeless at that, and all the instructions were in Taiwanese or something. Then it was Walkmen, I kept treading on the headphones, and them being bored all the time and leaving the bathroom like a marsh, how do people get towels so *wet*? Adolescents! Lying on the floor, great bare feet, flicking the TV channels with their horrible horny toes.'

She paused, panting. *Hotel Cipriani* rose and fell on her breast. Celeste stared at her. Asking Penny questions was like pulling the lever on a fruit machine—masses of money poured out. She couldn't be lonely, could she? A sophisticated woman like Penny. She couldn't feel the way Celeste did when she sat alone in her flat, listening to the sounds upstairs from Waxie.

Penny took a gulp of wine. 'And nicking my hair mousse. And cleaning their fingernails with my forks.' She screwed her eyes shut. 'And the *phone*. They were always on the phone, nobody else could get through, mumbling in monosyllables in their awful cockney accents. They live in Primrose Hill, you see. Everybody's children have cockney accents there.'

'Is it a poor area?'

She laughed. Flakes of the mask fell, like plaster. 'Christ, no! Full of rich, liberal parents. That's why they have these awful children. Luckily the boys didn't come round so much towards the end, they said it was so boring. They wanted to go out with their friends. Trails of silent friends, all in black overcoats like undertakers, sliding into the flat. Totally silent! Long, black coats. They'd all go off to Camden Lock, masses of them, like a great black oil slick. Honestly Celia, it's such a relief now.'

'Celeste.'

'Sorry. Celeste.'

'What was she like, his ex-wife?'

Penny groaned. 'Oh, God. Jacquetta.' There was a pause.

'Jacquetta.'

'She ended up marrying her shrink, you know. Saved on bills, I suppose. Like an alcoholic marrying their wine merchant. He's quite famous—Leon Buckman, heard of him?'

Celeste shook her head.

'He's always on the box. When I first met Buffy his TV was broken. He'd kicked it in when Leon was on some programme about sexual dependency.' She dipped her finger in her wine, lifted out a flake, and wiped it on her robe. 'It's funny, I can talk about her now. She doesn't mean anything anymore. It's like looking at a photo of Cliff Richard.'

'She looked like Cliff Richard?'

'No, no. It's just, years and years ago, when I was young, he used to bring me out in goosepimples, I lusted after him so much, and now he's just a creepy old Christian covered in Panstick. You can't believe these feelings could die, can you, they're so fierce at the time.'

'Jealousy, you mean?'

Penny nodded. 'You ever been jealous?' Celeste opened her mouth to reply, but Penny went on. She had gathered momentum now. She talked in a rush, as if she hadn't talked to anyone in a long time. 'I used to drive past her house.'

'In Primrose Hill?'

'That's right. Buffy's old house, where they used to live together. Where she still lives. If her car was parked outside I looked into it, at the stuff on the back ledge. Apple cores. Leaflets for holistic centres in Crouch End. Whatever they were, even her kids' stuff, they were sort of charged. They made me feel faint. You probably think I'm silly—'

'No, I don't actually.'

'I've never told anyone this. Funny, isn't it? I used to look up at the house and imagine their life in it. The bedroom was on the second floor. I'd look at the window and try to work out how many times they must've made love in there. Hundreds? Thousands? Seven years, 365 days, say, on average twice a week . . .'

'That's 728 times.'

'But say they'd done it more often the first couple of years. Say, five times a week for the first three months . . .'

'That's sixty times.'

'Gosh!' Penny grimaced. 'And, say, three times a week for the next eighteen months . . .'

'216,' said Celeste, 'which plus the sixty makes 276 in total, for the first two years.'

'Hey, you're fast!' Penny looked at her with admiration. 'A mathematical genius. What a surprising girl you are.' She laughed. 'If you knew Buffy you'd think how ridiculous, but I was in love with him then, you see. I thought: maybe he'd been a lot more vigorous then,

125

maybe she was marvellous in bed. I wondered whether he compared us. What her body was like.' She stopped. 'This is stupid. You're not interested in this.'

'I am. Go on. Hadn't you seen her?'

'Oh, yes. A few times. When I brought the children back. Gosh, this is fun. I'm glad Colin's not here.' She drained her glass. 'Don't usually drink, either.'

'What did she look like?'

'Rather beautiful, I must admit. I didn't want to admit it, of course. Though in a funny way it made Buffy more attractive, that he'd been married to a beautiful woman. She was sort of bony and soulful. Thick, curly mane of hair when mine had always been boring and straight. I couldn't see much of her body because she wore so many layers, awful arty clothes, cobwebby shawls, Miss Haversham meets the Incas. But I imagined it. I wondered if her thighs were slimmer than mine. If she was, you know, *tighter* inside because of all her t'ai chi.'

'What's that?'

'Chinese martial arts. Terribly seventies.' She refilled the glasses.

Celeste's head was swimmy. She tried to catch everything Penny was saying, but she talked so fast. Larger pieces of her face pack had now flaked off, revealing areas of skin beneath.

'It was much worse in the cottage, of

course,' said Penny.

'The place in Suffolk? With the carrots?'

Penny nodded. 'There were all these relics of her there, and I had to live with them. Things she'd planted in the garden, that always reminded me of her. Trees and things, that I couldn't pull up. I tried, once, but the roots were too deep.' She sighed. 'Curtains she and Buffy had chosen together. Stuff they'd got at auctions when they were probably happy, or as happy as you could be with such a self-absorbed cow as her. I had the whole place redecorated, of course—I did this feature on updating your second home, so I got it done for nothing. I even had the cesspit emptied. I said to Buffy *I don't want any old wife's droppings in there.'*

They sat in silence for a moment. Down in the street cars hooted, stuck in the traffic. Below them, people must be shovelling in pasta. Everyone was busy having an evening out. Celeste willed this Colin man not to come home yet.

'I threw out everything I found in cupboards and drawers, of course,' said Penny. 'Hairpins, boxes of Tampax, her dusty old packets of mung beans. Cassettes with her slopey handwriting on them. Joan Baez, honestly!'

'Who's she?'

'Soppy folksinger. Typical Jacquetta. You're too young to know about Joan Baez.' She paused, remembering. 'Shells from family holidays, and old espadrilles with sand still in them. Photos, of course. They're the worst.'

Celeste nodded. 'I know.'

'When Buffy was out one day, I found a photo of her sunbathing on the lawn. I burnt it. Then the next day I dug a vegetable patch there, to get rid of her.'

'Where you grew the carrots?'

'And later I got the conservatory built. The final exorcism. Fumigation. Whatever. But by then she'd sort of dissolved anyway, she'd lost her power, because I'd fallen out of love with Buffy.' Suddenly she jumped up. 'Gosh, I wish you'd taken notes. I must write all this down, before I forget.'

'Why?'

But Penny wasn't listening. 'Sally's gone to *New Woman*, hasn't she,' she muttered, searching for a pen, 'or was it *Woman's Journal*? She liked my thing on the Redundant Penis. Cut it to ribbons, of course, but still . . .' She grabbed a notepad. 'There's always Louise, she owes me one after that débâcle over the menopause piece . . .' She stopped. 'Shit, they've sacked her.' The peeling mask gazed thoughtfully through Celeste. '*Options* might want it. I gave them lots of names for that *How I Lost my Virginity* thing . . .' She tapped the Pentel against her teeth.

Celeste got up. 'Shall I just get on with it then?'

'What?'

'The recycling thing.'

'Sure, sweetie. Some more arrived this morning. I biked them round.'

Celeste made her way to the door. The floor rocked gently from side to side as if she were standing on a swing. 'Bye, then.'

'Wait!' Penny disappeared, and came back with a jacket. 'Have it. It's Saint Laurent.'

'I couldn't!'

'It's all right, it didn't cost me anything. We did some fashion shots. It'd look much better on somebody young.' She did, in fact, look ancient this evening, her face cracking like a monument.

'You sure?'

Penny put it on her. 'Boxy shoulders. I knew you'd look good in it. Power dressing!'

*   *   *

Celeste managed to climb onto the bus. The sliding doors hissed shut. Clinging to a pole, she swung herself into a seat. She thought: What's happening to me? I'm drunk. I'm wearing an ex-wife's clothes. I'm learning things I had no inkling of.

The man in the seat next to her leant towards her and said: 'Let's have a look at those titties.'

'Go fuck yourself!' she replied loudly.

He got off at the next stop and she sat there, blushing. How could she have said that? She had never sworn in her life. Where did those words come from? She started giggling and put her hand over her mouth.

She made her way up Kilburn High Road, past the boisterous Irish pubs and the glowing, rosy curtains of the Society Sauna and Massage. It was nine o'clock. A Rastafarian leant against a lamp-post, eating a drooping triangle of pizza. London alarmed her less, now. She was learning to deal with it. She stopped outside her flat and fished for her keys. I'm learning to lie, she thought, marvelling at herself. Well, I'm learning to keep quiet about the truth. I'm learning to drink Sancerre and wear power jackets.

In the hallway she stumbled over a large parcel. A note was Sellotaped to it: *Whose is this? Waxie.* She carried it upstairs and switched on the light. But she didn't open the package, or even look at the heaps of objects arranged around the floor like the items for some demented jumble sale. She went straight to the phone directory, and opened it at 'B'.

In one sense, things were becoming more confusing. But she was learning to cope. *Buckman, Leon.* She found the address, in Primrose Hill Road, and sat still for a moment. Her heart thumped. She looked down at her jacket; it was a rich midnight blue and beautifully cut, even she could see that. She had never worn anything like it. Back home the neighbours wouldn't recognize her; they would think she had come to do a survey or something.

She fingered the stiff lapel. This was what actors did; they dressed up and became somebody else. Buffy knew how to do it; that was his job.

Suddenly she was ravenous. She made some toast, heated up some baked beans and poured them over it. As she sat she looked at her new self, hanging over the back of the chair. She felt strong and resourceful. Shy? No, not now. Not any longer.

CHAPTER FIFTEEN

In his basement consulting room, Leon was listening to a patient. Outside, children whooped on Primrose Hill. Indoors, there was a long, shuddering breath.

'I'm ready to talk about my father now,' his patient was saying.

Leon nodded. 'What do you want to tell me?'

'I've kept it buried, you see, all these years. What he did to me. I *know* he did it to me because I can't remember it.' She took a drag of her cigarette. 'I've buried it, I realize that now. I've denied it to myself, because it's so painful . . .'

She sat, wreathed in smoke. *Here we go*

again, Leon thought. He wondered, for a moment, if the time would come when his two grown-up daughters in America would suddenly accuse him of sexual abuse, and take his protests as further proof of guilt. Everyone was muscling in on it now. Even Jacquetta had had a go, telling him she was sure now that her father, a mild, stammering academic, had fondled her in her bath when she wasn't looking. It reminded him of the sixties, when practically every woman he met had claimed some sort of sexual contact with Jimmy Hendrix.

'. . . he used to sit me on his knee, you see, and read me *Winnie the Pooh.* He used to read to me every night. I should have realized that was a danger sign. He wanted me close to him, he wanted power over me . . .'

The front door banged. There was a dragging noise along the ceiling. He and Jacquetta had the builders in. Well, Jacquetta had the builders in. They were building her a conservatory in the garden. A distant voice bellowed: 'Stavros! Where the fuck's those two-by-fours?'

His patient lit another cigarette. 'I see it now, of course, since I've been coming here. All my victim-dictated behaviour stems from that time when I sat there, his arms around me, giving me a hug and a kiss when he closed the book . . .' Her voice trembled.

Leon shivered. There was a draught in the

room. Had somebody left the back door open?

She started to cry. 'That hug. I know now it wasn't just a hug. Oh no. It was a sort of rape, an assertion of his power over me, his male power, abusing my trust, my little girl's trust . . .'

Leon looked up. A man had come into the room. He wore overalls and was covered in dust.

'Sorry, mate. Just looking for a plug for me extension lead.'

*   *   *

Leon and Jacquetta didn't quarrel; they talked things through. When he went upstairs for lunch she was pouring boiling water onto her ginseng tea-bag. He went up to her and kissed her lightly on her forehead.

'Sweetheart, we really must do something about the noise.'

'*I* should, you mean.'

A mixture of hammering and Capital Radio floated in from the garden. He opened the oven. Maria had heated him up some cannelloni. God bless the Portuguese. His wife was too spiritual to cook. Too spiritual to pay her parking tickets either, he thought, as he glimpsed another couple of them amongst the opened mail on the table. He put them into his pocket and sat down.

'The builders, they've been using the

patients' lavatory,' he said. 'The seat was up and there was a cigarette butt floating in it.'

'I knew you didn't want me to have the conservatory built. I knew you thought it was too expensive.'

'I didn't say that, actually.' At the time, he had just asked her if she was sure she wanted it. There had been a piece in the paper, only yesterday, about conservatories being a warning signal of marital unrest. On the women's page. Something about architects combining with divorce lawyers. He had only read it because it was next to an article about the dysfunctional orgasm, one of his specialities.

'You don't understand, Leon. You can seal yourself off in your, your . . .' She pointed towards the basement. '. . . your ivory tower. I'm a *woman*. I have children. Things are needed from me all the time, little pieces of me. It's give, give, give. This place . . .' She gestured around the expanse of the kitchen . . . 'I feel hemmed in, Leon. Closed in.' She pointed out of the window, to the green slope of Primrose Hill. '. . . that concrete jungle out there, all those people. I need to be just myself sometimes. I need somewhere to be alone, with growing things.'

'But you can't be alone in a conservatory. That's the point of them. Everybody can see you.'

She sighed. He noticed, for the first time,

134

the grey threads in her hair. Not for the first time, exactly, but it always gave him a shock to see them. She was still a handsome woman—strained, fine-boned—but there was no doubt that they were growing old together. His own mane of hair had turned grey quite suddenly soon after he had married her. But he still had a certain Norman Mailer glamour to him, one of his female patients had remarked on this only recently. She was still in transference.

Jacquetta turned away, her beads swinging. She was wearing a mulberry, knitted two-piece he had bought for her in Monsoon. After they had married he had tried, gently, to tone down her wardrobe. This was for her sake as much as for his, she surely didn't want to be seen as a wrinkled Flower Power child at some conference in Stockholm. But then it turned out that she had no intention of coming on his conference trips anyway. Not for her, the role of appendage. Or, to put it another way, the role of supportive wife.

'I know we're not supposed to exist up here,' she said. 'I know we're not supposed to have a life. *I* couldn't bear *you* having a life, when I was your patient. I remember hearing the radio through the wall. Your incredibly dreary wife listening to *The Archers*.'

'It wasn't her. She never listened to *The Archers*. It was the home help.' His ex-wife, in fact, was now a senior investment analyst on Wall Street but Jacquetta didn't like to be

135

reminded of this. Even now, after nine years, she never called his ex-wife by her name. Jacquetta had an awe-inspiring capacity for self-deception, something they were just starting to do some good work on when their relationship slid from the professional to the personal, he had joined her on his couch (the floor, actually) and the analysis had to be prematurely terminated.

Jacquetta was nibbling a piece of celery in her abstracted way, as if she wasn't really doing anything as boring as eating. Sometimes he found this endearing; it depended on his mood. He loved her, he was sure, but on the other hand he was a man of science. What was love? A muscular spasm? A reassurance of the self? A need for lit windows when you returned home in the dark? He couldn't talk about this because she would take offence. She was extremely touchy. *Fiery*, he had thought at first, *artistic temperament*, but now he thought, touchy. *Difficult* was only something other people said. Despite all sorts of things, he still found her lovable. Contrary, but lovable. If, after all this time, he knew what love was.

He had been through so many marriages and so had she. That at least was something they shared. It brought them close, like children of army parents who had been brought up in trouble spots all over the world. Of course he felt the odd tweak of jealousy, but by hosting a Channel 4 series on the subject he had finally drained it of meaning, even for himself. Sometimes he still felt uncomfortable, too, living in her old marital home and working in the bottom of it, like a miner digging away in the depths of its subconscious, digging away at his seam of gold. But it was in a prime location, crammed with money and neurotic wives, and she had managed to hold onto the property with her own vague sort of ruthlessness, as if it were humdrum and somehow demeaning for anyone else, in this case poor old Buffy, to battle over the vulgar subject of money. She had managed it the way she nibbled the celery, vaguely disclaiming responsibility for what she was doing. Being on the profiteering end of this—his own wife having kicked him out, subsequently sold the house and gone back to the States—he had failed to ally himself with Buffy in any us-men-together sort of way. He wasn't that sort of pubby chap anyway. He had always been better with women. Besides, he had been sleeping with the man's wife.

He scraped his plate clean and stacked it in the dishwasher. Jacquetta was standing at the window, peering at the building site in their back garden. She wasn't wearing her glasses; she was always losing them somewhere around the house. Hunting for her spectacles was the only indoor activity that all the family shared. The workmen had suddenly disappeared, the way workmen do. Maybe for lunch, maybe for weeks. She was twirling a piece of hair around her finger. She was either spoiling for a fight or just waiting for him to leave.

'I know India's being difficult,' she said, 'but you could be more supportive.'

'I'm very fond of India. I'm very fond of all your children.'

'You hate her using our bathroom.'

'Only because she's in there such ages.'

'She's insecure about her looks. That's why.'

'I just wish she'd be insecure in the boys' bathroom.'

'She can't. It's too disgusting.'

That was true. Even Maria, their treasure, wouldn't go into the boys' bathroom. She wouldn't go into their bedrooms any more, either. Last week, ignoring a *Quiet Please! Examination in Progress* sign Bruno had stolen from school and pinned to his door, she had gone into his room and found him in bed with the girl from the dry cleaners.

'She is trying to find a flat,' said Jacquetta.

India won't move out, thought Leon. Not if she has any sense. Nobody's children move out anymore. In fact he *was* fond of India. She was the product of Jacquetta's first marriage to a man called Alan. They had been hippies together in the sixties; Leon had seen some painful but hilarious snapshots of them in bellbottoms. Their daughter was called India because she had been conceived in an ashram near Bangalore. He sometimes wondered if

India's subsequent problems stemmed, in some measure, from this continuous reminder of the sexual activity that had produced her, twenty-three years previously. At the very least, it seemed embarrassing. Her father, Alan, had since gone into software.

'It's not India,' he said, 'it's the boys. One of them's been using my computer. I tried to call up a file yesterday—a patient's file, she was just about to arrive—and instead I got *The Pros and Cons of Bismarck's Foreign Policy*.'

Jacquetta twitched her shoulders, as if a midge were bothering her. She wasn't really listening.

He went on: 'For people who don't ever talk to us they make an extraordinary amount of noise. And we've got to do something about their rabbits.'

'We can't get rid of the rabbits. They're *theirs*.'

'But they never go near them,' he said. 'They never even go in the garden. They never even open their *curtains*. They've forgotten they *exist*.'

'They wouldn't if they went. They'd be terribly upset, you know that. Remember what happened with their stick insects.'

'That was Buffy's fault,' he said. 'Anyway, they could've been dead for years by then. They were mummified. Everyone had forgotten about them.'

'The boys were traumatized, Leon! I talked

it through with my group. I couldn't let it happen again.'

'But the things keep breeding, sweetheart, and getting out of their hutches. It's pandemonium out there, since the workmen arrived. Last week one of my patients was just starting to open up for the first time—five months it'd taken. She was just starting to talk—to freely talk—when this baby rabbit hopped into the room and started to wash its ears.'

Jacquetta gazed out of the window. 'All right. But we can't get rid of the original pair. Not for children of a broken home. That would be too symbolic.'

CHAPTER SIXTEEN

That night the temperature dropped. The wood next to Lorna's cottage, already so thin and wintry, closed in on itself. Water froze in the ruts. Nothing stirred; the place was locked. The first frost, when it arrives, locks the senses; it is impossible to imagine anything changing. But Lorna, lying in bed, knew otherwise. She had read the sheet of paper, plucked from the photocopier. She didn't need to sleep to start this particular nightmare, for it was starting right now, without her. *My wood, my secret wood*, she repeated to herself, *how can they?* She turned over, and stared at the ceiling. *How can they bulldoze it up and turn it into a Leisure Experience?*

*　　　*　　　*

Brenda was dreaming of leisurewear, the flip-flip of the catalogue pages. She never remembered her dreams, the next day. Well, there was so much to do, wasn't there? It was all go, go, go.

Beside her, Miles slept. He had spiralled airily down into a place she could never reach. Nobody could meet him there except his uninvited guests, each night so eyebrow-raising yet so inevitable. He lay, trapped by Brenda and released by his dreams; outside the drone of cars, the arc lights. Beyond the ring road, Swindon slumbered.

He slept, dead to the world. He dreamt from the store of his past; none of the people in this story were alive for him yet though, who knows, he may have brushed against the shoulder of somebody who had brushed against one of them; he himself might have brushed against one of them. A car carrying somebody who had made love to one of them might even now be circling the roundabout whose sodium lights filtered through the curtains and bathed Brenda's humped shape in a flat and shadowless glow.

Way above the starter homes, above the

orange glow of Swindon, the moon shone. It shone on the wood next to Lorna's cottage, its own reflection blurred in the frozen puddles. It shone on the white bones of Jacquetta's conservatory, curved like whale ribs over the black, matted garden. There is nowhere as secret as a London garden. Closed in by the cliffs of the surrounding houses, whose lights switched off one by one, it guarded its memories—of Buffy's children and the children before them, children who themselves had grown old and died. Beyond the houses, over in the Zoo, the wolves howled.

*   *   *

Jacquetta's dreams were incredibly vivid and powerful. She was proud of them, like a mother is proud of her surprisingly athletic children; the next morning she liked to recount them in detail to whoever she was living with at the time. Her first husband, Alan, used to roll his eyes and say 'Wow', but he said wow to everything. A man called Otto tried to interrupt and tell her his. Buffy, after they had been married for a while, used to get impatient. 'Bloody hell,' he would say, 'I've forgotten who everybody is. Hang on a bit. It's like some blooming Norse saga.' But then Buffy had never really understood her.

Leon did. Leon understood her creative unconscious, her needs and her insecurities, her fragile sense of self. He understood how, through her disastrous relationships with men, she was trying to make contact with the child in herself, the small girl trying to gain the love of the cold and distant father who had in all likelihood abused her in the past. Leon had explained it. How she needed constant reassurance from the men who she chose unerringly for the damage they would do to her. How she had to break those old childhood patterns. In the group she went to, they called it Rewriting the Family Script.

The problem with Leon, if there was a problem, was that he understood too much. This was something else they discussed in the group. She had once had an affair with her gynaecologist—she had gone to him about her painful periods—and quite apart from the fact that he had turned out to be yet another sadistic bastard she had had the feeling that he was more familiar with her erogenous zones than she was herself. This had left her feeling helpless and disempowered, as if she were a bystander while he and her sexual organs just got on with it. Sometimes she felt that Leon was doing this, with her head.

He was wonderful, of course. He was a suave and accomplished lover; he was a regular visitor to their local gym and unlike some men she had known he hadn't degenerated into an overweight slob. That he earned a large amount of money wasn't important to her, she wasn't into possessions, but his wordly success made him content and she was happy to see that because she was a giving and generous Sagittarian.

The trouble was, he understood everybody. That was his profession. He called himself an enabler, a locksmith. He didn't give people the keys, of course. He enabled them to forge the keys themselves; working out their own combination was part of the process. From the upstairs window she could see the tops of his patients' heads as they made their way down the steps to his consulting rooms. After fifty minutes they emerged white-haired; older and wiser. This was no doubt caused by the falling plaster dust—there were usually builders around, for one reason or another—but for a visual person like herself those departing white heads made a vivid symbolic statement.

He almost understood too much. This was a ridiculous thing to say, she knew that, but sometimes she felt like a struggling novelist living with somebody who knew how to write the story better than she did. He knew the main character so well; he was acquainted with all her early traumas and subsequent patterns of behaviour. She couldn't get angry with him for this—how could she? Besides, Leon never got angry. He would gently explain exactly what she thought and then ask, 'Are you comfortable with that?' Sometimes she remembered the rows she had had with other men and felt wistful, like a retired matador missing the stench of sawdust and blood.

No wonder she had such powerful sexual fantasies about her builders—priapic Greeks, ruddy young Geordies who would require nothing of her except her compliant, middle-aged body, who smoked roll-ups and talked about football teams she had never heard of. Who wouldn't understand her at all. Watching them toiling in her house, their chests slippery with sweat, made her insides melt. The rawness, the vigour, the muscles moving under their skin as they heaved up a floorboard! She was always thinking up ways of improving the house. She had had three bathrooms installed already and was going to get a fourth put in, for India.

This was one of the things she discussed with her group. There were six of them, all women, and they met in a room above a video shop in Muswell Hill. She could talk to them about Leon, her need for builders, everything. She didn't need to feel disloyal, because Leon understood why she went there. When she told him they did psychodrama—all of them acting him, in turn—he wasn't threatened, only interested. Besides, there were less and less opportunities to tell him things anyway because he was always so busy.

Sometimes she did something which she knew was just a cry for attention, a need for some sort of primal response. She was just recovering from a short but intense affair with her conservatory architect. He had the keys to a show flat in Battersea and they used to go there after hours. The place was exhilaratingly un*hers*—ruched curtains and interiors laid out on the coffee table. Freed from the needs of her children, the puppet-string pulls of her life, the total comprehension of her husband, she had felt thrillingly liberated. There was plaster fruit in the kitchen and she had felt like Hunca Munca in the Beatrix Potter story, lawlessly exploring a toytown home.

There had been other episodes, quite a few actually, mostly with the disenchanted husbands of women she knew, and once with her pottery teacher. When she tearfully confessed, Leon understood. He always did. He took her in his arms. He told her the thing with her architect was quite natural, that we all needed our own private show flats in our heads, that in fact he had written a paper on it and read it out to an audience of two thousand psychotherapists in Baden-Baden.

Buffy, of course, would have bellowed and spluttered and got raging drunk. Other men she had known would have hit her. Leon just stroked her cheek and went downstairs, where he was dictating his latest book to his secretary. He had written several best-sellers. *The Blame Game and How We Play It* had been translated into twelve languages and his latest, *Guilt: A User's Guide,* had just been published.

He was intensely proud of what he called his babies. Almost touchy, actually. Last Monday he had been on *Start the Week* and she had forgotten to tape the programme for him—she had been doing her postural meditation at the time—and he had almost got angry.

She had the vague feeling that he was going on TV this evening, in fact. Outside it was freezing cold. She could see the grey breath of the builders as they huffed and puffed in the garden, dragging panes of glass wrapped in brown paper. She was upstairs in her studio— her own room, her sanctum. This was her working time. She was working.

She sat at her desk. The trouble was, she had too many ideas. She had just been on a creative writing course and she thought she might write some prose-poems based on the seasons at their Tuscan house—a sort of contemporary *Book of Hours*—and illustrate them with drawings. The thing was, she had only been to their Tuscan house in the summer. Another idea that had been brewing for some time was an ecological children's story based on *The Tibetan Book of the Dead*, but she had to be in the right mood for this. Various projects connected with her aromatherapy course, maybe with dolphins featuring somewhere, had also been simmering. Maybe she should ask her group if she were ready for this.

She was interrupted by the ring of the

doorbell. Nobody else seemed to be around so she left her studio and went downstairs. She passed Bruno's bedroom door. There was a sign on it saying *STOP!!! DO NOT ATTEMPT TO MOVE THIS CAR!!!* It was one of those car-clamp stickers. They were always stealing things from the street—plastic cones, hideous objects like that—bringing them home and not knowing what to do with them. Adolescent boys . . . She couldn't begin to understand them. They were such an alien species that she sometimes forgot about them for days.

She negotiated the builders' planks, stacked in the hall, and opened the front door. A pale young woman stood on the step.

'Hello,' she said. 'I've come about the rabbits.'

*   *   *

Jacquetta was miles away. It took her a moment to gather her wits.

'The sign outside,' said the young woman. *'Baby Rabbits Free to a Good Home.* I was just, you know, passing by and I saw it. I love rabbits.'

'So do I. It's awful to get rid of them but my husband insisted.'

A waif on her doorstep! The girl looked freezing. Her face was blanched white; only her little nostrils were pink. Jacquetta led her into the kitchen where she stood in front of the

148

Aga, warming her hands. She was actually trembling with cold. Her coat fell open and Jacquetta noticed a tiny gold fish around her neck.

'It's the Year of the Fish,' she said, pointing to it. 'At least I think it is. Or maybe it's the Year of the Monkey. They go past quicker and quicker, the years, as one gets older. It's quite frightening.'

The young woman was still staring at her. Jacquetta wondered if she had a blob of paint on her nose. She took off her specs and the room blurred; she put them back on again. How dark and lustrous the girl's eyes were! Haunted. She had a delicate bone-structure too, like a ballet dancer. She would be marvellous to draw. The girl gazed around the kitchen as if she had never seen anything like it before—the dresser full of Jacquetta's pottery, the Georgia O'Keefe calendar. Despite the conventional clothes there was a vividness about her, an intensity, that Jacquetta felt she could identify with.

'Can I have a glass of water?'

Maybe she was going to faint. Jacquetta filled a glass and gave it to her. The girl's hand trembled; as she lifted it to her lips the glass dropped from her grasp and fell onto the floor.

'Oh, gosh, I'm sorry!'

Jacquetta picked it up. It hadn't broken; the builders' dust sheets had saved it. 'It's the last glass from a set I bought in Venice,' she said.

'On one of my honeymoons, actually.'

'One of them?'

For a moment Jacquetta couldn't remember which man it was. She adored Venice and had been so many times. 'Ah, yes. My second husband.' Russell. He had spent his whole time eating. In *Venice*. One didn't go to Venice to *eat*. She should have realized, then, that the two of them were totally incompatible.

'What was he like?'

What an odd thing to ask! 'A Taurus. Hopeless for me.'

Jacquetta put on her cloak and they went down the steps into the garden. It was freezing cold and the light was beginning to fade. The builders were packing up for the day.

'What a bore,' said Jacquetta, looking at the rabbit hutch. 'They've got out again.'

'They're under there somewhere,' said the oldest builder. She had an idea he was called Paddy. He was pointing at the frozen earth. 'They've made a burrow.'

'What shall we do?'

'Come on lads!' he said, 'Let's dig 'em out.'

The ground was frozen too hard, however. One of them suggested boiling a kettle, which they did. They poured it onto the earth. Steam rose. They started digging again.

The one called Paddy pointed to the ground. 'Know what we've got in there? Some hot cross bunnies!'

Jacquetta sighed, huddled in her cloak.

150

When one had children, everything was so complicated. Even disposing of their pets turned out to be a major operation. And then the boys would probably make a fuss, when they came home from school. She sometimes wished she could just pack her paints and go to Goa or somewhere, somewhere simple, and just *be*. She gazed at the flushed sky. The sound of the spades seemed far away.

'Steady on, Stavros! Don't want to hurt the buggers.'

She loved this time of evening. The light from the kitchen, shining on the struts of her conservatory, reminded her of the temple at Karnak. She had gone to a *son et lumière* there once, with a man called Austin. Just for a while, he had seemed the man she had been looking for all her life; she was prone to these romantic impulses. She had sat there, in the Egyptian twilight, with his arm around her. Suddenly Buffy's voice had boomed out. *'It is said that, long ago, when Thebes was at its zenith, when gods were men, when Isis, she of the mischievous eyes, was beloved of Osiris . . .'* What a shock it was, to hear his voice! How rudely it had shattered her mood! Even worse, she had been married to him at the time. *'Let us journey into the past, let us unroll the scrolls of time and consider again these avenues, built by Rameses II and restored by the Ptolemies . . .'* She'd had no idea he had recorded the soundtrack. How tactless of him! For a

151

moment she had thought he had planned it just to spoil her tryst amongst the ruins.

'Got one of them! Here, Mrs Buckman.'

A struggling rabbit was shoved into her arms. One of the men was lunging after another one which was hopping away in the dusk. Her husband, disturbed by the shouts and whoops, had appeared in the doorway of his consulting rooms.

'What on earth's happening?'

She had temporarily forgotten why they were doing this. Then she caught sight of the young woman. She sat like a spectre on the steps of the skeletal conservatory; her head swivelled from Leon to Jacquetta. She seemed to have no interest in the rabbits at all.

'Two down,' cried Paddy, 'one to go.'

'Don't catch the two big ones,' said Jacquetta, 'the parents. They're staying here.'

She looked at the girl again. I know, she thought. She's like a child, an unborn child, sheltered within the ribcage of an all-embracing mother. I shall paint that. I have been a child, a mother too. I shall paint her boldly, in acrylics. The struggling rabbit scratched her wrists but she only discovered this later. At the time she was so fired with creativity that she didn't notice.

*   *   *

The three baby rabbits were finally caught.

Jacquetta and the young woman carried them into the kitchen and put them on the table. They lolloped around, their whiskers sparkling. They raised themselves on their hind legs and sniffed the copper candlestick; they sat on the *Independent*, washing their faces with their paws.

'Look at the light shining through their ears!' cried Jacquetta. 'The tracery of veins. Aren't they beautiful! This is the end of my boys' childhood, the last of their pets to go. Really, I can hardly bear you to take them.'

'You've still got the mother and father. The big ones.'

'Don't you see how symbolic it is? The young leaving; just a sad old mother left behind.'

'We all have to leave home. I did.'

'How could you know about loss?' said Jacquetta. 'You're far too young.'

'I'm not.'

The girl was sitting in the Windsor chair, looking at her intently. How abrupt her voice was! With a funny flat accent. Jacquetta looked at the strong, raised eyebrows; the pointed face. In the room nothing stirred except the pendulum of Buffy's old grandfather clock, swinging from side to side, and the rabbits on the table. One of them had found a piece of apple rind, from lunch, and was nibbling it.

The builders clomped through the kitchen

153

on their way home. 'Cheerio!' they called. In the hall they addressed each other loudly. 'What're you having for dinner, Stavros?' 'Rabbit kebabs! And you, mate?' 'My old lady's cooking my favourite.' 'And what might that be?' 'Bunnyburgers and chips!' The front door slammed.

'I'm glad you came today,' said Jacquetta. 'You'll never realize how momentous this is.'

'What do you mean?' asked the girl.

'It's a turning point for me. It's important to mark these moments, validate them.' The young woman listened intently. It was nice. Sometimes, in the group, Jacquetta had the feeling that the other members looked as if they were listening, but they were really just waiting their turn. 'My whole life's been geared to my kids, you see. Dictated by their needs.'

'How many have you got?'

'What?'

'Children.'

Jacquetta thought for a moment. It was so complicated. 'Three, basically.'

'*Basically?* What do you mean, *basically*?'

'Well, there's all those stepchildren and things.'

'How many?'

'Oh, lots.' Jacquetta gazed at the apple rind disappearing into the rabbit's hinged mouth. 'But today I've been released. I'm starting the process of separation, you see, of returning to myself. After all these years of being seen in terms of other people.' She paused, and then she announced, 'Now, I'm sure, I'm going to be able to *paint*.'

CHAPTER SEVENTEEN

The front door slammed and two adolescent boys came in. They were dressed in black, and carried school bags.

'It's fucking freezing out there,' said one of them. 'What happened to global warming?'

For a moment Celeste didn't dare look at them. They stomped through the kitchen and opened the fridge.

'Half a tin of bleeding Whiskas. There's no fucking food in this place. There's never any fucking food.'

Buffy's sons. She looked at them now. They were poking their heads like crows into the fridge. They turned. Their faces were chalk-white, and spotty.

'You're a crap mother.'

'I've been working,' said Jacquetta.

'Oh yeah? You never work.'

One of them had his hair shaved at the back and a series of chains in his ear, looped together, like a little link fence. The other one had matted black hair tangled like a cat's coughball. Neither of them looked anything like Buffy, but then she hadn't known him when he was young. Their long skinny wrists protruded from their sleeves.

Jacquetta pointed to the table. 'This person, sorry I don't know your name, she's going to take your baby rabbits.'

'What rabbits?'

'Your pets.'

They looked at the baby rabbits, which now sat huddled together panting. There was a puddle on the newspaper.

'Don't be upset,' said Jacquetta.

'I'm not,' said one of the boys.

'Didn't know they'd had any babies,' said the other. He turned to his mother. 'Give us some dosh.'

'Why?'

'Going to get my nose pierced.'

The older one laughed—a startling, harsh sound like a corncrake. 'Nobody gets their noses pierced anymore. Only people who live in East Finchley.'

'The Tuaregs do,' said their mother.

'They live in East Finchley?'

'Africa,' she said. 'They're a tribe. Or maybe it's the Nubians. Incredibly statuesque and beautiful.'

'Tasmin Phillpott's got a ring through her nose,' said one of the boys. 'She looks like a pig.'

The other boy had opened a tin of grapefruit segments and was eating them with

156

a serving spoon. 'My teacher says, why didn't you come to Parents' Evening?'

'Parents' Evening?' asked Jacquetta.

'You never come.' He rummaged in his bag and pulled out a damp, partially disintegrated piece of paper. 'Here's the reminder.'

'Did your Dad go?'

'Buffy? Christ, no. We didn't tell him. Last time he took out his hip flask. Anyway, he never knows what subjects we do.' He poured some cornflakes into the grapefruit tin and stirred it up. 'Nor do you.'

'I do!' said Jacquetta.

'You're both hopeless. Anyway I'm glad you didn't come. You'd do something really sad, like last time.'

'What do you mean?'

He snorted into his Cornflakes, and wiped his nose on his sleeve. 'You wore that sequin, like, headband thing. Everybody *stared* at you. And then you told our headmaster you'd had an erotic dream about him.'

'Did I?'

He shovelled in the last of the Cornflakes. 'My teacher only wanted you to come in case you brought Leon. She saw him on TV; she's got the hots for him.' He flung the tin in the direction of the swing-bin. 'She's that pathetic.'

A dirty white cat sprang into Celeste's lap. It was surprisingly heavy. She stroked it; as it purred, rhythmically, its claws dug into her thighs. She didn't dare push it off; she didn't dare *move.* Only an hour ago she had been standing, shivering, outside this fortress of a house, this creamy cliff five storeys high. Just standing there, staring at it, like Penny used to do. *I used to look up at the house and imagine their lives in it.* Then she had seen the sign, *Baby Rabbits Free to a Good Home* and rung the bell. On impulse, just like that. So much had happened, with such swooping speed and a distracted sort of intimacy, that she felt queasy. How easy it had been! She had been like a burglar, discovering a door was unlocked. There was so much she needed to ask, but on the other hand she didn't want them to notice her sitting there. She felt like a surveillance camera in a crowded shop.

As they bickered, she looked around. It was a huge kitchen. There were a lot of abstract paintings hanging up—violent and splashy, as if someone had been stirring a pot too vigorously and some of it had been flung onto the walls. Every surface was crammed with things—how different from her own neat home in Melton Mowbray! She wondered how much had changed in this room since Buffy had lived here. But then she didn't know what Buffy's taste ran to, anyway. She hadn't visited his flat yet; she hadn't let him take her there. She was so confused, so emotional, that she suddenly felt exhausted, like an overloaded electricity grid blacking out. But now somebody seemed to be talking to her.

'What are you going to carry them in?' Jacquetta was looking at her, eyebrows raised above her blue-rimmed glasses. She was wearing a sort of peasant's scarf wrapped around her head, and a lot of beads. It was only now that Celeste dared to have a good look at her. She wore a baggy sort of garment covered in zigzags and a long red cardigan. With all that jewellery she looked like a high priestess.

'Carry them?' asked Celeste stupidly. She had forgotten why she was supposed to be here.

'She can take them in that,' said one of the boys. He pointed to a cardboard box. 'Leon's crap book came in it. His author's copies.'

'It's not crap,' said Jacquetta vaguely.

They put the rabbits into the cardboard box. It had a label on it: *Guilt: A User's Guide, by Leon Buckman. 8 Copies.* One of the boys fetched some Sellotape.

He was just taping down the lid when the doorbell rang. Jacquetta answered it. She returned with a big black man.

'Car for Mr Buckman,' he said. 'BBC.'

At the same moment a chunky young woman came down the stairs, yawning. 'What's happening?' she asked.

'Leon's going on TV,' said Jacquetta. 'Go and buzz him, somebody. He's downstairs. And this person's taking our rabbits.'

'You going to the White City?' the yawning

159

woman asked the driver. 'Can you give me a lift? Drop me off on the way?' she turned to Celeste. 'Hi. I'm India.'

Celeste said she was just taking the rabbits away. India asked if she had a car; Celeste shook her head.

'Which way are you going?' asked India.

'Kilburn.'

'Want a lift? He'll drop you off.' India lifted up the box. 'Come on,' she said. 'Leon'll just be putting the finishing touches to his *coiffure*. He'll be here in a minute.'

'Where're you going?' asked her mother.

'Oh, just to see a friend.' India, the box under one arm, grabbed a coat in the hallway. Celeste turned to say goodbye, but Jacquetta was talking to her sons. They, too, were putting on their coats.

'We're going carol singing,' said one of them.

'But it's not December yet,' she said. 'Anyway, you can't sing.'

He laughed his corncrake laugh. 'Yeah, but they'll be so scared of us they'll give us the money.'

*   *   *

Celeste and India sat in the limo, waiting for Leon. They had put the box of rabbits in the front seat. Celeste hadn't a clue what she was going to do with them. She felt utterly helpless,

160

swept up by events which were now beyond her control. One ex-wife, and now another! She had come in from the cold and sat in their rooms. Neither of them had thought it rude or odd. Children and step-children had appeared. So had rabbits—what on earth was she going to do with them? Buffy's past was like some complicated board game; she had opened it and taken out some of the pieces, but nobody had read her the rules. It was curiously exhilarating.

'Why are you called India?' she asked.

India took a card out of her wallet and passed it to her. 'I couldn't bear to tell anyone anymore, so I had this printed.'

Celeste read the card. It was printed in italic script. 'I see,' she said, reading it again. Conceived in an ashram in Bangalore. 'Gosh, how exotic.'

'That's what Mum thinks. I think it's fucking embarrassing.'

'Who's your father, then?'

'He's called Alan. He works in Strasbourg. He only talks to his computer.' She snorted. 'He doesn't communicate with me, I'm not IBM compatible.' She wiped her nose. 'Fathers! Who'd have them!'

Alan. Celeste hadn't heard of him. Where did Buffy come into this? She couldn't work it out yet; Leon would be arriving any minute.

They sat there, looking at the bulgy folds in the back of the driver's neck. He wore a peaked cap. She felt comfortable with India. She looked about her own age, for one thing. She looked straightforward too, in a pissed-off sort of way. She had a square, suetty face; she hadn't inherited her mother's looks. She wore a woollen bobble-hat and a black, man's coat. It smelt of mothballs. Her fingernails were bitten right down. Celeste gnawed her fingernails, but only round the edges. Still, she felt a bond.

India leaned forward and addressed the driver. 'So what's he wittering on about this time?'

'Mr Buckman? I just take him there, miss.'

'Probably blathering on about his book.' She pointed to the box in the front seat. 'That's it.'

The driver read the label. '*Guilt: A User's Guide.*'

'Listen to it.'

'Listen to it?' he asked.

'Go on.'

The driver bent over the box and listened. 'There's something moving about.'

India sniggered. 'Smells a bit funny too, doesn't it?'

The driver sniffed. 'Now you mention it.'

At that moment the front door opened and Leon appeared. He was the man Celeste had seen in the garden. He hurried down the steps and strode briskly towards the car.

'It's all right,' he called cheerfully, 'I'll sit in the front.'

162

The driver lifted up the box and put it onto the floor. 'What *is* it in there?' He tipped the box; there was a sliding sound.

They drove off. Leon leaned over the seat and shook Celeste's hand. 'Hi,' he said, 'and who are you?'

Celeste told him her name. Leon's hand remained in hers for a moment; it felt dry and sincere. Even in the dark she could see that he had a terrific tan; at this time of year too. No wonder Buffy had kicked in his face, on the TV.

'You're not from London, are you?' he asked. 'You look far too wholesome.'

Celeste told him she came from Leicestershire. She said she worked in a shop—she didn't say where—and that it was her day off.

'You have any family here?' he asked.

She shook her head, willing him to stop. After all these weeks, he was the first person who had actually asked her any questions. Buffy mostly told her how beautiful she was, the light of his life, how could he believe his luck, an old has-been like him. Or else *she* asked *him* questions—about his past, how he had met Gene Kelly once, the thousands and thousands of interesting things he had done and the people he had worked with, most of whom she had never heard of, or only read about in magazines. They sat in teashops for hours, until the waitresses cleared the tables;

163

they went to the theatre; they sat in pubs and talked until closing time. She had learned more, in the past few weeks, than she had learned in her whole life. Buffy had such a rich past packed into him, he was as concentrated as potted meat. Better, because he never ran out.

But Leon asked her questions. As the dark trees of Regent's Park flashed past he gazed at her with tender curiosity; she felt like one of the rabbits, mesmerized by the headlights of his eyes. No wonder his patients came back for more. She seemed to be telling him that she was an orphan. She must be careful. He would seek out any lies with his professional radar.

'So how do you like London?' he asked.

'Well, it's full of surprises.'

He smiled. 'Nice ones?'

She paused. 'More, like, unexpected.'

'If they weren't, they wouldn't be surprises, would they?'

The car stopped in the Edgware Road. Celeste and India got out, with their cardboard box.

'Let's meet again,' said Leon, leaning out of the window. 'I can see my family's taken to you.' The car drove off into the traffic.

India made a retching noise and pretended to vomit into the gutter. 'Isn't he creepy!' she said. 'Almost as awful as Mum. They deserve each other.'

'Why's he creepy?'

'See the way he leched all over you? He does that to everybody. He's always asking me about my sex life. I don't *have* a sex life but I make things up, really disgusting things to see if I can shock him.'

'Do you?'

She shook her head. 'He gets off on it. He's sex-obsessed. He's always touching me, ugh. He screws his female patients and pretends it's therapy.'

Celeste stared at her. 'Does your Mum know?'

India shook her head. 'She never knows what's going on. She's too busy going to her groups and talking about it.'

'How do *you* know?'

'I found his condoms. He keeps them in his *Dictionary of Dangerous Drugs*. I'd gone down there to look up something. I borrow the keys to his cabinet, see, I can get all sorts of stuff there, and I was just checking to see if I'd done something really silly this time.'

'What do you mean?'

'Oh, mixing them. You know.'

'You steal his drugs?'

'LSD and Librium or something,' said India. 'I can't remember. So I looked in his book and there were these packets of condoms, hidden between the pages. Must've been in the L's. About six packets too, the randy sod.'

They were standing on the pavement, the traffic rumbling past. Celeste held the box; it

165

was a lifebelt to stop her from drowning.

'You going this way?' India asked.

Celeste nodded. They started walking.

'They're such a fuck-up, aren't they?' said India. 'Parents.'

'Are they?'

'They make such a fuck-up of their lives. So bloody irresponsible.'

Celeste was about to argue, but she stopped. Hers had been too, in their own way. Their entirely different way. Strangely enough, her upbringing and India's had something in common.

'So bloody childish,' went on India. She walked, her hands thrust into her pockets, staring at the pavement. 'Mum used to nick Bunch to take to her Primal Therapy.'

'What was Bunch?'

'My teddy bear. She'd used him to help her regress. She'd regress to her childhood. But *I* was the child! It was *my* bloody teddy! He wasn't the same when he came back. One of his eyes was loose.' She veered left, sharply, and marched across the road. A van screeched to a halt. Celeste hurried after her and rejoined her, breathlessly, on the opposite pavement. 'Leon's a mega-wanker,' said India. 'Mega. Do you know, his answerphone has messages in English, German and Urdu? They think they're so trendy but both of them are really pathetic, lonely people.'

'Don't you like your Mum at all?'

166

'She doesn't know how to be normal. Parents should be normal. That's the point of them.'

'Mine were,' said Celeste. They weren't, of course. She realized that. But at the time she had thought they were normal. Boring, actually, though she wouldn't have used that word about them then.

'She's totally self-absorbed,' said India. 'She has to be the centre of bloody attention. She's always going on about her work. *My work,* she says in her suffering artist's voice. Any woman who talks about her work like that is bound not to do any. And if she does, it's bound to be awful. Have you seen her *paintings*? She just leeches off men, screwing them for alimony, screwing them for everything, and then going on about what a feminist she is. And sunbathing in the garden without any clothes on, every nipple on view. And asking bus conductors their birth signs, stupid things like that. And rushing off to Tunisia for three months. *Three months!* Leaving us with our nanny. Honestly, you're so lucky!'

'How do you know?'

'Because yours couldn't have been as bad as mine.' She stopped. 'God, I have been going on. Must be terribly boring.'

Celeste shook her head.

'This is where my friend lives,' said India. 'Where are you going?'

'I've got this flat in Kilburn.'

167

'Oh! I know somebody who lives round there.'

'Who?'

'He's called Waxie. He sells me coke.'

'Coke? You go all that way?' Celeste looked at her, puzzled. Was the whole family mad? 'Couldn't you just get it from a machine?'

India burst out laughing. 'A machine?'

'Or a shop or something?'

India paused. 'No, dearie. I mean Coke. Cocaine.'

Celeste didn't know how to reply. In their box, the rabbits were restless. They all slid one way, she could hear their claws scrabbling. Her fingernails used to make that sound, *scrabble-scrabble*, when she typed invoices on the Amstrad back at Kwik-Fit.

India put her arm around her, awkwardly. 'You make me feel awfully old.' She wiped her nose on the back of her glove; it was freezing cold. 'In my so-called family, all the kids are old. It's the grown-ups who're infantile.'

'Is that why you take drugs? You shouldn't, you know. Who's this friend you're seeing? Another drug-dealer?'

India laughed. 'No no. It's my stepdad. Well, one of them.'

There was a pause. They were standing outside a block of flats. Celeste looked up; the building loomed, heavy and monumental, against the suffused sky. The porch was lit. LOMFIELD MANSIONS, it said. The B was

168

missing.

Buffy! She nearly said the name out loud. She had been so distracted, she hadn't noticed where they were standing.

'I said friend because I want to keep Buffy separate,' said India. 'They'd just get all psychological otherwise.' She stood there, huddled in her coat. 'I like him, you see. We *are* friends, actually. My Mum led him an awful dance, I'm really sorry for him. At least he's *human*. At least if I have a problem he doesn't read me the bloody *I Ching*. He takes me to the pub. Anyway, he makes me laugh.' She paused. 'Listen, why don't you come up and meet him?'

'No!' Celeste backed away, clutching her box. 'I mean, he sounds lovely, but . . .'

She had to get away. Maybe he was looking out of the window! Maybe he could see them standing there together. How could she possibly explain?

She turned to India. But India had already left. Suddenly energetic, she was leaping up the steps of the block of flats, her coat flapping.

CHAPTER EIGHTEEN

'You old fool!' cried India, 'You old fart! What's her name?'

'I'm not telling,' said Buffy. 'Not if you take that tone.'

'How old is she?'

'Your age.'

India snorted with laughter and helped herself to one of his cigarettes. 'It's disgusting. Are you sleeping with her?'

'No. Unfortunately.'

'I should think not. How grotesque!'

'I adore her,' said Buffy. 'I've never felt like this before.'

'You always say that. You probably said that with Mum.'

'Don't I deserve a little happiness?' he bleated. 'After all these years? I've even given up drinking. More or less.'

They sat there, wreathed in smoke. She stroked his knee. 'I'm happy for you, Buff, I really am. Maybe this is the real thing. Does she know about all your repellent ailments?'

He nodded. 'Better than anyone. She knows about my piles and my constipation and my athlete's foot—'

'Gawd. She a doctor?'

Buffy shook his head. 'I'm not telling.'

India gestured around the room. 'Perhaps she can sort this place out. Look at it! When you're on your own you revert, don't you? Remember when you and Mum split up, and I came round after school to spring clean?'

'In your gymslip, with your little duster,' said Buffy. 'My angel of mercy. I remember. I burst

170

into tears.'

'You were probably pissed.' She looked around. 'This flat really pongs. You'll never get your leg over, not till you do something about it. You can hardly get the door open, let alone drag some woman through it.'

They were silent for a while. From the bedroom came the sound of cracking bones. George must have discovered last night's Kentucky Fried Chicken.

'What about you?' asked Buffy. 'My Dark Continent?'

'If there was anybody, you'd be the first to know. But there isn't.'

'Is everything all right?'

India gazed down at her hands. He noticed the nicotine stains on her fingers.

'I wish you didn't smoke,' he said. 'It makes me feel guilty.'

'Don't.'

'Don't what?'

'Feel guilty.'

'Heavens, nobody's ever said that to me. Why shouldn't I?'

India was sitting on the floor. She pushed some crumbs into a little pile. 'Remember when you and Mum used to have those awful, awful rows?'

Buffy nodded.

'And Bruno stood up in his cot and cried and rattled the bars,' she said. 'I used to lie in bed with my eyes tight shut, but it never did any good, you still went on yelling, I could still hear you.'

'Don't!'

'Just like Mum was with Dad, but worse somehow. Maybe because I was older and I could understand what you were saying.' She flattened the pyramid of crumbs with her finger. 'Then you came in. You closed the door and sat beside my bed. And you put on Hammy's voice—you didn't put it on, you *were* Hammy. Or Voley or whoever it was, all those stupid animals. You took me somewhere else, along with you. We went off on our adventures.' She looked up. 'You were the only one who could do it. You let me escape.'

He sighed. 'So did I.'

'You're lucky. You're an actor, you can do it all the time.'

'Too bloody much of the time. That's what they all said. Your Mum, and all the others.'

She squashed the pile of crumbs and stood up. 'I can't, you see. Not any more.' Abruptly, she pulled on her woolly hat and picked up her coat.

'Don't go!' he cried. 'Come out and have a spaghetti!'

But she was at the door now. 'Got to see someone.'

'Who?'

'Just a friend.' She pushed aside some plastic bags and opened the door.

Buffy got to his feet and followed her out.

172

'Who?'

She wasn't taking the lift; she was hurrying down the stairs. Her voice echoed, as it floated back to him. 'Someone called Waxie.'

And she was gone.

*   *   *

Buffy sank back into his chair. He suddenly felt terribly depressed. How he longed to see Celeste's bright young face! But he didn't know where she was. It was her day off but she had refused to go out with him; he had wanted to take her to the Tate and introduce her to Bonnard but she'd said she had something planned. Same with her day off the week before. He had rung her flat, twice, but there had been no answer.

Maybe she was seeing someone else, a young vigorous man who wasn't a hopeless failure, who hadn't had the *chance* to be a hopeless failure. Whose future disasters weren't even written yet. Whose inadequacies were still in embryonic form.

Celeste was changing. She was wearing quite assertive clothes nowadays, fashionable clothes in strong colours. Last week, when he had taken her out to dinner, she had worn an almost intimidating jacket and a really rather seductive black dress. Was she just adapting to her habitat, or was there some unwelcome significance to this?

173

He wished India hadn't rushed off like that. It was five to eight. The sun was well over the yard-arm; in fact, it had been pitch dark for hours. No harm in a small scotch. He heaved himself to his feet and padded into the kitchen. It was freezing cold. He peered into the boiler. The pilot light was out.

Blithering hell and damnation. Penny could fix the boiler but Penny wasn't here. When halted at various obstacles in life's path he suddenly missed the various women with whom he had cohabited, different ones according to the nature of the aggravation. When he couldn't work the camera he thought of Penny; *she* would have remembered to remove the lens cap when photographing the pavement. She could get the car started, too; it was now rusting away in the residents' parking bay, its battery long since dead. Any electrical mishaps reminded him of Phoebe, a costume designer with whom he had lived for a short and not entirely harmonious time but who had been surprisingly deft with a fusebox. When his houseplants withered—they had all withered—he thought of Jacquetta, who used to talk to them or something; whatever dotty methods she used, it did the trick. Lorna had had green fingers too . . . *Lorna.* Goodness, he hadn't thought about her for years. She would be a middle-aged woman by now. Lorna . . . didn't he say, once, that she was the love of his life?

He drained his glass and poured himself another scotch, purely as insulation. He should have learnt how to do these things, fuseboxes and so on, when he had the chance. Trouble was, you didn't think about it at the time and when the final explosion happened, the appalling bust-up, it didn't cross your mind to say: *By the way, before you go, could you just show me how to set the timer on the video recorder?*

What had they learned from him, and he from them? Popsi had showed him how to cook terrific mince, hers was the best of all his exes' mince. Lorna had known the names of lots of birds, linnets and so on, she was always pointing them out, but most of the time he hadn't been attending. A woman called Miriam had taught him the words of all the songs in *Guys and Dolls.* But it didn't seem a lot, when you looked back on it. In fact, it seemed pitifully little. Maybe what he had learnt from them had been so profound that he couldn't just at this moment put it into words.

He looked around the kitchen. On the shelf sat Penny's half-finished pot of Marmite. Lorna had loved Marmite too. So had nearly every woman he had known in a sufficiently domestic setting to discover this. No male acquaintance of his had liked Marmite, it seemed to be purely a female thing. He looked at the clutter of pots and jars. Would Celeste like Marmite? He would probably never know. He had been a failure, with his wives and his children and his step-children, how could he possibly crank himself up again for a lovely young creature like Celeste? How could he lumber her with someone like himself? If, that is, she wanted to be lumbered at all, which he was starting to doubt.

Why was she constantly disappearing, and with whom? Maybe his role had just been to get her going. It was like when you rented one of those holiday apartments in the Algarve. In your room there would be one of those starter packs—a couple of tea-bags, a bun, maybe an orange. That was him. She had eaten him up and now she had learnt the language she was launching off into an independent life of her own.

He made his way into the living room, knocking into India's tea mug and slopping its contents on the floor. She had hardly drunk any of it. What was wrong with her; was it his fault, like everything else? She had sort of implied that it wasn't, entirely; her words had deeply moved him.

He switched on the TV. Leon's face bloomed onto the screen.

'. . . *we must realize, Gavin, that for many people guilt is a fuel. They run on it, they can't function without it—*'

The smug git. Buffy switched it off. He no longer wanted to kick in the TV, however;

Leon's face—fleshier now, and even more irritatingly handsome—no longer had the power to enrage him. It had been defused. Oh, the expense of spirit . . . They had all been defused. Even Penny, who he had recently glimpsed hailing a cab in Tottenham Court Road, even Penny had almost reverted back into a smart, glossy woman in an unfamiliar black coat. Eight years of sleeping in the same bed, of squabbling over the map in the car— eight years of everything had vaporized just like that, wasn't it alarming? They had vaporized as if they had never happened. Or, more exactly, they had been drained of meaning, they were full of sound and fury, signifying nothing. He must never tell Celeste this, never. One must never tell such horror stories to the young; they would never get to sleep at night. Keep to the woodland creatures.

He wasn't inebriated. Just cosmic. He put a Brahms quartet on the record player; he put on his overcoat and sat in front of the dead TV. A man he'd met in New York had once been walking past a record shop with Mia Farrow. The window had displayed a collection of Frank Sinatra records; she had paused, and nearly gone in to buy one. It was only then that she had realized *she had been married to Frank Sinatra, once.*

He thought of all the women he had known. Of course he could remember them; the hot agonies might have vaporized but the memories remained. He could draw nourishment from them for years, like a camel with water stored in its hump. He remembered the way Popsi poured Nescafé into the lid, instead of taking it out with a spoon—a habit either endearing or irritating, depending on his mood. Did other people do this? He hadn't met any. Penny's schoolgirlish wriggle each morning as she pulled on her surprisingly puritanical cotton knickers. Carmella's deft and impressive card-shuffling; their happiest hours had been spent playing gin rummy, with Nyange asleep in her cot. Who was Carmella playing card games with now? Where was his daughter, Nyange? Was Penny wearing lacier and more interesting knickers for that awful photographer, and pulling them on in a more lascivious manner?

Sometimes he wondered if they knew what they had in common, these women whose only similarity was, to some degree, he supposed, temporarily loving him. He knew what life was like with each of them, that was his secret. He was like a computer database, with all this information stored in him. The way Jacquetta brushed her teeth, sucking moisture from the brush and spitting, never rinsing from a mug. Everybody he had lived with brushed their teeth in a different manner. Those intimate moments, in so many bathrooms! Lorna—yes, Lorna, now he remembered it—she used to dust herself with talc, a cloud of it, her hips thrust forward. She and Popsi, though they didn't know it, had shared a cheerful lack of inhibition in the bathroom, peeing while he shaved (he was beardless then), both wiping themselves daintily from the front rather than the rear, the only two women he had known who did it that way round. Popsi even used to insert her diaphragm when he was in the room, squeezing cream onto it with the skilled insouciance of a patissiere anointing a tartelet.

The temperature was dropping. He lit another cigarette, clumsily, with his gloved hands. Then there was the lovemaking, ah, the lovemaking. He shouldn't think like this but he couldn't help it. Even freezing cold, he blushed. The warm bodies, the chilly toes, the blind rapture and damp embarrassments . . . Jacquetta's thin, strenuous body, the way she climaxed whimperingly, turning her face away as if it were too precious to share. Penny's wholesomely gymnastic approach, at least during the early years, her smooth but hefty thighs gripping him like a vice, the surprisingly rude words she whispered into his ear, words she never used during daylight hours, like the louche company one only met in nightclubs . . . Popsi's boozy breath and gratifyingly multiple orgasms . . . Oh, the breasts he had known, the heaviness of them in his hand, the soft stomachs and hard shoulder-blades . . . the skin . . . the fingers . . . A girl called Annabel in

179

that hotel room in Rye . . . Desperate and adulterous copulations in the backseat of cars, the windows steaming up . . . the indignities, the bare buttocks . . . The marital companionability and giggles, the familiar adjustments of flesh against flesh, limb against limb, year after year, *ouches* on holiday when they were sunburnt, dear secret places where someone else was trespassing now, though they weren't of course, he himself had trespassed since . . .

Shut up. He could go on like this for ever. There was nobody, of course, that he could ever tell. And each woman he had loved, she held all those secrets locked within her, too— of other men who at the time he couldn't bear to contemplate, you blocked them out. What were they doing now, Phoebe and Annabel and Popsi and all the others? They stayed, fixed, at the age he had known them; such is the egocentricity of memory. In his head they were still young women though some of them would be grandmothers now. What were they doing—making tea for somebody else; opening a tin of cat food? Ten to one they weren't sitting in front of a blank TV thinking of *him.*

In some ways it was a relief, of course. It was a relief that he no longer had to visit Penny's testy old father in Ascot, that he no longer had to pretend to himself that Jacquetta's paintings were any good. These

180

were other people's responsibilities now, and sometimes he felt a grateful warmth towards his successors. It was like passing on a troublesome car which sooner or later would start making that funny knocking noise. This wasn't a sexist comment because he felt exactly the same about himself. My God, the complaints about *his* performance! Women had used him and passed him on, ruthlessly in many cases. They had ransacked him en route like departing soldiers, stripping him of his home and his children.

Sometimes, however, he had felt barely touched. Some women, Jacquetta for instance, hadn't really registered him at all. She had never looked at his childhood snapshots or shown the slightest interest in his past. She was either distracted or prickly. Coming home from a dinner party, for instance, he would make some mild remark like: 'Isn't it odd how people who're wonderful cooks often make awful coffee, and vice versa?' Instead of companionably agreeing or disagreeing she would bark: 'What do you mean? *I* can't cook?' Other women, less neurotic but as healthily egocentric, had blithely let him foot the bill and slipped from him into the traffic, into other arms. Sometimes he felt like a bottle of wine that travels from one party to another, passed from host to host, a bottle so undrinkable that nobody wants to open it. Hirondelle, say, or that stuff called *Red Table*

181

Wine: Product of More than One Country.

He topped up his glass. Penny had once said: 'You're just an old soak. You're not even brave enough to be an alcoholic!' A remark he had felt was both glib and deeply meaningless; typical of a journalist.

Lorna wasn't like that. What had happened to Lorna the country-lover, the bird-spotter? He had loved her once. He could get quite maudlin, thinking about those missed opportunities. The right woman at the wrong time, and—my God—vice versa. No point in it, really. He was alone now. There was nobody just to be around, somewhere in the flat, when he opened his income tax demands. At certain moments even an unsupportive woman was better than nothing. He'd better go and see the blasted porter about the blasted pilot light.

Buffy tried to raise himself from his armchair. George, who had been sitting beside him, thumped his tail and climbed to his feet. Buffy sat down again; the whole operation seemed too complicated, just now. George sank back to the floor.

Celeste . . . oh, Celeste . . .

CHAPTER NINETEEN

Celeste sat in the candlelight, drinking a glass of wine. She had got the idea of the candles from Jacquetta's house; she had bought them at the late-night shop and stuck them in saucers around the room. How magical! She could no longer see the damp patches on the wall, or the marks where the previous tenants had hung their pictures. Though she had put away her little crucifix, though the tentative faith she had once possessed had been rocked to its shallow foundations, the candles made her room feel sacred and somehow stiller than usual, even though the shadows danced elastically and the rabbits hopped around the carpet. Wine-drinking was a habit she had picked up from Penny. A glass or two in the evening, that was all. Sancerre, because that was what Penny had been drinking and Celeste didn't know any other kind. She tipped back her glass and drained it. If Buffy's exes could do all this, why couldn't she?

Since she had visited Penny, the week before, two more large boxes had been delivered. She had unpacked everything and laid out the objects on every available surface. She didn't know where these objects were going to be photographed, or when—nobody had mentioned this or indeed how much money she herself was going to be paid—but she needed to display them so that she could write down their descriptions and divide them into groups.

Growing Things was one. Flowerpots had been constructed from just about anything that

183

was vaguely cylindrical, lampshades included. Seedling trays had been made out of the paper cups from boxes of chocolates and the cut-off fingers of rubber gloves. By pricking holes in the bottom of a sports holdall someone had created a capacious Gro-Bag—*with handy travel handles* said the accompanying note, though it didn't explain why one should want to take tomatoes anywhere. *Safety Aids* was another group. This included a pair of child's waterwings constructed from the styrofoam shapes used to pack a hi-fi. Broken rubber bands, knotted together, provided the straps. *Handy Hints* was a general sort of title, used for things like coffee-cup cosies made out of discarded sweaters and a stamp-moistener made from an empty roll-on deodorant bottle.

Just looking at them made her feel obscurely weary. She was starting to realize that no classification was really possible, even by a mind as logical as hers. Some of the objects seemed to have three or four uses and some seemed to have no use at all. Even if they had a use, she could never imagine anyone actually using them. And she still hadn't worked out the thing with the colander. Ranged around the room in the candlelight, they resembled religious offerings donated by a deeply confused congregation. One of the rabbits was already nibbling at a bundle of cut-up tights, which had been accompanied by a long explanatory letter she seemed to have lost.

She had a suspicion that the whole business was getting out of hand. Besides, there was something else that disturbed her, some symbolic meaning to it all that she didn't want to examine. It seemed to be to do with Buffy, and her place in his life. What had Penny said about 100 uses for a discarded husband? Maybe he saw her as a new shoot growing from the rubbish tip of his past—a rubbish tip which daily grew in size as she discovered more about it. Old tights and all.

She mustn't think about this; not now. She missed him desperately; she longed to pick up the phone. But she mustn't; not yet. Instead she looked at his sons' rabbits. One of them was eating a digestive biscuit which she had laid out on a plate, along with some lettuce leaves and a bit of cucumber. Under the table stood their cardboard box. Its bottom was damp from their long voyage and littered with droppings like spilled raisins. The sticker saying *Guilt: A User's Guide* was peeling off. Not surprisingly, the rabbits showed no inclination to go back into it. If only somebody had sent something really useful, something that could be turned into a hutch! She would have to buy one tomorrow, in her lunch hour, if she could find a pet shop. The rabbits were all black, and larger than she had thought at first; they weren't really babies at all. But it was nice to have some company; she had always liked animals and had been devoted, as a child, to her guinea-pig Jonathan. His death had been her first acquaintanceship with grief. When she had needed to stop giggling—during school prayers, say—she only needed to picture his stiff little body to come to a shuddering halt.

She poured herself another glass of wine. She needed to talk to Buffy, soon. His voice was inside her head. He was so familiar that she felt she had known him all her life, that his voice had been there since she had sat in the armchair sucking her thumb. All the questions swimming around her brain, he could answer them or at least have a go. She loved him for that; she had never known a chatty man. Why do people's Walkmen always seem to be playing the same tune? Last summer she had wondered this, briefly; nobody she had met, then, would have been equipped with any sort of reply. Why does all French people's handwriting look the same? (Her whole class, at one time, had had French pen-pals.)

But there were questions much more urgent than these, questions so painful that her stomach clenched. The trouble was, she couldn't ask them. He would just think her insane—insane with jealousy. He wouldn't even be flattered. *Why are you so obsessed with my ex-wives?* She couldn't tell him the reason—not yet.

*　　　*　　　*

There was only one person she could ask: Jacquetta. Jacquetta would know.

She could phone. She knew the number. A rabbit, sitting on its haunches, was nibbling one of her spider plants. Celeste sat beside the phone, not moving. Nine o'clock came and went. Footsteps thumped up and down the stairs. India had come and gone but she didn't know that. Time passed. The ceiling creaked; music played. Her building was a-whisper with transactions.

Celeste didn't phone; she didn't dare. She blew out the candles and went to bed. In the house of secrets she lay, her eyes closed, vibrating gently to the underground trains. In the other room the rabbits were busy. At some point she heard the muffled thud of a plant pot, one of her spider plants no doubt, as it fell to the carpet.

*　　　*　　　*

The next day, energized by the bright shop, by being at work, she felt emboldened. There was a buzz in the air. Mr Singh's oldest daughter was sitting the exam for a private school, and he kept rushing to the phone to see if she was home yet. On their display stands the women's faces filled Celeste with courage. Such beauty, such miracles. Be a Vamp! Be a Blonde! Get

187

into private school! Shake a bottle and anything could happen. Each package was filled with possibilities. She could change her life, change her accent . . .

Mr Singh put down the phone. She asked if she could use it.

She paused, her hand on the receiver. Her courage drained away. What excuse could she use this time? At some point, surely, even Jacquetta might get suspicious.

It was then, as she stood there, that the door pinged and a long black figure entered the shop. Its matted hair stood up, like a surprised person in a cartoon.

It was Tobias. Or was it Bruno? One of Buffy's sons. Just for a moment, as he stood there in the harsh strip lighting, she saw the resemblance—the nose, the posture.

'Oh,' he mumbled, surprised. 'Hello.'

*   *   *

Tobias had been going to visit his Dad. He did this secretly, creeping out of the house like a married man committing adultery. It was not that his Mum and Leon disapproved. Far from it. Leon in fact encouraged him to maintain a relationship with his father—the main reason, of course, for him to never let on that he did. Leon! What a wanker.

His half-sister India visited Blomfield Mansions quite a lot, he knew that. But it was

188

only recently that he had begun to see why. His Dad's life was such a mess, that was partly why. It made even *him* feel sorted-out. There was something about his Dad's glaring inadequacies that made him, Tobias, feel miraculously mature. Besides, now Penny was gone he felt sorry for the old tosser. There was something sort of simple about his Dad's ramshackle life. At home everything was so muddy—his Mum so tricky and abstracted, his stepdad so fucking understanding. What do you do when a bloke gives you condoms? Where do you go from there? Didn't Leon realize that the point about being sixteen was to be *misunderstood*?

Oh, it was more than that. It was lots of things. He didn't want to analyse it, they had enough of that psychological crap at home. Basically, he was skiving off school and he needed some dosh. His Dad always lent him money—if he had any—because he was a soft touch and anyway he always felt guilty about being such a rotten father. There was a quid pro quo here.

So when Tobias rang the doorbell and just got the barking dog he felt disappointed, for several reasons, that his father wasn't at home. (In fact Buffy, who had a splitting hangover, was down at the BBC narrating a documentary about pygmies but nobody else knew that.)

Tobias took the lift to the ground floor, went out, and walked round the corner to the

189

local chemists. He needed to buy some Phisomed for his pimples. He opened the door and came face to face with the person who had taken his rabbits.

'Oh, hello,' he grunted. He wiped his nose with the back of his hand and shuffled his feet. How fucking embarrassing. The point of buying zit stuff at this shop was that nobody knew him. Now, if he were buying some spray, say, to curb the powerful sexual scent he gave off, something like that . . .

He edged towards the other assistant, the big plain one. She was sitting on a stool reading a women's magazine. He looked over her shoulder at the article: *The Pros and Cons of Stomach Stapling.* But it was no good; the other one came up to him.

'Hello.' She smiled at him. 'Your rabbits are doing really well. Bigger every day. Is there anything I can get you?'

Tobias felt his face heating up. You try to be cool and then what happens? You frigging *blush.* What a divhead! He liked her. She was older than the girls he knew, of course; she must be, like, early twenties. But it was the girls his age who seemed the old ones, with their boots and their loud dismissive voices and the way they looked bored all the time even when they were laughing about something he didn't understand. The way they wore badges saying *I Practise Safe Sex* and totally ignored him. He had grown up with some of them, he had been to primary school with them, but by now they looked as if they'd never been young at all.

He couldn't ask for the pimple lotion, not now. So he mumbled something he had heard the last time he had been listening to anybody at home.

'My Mum was talking about you,' he muttered. 'She said she wanted you to sit for her.'

'Sit for her? Where?'

'Like . . .' He rolled his eyes. He always did this when he talked about his Mum's work. 'Like, she wants to paint you.'

She stared at him. *She* blushed now—a pink glow that spread up her face and matched her overall. 'She does? Really?'

CHAPTER TWENTY

At the Happy Eater it was lunchtime all day, breakfast time too, anytime. Meals looped and repeated themselves like the Muzak, ravelling and unravelling. Lorna walked from the kitchen to the tables, the tables to the kitchen. Her head was swimming with the names of plants. Birds she knew about, but plants . . . plants she was just learning. Her legs ached. She was getting too old for this.

*   *   *

Way across England, somewhere near Swindon, Miles sat in a Little Chef. He was mopping up ketchup with a piece of bread. Outside, traffic droned. He swallowed the last mouthful and lit up a cigarette. He had started smoking again. He knew it was unfair, to blame this on his wife, but that's what he did. After all, there was nobody to stop him. His marriage was like a cot-death. Barely begun, it had turned over on its face and stopped breathing. Nobody noticed, least of all his wife. Around him people carried on shovelling in mouthfuls of peas.

*   *   *

Meanwhile, in London, Penny sat in the Groucho Club nibbling a goat's cheese pizza. She was interviewing a blockbuster writer. As he droned on she watched the looping ribbon of her cassette recorder. Round and round it went, filling itself with his words. He was telling her about his Cotswolds mansion. As he talked about his tennis court she suddenly thought: *Rich people never have to write their initials on their tennis balls.* This struck her as so true, so witty, that she thought: *Must tell Buffy tonight.* Then she realized that she couldn't. This sensation still hit her. Months, it had been, and it still hit her.

192

*　　　*　　　*

Outside, a wintry sun shone. A mile away, shoppers in Knightsbridge were heading for sandwich bars. One of them was a middle-aged woman Buffy had slept with a quarter of a century earlier, an incident forgotten by both of them. She was emerging from Harrods, where she had just bought a party dress for her grand-daughter. Her reflection flashed against the window; behind the glass stood the mannequins Quentin had arranged. Her reflection flashed, and was gone.

*　　　*　　　*

Nearby, Quentin himself sat in a cappuccino place. He often came here in his lunch hour. Black and chrome, sharp and stylish, it made everybody look well-designed. It drained them of their past and re-created them as fashion statements. Stirring his coffee, he remembered when he was a little boy and how he pretended he had a limp. His ma, Popsi, would get exasperated and walk on ahead. Passers-by would murmur *poor little mite* and glare at her — glare at his Mum, the most warm-hearted soul in the world. He knew he was making some sort of point, even then; that he was getting at her in some way. He closed his eyes, to concentrate. He must bring this up with his

193

therapist. Closing his eyes, he pictured a shadowy figure—a man, striding ahead with his mother, turning to bellow at him to buck up. Was this Buffy, or one of the fathers who had come after him?

Quentin folded the fluff into his coffee. Talbot, the man he lived with, he always scooped off the froth first. For some reason this was starting to be irritating. Like the way his own ma, Popsi, poured instant coffee into the lid and flung it into the mugs without measuring it out with a spoon.

Quentin looked up and met the eye of a tall, good-looking man with a box of photographic equipment. Nope. No blip on the radar screen. Besides, he was too young. Quentin was irresistibly drawn towards older men. He knew why, of course; he hadn't spent a fortune on therapy for nothing. *I'm looking for my father; all these years, I've been limping to get his attention.*

*　　*　　*

Across the room Colin gazed, briefly, at the bloke who sat with his eyes closed. Good bone-structure; light him well and he could be a model. He gazed with the same detached interest at the Gubbio coffee-machine and wondered if he could ever fit one into his kitchen. 'There's no room for anything!' Penny cried. 'There's no room for me! If only I was

194

hinged, you could fold me up and keep me in a box.' She was a tall woman, she needed to stride about. That's what had made her so attractive in the first place. Sometimes he wondered if he was going to be able to cope with her.

*   *   *

Buffy sat in his local, The Three Fiddlers. He was eating a Scotch egg. Well, a grey, loose piece of breadcrumbed cardboard that fell off a small, bluish, rubbery ball that had probably been hardboiled when he was still married to Jacquetta. Why hadn't he learned his lesson about Scotch eggs; why did he still order them? A bit like marriage really; you're hungry, you think it'll be different this time, it can't be as bad as the last one.

On the TV some satellite, Sky or something, was showing tennis. In November. Satellite TV, like central heating, rendered the seasons meaningless. Watching the ball fly, Buffy remembered watching a Wimbledon final long ago. Connors, was it? Or even Arthur Ashe? Years ago. Jacquetta was away, supposedly visiting her aunt in Dorset. Funny, then, that as he sat there he saw her quite clearly amongst the spectators in the Centre Court. Just to the left of the umpire. She was sitting next to a man. Their heads turning one way, then the other. And then turning to each

195

other.

And she didn't even like tennis. In fact, she hated it. That was the worst thing of all. Oh, where was Celeste, who knew nothing of these things? Celeste his innocent girl, his comfort and joy? Not in the shop. Mr Singh said it was her day off. Where was she? His old heart ached.

*   *   *

Celeste sat, hunched on the concrete. Her buttocks were numb. Here in the garden it was freezing; the wintry sun had slipped behind the house and the conservatory lay in shadow. Wind whistled through the skeletal struts; the place hadn't been glazed yet and the workmen seemed to have disappeared. According to Jacquetta they had been gone for days. 'Builders!' she sighed. 'They always let you down in the end. Believe me. I know.'

Jacquetta was painting. Her hair was pulled back in a rubber band; she wore a spattered pair of dungarees which she said had belonged to a plumber of her acquaintance. 'What a man!' she said. 'Built like a shire-horse!' Her face was pinched with concentration; her arm flicked the paint to and fro in bold brush strokes. As she worked she hummed—a low, tuneless sound which for a while Celeste couldn't locate. Then she realized that it stopped when Jacquetta rinsed her brush.

196

Behind her spectacles, Jacquetta inspected her. *If she knew what I was thinking!* But Celeste guessed that she herself was just an arrangement of shapes and colours. She was just an object to be painted.

With Penny, too, she was just as unknown— a willing pair of hands, a person to wear Penny's cast-off clothing and deal with other people's cast-offs. Both women wanted something from her but neither of them had the foggiest idea what *she* wanted from *them*. It was funny, the way neither of them questioned the way she had popped up into their lives. Instead they just found ways of making her useful. Which was lucky, of course. Their lack of curiosity made the whole thing easier. No, not easier. None of this was easy. But for the moment it made everything more possible to manage.

Celeste sat in the conservatory, as instructed, her arms around her knees. Behind Jacquetta reared up the family home. Buffy had lived in there. He had eaten thousands of breakfasts with this woman. She, Celeste, had never even *seen* him eat breakfast. She didn't want to think about it. Now he was so familiar to her the thought of his unknown lives, so many of them, was becoming horribly painful.

Her arms ached, from gripping her knees. 'I want you foetal,' Jacquetta had said. 'What I'm seeing is a child, waiting to be born in the ribcage of her mother.'

Through the ribs the wind blew. Far away, wolves howled. Now Celeste knew they were wolves it made the sound even more desolate. It echoed around the world. She was lost; more and more lost as time went by. She gazed at the cliff-face of the house; at the curtained French windows of Leon's consulting room down in the basement. It was all closed, to her. Nearby, in their hutch, the two remaining rabbits were mating. They had been at it for hours, judder judder, the hutch rocking. The female's eyes were glazed in an enduring-it sort of way, but at least they had each other.

I must talk to her. Celeste opened her mouth to speak, but just then Jacquetta said: 'You make me feel quite broody. I'd love to have had another daughter. Sons are so . . . well, so male.' The brush flicked to and fro. 'But then Leon says daughters are so *female.* He's got some, you see.'

He's got some. It sounded like cufflinks. He's got some somewhere, can't quite remember where. In the chest of drawers? To these people children seemed to be produced with the carelessness of rabbits and scattered God knew where. Was it being middle-class and educated that made people so profligate? They didn't have to hoard because there was always more where that came from. And here she was, using words like *profligate.* She was changing. Buffy and his world were changing her.

'Leon's put in a lot of time with them. His daughters,' said Jacquetta. 'He knows how important that is. He's seen so much damage, that's why. Dysfunctional relationships. That's his speciality. I was very damaged when I met him, you wouldn't believe. Well, if you'd met my then husband you would.' Jacquetta paused. 'Er, can you keep still?'

Celeste was staring over Jacquetta's shoulder. She stared at the basement curtains. They weren't quite closed. In the gap, inside the consulting room, something was moving.

'He works on the child within,' said Jacquetta. 'We all have a child within us, a child we need to reach. That's what I'm trying to reach too, in my own work.' She squinted at Celeste. 'You're leaning to the side. Can you sit straight?' She went on painting. 'He's wonderful with his patients. It takes a lot of work, of course. Years, maybe, with some of them. They can be so resistant, you see. So terribly defended.'

Celeste stared, mesmerized, at the gap between the curtains. A pale shape rose and fell, rhythmically, as if it were being pumped by a pair of bellows.

'He's very persistent, very sensitive. He thinks of himself as a locksmith, an enabler. He's there to help them help themselves. It can be very exhausting. He gives so much of himself, you see. He works incredibly hard. When he comes upstairs, sometimes, he looks

199

quite drained. The poor love.'

Frozen, Celeste watched. The pale shape was pumping up and down, faster now. She heard a faint cry, or was it just the wolves?

'Straighten up, can you lovey? You're leaning again.' Jacquetta's brush hesitated. She started to turn round. 'What is it?'

'Nothing!' Celeste pointed to the hutch. 'It's just the rabbits.'

'Ah. You're not embarrassed are you?' Jacquetta laughed. 'That's what I like about animals. They're so honest.' She paused. 'Excuse me, but could you open your eyes?'

Celeste had to get out of there. Anyway it was getting dark. When she opened her eyes a light had been switched on behind the curtains. They had been closed now; a mere slit of brightness shone between them, just a crack. Hadn't he realized that anyone was out here in the garden?

She couldn't ask Jacquetta questions now. She must have muttered something about it getting cold because the paints were being packed away and now Celeste was hurrying up the spiral staircase, clatter clatter, into the kitchen. She stood beside the Aga. How could she find out what she needed to know when at any moment Leon might come upstairs? He didn't know she had seen anything, of course, but *she* did and that was bad enough.

She was standing there when the front door banged and Bruno, the other son, came in. He was dragging a large, battered metal sign. It said BUSES ON DIVERSION.

'Yo,' he said. 'Want to help me get this up to my room? It's for my collection.'

She lifted up the back end of the sign—it was surprisingly heavy—and they started upstairs.

'What're you going to do with it?' she asked breathlessly.

'Dunno.'

'What's going to happen to the buses? Won't they go off in the wrong direction?'

They stood on the landing, panting. All over the city wolves howled, rabbits juddered and buses careered into blind alleys. How did anyone cope? Quite apart from the other, much more embarrassing thing. She should have been warned when India told her about the condoms.

They had reached Bruno's bedroom. He pushed open the door—he had to push hard, there was so much stuff crammed against it—and switched on the light.

For a moment she thought the place had been ransacked. Clothes and lager cans were strewn ankle-deep all over the floor. Half-open drawers spilled more clothes. *Have I got children? I must have left them somewhere, look in the chest of drawers.* She stumbled over an empty vodka bottle and knocked into a traffic cone. Though basically a rubbish dump, the traffic signs gave it the air of a London

Transport depot. There was a curious smell hanging in the air, too—a smell like burnt dung.

'Gosh,' she said. She thought: Buffy used to tiptoe into this room and kiss this boy goodnight. What earthquakes had happened since then! 'What a horrible mess!'

'Good, isn't it. Once I was asleep here for two days. There, under that stuff on the duvet. They couldn't find me. They ended up calling the police.'

In Melton Mowbray teenagers weren't like this. They didn't have his matted hairstyle and stupefied look. And, she was sure, his disgusting living quarters. The more money people had, it seemed, the more untidy they became. Back home people complained about their teenagers, of course, because they got on their mountain bikes and did wheelies around the phone kiosks. But overnight they turned into sober young wage-earners in Tesco's overalls. They had to.

'It's almost as good as my Dad's place,' he said.

'Really?'

'You should see it.'

'Should I?'

He smiled affectionately. 'He's hopeless, the old fuck-face.'

'You shouldn't talk about him like that.' She dumped the sign on the bed. 'Haven't you any respect?'

'With *my* parents?'

Just then there was the clump of boots on the stairs and the other one came in. Tobias.

'Hi,' he said. Then he sniffed and turned to his brother. 'What've you been smoking? Where did you get it?'

'Mum. I scored her some and she gave me a bit. My tithe.' He turned to Celeste and added, kindly: 'I know about tithes because we've been doing the Middle Ages.'

What was he talking about—his Mum giving him cigarettes? Celeste gazed at the walls. They were black. Skulls and posters of leather-clad women hung there, along with signs saying ALTERNATIVE ROUTE and POLICE NOTICE: ACCIDENT. She felt weak, but there was nowhere to sit down. Her life was sinking into chaos, signs sending her off in all directions, the wrong directions, one-way streets and cul-de-sacs, rabbits eating her belongings and people's husbands getting up to you-know-what in basement rooms. Her feelings about Buffy were getting more confused every minute.

Who could she talk to now? His boys, maybe. She had a feeling they were more intelligent than they pretended. But not here. Besides, they had put on some deafening music and her head was throbbing.

There was only one person left, only one hope. She shouted at them: 'Where's India?'

Tobias laughed his corncrake laugh. 'Go to

203

Pakistan and on a bit.'

'What?'

He turned down the noise. 'Just kidding. Sorry. She's out.'

'Where?'

'At work.'

'Where's that?'

*   *   *

Celeste, emerging from Leicester Square tube station, was assaulted by drunken yodelling and the smell of hot-dogs. A spotty youth was playing a saxophone. She walked briskly past him. Buffy had once said: 'Why does one only stop and listen to buskers when one's on holiday?' She stepped over a prone body; she hurried, bent double, past a Japanese man who was aiming with a video camera. By now she was learning the Londoner's duck and scurry, the swerves to avoid a drunk, the little skip over a puddle of sick. Only three weeks ago she had wandered dazed around Soho, flinching at the noise and smells. Only three weeks; how she had hardened up since then!

It was a big cinema, not one of the cupboards Buffy had complained about. She had meant to ask the manager if she could speak to India but *Citizen Kane* was showing, and Buffy had told her it was really good, so she simply bought a ticket and went in.

The ads were playing—a blue-jeaned rump

was swaying on the screen, accompanied by loud music. Celeste paused in the dark. Somebody took her ticket; it wasn't India. But in the darkness other torches were weaving and dipping, up and down the auditorium. Which one belonged to her?

Celeste was shown to a seat. Once her eyes had grown accustomed to the dark she saw that the cinema was only half full. The curiously meaty smell of popcorn was in the air. Up on the screen the film began; an iron gate, turrets against rushing black and white clouds. One or two people were still arriving; in the aisles the torches still swivelled, shining on an empty seat here, an empty seat there. They flashed like fireflies. Soon they would be gone; the usherettes would disappear to wherever usherettes went. Where did they go? They just melted away.

She had never thought about this. She had never thought about so many things. Up on the screen a voice spoke boomingly. The audience breathed; they sighed, *en masse*, like a great dark sponge, settling down. They had ceased to function; the actors lit their faces, dancing across their irises. Celeste didn't really watch the film. For the first time she wondered what it must be like to be an actor. She hadn't really thought about this before. This was what Buffy *did*. He put on fancy, dress and became somebody different. He escaped into it, leaving his various families in the dark, fumbling around while he entertained everybody else.

This wasn't fair. The seat next to her was empty. If only Buffy were here, he would explain. He would sit there, his bear-hand on her knee; he would feed her pieces of Bournville chocolate. He would lead her into the story, into an adventure. Perhaps he would protest that he wasn't escaping; that he was returning people to themselves. He was filling their heads with reflections of themselves, he was filling them with answers. If not answers, then dreams. Who knows? He wasn't here.

India was, somewhere. Celeste couldn't concentrate on the film; she got up and went to look for her. There was nobody in the lobby except a bored-looking man selling hamburgers. He lounged beside the bubbling tank of orange juice. She went up the wide, carpeted stairs to the upper floor.

India was standing in the doorway marked *Circle.* Celeste could recognize her from the back, even in her maroon uniform. She was watching the film. Celeste tapped her on the shoulder.

India turned. 'Hi,' she said. 'What're you doing here?'

Celeste shrugged. 'I heard it was good.'

'I've seen it about a zillion times. My stepdad—Buffy—ex-stepdad—he used to take me to the pictures all the time. Specially the old ones. He knew the names of the actors; he

206

used to whisper to me and everyone told us to shut up.' She tensed. 'Watch this bit.'

Celeste watched for a moment. India took her arm and led her to a seat. They sat down. There was nobody else up here, in the circle. India glanced around and took out a pack of cigarettes. 'Hope Mr Nathan doesn't see us. He's tried to sack me twice.' She lit a cigarette and sat back. She pointed to the screen, whispering: 'People don't really get old like that. Poor old Orson Welles had no idea what was in store. Bunged on a few wrinkles and whitened his hair.' She exhaled smoke. 'Little did he know that he was going to blow up like a balloon and his career crumble into pieces.'

Down below, actors bloomed on the screen. They lit India's face and her wreathing cigarette smoke. Celeste asked: 'So you came to these films with your stepdad?'

India nodded. 'It was our secret skive. *L'Atalante*, *Les Enfants du Paradis*, the only French I learnt was through subtitles.'

'When did he meet your Mum?'

India grinned. 'At a health farm. Mum was meditating in the garden, and he was creeping out to go to the pub. He was trying to squeeze under some barbed wire but his trousers got caught. She had to rescue him.'

'No, I mean how long ago?'

India put her feet up on the seat in front. 'She was married to my real Dad then. To Alan.'

'What about Buffy? Was he married?'

'Oh, Buffy's always married.'

'Is he?'

'He's such a romantic. Rather sweet really.' She inhaled deeply. She didn't seem to think it odd, Celeste questioning her like this. Maybe she was full of drugs and everything seemed natural. 'He was married to Popsi.'

'Popsi?'

'Popsi Concorde. Daft name, isn't it? Mum thought so, but I suppose she would.' She stopped, and gazed at the screen. Orson Welles was smashing up bedroom furniture. 'She was obsessed with her for a bit. As much as Mum can be obsessed with anybody except herself. Retrospective jealousy, I suppose. She kept on going on about how vulgar and brassy she was.' She blew out a plume of smoke. 'All I knew was Mum kept taking me to this pub.'

'What pub?'

'The pub Popsi worked at. She'd moved in there with her new boyfriend or husband or whatever.' The voice of Orson Welles boomed like Buffy's, boomed echoing from the past. It caressed the audience. India tapped the ash off her cigarette and turned to Celeste. 'Why're you so interested?'

'I just am. My life's so boring.'

'Don't you want to watch the film?'

'This story's much better,' whispered Celeste. 'Go on.'

'We'd take the tube to Sloane Square. Gosh,

208

I haven't thought about it for years. I was just little. Dunno why they let me in but Popsi was the easy-going type. It was called The Old Brown Mare, I remember the sign. I liked horses.'

They watched the film for a while. At least, Celeste pretended to watch it. Afterwards she couldn't remember a thing that had happened in it. She only remembered India sitting beside her, with the torch lying in her lap and the bluish light from the screen playing over her face. 'What was she like, Popsi?'

'Peroxide blonde, Barbara Windsor type. Buffy said she was the sort of woman who always had one too many buttons undone. I remember seeing her reflection in all the little mirrors around the bar. Mum would just sit there, watching her. She probably didn't even know who Mum was. I ate lots of crisps.' She laughed. 'The funny thing was, Mum doesn't even *drink*. She never goes to pubs. Not usually. But jealousy makes people do peculiar things, I suppose. They get unhinged.'

Celeste hadn't noticed that the film had finished. There was a stirring, downstairs. Just then a man appeared, in a dinner jacket. He seemed to be shouting something at India.

When Celeste turned round, India had gone. Just a gauzy layer of smoke remained, hanging in the air. And then the lights came up.

CHAPTER TWENTY-ONE

Miles pushed the trolley down the aisle. Muzak burbled, to sooth his troubled soul. Every now and then he consulted Brenda's list. Snicker Bars. Fiesta Kitchen Towels. Vosene Silk Hair Conditioner. Diet Tizer. He was never in the right aisle, but then her list wasn't in any sort of order. He kept retracing his steps and bumping into people coming the other way. Mostly women; it was the middle of the afternoon.

He was in a huge Tesco's just outside Chippenham. They were building a whopping Sainsbury's further up the road, too, in the middle of a field. They all had belfries and gables and clock towers; they were big brick leeches sucking the town dry. He'd said to Brenda: 'Just think. In hundreds of years archaeologists will say—what was that great religious revival? All those huge, huge churches. Vast car parks! We must have got it wrong, that it was a Godless age.' But Brenda hadn't listened, she had spotted a ladder in her tights.

Tesco Malted Wheats. He flung the packet into the trolley. Neither he nor Brenda ate Malted Wheats but that wasn't the point. He felt exhausted; his legs ached like a housewife's.

210

He made his way to the tinned fish. This was the big one, the one she had gone on about. Trouble was, they were clean out of pilchards. The word must have got around.

He loaded the groceries into his car and drove to Gateway's, the other side of Swindon. He searched along the maze of aisles. Pilchards. He almost whooped. He cradled the tin in his hand. To Brenda, this wasn't a can of Abbey Vale Pilchards in Tomato Sauce. It was a British Airways Round-the-World Trip of a Lifetime for Two, with £100,000 thrown in.

He must have spent hours shopping, driving along ring roads from one supermarket to the next. By the time he got home it was dark and Brenda was back from work. From the sound of it, she had her friend Gail with her. He heard their voices in the lounge.

'So we're sitting in the cinema,' said Gail, 'and he started sort of sliding his hand up my skirt. Just a bit at a time. He thought I wasn't noticing.'

'Was that your pleated skirt from Marks and Spencers?' asked Brenda.

He dumped the shopping on the kitchen floor. Brenda was beside him in a flash.

'Did you get the pilchards?' she asked breathlessly. He nodded. 'And the other things?' She kissed him on the cheek. As she did so he noticed that the sink was full of water. Bottles lay submerged in it, to soak off their labels.

She carried the tin of pilchards, like a trophy, into the lounge. Gail's voice rose. They started giggling.

He stood there in silence. In the water the labels uncurled; some of them had already risen to the surface. The plastic bags sighed as they settled themselves around his feet. More and more strongly, nowadays, he felt as if he had wandered into the wrong house. These little starter homes all looked the same, it was an understandable mistake. He had actually done it once; he had sauntered, whistling, into the house next door and surprised the Widdicombes eating a fondue. He could just walk into another front door and begin all over again.

Did other men feel like this? He hadn't been a husband for long, only two years. He should have got used to it by now, but in fact the opposite seemed to be happening. Maybe it was the inside-out nature of their lives, Brenda working and him not. That was the most reasonable explanation. But he had started to feel this some time before he had been made redundant.

He started to put stuff away in the larder. On the shelves sat rows and rows of tins, stripped of their labels. They glowed, dully. Large ones, smaller ones, flattish ones. Choosing something to eat made him and Brenda seem like a blind couple; there was a dotty sense of adventure to it. You opened a tin and what would it be? Sponge pudding? Butter beans? There were ten cans of Bachelor Mushy Peas amongst that lot which nobody was ever going to eat. Brenda had only bought them for their labels—ten, so she could send off a multiple entry.

The whole house was silting up with things they were never going to eat, or condition their hair with, or squirt the furniture with. By now the larder was so packed he could hardly close the door. It made him feel breathless and congested, as if he had indigestion. Her craze for competitions was getting out of hand; it was an addiction, really. She quite cheerfully admitted that. And how could he have the heart to stop her?

She had such a boring job. Eight hours a day she sat at a console, tubes plugged into her ears as if she were in intensive care, staring at a screen that gave her a headache. How could he cut off her escape routes? All her friends at work were compers. During their lunch hour they scratched away at their scratch-pads of magic numbers. They washed butter wrappers. They collected bottle-tops as proof of purchase and squashed them under their chair-legs to make them flat enough to send off. They dreamed of cars and dishwashers and holidays for two in Bali; they dreamed of trips to the stars. They dreamed of the Long White Envelope sliding through their letterbox; they spoke of this in hushed and reverent initials—*the LWE.*

In the evenings they sat in each others' lounges and made up slogans. *Hovis and Half-Fat Anchor taste so good together because . . . BP Lubricants are the sportsman's choice because . . . It Asda be Asda because . . .* If they were in his house he could hear the sudden bursts of laughter, the excited voices as one of them was suddenly possessed with what they called *Winspiration.* Before he met Brenda he had presumed that slogan-writing was a solitary activity, like masturbation, but she and her girlfriends did it together, a chaste orgy of voices chiming with insincere tributes to the goods they never used .

. . . *because their porkers are corkers . . . because it keeps your food eatable at a price that's unbeatable . . .* They were experts. They knew the combinations of flattery and humour that would win; they sneered at the tired old clichés like *Experts perfect them and connoisseurs select them.* One had to admire them for it. He did, actually. They won a lot. Only last September one of them, Phyllis, had calculated how many packets of Opal Fruits were piled up inside a Ford Escort GTi; she had won the car and all the sweets *and* had her photo in the local paper.

Oh, yes, they won. Brenda, in particular. That was the trouble. She was always hauling him off to presentations in hotels hundreds of miles away in the north of England, Stockport, places like that, where toupéed TV personalities whose programmes he had never seen put their arms around Brenda and called her *my love.* Then there were all the deliveries. Last week he had had the fright of his life when he had answered the doorbell to a man in green overalls who said: 'Hi there, I've come from Mars.'

That time it was a microwave cooker. Lucky he was home all day to take the stuff in. The house was filling up. At the top of the stairs was the little bedroom where he pictured their child would be; he had even papered it with a frieze of teddy bears. But they didn't seem to be able to have a baby and now the room was stacked with things he could never imagine anyone wanting, more and more of them, piled up: a thermos-gas barbecue, a Phillips foot spa, a digitally-controlled hostess trolley. In the corner was heaped £250-worth of Marley Cushion Flooring, consolation prize in the Shake'N'Vac competition. It was impossible to open the window anymore; it was wedged shut with a boxed set of Dunlop Maxfli golf clubs and balls. He had never played golf. 'Get on with you,' said Brenda, 'you could learn. I'll win you lessons!' She kept winning things for him; she thought they were in on this together and that they'd become Comping Couple of the Year. She didn't seem to notice his lack of interest. He had hidden some of the stuff in the cupboard—trouser presses, things like

215

that. There was £100-worth of Denim Men's Toiletries in there; he got a whiff of it sometimes, when he passed.

She didn't notice because, like an addict, she was onto her next fix. Where did this hunger come from? Was it his fault? Maybe he had disappointed her and she was trying to fill the void. Maybe it was his fault that she hadn't got pregnant. He didn't dare ask; she didn't like questions. If he asked: 'What's all this for?' she would gaze at him, her eyes blank. And then he would get that hollow, lonely feeling again.

*　　　*　　　*

That night, in bed, she snuggled up to him. 'Poor Gail,' she said, 'she's always going out with such awful men. They think she's desperate, just because she's living with her Mum.' She kissed his ear and pushed her hand inside his pyjama bottoms, caressing his buttock. 'Aren't I the lucky one? They all say so.'

Her bold familiarity made him sad. He willed her to go to sleep but her fingers were working on him, she was deft and businesslike. She could still arouse him even though his mind was miles away. He remembered the first time they had made love. They had just met, at a party. They were both drunk and fumblingly passionate, in bed at his flat. The local radio

216

station was playing rhythm and blues. Just as they were shudderingly reaching a climax the music had stopped and the 2 a.m. news came on: *In Belfast, a publican and his wife were killed when an IRA gunman shot them at point blank range.* Even this had not checked their ardour, not in those days.

When they had finished, she curled herself against his shoulder and told him about the treasure hunt. It was the competition on the can of pilchards. 'Tomorrow I'm sending off the entry form,' she said, 'just think of it— Hong Kong, Sydney, DisneyWorld! Just the two of us!'

She fell asleep abruptly, breathing into his neck, her leg hooked round his thigh. It was cold. He wanted to put on his pyjama bottoms but on the other hand he didn't want to wake her up. A dual-choice question: Was this because a) he was so nice, or b) he didn't want her to go on talking? If she won the prize, could he send her round the world all by herself?

That night, gazing at the sodium light glowing through the curtains, he realized quite clearly that his marriage was a mistake. It was such an alarming thought that he didn't quite put it into words, even to himself. Life was so chancy; it was chancier than any scratch-card, and much more terrifying. Looking back, he could pinpoint the exact moments when he had made the wrong choice and set in motion

217

a series of events he had been powerless to stop. One such moment had been standing at the school noticeboard and realizing that if he kept on with physics he could get out of games. The quickening momentum of this choice had propelled him into college and from there into the research labs of Glaxo's, six numbing years from which he had only just been rescued by redundancy. What on earth was he going to do now, with all his boats burned?

Another such moment had been bumping into an acquaintance called Neville Bowman at an off-licence one Friday night. Neville was buying a bottle of Hirondelle to take to a party, so instead of renting a video Miles had joined him and thus set ticking the count-down to that moment when he first glimpsed Brenda in the kitchen, nibbling a gherkin. She wore a strapless top-thing that exposed her plump, creamy shoulders. How lively she was! She chatted to him non-stop. Being shy himself, or maybe just lazy, he had always been attracted to bold, talkative girls and Brenda was certainly bold. By midnight they were pressed against the wall on an upstairs landing, kissing passionately as people squeezed past on their way to the loo. Briefly he had opened his eyes and seen her waving, over his shoulder, to one of her girlfriends.

Maybe even then it wouldn't have gone further. But when they paused for a breather he had felt obliged to back-pedal a bit and ask her about herself, what she liked doing in her spare time and so forth.

'Comping,' she had said.

'Really? So do I!' His heart had swelled. Suddenly she was dear to him. Not just sexy, but a friend too. He had never met a girl who liked camping. They could stride across the Berkshire Downs, ruddy-cheeked; she could help him carry his equipment, which had always been too heavy for one. They could bird-watch together and then, of course, there was that good old double sleeping-bag waiting. He had kissed her with real ardour then—with love, even. And by the time he discovered that he had misheard her—comping was a word unfamiliar to him then—it was really too late.

He lay there, his eyes open, visualizing drastic measures. A tornado swept up all the little houses in the Hazeldene Estate and blew them away, spinning, like Dorothy's house in *The Wizard of Oz*. His own house landed in such a distant land he could never find it, and Brenda would live happily there with someone else. The whole thing painless.

Or—he would simply go to sleep and realize that these past two years had been a dream. He would wake up and it would all be over. He had never gone to the party that night; he had rented the video and fallen asleep in front of the TV . . .

Or . . . or he scratched Brenda's back with his fingernail . . . under her skin, a message was revealed. What did it say . . . why couldn't he make out the letters? . . . Or was it numbers, a secret combination he must unlock . . . he tried to read it but he couldn't, and now it was blurring . . .

Miles slept, imprisoned and released, unaware that downstairs the can of fishes was going to take the decision out of his hands, just as the biscuit tin had done for Celeste, and that his life was already moving in a direction where everything would be changed, utterly; that in the future he would indeed look back on these years with the detached and vaguely affectionate curiosity of someone who had, in fact, simply dreamed them.

CHAPTER TWENTY-TWO

'So what did you do last night, my treasure, my pigeon?' asked Buffy. 'I missed you.'

'I went to *Citizen Kane*.'

'Who with?'

'Nobody,' said Celeste. 'I feel so ignorant, I want to catch up. I went by myself.'

Could he believe her? She smiled at him—such a clear, candid face!

'I wish I'd taken you,' he said. 'I love watching you watching things.'

Celeste didn't reply. They sat down in the stalls. He had brought her to the Barbican to see *The Winter's Tale.* She rearranged his back-support cushion, wedging him in. Sitting in a theatre with Celeste made him realize how old he was getting—how the seats were getting smaller and harder, how the actors' voices were becoming more mumblingly indistinct. Celeste's youth was like a light being switched on in a house—the twilit garden was immediately plunged into darkness, her brightness edged it towards night. He was the garden, of course.

They settled down. Normally nothing would induce him to come to the Barbican, it made him feel like a prisoner of Stalinism, but he thought that she might be moved by the play, with its magic and redemption, its possibilities of miracles. Besides, Leontes was being played by an old rival of his, a reformed hell-raiser called Dermott Metcalfe who was rapidly becoming a Grand Old Man of the Theatre—a title earned by anybody if they stuck at it long enough, had one lucky break and kept out of the boozer. Dermott and he had been rivals in love, too. Long, long ago, on tour with *The Voysey Inheritance*, they had both fallen for the DSM, a comely redhead called Serena, and though Buffy had briefly enjoyed her favours it was Dermott who had finally captured her—indeed, who had married her. Probably was married to her still. Somewhere in Sussex she would be ageing beautifully—she had a splendid bone structure—and serving tea to colour supplement journalists who had come down to interview her husband.

The lights went down; the play began. Buffy took Celeste's small, cool hand and pressed it to his chest.

'Too hot, too hot!' cried Leontes, *'To mingle friendship far is mingling bloods. I have tremor cordis in me: my heart dances; But not for joy; not joy . . .'*

He had always been irritated by Leontes—what a stubborn, blustering old fool! Fancy suspecting a wife like Hermione. Anyone could see she wasn't the sort to two-time him; *she* wasn't going to plaster herself with Sudden Tan and fornicate above a pasta shop.

'Inch-thick, knee-deep, o'er head and ears a forked one!' Leontes shook his locks. *'. . . many a man there is even at this present, Now, while I speak this, holds his wife by the arm, That little thinks she has been sluic'd in's absence, And his pond fished by his next neighbour . . .'*

Dermott was doing the business in a sonorous, look-at-me way that seemed to go down all right with the audience, but they looked as if they all came from Kansas. Buffy turned to gaze at Celeste—the stem-like neck, the choir-boy profile. She seemed entranced.

'Is whispering nothing?' bellowed Leontes. *'Is leaning cheek to cheek? Is meeting noses? Kissing with inside lip? Stopping the career of laughter with a sigh?'*

He wanted to tell her *it should be me up*

222

there! The trouble was, the dramas in his own life had effectively eclipsed those of his career. Too many bloody dramas on the domestic front. Rows and recriminations and, all right then, the odd blinder, but only when a chap was at breaking point . . . The chaos brought on by the defection of his various wives—Jacquetta, for instance, rushing off to Wales with that creepy Gestalt therapist when he was just preparing his Macduff. Her other escapade to Egypt. The hungover, cross-country trek to reclaim his sons from her mother, whose outrage seemed inexplicably directed at him rather than her nymphomaniac daughter . . . The bust-up with Popsi which sabotaged that film job. Only Popsi could barge into The Ivy, where he was lunching with the director, and manage to fling a bowlful of vichyssoise into the *director's* lap. Her aim had always been poor . . . The bloodsucking lawyers, barely out of their teens, who summoned him to court when he should have been in rehearsal, who bled him dry and forced him to turn down the BBC and take that mini-series job in L.A. that didn't survive the pilot. And yet nobody blamed the women. Well, they were women, weren't they? He was a brute, an egotistical bastard, an oppressor. *They* weren't, oh no! Their possession of fallopian tubes absolved them from any blame and to cap it all they stole his children too—

Buffy blinked. Up on stage, Hermione was

speaking.

'Take the boy to you: he so troubles me, 'Tis past enduring . . .'

She lifted up her son and gave him to one of her attendants—a slender, dark-skinned girl in an ochre gown. Buffy stared. Where had he seen that girl before? Waiting tables at the patisserie? She looked so familiar.

The girl put her arm around the child. *'Come, my gracious lord,'* she said, *'Shall I be your playfellow?'*

Working behind the counter at some shop he frequented? Where was it?

The girl turned, tossing her head. Buffy sat there, frozen. Oh, my God. Now he knew. Once, years ago, he had arrived at the place where she lived—a flat, three flights up, in the Elephant and Castle or somewhere. He had arrived to take her out to tea. She had opened the door to him—a skinny thing, pigtails, twelve or thirteen. She had turned, tossing her head like that, and called, 'Mum, there's a man here.'

'Bear the boy hence!' shouted Leontes. *'Away with him!'*

Nyange swept off-stage, taking the child with her. Buffy sat there, rigid, until the interval lights came up. He put on his spectacles and fumblingly leafed through the programme. There she was: *First Lady . . . Nyange Jamison.* His own daughter.

People were stirring. Beside him, Celeste

224

was asking a question.

'. . . wife,' she seemed to be saying. Something about a wife.

'Hermione,' he answered abstractedly. 'That's Leontes's wife. He thinks she's being unfaithful, the old paranoid.'

'No. Your wives.'

'What?' He tried to gather his scattered wits.

'Your wives,' she said. 'I didn't know you had so many.'

He looked at her. 'You never asked.'

She shrugged. 'It just seems rather a lot to me.'

'Me too! I didn't *want* it, you know. I didn't *choose* to be married to lots of wives.' He closed the programme. 'I didn't think—when I grow up I want to get divorced three times, what fun!' He put his arm around her awkwardly, wedged in his seat. 'One day you might understand, my darling girl.'

She got up. 'Let's get a drink.'

Her voice was thin and sharp, almost commanding. Maybe she had noticed his attention straying. She looked at him coolly, as if, when it came to women, he suffered from some form of incontinence. How could he tell her about Nyange now? He wanted to point out his daughter's name in the programme but this was hardly the time to spring upon Celeste yet another instance of his supposed lack of control. In fact it had been Carmella, Nyange's

225

mother, who had wanted a baby in the first place but it would doubtless seem churlish to point this out.

They moved towards the bar. He wanted to say: that was my daughter up there! Last time I heard she was a model but now look at her. Acting's in her blood, that's why; she got it from me. Oh, if only she had told me. I could teach her a tip or two, if she had come to me. She is my daughter, dammit.

If Celeste wasn't being so chilly he could put his arms around her and say: That was my daughter up there, I haven't seen her for years. I used to take her to the Soda Fountain at Fortnum's. I used to watch her shovelling in Knickerbocker Glory and telling me about her new stepfather, oh, the pain of it! I used to send her birthday presents until I got disheartened by the lack of response. I used to send her presents that were too young for her; I only realized that later. I sent her a box of magic tricks and the next time I saw her she was wearing lipstick. When you have lost your children you stay forever a step behind. All over the world, banished fathers are sending their children clothes that are one size too small. Maybe we want them to stay young forever. To stop the clock. Then we'll start again and get it right this time.

'What's the matter?' Celeste held his arm. 'Are you okay?' She sat him down; her voice had softened. 'You look awful.'

226

*   *   *

During the second half he decided to brazen it out. When the curtain came down he would take Celeste round to the Stage Door and introduce them. Who knows? Celeste might even consider him racy to have fathered this exotic, dusky creature. Out of wedlock, too, for he had never been married to Nyange's mother. Up on the stage Camillo was speaking.

'I have heard, sir, of such a man, who hath a daughter of rare note: the report of her is extended more than can be thought to begin from such a cottage.'

Of course they must meet. How piquant! Besides, he himself was longing to meet Nyange again—at last in a setting that both of them understood: the theatre. A world that could bond them together at last. Watching his daughter move across the stage, poised and solemn, he felt a curious warmth. It was such an unfamiliar sensation that for most of Act IV he couldn't identify it. Then he realized: it was pride. He was actually proud of one of his children. Would it be asking too much for them ever to be proud of him? Yes.

'You gods! Look down, and from your sacred vials pour your graces upon my daughter's head!'

The cast took their bows to loud applause. Buffy grabbed his back-rest and ushered

Celeste out.

'There's someone I want you to meet,' he whispered.

*　　　*　　　*

'Is this the way?' asked Celeste.

LEVEL 8, said the sign. TIERS 1/2.

They hurried along a sodium-lit corridor. At the end was a gate. EMERGENCY EXIT. He rattled the bars; it was locked.

He took her hand; they hurried down another corridor and emerged onto a windy walkway. It was freezing. Their feet clattered on the concrete.

'I'm sure this is wrong,' she panted.

They pounded up a flight of stairs. GATE 2. Again they were stopped by a locked door. Beside it was a metal plate of entryphone buttons. NORTH STAIR. FLATS 28–46. Buffy's heart pounded; he tried to catch his breath.

They hurried down a ramp. LEVEL 8. An arrow pointed one way. LEVEL 7. An arrow pointed another way. FOLLOW GATE TO YOUR DESTINATION. They hurried down another corridor and pushed open a door. A stream of cars thundered by, choking them with exhaust fumes. They seemed to be in some underground road. What a nightmare this place was! Where was the Stage Door? Signs and arrows pointed them in all directions, NO ACCESS TO VEHICLES. ADVANCE BOOKING LEVEL 5. SPRINKLER STOP VALVE INSIDE. How could he get to his daughter when everything conspired to confuse him? Once, when he was visiting his sons in Primrose Hill, he had been allowed to go upstairs to Bruno's room. On the door was a large metal sign saying NO ENTRY.

They hurried across the carpeted, orange expanse of wherever they were, some level or other. The Barbican building was emptying. Maybe he was losing his way on purpose. Maybe he was doomed to take the wrong turning, to find himself up a blind alley. To bang on the glass while one son, Quentin, slid out of sight, disappearing into Harrods. To gaze helplessly at Nyange, unreachable on a stage.

Celeste had stopped somebody and was asking them directions. She turned and grabbed Buffy's hand, pulling him along.

'This way!'

His chest hurt, his corns throbbed. Gasping, he followed her through a door. They emerged at the mouth of the underground car park. People were climbing into taxis and driving off in clouds of diesel smoke. Maybe he had missed Nyange; maybe she had already gone.

'There it is!' said Celeste.

Stage Door. Royal Shakespeare Company. One by one the actors were emerging, looking smaller than they had looked on stage. Buffy paused.

'Who are we looking for?' asked Celeste.

At that moment Dermott Metcalfe strode out. He was well wrapped up in an astrakhan coat and fedora.

'Russell, old cock!' He strode up to Buffy. 'Long time no see. Where've you been hiding? Enjoyed the show?' He turned to Celeste. 'Well, hello. This your daughter?' Buffy opened his mouth but Dermott was shaking Celeste's hand. 'Following in the family footsteps, eh?'

Not this one! Buffy wanted to shout. Not this one, the other one! But at that moment a car slid out of the mouth of the underground car park and stopped beside them.

'Darling.'

Serena's face, thirty years older but still recognizable, and indeed beautiful, smiled from the open window of the driver's seat.

'Russell Buffery, remember?' said Dermott.

She frowned for a moment, then her face cleared. 'Russell! Our children used to listen to Hammy. I told them, I used to know that man. Well, hamster.'

Dermott turned to Celeste. 'They were sweethearts once, these two. Before I staked my claim.'

Celeste stared at the woman in the car and turned to Buffy. '*Another* one?'

Dermott was talking. 'Every evening she

230

drives me in from Gerrards Cross, isn't she a jewel?' He kissed the tip of his wife's nose. 'A pearl beyond price. I'm a lucky bugger.'

Suddenly Celeste took Buffy's arm. 'Oh, he's a lucky bugger too, aren't you Dad? What with Mum and all of us.' She turned to Dermott. 'There's lots of us, you see, but we're one big happy family. Isn't that right, Dad?'

Buffy nodded, dumbly.

She squeezed his arm. 'Trouble is, Dad's just too much of a stay-at-home. He's spent his whole time with us, playing with us, being a good Dad, that he's hardly had time for his career. Isn't that true, Daddy? That's why nobody sees him around much. But it's been worth it. For all those happy memories and happy times together.' She pulled him away. 'Come on, Dad. Time for bed.'

*   *   *

'My God, Celeste!' Buffy gazed at her. They were sitting in a taxi, driving home. 'That was terrific. What an actress!' He cleared his throat. 'Er, why did you do it?'

She turned to look out of the window. 'He was such a creep, I suppose. I'm fed up with people going on about how happy they are. Then you see them messing around in basements.'

'Basements? Who's been messing around in basements?'

231

She didn't reply. She was sitting huddled in the corner. He moved closer.

'Did you really mean it? About it being time for bed?'

She shook her head. 'Just drop me off in Kilburn High Road.'

'Celeste.'

She turned to look at him. The street lights chased across her face. Her eyes, how dark they were!

'My darling girl, what's the matter? I never know, with you. That very first day, in the shop—your lovely face, it changes like the weather. Let me take you home.'

She sat there, gnawing her fingernails.

'I don't even know where you live!' he said.

'There's lots you don't know.'

He removed her hand gently. It was trembling. 'Tell me.'

'Not now. Not yet.'

CHAPTER TWENTY-THREE

Celeste emerged into the sunshine of Sloane Square. Each tube escalator, she was discovering, propelled her into a different London. One day she might piece them all together. No drunks here; even the air smelt more wholesome and expensive. Women in tweeds strode past, carrying bags from the

General Trading Company; one of them had a labrador in tow. A glossy Penny-type, wearing a designer suit, yelled 'Taxi!' in a carrying voice. Celeste herself felt smarter now; she had bought a new coat, russet red, from one of those shops she had once found too intimidating to enter. The coat had cost a lot—a whole month's rent from the people living in her old home, but that's the sort of thing she did now.

She consulted her map and walked down Sloane Gardens, past blocks of mansion flats which resembled Buffy's except there were BMWs parked outside. Her shiny new boots tap-tapped on the pavement; they sounded confident, but her heart was bumping against her ribs. Why had she been so stupid the night before? Buffy must think she was mad, suddenly jabbering on like that in front of other people. And what would he think if he saw her now? This was the third journey she had made into his past, the third and the deepest. Each one, she had thought, would be the last. How could anybody have had so many wives? Other women, too. She felt like an archaeologist, uninvited and illegal, digging through the foundations of an old building, through Victorian layers and then medieval layers and finally unearthing, way below, the broken mosaic of a Roman villa.

She was in an area called Pimlico. *Passport to Pimlico* was one of the old films Buffy loved;

he had appeared in it, he said, as a talented juvenile. He had told her a rude story about one of the actors but she was in no mood to remember it now. She turned left and walked down Pimlico Road. There it stood on the corner: The Old Brown Mare.

She crossed the street and approached the pub. The sun glinted on its windows. Drawing nearer, she paused. It didn't look like a pub anymore, not quite. It looked too airy and clean. There was fancy script above the window: *Wine and Tapas Bar.* She pressed her nose against the glass; inside, the place was empty. Just a lot of chairs and tables, with pink tablecloths on them.

She hesitated. Then she pushed open the door and went in. Behind the bar, the mirrors were still there; the mirrors which had reflected multiple images of Buffy's ex-wife. She smelt garlic. A woman appeared, carrying dishes of food. She was so tanned and stylish that Celeste felt drained. She put a plate of squid on the counter.

'Yes, what is it? We're not open yet.'

Celeste said: 'I'm looking for someone who used to run this place. When it was a pub.'

'Dominic!' she yelled.

A man appeared from the kitchen. He, too, was extremely good-looking. 'Where's the effing enchilladas?'

'Talk to this woman would you,' she said, wiping her hands on her apron.

Celeste explained again, adding: 'It was years ago. She was called Popsi Concorde.'

'What?'

Celeste blushed. 'She was, really.'

He gazed at her. She felt embarrassed on Buffy's behalf, that he had married somebody with such a silly name.

'We negotiated with the brewery,' he said. 'I've no idea who the landlord was. Never met him.'

They turned away. They were like two racehorses, tossing their heads and walking off while she stood there rattling her bucket.

*   *   *

Her knees felt weak. She stood outside; ridiculously, her eyes filled with tears. Nobody would talk to you like that in Melton Mowbray. If only Buffy were here; he would have bellowed at them. He would have thumped the counter, making the pimentos jump. She needed him so much that her chest hurt. She thought: I have no one else in the world.

Just then she looked at the row of shops opposite. One of them was a hairdressers.

A peroxide blonde. A peroxide blonde went to the hairdressers, didn't she? She needed frequent touchings-up. A peroxide blonde went to the hairdressers *a lot.*

Celeste crossed the street. Of course Popsi

235

could have used one of the many preparations she herself sold over the counter. But no harm in giving it a try. She stopped outside the shop. In the window, the colour photos of models had faded. The place looked as if it had been there for years; that was a promising sign. It said *Unisex* but she couldn't see any men inside; just an old dear being combed out. A plump woman, well into her fifties, was standing on a chair pinning up a string of gold letters: MERRY CHRISTMAS TO ALL OUR CUSTOMERS. When Celeste came in she stepped down and approached her, smiling.

She looked so friendly—such a change from the people across the road—that Celeste said, 'Hello. I'd like some highlights. Do you think they'd look nice?'

*   *   *

How soothing it was! Long ago her mother used to wash her hair, cradling her head in the bath, massaging in the shampoo and gently lowering her into the sudsy water. Then the rubber hose, the spray sluicing her head. The shell tiles, glimpsed through stinging eyes.

The hairdresser was called Rhoda. All through the highlights operation, which had taken ages, she had chatted to Celeste and the other stylist about how she was going to decorate her new flat in Lechworth. With each new customer, she started all over again. The lease had expired on this place and The Body Shop was moving in. 'It's the end of an era,' she said. 'My regulars are gobsmacked. What do they want with Peppermint Foot Lotion?' Celeste sat while she blow-dried her hair. 'I'm giving you the tousled look,' she said, 'it's all the thing.'

Once, Celeste had seen a TV programme of a butterfly emerging from a pupa. It had pushed out slowly, straining and splitting the sides of its strong brown envelope. She too was making an effortful transformation. Once, she had just washed her face with soap and water and put on a track suit. Now she was learning how to apply make-up; how to buy grown-up women's clothes. She gazed back at the streaky, tangled mop on top of her head. *Your own mother wouldn't recognize you.* Was she more herself, or less?

Puff-puff went the spray. She looked at Rhoda in the mirror. 'Remember when the pub opposite was a pub?' she asked. 'Do you remember the woman who worked there? Years ago, it might have been. Do you remember her?'

Rhoda nodded. 'Course. Eileen Fisher. Oh, we had some laughs!'

'Eileen Fisher?'

'She was a lovely person. Big-hearted. A warm, lovely person, wasn't she, Deirdre?'

'With that little ratty husband,' said Deirdre.

237

The place was empty now; she was fixing a paperchain onto the wall with a drawing pin. 'They put him inside, didn't they? Always thought he was dodgy.'

'It can't be the woman I mean,' said Celeste. 'Mine's called Popsi Concorde.'

'Oh, that was her stage name. She'd been in the theatre, see. Before she took up with what'shisname.'

'Terry,' said Deirdre. 'But give him his due, Rhoda, he was always nice to her little boy.'

'Little boy?' asked Celeste. The hairspray smelt so strongly of almonds and disinfectant that she almost swooned.

'Funny little thing, wasn't he,' said Deirdre. Her arms were full of tinsel. She gazed down at it. 'Never more, tinsel, will you embellish our walls. I think I'm going to blub.'

'Quentin,' said Rhoda. 'That was his name. She'd be sitting here, in this very chair, and he'd put on her shoes. High heels, she always dressed nicely. He'd put on his Mummy's shoes and stagger about. He did make us laugh.'

'Not forgetting the ostrich boa,' said Deirdre. 'He's probably a transvestite now.' She giggled. 'Or worse.'

They laughed, then suddenly stopped. 'Lord, I'm going to miss them all,' sighed Rhoda. 'Every one of them, even the ratbags.'

'Where did she go?' asked Celeste.

Rhoda inspected her in the mirror. 'There

238

you are. A small triumph, though I say it myself.'

'What happened to Popsi? Where is she?'

'This was years ago.'

'I know exactly where they went,' said Deirdre. 'When her old man was put away she got a job at that antique shop down the Fulham Road. She came back once, for her roots.'

'What antique shop?' asked Celeste.

'She said we mustn't lose touch. But you do, don't you?'

Celeste was standing at the till now, paying with her Barclaycard. 'Can you remember?'

Deirdre shook her head. 'But I go past it on the bus. It's next to that pizza place.'

Celeste signed the receipt. Her writing slanted; she couldn't control the biro properly. Her very name looked unfamiliar, as if it belonged to somebody else. She would have to get used to the hair too. 'Can you remember which one? You see, there were all these pasta places in Soho and I never found the right one.'

'Pardon?'

Celeste paused. It must be the hairspray. She really felt quite strange.

'I know,' said Deirdre. 'Pizza Hut.'

*   *   *

It was half past three. Celeste ate a whole

pepperoni pizza, deep-dish, she was that ravenous. Her hunger seemed to exist independently; it functioned, like a hospital generator, when everything else had broken down. The place was empty; outside the street lights were being switched on. She had already looked in the window of the antique shop next door, of course. There was no blonde woman sitting there; that would have been too much to hope for. Just a grey-haired old man and a lot of furniture.

She ate the crust; she always left the crust till last. Buffy had been married three times; each discovery made her feel she knew him less. Had he been a different man with each of them, somebody she wouldn't find familiar? Not just with the wives, with the other women too. He must have been really successful once, to have bought such an enormous house in Primrose Hill. How had he behaved in it, with Jacquetta? She herself had changed so much over the past few weeks, just by moving to London. The city had an unsettling effect on her. It was like living in a huge department store, not full of clothes but full of people. Maybe that was why its inhabitants married so many times. They couldn't resist going into the changing rooms to try on another person, and seeing how they fitted.

She paid up and went outside. The sun had long since gone; a light drizzle was falling. She stood outside the antiques shop. The man was on the phone. Some plates were displayed in the window. They didn't look any different from the plates back home. She thought of the ornaments on the mantelpiece, back in Willow Drive. One was a donkey with baskets on its sides; how she had loved it when she was little! Maybe it wasn't valuable, but it was valuable to her and that was the main thing. She had put away all the breakables, of course; packed them into boxes in the spare-room cupboard.

She peered through the glass. There was a big gloomy wardrobe at the back of the shop. Probably worth lots of money, but that didn't make it any prettier. Who had died, that their furniture had ended up here? The thought of people's pasts made her feel exhausted; she had had so much of that lately. Lumberyards of the past; children picking through the items, dressed in black like undertakers. Who was this Quentin? Was he another one of Buffy's children?

I'm not dressed in black, thought Celeste. I'm wearing a posh coat and I've just been to the hairdressers. Summoning up confidence, she pushed open the door. A bell tinkled and the man looked up.

She hesitated. She had seldom been inside an antiques shop, it wasn't her sort of place. But then Soho hadn't been, either, or Primrose Hill. The place smelt of polish. The man finished his phone-call. He was talking in German; she heard *deutschmarks*.

241

'Well, young lady, what can I do for you?'

He spoke as kindly as an uncle; she decided to brazen it out. She couldn't possibly pretend she had come in to buy something. 'I'm looking for a woman who used to work here. She's called Eileen Fisher. She had blonde hair.'

'Have a pastille,' he said, offering her the tin. 'There was an Eileen, but her hair was most definitely red.'

She put a pastille into her mouth. 'Are you sure?'

'Ah, Rodney. You can verify this.'

A young man had come in from the back room. He was tall and waxy-looking, with moles on his face. 'Seen the shipping forms?' he asked.

'My son, Rodney,' said the older man. 'Eileen Wingate, you remember. My eyes weren't deceiving me when I say she had red hair?'

'Wingate?' asked Celeste. Wasn't she called Eileen Fisher? 'Eileen Wingate? That was her name?'

'Dyed, Pops.'

Celeste stared. 'She's died?'

Rodney smiled. 'Not her. Just the barnet. *Sans doute* a bottle job. Definitely. Why're you looking for her?'

'It's a bit complicated.' A clock chimed; they waited until it had finished. 'Why was she called Wingate?'

242

'Must've been married to somebody called Mr Wingate. In truth, forsooth, I don't know. She nattered on but one didn't always take in every single word. Never get any work done.'

'What happened to her? Where did she go?'

Another clock chimed; a lower dong . . . dong . . . dong . . . dong. The father and son shook their heads. 'Moved out of London,' said the son, finally. 'She stayed in the business, I think, but not our line of the business. Where was it, Pops?'

'South coast?' he asked. 'That ring a bell?'

'I don't know!' Celeste sat down, heavily, on a spindly chair. 'When did she go?'

'Six, seven years. Haven't had a dickybird. Just a card at Christmas.'

'A card?' asked Celeste. 'A Christmas card?'

'Her son does them. Quentin. Frightfully artistic. Woodcuts and whatnot.'

'Have you got one yet?' asked Celeste. 'This year?'

The two men looked at her. Maybe she was behaving oddly, but she was past caring.

'Only got a few, so far,' said Rodney.

He took her into an office at the back of the shop. On the desk, a fax machine beeped; it hummed, and paper slid out like a tongue. Rodney was sifting through a small pile of Christmas cards.

'It might have her address on it,' said Celeste. 'On the envelope—you know, one of those little stickers. It might have her address

243

inside.'

He put down the pile. 'Not here yet. Maybe we'll get it at home.'

'Can I give you my phone number?' she asked. 'Will you phone me?'

*   *   *

She stood outside her flat, fumbling with the doorkeys. In one hand she carried a bag of cabbage leaves and carrots for the rabbits. After the beeswaxed order of the antiques shop the place next door looked chaotic— racks of coats, old saucepans, the female mannequin leaning against the wall as if she were drunk. MIND CHARITY SHOP, it said.

She felt deeply disorientated. How many names did this Popsi woman have? How many times had *she* been married? Upstairs, Celeste passed the mirror. A woman, topped with tousled hair, stared back. Who on earth was that?

She took the bag of food into the living room. She hadn't bought a hutch; she hadn't had time. Either she was working all day or else off on one of her voyages into the interior. The rabbits hopped up to her; they were becoming quite tame. She put the cabbage leaves on a plate and laid it on the carpet. Squatting there, she was suddenly aware of movement in the corner of the room. Just a tiny movement; something stirring.

It couldn't be a rabbit. All three were here, dragging the cabbage leaves onto the carpet and nibbling them. She climbed to her feet and walked across the room.

On the floor, jammed between the radiator and a box of recycled stuff she hadn't unpacked yet, was the bundle of cut-up tights. Half-hidden in it, she saw a squirming tangle of bald, pinkish-grey creatures. She gasped; just for a moment she thought they were maggots, but of course they were far too big.

One of the rabbits had given birth.

CHAPTER TWENTY-FOUR

It wasn't Lorna's wood, of course. It belonged to a local farmer called Vic Wheeler. He owned a lot of land, the whole secret valley and beyond, and was possessed of such entrepreneurial zeal that he was known in the village as Wheeler-Dealer Victor. Already, over at Barstone, a 2000-bed international hotel was being constructed, plus industrial units and an Asda superstore. One of his woods had already been bulldozed to create a roundabout and another had been sold to a Japanese firm which specialized in male bonding. Each weekend executives arrived from London, wearing flak jackets, and rampaged through the trees shooting each other with red dye and learning how to relate. That Vic Wheeler's son had married the daughter of the Chief Planning Officer had done no harm at all, squire.

It was mid-December. By now Lorna knew the full extent of the plans. Vic Wheeler had set up a consortium to build a Leisure Experience. It was to stretch over 300 acres. A theme park was planned, though the theme itself had not been decided yet. There was to be a bowling alley, skating rink, three fast-food outlets and, where her wood now stood, an eight-screen multiplex cinema. The pace was quickening. In the Happy Eater besuited men spread maps across the table and cockily bandied numbers to and fro; outside, their Ford Granadas were spattered with mud from their forays through the fields.

Lorna was a solitary person, an independent spirit. Various protest groups had been formed but she had devised her own plan. She had got the idea from a short story. She had read it, years before, in an old copy of *The Times* which she'd been using to wrap up chicken bones. In the story a woman, to save a local wood, had planted it with rare plants and filled its pond with an endangered species of newt. The wood had been declared a Site of Special Scientific Interest and nobody had built anything at all.

The plans were going to be put before the council in the spring. By that time the wood had to be planted up. Lorna felt surprisingly energised. It was like petty squabbles and complaints—who's going to do the washing up, say—vanishing the moment war is declared. Looking back, her whole life seemed to have consisted of botched relationships and missed opportunities—men, her acting career, the other thing she didn't want to think about. So much had slipped through her fingers for reasons that now seemed laughable, if they were not so sad. Now she could actually do something, something positive and complete.

It was a misty Sunday afternoon. She sat on her veranda, sorting through the catalogues that had arrived during the week. There was one from a wild plant nursery in Herefordshire; another from a specialist orchid-grower. With mild interest, she looked at her legs. She was wearing men's corduroy trousers; she had found them years before in the potting shed. They were tucked into mismatched woolly socks, one red and one striped, with another pair of socks on top. They didn't match either. She supposed she must look odd, but then oddness only exists in the presence of other people. The same applied to her age and her sex; she was both ageless and sexless, there was nobody to mirror her back to herself. She didn't know if she were amusing or not because there was nobody around to laugh. She simply existed. After all, human behaviour is only born in company; how does one know a burp is rude if there is nobody there to flinch? She had lived alone for a long time now. Stepping into the Happy Eater was like stepping into the world, like suddenly appearing on stage, but nobody really knew her there, customers passed through, staff came and went. It seemed like a dream and this was the real thing: the hazy sky, the tracery of trees, her cat rubbing its head against her trousered leg.

Some of the plants had already arrived and lay in a row, waiting to be planted, misting up their polythene bags as if they were breathing in there. They were her allies, her limp, green troops. She had bought some more plants at garden centres, and had even found a rare species of poppy at a Texaco station. Suddenly she thought of Buffy. He would say: *Funny, isn't it? Garden centres are full of furniture and garages are full of plants. And tandoori chicken sandwiches. And bags of potatoes. Amazing one can get any petrol in them at all.* She hadn't thought about him for ages. His voice spoke to her sometimes; other people's voices too. They were all there, even if she didn't hear them, like a radio that happened to be switched off.

She shook her head, to clear it. She put on her overcoat, tying it around her waist with string, and fetched her spade. She must get going; weeks of planting lay ahead of her. The sun was sinking; soon it would be dark. She worked in the dark, when nobody could see

248

her.

There had been no frost for days; the ground was soft and ready for her. Beyond the garden lay the wood; thin and airy except for its fir trees and the clotted, dark ivy thickening the trunks. She only noticed the ivy in the winter; it was revealed, now, like a silent person at a party one only notices when the other guests have gone.

CHAPTER TWENTY-FIVE

They were one big, happy family. That's what they said, Popsi and the traders in the antiques arcade. Always a laugh somewhere; always a drama. They helped each other out; they minded each other's stalls when one of them went to spend a penny. Nobody went upstairs to get a bacon butty without asking if their neighbour fancied one too. They knew each other's life stories and what stories they had! Even Popsi's ups and downs—and she had had a few—even her ups and downs were par for the course here. Put it on the TV, they were always saying, and who would believe it? Take Margot, who had the china stall opposite; who would believe, looking at her now, that she had once been principal trapeze artiste with Gerry Cottle's Circus? Not only that, but she had won a battle against ovarian cancer and spent three years living in a caravan with a manic depressive? That was a long time ago, of course, before she had put on the weight. She had seven grandchildren now, but she didn't look a day over forty-five.

That's what they said about Popsi, too. People took them for sisters, in their matching sheepskin coats. She and Margot had both done their hair the same colour too—Plum Crazy. Popsi had always believed in ringing the changes, hairwise. They both believed in making the best of themselves, in keeping time's winged chariot at bay. Live life to the hilt, that was their motto. Popsi fondly watched her, across the aisle, talking to a customer. 'It's a very rare piece,' Margot was saying, 'it's very unusual, of course, for it not to have a handle.'

Popsi loved it here. Their little band—it was like being in rep. Better really, because nobody went away. Every Thursday to Saturday here they were sitting in their stalls, blowing on their hands, their little heaters glowing. Every week she looked forward to it. The rest of the time she would be away on buying trips— antiques fairs in conference hotels, places like that. Sometimes a call came and she had to drop everything. They were only walk-on parts, of course, but it was good to keep your hand in. Unlike her, producers were getting younger and it was sensible to keep in the swim. Only the week before she had been a '*harassed shopper*' in *Inspector Morse*.

But at the end of the week, when she drove along the promenade and unloaded her car, when she came into this chilly hall with *hellos* all round and its low beams saying DUCK OR GROUSE, each week she felt she was coming home. She felt herself here. That was why she had called herself Popsi again. Women's Lib, she had always been for it though she hadn't known at the time. Get out of life what you put into it, that was another of her mottoes, and have a laugh on the way. She had always felt like a Popsi, that was why she had given herself the name in the first place. She had only changed her name to please her husbands and now she didn't have one anymore she was staying Popsi Concorde until she dropped off her perch.

It was even jollier now, with Christmas coming. Trade had picked up; it was really quite brisk, with people coming to find that special present, that personal something that showed you cared much more than a gift pack from Boots. *You're buying a little bit of history,* that was what she told people, *a little bit of someone's life. Recycling's all the rage, isn't it?* When she thought of all the things she had thrown out, all those times she had moved, she wanted to weep.

Down the aisle Walter, who sold military paraphernalia, was playing *I'm Dreaming of a White Christmas* on his wind-up gramophone.

251

He lived with his mother in a bungalow up on the Downs. He had taken Popsi to a traction engine rally once but he really wasn't her type. When he had tried some hanky-panky on the way home, in the back of his vintage bus, she had patted him on the head and told him to find a nice girl more his age.

Customers tried to pick her up too—men had always tried it on with her, God knows why. Only the week before, one joker had lifted the receiver off one of her phones and pretended he was ringing her: 'How about coming out for a swift half, you voluptuous pussycat?' She would have, once—give her a drink and she was anybody's—but now all she wanted to do was put her feet up in front of the TV. Her joints were playing up. They ached more this time of year, with the fog rolling in off the Channel. In fact, they ached more *each* year. Sooner or later it would be hip replacement time; everybody here swore by them.

Margot was doing very well. 'It's only a hairline crack,' she was telling a customer as she wrapped up a sugar bowl, 'put on a spot of Araldite when you get home.' She had run out of carrier bags and Popsi had given her a few from her stock of Sainsbury's ones. It was quieter in her stall. She sold period phones and radios. Her line wasn't so seasonal; she catered more for the bona fide collectors and they didn't believe in Christmas. In between

252

customers she and Margot nattered all day, only pausing briefly to make a sale and then carrying on where they had left off. They didn't stop for browsers, of course; china-teases, Margot called them. From long experience they could both spot one of those and Margot could deal with them as she went along. '. . . so then he really started getting violent—*yes it is pretty isn't it*—he got me down on the settee, the kiddies yelling their little heads off, I thought he was going to *kill* me— *no dear, I'll be making a loss on it as it is . . .* when they got me to Casualty they'd never seen such bruises . . .'

A lot of the people here were browsers, actually. On holiday, maybe, and just getting out of the rain. Because it was a seaside town they got a lot of retired folk, too, who didn't like the new shopping centre because it was full of lager louts. They fetched up here, sucking in their teeth when they saw the prices on the old biscuit tins and spinning out the morning over a cup of tea in the café. Just occasionally real dealers visited: Germans and Swiss, in fur-collared coats, with Mercedes estate cars parked outside. They knew exactly what they wanted. When they walked down the aisles everybody else looked amateurish and dowdy; a hush fell, as it does in a hospital ward when the consultants sweep in.

She was expecting one now, actually: a Mr Fleischmann, but he hadn't turned up yet. She had met him in an antiques fair in Birmingham and she had found him the items he wanted. Dealing with him made her feel suave and international, part of a network. Most of her customers were ordinary nostalgia-buffs who just liked bakelite—young blokes with gelled hair, probably designers, or else anonymous, solitary collectors who wore anoraks and looked like train spotters. She imagined them alone at night, sitting next to their collection of valve radios. It made her feel motherly.

She would kill for a coffee but Margot was busy and Duncan, the clock specialist in the next booth, was talking to a testy-looking customer. 'Well, it was working this morning,' said Duncan.

Just then Elsa appeared. She ran a period clothing stall and believed in an Afterlife. She was always trying to tell Popsi hers but Popsi said no thanks, this one kept her busy enough.

'I saw this piece of watered silk and I thought *Quentin*,' said Elsa.

'You are a dear.'

'Well, it's Christmas, isn't it?'

See? That was what they were like. Elsa left and Popsi put the piece of material into a carrier bag. Margot, who was wrapping up a teapot, was telling a customer about one of her grandchildren. Sometimes it irked Popsi, that Margot treated complete strangers to the intimate details of her family life, grabbing them with the same breathless confidentiality

254

with which she grabbed Popsi. Did five years of friendship count for nothing? Or maybe Popsi was just irked by the knowledge that, things being what they were, it was unlikely she herself would ever be a grandmother at all. Quentin was you-know-what (she said the word quite openly to other people, she was quite broadminded, but it still pained her to say it to herself) and her daughter Maxine, a big girl, had gone to veterinary college and showed far more interest in horses.

How did Quentin get that way? It certainly wasn't inherited. She herself had always been healthily heterosexual and though Buffy said he had been something of a tart at boarding school—according to him he had been angelically beautiful and passed around the sixth form like a plaything—when he left he had soon reverted to a lifelong interest in the opposite sex. She blamed the whole thing on the carrier bag episode; that had been the turning point.

Even now she blushed to think of it. Remembering moments like this warmed her up better than any electric blower. She had been living with Terry, above the pub. However, she had also been having a little hows-your-father with a lovely man who lived in Chelsea. He like to see her dressed up. So two afternoons a week she crept off to his flat, with her carrier bag. Quentin was at school then. Trouble was, one day she had picked up

255

the wrong carrier bag. Arriving in the gentleman's bedroom, she had unpacked it: out came some muddy shorts, a packed lunch and a stout pair of football boots.

Margot had hooted with laughter at this but it really wasn't funny. 'What about little Quentin?' said Popsi. 'There he is, in the changing room, opening his carrier bag and taking out my suspender belt and my satin corset.' 'Don't forget the split-crotch panties!' shrieked Margot, who liked to hear this story again and again, 'and the whip! Don't forget the whip!' Quentin had always been a sensitive boy; sometimes she felt this had sent him right off the tracks.

She had come to terms with it now, of course. In fact she had become very fond of some of his menfriends and one or two of them still came down to visit her long after they had split up with him. She was devoted to Talbot, who currently lived with him. Maybe she was a sort of Judy Garland, a fag-hag. From long heart-to-hearts with them she discovered the problem usually stemmed from the father anyway, so she could always blame it on Buffy. He had been a hopeless example to a son.

Margot was still busy. A customer was holding a cruet. 'Think it over dear,' said Margot 'but it probably won't be here next week. They go very fast, particularly if they're missing the pepper pot. That makes them a collector's item.'

Irritated, Popsi called 'Margot!' and tapped her tooth. It had an immediate effect: Margot stopped talking and whipped out her mirror. The two of them had an agreement: Margot rationed Popsi's cigarettes and Popsi told Margot when she had lipstick on her tooth. Margot's front teeth stuck out, that was why, and she always put on too much lipstick in the first place.

When she turned back, Popsi noticed a young woman standing near her stall. She wore a reddish coat and a black scarf. Her hair was streaky. Maybe I should try streaks, thought Popsi. She had dyed her hair for so long she could no longer remember what colour it was. Then she realized: of course, it would be grey. This gave her such a jolt that she came to a standstill.

The young woman stepped closer, picked up the receiver of one of the phones, looked at it, and put it down again.

'Nice, isn't it?' said Popsi. 'That's a Pyramid, Second Series. I've got one in red, too.'

She didn't look like a browser. Nor did she look like a customer. She looked fidgety; Popsi's children used to look like that, fiddling around with things, when they wanted to ask her for some money.

'This one's nice,' said the young woman. 'I've seen them in old films.'

'That's a Candlestick, pet. An early one,

probably 1920. Interested in period phones?'

She pointed. 'We used to have one like that at home.'

'Yes, my love, they're the most usual. Cheeseboards. Made right through the forties. You wouldn't remember those days of course, fresh young thing like you.'

'Do the radios work?'

'Do the radios work, she asks! Of course they work. Need to warm up, but then don't we all? Lovely tone; warm and brown.'

'I used to listen to the radio.' She touched the walnut veneer of a Ferguson; her finger made a mark in the dust. 'I used to think there were real people in there.'

'Well they are, aren't they? In a manner of speaking.' She laughed. 'Only too real, some of them.'

'What do you mean?'

'You really want to know?'

The girl nodded.

Popsi looked at her. 'How long have you got?'

*　　　*　　　*

'I was playing Doll Tearsheet. First day of rehearsals the director, what was his name? Lovely man. He came up to me and said, *Darling, this is Russ Buffery, our Hal.* And there was this fellow, black polo neck, very racy in those days, very debonair, and he took my

258

hand and kissed it. Something clicked. My knees turned to jelly. I thought: *can't wait to see you in tights!* It was danger ahead, I knew that. Spontaneous combustion. Ever felt it?'

Celeste didn't reply. They were sitting in the little booth; smoke wreathed up from their plastic coffee cups. Popsi took out a packet of Silk Cut. The woman in the stall opposite called, 'Popsi!'

'Just telling her about my first.'

'That's your fourth,' called the woman.

'*Husband,* I mean,' said Popsi. She lit the cigarette, holding it in her mittened hand, and turned to Celeste. 'Have to smoke when I talk about Buffy. I called him Buffy, there and then, and it stuck. Oh, he was charming, the rogue! We were both so young, of course, your sort of age, pet. We had our lives ahead of us, or so we thought.' She inhaled, and blew out smoke. 'You don't want to hear all this.'

'I do!'

The other woman shouted across. 'She doesn't, lovey. She's just being polite.'

'I'm not,' said Celeste. 'Honestly.'

'Don't tell her the rude bits!' called the other woman. 'Not till I can listen! I've heard it all before but I still like it.' She turned to her customer. 'Sweet, isn't it? Very unusual pattern.'

'Well, we fell for each other,' said Popsi. 'We fell in love. I've never been happy like that before or since. We toured all over Britain, he

259

got lovely notices, he was a lovely Prince Hal, and, oh, he made me laugh! I adored him. So did everybody—the cast, the landladies, he could wrap them round his little finger. See, like the Bard said, he was not just witty in himself, he was the cause of wit in others. Oh, we heard the chimes at midnight all right.' She stopped for a moment, coughing her gravelly smoker's cough. 'Course later, when he put on weight, he could've played Falstaff himself. But then . . . I thought this is my man, for life . . .'

Celeste was sitting on a camp stool. The aisles were full of people; sometimes somebody bumped against her but none of them stopped at the telephones. Over the other side of the hall somebody was playing *I'm Dreaming of a White Christmas.* She seemed to have heard it before; or was it just this story that seemed so familiar?

'So we're married now, two rooms in Bloomsbury, it was a palace compared to where I'd grown up. And then our little boy was born and, well, it all started going to pieces. You know what it's like.'

'No I don't.' She gazed at Popsi's rouged face. As she travelled back in time she was discovering progressively older ex-wives. Popsi, however, though the oldest, was holding out gamely against the ravages of the years. She wore a thick layer of orangey make-up and her hair was dyed an interesting colour Celeste had never seen before—if forced to pin it down, she would say mulberry. Her face was still very attractive.

'Maybe it wasn't the kid,' she said, 'maybe it happens. You think it's the end of the world at the time. Anyway, Buffy and me, we started making other friends.'

'Hadn't you got any already?'

'I mean, special friends.'

Celeste paused. 'Oh.'

'We did misbehave, I admit it. Lord, the boozing and the screaming matches, and one of us slamming out, and me picking him up next morning from Bow Street station, drunk and disorderly. Then one of us moving out and going to live with someone else, then coming back and having another bash. It was the sixties, see. Everything was hanging out, hanging loose, whatever, everything was up for grabs. Didn't know what we were doing, half the time.'

'Why not?'

'You wouldn't understand, my love. You were just a twinkle in your mother's eye.'

The woman opposite stepped across. 'Got any more carriers, ducky?'

Popsi rummaged under her chair. 'What's your name again, pet?'

'Celeste.'

She said to the other woman: 'Just telling Celeste about what we got up to in the Swinging Sixties.'

261

'Don't listen. X certificate!' The woman clapped her hands over Celeste's ears. Celeste wobbled, on her camp stool. When the hands were removed *I'm Dreaming of a White Christmas* was playing again.

The other woman went back to her customers. Celeste looked at Popsi's face, her rouged cheeks and bright blue eyeshadow. The whole thing felt unreal. Outside it had grown dark; in the roof, the skylights were black. The little booths, cluttered with their props, looked like stage sets. She felt she was a child watching an incomprehensible pageant of ex-wives, a costume drama in three acts. They had been paraded before her: Penny, Jacquetta, and Popsi—the Career Woman, the Neurotic, the Good-Time Girl. So quietly did she sit, an audience of one, that nobody noticed her. What were those lines from school? *They strut and fret upon the stage.*

Popsi was massaging her legs. 'It's the circulation that goes,' she said. 'Still, cold hands warm heart.' She wore a sheepskin coat and fur-lined boots; still she shivered. 'Funny to think of it, how it just goes. Just like that. We met off and on, of course, for Quentin's sake. No hard feelings really, there was fault on both sides, I'd be the first to admit that. But all you have left is a few memories, and the kids.'

'Kids? Was there more than one?'

'Nyange was born by then, by the time we

262

split up.'

'*Nyange?*'

'Buffy's little girl. Weird name, isn't it? He'd had a short sojourn with somebody called Carmella. Way out of his league, I told him so at the time.'

Celeste paused. She fiddled with the dial on a radio, turning it to and fro. Nothing happened, of course. 'What happened to her? Nye . . . ?'

'Nyange. I see her sometimes. On packets of shampoo and things.'

'What do you mean?'

'She's a model. She was, anyway. Ever so gorgeous. But then they often are, aren't they?'

Behind Celeste, a man cleared his throat. 'Those work?' he asked, pointing to the shelves full of phones.

'Of course,' said Popsi, 'just plug them in.'

'Oh,' he said, and went away.

Celeste asked: 'What do you mean, they often are?'

'Half-coloured people. See, they get the best of both worlds.'

'Her mother was—'

'Black, dear. She was a dancer, legs up to her neck. Way out of his league, like I said.' She sighed. 'Wonder what happened to her. She was in the chorus of *Hair*. What happened to them all. Mine, his, everybody's. You can't help wondering, can you?'

'What happened to you?'

Popsi laughed; it sounded like pebbles being shaken in a jar. 'You got all week?'

Celeste looked at her watch. 'Got to get back to London, actually.' She looked up. 'You had any more children?'

'Depends what you mean, *had*.'

There was a silence. Down the aisle some thin, reedy voices were singing *Good King Wenceslas*. She heard the rattle of a tin.

'I don't see,' she said, 'I don't understand!'

'I've got Maxine, of course. I had her with Terry, that's my second husband. And there's Quentin. But my little boy.' Quite suddenly, her eyes filled with tears. 'My little boy, he'd be a grown man by now.'

The tears spilled down her cheeks; they literally spilled, as if someone were tipping a cup. Behind them the voices grew louder; the tin rattled. They were singing *Oh, Come all ye Faithful* now. Celeste didn't turn. For an alarming moment she thought Buffy's two sons might be standing there, dressed in black and glaring at her. All his children, rattling tins and demanding God-knows-what.

'He'd be forty this year,' said Popsi. Her mascara was sliding down her cheeks. 'When I see a middle-aged bloke in the street, I think *that could've been him.*'

'You mean you don't know where he is?' Celeste had to raise her voice above the noise.

Popsi shook her head. 'I had a you-know-what when I was sixteen.' She rubbed her eyes; the mascara smudged. 'He's still there, in my heart. And all my little unborn grandchildren. Sorry, love. When I think about him I just start to blub. I remember, once, in John Lewis's . . .'

A tin was thrust in front of Celeste's face. A small girl looked at her coldly. 'It's for battery chickens,' she said.

Celeste searched in her bag. Popsi seemed in a dream. She looked at the little girl. 'Aren't you a poppet,' she said, vaguely.

Celeste gave some money to the little girl, who went away. Popsi woke, and fumbled for her purse. 'Wait!' she called. She heaved herself to her feet and went off down the aisle, after the carol-singer. The singing grew fainter.

*   *   *

Just then the phone rang. Celeste stared at the shelves of telephones. There were at least thirty of them—cream ones, black ones, the things called candlesticks, with a separate mouthpiece on a string, like the ones you saw in Westerns. The ringing continued. She stared, panic-struck. Which phone was ringing? She lifted up the nearest one—a brown thing, covered in dust—but it was dead.

Popsi hurried back to the stall and rescued her. She grabbed a modern phone, hidden amongst the others, and spoke into the receiver.

'Ah! *Guten morgen* or whatever.' She blew her nose. 'Pardon, *guten tag.*' She listened. 'London? You can't come down here?' She paused, thinking. Her tears had dried now, though her face was still a mess. 'Wait. *Uno momento.*' Putting her hand over the receiver, she turned to Celeste. 'You going back to London? Can you do me a favour?'

'What is it?'

'It's this dealer, see, and he's flying to Hamburg tomorrow. There's a couple of phones for him here. Could you take them to London and he can pick them up from your place?'

'But you don't know me.'

'Oh, I'm a trusting soul,' she said. 'Always have been. That's the trouble really.'

CHAPTER TWENTY-SIX

Celeste sat in her room, waiting for the phone to ring. The German man, she had forgotten his name, was supposed to be phoning before ten; he was going to come round, give her a cheque and take delivery of his two Pyramid phones, one brown and one black.

At 10.15 the phone rang. It was Buffy.

'Light of my life,' he cried, 'my little plumcake. Oh, I've been missing you!

266

Where've you been all day?'

'Just out.'

'What's happening? What have I done wrong? Can I come and see you?'

'Not really. I'm expecting a call.'

'Who from?'

'Just somebody. I'll be in the shop tomorrow.'

She put down the phone. Her hand was trembling. It was so painful, hearing his hurt voice, but she couldn't talk to him yet. Not yet.

*   *   *

Buffy put *Death and the Maiden* on the record player; the slow movement always made him cry. He gazed at his glass of wine. His latest method of cutting down drinking was to buy such disgusting stuff that even he couldn't finish the bottle.

Why was Celeste being so cold? Christmas was only ten days away and she still wouldn't say if they were going to spend it together or not. She had nobody to go back home to; nor did he. They were both orphans in this big, blustery world. They loved each other, didn't they? He constantly told her how much he adored her. She never actually said she loved him but she hugged him, she sat on his knee and picked little bits of fluff out of his beard; she laughed at his jokes and she showed an all-consuming interest in his previous marriages.

For the time being, this was enough. That events had not yet taken a more carnal turn had something to recommend it—after all, look what had happened to Humbert Humbert. Just sitting next to her in a tea shop filled him with joy. If for once in his life he had an unconsummated love affair, surely that meant it need never end?

December was the cruellest month, with Christmas looming. It was a month of gathering pain. Soon the day of reckoning would arrive, the day when it became all too clear that nobody else wanted him anyway. The rest of the year he could fool himself, but not on December 25th. He was an outcast, shivering in the cold whilst all over Britain loving families sat beside the fire opening presents and playfully trouncing each other at board games.

That it had never really been quite like this, even when he had been secure in the bosom of his various families or allied arrangements, didn't tarnish the nostalgia with which he gazed back to the past. If he were honest, he could remember the most monumental rows. They were often sparked off by something small, but then the whole day was a tinder-box, wasn't it, ready to flare up at any minute. Only the previous Christmas, when he had actually been allowed to have his sons (and that only because Jacquetta and Leon had gone on a second honeymoon to Israel), only the previous year the meal had disintegrated when he had, whilst berating Tobias for his table manners, leaned across him to grab a roast potato. Not a venial sin, surely, but something must have been bottled up in Penny for her to yell at him about his appalling double standards, what a pathetic example he was, how belligerently self-righteous and he could at least have used a spoon rather than his hand. This had led seamlessly into what was known as a lively discussion on his short-comings as a parent, even his sons chiming in—which was an improvement, he supposed, on their usual mutinous silence.

His various Christmases had come in all permutations, most of them uncomfortable and some so disastrous that he would have preferred to have spent the day in a Salvation Army hostel. At times like that, how preferable was the charity of strangers to anything muddier! In fact, looking back, the more tenuous the link the more successful the day. This was no doubt because expectations weren't that high to begin with. After Jacquetta had left him, and he was at one of his lowest ebbs, he had actually spent a surprisingly happy Christmas with an old lesbian aunt of hers who he had always liked and who, oh, bliss, demanded nothing of him except an inexhaustible stamina for a card game called Spit.

Then there were the various bizarre times

when he had, as it were, gone back a notch, shunting excruciatingly into his former life with a slight change of cast. This happened after a few years when the wounds had healed, or were supposed to have healed, and it was considered beneficial for the children to have some seasonal get-together. On one occasion Leon had flown to America to spend Christmas with his ex-wife, shunting back a notch himself, and Buffy had returned to his old home for a parody of Christmases past—a grand-guignol occasion which had effectively squelched any future shenanigans with the girlfriend he had brought along with him, he supposed as an act of bravado. Mercifully he could remember little of the day, except his drunken ransacking of the Christmas cards on the mantelpiece to see which of their mutual friends had sent a card to Jacquetta and whether they had included Leon in their message of goodwill.

Another occasion, almost more desolating, was long ago when Jacquetta had temporarily deserted him and he had looked up Carmella, the Caribbean dancer with whom he had had a brief affair. After all, she had borne him a daughter. Christmas with these two comely near-strangers, in a shawl-festooned room in Deptford, had been unbolstered even by alcohol for there was nothing in the place except apple juice. They were vegetarians, too, and though Carmella had cooked him a pheasant wing Nyange kept saying, 'poor little bird, just think it could be flying around the woods'; in the end he had had to barricade his plate from her offended eyes, propping up the book Carmella had given him as a Christmas present—a volume called *Women's Woes: A Look at Gender Tyranny.*

It was better, really, if these sorts of gatherings didn't take place on the day itself; it placed too much of a strain on everybody. Such was his network of ex-families that he had sometimes eaten several dinners on the evenings leading up to Christmas—two or three of them, like dress rehearsals for a performance from which he himself would be absent. Though reasonably festive, salmon would be served as a stand-in for turkey and fruit salad as a stand-in for the Christmas pudding; there was the unmistakable sense of everybody else eating lightly in preparation for the blow-out to come, the next day or the day after that. Unopened boxes of crackers would be waiting on the sideboard, tactlessly in full view. The children's hand-made table decorations would only partially be finished. As he opened his small—sometimes very small—gifts, he could see the larger, more lavish parcels stacked around the base of the Christmas tree, ready for the big day when he himself would be absent.

The problem with this, of course, was that Christmas Day itself would be left gapingly vacant, though India had once come round with a doggy bag, saying she would much rather have spent it with him. Besides, there were worse things than being alone. During his marriage to Penny he had been forced to spend the day with her parents in Ascot, an experience that had made the whole trauma of his divorce worthwhile.

Buffy lifted up the phone. It was eleven o'clock. He couldn't ring Celeste again. She had sounded so dismissive. Who was phoning her, that she expected their call so keenly? Her new hairstyle was a worrying sign. She looked fetching, but more tousled and beddable somehow. Almost randy, in fact. She had acquired a new mannerism to go with it—she shook her head, like a dog emerging from a pond, and then ruffled up her hair with her fingers. He didn't trust that.

George had farted. Buffy hurried to the window and struggled with the catch. The trouble with dogs was that, unlike humans, the process was totally silent. This meant one only became aware of it gradually and by then it was almost too late to take any action. He flung the window open and gazed across the Edgware Road at the block of flats opposite. In the windows, festive lights pinpricked the darkness. Where the rooms were lit he could see the shapes of the Christmas trees themselves, placed squarely in view to make him feel unloved. What was she doing? If he

272

knew where she lived he could jump into a taxi and accost her, flinging himself at her feet. But what happened if he looked up, and there was a man standing beside her?

*   *   *

He hadn't rung. He wouldn't now, it was 11.30, far too late. He had obviously decided to forget about the whole thing and go back to Germany.

What did it all mean? What did anything mean? Celeste hadn't moved for some time. She was sitting on the carpet, freezing cold. Already, her afternoon seemed as lurid and unlikely as a dream. Had she really been in Hastings? She could have been to the moon. Events were so out of control that she felt paralyzed. Another batch of baby rabbits had been born. She had put cardboard boxes on either side of the room, like hi-fi speakers, and filled them with torn-up newspaper. Bits of paper had already spilled onto the carpet; within the boxes the bedding moved as the babies stirred. The first lot—six of them—were stronger now, lifting their blind blunt heads. Soon they would be shakily venturing forth.

Along the edges of the room were stacked the recycled items—a jumble of plastic containers, lampbases, hair curlers—like an insane obstacle course. The room was starting to smell. What was she doing with all these relics from Buffy's past? The rabbits, the colander, the two silent phones—what meaning was locked within them? Her life was slipping into confusion and squalor. Her heart beat fast and she could scarcely breathe; she felt as if she were underwater, trying to swim to the surface. The water pressed down on her, filling her lungs.

She struggled to her feet, put on her coat and left the flat. Music thumped from behind a closed door. Why, when the place was so obviously full of tenants, did she never see anybody? She hurried into the street. The cold air hit her. Suddenly she was wide-awake.

CHAPTER TWENTY-SEVEN

Buffy opened the door. He was wearing pyjamas and a very old dressing-gown.

'Celeste, my love!' He put his arms around her. It was midnight; he looked surprised but delighted. 'How wonderful to see you!'

She disentangled herself and inspected him. How seedy he looked! Grey and unshaven—even though he was bearded he managed to look unshaven.

'So this is where you live.' She looked around. 'Crikey.'

'I would've tidied it up if I'd known.' He

hugged her again. 'My tonic, my life! My heart implant, you little ticker.'

'Don't be silly. Can I have a drink?'

'Don't try that wine, it's disgusting. Let's have a scotch.'

She negotiated her way into the room. It was a terrible mess; worse, even, than his sons'. There were things all over the floor. It looked as if he were camping here. Perhaps that was all he had ever done—just camped. She cleared away some newspapers and sat down in an armchair. Dirty grey dog hairs were matted into the fabric.

'There's a funny smell in here,' she said.

'I know. Don't know where it comes from. I need somebody to look after me.'

'Aren't you old enough to look after yourself?'

'Nobody's old enough to look after themselves.'

Women must have said that to him so many times. She thought of all the quarrels he must have had—everything she accused him of must be so familiar to him by now. How exhausting it must be! No wonder old people looked so old. It was all the repetition. She herself had had hardly anything duplicated yet—words of love or words of blame.

He gave her a glass of whisky. 'I want to sit close to you and lay my head on your knee, but my back hurts.' He sat down in the other chair; beneath him, the stuffing had disgorged onto the floor. He patted his knee. 'Come and sit on mine, you little sparrow.'

She didn't budge. She looked at him, across the littered hearthrug. 'Who did you love the most?' she asked.

'What?'

'Of all of them?'

He got up and came over. He pulled her to her feet. 'You silly.'

'Tell me about them.'

'They don't mean anything.'

'Well they should!' Her loud voice startled her. The dog pricked up its ears. 'You married them, didn't you?'

'Who have you been talking to? What have they been saying about me?' He put his hands over her ears, like the woman had done that afternoon. 'Don't listen to them,' his muffled voice said.

She removed his hands. Everyone seemed to be treating her like a baby. He gripped her; they collapsed into the armchair.

'Did you tell them all the same things?' she asked. 'Are you just a clever actor?'

'My dear girl, if I was a clever actor I'd be getting some work.'

They were wedged awkwardly in the chair; he was a big man. She spoke to an egg stain on his dressing-gown. 'I don't know what to believe anymore.'

'Don't be jealous of anybody. Ever. *This* is important. *This*. *Us*.' He lifted her face and looked at her. 'Nothing else matters.'

'But don't you see? It should! I want them to matter. I want all of them to matter! Else, what's the point?'

She had never really needed a drink in her life, or known she had needed it, until tonight. Trouble was, she couldn't reach her glass. She was wedged in. Oh, the great breathing bulk of him, smelling of warmth and tobacco. When he talked she could feel the reverberations, like the tube running beneath her room.

He said: 'Everything matters, but nothing matters that much. You'll learn this, one day. It's not depressing, sweatheart, it's not depressing at all. But you might not understand yet. When I die, I want you to put it on my gravestone—*Everything matters, but nothing matters that much.* Will you promise?'

'That's not fair, talking about dying.'

'Looking at you makes me think about it. Since I met you I think about it all the time.'

She struggled out, from under him, and walked to the mantelpiece. She suddenly felt stagey, as if a director had told her to stand there.

'All right,' she said. 'Let's just talk about the *everything matters* bit. If that's the case, who were you with, say, in the summer of 1968?'

'Who? You mean, a woman?'

She stared at her reflection in the mottled mirror—her set jaw, the floppy mop of hair. She nodded.

'Well,' he said. 'I was sort of married to Popsi.'

'Sort of. What do you mean, *sort of*?'

'Sweetie-pie, you've never been married.'

'No.'

'Well, then.'

'*So sort of* means somebody else,' she said. 'Who was it?'

He sat there. His eyebrows went up and down, as he frowned. He was thinking.

'I know,' he said. 'I was married to Popsi, but I was vaguely with Lorna.'

She turned from the mirror and stared at him. 'What do you mean, *vaguely with Lorna*?' *Basically*, that was what Jacquetta had said: *Basically I've got three children.* What had Popsi said? *How many children? Depends what you mean.* 'Vaguely! Basically! What on earth do you all mean?'

He sat, slumped in his chair. 'You're young,' he said. 'Certainty is the luxury of the young. When you get older there's no such thing as a straight sentence. It's all qualifiers. Parentheses sprout out all over the place.' He pointed to his ears. 'Like hair, sprouting out of these.'

'I just want to know what vaguely means. Who was she?'

There was a pause as he lit a cigarette. 'She was a lovely girl. Very young, younger than you. Very ambitious.' For a moment, his face was obscured by smoke.

278

'Ambitious for what?'

'For the same thing I was. Fame, success, all that. She was going to be a great classical actress.'

'Was she? Is she?'

He shook his head. 'The world's full of people who're going to be great actors. Now they're, I don't know, running country hotels and writing cookery books and . . .'

'Selling antiques.'

'Selling antiques. And getting divorced and doing all the things everybody does.' He smiled at her. 'Trying to make beautiful young girls fall in love with them. Life's a very time-consuming business. You have to be super-humanly talented or ruthless to push through all that. If you're not superhumanly talented or ruthless, but only a bit, then everything else comes flooding in. All the parentheses. The *vaguelys* and *sort ofs*. If you see what I mean.'

There was a silence. She took a sip of whisky; it burned her throat. She looked across at him. He raised his eyebrows. His hair was greying, his beard even more so, but his eyebrows were still black. His thinking bits, moving up and down to the fluctuations within. Puppet eyebrows, worked from machinery that was dear to her. She loved him very much, but she didn't move towards him; she stayed at the mantelpiece. She hadn't finished with him yet.

'What was her whole name?'

He had to think for a moment. 'Lorna Kidderpore.'

'Lorna Kidderpore.'

'Her father was a distinguished something or other. Mathematician.'

'How long did you know her?'

'Just a month or two.'

'Did you love her?'

'Of course,' he said. 'I'm not a womanizer, darling, I'm a romantic. A romantic falls in love for life. Trouble is, they know no past and no future. They learn from nothing and anticipate nothing. That's what they share with the very stupid, who in many ways they resemble. A romantic actually believes in possibilities. That's why my life's been such a mess.'

'What happened?'

'She was offered a job. Touring Europe with some theatre company. She had to choose between the job and me and she chose the job.'

'What happened to her?'

'I don't know.'

'Did you ever see her again?'

'Once. I saw her once.' He flung his cigarette into the grate. It was full of old cigarette butts.

'When?'

'Five, six years ago. In Dover. Penny and I were taking my boys on holiday, to France. Not a great success. In fact, an unmitigated disaster. Penny got food poisoning and Bruno got into trouble with this gendarme, and then the car broke down—'

'Get back to Dover.'

He smiled. 'That's what I always imagined my children saying.'

'What children?'

'The ones I never met. The ones who listened to me on the radio. You should've seen all the letters I got, the cards coloured with crayons, hundreds of them! They loved me much more than my own kids did, but that's because they didn't know me.'

'We did! You made us feel we did. You told us stories. Our parents just told us to mind our table manners. Tell me the story. Tell me about Dover.'

The dog got to its feet, padded over to Buffy and sat down again, next to his bedroom slippers. 'Are you sitting comfortably?' said Buffy.

'Yes,' said Celeste, though she was standing.

'Then we'll begin. It was a bright sunny morning and Buffy and his family were going on holiday. Gosh, what an adventure! They were off to meet the frogs. The two little animals in the back were fighting as usual. *"Stop it, you little scallywags!"* said Buffy, with a twinkle in his eye. Just then, as they were driving through Dover Town, lo and behold! Bless my cotton socks! There was his ex-mistress, coming out of a greengrocer's shop.'

'What happened?'

He took a sip of whisky. 'I shouted at Penny to stop and she did, but everybody hooted at us. And by the time she had found somewhere to park and I'd rushed out, well, Lorna had gone. Disappeared.'

Celeste yawned, though her heart was thumping. 'That was a lovely story,' she said. 'Now it's time for beddibyes.'

Buffy jumped to his feet. 'Yes, yes!' He put his arms around her. 'Oh, I've been longing for you to say that for the past six weeks. Ever since I saw you in your little overall.'

'Not here.'

'Look, I promise not to do anything. Scout's honour. I probably couldn't anyway. I peak at about ten and by five past it's all over.' He rubbed his beard against her cheek. 'We can just sleep together. I washed the sheets last week. Last month, anyway.'

'No, I must go.' She pulled away from him.

'But it's half past two!'

'I'll find a cab.'

'You can't go alone, it's not safe.'

She grabbed her coat and made for the door, tripping over a carrier bag. It tipped over, clankingly, and empty bottles fell out.

'I want to talk to you about Christmas!' he cried.

She kissed him, and ran downstairs.

'What about Christmas?' His voice echoed in the stairwell, fainter and fainter.

Back in the flat, the three phones sat in a row. She picked up the receiver of her own phone, the one that worked. Music was still thumping through the walls; she heard a banging door and muffled laughter. People here stayed up all night.

So did the people at directory enquiries. 'Which town?' asked the girl.

'Dover,' said Celeste.

'What name?'

'Kidderpore, L.' Celeste spelt it out. There was a pause. She waited, tensely. This Lorna woman had probably changed her name about three times since then. Everybody else had.

But then the voice answered.

CHAPTER TWENTY-EIGHT

London was revving up for Christmas. There was a quickening in the air, a Friday night quickening but every day of the week now. People double-parked their cars and dashed into shops; restaurants were crammed with secretaries in paper hats. Postmen, opening postboxes, stepped back at the avalanche of envelopes and children in nativity plays squirmed inside their sheets. All this and more, dread and joy and loneliness. Stalls appeared in Kilburn High Road, selling wrapping paper, and in the shops CD players were strewn with tinsel. Buffy's wine merchant was doing brisk business. Buffy himself had bought two bottles of Leoville Lascalles, but was Celeste going to drink it with him? He had bought her a pair of silver earrings for her dear pierced ears but when was he going to give them to her? Just as he and Celeste had become more intimate—the events of that night had shifted them into something more raw and personal, something that more resembled a love affair—she seemed to have gone to ground.

The next couple of days she hadn't been in the shop at all. Mr Singh said she was doing his VAT. 'She's too good for this place,' he said, 'she has a brain, that girl.'

'I know that!' said Buffy. 'Please get her to call me.'

He had phoned her, and got no reply. He had sat beside his phone like a teenager, waiting for her to ring. The next day there she was in the shop. His heart lurched.

'Please bear with me,' she said. 'I've got something to sort out first.'

That evening he put on the answerphone and went to a Christmas party, at which he had hoped to show her off. When he lurched home the machine said 0. What was happening; why was she being so mysterious? From long experience, of course, he knew the answer.

All Sunday he fretted. He bought all the papers, as a displacement activity, but he couldn't concentrate. Listlessly, he turned the pages. A treasure hunt competition had grabbed the public's imagination, with thousands of people haring all over the country searching for the prize. *My Room* was a concert pianist, with a wife and a brood of blond, smiling sons. They sat in an immaculate lounge, looking safe. The woman said '*My husband is my best friend,*' one of those statements that for some reason had always filled him with rage.

He took the dog for a walk, shuffling past the columned villas of Little Venice. Range Rovers, the ultimate fuck-the-rest-of-you vehicles, were parked outside; as he passed, people drew their curtains closed. He stood on the bridge, gazing down into the canal. If he threw himself in, would she care? Would any of them care? Would they even notice?

His eyes filled with tears. Does anyone love me enough, he wondered, to look in the paper when I'm abroad and see what the weather's like in the place I'm staying? That sort of thing? Have they ever?

*   *   *

Christmas was coming and Quentin was alone. Alone in his flat with a *Serves One* Tagliatelle.

285

Back to serves one, back to square one. Talbot had moved out. Quentin gazed at the swagged and beribboned room, its damasks and velvets. It was his own place again; his home had been returned to him and no trace remained of Talbot—nothing, after two whole years. At the moment this was deeply disorientating; one day, when he was feeling better, maybe he could find it invigorating. He had in the past.

The split-up had been a mutual decision really, if such things could ever be mutual. The moment someone voiced their doubts Quentin always convinced himself he had been feeling this way too, all along. He did this for self-protection. The moment someone said 'It's not working, is it?' or 'We've got to talk,' things were changed for ever. This happened in other spheres too. Somebody once said his wallpaper was vulgar and he had never been able to look at it in the same way again. In the end he had stripped it off and redecorated the entire flat.

Quentin switched on the microwave. He hadn't told his Ma yet. He dreaded her disappointment; she had liked Talbot. 'This one'll last,' she had said. But nothing lasted, not in his family. No wonder he found it difficult to sustain relationships; with his parents' example, who could? His past resembled some ramshackle lodging house, people coming and going, strangers installing themselves at the breakfast table and then inexplicably disappearing. His therapist called it, 'emotionally rented accommodation'. He said that Quentin's failure to sustain relationships was his way of staying close to his father and mother. By repeating the pattern he stayed their child forever, bonded to them. And it was true. Each time he broke up with somebody he thought about his father and wondered how he had felt. It was like an accident making you aware of all the other people who must be in hospital.

Quentin laid the table for one—he always did this properly—and uncorked a bottle of Chardonnay of which he would only drink half. Popsi, his Mum, said, *look on the bright side.* She said, *every person you meet, you learn a little something.* He tried to remember what he had learnt from the men with whom he had lived. Derek? Derek had taught him how to make marmalade. He had also taught him more than he really wanted to know about old blues singers, Blind Somebody This and Blind Somebody That, to tell the truth they all sounded exactly the same to him. Talbot? Talbot had taught him the rules of American football and how to play *Take my hand, I'm a Stranger in Paradise* on the piano with one finger. Quentin was sure there must have been more than this, but the thought of Talbot was still too raw.

What had his Dad learned, from all his wives? How had he coped? He would like to see him, but by now a meeting would be so strange and artificial that he didn't want to risk the terrible sense of loss such an encounter might cause. Maybe his father was disappointed in him because he was gay. But he didn't even know that. Big things like that, let alone the little things. A whole universe of little things which, even if they met now, it would take a lifetime to bring up in conversation.

Long, long ago his Dad used to visit. This was during the Pimlico period, when Quentin was little. When he lived above The Old Brown Mare. In retrospect, maybe his father only visited because it was a pub; maybe it was less to do with parental love than with the magnet pull of the booze. He and Ma had the most appalling rows. Then Terry, his stepdad, would storm across from the Saloon Bar and throw his father out. The bellowings in the street! The shape behind the frosted glass, banging on the window! The fist, battering against the inlaid lettering, PUBLIC BAR written the wrong way round, RAB CILBUP. The bellowings fainter and fainter as the years passed.

The visits petered out. As time went by, each meeting became a paler repetition of the one before, each one more indistinct until the image of his father almost faded away. Maybe his Dad felt the same, that Quentin gave less of himself each time, said less, until they were like two near-strangers exchanging small talk. Barely remembering, after the event, what the other person looked like. His Dad was like a rubber stamp which was never dipped in the ink pad. Stamp, stamp, each time fainter.

Quentin sat down with his tagliatelle. What was he going to do for Christmas? Each year he dreaded it. Each year the friends his age dispersed to their families in Northumberland or Surrey; temporarily they became dutiful sons, people he would hardly recognize if he saw them, chaps who hadn't brought home a girlfriend yet but there was plenty of time for that, wasn't there dear? The men with whom he had lived, who were mostly older, had sometimes taken him somewhere hot, Morocco or somewhere, but this had often ended in tears.

Sometimes there had been nobody at all in his life and he had simply gone home to his Mum. These Christmases, though cheery and alcoholic, had often ended in tears too. It never failed to amaze him that, considering she was such a simple woman, their relationship was so complicated. Had his Dad ever felt this? Being a son was a peculiar condition with its own network of snares and traps, but then, no doubt, being a husband was a peculiar condition too. He himself had been a sort of husband to Talbot, who had been rather female in his moods. He would like to discuss this with someone. His Ma wouldn't understand. He adored her really, despite the tears, but she would take it personally; she wouldn't understand.

His Dad would. This year, for the first time, he didn't just wonder: what will Buffy be doing? He always wondered that, briefly. This year he thought: wouldn't it be interesting if we met?

* * *

Christmas was a time of miracles. That was what Miles had been brought up to believe. Brenda believed in it too. Beneath the tree, in their little house near Swindon, the floor was spread with Ordnance Survey maps. She crouched there, muttering under her breath. How dumpy she was! Once he had considered her curvacious but his inner vocabulary had changed. *Curvacious* to *dumpy, vivacious* to *wittering.* It was the same thing, really, just lit from the other side. He wished he weren't voicing this, even to himself. It was a terrible thing to put into words.

'Framshill . . .' Her stubby finger moved across the map. 'Six-Mile Bottom . . .' She looked up at him, her face flushed. 'Gail thinks it's in the Peak District but I'm keeping my trap shut.'

A gold key. That's what lay buried somewhere or other. The key to a trip of a lifetime, to a fortune, to happiness. Brenda

290

didn't look happy; she looked flustered. Already, all over Britain, people were tramping over ploughed fields. They were armed with torches; they went out after dark, when nobody could see them, to dig for the treasure.

'Where's Tiverton?' she muttered. 'Devon. Blast.' She tapped her biro against her teeth. 'What's an anagram for *sepia*?'

'Despair.'

'Don't be silly, there's no town called Despair. Anyway, that's got a *d* in it. And an *r*.'

*   *   *

Celeste was spending the night with somebody. How did he know? Because she looked flushed and radiant—her actual features looked subtly different—and under her overall she wore the same sweater two days running. Because when he phoned her, first thing in the morning, there had been no reply. When questioned she had shrugged her shoulders—assumed nonchalance, he knew it well—and said: 'I must've just popped out to get some milk.'

Red alert! Warning bells! *Popping out* always meant trouble. That airy, throw-away phrase, what betrayals it had concealed! Jacquetta just *popping-out* to the shops. Such housewifely diligence, how very uncharacteristic! Him running out to remind her to buy a bottle of soda and seeing her at the end of the street, in the public call box.

He was sixty-one, with a lifetime of *popping-outs* behind him; he was something of an expert on the subject. He knew when a woman was having an affair, just as he knew when a woman was pregnant. He had heard the ping of the phone extension, that tiny chime at midnight. He had seen that closed, secret look on her face; that look a child has when they have got a forbidden sweet in their mouth and stop chewing when a grown-up comes into the room. Oh, the over-elaborate explanations of where they had been! (He should have smelt a rat with Penny's trips, he had slipped up there.) The fact that they always seemed to be having a bath when he came home from work. The sudden and totally uncharacteristic acts of generosity—*no you go, you'll have a lovely time*—and lunches in town with female ex-schoolfriends whose name he didn't quite catch. The sudden alertness when the phone rang, like a fox stiffening at the sound of a hunting horn.

Oh he could go on for ever, he could give master classes in it. And here it was, starting all over again. In the season of goodwill, too.

*   *   *

Come and Behold Him, Born the King of Angels . . .

Five days to go. In Blomfield Mansions,

Buffy was sleeping. Down the road, in one of the large houses with ruched curtains, one of the houses he passed in his walks, Annabel lay sleeping too. Annabel, from the hotel room in Rye. He hadn't met her since; indeed, he never would. But what did it matter now? Women he had touched; women he had wanted to touch. Women who had arrived too early or too late, just missed on the stairs, just missed at the bus-stop. Women he had just glimpsed in a swing door and dreamed about later, waking in the night damp with desire, with evaporating conversations. Who cared if it never happened, what was the difference? He was alone now, asleep, with his dog snoring beside him.

*　　　*　　　*

While he lay dreaming, India and Nyange were emerging from the Subterranean Club. It was a smoky basement near the Charing Cross Road, its floor slippery with beer and flyers. They emerged, their eardrums singing. Downstairs the music thumped; muffled, now, like heartbeats.

They met occasionally in the West End, when India finished work at the cinema. They were fond of each other; after all, they were sort of family.

'Your Dad's been very strange recently,' said India.

'Which dad?'

'Your real one.'

'Oh. Him.'

'He's obsessed with somebody half his age.'

'Not with me though. Oh, no.' Nyange tossed her head. 'He hasn't even come to see the show.'

'How could he, when you've never told him about it?' They stood at the stop, waiting for the night bus. 'It's up to you, too,' said India.

Men, passing, turned to stare at Nyange. She turned her head away. An empty Marks and Spencer's carrier bag bowled along the pavement, its handles raised like arms. A gust of wind blew it into the air, up, up above the parked cars.

'What're you doing for Christmas?' India asked.

'Mum's going to Kingston, but I can't go because I'm working.'

'Kingston's not far.'

'Kingston Jamaica, peabrain. Visiting the grandparents. Doing some consciousness-raising amongst the women. She's really boringly political now.'

'Go and see Buffy.'

'I can't,' said Nyange. 'I haven't seen him for years. Last time it was really depressing.'

'Why?'

'He smoked all through Christmas dinner.'

'Perhaps he was nervous,' said India.

'Mum had to cook him pheasant, yuk. He

294

bit on a shotgun pellet and cracked his tooth, blimey he made a fuss. We said poor little bird, it didn't want to get shot. It would rather be flying round the woods and things, wouldn't it? And then he gave half of it to his dog.'

'Maybe you'd put him off. Maybe it was disgusting.'

'Then his dog was sick on the carpet.'

'Exactly.' India's bus hove into sight, its interior blazing with light. 'Actually, I like him better than my real parents.'

'That's because he's not your real parent,' said Nyange.

The bus slowed down. India rummaged for her purse. 'It's the season of forgiveness. Whatever your Mum's been saying about him, all these years, that's not to do with you. He's in quite a state.'

'I *can't.*'

The bus doors folded open with a hiss. 'Come and have Christmas with us then,' said India. She hugged her and stepped on the bus. 'I wish you would. It'll be much more fun if you're there.'

The doors closed, with a sigh. India sat down. The bus was empty. DO NOT SPEAK TO THE DRIVER, said the sign.

As the bus carried her home, India dozed. She dreamed it was Buffy up there, sitting at the wheel. The bus wasn't empty now, it was crammed with children and ex-wives. DO NOT SPEAK, it said, but they were all

295

speaking at once, their voices deafening. They were shouting that he hadn't a clue where he was going, he hadn't passed his test and how could he take them home when he didn't live there anymore?

*   *   *

O Come, All Ye Faithful . . .
Three days to go. When Buffy went into the shop, Celeste was on the phone. She muttered something into the receiver and put it down quickly.

'Who was that?' he asked, a pleasant smile stretching his lips.

'Nobody.'

He tried to rally. 'Let me take you out tonight. *The 39 Steps* is on at the Everyman.'

'Oh, dear.' She reddened. 'Sorry, I can't.' She stood behind the counter, gnawing her fingernail.

'Know what Picasso said? One starts to get young at the age of sixty, and then it's too late.'

'Don't be silly,' she said, smiling.

He paused, then he said casually: 'Would you believe, I don't even know your address! What happens if I want to send round a little Christmas something?'

'How lovely!' She told him her address. 'I'm up on the second floor.'

*   *   *

When the snow lay round about, deep and crisp and even . . .

Three days to go . . . but no snow lay. The weather was mild. The ground was soft, perfect for digging.

In the dark, solitary figures toiled. The moonlight caught the flash of their spades. One on Dartmoor; one in a field just outside the glow of Basingstoke. All over England people were digging for treasure.

In Bockhangar Wood, in deepest Kent, two figures were digging, side by side. They weren't digging for treasure; they were planting, hoping for their own miracle.

*   *   *

Last winter I went down to my native town, wrote Dr Johnson, *where I found the streets much narrower and shorter than I thought I had left them, inhabited by a new race of people, to whom I was very little known. My playfellows were grown old, and forced me to suspect that I was no longer young.*

Added to that, thought Buffy, a drowsy numbness brought on by duplicity and drink. At his age it was hard to stay awake until the small hours. He managed to, until two in the morning. Then he went downstairs and hailed a cab.

It was a tired-looking street. His darling

angel lived here; his darling, treacherous angel. There was nobody about. He got out, telling the taxi-driver to wait, and crossed the road.

There was a junk shop, at street level. Up above music thumped. Pink light glowed through a torn blind. But on the second floor, Celeste's floor, the room was dark. The curtains hadn't even been closed. Nobody was there. And by this time of the night, nobody would be.

He stood there, shivering in his bedroom slippers. There was a note stuck with Sellotape to the front door. *Liam, I'm at Chog's.* Behind, the *mutter-mutter* of the taxi-engine. *Mutter-mutter, cuckold-cuckold, that'll be £3.50 squire, from Heathrow ho-ho, mutter-mutter, bit of a wally aren't you? Always have been, eh?*

*   *   *

God rest ye merry gentlemen, Let nothing you dismay . . .

The Three Fiddlers was festooned with streamers, the ceiling practically groaned with them. The lunchtime roar was swelling in volume; beside the fire the two old girls, Kitty and Una, were singing. Behind the bar the impossibly young Australian was wearing a Santa Claus hat.

Buffy was having a drink with Celeste. Men leered at her—even more so, with the new haircut. Oh, my God, did *he* look at her like that?

'Who're you seeing?' he asked.

'Who?'

'What's his name?'

'Buffy, I told you!' She patted his knee. 'He doesn't exist.'

'Is it Liam?'

'Who's Liam?' she asked.

'Or Chog?'

'Who're you talking about?'

She got up and went out to the loo. Or was she making a phone-call? While she was gone he rummaged inside the pockets of her coat. The things he had discovered, in his previous lives! Train tickets to Bristol Temple Meads; a screwed-up note, in unfamiliar writing, saying *Bell broken, bang on door, xxx.* No actual love letters, he had never slept with a woman that stupid.

He pulled out her darling woollen gloves and a packet of Polos. He felt around in the bottom and pulled out some empty, earthy polythene bags and a plant tag. *Cypripedium calceolus,* it said. *Lady's Slipper Orchid.*

He bundled all the stuff back. Who was she having an affair with—a gardener? She returned.

'I am coming for Christmas, aren't I?' he bleated.

'Of course. I said so.'

'I've bought the turkey.' He had insisted on

299

this. He hadn't bought one for years; it made the whole thing seem more domestic—more possible, somehow.

'I'll come and fetch it on the morning,' she said. 'Then you can come to my flat. I'm cooking us all Christmas dinner.'

'What do you mean, *all*?'

She blushed. Whoops, a slip-up there. What was she envisaging, some ghastly show-down?

'Who're you talking about?' he asked.

She said: 'I've got a lot of rabbits.'

'Why?'

'I'll tell you some day.'

He put his arm around her. 'Let's have lunch tomorrow. It's Christmas Eve. Let me take you out somewhere swish.'

She stroked his knee, running her finger down the lines of the corduroy. 'I can't,' she said. 'I'm getting off work early.'

'When?'

'One o'clock,' she said.

'Why?'

'I've got to go somewhere,' she said.

CHAPTER TWENTY-NINE

Christmas Eve and the streets were crammed. People were leaving, their cars piled with gifts. *Better fill up now, no petrol tomorrow.* People were going home, gathering in their children, battening down the hatches. People were rushing out making last minute forays—cranberry sauce, paper napkins. Oh, God, some Ferrero Rocher chocolates for Thingy. The rustling of wrapping paper behind closed doors, whispers, giggles. In heated rooms trees silently dropped their needles, and unwatched TVs announced that snow was forecast.

*   *   *

It is not just what you wear, it's the way you wear it. This was Buffy's profession, of course. Still he was taking no chances. Shaving off the beard was the obvious thing but he couldn't bear to do that. God knew how many chins lurked under there by now; that was one of the reasons he had grown it in the first place. But he wore a black trilby hat; he had purloined it, long ago, from the BBC costume department and nowadays he only wore it to visit his bank manager. He wore dark glasses. Christmas Eve had dawned cold but sunny too, so they didn't look too ridiculous. He had wrapped a black scarf around his face; as he hid in the bushes, waiting, his hot breath breathed back into his face, dampening it with the condensation of his anxiety. His coat—well, Penny had given it to him, say no more. Charcoal-grey, satin-lined, from Aquascutum. *Her* sort of thing, like all her presents. One look at the coat and you could see why his marriage had failed. He

301

hadn't worn it for years; Celeste, of course, had never seen it.

Through the sooty leaves he could see the corner shop. At one o'clock sharp Celeste emerged, putting on her coat. She called 'Happy Christmas!' as she closed the door and hurried into the Edgware Road, crossing when the green man was lit.

His old heart was thumping. He sidled out, through the shrubbery. A bus was approaching. He crossed the road, saunteringly, like a stockbroker. Or was he a bit of a spiv, with the shades? Whatever, she didn't notice because she had shuffled in, with the rest of the queue, and by the time he climbed in she had gone upstairs.

She liked sitting on the top of buses. How painful it was, to remember her childish confidences now! He mustn't think of that, it was too upsetting; he had to keep alert and keep in character. His skin tingled with the old actor's adrenalin—it had been so long since he had done any proper work. Down here he was in a good position to see her leave. The woman next to him had a pile of parcels on her knee. 'They all want those Nintendo things, don't they?' she said.

Celeste got out at Victoria Station. He got out, following her through the crowds. The place was packed. Everyone was fleeing the city; they carried suitcases and Christmas presents. Just for a moment he lost sight of her, then he glimpsed her standing in line for a ticket. She stood motionless, her face blank. What was she thinking? He felt uncomfortable, watching her. When people are amongst strangers they revert to themselves, they look smaller. Her breathless charm, her very Celesteness, had drained away; she was just a slim, abstracted girl consulting her watch. She could be visiting an aged aunt, instead of setting off to meet her lover.

She got her ticket and hurried across the concourse. On the way she stopped at W H Smith; he watched her buy a magazine. She had no luggage; she must be returning that night. Besides, she had to cook him dinner the next day. She had said she would come round in the morning to fetch the turkey.

All of a sudden, such domesticity seemed utterly unlikely. She was leaving him for ever. She was taking the boat train; she was travelling to Gatwick. She was going to fly away and he would never see her again.

She hurried towards the platforms. Blithering hell, he hadn't bought a ticket. He didn't know where to buy a ticket *for*. Too late now. Too late to go to the ticket office and ask the man her destination. He should have thought of this, but his own boldness in this enterprise and his growing sense of unreality had paralysed him. Quick! Action stations! He hurried after her. He would have to pay on the

303

train. He was swept up in a hurrying surge of people; thank God he had told the porter to take the dog around the block, if he wasn't home by six.

*   *   *

'But it's Christmas Day!' Miles stared at her.

'Not till tomorrow.'

'It's Christmas Day tomorrow. All your family's coming!'

'We'll be back by then. Come on.' Brenda already had her coat on.

'But it's miles!' he said. 'It's hundreds of miles. It's East bloody Kent!'

She was trembling—actually trembling. He had never seen anything like it. The woman was mad. 'If we don't get there first, somebody else'll find it.' She switched off the Christmas tree lights. She dashed to the window and checked the catch. 'Don't you see, nobody'll go out tonight!'

'No, because they're not totally insane.'

She switched off the light in the little crib above the fireplace. She turned round to face him. 'I've found it, Miles. I've worked out the place where the treasure is. If you're not coming, I'll just go by myself.'

*   *   *

Celeste was in the next carriage. Through the

interconnecting door, Buffy could see the top of her head. He had bought the *Standard;* he pretended to read it, but he had forgotten his spectacles. Outside the suburbs slid past. The sun was already sinking; poplars cast long shadows across a wintry sports field. Next to him, a woman nudged her child: 'Stop that, Lottie, or there'll be tears tomorrow.'

He was Gervais, a crooked merchant banker. He had been involved in some dubious insider dealing. The dark glasses were to conceal his identity; he was fleeing the country—Dover-Calais-Basle. The climax of the episode was a fight to the death in the snow-covered Alps. It was a European co-production, Klaus-Maria Brandauer, the works.

'Don't stare!' hissed the woman. 'It's rude.'

He smiled at the child, and rewound his scarf. *Close-up*, here, of his noble profile.

This is why I love acting, he thought. Anything's better than being me.

*   *   *

The car, with Miles and Brenda in it, sped along the M4. They had left their home, which was already in shadow. Miles was trying to remember Christmases past but he couldn't manage it. Unhappiness plugs our ears, it presses its fingers into our eye sockets. He was a lump of matter, no better than putty. He had no past and no future. Only the car was moving.

*   *   *

The train stopped at Dover Priory. Celeste got off. Outside, people greeted each other with open arms. Nobody was meeting her, however. He followed the rust-coloured coat as it made for the taxi-rank.

She drove off. Ducking into a taxi, he leant across to the driver and repeated the line from a thousand movies.

'Follow that cab.'

*   *   *

The sun was sinking. Beside Miles, in the passenger seat, Brenda leaned forward. 'Oh, hurry!' she said. She looked like the witch in *The Wizard of Oz*, leaning forward on her bicycle. The sharp nose; the sharp voice. They were hurtling through Kent. He was driving so fast that soon, surely, they would spin off into the sky.

*   *   *

Buffy had removed his dark glasses. He was in the middle of the countryside, the middle of nowhere. He stood shivering in the lane, watching the cab leave. The driver hadn't

306

switched off his inside light; it glowed, a bright lozenge against the flaming sky. For a mad moment he wanted to shout *stop*! Civilization was driving away, leaving him totally alone. He was freezing cold.

Celeste had disappeared down a muddy track. She hadn't seen him; he had told his taxi to stop further up the lane. What on earth was she doing here in the wilds of nowhere? Who was she seeing? It was getting darker by the minute. Why did it always get so dark in the country, so soon and for so long? How did anyone stand it? Near him, something was rustling in the hedge—something bulky. Far away, across the fields, a dog barked; the loneliest sound in the world.

Buffy had always had an equivocal relationship with the countryside. It was best experienced—indeed should only be experienced—during a hot June afternoon with a glass of Chablis in one's hand. The cottage in Suffolk had been bought for Jacquetta's sake; she had said she felt trapped in London and at that time he would have done anything to please her. He had had visions of the boys romping through the woods and returning home with sticklebacks in jam-jars; of Jacquetta transformed into a smiling, wife-type person. Of himself transformed into a manly paterfamilias, chopping wood and presiding over games of charades during their TV-free evenings. It hadn't turned out like that, of course. It hadn't turned out into anything remotely resembling that.

He walked along the lane—even that made him breathless—and stopped at the track. It led downhill, between thick hedges. There was still enough daylight to see that it was muddy—tyre-ruts glinting with water. On the other hand it was too dark to see with any accuracy how to step around the muddiest bits. At the end of the lane—far away, impossibly far, in his condition—he could see the lights of some sort of habitation. Celeste's love-nest. He felt suddenly, achingly, lonely. If only she were here, to keep him company! Impossible, of course. She was his enemy now; the very person he was stalking. Another treacherous woman. His darling Celeste, she had turned out to be just like the others. Oh, the weariness of it, the plummeting predictability!

He listened to the silence. Far away, there was the hum of the main road. No other signs or sounds of human activity. On the other side of the hedge, startlingly close, something coughed. It sounded horribly human. What a cold, wet, horrible place the countryside was! And there was so much of it, miles and miles of it, going on forever. Oh, to be back in London, in his cosy flat!

Stumbling and slipping, he inched his way down the track. His feet sank into the mud. He heard the bronchial cough again, then a rustling noise and some bleating. There must be sheep in there. Christmas Eve: in other circumstances the whole thing could be quite Biblical.

Who on earth lived down there, and what exactly was he going to do? All he knew was that his socks were sodden; his shoes were hopelessly inadequate for this sort of thing. If he had known, he would have brought a pair of wellington boots.

*   *   *

It took Buffy a long time to inch his way down the track. It was quite dark by now, though a moon had risen. Through the trees he could see the lit windows of a dwelling, nearer now. The yellow rectangles reminded him of an advent calendar, of years of children squabbling about whose turn it was to open the next little window and then, quite suddenly, growing too old to bother. An arctic wind sliced across his cheeks; it sliced through his thin, city coat. Was that a twinge of angina? Faintly, very faintly, he heard the sound of music. He slithered and grabbed at the hedge, tearing his hand.

Maybe he should turn back. What had knowledge ever brought him but pain? So many betrayals. Was there anyone one could grasp, in this world, and hold close to your heart?

He couldn't turn back, of course. He was

lost in the windy night. There was nowhere to go, and nobody to take him there. And it was too late now. Sodden and scratched, he was standing on someone's spongey lawn.

The black bulk of a building loomed up. It looked like a cottage. The front door opened, with a blaze of light. *Donna e mobile* swelled out, Pavarotti, and spilled across the lawn. The light shafted across the garden, illuminating the trunks of trees. He heard laughter.

Celeste came out. She was with a man, who was muffled up in a hat and greatcoat. They were laughing together. Arm in arm, they hurried off down the garden; they seemed to be carrying bags.

He watched them, in the moonlight. They crossed the garden, the lit, theatrical set; they climbed over a fence. And then they were gone.

The blood drained from him. Tears filled his eyes. Another man—he had guessed, of course. But no amount of steeling himself could prepare him for the staggering voltage of the truth.

*   *   *

Miles, obeying Brenda's instructions, stopped the car outside a Happy Eater.

'Can't we have something to eat first?' he asked. Through the window he saw Christmas decorations, brightly-lit tables, and people

310

putting food into their mouths. We may not be happy, he thought, but we could at least eat.

'You've had your sandwiches,' said Brenda. Shaking, she pulled open the Ordnance Survey map, yet again. 'Three fields, and we're there! Come on!' She got out of the car and pulled out the spade and the trowel. 'It's a full moon!' she whispered. 'A hunter's moon! Get the torch!'

He got out. The wind slapped his face. They seemed to be on some sort of ridge, miles from anywhere. A large elephant stood nearby, its back silvered by the moonlight. Beside him the parked cars were dimmed by condensation. Brenda pulled his arm; he stumbled across the tarmac.

*　　　*　　　*

Buffy stumbled blindly across the garden. He collided with a barbed-wire fence. Breathing hoarsely, he wriggled through it, tearing his coat. He seemed to be in a tangle of brambles now. Trees reared up above him. The moon was hurtling through clouds. Lower down, an orange glow seeped up, like a stain, from the horizon. That must be Dover—civilisation. A thousand miles away. Now he was deeper into the wood he could hear the traffic on the main road, louder somehow. Why? A trick of the air. Amongst the trees some creature—a bird? How the hell did he know?—something made

311

a scraping sound, again and again. The sound of a knife being pulled through a sharpener. Himself, sharpening a knife for the Sunday roast. So many roasts, so many Sundays. Through the trees, in the moonlight, he could see the two figures. They were walking together, close to each other. His brain roared. He stumbled towards them.

*   *   *

Miles stumbled after his wife. She was galloping down the hill. On either side of her, rocks detached themselves from the ground and scampered away, bleating. He heard her voice. 'That's it! There it is!'

She pointed. A wood rose up, ghostly in the moonlight.

'Fifty feet inside the perimeter,' she called, 'due south!'

I'm not here, he thought. This is a dream. I'm asleep, in Swindon. In a moment I'm going to wake up. There'll be no Brenda; nothing.

She was running down the hill towards the wood. He heard the thump thump of her gumboots. The moon was so bright he could see her breath, puffing.

*   *   *

Buffy pushed through the brambles. A thorn caught his scarf and pulled him back, temporarily throttling him. The sky had cleared. Above, the moon shone in a vaulted dome of stars.

*   *   *

'Oh, shit!' hissed Brenda. She pulled Miles behind a fir tree. 'Look!' she whispered.

He peered out. Between the trees, fifty feet away, something moved. It was two figures, a man and a woman. He could see them quite clearly. They were toiling, amongst the trunks. Digging. He saw the glint of a spade.

'Oh, no!' gasped Brenda. 'Somebody's there already!' Her voice broke. 'I can't bear it!'

Suddenly she launched herself off, crashing through the undergrowth.

'Brenda!' he hissed. Slithering and stumbling, he followed her.

*   *   *

Buffy stared. What was happening? There seemed to be four people now. He heard the faint sound of voices. Through the trees, in the moonlight, the couples looked quite Shakespearean. Lovers in the Forest of Arden. And what bloody part was he supposed to play? He stood there, numb with cold. He had been thrust upon this stage; he had forgotten his lines.

A fight seemed to have broken out; two of

313

the people were struggling. He heard a shout.

*   *   *

Brenda was wrestling with the overcoated figure, trying to pull the spade out of its hand. Miles heard it shouting: 'We're not digging things up! We're putting things in! We're putting plants in!'

'Stop her, can't you?'

A girl stood in front of him. She grabbed his arm.

'Stop that horrible woman!' she said. 'Who is she?'

'It's my wife.'

He stared at the girl. Moonlight shone on her wild eyes and tangled hair. She was utterly beautiful—the most beautiful woman he had ever seen. Gazing at her, he felt a curious sensation. It was as if his body was being both drained and refilled—a tender transfusion. He woke up from his long hibernation. It was as if he were suddenly face to face with the lost half of himself, with somebody so utterly familiar he didn't have to speak. His heart swelled, filling him, blocking his throat. Gently, he pushed the hair off her forehead.

'What's your name?'

'Celeste.'

He couldn't speak. He wanted to put his arms around her. He wanted to open his coat, pull her in and button her up close to him; he

314

wanted to press her against his beating heart.

*   *   *

At that moment there was a crashing noise, like an elephant approaching. A bulky figure was charging towards them. It wore a black hat and a black coat; it was trying to push through the undergrowth but a fallen tree blocked its path.

The girl turned. 'Buffy!' she cried.

The man was squeezing under the bough of the tree, trying to crawl through. Suddenly he bellowed—a bellow that echoed through the wood, silencing them all. With a flapping sound, birds flew off.

He lay on the ground, groaning. 'My heart!' he groaned. 'My back!'

They approached him. He lay there like a beached whale, moaning with pain.

'It's a heart attack!' he moaned.

Celeste knelt down beside him. 'Buffy! What are you doing here?'

'What the hell are *you* doing here?' he yelled. He lifted his head, grunting, and pointed to the figure bundled up in the greatcoat. 'Who's that tramp?' His head fell back.

'That's not a tramp,' replied Celeste. A twig snapped as they all stepped nearer. The wind had died down; far away, there was the sound of singing.

She shone the torch onto the face of her companion. No, it wasn't a tramp. It was a middle-aged woman. She wore a woolly beret thing pulled over her ears. She stared down at the figure lying at her feet. He stared up.

'My God,' he said. 'Lorna.'

'That's not a tramp, you silly billy,' said Celeste. 'That's my mother.'

CHAPTER THIRTY

It was Christmas Day. Freezing cold, heavy grey clouds, the first flakes of snow falling. The trees were locked like iron in the grip of winter; the only movement was the flutter of birds, swinging on the strings of bacon rind. Outside Keeper's Cottage, in deepest Kent, several cars were parked.

In the cluttered little living room Buffy was laid out on the floor, his head resting on a cushion. He was surrounded by his ex-wives, all three of them. Lorna was rummaging in the cupboard, looking for some sherry. Celeste was bringing in some glasses.

'We thought you were dying,' said Popsi.

'So you care!' cried Buffy. 'You all care!'

Nobody replied to this. Celeste put the glasses on the table, removing a pile of gloves and scarves. 'I didn't realize it was only his back,' she said. 'He seemed in such a state.

That's why I phoned you all.'

'I am in a state,' said Buffy. 'It's agony. It's completely locked.'

'It did that in Kendal, remember?' said Popsi. 'On our honeymoon. You were as helpless as a baby.'

Penny looked down at him. 'It did that when we were supposed to be going to Daddy's seventieth birthday party. Purely psychosomatic.' She nudged him with her boot. 'What an old hypo,' she said. 'Buck up, you self-pitying old buffoon.'

'Don't be so heartless!' said Popsi. She ruffled his hair. 'You poor old sausage. Shall I light you a cigarette?'

Jacquetta gazed at him vaguely. 'You should centre your spinal fluid,' she said.

The room was so crowded it was difficult to move without bumping into somebody. Tobias and Bruno were jammed between the sofa and the bookshelves; like all adolescents, they seemed to take up more space than fully-grown people. They were sorting through Lorna's pile of cassettes.

'Rough!' said Bruno. 'It's all bleeding opera.'

'You can thank me for that,' called out Buffy. 'I taught all these women to love opera.'

'No, actually,' said Lorna. 'I taught you.'

'Oh, oh, he's re-writing history again,' said Penny. She looked down at Buffy. 'He's good at that.'

317

'I am here, you know,' said Buffy. 'You can address me. I'm here, I'm in pain.'

Eleven people were squashed into the room. Some of them had never met before; most of them had never met Lorna. Summoned from their various Christmases and thrust into this cottage, miles from anywhere, they still wore a dazed look. But they were starting to settle down. Quentin and Nyange sat in the window seat. He was holding a skein of her hair as she demonstrated how to plait cowrie shells into it.

Penny gazed at the brown-skinned girl and the homosexual, sitting side by side. 'Very Channel 4,' she remarked. 'All we need is somebody who is physically challenged.' She stopped, and looked down at Buffy. 'Whoops! Forgot. We've got one. In fact, looking back on it, he was frequently physically challenged.'

'Just what do you mean by that?' demanded Buffy.

Penny laughed. So, disconcertingly, did some of the other women.

'Sherry?' asked Celeste, handing round glasses.

'I'm dying for a pee,' said Buffy. 'I've said it about eight times. Will somebody please carry me to the lavatory?'

There was a silence.

'Come on!' said Buffy. 'Who's going to volunteer?'

'Not me,' said Penny. 'No fear.'

Popsi said: 'Last time I carried you, remember, when you were drunk? I did me back in. And—well, pet, there's a bit more of you now, isn't there?'

Penny looked around. 'Any offers? Jacquetta?' But Jacquetta didn't seem to hear.

'For God's sake!' cried Buffy. 'After all these years. Is it a lot to ask?'

'Yes,' said Penny.

India got up from the floor. 'We'll do it. Come on, Celeste.'

*   *   *

All over Britain, families were sitting down to Christmas lunch. In Buffy's flat, George had found the turkey. The fridge door hadn't closed properly for months; the dog had simply nudged the door open with his nose and dragged the turkey out. Half-chewed portions of it were strewn over three rooms.

In Celeste's flat the rabbits had found the vegetables. Bits of carrots and Brussels sprouts lay scattered over the carpet. The rabbits sat there, munching; they vibrated to the trains below and the thumps of the music above.

*   *   *

The fire blazed in the grate. Penny, sipping her sherry, was looking with interest at the other women. 'Isn't this fascinating! We're like a

319

reunion of old girls who've been to a particularly ghastly boarding-school.'

'Thanks!' said Buffy, who was back in position on the floor.

Popsi laughed her gravelly laugh, and ended up coughing. She was wearing a gold lurex sweater, cut perilously low. She had sprayed glitter onto her hair; she called it her Christmas decorations.

Penny gazed at Popsi. 'I always wondered what you looked like,' she said, 'but you were so much before my time. You were just a lot of crossings-out in Buffy's address book.'

'Oh, the places I've lived,' said Popsi. 'Gypsy isn't in it. Had two husbands after him, Terence and Ian, but he was the nicest.' She lifted Buffy's head and inserted a cigarette between his lips. 'You were, you know. Course you were slimmer then.' She lit the cigarette for him. 'But so was I.'

She sat back in her chair, panting. Whenever she moved, glitter scattered.

Jacquetta waved her hand. 'All this smoke . . .' She vaguely batted it away.

Lorna and Celeste, the hostesses, refilled glasses. 'Sorry there's only this,' said Lorna. 'I'm sure there's some Twiglets somewhere. I wasn't expecting company, you see. I was supposed to be going up to London, with Celeste. After we'd done some planting. We were going to go up to London and give Buffy a surprise.'

'Oh, you've done that all right,' he said.

'This is much more fun,' said Penny, holding out her glass. 'I wouldn't have missed it for the world. Better than going to visit Colin's father in Nantwich. I've got a feeling he's just like Colin, only more so.'

It was a crowded little room, even with no people in it. Plants and old sheeps' skulls crammed the window ledges. Holly had been thrust behind picture frames. The curtains were closed against the cold grey day.

Quentin fingered the fabric. 'Damask would be super here. Gold and russet, can't you see it?' He turned to Lorna. 'I can get you some with my discount. I work at Harrods.'

'Harrods?' replied Lorna. 'Last time I saw you, you were in your pram. I just sneaked a look. You were a lovely baby.'

'Wasn't he just!' said Popsi. 'When was that, dear?'

'I was meeting Russell in a tea shop,' said Lorna, 'and he was looking after him.'

Popsi looked down at Buffy. 'You never looked after Quentin.'

'Of course I did!' said Buffy. 'I looked after him all the bloody time, while you were off with your fancy men. Now who's re-writing history?'

Nyange ran her finger along a beam. 'I've always dreamed of a place like this. A little cottage. A place with roots. Mum and me, we've been all over.'

321

'Emotionally rented accommodation,' said Quentin. 'Join the club.'

'Don't blame me,' said Buffy. 'Blame your mothers. There's two sides to this, you know. You've never heard mine.'

'Yes,' said Nyange, 'because you were never there.'

'Whose fault was that?' demanded Buffy.

Popsi raised her glass. 'He's here now. We all are. Better late than never.'

They drank. Jacquetta gazed around. 'This house has an incredibly strong sense of history.'

Popsi said: 'We're history, aren't we? All of us.'

'You're my history,' said Buffy.

'That's it in a nutshell,' said Penny, 'the Russell Buffery World View.'

'Oh, shut up!' he said.

'Did you colour wash these walls?' asked Jacquetta. 'I'm thinking of getting the builders back in. I've just found a marvellous decorator. He's called Kevin. I thought I'd get my kitchen done.'

Lorna looked around. 'That's not colour wash,' she said. 'That's patches of damp.'

Penny turned to Jacquetta. 'I had the cottage repainted, after you. I was so jealous.'

'Really?' asked Buffy. 'How gratifying!'

'Oh, it didn't last,' said Penny. She looked at the women. 'Funny old harem, aren't we.'

'A roomful of women, what bliss,' said Buffy.

He tried to raise his head, groaned, and relapsed onto the cushion. 'Wouldn't it be wonderful if you all started fighting over me.'

Penny nodded. 'Like, last one to leave has to take you home.' She took another sip of her sherry. 'Three wives, one for each decade. A sixties one, a seventies one and I suppose I was the eighties one.'

'Don't you dare write a piece about it, you bloodsucker,' said Buffy. 'This is Christmas. A sacred day. A private, family occasion.'

'Ex-family, thanks very much' said Penny.

'Not for me,' said Buffy. 'I've found a daughter!'

Penny laughed. 'I know. The way you've been going on, anyone would think you'd given birth to her yourself.'

'It's a miracle. A miracle birth!' Weakly, he patted the carpet beside him. 'Come and sit here, Celeste. Can I call you daughter? Budge up, everybody.' Celeste sat down beside him, wedged in. 'Look at this beautiful young woman,' he said. 'A new slate, a clean broom. We're starting today, from scratch.'

'Yes. And you won't have to go to all the trouble of traumatising her childhood,' said Jacquetta. 'Running off with other women—'

'Me?' shouted Buffy. 'What about you? Rushing off to Tunisia with your art teacher, creeping off to Egypt with that asshole Austin, shagging your shrink when I was paying for the sessions, know how much they cost—?'

'Children, children!' said Popsi. She turned to Lorna. 'Go on, lovey, show it to us again.'

Lorna had been sitting beside the fire, feeding it with logs. There had never been so many people squashed into this room. She had been turning from one to another, her head swivelling as if she were at some marital Wimbledon, the ball of blame flying to and fro. She felt oddly detached from it all; so used was she to being alone that she needed to be by herself to catch up with it all. Though she had changed into a skirt for these ex-rivals or whatever they were, though she had tidied herself up for the arrival of these various sort-of-siblings of her own astonishing daughter, she was still wearing a lot of clothes. She reached down inside her sweater, inside the layers of thermal underwear; she rummaged around and pulled out a chain. Hanging from it was a little gold fish; it glinted in the firelight.

'Pisces,' said Jacquetta. 'Mutability and magic.'

'Your little fish, and her little fish,' said Popsi. 'Separated at birth. Go on, tell us again. It makes me cry.'

Lorna smiled. In the firelight she looked younger. For a moment they could glimpse the resemblance between mother and daughter—the wide cheekbones, the tapering face—though the lines of her pointed chin were heavier now. She threw another log on the fire.

'I was on tour in Greece, playing Juliet, when I found out I was pregnant. At first I just thought my costume had shrunk. Then I realized.'

'Why didn't you tell me?' demanded Buffy.

'Ssh!' said Popsi.

'I knew it was Russell's, of course. But he was older than me. He was married.'

'Sort of,' said Celeste.

Popsi nodded. 'Sort of.'

Lorna felt she was giving a speech. Until Celeste had knocked on her door, ten days ago, she had never even rehearsed it. Now, however, the words had sorted themselves out into some kind of order. This small segment of history had become solid, by repetition; beyond it lay the unknown years that so far belonged only to Celeste. 'When I got back to England I didn't know what to do. It was different in those days, my parents would have been appalled. My father was running the Institute of Statistical Research.' She turned to Celeste. 'That's where you get your head for figures, I forgot to tell you that. He was frightfully old-fashioned. He'd always been against me going on the stage in the first place. And Russell—'

'I adored you!' cried Buffy. 'If I'd known—'

'I knew it wouldn't work, honestly,' she said. 'Even that young, I could tell. You could tell too, I'm sure you could. We'd had the best of each other. Well, I'd certainly had the best of you—'

'All three inches of it,' said Penny.

'For God's sake!' yelled Buffy.

'She's only joking, love,' said Popsi, patting his knee. 'We all know it's three and a half.' She and Penny started giggling.

'Is this the way women talk when they're alone?' asked Buffy.

Celeste turned to Lorna. 'Go on.' She nearly added Mum, but she couldn't quite say it, not in front of everyone. She didn't know if she quite *felt* it, yet. *Kidderpore* was something she would have to get used to. She had already practised it in the mirror, *Celeste Kidderpore, Celeste Kidderpore,* like a girl does when she is going to get married.

'Are you sitting comfortably?' asked Lorna.

'Not with this great porpoise hogging all the space,' said Penny. 'I've never known anyone take up so much room.'

'I'm in pain!' Buffy cried. His feet were wedged against the fire grate and his chest was sparkling with glitter from where Popsi had been leaning over him.

'So I didn't tell anyone,' said Lorna. 'When she was born I was offered Electra, in Glasgow. I desperately wanted to do it.' She gazed into the flames. 'I was very ambitious then. I suppose you'd say liberated and independent but it all boiled down to egocentricity. Actors are the most ruthless people in the world. They have to be, to do their job. That's why they make such awful parents.'

'Hear hear,' said somebody.

'Shut up,' said Buffy.

Lorna turned to Celeste. 'So I put you up for adoption. They took you away very quickly. All I gave you was the little fish, my other half, because you were Pisces. And I called you Celeste, just because I loved the name. And that was that.'

There was a silence. Outside, dusk was already falling but nobody had noticed. Lunchtime had long since come and gone.

'Any more of that sherry?' asked Popsi, the tears sliding down her cheeks.

Celeste emptied the bottle into her glass. There was a silence. Even the boys were listening. They sat hunched beside the fire; in their ears, the rings and studs glinted. Bruno had rolled up some newspaper and shoved it into the flames. All that news, all those words, history now, they burned as brightly as the logs. Old wood and old words, they both gave off heat and brought a flush to people's cheeks. What did it matter, the cause of the heat, when it was warming them now?

Celeste had heard this story by now, of course—many times, during the past ten days. She had heard a lot more from this woman she was slowly trying to recognize as her mother. The main events were taking on the glazey feel of a fairy story, a myth for others to repeat during the dark winter evenings. Buffy lay on the floor like a silent radio, waiting to be switched on. He would be telling the story soon, embellished with his own indignant and colourful punctuation. With that honeyed voice he would make it history. His voice was so authoritative, it had such power and resonance and seduction in it. It existed independently from his own muddled life, and soon she was to become part of his repertoire. This gave her a warm, swelling feeling of importance.

She drained her sherry. Melton Mowbray was far away now, back in another life. The girl she was then—she could hardly recognize her. *Celeste.* Her very name had never seemed to fit her, she had never quite fitted in. She had always felt solitary and out of step, though in those days she didn't have the words to voice this, even to herself. Such thoughts would have seemed alarming and ungrateful. Back home you didn't think of your parents as *not your sort.* In London you did, by gosh you did, but not up there. You didn't blame it on *them* if you felt somehow amorphous and undefined, like an out-of-focus photograph. If you felt terribly lonely.

Popsi was talking to Lorna. 'What happened to your career, love?' she asked. 'I saw you on the stage once, you weren't half bad. Course I didn't like to admit it then, because I was a teeny bit jealous.'

'Were you?' asked Buffy hopefully.

'Not for long. I had my own hands full at the time.' She turned to Lorna. 'Course, I might have felt differently if I knew you'd had a *child* with him. But I didn't.'

'Nor did I!' said Buffy.

'I carried on for a while,' said Lorna, 'but something had withered. Oh, I don't know. Something died. Like I was a fire without fuel, know the feeling?'

'I always had too much fuel,' said Buffy. 'That was my trouble. So much bloody fuel I couldn't get the flames to start.'

Penny said: 'The trouble with you—'

'Oh, oh, here we go,' said Buffy. 'The trouble with me. Why don't you just record it onto a cassette to save yourself the bother?'

'The trouble with you is that you were so busy making up your own dramas you didn't have any left for your work. Like you played this role—old and cuckolded and broke, poor old Buffy. For a start, you're not even old. You're only sixty-one!'

'Sssh, love,' said Popsi, and turned to Lorna. 'Go on.'

'I was just making empty gestures,' said Lorna. 'I felt it. I knew I was doing it.'

'The women I know, they're always going on about how children ruined their careers,' said Buffy. 'Now you're saying not having one ruined yours. You lot want it both ways.'

'Do shut up,' said Penny.

Lorna said: 'I wanted to be doing it for someone else, and there wasn't anyone else to be doing it for. From then on I sort of drifted. In and out of things. Jobs, everything. If you don't have any complications, then you feel quite lost.'

'Or quite free,' said Penny. 'Maybe it's the same thing.' She moved Buffy's leg off her foot. 'You're the most liberated of us all. We just got married.'

'We've just seen ourselves in terms of men,' said Jacquetta.

'And their bank accounts,' said Buffy bitterly.

'Just going to make my camomile tea,' said Jacquetta, drifting out to the kitchen.

'That's what she always did,' said Buffy. 'Make tea.'

'This is such heaven,' said Penny. 'I wish I had my tape recorder.'

'We're not a mini-series, dear,' said Popsi.

'No, we're much better.'

Buffy said: 'You could do us on *Penny For Them. Is your family getting hard and stale? Try adding some Celeste and stirring it up!*'

Popsi wasn't listening; she was staring at Penny. 'You're Penny Warren?'

Penny nodded.

'The journalist? I sent you something and you printed it! About how, if you want to get rid of fish smells, you can boil up coffee beans in the saucepan.'

330

'Did you?' said Penny. 'I've forgotten.'

'For goodness sake!' said Celeste suddenly. 'This is my life you're talking about! It's not fish smells!' She sat rigid, staring at them all. 'Everything—all my past—I grew up thinking that was the truth! My parents, everything. I trusted them all—when you're a child you trust everyone. Don't you see—all these years, everybody's been lying to me!'

'Join the club,' said Buffy.

Lorna got up. 'I think we all need another drink.' She opened the cupboard. She took out a bottle and peered at the label. 'Madeira. That'll have to do.' She unstoppered the bottle and sniffed it.

Buffy tried to put his arm around Celeste. He fell back, yelping with pain.

'You're so cynical!' Celeste said. 'All of you. If you knew what you sounded like!'

'My dear,' said Buffy. 'If we're talking about lying, what've you been doing to *me* these past two months?'

Celeste reddened. There was a silence. Lorna inched her way around the room, filling glasses.

Celeste said: 'I didn't lie. I was acting.'

'Ah, a chip off the old block,' said Buffy. 'I don't mind. Lucky my overpowering sex drive didn't carry me away.' Penny hooted with laughter; he ignored her. 'Else I might've done something we would all have regretted.'

Jacquetta wandered in with her cup of

camomile tea. 'That's what happened with *my* father, I'm sure of it.'

'You still going on about that?' said Buffy. 'Your poor old Dad.' He turned to Celeste. 'It's a relief, really. My darling girl. I knew I loved you, but this is better.'

'Why?' asked Celeste.

'Because it need never end. In fact, it's just starting. One can divorce a wife, but one can never divorce a child.'

'No,' said Jacquetta, 'but you can hardly ever see them.'

'Whose fault was that?' he bellowed, twisting round. 'Every Saturday you kept saying they had to go to the dentist, they had to buy clothes for school, every Saturday you were suddenly this diligent mother—'

'Children!' Popsi put up her hand. 'Water under the bridge, dears.'

Tobias said: 'It's all Mum's fault. We wanted to come and see you.'

'And our stick insects,' said Bruno.

Buffy gazed up at him. 'You remember them?'

Popsi said: 'Quentin always spoke fondly of you.'

Quentin nodded. 'When I was at St Martins I painted an entire "Saint Sebastian Pierced with Arrows" while you were reading *Rogue Herries* on the radio. I said to my friend, that's my father. Your voice was very comforting when I was doing the bloody bits—you know,

332

the punctured flesh. I'll show you the painting one day. It's in my flat.'

'I banged on the window once, but you didn't hear me,' said Buffy.

'At the flat?'

Buffy shook his head. 'At Harrods.'

Popsi put her arm around her son, spilling glitter onto his shoulder. The lurex top slipped lower. 'Now we've broken the ice we can all be friends. Come and have a meal with Quentin. He's a tip-top cook.' She turned to Celeste. 'Your half-brother! My head's reeling.'

Everyone was quiet, trying to work it out. Madeira on top of sherry didn't help. Was India an actual relative? No, but she was about the same age. Nyange was, though. She was a half-sister. She sat in the window seat. She had stuck a sprig of holly in her braids, twining it amongst the shells and coloured threads. She looked as startling and exotic as a votive goddess.

'Tobias and Bruno,' said Buffy, 'they're your half-brothers.'

'Maxine isn't,' said Popsi. 'I had her with Terry. Didn't I?'

Celeste had sorted it all out some time before, when she had first discovered the truth. This lot were experts, but it was still taking them a moment or two. It was like watching a group of crossword-puzzle champions tackling a really difficult one, one of those big-prize ones with cryptic clues.

Suddenly she felt overcome with affection for them all. How her moods see-sawed today! Buffy was right. In a sense, of course, she had lied to them too, or at least concealed the truth, and one always feels responsible towards people one has put at a disadvantage.

Penny, the sharpest of the three, was looking at her. 'All those questions about Buffy, after you'd accidentally-on-purpose bumped into me, you wily girl . . .'

'Oh, ho, the penny's dropped,' said Buffy.

'. . . I sort of wondered why you were so interested.'

'So did I,' said Buffy. 'Poor foolish me, I thought you were jealous.'

It wasn't totally dissimilar to jealousy, was it? The same hot, overpowering hunger for every detail, a similar pain?

Penny was gazing at her, her head tilted. 'You were working out if I could be your mother.'

'And me!' said Popsi. 'Wish I was, you're a real poppet. And I thought you were only interested in telephones.'

'The man never came,' said Celeste.

'Oh well—win some, lose some.'

Jacquetta was cleaning her spectacles with the hem of her shawl. She put them back on, and gazed at Celeste. 'I finished the painting yesterday. I called it *The Lost Child. I* must have had some sort of premonition. Subconsciously, of course. You have his

334

eyebrows, that's what I noticed.'

'I noticed them too,' said Penny. 'Buffy's thick black eyebrows. I remember thinking you ought to pluck them.'

Buffy weakly raised his glass. Celeste refilled it. He looked at Lorna, who sat beside the fire in her darned jumper, woolly skirt and bright red tights. She wore striped socks too, but today they matched. He said: 'This is our child. It's only just sinking in. All last night, after you'd tenderly tucked me in here, under my simple blanket, all last night I lay awake, gazing at the embers of what might-have-been. And yet marvelling that here she is. I didn't sleep a wink.'

In fact both Lorna and Celeste, upstairs in the bedrooms, hadn't been able to sleep a wink themselves. They had been kept awake by the stentorious snores downstairs in the living room. But they didn't like to break the mood.

Lorna looked at her daughter, who sat on the floor next to Buffy's prone body. She herself didn't feel like a mother; not yet. There hadn't been time. It was something she would have to learn from a standing start, like a Berlitz crash course in some foreign language. But maybe neither of them wanted this, by now; maybe it was no longer appropriate. They had missed the mothering years, and were starting out as grown-ups together. Already Celeste felt familiar to her—lovable, even—but they had a long way to go. Oh, it

335

was too complicated to think about, with all these people here, and Penny was talking.

Penny was saying, to Celeste: 'What I don't understand, sweetie, is why didn't you just ask Buffy? Why didn't you just ask him how many children he had?'

'Because of the letter,' said Celeste.

'What did the letter say?'

Celeste paused. Everyone was looking at her—even Jacquetta, who sat huddled on the floor, swathed in a shawl, nursing her tea. *I'm an actor's daughter,* Celeste realized. For twenty-three years I thought my father repaired washing machines. For twenty-three years—oh, I must turn every event around in my hands, lift it painfully and examine it all over again. I've hardly started; it will take for ever.

She turned to her mother. 'Can you pass me my shoulder bag?' Lorna passed it to her. Celeste opened it, unzipped her wallet and took out the letter. She kept it there, between her phone card and her bus pass. She unfolded the paper; the letter was disintegrating at the creases, from re-reading. She cleared her throat, and read to her audience.

'My dearest Celeste,' she read, *'This is a difficult letter to write but it must be done. Now that we are both gone I have to tell you something that concerns you. It is a secret that Donald and me have kept from you for all these years past, and you might not agree with that but*

336

we did what we thought was best. We have loved you like a daughter, but that is not the whole truth. You were chosen. We chose you because we thought you were the one for us, and God had decided in His wisdom not to give us a child of our own. Except that he did. He gave us you. All these years you have bought us nothing but happiness, and I want to thank you for that. I don't know anything much about your real parents but maybe one day you will be wanting to find out more about yourself. So here is what I know. Your mother gave you this fish, which I leave for you enclosed. I think you are the daughter of a man called Russell Buffery but I am not sure about this. Maybe he would know, were you to find him. Maybe he was married to your mother, but I would think not. Probably he does not know about your existence and in my opinion it is best to let sleeping dogs lie. God bless you, and thank you for being such a joy to us all these years. There is £800 cash for the arrangements in that plastic tub thing with a lid on it, the thing Annie gave us and we never used, that you dry lettuces in. Should you have problems with the plumbing the mains stopcock is in the front garden to the right of the gate, I don't think you ever knew. All my love my darling, Connie.'

There was a silence, broken by a sob from Popsi. 'Oh, that's so beautiful!' she cried. She sat there like a large fairy, her glitter scattered over the people she had touched—Buffy,

Celeste. 'Oh, if only *I'd* done that. Had my boy adopted. He might be here right now, with us.'

Even Penny was sniffing. She wiped her nose and said, briskly: 'You could have found them out much more easily, you know. You could have gone to Somerset House and asked to see the records. Children's Act, 1975. Adopted children have a right to trace their real parents.'

'I didn't know that,' said Celeste. 'Anyway, I wanted to see what he was like.'

'So you came to London . . .'

Celeste nodded. 'I tracked him down—I just found him in the phone book—and got a job nearby. And by that time it was too late. Each time I found one of you, I found there was another one of you before that.'

'And then another one on the side,' said Penny.

'And by that time it was too late to tell the truth,' said Celeste. 'It had sort of got too complicated.'

'Exactly,' said Buffy. 'One never lies. One just grows up.'

'In her case, pretty fast,' said Penny. 'She'd hardly got her skis on and whoosh! She was off down the Black Run.'

*　　　*　　　*

There was a general stirring. It was six o'clock and the three exes were preparing to rejoin

338

their other lives. Back at their homes food was waiting to be cooked, presents to be unwrapped. Their Christmases, stilled by Celeste's urgent phone-call, were waiting to be re-activated. Buffy tried to get to his feet, bellowed with pain, and flopped back on the floor.

'Happy Christmas to you all, my dears,' he said, waving them goodbye. 'My loves, my better halves, my lost delights . . .'

'All right, all right,' said Penny.

One by one they filed into the little hall, and started putting on their coats. Lorna opened the door. Snow blew in and swirled around. She flinched back.

Outside, in the darkness, the garden was deep in snow. A foot, at least. It had fallen while they were busy talking; it must have been falling for hours. There were mounds where the bushes had been; in the distance, larger humps where the cars were parked. It was eerily beautiful, and utterly, utterly silent. No murmur, even, from the main road beyond the hill.

There was no way they could get out. They couldn't possibly drive their cars up the track in these conditions. They were snowed in.

CHAPTER THIRTY-ONE

They went back into the living room and took off their coats.

'What are we going to do?' asked Lorna.

'This is what Catholics must feel,' said Penny, looking down at Buffy. 'When they want to get divorced. Permanently snowed in. For life.'

'There's hardly anything to eat,' said Lorna. 'There's hardly anything in the larder.'

'We could always cook Buffy,' said Penny. 'There's enough of him.'

'Shut up!' he yelled.

'Char-grill him over the fire,' she said, 'and save one little piece for the doggy bag.'

'Shut up!' He struggled to move. 'This isn't some avant-garde feminist film.'

Penny laughed. '*Lord of the Flies*, divorce style.'

Jacquetta said: 'Can't we phone for help? Leon'll be worried.'

'Oh, no he won't,' said India, 'he'll be too busy. Don't you remember? Christmas is so traumatic all his patients phone him up.'

'That's true,' said Jacquetta.

India went on: 'Sometimes they're in such a state he has to open up his consulting rooms for a special session.'

Celeste nudged her. 'Ssh!' she whispered.

Lorna lifted the phone but the line was dead. 'Oh, Lord. The wires must be down.'

The kitchen was crammed with women. They opened cupboards and pulled out drawers.

'There's some fish fingers in the fridge,' said Lorna.

'Have you got a wok?' somebody asked.

'There's some sausages somewhere,' said Lorna. 'I got them from work, but I think they're date-expired.'

Popsi sighed. 'I know the feeling.'

'There may be some hamburger stuff,' said Lorna.

'I'm a vegetarian,' said Jacquetta.

'You would be,' said Penny. 'Why are difficult people always vegetarian?'

Popsi had put on an apron. 'Come on girls, its loaves and fishes time.' She looked in the fridge. 'A bit of cheddar cheese, one strawberry yoghurt, Lordy, these sausages are old.' She turned to Penny. 'Penny for Them?'

'Want to add some zip to that tinned cannelloni? Try mixing it with a little boot polish!'

'Want to stretch that tagliatelle a little bit further? Try adding kitty litter, for a real family treat!'

'And the left-overs make a super potting-compost!'

Jacquetta peered in the larder. 'Here's some chick peas, but they take three and a half

341

hours.'

Lorna stood there helplessly. 'I'm afraid I'm not very domesticated.'

'Lucky you,' said Penny, 'you haven't had to be.'

Popsi was rummaging amongst some vegetables. She pulled out a small, wizened carrot. 'Remind you of anyone, girls?'

They burst out giggling, even Jacquetta. Nobody had ever heard her laugh before; they all turned and stared.

At that moment Quentin came in, rolling up his sleeves. 'Leave it to me, dears,' he said.

*   *   *

Outside, the windows shone in the dark. In the garden Bruno and Tobias were having a snowball fight. They had lost their teenage languor, they were children again. Whooping and shrieking, they clawed up the snow, handfuls of it, and flung it at each other.

India opened the cottage door. Light spilled out onto the snow. 'Come in!' she called. 'Mum says you'll freeze!'

But they didn't hear. Suddenly she waded out. 'Nyange!' she called. 'Come out! It's wonderful!'

*   *   *

Buffy and Celeste were alone in the living

room. She sat, propped up against his stomach. Outside in the garden they could hear whoops and yells. From the kitchen came bursts of laughter.

'Sounds like Dorm Night in there,' said Buffy.

'They seem to be getting on pretty well,' said Celeste.

'They shouldn't. It's unseemly.'

'They do have something in common.'

'I know.' He paused, listening to a burst of raucous laughter. 'That's what worries me.' He tried to sit up, to listen better, and fell back. 'Pass me my cigarettes, sweetie.'

'You shouldn't smoke.'

'Do you mind? Do you really care?'

She stroked his beard. 'Of course I do, silly.' It was painful, to watch him making this huge readjustment towards her. She had known for months that it lay ahead of him, like a major operation he was unaware that he had to face. She had meant to prepare him for it more gradually—more ceremoniously too, with a gentle talk culminating in a Christmas dinner *à trois*, back at her flat—but the unexpected events in the wood had thrown the whole thing into disarray. 'Look, I'm awfully sorry.'

'I adore you. You know that.'

'I adore you, too,' she said. 'So is that all right?'

He nodded. He took her hand and kissed the fingers, one by one. He laid her palm against his cheek. In the kitchen the bursts of laughter and the clatter of pans seemed far away. Here there was no sound except the shifting of a log as it settled in the embers of the fire.

'You've got glitter in your beard,' she said.

'You've got some on your jumper.'

'You know I'll never be able to call you Dad. It makes me feel too funny.'

'That's fine by me. Hasn't done me much good up to now.'

She pulled away. 'Listen!' She glared at him. 'You're not a failure! I've seen your boys with Jacquetta, they're just as horrible with her. They're adolescents! I've been in all your lives. I've heard how they all speak about you, your ex-wives, India, everybody, I'm probably the only one who has. I've been like a fly on the wall. Don't you understand? They wouldn't be so rude about you if they weren't fond of you. It's a compliment, in a funny way.' She paused for breath. She had been meaning to say this all day. 'You've not been a failure, Buffy! You've just had more of a past to be a failure *in*! And look—they're all here, aren't they? All your exes. They all rushed down, on Christmas Day too! Listen to them. And your children too.'

They paused. A snowball thudded against the window. Outside, yells echoed over the countryside—all the Christmases he had never had, they were happening here, now. They echoed across the dark, locked countryside.

'You've brought them all together, bless you,' he said. 'You're the only one who could do it.'

'That's not true! I just helped it happen. Don't you see, you silly? I think the reason you can't act anymore is that you're too busy acting out this, this, *scenario*.'

'What scenario?'

'Of poor old Buffy. Poor old battered Buffy, all abandoned and divorced. Penny's right. You've got sort of locked into it and it's not really true! You're not that old. You haven't even got anything wrong with you, not really. It's, like, you've written a part for yourself and those are the only lines you know.'

Just then Jacquetta came into the room. She wore his trilby hat, at a rakish angle, and she had tucked a *Historic Sights of Kent* tea towel into her waistband. She was still giggling. 'Sorry to interrupt,' she said, 'but do you two want baked beans with yours?'

*   *   *

Afterwards they all said, to whoever would listen, that it was certainly the most bizarre Christmas dinner they had ever had, and they should know—they had had some bizarre ones in the past. They ate a concoction of stir-fried tinned ravioli, cabbage, onions, sausages and baked beans with, as Lorna said in her supervisor's voice *your choice of tomato ketchup or piccalilli.* This was washed down with half a bottle of tawny port, a litre bottle of Cinzano somebody had discovered in the back of the larder and three cans of date-expired Budweiser Lorna had bought for some men who came a long time ago to fit her new boiler.

They ate on Buffy. One of his hundred uses, as an ex-husband, was to provide a convenient dining-table. He wasn't allowed to laugh or move, however, or the plates slipped off. Celeste fed him. They sat around on the floor, eating off their laps and off Buffy. They all had Happy Eater napkins, there were plenty of those. Popsi had put a sprig of mistletoe in her hair. Lorna had found, hidden away, a Dizzy Gillespie record. She put it on. Nearly a quarter of a century earlier she had danced to this with Buffy, little knowing that their embraces would lead, after such a long hiatus, such a long, waking sleep, to the presence of this flushed young woman tenderly lifting his grizzled head and shovelling food in. A daughter, popped up from nowhere! As they all became drunker this fact struck them as both wonderfully strange and utterly inevitable.

Even Jacquetta had drunk a tumblerful of Cinzano. She looked down at Buffy. 'Remember those picnics in Provence, when Bruno and Tobias were babies? Remember the smell of lavender and camembert?'

346

'I remember everything,' said Buffy.

'Even when you were too drunk to remember,' said Penny.

He tapped his head. 'It's all in here. In my as yet unwritten memoirs. Even as you sit here, like hyenas around the carcass of an old water buffalo.'

Celeste looked at the three ex-wives. 'Say it was worth it! You can't just switch it off, can you? Say it was all worth while!' She drained her glass; her brain buzzed. 'Say you miss him.'

Penny raised her hand. 'Only if we don't have to have him back.'

'I just want to know,' said Celeste. She had such a long, laborious past to recover, it had to mean something. All of it. Otherwise what was the point?

'I miss you.' Penny looked down at Buffy. 'I miss you when I want to go to the theatre. Thingy never goes to the theatre. I miss you when I've got something to say that only you'll understand. Something about tennis balls, for instance; I was thinking about rich people's tennis balls the other day. There are things I'll never have a reply to, now.' She munched, thoughtfully. 'I don't miss your dog, though.'

Popsi said: 'I was thinking about you only last week, pet. They'd pinned up this sign saying *More Stalls Upstairs*. You once said to me that there were two signs that always made you feel depressed, though you didn't know why. One was *More Stalls Upstairs* and the

347

other was *Light Refreshments will be Served.'*

'You remember that?' asked Buffy.

She nodded.

'I don't,' he said.

'You weren't even that bad in bed,' said Penny. 'We were only joking, about the carrot.'

'What carrot?' demanded Buffy.

'We had our moments, didn't we?' she said. 'At least you *talked* afterwards. And during. Sometimes you talked so much we had to stop.'

'Ssh!' said Popsi, 'not in front of the children.'

Jacquetta gazed at a piece of ravioli, stuck on the end of her fork. 'I miss the person I was, with you. When somebody goes, the person you were, with them, that person disappears too. Nobody else can bring that person back. When a marriage breaks up, it's two people you've lost.'

There was a silence. 'That's deep,' said Popsi. The mistletoe had slid below her ear.

'It doesn't end, does it?' asked Celeste. 'Look, we're here! We're here now!'

They sat there, in tipsy contemplation. The meal was finished. They screwed up their napkins and threw them into the fire; the flames flared. They lifted their plates off Buffy's stomach. Celeste turned to her mother. 'Did you miss him?'

Lorna stood up, holding a handful of plates. Behind her, a piece of holly slipped beneath

348

the picture frame and fell to the floor. She shook her head. 'Not really.' She stepped over Buffy, on her way to the kitchen. 'But I missed you.' She turned to Celeste. 'I missed you all the time. When I worked in Selfridges I thought you'd come in to try on a jumper. Then I moved to Dover and started a little flower shop. Weddings and christenings, we made up these bouquets. I thought—who knows? One day? Silly really, but I always hoped. Then they knocked us down to build a car park and the only job I could get round here was in catering. Not my thing really, but I thought—all those people passing through, surely one of them might be you? All those years, feeding other people . . . I thought you'd walk in the door and somehow I'd recognize you. I thought you'd be wearing the same sort of clothes I liked wearing, even the shoes. Which was ridiculous. I just thought I'd know who you were.' She paused, at the door. 'Oh, I missed you all right.'

*   *   *

Outside stood a snowman. Large and shapeless, it stood in the middle of the lawn. It wore Buffy's trilby hat and his overcoat. It stood facing the glowing curtains of the cottage. The conker eyes gazed sightlessly as the snowman stood facing the music. Dizzy Gillespie played, echoing down the years.

Music to dance to, to fall in love to; music for sex and for love. The snowman stood there, freezing hard. Around it, the ground was scuffed and muddied by the children's feet.

*   *   *

The Dizzy Gillespie record finished with a click. They sat there in the silence. After a moment they realized it wasn't completely quiet; there was a low humming sound. Maybe it was the record-player motor.

They sat very still. Popsi belched. 'Whoops,' she said, 'pardon.'

They listened. There was a far rumbling sound, the sound of an engine. They held their breath; they felt like castaways, hearing the drone of an approaching airplane.

It was getting louder. Suddenly they jumped up and hurried to the window. Crowding around it, jostling each other, they pulled open the curtains. A sheep's skull fell to the floor.

They pressed their faces against the glass. Outside, a pair of headlights shone in the darkness.

'It's Leon,' said Jacquetta. 'Just when I was starting to enjoy myself.' She turned round and said to Buffy, 'He's always been jealous of you.'

'He hasn't!' said Buffy, from the floor. 'Has he?'

'Why do you think he writes all those

books?'

Penny stared into the dark. Torchlight was approaching, bobbing across the garden. 'It's Colin, being all manly,' she said. 'Do you know, he's never said he loves me. This is his inarticulate way of showing it.'

'I used to say I loved you!' said Buffy. 'All the time.'

Quentin nudged Penny aside and pressed his nose against the glass. The torchlight was closer now, dazzling him. 'Maybe it's Talbot,' he said. 'But I don't think so somehow. Anyway he can't drive.'

The doorbell rang. Lorna went out to answer it. The other women waited. For some reason they looked sheepish, as if they had been caught *in flagrante*. They heard a man's voice, in the hall. They heard the rumble of motors and more men's voices, out in the garden. They smelt exhaust fumes.

Lorna came back in. She spoke to Celeste. 'It's that man we met in the wood last night.'

Celeste stared at her. 'What?'

'That man who took such a fancy to you. The man with the awful wife.'

'He's here?'

'What an angel,' said Lorna. 'He's come to rescue us. He's got them to bring the snowplough down the lane.' She turned. 'Celeste?'

But Celeste had gone. She had stumbled over Buffy and rushed out into the hall.

351

CHAPTER THIRTY-TWO

The next day the snow melted. In the wood the trees dripped; secret sighs and creaks. A soft thud as the snow loosened and fell from a bough. In Lorna's garden the snowman was melting. Gradually, Buffy thawed. The burly shape dwindled, perspiring in the sunshine. The overcoat sagged; the hat sank into its shoulders. As the hours passed it subsided gently into its own pool of water.

The next day, all that remained was a bundle of empty clothes on the scuffed and muddy grass. A puddle, surrounded by the skiddy footmarks of its children.

CHAPTER THIRTY-THREE

Later, months later, when Celeste and Miles were living together, he said to her: 'Just think. A little tin of fishes led me to you, my gorgeous. Pilchards! I don't even like them. Do you?'

She shook her head. A little gold fish had led her, too—back into the past and forward into the future. Sometimes, when she looked back to the events of that winter it all seemed like a fairy story. If she went back to the antiques arcade Popsi's booth would be shuttered up with a metal grid. *Who? Nobody of that name here. Who has a name like that anyway?* If she opened the paper and read a travel piece by Penny who could believe it? Had Penny really sipped a daiquiri in Barbados or was she lying on somebody's floor spinning her own dreams? The recycling book was never published; the Leisure Experience was never built.

Waxie and the other squatters had long since moved into her flat and changed the locks. In fact she had never gone back at all. The rabbits and telephones and colanders; they had never really belonged to her. They were just props that had helped her form this new character, Celeste; props that seemed to mean something at the time, if only she had understood.

What did it all mean, and did it matter anymore? Everyone she loved, she had them now, and they had her. She had joined them. She had even helped create an ex-wife of her own—Brenda, languishing in Swindon. She felt so guilty about this that she had started to read Leon's book. She had joined them all right, her tumultuous new family.

And that afternoon she was meeting Buffy for tea. They were going to plan his delayed sixtieth birthday party, to which everyone was invited. They had to meet early because he was working that night. He was playing Mr

353

Hardcastle in *She Stoops to Conquer* and, what with the wig and whatnot, the make-up took ages.